NETWORKS OF NAZI PERSECUTION

Studies on War and Genocide
General Editor: Omer Bartov, Brown University

Volume 1

The Massacre in History
Edited by Mark Levene and Penny Roberts

Volume 2

National Socialist Extermination Policies: Contemporary German Perspectives and Controversies
Edited by Ulrich Herbert

Volume 3

War of Extermination: The German Military in World War II, 1941–1944
Edited by Hannes Heer and Klaus Naumann

Volume 4

In God's Name: Genocide and Religion in the Twentieth Century
Edited by Omer Bartov and Phyllis Mack

Volume 5

Hitler's War in the East: A Critical Assessment
Rolf-Dieter Müller and Gerd R. Ueberschär

Volume 6

Networks of Nazi Persecution: Bureaucracy, Business, and the Organization of the Holocaust
Edited by Gerald D. Feldman and Wolfgang Seibel

NETWORKS OF NAZI PERSECUTION

Bureaucracy, Business, and
the Organization of the Holocaust

Edited by
Gerald D. Feldman and Wolfgang Seibel

Berghahn Books
New York • Oxford

First published in 2005 by
Berghahn Books
www.berghahnbooks.com

© 2005 Gerald D. Feldman and Wolfgang Seibel
First paperback edition published in 2006

All rights reserved.
Except for the quotation of short passages for the purposes
of criticism and review, no part of this book may be reproduced in any form
or by any means, electronic or mechanical, including photocopying, recording,
or any information storage and retrieval system now known or to be invented,
without written permission of the publisher.

Library of Congress Cataloging-in-Publication Data

Networks of Nazi persecution : bureaucracy, business, and the organization
of the Holocaust / edited by Gerald D. Feldman and Wolfgang Seibel.
  p. cm. -- (Studies on war and genocide)
  Includes bibliographical references.
  ISBN 1-57181-177-X (alk. paper)
  1. Holocaust, Jewish (1939-1945)--Causes. 2. Holocaust, Jewish
(1939-1945)--Economic aspects. 3. Germany--Economic policy--1933-1945.
4. Bureaucracy--Germany--History--20th century. 5. World War, 1939-1945--
Confiscation and pillage--Europe. 6. Nationalsozialistische Deutsche Arbeiter-
Partei. Schutzstaffel. 7. Jewish property--Europe. I. Feldman, Gerald D. II.
Seibel, Wolfgang, 1953- . III. War and genocide ; 6.

D804.3.N483 2004
940.53'181--dc22   2004043734

British Library Cataloguing in Publication Data

A catalogue record for this book is available
from the British Library.

ISBN 1-57181-177-X hardback
ISBN 1-84545-163-5 paperback

Printed in the United States on acid-free paper

Dedicated to the Memory of Roger V. Gould,
1962–2002

Contents

List of Figures ... ix

List of Abbreviations ... xi

Introduction

    The Holocaust as Division-of-Labor-Based
    Crime—Evidence and Analytical Challenges ... 1
    Gerald D. Feldman and *Wolfgang Seibel*

Part I – Rivalry and Competition

1. Introduction: Rivalry and Competition ... 13
Christian Gerlach

2. The SS Security Service and the Gestapo in the National
Socialist Persecution of the Jews, 1933–1939 ... 20
Wolfgang Dierker

3. "Aryanization" and the Role of the German Great Banks,
1933–1938 ... 44
Dieter Ziegler

4. The Looting of Jewish Property and Franco-German Rivalry,
1940–1944 ... 69
Philippe Verheyde

5. Seizure of Jewish Property and Inter-Agency Rivalry
in the Reich and in the Occupied Soviet Territories ... 88
Martin C. Dean

6. The Polycratic Nature of Art Looting:
The Dynamic Balance of the Third Reich ... 103
Jonathan Petropoulos

7. The Holocaust and Corruption ... 118
Frank Bajohr

Part II – "Smooth Cooperation"

8. Introduction: Cooperation and Collaboration 141
   Gerhard Hirschfeld and Wolfgang Seibel

9. The Looting of Jewish Property and the German Financial Administration 148
   Alfons Kenkmann

10. Organized Looting: The Nazi Seizure of Jewish Property in the Netherlands, 1940–1945 168
    Gerard Aalders

11. Perpetrator Networks and the Holocaust: The Spoliation of Jewish Property in France, 1940–1944 189
    Marc Olivier Baruch

12. "Ethnic Resettlement" and Inter-Agency Cooperation in the Occupied Eastern Territories 213
    Isabel Heinemann

13. The *"reibungslose"* Holocaust? The German Military and Civilian Implementation of the "Final Solution" in Ukraine, 1941–1944 236
    Wendy Lower

Part III – Decentral Initiative and Vertical Integration

14. Introduction: A Bureaucratic Holocaust – Toward a New Consensus 259
    Michael Thad Allen

15. Local Initiatives, Central Coordination: German Municipal Administration and the Holocaust 269
    Wolf Gruner

16. The *Reichskristallnacht* and the Insurance Industry: The Politics of Damage Control 295
    Gerald D. Feldman

Part IV – "Structure," "Agency," and the Logic of Radicalization

17. More than Just a Metaphor: The Network Concept and Its Potential in Holocaust Research 321
    Jörg Raab

18. Restraining or Radicalizing? Division of Labor and Persecution Effectiveness 340
    Wolfgang Seibel

Notes on Contributors 361

Index 367

List of Figures

4.1	Economic "Aryanization"	73
4.2	Patterns of intervention in small firms	75
4.3	Patterns of intervention in large firms	75
4.4	German interference in forty-one firms	81
9.1	Oberregierungsrat Heinrich Heising	151
9.2	The Baer Family	153
9.3	Control of possessions	159
10.1	The hierarchy of looting in the Netherlands	186

List of Abbreviations

AG	Aktiengesellschaft
AOK6	Armeeoberkommando 6
BdS	Befehlshaber der Sicherheitspolizei und des SD
CDC	Caisse des dépôts et consignations
CDJC	Centre de documentation juive contemporaine
CDU	Christlich Demokratische Union
CGQJ	Commissariat Général aux Questions Juives
DAW	Deutsche Ausrüstungswerke
Dego	Deutsche Golddiskontbank
DFG	Deutsche Forschungsgemeinschaft
DNB	De Nederlandsche Bank
DSK	Devisenschutzkommando
DVL	Deutsche Volksliste
EK5	Einsatzkommando 5
ERR	Einsatzstab Reichsleiter Rosenberg
EWZ	Einwandererzentralstelle
FA	Finanzamt
FK	Feldkommandantur
FRG	Federal Republic of Germany
GDR	German Democratic Republic
GFP	Geheime Feldpolizei
GG	General Gouvernement
HJ	Hitler Jugend
HSSPF	Höherer SS- und Polizeiführer
HTO	Haupttreuhandstelle Ost
HTW	Handelstrust West
IfZ	Institut für Zeitgeschichte

Liro	Lippmann, Rosenthal & Co.
MBF	Militärbefehlshaber in Frankreich
NKVD	People's Commissariat of Internal Affairs
NS	Nationalsozialistisch
NSBO	Nationalsozialistische Betriebszellenorganisation
NSDAP	Nationalsozialistische Deutsche Arbeiterpartei
NSV	Nationalsozialistische Volkswohlfahrt
OFP	Oberfinanzpräsident
OK	Ortskommandantur
OMGUS	Office for Military Government (U.S.)
OT	Organisation Todt
PA	Provisional Administrator
PK	Propagandakompanie
POWs	Prisoners of War
RFM	Reichsfinanzministerium
RFSS	Reichsführer SS
RJM	Reichsjustizministerium
RKF	Reichskommissar für die Festigung Deutschen Volkstums
RM	Reichsmark
RSHA	Reichssicherheitshauptamt
RuSHA	Rasse- und Siedlungshauptamt
RV	Reichsvereinigung der Juden in Deutschland
RWM	Reichswirtschaftsministerium
SA	Sturmabteilung
SCAP	Service du Contrôle des Administrateurs Provisoires
SD	Sicherheitsdienst
SDHA	Sicherheitshauptamt
Sipo	Sicherheitspolizei
SK4a	Sonderkommando 4a
SNCF	Société Nationale des Chemins de fer français
SS	Schutzstaffel
SS-WVHA	SS-Wirtschaftsverwaltungshauptamt
UGIF	Union générale des Israélites de France
UWZ	Umwandererzentralstelle
VVRA	Vermögensverwaltungs- und Rentenanstalt

INTRODUCTION

THE HOLOCAUST AS DIVISION-OF-LABOR-BASED CRIME— EVIDENCE AND ANALYTICAL CHALLENGES

Gerald D. Feldman and Wolfgang Seibel

Division of Labor, Networks, and Organized Mass Crime

Organized mass crime is unthinkable without division of labor. The Holocaust is no exception to this rule but, rather, its most horrifying manifestation. Evidence related to the role of government bureaucracy was, to be sure, already part of classic Holocaust research.[1] Meta-theories of the Holocaust have drawn on the nature and consequences of modern bureaucracy as a tool of persecution and mass murder, the most prominent being Hannah Arendt's banalization theory.[2]

Both the planning and the implementation of genocide were carried out in accordance with conventional division-of-labor principles. From 1939 on, the Amt *IV*, "Gegnererforschung und Bekämpfung" (Researching and Combating the Enemy) of the Reichssicherheitshauptamt (Reich Security Main Office) with its Department IV B 4, run by Adolf Eichmann, was in charge of anti-Jewish policy. The enforcement of the persecutory measures was delegated to the Staatspolizeileitstellen (State Police Head Offices) or, in the German occupied territories outside the Reich, to the Befehlshaber der Sicherheitspolizei und des Sicherheitsdienstes (SD) (Commanders of the Security Police and Security Service) (BdS). These core institutions, however, were dependent on numerous other institutions and individual participants, state and private, German and, in the occupied territories, domestic agents, for the implementation of the "final solution." In the occupied territories in particular, anti-Jewish policy implied resource dependency of the occupation administration and the Berlin central offices.[3] Vertical division of labor was eclipsed by the rivalry between different agencies, both German and domestic, resulting in "polycracy" or even "organized chaos."[4]

Thus, anti-Jewish policy and the persecution apparatus were obviously not just an SS and Gestapo matter. What is more, coordination of the complex persecution apparatuses could not be accomplished in an exclusively hierarchical manner. As the chapters in this volume reveal, coordination took place in a hierarchical as well as a cooperative way and, just as the differentiation of power within the regime or between the occupying power and domestic authorities played a role, so did the interdependence of a variety of agencies beyond formal rules of cooperation. To a large extent, the persecution apparatus was made up of inter-organizational networks as they have been described in political science and organization sociology literature.[5]

This perspective is supported by three strands of recent Holocaust research findings.

The first aspect concerns the situation of the SS and police apparatus, without question the core institution of the persecution apparatus. The degree of hegemony of the SS and police apparatus—abundantly described in the literature[6] —as it had been emerging in Germany since 1933 through the fusion of party organizations (SS, SD) with the state police and its independence vis-à-vis the general public administration, was, in the occupied areas, again dependent on the formal structure of the occupation regime. This, in turn, was shaped by the strategic goals of the occupying power, but it did not follow a standardized plan within these goals as is revealed by the situation even in a region so highly homogenous as German occupied Western Europe.[7] In one way or the other, however, division of labor meant collaboration of indigenous institutions and individuals.

The second aspect concerns the range of the anti-Jewish measures, mainly the relationship between economic and repressive police persecution. The "Aryanization" of Jewish-owned businesses was not controlled by the SS and Gestapo but instead took place under the jurisdiction of the Gauwirtschaftsberater (Regional Economic Advisors) of the Nationalsozialistische Deutsche Arbeiterpartei (NSDAP) in cooperation with the self-administrative chambers of industry and commerce and the free professions, as well as the local governments, law firms, banks and insurance companies.[8] In German-occupied territories, the jurisdiction for "Aryanization" and the spoliation of Jewish assets in general lay with the regular civil or military occupation administration, which was again decisively dependent on domestic agencies.[9]

Finally, the destruction of the economic existence was inseparably connected to the physical extermination of the Jews. Although organization of the deportations was the exclusive domain of the Gestapo, the plundering of the last personal assets and belongings prior to deportation required cooperation with a large number of regular authorities, for instance, as has been reported for Germany proper, with the residential registration offices (Einwohnermeldeämter), fiscal authorities, housing offices, district courts, employment offices, and further with the chambers of trade and commerce, trade guilds, savings banks and other banks, and, last but not least, with the Reichsbahn (state railroad).[10] In the German occupied territories, this pattern was repeated, despite considerable regional differences. In the final phase of the victims' complete defenselessness, there was a downright "enrichment race"[11] in both the "Aryanization" and the plundering of household and other personal belongings between the Gestapo and the finance administration[12] and, under the supervision of public authorities, between companies, private individuals, and banks.[13]

The third aspect concerns the interrelation of the differing segments of tactical and strategic German warfare and occupying politics with the mass murder of the European Jews. The studies by Aly,[14] Dieckmann,[15] Gerlach,[16] Gutberger,[17] Heim and Aly,[18] Herbert,[19] Müller[20] and Friedrich[21] describe the interlocking of varying logics of action and interests within German warfare and occupation politics and their effects on the initiation and implementation of the Holocaust. This reflected the "polycratic" conglomerate of, for instance, health policy, population politics, economic planning, agriculture and nutrition, and warfare. Toward the representatives of the respective spheres of interests, the SS and Gestapo apparatus acted partly as a partner in cooperation and yet partly as an opponent within the sphere of their respective interests.

However overwhelming the diversity of actors and institutions involved in the persecution, the ways in which division of labor was linked to perpetrator agency have, by and large, remained unexplored. The present volume focuses on these issues.

One important fact to be acknowledged is that the formal status of division of labor varied substantially. It ranged from highly formalized and tightly coupled relationships between participating agencies to ephemeral and loosely coupled linkages between individual actors. Weberian bureaucracy with rigid rules and hierarchies did play a crucial role in the preparation and execution of persecution and mass murder. German fiscal administration with its endeavor to confiscate as much of the Jewish assets as possible is a prominent example.[22] It would be misleading to assume, however, that the machinery of public administration always acted in accordance with the conventional rules of hierarchy and regulated cooperation as far as the persecution of the Jews was concerned. A striking phenomenon is the self-initiative of local and regional authorities, which often took independent steps of anti-Jewish discrimination and persecution years ahead of central Reich regulations, and then asked for central coordination for the sake of homogeneity.[23] While this largely reflects the influence of local Nazi leaders in municipal administration, state administration, too, rigidly implemented anti-Jewish regulation without central initiation or coordination.[24] Moreover, public authorities and the Nazi party organization were not just acting as law-abiding agencies. Bribery and corruption were an integral part of the persecution.[25]

Other organizational forms of persecution were much more informal, and yet at least as effective as public bureaucracy. The spoliation of Jewish assets, the "Aryanization" of Jewish-owned firms in particular, required a vast array of expertise and institutional assistance. Banks, brokers, law firms, investors (often former competitors), and intermediaries of the Nazi party as well as local and regional administration formed networks of spoliation and persecution whose extension and structure are illustrated in several chapters in this volume.[26] What made those networks stable and effective was, above all, the mutual benefit of those involved.

Networks and the presumptive source of their formation and stability make us aware that, although individuals persecuted the Jews in obedience to orders and in accordance with their own anti-Semitism, neither hierarchy nor ideology was an indispensable prerequisite for the active involvement in mass crime. As the chapters in this volume illustrate, individuals contributed to the radicalization of anti-Jewish policy without following orders or a particular commitment to anti-Semitism. Apparently, the motivational basis of persecution was much more encompassing. However extended the variety of motives of persecutors and their helpers, motivation was not just contingent. What several chapters of this book reveal is the coordinating and legitimizing role of professions and institutions. The looting of Jewish property or the "Aryanization" of Jewish businesses, for instance, was certainly stimulated by crude enrichment. But many accomplices had only limited opportunities—if any—to enrich themselves personally. Rather, they fulfilled what they perceived as an obligation toward professional standards and institutional roles as bankers, insurance representatives, lawyers, civil servants of the fiscal administration, etc. Those roles and standards, however, were not strictly binding. They certainly provided strong incentives but also left considerable leeway for personal choices.

It is here that anti-Semitism did play a crucial role in two dimensions. One is that many peripheral but indispensable actors within the persecution apparatuses shared anti-Semitic stereotypes and approved anti-Jewish measures in general. Removing Jews from entire industries and combating them as a group of uncertain loyalty to the Reich were what many outside the orbit of the SS and Gestapo perceived as justifiable and appropriate even if they did not share the idea of physical extermination. Once anti-Jewish stereotypes had been adopted, principled resistance against more radical steps of persecution was very unlikely. A second function of anti-Semitism as state ideology was coordination regardless of personal conviction. The anti-Jewish agenda produced signals that were unmistakably simple and unambiguous and, thus, could be taken into account independently of individual persuasion. In combination with the permanent threat of violent coercion, state anti-Semitism played a powerful role in homogenizing the action of tens of thousands of "helpers" who would not have taken the initiative to persecute the Jews themselves but did not hesitate to comply with the persecution once it was initiated by those in power.

The Structure of Organized Mass Crime and Moral Responsibility

Regardless of its uniqueness in history, the Holocaust shares crucial characteristics with organized mass crime in general, of which the present volume stresses networks and division of labor as predominant structural features. Organized crime is obviously a structural phenomenon, but a merely structural perspective entails obvious risks of misinterpretation. Criminal action, like any kind of human agency, is embedded in social structures in the sense of regularities of interindividual relationship, but crime as such is committed by responsible individuals. Assessing the degree of personal responsibility is what the structural analysis of organized crime should be ultimately aiming at. As the sense of moral obligation remains the very basis for distinguishing between right and wrong, the analysis of formal and informal structures of human agency can never exculpate individuals whose wrongdoing is beyond any doubt. But the analysis will nonetheless reveal regularities of interindividual and interorganizational relationship that enhance or reduce the risk of individual wrongdoing.

Networks are a particular case in point. Interindividual and interorganizational networks are portrayed in the relevant literature as an alternative to conventional governance in terms of public and corporate bureaucracy.[27] Deeper insight into the nature of organized crime, however, challenges such appraisals. The evidence presented in this volume, both empirical and theoretical in nature, supports the assumption that informal, network-type mechanisms of governance on the one hand and traditional bureaucracies on the other hand were equally effective in mobilizing human resources for evil purposes during the Holocaust. Certainly, one important difference between "good" and "evil" networks resides in the macro-political order in which they are embedded. But networks as a type of organized crime per se represent issues of judgment, leadership, and morality. The leadership of network elites may be designed either to mobilize or to demobilize human resources. The mobilization of networks of persecution, for instance, was dependent on intellectual capability, moral judgment, and ideological zeal.

However, when it comes to organized mass crime, moral judgment is obviously not only a matter of the leadership of criminal elites but also a matter of the compliance and support of rank-and-file participants. Support of participants and organizational cohesion, as described in organization-theory classics,[28] are fundamentally ambivalent phenomena based on an interplay of selfishness and legitimacy. On the one hand, it is precisely *not* the willingness to cooperate for the sake of common goals which makes organizations stable, powerful, and effective. Rather, individuals use organizations for personal purposes such as income, career promotion, etc. The decoupling of organizational performance from personal commitment to organizational goals makes organizations much more effective than cooperation on the basis of shared goals, the reason being the enormous diversification of motivational sources. Networks, reaching far beyond the boundaries of formal organization, even enlarge this diversity. On the other hand, despite the dominant role of personal purposes, individuals are not unaware of organizational goals and no sustainable integration or true leadership can be based on immoral organizational purposes.[29] That is why organized mass crime is intrinsically connected to legitimating concepts and ideological rationalizations.

The very ambivalence of organizations as such makes the structure of organized mass crime robust and vulnerable at the same time. The robustness stems from the decoupling of individual motivation from organizational goals, which makes "organized evil" decisively more dangerous than mobilization through shared goals or beliefs. The reason is, again, the enormous diversification of motivational sources.[30] The opacity and blurriness of networks do not help to reduce those risks. The fact, however, that individuals (accomplices, "willing executioners," "collaborators," etc.), in spite of all their selfishness, remain aware of organizational goals implies, first, that accomplices remain accountable for what they are doing even when they act in networks that are fluid and opaque in nature and, secondly, that the separation of organizational goals and individual motivation is limited by the quest for legitimacy and identity.[31]

If there is good sense in acknowledging that moral indifference is basically an unstable mind set,[32] this will also affect the moral indifference of accomplices: Hence the potential influence of moral standards and, not least, examples of civil courage and moral leadership.[33] Raising moral costs for accomplices can make the decisive difference and, therefore, is an important element of public awareness and policy. What Holocaust research reveals is not just the structural complexity of the persecution machinery but also the failure to observe the most elementary moral imperatives. Sustaining those imperatives remains as much an obligation as analyzing the linkage between "agency" and "structure," without which even the highest moral standards will fail in a world of complex organizations.

Organization of the Volume

The present volume is organized according to three principal configurations of division of labor and mobilization of individuals and agencies for persecution. The three thematic parts are introduced by prominent scholars in the field, Christian Gerlach, Gerhard Hirschfeld and Wolfgang Seibel, and Michael T. Allen. A concluding part is devoted to general issues of network analysis and division of labor when it comes to Holocaust research.

Part I with chapters by Wolfgang Dierker, Dieter Ziegler, Philippe Verheyde, Martin Dean, Jonathan Petropoulos and Frank Bajohr, refers to rivalry and competition as intensifying rather than impeding forces of persecution. Precisely because the persecution machinery was neither monolithic nor exclusively hierarchical, distribution of jurisdiction and power remained often blurred and contested. However, competition among individuals and agencies and eagerness to conquer or to defend jurisdiction in *Judenangelegenheiten* (Jewish affairs) rarely caused persistent friction. Rather, as with competition elsewhere, the result was a growing effort to outperform rivals, which crucially radicalized the persecution.

Part II with chapters by Alfons Kenkmann, Gerard Aalders, Marc-Olivier Baruch, Isabel Heinemann and Wendy Lower provides an alternative view on the consequences of division of labor. The chapters in this section analyze how perpetrators aptly coordinated their respective interests and strategies. This may prevent us from overstating the image of "organized chaos" as an ingredient of Nazi rule. Persecuting and annihilating the Jews were at the core of Nazi Germany's policy in all of Europe during World War II. While it is undeniable that division of labor and the network-type blurriness of jurisdiction and competencies had a particular impact on the implementation of the Holocaust, the perpetrators often were smart and energetic enough to overcome the disadvantages of administrative fragmentation.

Part III with chapters by Wolf Gruner and Gerald D. Feldman, sheds new light on the relationship between decentralized initiatives and central coordination when it comes to anti-Jewish policy in Nazi Germany. In the domains of both police repression and the economy local or non-governmental actors either initiated measures against the Jews or skillfully anticipated and operationalized what they perceived as the will of the ruling clique. The vertical axis of division of labor and reintegration is of particular interest. In some instances, as in the case of the municipal administration, decentralized agencies used traditional techniques of self-coordination in an effort to homogenize and thus radicalize anti-Jewish policy. In other instances, as in the case of the German insurance industry, anticipatory obedience led to flexible adaptation vis-à-vis the regime's anti-Jewish agenda at the expense of moral and professional standards.

In the concluding part IV, Jörg Raab and Wolfgang Seibel provide a discussion of networks, division of labor and the Holocaust from a social science perspective. Networks are more than just a metaphor. In recent decades, research has made considerable progress in the measurement and visualization of the informal relationship between individuals and institutions. Making networks of persecution measurable and visible is a most challenging task. Moreover, taking individual intention and its impact on the persecution seriously requires a reconciliation of methodological individualism with structural analysis. This implies building hypotheses on how division of labor and the differentiation of power within the persecution apparatus affected both the room to manoeuvre and the incentive structure of the perpetrators and their "helpers." Building and testing those hypotheses remains a challenge to future interdisciplinary research.

Acknowledgments

This volume originated from an international conference held at the University of Konstanz, Germany, in September 2000, which was generously supported by the Deutsche Forschungsgemeinschaft (DFG). The University of Konstanz sponsored the preparation of the present publication, including the translation of several contributions into English, through additional research funds. Final editing was made at the Institute for Advanced Study, Princeton, where Wolfgang Seibel was a member of the School of Historical Studies in the second term of the academic year 2003–2004. The editors wish to thank James Fearns for translating the German papers selected for publication. Jürgen Klöckler and Insa Meinen, with the assistance of Anja Bertsch, Till Blume, Julia Galka, Katrin-Isabel Krähling and Tina Schmidt-Böhringer, assumed the tedious task of revising the manuscripts according to the publisher's formal demands.

The volume is dedicated to the memory of Roger V. Gould (1962–2002), a pioneer of historical network analysis, who served admirably as a general commentator to the conference from which this book emerged.

Notes

1. Raul Hilberg, *The Destruction of the European Jews*, 3 vols. (New York, 1985); Uwe Dietrich Adam, *Judenpolitik im Dritten Reich* (Düsseldorf, 1973); Hans G. Adler, *Der verwaltete Mensch. Studien zur Deportation der Juden aus Deutschland* (Tübingen, 1974); Lucy S. Dawidowicz, *The War Against the Jews 1933–1945* (Toronto/New York, 1975); Gerald Reitlinger, *The Final Solution. The Attempt to Exterminate the Jews of Europe, 1939–1945* (London, 1953).
2. Hannah Arendt, *Eichmann in Jerusalem. A Report on the Banality of Evil* (New York, 1963); see further Guy B. Adams and Danny L. Balfour, *Unmasking Administrative Evil* (London, 1998), pp. 15–19, 53–72; Zygmunt Bauman, *Modernity and the Holocaust* (Ithaca, 1989); Hans Mommsen, "Die Realisierung des Utopischen. Die Endlösung der 'Judenfrage' im Dritten Reich," *Geschichte und Gesellschaft* 9 (1983): 381–420; J.C. Scott, *Seeing like a State: How Certain Schemes to Improve the Human Condition Have Failed* (New Haven London, 1998), pp. 76–83.
3. Cornelis J. Lammers, "The Interorganizational Control of an Occupied Country," *Administrative Science Quarterly*, 33 (1988): 438–457; idem, "Macht und Autorität des Deutschen Besetzers in den Niederlanden während des Zweiten Weltkrieges. Ansätze zu einer Soziologie der Besatzung," *Journal für Sozialforschung*, 31 (1991): 401–415; idem, "Levels of Cooperation: A Comparative Study of German Occupation Regimes during the Second World War," in Robert Bohn, ed., *Die deutsche Herrschaft in den 'germanischen' Ländern 1940–1945* (Stuttgart, 1997), pp. 47–69.
4. See Wolfgang Seibel in the present volume.
5. Patrick Kenis and Volker Schneider, "Policy Networks and Policy Analysis: Scrutinizing a New Analytical Toolbox," in Bernd Marin and Renate Mayntz, eds., *Policy Networks* (Frankfurt on Main/New York, 1991), pp. 25–59; David Knoke, *Political Networks: The Structural Perspective* (Cambridge/New York, 1990); Renate Mayntz, "Policy-Networks und die Logik von Verhandlungssystemen," in Renate Mayntz, ed., *Soziale Dynamik* (Frankfurt on Main/New York, 1993), pp. 239–262; Walter W. Powell, "Neither Market Nor Hierarchy: Network Forms of Organization," *Research in Organizational Behavior*

12 (1990): 295–336. For an example of empirical network analysis applied to Holocaust research see Wolfgang Seibel and Jörg Raab, "Verfolgungsnetzwerke. Zur Messung von Arbeitsteilung und Machtdifferenzierung in den Verfolgungsapparaten des Holocaust," *Kölner Zeitschrift für Soziologie und Sozialpsychologie* 55(2003): 197–230.

6. Jens Banach, *Heydrichs Elite. Das Führerkorps der Sicherheitspolizei und des SD 1936–1945* (Paderborn, 1998); Richard Breitman, *The Architect of Genocide. Himmler and the 'Final Solution'* (London, 1991); Ruth Bettina Birn, *Die höheren SS- und Polizeiführer. Himmlers Vertreter im Reich und in den besetzten Gebieten* (Düsseldorf, 1986); George C. Browder, *Foundations of the Nazi Police State: The Formation of Sipo and SD* (Lexington, 1990); idem, *Hitler's Enforcers. The Gestapo and the SS Security Service in the Nazi Revolution* (New York/Oxford, 1996); Hans Buchheim, Martin Broszat, Hans-Adolf Jacobsen, and Helmut Krausnick, *Anatomie des SS-Staates*, 2 vols. (Munich, 1967); Robert Gellately, "Situating the 'SS-State' in a Social-Historical Context: Recent Histories of the SS, the Police, and the Courts in the Third Reich," *Journal of Modern History* 64 (1992): 338–365; Gerhard Paul and Klaus-Michael Mallmann, eds., *Die Gestapo. Mythos und Realität* (Darmstadt, 1995); Friedrich Wilhelm, *Die Polizei im NS-Staat. Die Geschichte ihrer Organisation im Überblick* (Paderborn, 1997); and the contribution of Wolfgang Dierker in the present volume.

7. Wolfgang Seibel, "The Strength of Perpetrators—The Holocaust in Western Europe, 1940–1944," *Governance—An International Journal of Policy, Administration, and Institutions* 15 (2002): 211–240.

8. Johannes Bähr, *Der Goldhandel der Dresdner Bank während des Zweiten Weltkriegs* (Leipzig, 1999); Avraham Barkai, *Von Boykott zur 'Entjudung'. Der wirtschaftliche Existenzkampf der Juden 1933–1943* (Frankfurt on Main, 1987); Frank Bajohr, *"Arisierung" in Hamburg. Die Verdrängung der jüdischen Unternehmer 1933–1945* (Hamburg, 1997); Gerald D. Feldman, *Allianz and the German Insurance Business, 1933–1945* (Cambridge, 2001); Helmut Genschel, *Die Verdrängung der Juden aus der Wirtschaft im Dritten Reich* (Göttingen, 1966); Harold James, *Die Deutsche Bank und die "Arisierung"* (Munich, 2001); Gerhard Kratzsch, *Der Gauwirtschaftsapparat der NSDAP. Menschenführung, "Arisierung", Wehrwirtschaft im Gau Westfalen-Süd. Eine Studie zur Herrschaftspraxis im totalitären Staat* (Münster, 1989); Johannes Ludwig, *Boykott, Enteignung, Mord. Die "Entjudung" der deutschen Wirtschaft* (Hamburg, 1989); Jonathan Steinberg, *Die Deutsche Bank und ihre Goldtransaktionen während des Zweiten Weltkrieges* (Munich, 1999); Dieter Ziegler, "Die Verdrängung der Juden aus der Dresdner Bank 1933–1938," *Vierteljahrshefte für Zeitgeschichte* 47 (1999): 187–216; and contributions by Dieter Ziegler, Philippe Verheyde, Martin Dean, Jonathan Petropoulos, Frank Bajohr, Alfons Kenkmann, Marc Olivier Baruch, and Gerald D. Feldman in the present volume.

9. See for France Commission Mattéoli [Mission d'étude sur la Spoliation des Juifs de France], *Rapport final de la "Mission d'étude sur la spoliation des Juifs en France,"* (Paris, 2000); for Belgium Commission Buysse [Commission d'étude sur le sort des biens des membres de la communauté juive de Belgique spoliés ou délaissés pendant la guerre 1940–1945], *Rapport final: Les Biens des victimes des persécutions anti-juives en Belgique* (Brussels, 2001); for The Netherlands Gerard Aalders, *Roof. De ontvremding van joods bezit tijdens de Tweede Wereldoorlog* (The Hague, 1999).

10. See Adler, *Mensch*, pp. 323–437; Wolfgang Dreßen, *Betrifft: "Aktion 3". Deutsche verwerten jüdische Nachbarn* (Berlin, 1998); Michael Zimmermann, "Die Gestapo und die regionale Organisation der Judendeportationen. Das Beispiel der Stapo-Leitstelle Düsseldorf," in Paul and Mallmann, *Gestapo*, pp. 357–372.

11. Bajohr, *Arisierung*, p. 265.

12. Barkai, *Entjudung*, pp. 189–198.

13. Adler, *Mensch*, pp. 589–644; Bajohr, *Arisierung*, pp. 265–324; Barkai, *Entjudung*, pp. 189–203; Franziska Becker, *Gewalt und Gedächtnis. Erinnerungen an die nationalsozialistische Verfolgung einer jüdischen Landgemeinde* (Göttingen, 1994); Alex Bruns-Wüstefeld, *Lohnende Geschäfte: Die "Entjudung" der Wirtschaft am Beispiel Göttingens* (Hanover, 1997); Dreßen, *Aktion 3*; Genschel, *Verdrängung*, pp. 249–255; Bob Moore,

Victims and Survivor: The Nazi Persecution of the Jews in the Netherlands 1940–1945 (London, 1997), pp. 104–106; Zimmermann, "Gestapo", pp. 357–372.
14. Götz Aly, *"Endlösung". Völkerverschiebung und der Mord an den europäischen Juden* (Frankfurt, 1995).
15. Christoph Dieckmann, "Der Krieg und die Ermordung der litauischen Juden," in Ulrich Herbert, ed., *Nationalsozialistische Vernichtungspolitik 1933–1945. Neue Forschungen und Kontroversen* (Frankfurt on Main, 1998), pp. 292–329.
16. Christian Gerlach, *Krieg, Ernährung, Völkermord. Forschungen zur deutschen Vernichtungspolitik im Zweiten Weltkrieg* (Hamburg, 1998); idem, *Kalkulierte Morde. Die deutsche Wirtschafts- und Vernichtungspolitik in Weißrußland 1941 bis 1944* (Hamburg, 1999).
17. Jörg Gutberger, *Volk, Raum und Sozialstruktur. Sozialstruktur- und Sozialraumforschung im "Dritten Reich"* (Münster, 1996).
18. Susanne Heim and Götz Aly, *Vordenker der Vernichtung. Auschwitz und die deutschen Pläne für eine neue europäische Ordnung* (Frankfurt on Main, 1991).
19. Ulrich Herbert, "Die deutsche Militärverwaltung in Paris und die Deportation der französischen Juden," in Herbert, *Nationalsozialistische Vernichtungspolitik*, pp. 170–208.
20. Rolf-Dieter Müller, *Hitlers Ostkrieg und die deutsche Siedlungspolitik. Die Zusammenarbeit von Wehrmacht, Wirtschaft und SS* (Frankfurt on Main, 1991).
21. Jörg Friedrich, *Das Gesetz des Krieges. Das deutsche Heer in Rußland 1941–1945. Der Prozeß gegen das Oberkommando der Wehrmacht*, 2nd ed. (Munich, 1996).
22. See contributions by Martin Dean and Alfons Kenkmann in the present volume.
23. See contribution by Wolf Gruner.
24. See again Alfons Kenkmann in this volume.
25. See contribution by Frank Bajohr.
26. See contributions by Gerald D. Feldman, Jonathan Petropoulos, Philippe Verheyde and Dieter Ziegler.
27. See H. Brinton Milward, "Governing the Hollow State," *Journal of Public Administration Research and Theory* 10, no. 2 (2000): 359–379; Mark Thatcher, "The Development of Policy Network Analysis," *Journal of Theoretical Politics* 10 (1998): 389–416, for recent overviews.
28. See Chester I. Barnard, *The Functions of the Executive*, Thirtieth Anniversary Edition (Cambridge, 1968); Herbert A. Simon, *Administrative Behavior. A Study of Decision-Making Process in Administrative Organization* (New York, 1945).
29. Philip Selznick, *Leadership in Administration: A Sociological Interpretation* (New York/Evanston/London, 1957), as the classic reference and Steven P. Feldman, *Memory as a Moral Decision: The Role of Ethics in Organizational Culture* (Somerset, 2002) for a recent account.
30. A similar point, emphasizing the role of exchange and interorganizational competition, is made by James Buchanan, "A Defense of Organized Crime?" in Simon Rottenberg, ed., *The Economics of Crime and Punishment* (Washington D.C., 1973), pp. 119–132, with respect to organized crime in general and by Albert Breton and Ronald Wintrobe, "The Bureaucracy of Murder Revisited," *Journal of Political Economy* 94 (1986): 905–926, with respect to the Holocaust in particular. Ian Kershaw, *Hitler: 1936–45: Nemesis* (London, 2000), pp. 1–60 ("Ceaseless Radicalization"), gives a rich account of the disastrous dynamics resulting from the diffuse linkage between the various motives at the grass-roots level that made ordinary Germans comply with dictatorship and the overarching goals of Hitler and his clique. In a similar vein, Wolfgang Seibel, "A Market for Mass Crime? Inter-Institutional Competition and the Initiation of the Holocaust in France, 1940–1942," *Journal of Organization Theory and Behavior* 5 (2002): 219–217, analyzes French-German collaboration in the preparation of the Holocaust in France.
31. Harrison C. White, *Identity and Control. A Structural Theory of Social Action* (Princeton, 1992), for identity and control in interorganizational networks.
32. Thomas M. Scanlon, *What We Owe to Each Other* (Cambridge, 1998).
33. See Martin Gilbert, *The Righteous. The Unsung Heroes of the Holocaust* (New York, 2003).

Part I

Rivalry and Competition

CHAPTER 1

INTRODUCTION: RIVALRY AND COMPETITION

Christian Gerlach

Research about National Socialism in the 1970s and early 1980s showed results on the structures of the regime that were surprising at the time. It turned out that instead of a monolithic bureaucratic machinery working from top to bottom there were several sources of political power. An increasing number of rival agencies, institutions and organizations had overlapping or unclearly defined responsibilities. According to the theory of polycracy, they competed for influence and more competence.[1] In the absence of clear legal and administrative norms, high-ranking Nazis struggled for Hitler's favor, one trying to outdo the other in what they thought was expected. According to the interpretation of "structuralist" or "functionalist" scholars, it was more this struggle than Nazi ideology that brought about a radicalization of Nazi policy, leading ultimately to the Holocaust. And Hitler in fact supported the most radical figures.[2] One of the effects of the Nazi system, as seen by this school, was consequently that rivalry absorbed political energies, led increasingly to inner tensions, and favored a tendency of the system toward self-destruction, which may have accelerated its end.[3]

Some aspects of this model have turned out to be too simple or overly theoretical. There was criticism that the importance of ideology had been neglected, that the impression of a paralyzing chaos was misleading, and that "radicalization" was sometimes imagined as having been produced by anonymous structures in a process in which any real actors had vanished. New empirical studies, based on much richer source material, have demonstrated that historical dynamics were much more complex. It has been underscored that different German institutions acted in a much more consensual way, especially in the occupied territories, where lack of manpower forced them to cooperate. One could even say that the crucial focus of recent works has been on cooperation rather than competition (see part II of the present volume). While there is no doubt about the correctness of the idea that the rivalry of different institutions did spur on German mass crimes, it has to be kept in mind that this was no more than one of the roots of violence.

All the chapters of the following section except one deal with the expropriation, the plundering and the utilization of property, focusing on Jewish property. Thus it seems to be appropriate to discuss the issue of rivalry, competition, and efficiency primarily with regard to the looting of property only—all the more so because wealth, money, and valuables are among the strongest incentives for competition that can be imagined (and among the strongest incentives for violence).

In recent years there has been a wave of research on the plundering of Jewish assets (as well as forced labor), fueled by growing public interest. National governments, several banks, and business companies employed historians in order to explore their past when they came under pressure. An increasing number of the resulting works have become part of the current debate in the scholarly field. However, the contributions to the present section view the issue of competition for Jewish property from different angles. Martin Dean emphasizes official cooperation and control of expropriated assets, while Frank Bajohr stresses individual gains and corruption. Where Jonathan Petropoulos sees a race between several institutions and organizations for works of art with an open ending, Dean analyzes an exclusive conflict between the SS and state financial institutions. Dieter Ziegler argues that big German private banks competed in the "Aryanization" business, struggling for shares of the market, whereas Philippe Verheyde comes to the conclusion that, despite efforts of German private firms, German occupational institutions in France restricted their attempts to take over French-Jewish capital. Ziegler points to state influence on big business as a result of the global economic crisis of the early 1930s; Verheyde and Dean see state and party institutions in control of the expropriation process, while Bajohr and Petropoulos argue that individual or particularist initiatives made any control an illusion. This reflects the complex and contradictory picture of recent Holocaust research. Especially if one changes the perspective and tries to take on the view of the victims, competitive initiative from below contributed to a complete and merciless persecution. This point is stressed by Petropoulos, Bajohr and Wolfgang Dierker below. It is particularly obvious in Martin Dean's analysis of the cooperation between tax offices, the Gestapo and private banks when robbing Jews who wanted to emigrate by using the instrument of the "Flight Tax" (*Reichsfluchtsteuer*).[4] Also, Dierker's analysis of the rivalry between the Security Service of the SS (Sicherheitsdienst or *SD*) and the Gestapo demonstrates that inter-agency competition had an radicalizing effect even in the inner circles of the persecutors.

The issue of corruption recently discussed in an important study by Frank Bajohr[5] is an aspect crucial to the understanding of the process of redistribution of Jewish property. Corruption contradicted the principal interest of state authorities in seizing the property of "enemies" for the state and, from 1939, for the support of the war effort. Bajohr suggests that a clear distinction between what he calls official, tolerated, and prosecuted corruption is hardly conceivable; the official reaction to, say, black-market activities could change over time and furthermore depended on place, on the persons involved, and on the situation. This means that the system tolerated several exceptions to state control over expropriated assets. Bajohr presents impressive material, emphasizing how common personal gain was and how big the sums of money involved were. Bajohr can even point to several cases in which functionaries pressed for the Jewish victims of their blackmail to be killed or deported to be sure that they would not claim their money back. He presents the Nazi Party as an important driving force behind corruption, calling their activities an "economic assistance program" in which "Aryanization," corruption, and the Party's illegal funding could hardly be distinguished. The Reichsrechnungshof (German Auditor General) could not prevent large sums being embezzled. It is sadly ironic and an absurd example of German bureaucracy that in July 1945, when the city of Potsdam, where this institution was located, had already been under Soviet administration for two months, the Reichsrechnungshof considered investigating the activities of Eichmann's Reichszentrale für jüdische Auswanderung (Reich Central Office for Jewish Emigration), once again because of indications of financial irregularities.[6]

Still, the question remains how useful it is to define "corruption" in such a broad way that it includes, for example, no less than much of the financing of the Nazi Party.[7] This normative term, which is commonly associated with chaos and devious practices, may obscure the view on negotiations to balance out different group interests. In principle, the assets of persons who were expropriated in Nazi Germany were to be appropriated by the state, which was to utilize them for the benefits of the "national community." Four types of competitors could come into conflict with national interests defined that way: first, private individuals (including, most importantly, public officials trying to set aside their personal share) and companies; secondly, nongovernmental organizations pursuing their particular interests, that is, mainly Nazi Party suborganizations; thirdly, public institutions (for example, regional bodies) that placed their institutional interests above the "national" interest; and, fourthly, foreign institutions, groups, or individuals whose demands were to be met.

The most important nongovernmental organization involved in the plunder of Jewish property, aside from regional Nazi Party offices inside Germany, was, not surprisingly, the SS. Correcting outdated images of an SS "victorious" in the administrative struggle in the East, Martin Dean concludes in this section that finally, by and large, the civil administration in the German-occupied Soviet territories achieved the control over the property of Soviet Jewry that it had claimed from the very beginning. The idea that the property of Jews was to be secured for the Reich remained stronger than particularism, though only after a long struggle on the upper administrative levels (whereas cooperation usually worked better at ground level). A similar development could be observed in the General Government of Poland, where the civil administration kept their hands on the real estate of murdered Jews, which the SS tried to get at least until early 1944.[8] This was a setback for the ambitions of the Reich Commissioner for the Strengthening of Germandom, an organization under the control of the SS, to organize a more systematic settlement policy in the General Government than the civil administration endorsed. The latter went to the limit in robbing the Jews. On 28 July 1942, six days after the huge deportations from the Warsaw ghetto to the Treblinka death camp had started, the Finance Department of the General Government even tried to collect the tax arrears of the murdered Jews from the organizer of the deportations, the SS and Police Leader of the District of Lublin, Odilo Globocnik. The Finance Department blackmailed Globocnik with demands that otherwise he would have to pay sales tax in retrospect for the SS-owned industrial enterprise Deutsche Ausrüstungswerke (DAW) at Lublin.[9]

Another example of rivalry between different public institutions is presented by Jonathan Petropoulos. After the annexation of Austria and the nationwide pogrom in 1938, the German state tried to control the plunder of art. But the many rival agencies—often acting in the name of highest-ranking Nazis, such as Hitler, Göring, and Himmler, but also including municipal museums—competed for the best booty in the occupied territories too. Cooperation or even "alliances" between agencies were often necessary to succeed. Art historians and art dealers constituted a network, one knowing the activities of the other and all of them gaining much for themselves. In the absence of a central institution organizing the robbery and distribution of art, such rival networks determined the outcome.

Corruption was indeed part of the Nazi system. But it would be misleading to conclude that this made it impossible for German politicians or functionaries to pursue ideological or economic plans—in regard not only to mass murder but also to the control and redistribution of property. Corruption both limited and increased the efficiency of "Aryanization." It is correct that very many of the German representatives, soldiers, police, and others in the occupied territories tried to profit for themselves, hunting for money or valuables. This is of special importance here because 95 percent of all victims of the extermination of European Jewry lived outside Germany and Austria. What happened in many places resembles the story of the Spanish forcing Inca Atahualpa to fill a room with gold items three times before killing him.

Yet the lion's share of the loot from the Holocaust consisted of real estate and land property, confiscated bank accounts, shops and factories, furniture, and household equipment. Most of this remained out of reach for corrupt officials. There was a general German policy according to which the bulk of Jewish property was to fall into the hands of the national administration, at least in most occupied countries, rather than directly into German hands, in order to cushion the burdens of the occupation and maintain some social stability. The case of French-Jewish businesses analyzed by Philippe Verheyde in this section is one example. From his sample of 175 big business companies, there was German interference in 41 cases, and only 4 percent of the capital of his sample actually fell into German hands. The reason was, Verheyde argues, "not only French [passive, C.G.] resistance ... but also a sort of self-limitation of German greed." The expropriation was based on French anti-Jewish laws of 1940–1941, stimulated or inspired by the Germans, who noted that such a policy strengthened participation in anti-Jewish persecution. Verheyde notes that, while the Germans determined the actions or gave the impulse, it was the French who organized the expropriation, creating an institution of more than 1,000 employees in 1944. Following a pattern observed in other occupied European countries as well, 97 percent of the small Jewish enterprises in France were closed to the benefit of their "Aryan" competitors.

Another example of this approach can be found in Borisov, Byelorussia, in the German-occupied Soviet territories: after the 8,000 Jews of this town with an overall population of 30,000 had been shot in October 1941, clothes, shoes, and furniture were distributed among the local Byelorussians, who lived in disastrous need of such articles. Nearly 70 percent were not given away freely but sold in order to absorb purchasing power. Finally, the German Economic Inspectorate of the Army Group Center received the proceeds of 300,000 rubles, whereas the local Byelorussian financial administration received 1.57 million Rubles.[10] The inhabitants of Borisov also benefited from empty flats and houses where the Jews had lived. In many European countries parts of the local population profited from and were corrupted by taking over large parts of the Jewish property.

The example of Hungary under German occupation in 1944 demonstrates that some dimensions of the problem of mass involvement in the Holocaust can hardly be understood if one does not take these beneficial effects into consideration. Especially the role of the state—in this case the Hungarian and, indirectly, the German state via the occupation costs —has often been neglected, a role that was invisible from the victim's perspective and for most other observers. The Hungarian state redistributed property by selling the belongings of Jews, absorbing purchasing power, and taking land and real estate to include in its budget, thus considerably contributing to the funding of the war effort, combatting imminent inflation, expanding social services for non-Jews, and mobilizing the population, satisfying it with accommodation and consumer goods. Only when the SS took over 51 percent of the shares of Hungary's biggest armament company, through blackmailing the Jewish owner family, did a substantial conflict with the Hungarian government occur, which forced Hitler personally to require Himmler to cooperate with the Hungarians.[11] In other words, the Nazi state—though not in total control—was partly able to accept and integrate corruption of its own officials, able to corrupt many people in occupied countries, and still able to take massive financial benefits from Jewish property for itself. Corruption and the ideological aims of the Nazis represented less of a contradiction than one might think, and, by and large, it seems that corruption did not paralyze the system. New questions in this direction will be needed in future research.

A comparative view on genocide and its economic underpinning may help to further elucidate the peculiarities of the Nazi system of appropriation, as well as that of one of her allies (Hungary). The expropriation of Armenian property was one of the driving forces behind the destruction of the Armenians in the Ottoman Empire during World War I. As in the cases of Germany and Hungary—and in fact with measures that were amazingly similar to those of the Hungarians—the Ottoman government tried to lay hands on all of the Armenian property. However, the ability of this state to take control, to collect, to register, and to protect the loot was much more limited. It did use Armenian farms to resettle hundreds of thousands of refugees and put former Armenian hospitals or schools at public disposal. And yet the idea of utilizing such values for general social policy purposes was less influential. Instead, the Ottoman government supported the redistribution of the most important part of Armenian property—businesses in commerce, finance, and trade—to local elites, which consisted of Muslim businessmen, party members of the Committee for Union and Progress, and the traditional elites (dignitaries and big landowners) in order to create a new commercial Muslim bourgeoisie that was considered "reliable." The method of achieving this was channelized corruption, with some control exerted by local party bureaus and new business associations.[12] By contrast, in Hungary and in Nazi Germany, economic elites took their profits from the expropriation of Jews, too, yet both states – commanding much stronger bureaucratic machineries and equipped with a different philosophy on social policy – redistributed larger sums to workers and the petite bourgeoisie in order to keep the lower classes under control.

In what has been the most extreme argument made about this to date, Götz Aly has recently argued that Nazi Germany's tax policy tended to burden the wealthy and benefit the socially weak, making use of resources gained through mass murder, the expropriations of Jews, and exploitation of occupied countries. According to Aly, who plays down the responsibility of big business for exploitation and expropriation, this made Germany Hitler's "*Volksstaat*", or a "redistributive state par excellence" (*Umverteilungsstaat*).[13]

A further important task for future research is reflected in Frank Bajohr's and Dieter Ziegler's demand that the usual administrative perspective on persecution and expropriation of the Jews be enlarged by the dimension of social history. It is necessary to reconstruct the perspective of more or less ordinary individuals, to differentiate between the opportunities they had for action and all the—perhaps contradictory—motives for the way in which they finally acted. The empirical basis for this undertaking, however, is problematic. New sources and a new look at them will be needed for a comprehensive understanding of the plunder of Jewish property and of the Holocaust, in order to understand it as a process created and sustained by individuals.

Notes

1. See Peter Hüttenberger, "Nationalsozialistische Polykratie," *Geschichte und Gesellschaft* 2 (1976): 417–442.
2. Hans Mommsen, "Hitlers Stellung im nationalsozialistischen Herrschaftssystem" and "Die Realisierung des Utopischen: Die 'Endlösung der Judenfrage' im 'Dritten Reich'," in Hans Mommsen, *Der Nationalsozialismus und die deutsche Gesellschaft* (Reinbek, 1991), pp. 67–101 and pp. 184–232 (the articles were first published in 1981 and 1983, respectively).
3. One recent example is in Ian Kershaw, *Hitler: 1936–1945: Nemesis* (London, 2000).
4. See also Susanne Heim, "Vertreibung, Raub und Umverteilung: Die jüdischen Flüchtlinge aus Deutschland und die Vermehrung des Volksvermögens," in *Flüchtlingspolitik und Fluchthilfe* (Beiträge zur nationalsozialistischen Gesundheits- und Sozialpolitik, vol. 15, Berlin, 1999), pp. 107–138; Hans-Dieter Schmid, "'Finanztod': Die Zusammenarbeit von Gestapo und Finanzverwaltung bei der Ausplünderung der Juden in Deutschland," in Gerhard Paul and Klaus-Michael Mallmann, eds., *Die Gestapo im Zweiten Weltkrieg: "Heimatfront" und besetztes Europa* (Darmstadt, 2000), pp. 141–154.
5. Frank Bajohr, *Parvenüs und Profiteure: Korruption in der NS-Zeit* (Frankfurt on Main, 2001); see also Bajohr's contribution to this section.
6. See German Federal Archives (BA) file R 2301, No. 8420.
7. See the definition in Bajohr, *Parvenüs und Profiteure*, pp. 7–11.
8. Peter Witte et al. eds., *Der Dienstkalender Heinrich Himmlers 1941/42* (Hamburg, 1999), p. 647, n. 77.
9. "I refer to our conversation on 28 July 1942, and ask you to pay the tax arrears of the Jews (especially of the Jews from Warsaw) from the assets seized during their resettlement. Then I shall decide about an exemption [of the DAW, C.G.] from the sales tax for the period from 1 January 1942 to 30 June 1942." Copy of an undated letter to Globocnik; see also Globocnik to Finanzamt Lublin, 21 July 1942; Generalgouvernement, Stadthauptmann Lublin, Finanzinspekteur, to Regierung des Generalgouvernements, Abteilung Finanzen, 24 July 1942; and Regierung des Generalgouvernements, Hauptabteilung Finanzen, 29 August 1942, all in Archivum Akt Novych (Warsaw), 111, no. 1188, pp. 155, 158–159 (back side). Globocnik had requested a tax exemption for the DAW because they were a "political" and "armaments" institution rather than a business run for profit. It had been decided that the DAW had to pay the tax for the period after 1 July 1942, in any case.
10. Rayon-Leiter Borissow to Wirtschaftskommando Borissow, letter of 5 May 1942 and account 8 September 1941 to 1 April 1942, Oblast Archive Minsk 624-1-8, p. 128 and p. 131; Economic Inspectorate Center, Situation Report of 7 March 1942, German Federal Military Archive Freiburg (BA-MA) F 42858, p. 824.
11. Christian Gerlach and Götz Aly, *Das letzte Kapitel: Realpolitik, Ideologie und der Mord an den ungarischen Juden 1944/45* (Stuttgart/Munich, 2002), pp. 186–239, 319–321.
12. See Christian Gerlach, "Nationsbildung im Krieg: Wirtschaftliche Faktoren bei der Vernichtung der Armenier und beim Mord an den ungarischen Juden," in Hans-Lukas Kieser and Dominik Schaller, eds., *The Armenian Genocide and the Shoah* (Zurich, 2002), pp. 347–422.
13. Götz Aly, "Hitlers Volksstaat," *Süddeutsche Zeitung*, 10 May 2002.

CHAPTER 2

THE SS SECURITY SERVICE AND THE GESTAPO IN THE NATIONAL SOCIALIST PERSECUTION OF THE JEWS, 1933–1939

Wolfgang Dierker

The SS and the police under the command of Heinrich Himmler were among the chief actors in National Socialist extermination policy. Historians of the Holocaust often tend to regard the two different parts of the SS and police apparatus, the Security Service of the Reichsführer-SS (Sicherheitsdienst—SD) and the Gestapo (Geheime Staatspolizei—Secret State Police), as a single unit.[1] This is entirely justified for the Second World War. The union of their central offices in the Reich Security Main Office (Reichssicherheitshauptamt—RSHA) on 27 September 1939 and their operations in the conquered areas of Europe led to a fusion of SD and Gestapo personnel and institutions; the respective memberships, offices, tasks, and activities became increasingly difficult to separate. But in the prewar years it was a different matter, and the present contribution consequently takes a step back in time. Studies of the ideological policy of the SD Main Office are used[2] to show how the combination of the SD and the Gestapo crystallized and then developed into an instrument of surveillance and coercion based on a division of labor by the beginning of the Second World War. The example of SD Jewish policy shows especially clearly how specific functional assignments and organizational forms influenced both the relationships of the two persecutory organs and the fundamental ideological motivation of persecutory praxis.[3] Within a few years the SD became the most efficient, sober, and radical advocate of the "dejewification (*Entjudung*) of Germany."[4] A complex relationship to the Gestapo, characterized by both conflict and cooperation, was constitutive of the Security Service. The development of the SD in the pre-war period will be examined from this viewpoint: first the specific features of its functions and organizational structure (I), then its working relationships with the Gestapo

(II), and finally the relationship of National Socialist ideology and political practice in the Jewish policy of the SS Intelligence Service (SS-Nachrichtendienst) (III).

I

In August 1931 the retired lieutenant (Oberleutnant zur See a.D.), Reinhard Heydrich was appointed to take over intelligence duties in the SS Reich High Command (Reichsführung SS).[5] Filled with ambition and a thirst for action, he built up an independent, centrally organized intelligence service and in July 1932 was appointed by Himmler to serve as head of what then was called the "Security Service" (Sicherheitsdienst).[6] As part of the SS, which was based on principles of racial-biological selection, political-ideological radicalism, and military orientation,[7] the Security Service's mission was to ferret out actual and alleged adversaries of National Socialism. The "enemy's fighting methods" were already a central issue in a speech given by the newly commissioned Intelligence Officer Heydrich to SS leaders on 26 August 1931. He warned against the treasonous subversion and spying by the Party's enemies and called for "extreme caution in the way members spoke among themselves about matters of concern to the Party."[8] The Intelligence Officer fanned his audience's fears of hidden traitors in their ranks and simultaneously drew their attention to the need for an effective counterintelligence service such as the one he had just taken over.

In the early period of NS rule the Security Service was politically rather unimportant. Its most important allies were Rudolf Hess, the "Deputy of the Führer," his Chief of Staff, Martin Bormann, and a few NSDAP Reich leaders, who had come to appreciate Himmler's intelligence service as a useful instrument in disputes with the Gauleiter (regional party leaders) and other forces struggling for autonomy in the NSDAP. The regime crisis of early 1934, fostered by dissatisfaction brewing in the SA, assisted the political establishment of the SD. On 9 June 1934 Hess named it the party's sole intelligence and counter-intelligence service and instructed the Gauleiter to pay a certain sum to the Reich leadership to finance it.[9] Three weeks later the alliance of the Party leadership with Himmler's security organs proved its value, as they played a considerable role in the murders of 30 June 1934.[10] After the "Röhm affair" the Schutzstaffel ("Protection Squad"), formerly subordinate to the SA, was elevated to an independent NSDAP organization, and in the following years it enjoyed a vast expansion in its political power. This finally led to the building up of a huge system of concentration camps and industrial enterprises, its own auxiliary army in the form of the Waffen-SS and a unified Reich Police, linked together with the SS and SD. Against the resistance of NS leaders like the Reich Minister of the Interior, Frick, who stood up for the primacy of regular state authorities, Himmler succeeded in establishing a vast power apparatus, which he increasingly detached from traditional government and administrative networks.

Himmler managed to prevail because his political maneuvers were always tied to ideological goals. The persistent expansion of his power was inseparably linked with a conviction that National Socialism was engaged in a secular struggle with its adversaries, with "ultra-Montanism" and "Bolshevism," Jews and Free Masons. "Germany stands at the beginning of a conflict which will perhaps continue for centuries," he prophesied in March 1936 to the Prussian State Councilors (Staatsräten)—"perhaps the deciding world conflict with these forces of organized sub-humanity."[11] In his basic conviction, Himmler knew he was of one mind with Hitler, whose boundless sense of mission led him to believe that he must lead the German people to new greatness by pursuing inner consolidation of the nation and external conquests. Hitler strove by means of military conquest to expand the German people's "*Lebensraum*" and at the same time to destroy its adversaries, Jewry and Bolshevism. In the end, however, he was driven by extravagant visions of worldwide domination, racial-biological "cleansing," and a perfect "ethnic community" (*Volksgemeinschaft*) which would bring all historical change to an end.[12] Hitler and Himmler agreed that Safeguarding the Reich from within against the alleged enemies of the National Socialist new order— Hitler and Himmler agreed on this was thereby of the greatest significance— a consequence of defeat in World War I, which was falsely attributed to a "stab in the back" by enemies at home. Himmler was determined to ferret out all the enemies of National Socialism in advance, learn everything about them, and fight them ruthlessly. It appeared that only a new security concept could guarantee this, one going beyond previous approaches and which was soon referred to as a State Security Corps (Staatsschutzkorps).[13] The entire State Police and the Schutzstaffel were to be merged to form a reliable ideological apparatus free of all the constraints of the constitutional state and directly responsible to the Führer. Despite recognizable reservations about the growing influence and limitless zeal of the Reichsführer-SS, Hitler gave him the decisive backing he needed to consolidate his authority continually.[14]

In this process the Security Service acquired a key role. On 4 July 1934 it was recognized by the leaders of the Political Police as the sole Party intelligence service, as it already had been four weeks previously by the NSDAP leadership. Its function was officially termed an "essential complement" to the state executive organs.[15] That the enemies of National Socialism could only be effectively combated by the two organs working together was affirmed by Himmler and Heydrich in December 1934, who agreed that as a "principle for a clear separation of the operational spheres" the police had to "fend off and counter the enemies of the National Socialist state," while the "SD keeps track of the enemies of the National Socialist idea and encourages the state police authorities in their struggle against them."[16] To dispel any reservations of the ministerial bureaucracy and suspicious Party leaders, they expressly emphasized that executive measures were exclusively the responsibility of the police and were denied to the SD, whose activities were restricted to intelligence-service tasks. This affirmation of a basic division of the terror apparatus into two parts secured the Reichsführer-SS and

Heydrich a basis of political power, in regard not only to the Party, but also to the state. According to the intention of its creators, the Security Service was to function as an ideological leadership, as an "inner elite,"[17] so to speak, of the state security corps that was being set up. As the sole counter-intelligence service of the NS movement, lacking the executive powers of the police, the SD was to operate "with the calm of an intellectual corps,"[18] to grasp the current and future political situation, and to track down the covert ideological counter-forces.

After the Security Service had proved its worth in the course of the "Röhm affair," Heydrich transferred his headquarters to Berlin in late summer 1934.[19] There the Security Office moved into the Prinz-Albrecht-Palais at Wilhelmstrasse 102, an imposing building in the immediate neighborhood of the Secret State Police Office (Gestapa).[20] On 30 January 1935 the SD was elevated to the status of an SS main office, the Main Security Office (Sicherheitshauptamt—SDHA),[21] and at the same time a basic reorganization began, which was completed a year later with a series of central decrees. So that the Security Service could function effectively during the years in which it was being built up, its leaders created a rigidly centralized, inflexible organizational structure. Only in this way did it appear possible to master its heavy workload in a reliable fashion, especially since the Security Service was a new, chronically underfinanced institution whose hastily thrown together staff could at first hardly keep step with the Gestapo's superior bureaucratic apparatus. An important organizational aid was a detailed division of responsibilities that regulated the systematic structure and relative status of all departments, even though it only described the actual tasks and competencies to a limited degree. The earliest surviving plans for the division of responsibilities from 1933/34 already list, although in different order, nearly all later SD surveillance areas. Dealt with were the National Socialist and ethnic German opposition, the churches under the heading "religion and ideology," Marxism and the Jews, separatism and pacifism; for Free Masonry there was even a separate department with a library, card index, archive, and museum. The surveillance of the most diverse sociopolitical domains, the later "spheres of life" (*Lebensgebiete*) of education and science, art and culture, law and economy, were also included, as well as foreign surveillance areas and counter-espionage as the nucleus of the foreign intelligence service.[22]

On 15 January 1936 a new division of responsibilities was introduced for the Security Service, which remained valid over the next few years.[23] Within the SD Main Office (SD-Hauptamt) there were now three offices, which were designated with Roman numerals. The most striking innovation was the broader distribution and finer differentiation of the individual surveillance areas, with no less than four further levels being created within individual offices. They ranged from the central department through the main department and department to the individual sections (Referate) and they were designated with up to four additional Arabic numerals. Thus Referat II 1121 (Zionists) was grouped with further sections under Department II

112 (Jewry), this in turn coming under Main Department II 11 (ideology), which was again incorporated into Central Department II 1 in Office II of the SD Main Office. This complex, multilevel structure, which at times irritated even the employees at the SD Main Office,[24] was not a sort of "number cabalism" (*Zahlenkabbalismus*) intended to confuse outsiders.[25] Rather, it contributed to a still more detailed management of intelligence-service work, by transferring the various administrative functions to separate levels. At the same time, it was intended to facilitate the systematic combination of the countless individual observations of all enemy groups and spheres of life into a comprehensive overall picture of the political and ideological situation. The spectrum of the operational areas was so wide and differentiated that initially it greatly exceeded the capacity of the SD and could only be regarded as an ambitious declaration of intent. It nevertheless reflected the claim, shaped by ideological images of the enemy, to become a comprehensive intelligence service: if the adversaries of National Socialism were simultaneously active in worldwide networks and operating covertly in all spheres of life, the intelligence service must be equally omnipresent, networked and covert in its work of identifying and combating the enemy. The perception of the totality of the enemies of National Socialism, itself a consequence of unbounded ideological conceptions of its aims, seemed to make the totality of SD surveillance and reporting absolutely indispensable. The director of the SD Domestic Intelligence Service (SD-Inlandsnachrichtendienst), Franz Alfred Six, proclaimed in July 1937

> that intelligence-service work should be activated in the entire area of II 1. The Intelligence Service must adapt itself to the nature of the adversary. Since, however, the various adversaries are all mutually interlinked, intelligence-service activity cannot exclude a priori a single adversary. The intelligence service must of necessity be total.[26]

II

Of the greatest importance for the activities of the security organs was the relationship between the SD and the Gestapo. According to a widespread opinion the situation was characterized by an uncomfortable and laborious coexistence, even antagonism, because the same tasks were assigned to both the Party Intelligence Service and the Secret State Police. This apparently led to the Decree on Functions (*Funktionserlass*) of 1 July 1937 through which the different duties and areas of competence of the services were demarcated.[27] However, studies of SD Jewish and church policy show that up to mid 1937 the relationship to the State Police was more complex than previously assumed and can best be described as conflict-prone complementation. The Gestapo and Security Service cooperated with and complemented each other effectively when they investigated the suspect activities of members of Catholic orders, took measures against Jehovah's Witnesses,[28] or monitored

Jewish assemblies in synagogues and cultural centers.[29] In its Jewish policy specifically the SD managed to establish itself as an ideological intelligence service, because unlike the Gestapo it was not obliged to justify its measures as responses to violations of legal provisions such as the Nuremberg Laws.[30] Compared with other state organs of the Third Reich the Gestapo was far better trained ideologically and politically radicalized, but it still acted in a more predictable and moderate manner than the SS Intelligence Service, as it took the political consequences of its coercive measures for the state into consideration.[31]

In progress reports the relationship of the SD and the Political Police was generally regarded as good and this was supported by ongoing discussions among the officials concerned, in which they exchanged information gleaned from previous work and made suggestions for future measures.[32] Nevertheless, the record of the years between 1933 and 1937 gave the lie to all greater expectations that the Security Service would establish itself as a total intelligence service for party and state and would operate "with the calm of an intellectual corps" to guide the regime's struggle against its ideological enemies. In lengthy memoranda SD experts developed political solutions and strategies, but they met with little response in important places.[33] At the same time, in order to achieve tangible success and to legitimize its activities, the SD turned to the same fields of work as the Secret State Police. It investigated actual or alleged violations of the law by enemies in the hope of finding points at which it could actively intervene.[34] But it continued to be at a disadvantage in comparison with the Gestapo with its monopoly over the implementation of direct coercive measures and its well-developed bureaucratic apparatus. Members of the Security Service could of course suggest measures of implementation and also participate in them, but usually they could not carry them out independently. The Secret State Police, however, was not willing to waive its competence voluntarily in particular areas. It did not limit itself by any means to combating the adversaries of National Socialism "with direct executive means," but made an effort to acquire the "necessary intelligence and surveillance capacities to prepare for this defensive struggle."[35]

The different understanding of their duties in the Security Service and Secret State Police contributed greatly to the tensions that existed despite all complementation and cooperation. Even though the officials of the SD Main Office and the Gestapa were still striving for smooth working relationships, in the provinces open differences of opinion and conflicts often prevailed. Here the institutional and conceptual dualism laid down by the respective headquarters had to be harmonized with specific local conditions and requirements, at times even affecting interpersonal relationships. Thus at the SD local office (Unterabschnitt) in Koblenz a small number of employees faced a far larger Gestapo apparatus and found it extremely hard to assert themselves in their field against Secret State Police competition. It was not without a certain plaintive tone that they complained about the "uncomradely" behavior of the State Police officials, who ignored the results of their work, did not let them take part in measures of implementation, and once, after a joint nightly interrogation operation even refused to drive an SD leader home in a police car.³⁶ In the Palatinate an acrimonious dispute arose in March 1936 about a former SD informer whom the Bavarian Political Police had arrested, at the instigation of the local Gau leadership, because of false and insulting reports. The Gestapa took over the investigation and, despite several SD admonishments, evidently made sure that the documents confiscated from the informer were not released.³⁷

Such tensions can in the end be traced back to the continued existence of the two separate security organs desired by Himmler and Heydrich. They were well aware that this sowed the seeds of interminable disputes over competence. This is shown by numerous decrees and orders in which members of both "branches" of the oppression apparatus were admonished to cooperate more closely and more amicably.³⁸ Despite all the duplication of work and competition, the surveillance of ideological adversaries was continued by both branches with the greatest energy. It was often precisely because of this overlapping that their work achieved considerable depth. Both at the center and in the regions the institutional parallelism resulted in the Gestapo and SD monitoring and goading each other on. The SS Intelligence Service used the task assigned to it of supporting the investigative work of the Gestapo in order to examine its ideological orientation and consistency and to send on any complaints to headquarters. Often the Security Service postured as the guardian of ideological correctness and fielded its ideological "competence" as a counter-weight to the organizational superiority of the Gestapo. Thus Theodor Dannecker, responsible in the SD Jewish Affairs Department for assimilated Jews, complained that the Gestapo was carrying on the struggle against the Jews "in an exclusively administrative fashion," lacked the required professional expertise, was completely ineffective in Jewish policy, and acted without the necessary sense of the ideological implications.³⁹ Conversely, SD officials had to endure Gestapo lecturing when they failed to fulfill their intelligence-service duties. Should the Security Service fail to set up a network of informers in various different enterprises, the Director of the Domestic Policy Department of the Gestapa, Heinrich Müller, threatened in March 1937 that "he would have to make the necessary arrangements within the State Police." The department head concerned, Wolf, thereupon obligingly assured him that this would be "worked on energetically."⁴⁰

The competition between the Gestapo and the SD to avoid being outdone by each other in their intelligence-service professionalism and ideological resolve increased the effectiveness and radicalism of the overall apparatus. This was the desired but not purposefully pursued result of the simultaneous existence of two parallel institutions and made supervision and administration easier for Heydrich. He let both security organs work according to their own principles and this kept the dualism alive, which suited his own power-seeking political and ideological intentions. These advantages were accompanied by considerable disadvantages, however. Among them was, above all, the widespread duplication of work and wasted energy caused by continuing friction among regional offices. Especially problematic was the situation of the SD departments responsible for "adversaries" like Communists, Jews, or "political churches." Here the function of the SD as a mere auxiliary of the State Police was not only questionable in itself but clearly becoming obsolete, because these adversaries had already been largely eliminated or seldom acted as social groups capable of united action. Their presence was consequently often only manifest in the actions of individuals in various spheres of life such as schools and universities, culture, administration, and the economy. Dieter Wisliceny and Herbert Hagen, officials responsible for Jewish matters, ascertained in 1937 "that in the future the main activities of enemies will be increasingly concentrated in their spheres of life."[41] Their intelligence-service surveillance, and also the pseudo-scientific research on the historical development and ideological foundations of "adversaries," as practiced by Franz Alfred Six in the SD Main Office,[42] increasingly moved into the foreground. This gradual change of function was favored by the Gestapo practice of leaving to the Security Service documents not directly useful in executive actions and also of providing it with information on current events for ideological evaluation. For the Jewish Affairs department of the SD Main Office, Wisliceny and Hagen concluded from this that the State Police recognized "a certain intellectual leadership of the SD."[43]

Continuing conflict and the costs of friction prompted Heydrich in July 1937 to define once again the principles underlying the relationship between the Gestapo and the SD. The impetus apparently came from the operational field of Marxism, where, after the rapid containment of Communist resistance, the duplication of effort had become most clearly apparent. The Security Service did of course insist on its claim to work on the intellectual roots of this enemy, its historical development, and its relationships to other hostile groups.[44] All efforts to coordinate the activities of the departments involved, Department II 121 of the SD Main Office and Office II 1 A of the Gestapa, failed due to the "impossibility of separating the intelligence service and the executive agency in the fight against illegal Marxism."[45] The directors concerned, Martin Wolf and Heinrich Müller, finally reached an agreement in early 1937 "that the previous situation is unacceptable."[46] When Müller then tried to persuade Heydrich to detach Department II 121 from the Security Main Office without more ado and to place it entirely under the Gestapa, Wolf responded with a counter-proposal for fundamental reorganization. Both security organizations would have to continue to operate side by side, he explained, but in the future the SD should concentrate on intelligence-service work in the spheres of life, while the Gestapo alone should be responsible for the surveillance and combating of individual enemies.[47] Heydrich, however, was as much opposed to the complete dissolution of the SD department dealing with enemies desired by Müller as he was to Wolf's ideas on extensive reorganization. Instead, on 1 July 1937 he issued a "Joint Directive for the Security Service of the Reichsführer-SS and the Secret State

Police," which adopted elements of both proposals but left everything essentially as it had been.[48]

The so-called Decree on Functions divided all the operational areas into three categories. Above all the "spheres of life" and the politically rather secondary questions of Free Masonry, foreign countries, and associations were placed under the SD's exclusive jurisdiction. In contrast, the Gestapo received exclusive jurisdiction in three sensitive security-policy areas: Marxism, treason, and emigrants. Finally, the areas of joint responsibility, in which the SD was to deal with "all matters … that are general and fundamental (whereby active intervention by the State Police is ruled out)" and the Gestapo was to deal with all individual cases, including most enemies—churches, sects, other religious and ideological groups, pacifism, Jewry, right-wing movements, and other groups hostile to the state—as well as the economy and the press. In principle, all offices of the Gestapo and the SD were expected in future to turn over to their respective counterparts all the proceedings for which, because of the subject matter or for technical reasons, they were no longer directly responsible. This principle was considerably broadened and complicated by the various stipulations on the need for countersignatures, the evaluation of all Gestapa procedures in the joint areas of responsibility by the SD Main Office, and recourse to the State Police for implementation measures in areas falling within the exclusive competence of the SD.[49]

In Security Service praxis the stipulations of the Decree on Functions produced only a few fundamental innovations. Department II 121 did keep the assignment to deal "intellectually and scientifically with Marxism,"[50] but lost its entire institutional substructure, including the undercover agents (*V-Männer*), and had to hand over the greater part of its files.[51] As a result of the Decree on Functions, the Church Department of the SD Main Office received still greater quantities of older and, for executive purposes, useless Gestapo files, which reinforced its commitment to the ideological research on enemies of the system advocated by Six. The Jewish Affairs Department of the SD Main Office, on the contrary, managed to expand its area of jurisdiction. On Six's orders, Hagen had already examined the entire file material of the relevant Gestapa Office in June 1937, and now Department II 112 took over even currently open investigation files from the State Police.[52] The self-confidence of the SD "Jewish experts" grew. They had forged links with the Reich Ministry of the Interior and the Foreign Office, announced Hagen, who continued: "The ultimate goal, which will be presented in more detail in a report to C [Heydrich] still in preparation, is the centralization of the entire processing of the Jewish question in Germany in the SD and Gestapa."[53]

The Decree on Functions produced neither a reformulation of previous duties nor a clear demarcation of areas of competence. It reinforced the former assignment of functions to the Gestapo and Security Service, called on their officials to cooperate on good terms and to this extent had, above all else, the character of an appeal. Both branches of the security apparatus continued to be entrusted with the task of combating the enemies of National

Socialism, the one as a police executive organ, the other as an intellectual and ideological intelligence service. To this end both continued to work in almost all operational fields, both in their formerly "exclusive" areas of competence, which in the past had often been breached by changes in the right to evaluate or to countersign documents, and in the fields of shared jurisdiction. It was precisely the adversaries considered to be long-term threats who continued to fall within the competence of both branches, in order to guarantee their being dealt with "fundamentally," i.e., intellectually and ideologically by the SS Intelligence Service and practically by suppression on the part of the State Police.[54] The internal relationship of the SD and the Gestapo "is determined neither by competition nor by hierarchies of superior and inferior standing," as the introductory sentence of the Decree on Functions summarized, "but rather by complementation and avoidance of all duplication."[55] The Reichsführer-SS and the head of the SD rejected a fundamentally new organizational arrangement and preferred to leave everything in a state of suspense. In this way they took the conception of a twofold state security corps into account, which would guarantee the "total struggle against enemies" and at the same time preserve the politically advantageous dualism of party and state. That Heydrich was by no means consciously and cynically playing the two security organs off against each other[56] is shown by his numerous calls for peaceful cooperation, which he also repeated the day the Decree on Functions was promulgated.[57]

With the Decree on Functions, Himmler and Heydrich had avoided a fundamental reorganization of the difficult relationships of the Security Police and the SD. For numerous reasons, however, the problems and the pressure continued to increase. Immediately after the start of the war an internal and external reorganization began whose most outstanding expression was the newly founded Reich Security Main Office. The closer integration of Gestapo, Kripo (Police Criminal Investigation Departement), and SD, as well as other organizational changes, lasted until early 1941 and hastened the unification of the security organs led by Heydrich. The immediate reason for the reorganization was a variety of problems, which, again, affected above all the Security Service. The intelligence-service apparatus had long suffered from a great scarcity of suitable employees, because the career prospects in the SD, salaries, benefits, and professional advancement opportunities were relatively unattractive.[58] The head of the Church Policy Department of the SD Main Office had to confess in late 1938

> that many employees see no further advancement opportunities in Department II 113 for themselves at the age of about thirty years and are therefore trying to return to their former profession outside state service or to transfer to other party offices where there is a sufficient economic basis for founding a family.[59]

After the "annexation" of Austria, the shortage of personnel again grew considerably due to numerous special assignments and the creation of new offices.⁶⁰ The question arose more urgently than before whether the multi-layered and complex SD intelligence apparatus could be preserved in its entirety. It required an enormously large expenditure of labor but was maintained for the sake of "total comprehension" and the surveillance needs of the headquarters. The relationship with the Gestapo, inadequately regulated by the Decree on Functions, continued to be problematic because of the duplication of labor in many areas. Finally, the degree of penetration and repression of the various enemy groups achieved up to that point cast doubt on the SD's previous working methods. The officials of the Jewish Affairs Department had for years evaluated the relevant publications and files, spied on Jewish personalities and assemblies, and built up conspiratorial ties to Jews at home and abroad. In early 1938 this intelligence-service investigation of the ideological enemy seemed to have been completed. In annexed Austria the SD experts for Jewish affairs could find no additional material that promised further insight: "The entire material is scarcely worth evaluating for intelligence-service purposes," stated the SD leader concerned in summing up his assessment of the confiscated files: "It can, however, still be drawn on for historical work."⁶¹ The limitation of the SD to the surveillance of the "spheres of life" and the tasks of a "scientific" research institution seemed to be an inevitable development, and the further exclusion and persecution of the Jews could just as well be taken over by the Gestapo. From early 1939 far-reaching organizational changes were in the offing, which disturbed SD officials, because in the given state of affairs these could only work to their disadvantage.⁶² A conference of the heads of the Jewish departments held in February 1939 decided that the previous strategy, especially the concentration of Jews in large cities, should of course continue, but that the staff of the SD offices should be considerably trimmed. Stricter qualification requirements for SD staff following the model of the Gestapo or even transfers from previous positions were not, however, planned.⁶³

Ultimately the new order aimed at by Heydrich and his deputies was formally realized at the moment the war began, as part of the mobilization of the SS and the police. On 1 September 1939 a "mobilization order" already stipulated numerous organizational, technical and material restrictions.⁶⁴ Ideological enemies were no longer to be dealt with by the SD using intelligence-service methods at all, and should only be taken into consideration in the context of the surveillance of the "spheres of life." Two days later, however, these stipulations were relaxed. "Political churches," emigration, pacifism, and reaction would continue to be dealt with to a limited extent by the offices previously responsible, since here the "seriousness of the threat and the systematic nature of enemy activities" did not permit "their influence to be determined solely in the spheres of life."⁶⁵ Internal RSHA investigation of enemies such as "Jewry," "Free Masonry," and "Bolshevism" using intelligence-service methods was, however, transferred to the corresponding Gestapo offices. Frequent reporting of morale and the general state of affairs was declared to be the major task of the domestic intelligence service in the future. In the form of "Reports from the Reich," it became the most important field of activity of the domestic SD.⁶⁶

In order to maintain the appearance of separate party and state organizations, Himmler and Heydrich's fundamental decrees of 27 September 1939 created an institution that could be referred to only internally as the Reich Security Main Office (Reichssicherheitshauptamt), but externally was to be referred to as the Head of the Security Police and the SD (Chef der Sicherheitspolizei und des SD) or using the previously customary terms.[67] In this umbrella organization the individual branches were retained in the form of departments (Ämter), among them the former counter-intelligence service of the SD in Amt II under Franz Six and the intelligence service for the "spheres of life" as Amt III under Otto Ohlendorf. For the assignment of work to the different departments a unified classification into department, group and section (Amt, Gruppe und Referat) was set up, which considerably simplified the SD's complex, five-level organizational scheme by replacing three hierarchical levels of the SD Main Office—central department, main department and department—with a single one in the form of the sections.[68] Now the external change of function in the SD began, leading by spring 1941 to the full transfer of its intelligence-service activities against the enemies of the Reich to the Gestapo. This was merely a precondition for the rapidly progressing fusion of both organizations during the Second World War. Even if Heydrich continued to defend the duality of the security apparatus, which alone could effectively research, investigate, and fight the enemies of National Socialism,[69] the Security Service had already largely fulfilled its task as the "inner elite" of the state security corps. As the crimes of the Einsatzgruppen (mobile killing squads) in the Soviet Union show, the Security Police and the SD had long since become a unified, ideologically oriented and violence-prone state security corps.[70]

III

By the start of the war the Security Service and Secret State Police had merged to form a single organ, which in the following years persecuted its victims with unequalled brutality and ruthlessness. Conflict and complementation characterized the relationship of the two organs and radicalized their actions. In the case of the SD the concrete power-seeking political aspect, which was also attributable to the SD's particular sense of mission and organizational network, was also imbued with somewhat abstract ideological motives. Ideological models, on the one hand, and institutional constraints and concern with power, on the other, interacted and contributed decisively to the radicalization of the entire apparatus. This tense relationship is treated in numerous historical studies of the National Socialist persecution of the Jews. The essential question is whether the SD and Gestapo members involved acted chiefly on the basis of their ideological convictions or because of political interests and constraints. Put pointedly: Should we regard the SD leaders concerned as ideological planners and strategists, or were they primarily motivated by concern for power?

The major finding of research, that National Socialist genocide stemmed largely from Hitler's universal racial ideology and was purposefully implemented by the NS leadership clique,[71] has been challenged by historians with a structural orientation, who support the notion of "cumulative radicalization."[72] According to this view, it was the Führer's propagandistic rather than programmatic statements of intent, the violent power-seeking political rivalries of his followers, and the self-propelling mechanisms of the bureaucratic apparatus that ultimately led to an unbounded definition of the enemy and the attendant escalation of violence. In the unconstrained expansion of the NS regime, Hitler's ideological metaphors became the sole reliable legitimization, from which the agencies of persecution derived increasingly abstract, even fictitious, conceptions of the enemy that finally plunged them into an orgy of mass murder.[73] In recent studies this model has been refined and modified; above all, historians have worked out the significance of the local authorities, which tried to resolve conflicts of interest and overcome self-created situational constraints by introducing increasingly draconian solutions.[74] Finally, studies of National Socialist "ideological elites" have introduced the convictions and mentalities of the actors responsible as key factors in the analysis of the radicalization process.[75] According to Ulrich Herbert, the ideological legitimization and motivational strategies of the perpetrators were of decisive importance precisely because the extermination policy was a cumulative process influenced by many actors and not simply a long-planned and centrally orchestrated mass-murder program.[76] As the "core group of the genocide," the members of the Security Police and the SD justified their actions to themselves and others with the claim that they were contributing to the realization of the ethnic, sociobiological reform plans of National Socialism. This motivating and legitimating ideology was supposedly based on the arbitrarily postulated highest "life value" (*Lebenswert*) of the people rather than a "catalogue of fundamental values" and in the end it served no concrete, positive objectives, but solely the acquisition and expansion of political power: "[And] since the final state striven for, even if not exactly defined, failed to materialize, a dynamic process was set in motion which made more and more groups responsible for this failure and worked for their 'elimination.'"[77]

Ideological elements doubtless exerted great influence on the political actions of SD leaders. They were convinced that the elimination of ideological enemies was merely a precondition for creating a completely new order of man and society, which they worked for confidently, aware that they knew the laws of historical development and the final purpose of history. The images of the enemy and the sense of mission of the SD ideological warriors were as sweeping and comprehensive as this vision of a new order, and any compromise seemed correspondingly unacceptable. Adolf Eichmann referred to the Jews as the "eternal enemy" and rejected any conceivable doubt about this identification of the adversary: "All objections and proposals for an understanding of them which can be foreseen must be rejected in advance as invalid because we know that the Jew is one of the most dangerous enemies—because he will never be entirely understandable."[78] Such unrestrained conceptions of the enemy and the goals to be pursued contributed to the incessant demands for a political praxis involving more radical and systematic exclusion and persecution of the Jews. In a November 1937 report on "inner-German Jewry," Dannecker insisted that the SD's chief task consisted "in the total exclusion of assimilated Jews from Jewish political life in order to bring the Jewish question in Germany closer to its final solution."[79]

Saul Friedländer regards "redemptive anti-Semitism" as the key to understanding National Socialist persecution of the Jews. Hitler and his followers accordingly understood the most important precondition for a superior culture and powerful state to be the "racial purity" of the German people. The presence of the Jewish "race" in its midst threatened the survival and claim to domination of the German nation and made their violent expulsion and extermination the sole means of warding off this danger.[80] Friedländer sees in this unique form of anti-Semitism a "vision of world history in which the rescue and salvation of the Aryan race depended solely on eliminating an evil force whose dangerousness allegedly grew with each passing day: the Jews."[81] But even if the persecution of the Jews dominated during the Second World War, especially in retrospect, in the 1930s other enemies were assigned a similarly high status by the SD. This is shown by the conflict with the Christian churches and religious communities, where the definition of the enemy and "research" alone were more demanding and laborious than in the case of Jewish "adversaries." It was not for nothing that after its establishment the department for "political churches" (SDHA II 113) remained by far the largest in the SD Main Office; in mid 1938 it had a staff of sixteen, while the Jewish Affairs Department had only seven.[82] The ideological foundation of National Socialist policies of violence was broader than it seems in view of the widespread concentration of contemporary historians on the persecution of the Jews. This is demonstrated precisely in Reinhard Heydrich's programmatic text quoted by Friedländer, Transformations of our Struggle (*Wandlungen unseres Kampfes*), which is mainly based on preliminary work by the SD Main Office.[83] The head of the SD names not merely the network of Jewish organizations, but also convinced Communists, Catholics, and Free Masons as the greatest threats to National Socialism, which as a political movement depended on its world view.[84] Besides the Jews, Heydrich regarded the "political churches" as the most dangerous adversaries. An "entirely political clerical bureaucracy with secular ambitions," he explained, appeared outwardly to accept the "spiritual and racial values of our people," in order to "systematically undermine the character and spirit of the German people."[85] The high value assigned to ideologically based images of the enemy can be inferred from the written statements of leading National Socialists and their political actions, but not the primacy of any one enemy group.

The "police version" of redemptive anti-Semitism, Friedländer continues, also explains the in itself inexplicable process by which the Security Service and Gestapo transformed the manifestations of life of a small social minority into an omnipresent Jewish conspiracy. No detail and no individual organization was too insignificant to be recorded and documented by SD Jewish experts: "Jewish organizations were identified, analyzed, and studied as parts of an ever more complex system; the anti-German activities of that system had to be discovered, its inner workings decoded, its true nature unveiled."[86] The images of the enemy and the violent measures are only explicable in their unconstrained radicalism if the underlying visionary conceptions of an absolute new order are taken into account. Hitler, Himmler and other NS leaders dreamed of "new men," of German world domination, "ethnic purification" and a perfect "ethnic community", and the Security Service acted with them in the name of this ethnic utopia.[87] "The world conspiracy scenarios, as presented for example by Eichmann, are consistent ideological constructs whose unreal contents in no way diminished their real power," Michael Wildt concludes: "The SD Jewish experts believed in their constructions."[88] The surveillance and persecution of ideological enemies by the Security Service was not understood as a merely negative and destructive task, but as an indispensable part of a "positive" ethnic restructuring of Germany and Europe.[89]

Ideological motives alone do not explain the radicalism and ruthlessness of SD Jewish policy, however. It was more than the linear, exclusive result of anti-Semitic intentions, as it simultaneously derived from the complex power politics and structural conditions under which political praxis unfolded. The Security Service was a newly created institution lacking any traditions, which first had to develop its own sense of mission and win a place in the power system of the Third Reich. The relationship to the Gestapo, marked by both conflict and complementary action, motivated the Party intelligence service to try to outdo its competitor through its ideological ruthlessness and cruelty. To this was added the precarious status of its officials and apparatus, as the chronically overburdened and underfinanced SS and Party Intelligence Service were confronted by the professional superiority of the state bureaucracies. Finally, the departments of the Main Office responsible for enemies of the state were staffed by remarkably youthful and politically active SS leaders, marked by different critical experiences, who, in contrast to the Gestapo officials, saw themselves much more clearly as members of an ideological elite.[90] It was mainly clerks and unsuccessful students, men such as Eichmann, Dannecker, and Hagen, who worked their way up to the top of the Security Service and later became key figures in the Holocaust.[91]

The influence of politico-structural factors is particularly clear from the way SD perceptions of the enemy were influenced by Jewish reactions to repression. In the pre-war years the coercive measures of the regime had noticeably stimulated Jewish religious and cultural life, which was expressed in a growing number and variety of organizations and activities.[92] Thus Kurt Singer, former Deputy Director of the Berlin City Opera, founded the "Cultural League of German Jews" to provide for Jewish artists excluded from the established cultural activities, and to offer the Jewish public "private performances" of numerous plays, operas, concerts, readings, and films.⁹³ Such developments were interpreted by the Security Service as an additional danger, because "hostile" influences appeared to be preserved in indirect and mediated forms in them. For 1937 the SD Main Office registered an increasing "flight into religiosity" and an "ever stronger participation in Jewish cultural activities."⁹⁴ To the SD observers this seemed ominous, as it could reinforce the tendency of German Jews to remain in the Reich, which was contrary to the political aim of increasing Jewish emigration.⁹⁵

In Jewish policy and other SD operational areas ideological motives and the determining politico-structural factors were interwoven, which served to intensify both the ideological images of the enemy and practical action in like manner. There was a union of theory and praxis here, which Hitler had already formulated in *Mein Kampf*,⁹⁶ and which the Security Service leaders took as a guideline for their actions.⁹⁷ According to this view, ideology had no value if it was not realized by the executive agencies of the state, and, conversely, state and party were worthless if they were not founded on an ideological "idea." SD experts were therefore urged not to lose sight of the "great tasks" in the course of their everyday routines and nevertheless always to have "implementation," the priority of praxis, in their minds.⁹⁸ Himmler concisely summed up this understanding of the unity of theory and praxis when he called on SD members to be both fanatical and action-oriented: "Therefore we will never be Jesuits, because we despise this,"⁹⁹ he proclaimed at the inauguration of Ernst Kaltenbrunner as Heydrich's successor in January 1943, alluding to supposed "Jesuit morals," according to which religious principles could at any time be sacrificed for the sake of political goals. But the Security Service was not only to guard against becoming a powerful organization without convictions; it was also to avoid becoming a group of ideological fanatics unmindful of power. "We will never become sectarians," added the Reichsführer-SS, casting a glance at the adherents of smaller religious communities like the Jehovah's Witnesses, to whom the uncompromising profession of belief meant everything, social influence very little. He continued, "I know that as yet the question whether we are a dying or a growing people has by no means been answered ...[and] that only a religious approach to these matters, an inner conversion, can help."¹⁰⁰

The semantic field of religion can possibly contribute to the clarification of the specific interaction of ideology and praxis in the Security Service. Among the approaches to an understanding of National Socialist rule already developed by contemporary observers, the concept of "political religion" has recently attracted increased attention.¹⁰¹ Three of the earliest and most important representatives of this approach were the German philosopher of history Eric Voegelin, the French sociologist Raymond Aron and the British journalist Frederick A. Voigt.¹⁰² They employed the concept of religion to describe the hitherto unknown extent of political violence and its justification by means of "final" aims that characterized the Nazi dictatorship and other despotic regimes of the time. All three authors viewed modern dictatorships not as mere counterpoints to liberal democracy, but rather as a consequence of secularization and an expression of a deep spiritual crisis of the epoch.

Eric Voegelin defined a "political religion" in 1938 as the deification of individual components of the world—state, race, or class—by political mass movements, so that the ultimate goal became "an earthly state of perfected humanity" and not perfection in the hereafter.[103] Aron, in contrast, saw National Socialism and Stalinism as religious phenomena in that they abolished the modern confinement of religion to the private sphere and justified their actions with a secular, final, and absolute promise of salvation; what was really new was their amalgamation of political violence and religious models of legitimization.[104] Whereas Voegelin thus interpreted the dictatorships from a Christian perspective, critical of secularism, as a consequence of the loss of religious convictions, and Aron conversely viewed them from an enlightened perspective, sympathetic to secularism, as resulting from the "loss of modernity," Voigt tried to synthesize these views. In his book published in 1938, *Unto Caesar*, the former Socialist and now religiously minded author, who had served as German correspondent of the *Manchester Guardian* until the "seizure of power," described the rise of "secular religions" as a consequence of the simultaneous decline of the Christian religion and secular bourgeois society.[105] In the title of his work, Voigt alluded to Jesus' distinction between obedience to God and the state,[106] thereby indicating his view that Communism and National Socialism no longer respected the distinction between the divine and earthly spheres. Instead they deified their secular collective social conceptions and at the same time ignored the Christian doctrine that man is sinful and needful of salvation by linking their actions with a promise of salvation in this world:

> Both have enthroned the modern Caesar, collective man, the implacable enemy of the modern soul. Both would render unto this Caesar the things which are God's. Both would make man master of his destiny, establish the Kingdom of Heaven in this world. Neither will hear of any Kingdom that is not of this world.[107]

For all the differences in the details of their approaches, Voegelin, Aron, and Voigt worked out certain essential defining attributes of political religions. They promised a salvation in this world that is ultimately inaccessible to reason and can only be experienced as "faith." At the same time their adherents presumed to know and to be able to influence the laws of historical development. They divided the world up into irreconcilable forces of good and evil, friend and enemy, in order to persecute violently and ruthlessly the actual or presumed adversaries of their absolute aims.

The description of political movements and tyrannies with the aid of the concept of religion has met with objections. Central to the critique are the redefinition and expansion of the concept in Voegelin's distinction between "other-worldly" and "inner-worldly" religions (*überweltlich* vs. *innerweltlich*),[108] which seems to contradict the guiding principle of Christianity as a religion founded on revelation, thus postulating a fundamental difference between God and man. In regard to National Socialism, Hans Buchheim distinguished between religions based on transcendental doctrinal truths and the "political belief" of National Socialism, which was "a false belief in terms of contents, intention, and manner."[109] For Hitler had merely used people's religious needs to lend his political goals absolute validity, although they were in no way related to divine revelation and thus lacked value and veracity.[110] Hannah Arendt even felt that the application of the concept of religion to totalitarian dictatorships was an "undeserved compliment."[111] Their true nature was defined by terror, whose "iron band" gave modern man, an abandoned being without ties or commitment, a final hold on life.[112] Finally, according to Hans Mommsen, National Socialism was not a political religion, because as a "simulative movement" it lacked that "ideological rigor and coherence" which must be regarded as an essential defining element of every true world view or religion.[113]

Whether the concept of political religion is affirmed or rejected depends ultimately, therefore, on the concept of religion used. Obviously, however, many reservations rest, as does the radicalization model of Ulrich Herbert, on two key assumptions: The rulers concerned had no value-oriented principles on which to base a "positive" new order and their ideological models of legitimization and motivation lacked a systematic dogmatic form in the sense of Christian theology. This fails to do justice to the mutual interaction of ideology and praxis in the Security Service, however. As cynical as National Socialist ideology appears in retrospect, it still offered SD members intrinsically logical interpretive models and concrete conceptions of a new order that were expressly understood not merely as a theoretical structure, but rather as a guide to political action. The concept of "redemptive anti-Semitism" is also too limited insofar as the National Socialist project of a new ethnic order was not only determined, in its universal dimensions, by racial biology. In both Jewish policy and other operational fields the SD clearly strove to overcome the "difference between dominion and salvation."[114] On all sides decisions and action were marked by fundamental ideological assumptions, which in turn were reinforced by institutional constraints and the interests of power politics, and this made the Security Service one of the most fanatical and dangerous exponents of National Socialist tyranny. The Security Service was not characterized by hierarchies of superior or inferior standing, but rather by a persistent interaction, a dialectical unity of ideology and politics, and this can fittingly be described as a political religion.

Notes

1. See, for example, Raul Hilberg, *The Destruction of the European Jews* (New York, 1961); Götz Aly, *"Endlösung". Völkerverschiebung und der Mord an den europäischen Juden* (Frankfurt on Main, 1995); Hermann Graml, *Reichskristallnacht. Antisemitismus und Judenverfolgung im Dritten Reich* (Munich, 1988).

2. Based on my dissertation: W. Dierker, "Himmlers Glaubenskrieger. Der Sicherheitsdienst der SS und seine Religionspolitik 1933–1941" (Paderborn , 2001).
3. On the Jewish policy of the SD see Michael Wildt, ed., *Die Judenpolitik des SD 1935 bis 1938. Eine Dokumentation* (Munich, 1995); Ulrich Herbert, *Best. Biographische Studien über Radikalismus, Weltanschauung und Vernunft, 1903–1989* (Bonn, 1996); Peter Longerich, *Politik der Vernichtung. Eine Gesamtdarstellung der nationalsozialistischen Judenverfolgung* (Munich/ Zürich, 1998), pp. 135–146; Klaus Drobisch, "Die Judenreferate des Geheimen Staatspolizeiamtes und des Sicherheitsdienstes der SS 1933 bis 1939," in *Jahrbuch für Antisemitismusforschung* 2 (1992): 230–254; Saul Friedländer, *Das Dritte Reich und die Juden. Die Jahre der Verfolgung 1933–1939* (Munich, 2000), pp. 213–222.
4. Memo "Zum Judenproblem," probably written by Eichmann, January 1937, in Wildt, *Judenpolitik*, no. 8, p. 96.
5. Himmler to Heydrich, 10 August 1931, BAB/BDC, SS-O Heydrich. On the early history of the SD see Shlomo Aronson, *Reinhard Heydrich und die Frühgeschichte von Gestapo und SD* (Stuttgart, 1971); George C. Browder, *Foundations of the Nazi Police State: The Formation of Sipo and SD* (Lexington, 1990); idem, *Hitler's Enforcers. The Gestapo and the SS Security Service in the Nazi Revolution* (New York/Oxford, 1996); Herbert, *Best*, pp. 133–147; Alwin Ramme, *Der Sicherheitsdienst der SS* (East Berlin, 1970), pp. 29–49.
6. Himmler to Heydrich, 22 July 1932, BAB/BDC, SS-O Heydrich.
7. Joseph Ackermann, *Heinrich Himmler als Ideologe* (Göttingen, 1970), pp. 141–156; Joachim C. Fest, "Die andere Utopie. Eine Studie über Heinrich Himmler," in J.C. Fest, *Fremdheit und Nähe. Von der Gegenwart des Gewesenen* (Stuttgart, 1996), pp. 138–166; Heinz Höhne, *Der Orden unter dem Totenkopf. Die Geschichte der SS* (Augsburg, 1995); Bernd Wegner, *Hitlers politische Soldaten. Die Waffen-SS 1933–1945. Leitbild, Struktur und Funktion einer nationalsozialistischen Elite* (Paderborn, 1997), pp. 25–75.
8. "Aktennotiz über das anläßlich einer Besprechung Münchner SS-Führer am 26.8.1931 im Braunen Haus von Heydrich gehaltene Referat über die 'Kampfmethoden der Gegner'", Aronson, *Heydrich*, no. 7, p. 318.
9. Decree of the "Stellvertreter des Führers," 9 June 1934, BAB NS 6/217, fol. 1f.
10. Aronson, *Heydrich*, pp. 191–195; Browder, *Foundations*, pp. 141–144; Herbert, *Best*, p. 143f.
11. Rede Himmler Speechs, 5 March 1936, BAB NS 19/4003, fol. 11.
12. Adolf Hitler, *Mein Kampf* (1925/27) (Munich, 1940); Gerhard L. Weinberg, *Hitlers Zweites Buch. Ein Dokument aus dem Jahre 1928* (Stuttgart, 1961). See also Joachim C. Fest, *Hitler. Eine Biographie* (Frankfurt on Main, Berlin, 1987), pp. 147–151; Klaus Hildebrand, *Das vergangene Reich. Deutsche Außenpolitik von Bismarck bis Hitler 1871–1945* (Stuttgart, 1995), pp. 567–578; Eberhard Jäckel, *Hitlers Weltanschauung* (Stuttgart, 1981); Ian Kershaw, *Hitler. 1889–1936* (Stuttgart, 1998), pp. 678–681.
13. Himmler Speech, 11 October 1934, BAB NS 19/4002, fol. 13; Reinhard Heydrich, "Wandlungen unseres Kampfes," *Das Schwarze Korps*, 13 (1935): 9. See Browder, *Foundations*, pp. 16f., 33, 73; Johannes Tuchel, *Konzentrationslager. Organisationsgeschichte und Funktion der "Inspektion der Konzentrationslager" 1934–1938* (Boppard, 1991), pp. 297–307.
14. Browder, *Foundations*, pp. 165–171, 187f., 205–207; Herbert, *Best*, pp. 153, 158, 161; Tuchel, *Konzentrationslager*, pp. 307–317, 346–359.
15. "Verfügung des Politischen Polizeikommandeurs und Inspekteurs der Geheimen Staatspolizei" of 4 July 1934, mentioned in "Runderlaß des Staatsministeriums des Innern, Politischer Polizeikommandeur Bayerns," 7 December 1934, BAB/BDC, Ordner 457, fol. 106f.
16. Ibid.
17. Wildt, *Judenpolitik*, p. 10f.
18. Himmler Speech, 5 March 1936, BAB NS 19/4003, fol. 45.
19. The move took place in August or September 1934. Best/Sicherheitsamt (Munich), 6 August 1934 to Heydrich, BAB/ZDH, ZB I/719, fols. 166–169, and Sicherheitsamt (Berlin) to Darré, 19 Sepember 1934, BAB/ZDH, ZB I/920, fol. 259.

20. Reinhard Rürup, ed., *Topographie des Terrors. Gestapo, SS und Reichssicherheitshauptamt auf dem "Prinz-Albrecht-Gelände"* (Berlin, 1987), pp. 11–15; Johannes Tuchel and Reinold Schattenfroh, *Zentrale des Terrors. Prinz-Albrecht-Straße 8: Das Hauptquartier der Gestapo* (Berlin, 1987), p. 96.
21. RFSS, "SS-Befehl 2," 25 January 1935, cited in Browder, *Hitler's Enforcers*, p. 175.
22. "Geschäftsverteilungsplan des Sicherheitsamtes," undated, George C. Browder, "Die Anfänge des SD. Dokumente aus der Organisationsgeschichte des Sicherheitsdienstes des Reichsführers SS," *Vierteljahrshefte für Zeitgeschichte* 27 (1979): 309–311; "Registraturverzeichnis," undated, ibid., 323f.
23. "Befehl des Chefs des SDHA zum organisatorischen Aufbau," 1936 [8 January 1936], Wildt, *Judenpolitik*, no. 4, pp. 73–80.
24. See Kunze/Sicherheitshauptamt [hereafter: SDHA]/SDHA II 1131 an alle SD-Oberabschnitte (außer Donau) (Verfügung), "II 23 zur Kenntnis," 13 May 1938, written comment by Six ("Herr Kunze probably does not know the difference between II 23 and II 223"), BAB/ZDH, ZB I/679, fol. 268f.
25. Höhne, *Orden*, p. 200; Heinrich Orb, *Nationalsozialismus. 13 Jahre Machtrausch* (Olten, 1945), p. 67 f.
26. Wolf/SDHA/II 121 to Ehrlinger, 5 August 1937, ZAHDS Moscow, 500/4/30, fol. 1f.
27. Aronson, *Heydrich*, p. 251; Heinz Boberach, ed., *Meldungen aus dem Reich 1938–1945. Die geheimen Lageberichte des Sicherheitsdienstes der SS 1938–1945*, vol. 1 (Herrsching, 1984), p. 13f.; Hans Buchheim, "Die SS—das Herrschaftsinstrument," in Martin Broszat, Hans Buchheim, Hans-Adolf Jacobsen, Helmut Krausnick, eds., *Anatomie des SS-Staates*, vol. 1 (Munich, 1989), p. 62f.; Robert Gellately, *Die Gestapo und die deutsche Gesellschaft. Die Durchsetzung der Rassenpolitik 1933–1945* (Paderborn, 1993), p. 84f.; Höhne, *Orden*, p. 210; Klaus-Michael Mallmann and Gerhard Paul, *Herrschaft und Alltag. Ein Industrierevier im Dritten Reich* (Bonn, 1991), p. 271f.
28. Dierker, "Himmlers Glaubenskrieger", part VI149–215.
29. SDHA/II 112, "Bericht über den Stand der Arbeiten der Abtlg. II 112 in der Bekämpfung des Judentums," 28 August 1936, Wildt, *Judenpolitik*, no. 8, p. 95; SDHA/II 112, "Tätigkeitsbericht" 16.02.1937–05.06.1936, BAB R 58/991, fols. 72–77. See Browder, *Hitler's Enforcers*, p. 190f.; Drobisch, *Judenpolitik*, p. 242t.; Wildt, *Judenpolitik*, p. 35.
30. See Browder, *Hitler's Enforcers*, p. 189.
31. Ibid., pp. 53–63; Christoph Graf, *Politische Polizei zwischen Demokratie und Diktatur* (Berlin, 1983), pp. 207–220; Gerhard Paul, "Ganz normale Akademiker. Eine Fallstudie zur regionalen staatspolizeilichen Funktionselite," in Gerhard Paul and Klaus-Michael Mallmann, eds., *Die Gestapo. Mythos und Realität* (Darmstadt, 1995), pp. 238–244.
32. SDHA/II 113, "Tätigkeitsbericht" 01.11.1936–15.02.1937, BAB/ZDH, ZB I/1681, fol. 74; SDHA/II 121, "Besprechung über Zusammenarbeit [mit Gestapa/II 1 A]", 19 February 1936, ZAHDS Moscow, 500/1/5, fol. 2f.; SDHA/II 112, "Richtlinien und Forderungen an die Oberabschnitte," Wildt, *Judenpolitik*, no. 12, p. 114f.; "Bericht Hagens über die Zusammenarbeit zwischen II 112 und Gestapa II B 4," 29 June 1937, ibid., no. 13, pp. 115–118; Gahrmann/SDHA/ II 1133, "Besprechung zwischen SD II 113 und Gestapa II 1 B 1," 30 June 1937, BAB/ZDH, ZB I/1256, fols. 566–569.
33. Herbert, *Best*, p. 186; Longerich, *Politik der Vernichtung*, pp.136–138; Wildt, *Judenpolitik*, pp. 32–37.
34. See Vermerk Wislicenys zur "Judenfrage," 7 April 1937, Wildt, Judenpolitik, no. 11, pp. 108–115.
35. Werner Best, "Die Geheime Staatspolizei," *Deutsches Recht* 6 (1936): 125.
36. Documents on the cooperation of Security Service and Gestapo 1935–1943, Landeshauptarchiv Koblenz, 662/332.
37. ZAHDS Moscow, 500/1/428.
38. Browder, *Hitler's Enforcers*, p. 63; Mallmann and Paul, *Herrschaft und Alltag*, no. 20, p. 468.
39. Notes by Dannecker/SDHA/II 112, spring 1937, see Wildt, *Judenpolitik*, no. 145, p. 39.
40. Note by Wolf/SDHA /II 121, 15 March 1937, BAB R 58/2476a, fol. 40.

41. Wisliceny and Hagen/SDHA/ II 112, "Richtlinien und Forderungen an die Oberabschnitte," 21 April 1937, Wildt, *Judenpolitik*, no. 12, p. 114.
42. See Dierker, "Himmlers Glaubenskrieger", part IX 248–259; Lutz Hachmeister, *Der Gegnerforscher. Die Karriere des SS-Führers Franz Alfred Six* (Munich, 1998), pp. 144–198.
43. Wisliceny and Hagen/SDHA/II 112, "Richtlinien und Forderungen an die Oberabschnitte," 21 April 1937, Wildt, *Judenpolitik*, no. 12, p. 115.
44. Wolf/SDHA/II 121, "Aufgabenteilung zwischen SD und Gestapa," 4 June 1936, ZAHDS Moscow, 500/1/6, fol. 6f. and BAB/ZDH, ZR/921 Akte 1, fol. 24f.
45. Wolf/SDHA/II 121 to SDHA/II 1, "Umbau der Abteilung II 121 seit dem 1.4.1937," BAB R 58/2436, fol. 41.
46. Wolf/SDHA/II 121 to Behrends/SDHA/II 1, "Arbeitsteilung zwischen SD-Hauptamt und Gestapa," 18 March 1937, ZAHDS Moscow, 500/1/6, fol. 1f. and BAB/ZDH, ZR/921 Akte 1, fol. 22.
47. Ibid.
48. Wildt, *Judenpolitik*, no. 14, pp. 118–120.
49. Ibid., p.119f.
50. Wolf/SDHA/II 121 to SDHA/II 1, 19 July 1937, ZAHDS Moscow, 500/4/30, fols. 4–7.
51. Wolf/SDHA/II 121 to SDHA/II 121, 1 November 1937, BAB R 58/2436, fols. 58–60; Wolf/SDHA/II 121 to SDHA/II 1, "Umbau der Abteilung II 121 seit dem 1.4.1937," 8 December 1937, BAB R 58/2436, fols. 41–43.
52. Wildt, *Judenpolitik*, pp. 38–40.
53. Hagen/SDHA/II 112, "Report on the Restructuring of the Departments in II 1" (Bericht über den Umbau der Abteilungen bei II 1), 7.12. December 1937, Wildt, *Judenpolitik*, no. 26, p. 161. See Browder, *Hitler's Enforcers*, p. 191f.; Longerich, *Politik der Vernichtung*, p. 140f.; Claudia Steur, *Theodor Dannecker. Ein Funktionär der "Endlösung"* (Essen, 1997), p. 22.
54. This in my opinion is how the decree's wording should be understood, and not in the sense that Heydrich assigned leadership tasks (*Federführung*) to the SD, while the Gestapo received "the function of an executive organ" in Jewish policy, as Steur thinks, *Dannecker*, p. 22.
55. Steur, *Dannecker*, p. 118. See Browder, *Hitler's Foundations*, pp. 191–193; Lawrence D. Stokes, *The Sicherheitsdienst of the Reichsführer SS and German Public Opinion, Sept. 1939–June 1941* (Baltimore, 1972), pp. 112–114.
56. Hachmeister, *Six*, p. 146; Stokes, *Sicherheitsdienst*, p. 109.
57. "Runderlaß des Chefs des SDHA und der Sicherheitspolizei," 1 July 1937, BAB R 58/239, fol. 196f. See also note by Zapp/SDHA/II 1131, 6 September 1937, handwritten note by Heydrich ("ich vermisse sehr häufig die befohlene Mitzeichnung des Gestapa!!"—I often miss the mandatory counter-signature of the Gestapa!!), BAB/ZDH, ZB I/1257, fol. 184; Six/SDHA/II 1, "Rücksprache mit C. (Heydrich)," 23 December 1937, ZAHDS Moscow, 500/3/322, fol. 248f.
58. Dierker, "Himmlers Glaubenskrieger" Religionspolitik, part II 45–55.
59. Hartl/SDHA/II 113 to SDHA/II 1, "Division of labor in Department II 113" (Arbeitsverteilung in der Abteilung II 113), undated (1938/39), ZAHDS Moscow, 500/1/615, fol. 19v.
60. SDHA/II 1, "Tätigkeitsbericht" 01.01.1938–30.06.1938, p. 44f., BAB R 58/7082.
61. Stein/SDHA/ II 112, "Abschlußbericht ÖAK [Österreich-Auswertungs-Kommando]," 28 October 1938, ZAHDS Moscow, 500/1/617, fol. 4.
62. Schellenberg/SDHA/ I 11, "Reorganisation des Sicherheitsdienstes des Reichsführers SS," 24 February 1939, BAB R 58/826, fol. 119.
63. Memo by Hagen/SDHA/II 112, 28 February 1939, ZAHDS Moscow, 500/1/619, fol. 2f.
64. CdSDHA/I 1113, Befehl für den SD No. 36/39, "Arbeitseinschränkung als Maßnahme in Spannungszeiten bezw. im Mob-Falle," 1 September 1939, BAB R 58/7088, fols. 85–92.
65. Knochen/SDHA II, "Arbeitseinschränkung als Massnahme in Spannungszeiten bezw. im Mob-Falle," 3 September 1939, BAB R 58/7088, fol. 95.

66. Rauff/SDHA/ I 11, "Amtschefbesprechung am 19.9.39," BAB R 58/825, fol. 15. See Boberach, *Meldungen*, vols. 2–17.
67. RFSS und Chef der deutschen Polizei. "Die Zusammenfassung der zentralen Ämter der Sicherheitspolizei und des SD," 27 September 1939, in *Der Prozeß gegen die Hauptkriegsverbrecher vor dem Internationalen Militärgerichtshof*, vol. XXXVIII, Nuremberg 1949, no. 361-L, 102–104; Runderlaß des CdSudSD, 27 September 1939, in ibid., p. 105f.
68. Best/RSHA I to Amtschefs II–VI, 12 October 1939, BAB R 58/7044, fol. 6f.
69. Reinhard Heydrich, "Der Anteil der Sicherheitspolizei und des SD an den Ordnungsmaßnahmen im mitteleuropäischen Raum," BAB R 58/844, fols. 245–247.
70. See Christian Gerlach, *Kalkulierte Morde. Die deutsche Wirtschafts- und Vernichtungspolitik in Weißrußland 1941 bis 1944* (Hamburg, 1999), pp. 180–196, 536–555; Helmut Krausnick, *Hitlers Einsatzgruppen. Die Truppe des Weltanschauungskrieges 1938–1942* (Frankfurt on Main, 1985); Dieter Pohl, "Schauplatz Ukraine: Die Ermordung der Juden in den Militärverwaltungsgebieten und im Reichskommissariat 1941–1943," in Norbert Frei et al. eds., *Ausbeutung, Vernichtung, Öffentlichkeit. Neue Studien zur nationalsozialistischen Lagerpolitik* (Munich, 2000), pp. 135–173.
71. Hildebrand, *Das vergangene Reich*, pp. 750–760; Andreas Hillgruber, "Der Ostkrieg und die Judenvernichtung," in Gerd R. Ueberschär and Wolfram Wette eds., *Der deutsche Überfall auf die Sowjetunion. "Unternehmen Barbarossa" 1941* (Frankfurt on Main, 1991), pp. 185–205; Eberhard Jäckel, *Hitlers Herrschaft. Vollzug einer Weltanschauung* (Stuttgart, 1986).
72. Hans Mommsen, "Hitlers Stellung im nationalsozialistischen Herrschaftssystem," in H. Mommsen, *Der Nationalsozialismus und die deutsche Gesellschaft. Ausgewählte Aufsätze* (Reinbek, 1991), p. 84.
73. Hans Mommsen, "Die Realisierung des Utopischen: Die 'Endlösung der Judenfrage' im Dritten Reich," in H. Mommsen, Nationalsozialismus, pp. 184–232; Martin Broszat, "Hitler und die Genesis der 'Endlösung': Aus Anlaß der Thesen von David Irving," in M. Broszat, *Nach Hitler. Der schwierige Umgang mit unserer Geschichte* (Munich, 1988), pp. 45–91.
74. Aly, *"Endlösung"*; Hans Safrian, *Eichmann und seine Gehilfen* (Frankfurt on Main, 1995); Thomas Sandkühler, *"Endlösung" in Galizien. Der Judenmord in Ostpolen und die Rettungsinitiativen von Berthold Beitz 1941–1944* (Bonn, 1996). Stressing the ideological and political preeminence of NS leaders, see Richard Breitman, *Der Architekt der "Endlösung": Himmler und die Vernichtung der europäischen Juden* (Paderborn, 1996); Christopher R. Browning, "Beyond 'Intentionalism' and 'Functionalism': The Decision for the Final Solution Reconsidered," in C.R. Browning, *The Path to Genocide. Essays on Launching the Final Solution* (Cambridge, 1992), pp. 86–121; Dieter Pohl, *Nationalsozialistische Judenverfolgung in Ostgalizien 1941–1944. Organisation und Durchführung eines staatlichen Massenverbrechens* (Munich, 1996).
75. Jens Banach, *Heydrichs Elite. Das Führerkorps der Sicherheitspolizei und des SD 1936–1945* (Paderborn, 1998); Browder, *Hitler's Enforcers*; Wildt, *Judenpolitik*.
76. Ulrich Herbert, "Vernichtungspolitik. Neue Antworten und Fragen zur Geschichte des 'Holocaust,'" in U. Herbert, ed., *Nationalsozialistische Vernichtungspolitik 1933–1945* (Frankfurt on Main, 1998), pp. 9–66.
77. Herbert, *Best*, p. 203f.
78. Memorandum "Zum Judenproblem," probably by Eichmann, January 1937, Wildt, *Judenpolitik*, no. 9, p. 96.
79. Dannecker, "Das innerdeutsche Judentum: Organisation, sachliche und personelle Veränderungen, geistiges Leben und die Methodik seiner Behandlung," 1 November 1937, Wildt, *Judenpolitik*, no. 21, p. 150.
80. Friedländer., *Das Dritte Reich und die Juden*, pp. 45f., 101f.
81. Ibid., "Von den Ursachen der Gefühllosigkeit," *Frankfurter Allgemeine Zeitung*, 7 October 1998, p. 44.
82. SDHA/II 1, "Tätigkeitsbericht" 01.01.1938–30.06.1938, p. 5, BAB R 58/7082.

83. Heydrich, "Wandlungen unseres Kampfes."
84. Ibid., 9/p. 9.
85. Ibid., 9/p. 10.
86. Friedländer, *Das Dritte Reich und die Juden*, p. 218f.
87. See Dierker, "Himmlers Glaubenskrieger" *Religionspolitik*, part IV100–118.
88. Wildt, *Judenpolitik*, p. 48.
89. Ibid., p. 63.
90. Ulrich Herbert, "Weltanschauungseliten. Ideologische Legitimation und politische Praxis der Führungsgruppe der nationalsozialistischen Sicherheitspolizei," *Potsdamer Bulletin für Zeithistorische Studien* 9 (1997): 4–18.
91. Banach, *Heydrichs Elite*; Browder, *Hitler's Enforcers*; Steur, *Dannecker*; Friedrich Zipfel, "A Sociographic Profile of the Organizers of Terror," in Stein Ugelvik Larsen, eds., *Who Were the Fascists? Social Roots of European Fascism* (Bergen, 1980), pp. 301–311.
92. Volker Dahm, "Kulturelles und geistiges Leben," in Wolfgang Benz (ed.), *Die Juden in Deutschland 1933–1945* (Munich, 1988), pp. 75–267; Friedländer, *Das Dritte Reich und die Juden*, pp. 183–191.
93. See Paul Mendes-Flohr, "Jüdisches Kulturleben unter dem Nationalsozialismus," in P. Mendes-Flohr and Avraham Barkai (eds.), *Deutsch-jüdische Geschichte in der Neuzeit. Vol. IV: Aufbruch und Zerstörung 1918–1945* (Munich, 1997), pp. 273–281.
94. "Lagebericht der Abteilung II 112 für das Jahr 1937," Wildt, *Judenpolitik*, no. 27, p. 162.
95. "Referat Hagens auf der Hauptabteilungsleiter-II-Tagung am 09.06.1938", Wildt, Judenpolitik, no. 30, p. 191.
96. Hitler, *Mein Kampf*, p. 419.
97. "Bericht über den Umbau der Abteilungen bei II 1," written by Hagen, 7 December 1937, Wildt, *Judenpolitik*, no. 26, p. 160f.; "Referat Hagens auf der Hauptabteilungsleiter-II-Tagung am 09.06.1938", Wildt, *Judenpolitik*, no. 30, p. 190.
98. Hagen/SDHA/II 112, "Die bisher vom Sicherheitsdienst auf dem Gebiete der Judenfrage geleistete Arbeit und die zukünftigen Aufgaben von II 112," 1.11.1937, Wildt, *Judenpolitik*, no. 17, p. 124.
99. Himmler Speech, 30 January 1943, Richard Breitman and Shlomo Aronson, "Eine unbekannte Himmler-Rede vom Januar 1943," *Vierteljahrshefte für Zeitgeschichte* 38 (1990): 346.
100. Ibid.
101. Markus Huttner, *Totalitarismus und säkulare Religionen. Zur Frühgeschichte totalitarismuskritischer Begriffs- und Theoriebildung in Großbritannien* (Bonn, 1999); Michael Ley and Julius H. Schoeps, eds., *Der Nationalsozialismus als politische Religion* (Mainz, 1997); Hans Maier, ed., *"Totalitarismus" und "Politische Religionen". Konzepte des Diktaturvergleichs* (Paderborn, 1996); Hans Maier and Michael Schäfer, eds., *"Totalitarismus" und "Politische Religionen". Konzepte des Diktaturvergleichs*, vol. II (Paderborn, 1997).
102. The concept of "political religion" has been used by various authors since the seventeenth century, although direct lines of continuity to the conceptions relevant here are not demonstrable. See Huttner, *Totalitarismus*, no. 169 p. 145.
103. Eric Voegelin, *Die politischen Religionen (1938). Hrsg. und mit einem Nachwort versehen von Peter J. Opitz* (Munich, 1993), pp. 17, 51.
104. Raymond Aron, "L'avenir des religions séculières," *La France libre* 7 (1944): 210–217, 269–277. Reprint: *Commentaire* 8 (1985): 369–383.
105. Frederick A. Voigt, *Unto Caesar* (London, 1938).
106. Mt 22, 21. In the 1611 King James Version of the *Bible*, "Render therefore unto Caesar the that are Caesar's, and to God the things that are God's." Huttner, *Totalitarismus*, no. 67, p. 110.
107. Voigt, *Unto Caesar*, p. 37.
108. Voegelin, *Die Politischen Religionen*, p. 17; see also Aron, "L'avenir", p. 370.

109. Hans Buchheim, *Glaubenskrise im Dritten Reich. Drei Kapitel nationalsozialistischer Kirchenpolitik* (Stuttgart, 1953), p. 17.
110. Ibid., pp. 9–39.
111. Hannah Arendt, *Religion und Politik* (1953), cited in Brigitte Gess, "Die Totalitarismuskonzeption von Raymond Aron und Hannah Arendt," in Maier, ed., *"Totalitarismus" und "Politische Religionen,"* p. 270.
112. Hannah Arendt, *Elemente und Ursprünge totaler Herrschaft* (Munich, 1986), pp. 710–730.
113. Hans Mommsen, "Nationalsozialismus als politische Religion," in Maier and Schäfer, eds., *"Totalitarismus" und "Politische Religionen,"* p. 181.
114. Hans Günter Hockerts, "Mythos, Kult und Feste. Münchenunich im nationalsozialistischen 'Feierjahr,'" in Richard Bauer , ed., *München – "Hauptstadt der Bewegung". Bayerns Metropole und der Nationalsozialismus* (Munich, 1993), p. 331.

CHAPTER 3

"ARYANIZATION" AND THE ROLE OF THE GERMAN GREAT BANKS, 1933–1938

Dieter Ziegler

When, at the end of World War II, the American occupying forces examined the role played by the great banks in National Socialism, they interpreted their participation in the spoliation of the German Jews and of the Jewish and Slav populations of the occupied territories as an unscrupulous exploitation of National Socialist (NS) expansionism for their own ends.[1] Apart from their attempts to play down the participation of the banks in the crimes of the NS regime, the representatives of the banks pointed out again and again in their defense that the legal situation and the terror of the National Socialists had left them no other choice.[2] The question of the room for maneuver of those in positions of responsibility in the corporations was, consequently, from the very beginning a central issue in the evaluation of the role of the great banks in National Socialism.

After the break-up of the great banks the question of their share of responsibility seemed at first sight to have been answered. Never again were great banks (or big industry in Germany) to be allowed to achieve a position from which they could prepare a war of aggression. At the same time, however, the question of the individual responsibility of the decision-makers was taken off the agenda. There were no prosecutions or convictions in any of the trials following the Nuremberg Trials, except in the case of one board member of the Dresdner Bank. The conditions at the time, after the foundation of the Federal Republic of Germany, were anything but favorable for a discussion of the room for maneuver of those managers of the great banks who participated in the persecutory measures. In the first place, the Nuremberg Trials were branded quite outspokenly as "victors' justice" by German public opinion; secondly, the interest of the Western allies in punishing war criminals had declined significantly because of the Cold War; and, thirdly, most of the surviving executive members of the great banks had acquired good reputations because of their contributions to the reconstruction of an efficient banking system in the young Republic.

Although the behavior of businessmen in the National Socialist period was discussed again and again in the following decades, a systematic debate on the room for maneuver of the decision-makers in German industry and German banking began only in the recent past as a result of the growing interest in everyday history. The greater weight attached to the actions and the responsibility of individuals in recent historical research has inevitably led, as Nathan Stoltzfus states, to a reevaluation of the role of ordinary people and their potential.[3] In this sense Frank Bajohr also pleads for "a sociohistorical expansion of the classical perspective of 'Jewish policy' which presents the economic exclusion and persecution primarily as a series of legal and administrative measures." After all, "German society contributed in a wide variety of ways to this process."[4]

A seemingly clear answer to the question why a considerable part of German society took part in the persecutory measures against the Jews was provided some years ago by the political scientist Daniel Goldhagen, who, in his book *Hitler's Willing Executioners*, hypothesized "that the will to kill Jews of both Hitler and those who implemented his murderous plans stemmed primarily from a single common source, namely evil anti-Semitism." Motivated by this kind of anti-Semitism "ordinary Germans" came to the conclusion "that the Jews *ought to die*."[5] This "eliminatory" character distinguished the anti-Semitism of the Germans from that of other European peoples and apparently provided a sufficient explanation for this crime against humanity.

Historians today largely agree that this explanation cannot be upheld, but a satisfactory answer to Goldhagen's question has not as yet been found. A first theoretical starting point is, however, provided by the analytical framework developed by Wolfgang Seibel, with which an attempt is made to explain the cumulative radicalization of the measures of economic persecution against the Jews, taking as an example the events in France in the years 1940 to 1942.[6] Seibel by no means denies that the ideological factor of anti-Semitism played its part: "where it was not present as an 'intention' it provided an attitudinal climate in which existing scope for decisions was regularly used to the disadvantage of the Jewish victims." Like Hans Mommsen, however, he argues that ideological intentions do not provide a sufficient basis for the explanation of the growing persistence and continual intensification of the process of persecution.[7] This is particularly clear in view of the success of persecutory measures in the occupied territories and in unoccupied France, where, according to Goldhagen's viewpoint, the anti-Semitism of the local inhabitants ought to have been significantly different from the anti-Semitism of the occupying forces. A logic of action based solely on anti-Semitism quickly came into conflict, however, with other rationalities justifying action so that the guidelines for action of those participating in the persecutory process must have been more robust than an ideology whose "eliminatory" character is in any case more than dubious. Seibel assumes, therefore, that structures and intentions interlock and that a variety of rationalities guiding action come together and must be held together in the institutions in order to achieve a growing persistence and radicalization of the persecutory process. At the level of intentions anti-Semitism could, for example, be linked with values and behavioral orientations that derived from the professional day-to-day life of the participants. In the case of civil servants these would be their duties toward the state and in the case of those employed in the private sector of the economy their duties toward their company. At the level of structures the professional values "had to be 'charged' with interests which resulted from the institutional position of the actors." It could, for example, be concern for the protection of the autonomy of an organization (public office, commercial enterprise) against competing organizations or the exploitation of unusual opportunities for utility maximization. The latter applies both to companies and individuals.

This analytical framework seems to provide a highly suitable basis for an examination of the participation of the great banks in the measures of economic persecution taken against the Jews in the Old Reich during the early phase from 1933 to 1938. The situation is obviously different from that of Seibel's case study. In the economic sector of the Old Reich until about 1937 the role of the state machinery was largely restricted to the setting up of the legal framework. Even the party could only intervene sporadically, if one disregards its propagandistic "drumbeating," and the terroristic apparatus of the regime only took action in exceptional cases. Consequently the non-Jewish economic subjects had a substantially greater freedom for maneuver than during the war. On the other hand, anti-Semitism as the ideology of the state was still something completely new and, accordingly, the deviation from the hitherto normal moral standards in business and social transactions with the Jews required acclimatization. Both cases have one thing in common, which distinguishes them from the final phase of the persecutory process, namely that all the measures were carried out in full view of the public and that every "national comrade" knew exactly what was happening to the Jews.

The empirical foundations for a comparative study of the participation of the German great banks in the measures of economic persecution during the 1930s do not yet exist. A fair amount of work in this direction has, however, been done in the last few years. In this context the pioneering study published by Christopher Kopper in 1995 on banking policy in the Third Reich deserves special mention, although it is based primarily on sources in public archives.[8] The chapter on anti-Semitism and the German Banks published in the same year by Harold James in the Festschrift of the Deutsche Bank[9] deals with the entire complex of the participation of the bank in the economic persecution of the Jews in a very cursory manner. For this reason the Deutsche Bank has in the meantime commissioned the same author to produce an in-depth study of the whole topic, which has recently been published.[10] A parallel study on the participation of the Commerzbank in the "Aryanization" of industrial property in the Old Reich by Bernhard Lorentz has also recently been published.[11] A study on the "Aryanizing" activities of the Dresdner Bank has not yet appeared. For the Dresdner Bank there is, however, a work available on the treatment of Jewish employees and pensioners.[12] In addition, it was possible for me to consult the as yet unpublished chapters of two dissertations, Ingo Köhler's chapter on the "Aryanization" of the Dresden private bank Gebr. Arnhold by the Dresdner Bank and its subsidiary Hardy & Co. and Thomas Weihe's chapter on the ejection of Jewish employees from the Commerzbank.

In what follows the measures of economic persecution against the German Jews and the extent of the participation of the three great banks, Deutsche Bank, Dresdner Bank, and Commerzbank, in them will at first be summarized, as far as the present state of research allows. Then an attempt will be made to assess the room for maneuver of the banks as institutions and of the individual decision-makers and to explain the causes of the smooth functioning of the banks within the machinery of economic persecution, using the analytical framework discussed above.

The German Great Banks and the "Dejewification" of the German Economy

The concept of "Aryanization" with which the National Socialists summarily characterized the economic persecution of the Jews encompasses a wide range of measures. The concept was already widely used in the 1920s in national anti-Semitic circles and it stood for a substantial or complete exclusion of the Jews from economic life. In this general unspecific meaning it found acceptance in the jargon of the public authorities and the general language use of the population around the middle of the 1930s. Often used synonymously with the concept of "dejewification," it now characterized both the ongoing process of expulsion and the destruction of economic livelihood and the transfer of property from "Jewish" to "Aryan" possession. An official or even semi-official definition from the Nazi period does not exist.[13]

Modern research continues to use the concept of "Aryanization" in order to characterize the full extent of measures of economic persecution. It does so for good reasons. First, there is no alternative concept in German, and, secondly, it expresses the unique historical nature of the complete spoliation of a racially defined minority involving a division of labor between a modern state and private individuals. But for the purposes of scientific analysis the contemporary concept of "Aryanization" is too unspecific. A differentiation between the various measures of economic persecution adopted is for this reason necessary.

The participation of the banks occurred in the following manner. The first step taken in the process of economic persecution aimed at the ejection of self-employed and wage-earning persons of Jewish origin from their occupations. Civil servants, journalists, doctors, lawyers, estate agents, senior executives of business corporations, and their boards of directors were all affected. The second step was the transfer of business property from private "Jewish" to private "Aryan" possession. For the purposes of the present study this process is again differentiated in accordance with the kind of property involved (banks/non-banks, partnerships/limited companies). The final step in the process of economic persecution is the confiscation of private property by the state authorities. This process does, it is true, start quite early with the instrumentalization of the Reich Flight Tax and currency regulations for the expropriation of Jewish emigrants.[14] But it acquires greater quantitative significance only as a result of a special tax, the Atonement Tax, on Jewish property after the pogrom of November 1938. This third step will not, however, be dealt with here, as the banks were only marginally concerned in the expropriation of emigrants and the implementation of the Atonement Tax lies outside the period under study. I have also omitted a comparative treatment of the developments in the territories (Austria, Sudetenland) annexed by the end of 1938, as this would also exceed the limits of a study of this kind.

The Great Banks and their Jewish Employees, and Members of the Managing and Supervisory Boards

The percentage of employees of Jewish origin in the private banking sector was traditionally above average,[15] and the higher the position in the hierarchy, the greater the percentage was. There were members of Jewish origin on the managing and supervisory boards of all three great banks at the time of the seizure of power by the National Socialists. In the Dresdner Bank no fewer than nine of the fourteen members of the executive were of Jewish origin, and among the branch managers their share was almost 20 percent.

The National Socialists were keenly interested in the purging of the banks, which were regarded as "jewified." But the National Socialist leadership was at first in a dilemma. On the one hand it had to taken into account the expectations of the "Old Fighters" (party veterans) for a "National Socialist Revolution," which, from their point of view, would have involved a complete transformation of the banking system. On the other hand, the banking crisis of 1931 had shown particularly clearly the catastrophic economic consequences that a collapse of the banking system would have. In early 1933 the banks had by no means recovered from the crisis and even smaller experiments could have quickly endangered their existence. It had to be the chief aim of the government, however, to overcome the economic depression as quickly as possible and to reduce significantly the number of unemployed. This was essential if the regime was to be stabilized politically in the medium term. For this reason radical interventions in the economy were out of the question right from the start. In fact, the great banks at first reacted very reservedly toward the National Socialist-led government. The only Jew to leave a managing board was Wilhelm Kleemann, a member of the executive of the Jewish community in Berlin, who left the Dresdner Bank on 31 March 1933. How unimportant the anti-Semitism of the National Socialists was for the Dresdner Bank in the first few weeks after the seizure of power is revealed by the fact that a "half-Jew," Reinhold Quaatz, was appointed as Kleemann's successor.[16]

In the spring of 1933, however, the pressure was massively increased when, probably by chance, a highly effective division of labor between the National Socialist mob and the government crystallized, with the help of which the first anti-Jewish measures could be effectively implemented. By forbidding, on the one hand, the often brutal attacks of the storm troops (SA) and the Nazi factory cell organization (NSBO) on Jewish businesses and shops, the government was able to win a reputation as the guarantor of law and order in the eyes of many contemporaries. On the other hand, however, it could use "pressure from the street" as an effective argument for "voluntary" concessions by the potential victims of such attacks.[17]

For this reason the Deutsche Bank showed a kind of "obedience in advance" in May 1933 and decided that two practicing Jewish members of the executive, one of them the spokesman for the managing board, Oscar Wassermann, would have to leave the board, not least because of pressure from the President of the Reichsbank, Hjalmar Schacht.

Although cultural anti-Semitic prejudice was very widespread precisely among the conservative economic elite,[18] there is no indication that members of managing or supervisory boards used the opportunity to drive out their Jewish colleagues. This is also true of the Commerzbank, although its board seems to have had closer connections with the new regime than the boards of its two competitors.[19] In the spring of 1933 the two Jewish members of the management were at first left undisturbed.

The Law for the Restoration of the Professional Civil Service, however, created a new legal situation by which the great banks were also affected. This law determined at first only that "civil servants who are not of Aryan descent must be retired," "non-Aryan" being defined as applying to all those persons with one parent or grandparent who was not "Aryan."[20] But only a short time later the scope of the law was extended to include "salaried employees and workers...of state-owned corporations and equivalent institutions and enterprises."[21] As a result the great banks became subject to the law, as, at this time, a large part of their share capital was in the hands of the public authorities. The Reich in fact held a majority of shares in the Dresdner Bank and, through its subsidiary, the Golddiskontbank, in the Commerzbank.

The provisions of the Professional Civil Service Law were by no means restricted in their application to board members or top managers, but applied to all employees of the great banks. Unlike the civil servants, however, the "non-Aryan" employees were not to be retired but dismissed after being given the notice legally due to them. According to the Professional Civil Service Law exemptions were only possible for those who had been employed since 1 August 1914, and those "who had fought for the German Reich or its allies in the World War" or whose fathers or sons had lost their lives in the war. If employers requested further exemptions they had to be approved in each individual case by the Reich Economics Ministry and were then only granted on a short-term basis.

In the case of the Dresdner Bank, in which almost 600 persons were classified as "non-Aryan," over 400 persons were dismissed by the middle of

1934, among them seven of the nine "non-Aryan" members of the executive, including the only recently appointed board member Quaatz. Exceptions were made for only 125 persons (or 20 percent of all "non-Aryans"), among them a member of the board and a deputy board member.[22] Unfortunately, no figures are yet available for the Deutsche Bank. Only the changes in the composition of the managing and supervisory boards are known. The two practicing Jewish members of the executive who had left the bank in spring 1933 were followed by Georg Solmssen as the last remaining "non-Aryan" member of the executive in 1934, although, as a baptized "non-Aryan," he was for the time being co-opted onto the supervisory board. In the Commerzbank the Professional Civil Service Law was not applied to the "non-Aryan" employees, whose number is estimated by Weihe to have been around 115 to 150 persons (or 1.5 percent to 2 percent of the entire staff). Apparently the majority shareholder and subsidiary of the Reichsbank, the Golddiskontbank, did not follow the example of the Reich Economics Ministry in the case of the Dresdner Bank and decided not to apply the provisions of the Professional Civil Service Law to the employees of the Commerzbank. Nevertheless, the Commerzbank did dismiss about 40 percent of its "non-Aryan" employees by the middle of 1935, among them the only Jewish member of the managing board, Ludwig Berliner, who, however, switched to the management of the Amsterdam subsidiary, Hugo Kaufmann.

The supervisory boards were not subject to the provisions of the Professional Civil Service Law and, consequently, most of the Jewish members were able to keep their posts. In the Dresdner Bank Fritz Andreae, a "half-Jew," was the chairman of the board until 1935, and even the Reich Economics Ministry kept a person of Jewish descent as its representative on the supervisory board of the bank. At the Deutsche Bank, which had in the meantime been completely reprivatized, Georg Solmssen remained on the supervisory board until as late as 1938 and only left after the Deutsche Bank had been classified as a "Jewish enterprise" because of his board membership.[23] However, the Deutsche Bank behaved completely differently towards the oldest member of its supervisory board, Max Steinthal, who not only was a practicing Jew but was also regarded as a liberal. Steinthal was a member of the managing board from 1873 to 1905 and then switched to the supervisory board. He remained formally a member of the board until November 1935, but from 1933 he is no longer mentioned in the business reports. The bank seems to have ignored him completely in other respects too. He was apparently too old to emigrate and died at the end of 1940 in a hotel room, after his house had been confiscated on the outbreak of the war.[24]

The "non-Aryans" protected by the exemptions of the Professional Civil Service Law were able to maintain their positions only for a time. Most of them were dismissed after the promulgation of the "Nuremberg Laws." According to the First Decree on the Implementation of the State Citizenship Law of November 1935 "Jewish" civil servants who had hitherto been protected by the exemptions of the Professional Civil Service Law also had to be forced to retire.[25] Although this regulation was never specifically applied to the salaried staff and the workers in companies predominantly controlled by the state and although by this time the reprivatization of the Deutsche Bank had been accomplished, the three great banks agreed to dismiss the hitherto "protected non-Aryans" by 31 January 1937.[26] The last remaining "non-Aryans" on the managing boards, Samuel Ritscher at the Dresdner Bank and the deputy board member at the Commerzbank, Georg Lust, now had to leave, along with the surviving "non-Aryan" members of the supervisory boards.

As far as the "dejewification" of the rest of the workforce was concerned, the three banks could not meet the deadline they had fixed. But by the end of 1937 there were only very few "non-Aryans" still working in the banks and by the middle of 1938 at the latest the last Jewish employees had left. In the case of the Dresdner Bank the majority of the employees who remained until 1935 were not dismissed but "pensioned off." There are two probable reasons for this. First, the majority of those who benefited from the exemptions of the Professional Civil Service Law had been in the service of the banks for a long time and had acquired a claim to a pension. Secondly, the plant manager of the Dresdner Bank, Hans Schippel, did at least recognize that "it is difficult for non-Aryan employees to find positions elsewhere."[27]

The "Aryanization" of Business Property

After numerous senior executives of Jewish origin had been driven out of their positions and the majority of the supervisory boards had been "dejewified," only self-employed businessmen continued to occupy "influential" positions in the economy from the point of view of the National Socialists. At first no legal measures were taken to infringe upon private industrial property. This did not mean, however, that the attacks of the SA and the NSBO had no direct effect. In some cases they certainly did lead to a "voluntary Aryanization" of the firms affected and occasionally the state of affairs illegally created by the attacks was subsequently legalized (as in the case of the Charlottenburger Wasser- und Industriewerke).[28] But this was not the rule.

On the other hand there is agreement in recent research on the fact that Jewish businessmen and manufacturers were uninterruptedly subject to massive pressure from 1933 on, even after the number of attacks had declined. At the time of the seizure of power the German economy had not yet overcome the crisis and many companies and businesses were already so shaky that the slightest fall in turnover as a result of boycotts or the loss of contracts from the public authorities would have meant ruin. In such cases an "Aryanization" of the business was usually out of question. But the non-Jewish competitors profited nonetheless when the Jewish businesses were liquidated, as the reduction of competition slightly improved their chances of surviving the recession. All in all, therefore, the legislation alone is not a good indicator of the practice of "Aryanization."[29]

Whenever a larger or an export-oriented company was "Aryanized" the great banks were entrusted from the start with the implementation of the property transfer. The role they played has not, however, been clearly established yet and must be examined in each individual case. Fundamentally the same behavioral typologies are conceivable as those found by Frank Bajohr in his study of the buyers of "Jewish" businesses. First, the banks could operate as unscrupulous profit-makers who went beyond the given discriminatory conditions and take the initiative against the Jewish owners. Secondly, they could profit from the persecutory measures as "sleeping partners," who carried out the transactions in a superficially correct way but worked against the interests of the Jewish victims, particularly in questions of evaluation, cooperating when the occasion arose with the authorities responsible for approval of their actions. Finally, it is also conceivable that they acted as willing partners of the Jewish victims, helping them to find fair buyers and, as foreign-exchange banks, assisting the emigrants in transferring as much of their remaining property abroad as possible.[30]

When examining the behavior of the banks the conditions must first be taken into account under which the "Aryanization" was carried out. Apart from the fact that, from 1936/37 on "Aryanization contracts" had to be presented to the Regional Party Economic Advisor and from 1938 to state institutions for approval, which clearly limited the autonomy of the banks in choosing buyers and setting prices,[31] the interests of the banks were not always the same. To start with, three types of activity need to be distinguished.

The first type can be characterized as "Aryanization on one's own account." In this case a private bank whose owners are of Jewish origin is taken over by the great bank itself or one of its subsidiaries. The liquidation of such private banking houses can also be included here, as the great bank entrusted with the liquidation often took over the clientele of the liquidated bank.

The majority of the estimated 345 Jewish private banks in existence at the end of 1935 had been liquidated by the beginning of 1939.[32] In many cases, however, the Jewish owners left and were replaced by new, non-Jewish owners.[33] The cases of "Aryanization" of private banks were very small in number and spectacular in nature. The two most significant examples of a takeover of a private bank regarded as "Jewish" by a great bank were the "Aryanization" of the Berlin banking house Mendelssohn & Co. by the Deutsche Bank in 1938 and the "Aryanization" of Gebr. Arnhold, whose headquarters in Dresden were first taken over in 1935 by the Dresdner Bank and its Berlin branch office in 1938 by the Dresdner Bank and its daughter company Hardy & Co. The Commerzbank did not participate in the "Aryanization" of private banks.

It is not known how many private banks owned by Jews were liquidated by the great banks. In the case of the Dresdner Bank at least twenty cases can be assumed.[34] The Commerzbank liquidated at least its partly owned subsidiaries Markus Schiff-Markus Nelken & Sohn (1935) and Siegfried Falk

(1937), and took over their clientele and business and probably the non-Jewish part of the staff.[35]

In the case of the Berlin private bank Mendelssohn & Co. the takeover by the Deutsche Bank is generally assumed by historians to have been a so-called "friendly Aryanization," in view of the concurring statements of the Deutsche Bank representative Hermann Josef Abs and Rudolf Loeb, one of the owners on the Mendelssohn side. Both confirm that the owners of Mendelssohn asked the Deutsche Bank for help because the state-owned Reichskreditgesellschaft announced its intention to buy the bank, whereas, at the same time, the NS factory cell was working for the continuation of the bank as an independent enterprise. The second solution in particular, which was also favored by the Reich Economics Ministry, was rejected by the owners because they feared that they might be held personally responsible by the foreign standstill creditors of the bank. Unlike the Reichskreditgesellschaft, the Deutsche Bank declared its willingness to clarify the question of the standstill credits in the interests of the owners. The "friendly" character of this takeover was confirmed after the war by the OMGUS (Office of Military Government for Germany, United States) investigations, which reveal that the participants in the negotiations always agreed that Mendelssohn & Co should be re-established as an independent banking house as soon as the economic and political conditions permitted.[36]

An important precondition for the comparatively favorable circumstances of the "Aryanization" of Mendelssohn & Co. was the fact that only about a quarter of the capital was in "Jewish hands." Consequently, until 1938, only limited pressure could be put upon the owners. The situation was completely different in the practicing Jewish, liberal and cosmopolitan Arnhold family.[37] It was not only the practice of religion, however, which made their situation different from that of the Mendelssohns. One of the partners, Walter Frisch, who participated in the negotiations on the Arnhold side, did, it is true, claim that they were fair. But this statement is not entirely plausible, as Frisch had been a member of the managing board of the Dresdner Bank until 1933 and, as a non-Jew, joined the Dresdner Bank private banking subsidiary Hardy & Co. after the "Aryanization" of Gebr. Arnhold.

The starting point for the "Aryanization" of the Dresden head office of Gebr. Arnhold was, however, the harassment of the family by the Party Regional Leader of Saxony, Martin Mutschmann, who at least wished to drive them out of his region. After interrogations on account of supposedly irregular financial transactions in the spring of 1933 had come to nothing, a charge of fraud was brought in January 1934, and, finally, in April 1935, an inquiry was opened against the owners because of currency offenses. Mutschmann was forced to adopt such methods because the clear directives of the Reich government did not permit him to take action against the bank by legally acceptable economic and political means.

Up to this point in time the Dresdner Bank was not involved in the process. But it now approached the Arnhold family to see whether they were interested in selling. After the owners had agreed, Frisch entered into takeover negotiations with his former colleagues and brought them to a swift conclusion. Although the Reich Economics Ministry assessed the conditions as favorable for the great bank, there is no indication that additional pressure was exercised on the family in this phase. After the "Aryanization," however, the Dresdner Bank changed its hitherto passive attitude and took legal steps to force through several "improvements" of the takeover conditions.

When in the course of 1937 the situation worsened for the Jewish banking houses in Berlin as well, the Dresdner Bank approached Frisch again in order to sound out the possibilities for a takeover of the Berlin branch. According to statements of the former lawyer of the Arnhold family, the negotiations took place under inauspicious conditions, and it is indeed scarcely conceivable that the family would have entered voluntarily into negotiations with a business partner who had just taken them to court. From this point of view the arrest of Kurt Arnhold by the Gestapo while the negotiations were in progress does not seem to have been pure coincidence. There is, however, no evidence that the Dresdner Bank took advantage of the custody, which lasted several weeks, and this was also denied vehemently by the bank during the restitution negotiations after the war. But, even if there were no actual agreements reached between the Dresdner Bank and the relevant authorities to increase the pressure on the Arnhold family, this example nevertheless reveals quite clearly how the division of labor in the process of economic persecution functioned. A wide variety of measures were taken to force Jewish businessmen to give up long before the "elimination" of Jews from the economy at the end of 1938, ranging from social isolation, as expressed, for example, in the application of the "Aryan paragraph" to association statutes, and official and commercial harassment, to charges of economic (and increasingly even sexual) offenses[38] and, finally, arrest and imprisonment. Even if they did not take the initiative themselves, the buyers—and these included the great banks—could simply stand aside and wait until the circumstances played into their hands. In accordance with the typology of the buyers of "Aryanization property" sketched above, the Dresdner Bank can at most be classified as a "sleeping partner" in the case of the Arnhold banking house.

The second type of bank "Aryanization" activity involved the procurement of small and medium-sized companies, usually private partnerships, in the process of "Aryanization." In these cases the banks did not take over the businesses that were to be "Aryanized" themselves, but arranged the sale in return for a commission. They either sought a suitable buyer among their clientele on behalf of a Jewish seller, or they sought suitable "Aryanization property" on behalf of an interested non-Jewish client. As the buyer was not usually in a position to supply the capital for the acquisition of the property in spite of a selling price that from the buyer's point of view was extremely favorable, the arrangement of an "Aryanization deal" usually went hand in hand with the arrangement of a credit agreement. Although the Jewish sellers were usually debtors to the bank—normally the decisive factor in the bank's access to the property—the need of the buyer for credit was almost always considerably greater than that of the previous owner. Particularly after the intervention of the Regional Party Economic Advisor in the process of "Aryanization" from 1936 on, the buyers were primarily holders of a party card and only secondarily, if at all, experienced businessmen. Knowledge of the sector concerned could not always be assumed, and capital of their own was the last thing the buyers had at their disposal.

The activities of the banks in this area probably started as early as 1933, but they had not reached a quantitatively significant amount by the end of the year 1937. The individual properties were usually so small that the sale could usually be arranged by the provincial branches or the Berlin deposit offices of their own accord. In the case of the Commerzbank and the Deutsche Bank the headquarters were only involved through the branch offices, which concerned themselves with "Aryanization credits" as part of their regular control of the credit transactions of the branches and deposit offices.[39] It was only when the credit needed for the "Aryanization" exceeded the amount which the branch manager could approve on his own responsibility that the head office intervened directly in the process of "Aryanization." When, however, at the beginning of the year 1938, the concept of a "Jewish business enterprise" was defined by the Reich Economics Ministry and, a few months later, the compulsory identification of Jewish businesses was introduced, the arrangement of "Aryanization deals" became large-scale business. The Dresdner Bank then established a special subdepartment within its Syndicate Department for such "Aryanization deals" and coordinated from there the activities of the branches and the deposit offices. In this "Aryanization Department" those orders of customers were collected in particular which could not be dealt with in the branch area. In such cases the branches reported to the "Aryanization Department," which itself, from spring 1938 on, sent regular circulars to the branches on reported "Aryanization property" and on customers interested in certain properties. In this way the buyers and the sellers of "Aryanization property" were to be brought together quickly even beyond the boundaries of the branch areas. For in these weeks of the "Aryanization race" speed was extremely important. It was, after all, essential to procure the company or business of a Jewish credit customer for a non-Jewish buyer who belonged to the clientele of the bank, so that credit customers were not lost. On the other hand, this massive change of ownership provided a unique opportunity to improve the bank's share of the market within the branch areas by procuring "Aryanization property" whose Jewish owner was a customer of a competing bank for the bank's own clientele. Apart from the swift and effective flow of information, good connections with the authorities and particularly with the Regional and District Party Economic Advisors were necessary. The banks had to reach an agreement with them not only on the selling price but also on the buyer. If this did not succeed immediately, a customer of a competing bank might be accepted.

Under these general conditions the banks had to weigh up the merits and demerits of two conflicting lines of action. Either they could opt for a buyer with a solid knowledge of the line of business and the corresponding business experience, so that the chances were as great as possible that the conditions of the "Aryanization credit" would be reliably met, or they could choose a politically reliable buyer, who however – as was very often the case with the "Old Fighters" – lacked the necessary business skills and was actually an inordinately high credit risk. If the bank proposed an "Old Fighter," it could be fairly sure of the approval of the authorities. But, if it proposed a customer who was not a card-holding member of the party, it would have to reckon with the competition of candidates from within the party. If another bank then supported such a candidate, the transfer of property could then be made to the disadvantage of the first bank.

The fact that the Dresdner Bank centralized the "Aryanization business" of its branches can be interpreted as a sign that it wished to use the chances offered by the "Aryanization business" as widely as possible by maximizing the flow of information within the bank. This does not necessarily mean, however, that it was more "aggressive" than its competitors on this account. For, although the Deutsche Bank and the Commerzbank did not centralize their "Aryanization business" in the same way, leaving it within the competence of the branches and the branch offices at the head office, both the Commerzbank and the Deutsche Bank were actively involved in this "race" Both banks included "Aryanization property" in the circulars with which they informed the branch managers of firms that were up for sale.[40]

In an evaluation of the "Aryanization negotiations" of the great banks, the fact must be taken into account that this service was often extremely useful for the Jewish owners. For, if the owner failed to find a buyer and he had to leave the country quickly because of the threat of arrest or other reasons, his firm would be placed under compulsory administration and he would receive nothing at all. However, even the fact that a Jewish customer approached his bank requesting support in the search for a buyer cannot be automatically interpreted to mean that the bank would then actually make an effort to represent the interests of its customer. As a general principle it can be stated that the further away from the decision-maker the Jewish customer was and the more anonymous the consequences for the decision-maker, the more ruthlessly the latter proceeded.

The Mendelssohns were close to the decision-makers, the "petty customers" of the provincial branches far way. The Berlin headquarters of the Deutsche Bank, for example, required the manager of the Freiburg branch to explain whether an "Aryanization property" put up for sale should be included in the bulletin "simply as a favor to your customers," as the bulletin is to be made "available only for the sale of objects in the realization of which we have a direct interest, e.g., using the proceeds to cover or reduce debit balances held with us." It was only after such an "interest in the realization" of the transaction was confirmed by Freiburg that the property was included in the bulletin.[41]

The scope of the "Aryanization business" can hardly be quantified. After the war the banks were, it is true, obliged by two allied military decrees to name all "cases of Aryanization" in which they had participated, whereupon, for example, the Mannheim branch of the Deutsche Bank listed 83 names and the Hamburg branch of the Deutsche Bank 147 names. The branches of the Commerzbank in Munich, Nuremberg, Fürth, and one Berlin deposit office alone participated in 70 cases of "Aryanization."[42] But in many of these cases the "participation" meant solely that the firm concerned had kept an account with the particular branch.

Even more problematic than the assessment of the scope of the "Aryanization business" is the attempt to determine the profits from it. Harold James rightly emphasizes that the "Aryanization" of industrial property was not "good business" for many of the branches of the great banks in spite of the commission they earned. He quotes the case of a deposit office of the Deutsche Bank in Stuttgart, that lost 70 percent of its credit totals within two years. A contemporary calculation for the Deutsche Bank as a whole estimated the "non-Aryan" share in its credit business at 13.6 percent in 1935. This share fell by the end of November 1938 to just 3percent. Even if the consequent drop in the credit business of around RM 70 million was softened or even compensated for by the new credits granted to the buyers of "Aryanization property," the average quality of the debtors had noticeably worsened. As early as November 1936 a member of the Rhenish-Westphalian Advisory Board of the Deutsche Bank warned the executive to "exercise great caution" in selling Jewish firms, as, in many cases, "'Aryanizations' have sometimes led to firms falling into weak hands."[43]

When the Deutsche Bank did in many cases become actively involved in the "Aryanization business," it often did so in order to demonstrate its willingness to cooperate with the local party offices or because of competition with the savings banks, the branches of regional banks, and the other great banks. For, if the economic damage caused by "Aryanization" could not be avoided, it wanted at least to reduce the harm done by winning the favor of influential party officials and collecting its commission. Anti-Semitism cannot be excluded as the motivating force behind the activities of some branch managers. But ideological motives do not seem to have played any part in the fundamental policies of the Deutsche Bank, the Commerzbank or probably the Dresdner Bank in the business they did as the "negotiators of Aryanization." This was presumably a matter of indifference for those in power, for as a rule the differences in motivation led to no differences in the results.

Between the two types of activity described above stands, as the third type, the "Aryanization" of bigger enterprises, usually joint-stock companies. In these cases the bank usually operated at first as an "Aryanizer" on its own account, not, however, with the intention of keeping the shares it acquired over a longer period of time; they were usually sold again in the medium term, care being taken, however, to keep the company concerned as a customer. As a general rule big companies were not encroached upon by the National Socialists in the first few years after the seizure of power. The existence of such companies was not to be endangered, in order to prevent a further increase in the army of the unemployed. Moreover, on account of their export business the big companies were often important sources of foreign currency for the Reich. There were, however, individual cases of "Aryanization" of big companies even in the early period of National Socialist rule. Those usually affected were companies that either depended heavily on public contracts (like the road-building company Johannes Jeserich AG) or, as producers of consumer goods, were seriously hit by the boycott measures taken by non-Jewish retailers (like the Beiersdorf AG). In such cases the great banks were often represented on the supervisory boards as major creditors and were thus in a position at least to influence the course of events. When changes in the management were called for, no resistance on their part was, of course, to be expected. After all, the banks treated the "non-Aryan" employees in their own houses no differently.

For the Dresdner Bank it can even be assumed that in some cases the representatives of the bank on the supervisory boards were among the driving forces behind the elimination of the Jewish members of the executives or of Jewish shareholders. The surviving files of the "Consultant for Special Economic Assignments" and later director of the head office in Berlin, Erich Niemann, point at least in this direction. Between May and December 1933 Niemann was delegated by the bank as its representative on eleven supervisory boards. All of the companies either were in need of reorganization or were to be "Aryanized" a short time later. The latter is true of the Orenstein & Koppel railway-carriage construction company, the H. Fuld & Co. telephone and telegraph works, the EPA Einheitspreis AG, the Dr. Cassirer & Co. cable works and the Julius Berger Tiefbau AG, civil engineering company. In all of these cases Niemann himself states that he "worked for the elimination of the non-Aryans," which is the probable reason for his delegation to the supervisory boards in the first place. Apart from Niemann, the Dresdner Bank also had a second "man for the dirty work," Hilarius Giebel, who was also formally an independent consultant. Giebel played a prominent part in the "Aryanization" of the Engelhardt brewery group.[44]

When shares in a commercial corporation were taken over the margin of profit between purchase price and selling price was as unimportant a motive for the commitment of the great banks as the commission they earned. Their main interest was, rather, in keeping the company concerned as a customer after its "Aryanization" and in securing influence over the companies by selling shares to their own clientele. Occasionally the pressure to "Aryanize" was exploited by a great bank in order to get rid of the management of a credit customer that was regarded as incompetent or uncooperative.[45]

To ensure the influence of a bank in a joint-stock company, there were (and are) numerous instruments. The most important is the dispatch of a representative of the bank to the supervisory board of the customer, usually backed up by a relevant number of votes in the general meeting. It was a specialty of German company law that the commercial banks also had votes in the general meetings not only for their own shares but also for those of their customers.[46] To this extent it was of the greatest importance for the industrial relations of all banks that the shares of joint-stock companies went to their own clientele, so that the proxy voting rights could be exercised. If a substantial block of shares of a Jewish customer was deposited at a competing bank after its purchase by a non-Jew, the new bank could try to force the representatives of its competitor off the supervisory board, as a result of which they would be deprived of important insider information about the affairs of the company. Such a shift would necessarily have left its mark on debtor—creditor relations.

Room for Maneuver, Structures, and Motives

At the time of the seizure of power all three great banks were either partly (Deutsche Bank) or with a majority interest (Commerzbank, Dresdner Bank) in the possession of the public authorities. Even before the seizure of power the Reich had intervened massively in the affairs of the banks. This was the case both in business policy, as when the Reich compelled the merger of the Dresdner Bank and the Danat Bank against the declared will of the managing board, and in personnel policy, as when Reichskanzler Brüning forced several executives of the Deutsche Bank and the Dresdner Bank to resign and replaced them with members whom he trusted. The freedom of action of the banks was, therefore, considerably restricted from 1931/32 on. A further threat to the freedom of action of the banks can hardly be overestimated in its significance as a motive for the bank executives in the first few years after the seizure of power. The application of the Professional Civil Service Law to their own staff by the Dresdner Bank could not, in principle, be avoided. The situation was rather less clear in the case of the Deutsche Bank, as there not only was it the state-owned Golddiskontbank—and not the Reich—that held a block of shares, but this also comprised only 30 percent of the total share capital. Particularly after the Golddiskontbank had begun to sell its block of shares back to the Deutsche Bank in November 1933,[47] the latter could theoretically have stopped "halfway" with the dismissal of its Jewish employees. It did not do so, usually putting forward "compelling business reasons" as a pretext. This could, for example, possibly refer to the fact that the local branches of their competitors had dismissed their employees of Jewish origin and that the Deutsche Bank feared disadvantages as a result. For this reason the branches of the great banks occasionally reached an agreement on a common procedure in the process of "dejewification" of particular branches, in spite of the tough local competition.[48]

The dismissal of the "protected non-Aryans" after the promulgation of the Nuremberg Laws was also not absolutely necessary, as the regulations for the dismissal of civil servants in the decree on the implementation of the law did not follow the Professional Civil Service Law in extending its application to companies equivalent to the statutory companies. Nevertheless, the great banks agreed on a timetable for the dismissal of those "non-Aryan" employees who had hitherto been protected by the exemptions of the Professional Civil Service Law. There does not seem to have been any difference between, on the one hand, the Commerzbank and the Dresdner Bank, which were only privatized in 1937, and, on the other hand, the Deutsche Bank, which had already been reprivatized. There is no question, therefore, that the banks had room for maneuver in the "dejewification" of their staff. There was room for maneuver, even if it only arose after the process had already got under way. But it was almost invariably used to the disadvantage of the persecuted.

As regards the transfer of business property the banks even had a completely free hand in deciding whether to participate or not. As the example of the Commerzbank demonstrates, the great banks could refrain from participation in the "Aryanization" of the private banks. But what is true of the private banking houses, however, is also true of other companies. Theoretically the great banks could have adopted a completely passive stance and have only intervened if they were asked for help by a Jewish owner. In such cases they could then have unselfishly pursued the interests of their client. There may well have been cases in which the banks behaved in this way, but all the indications are that this was not the rule.

When the banks used their theoretical room for maneuver in "Aryanization deals" exclusively or predominantly to the disadvantage of the victims, this can in all probability be attributed primarily to utility maximization. The survival of a company can also depend on this. Hence, such a motive can in the extreme case be evaluated as a not only subjective but also objective limitation of the freedom of action of a managing board. There can be no doubt, however, that the banks were willing to pursue business policies against Jews that were not generally practiced (why else should the Dresdner Bank have delegated a "man for the dirty work" instead of a normal board member as hitherto, to represent it on the supervisory boards of "Aryanization properties"?); secondly, forgoing "Aryanization deals" may well have cost a share of the market and so reduced the profits of the great banks in the short and medium term, but such a practice would not have endangered their existence. One would, of course, have to face unpleasant questions from shareholders at general meetings. But such a subjective limitation of freedom of action must be evaluated in a qualitatively different way than a breach of the law, such as a theoretically conceivable disregard of the regulations of the Professional Civil Service Law.

The situation is similar when one regards the room for maneuver of individual decision-makers within the banking organisms. I have already cited the example of the Dresdner Bank elsewhere to demonstrate that the range of individual behavior of those responsible for the "dejewification" of the staff was enormously wide.[49] In a number of cases it was possible to prove that leading members of the Dresdner Bank actively helped individual Jewish colleagues. This is true, for example, for the placement of top managers in "friendly" enterprises abroad, which occurred in all three great banks.[50]

Such persons were certainly in the minority, and it is also undisputed that the presence of more decision-makers who showed the courage of their convictions in the bureaucracy of the great banks would not have prevented the ousting of their Jewish colleagues. But the fact that the careers of none of the persons examined were endangered at any time on account of their attitude toward "Jewish policy" shows that the room for maneuver of the individual decision-makers would certainly have permitted them to throw a spanner in the works of the machinery of persecution.

An important reason why so few decision-makers took the initiative in using their room for maneuver to help the victims of persecution was probably anti-Semitic prejudice, which was very widespread in the German petite bourgeoisie. Radical anti-Semitic attitudes of employees of great banks are indeed known, but, in view of the evidence given by employees with a clean record during the denazification trials of hotheads of the NS factory cells after the war, it can be assumed that the majority of the staff of the Dresdner Bank were not radical anti-Semites. Tolerance of the supporting measures taken in support of dismissed Jewish employees, which were by no means always kept secret, and the obvious reserve of the Dresdner Bank company magazine in the question of anti-Semitic propaganda permit, furthermore, the conclusion that radical anti-Semitism as part of the "corporate identity" was regarded as undesirable.

Even the National Socialists who had moved into the management of the Dresdner Bank from 1934 on obviously took a pragmatic line, as they tolerated the continued employment of Jewish colleagues in responsible positions for a very long time in, of all places, the stock-market departments. It is difficult to imagine a more impressive proof of the fact that the anti-Semites in the management believed their own ideology in regard to the "avaricious spirit" of the Jews. From this point of view the Jews were predestined for the stock-exchange business, whereas the employment of "Aryans" was a business risk as long as competitors continued to employ Jews in this area. But if it was quite feasible that the decisive factors determining the actions even of National Socialists did not lie in their anti-Semitic ideology, this is doubly true of their conservative colleagues.

It is difficult to prove the existence of anti-Semitic attitudes of individual decision-makers. The idea that there were too many Jews in the financial sector and particularly in the top echelons of the banks was certainly widespread. The same is true of a racial definition of "Germanness." In principle, therefore, the Professional Civil Service Law and other legal measures of persecution corresponded entirely with bourgeois and conservative ideas.[51] It can be assumed that a substantial part of the staff, including some members of the management, approved the application of the Professional Civil Service Law to the great banks on principle. But here too ideologically based motives soon came into conflict with other rationalities guiding action. This is shown by an application of a manager of the Dresdner Bank who sympathized with the National Socialists to the Economics Ministry requesting approval for the appointment of Jewish employees at a general rate of 1 percent.[52] This would correspond to the share of the Jews in the overall population. If this application had been approved, the bank would then have been able to keep those Jewish employees who were most difficult to replace. The "dejewification" could then have been carried out in accordance with strictly commercial principles. Here, therefore, a rational logic guiding action overlies the irrational anti-Semitism, but without at the same time eliminating it.

Consequently, the anti-Semitic convictions of the decision-makers in the great banks are no more adequate than their restricted room for maneuver as an explanation of their involvement in the measures of economic persecution taken by the regime. Anti-Semitism as an "attitudinal climate" (Seibel) probably makes it easier to make decisions in favor of such measures, which had not hitherto been recognized as normal business conduct. But as a motive anti-Semitism was not "robust" enough. The professional logic that permitted the "Aryanization business" to appear as a normal banking service is clearly revealed in the composition of the bulletins of the Commerzbank and Deutsche Bank headquarters to their branches. In both cases the lists of "Aryanization property" were intermixed with those of non-Jewish companies for whom a buyer was being sought on behalf of the customer. Internally, therefore "Aryanization deals" were placed functionally on the same footing as the "normal" business transactions. Those responsible could, consequently, adopt the standpoint that the reasons for the sale of a company were none of the bank's business. It made no difference to them whether a family business lacked an heir or whether an owner needed capital to pay his Reich Flight Tax. Conversely, the example of the Commerzbank has served to prove—and this is confirmed by the credit files of the Dresdner Bank—that in spite of the social climate Jewish businessmen were regarded as creditworthy customers as long as they were solvent. The moment doubts arose as to their creditworthiness the great banks reacted very quickly, as they could safely assume that in view of the overall unfavorable conditions for "non-Aryan" companies the recovery of a business that was in trouble was highly unlikely. To this extent it was only logical that in November 1938 credits to Jewish customers were subjected to severe controls. Lorentz draws the conclusion that "the economic effects of racism…were thus in a way integrated as premises into the business principles of one's own economic activities."[53]

The detachment of the "Aryanization negotiations" from their discriminatory overall context and their treatment as "perfectly normal" business probably made it easy for many of those involved to hide their bad consciences behind a façade of professional logic. Corresponding personal testimonies are of course very rare. But the argument with which the chairman of the supervisory board of the Deutsche Bank, Franz Urbig, justified the exclusion of a Jewish colleague points in this direction. "The business aristocracy which you emphasize had, from the year 1918 on, lost a lot in our circles as well, and we were often forced to do something which, in the opinion of others, promoted the interests of the state, but contradicted our personal views."[54] Urbig thus presents the interventionism of National Socialism, in principle, as an unbroken continuation of the interventionism of the Weimar Republic. This maneuver also serves primarily the purpose of self-deception and justification. As has been mentioned already, there was, in fact, a tradition of seemingly similar interventions in the freedom of action of the great banks stemming from the Brüning era. The banks were accustomed to interventions in the choice of personnel and even in the form of employment contracts in this period. It did not require much in the way of self-deception to interpret the application of the Professional Civil Service Law as a continuation of the emergency enactment policies of the late phase of the Weimar Republic. The right of the government to dismiss undesired members of managing and supervisory boards and to appoint new members sympathetic to the government could not be disputed in view of its status as an owner, and that the new government also claimed this right for itself was at first sight a matter of course.

The Dresdner Bank had, moreover, carried out profound changes in its personnel at all levels on the occasion of the merger with the Danat Bank. The new measures seemed scarcely any different, except that now, instead of older employees being sent into (early) retirement, Jews were dismissed. The impact of the reduction in personnel of around 20 percent probably also contributed to a not inconsiderable degree to the loss of solidarity among the staff. Almost all employees had been living for years under the threat that professional failure would very quickly lead to incorporation in the army of the unemployed. Because the poison of anti-Semitism had penetrated society so deeply, many of the employees of the Dresdner Bank were probably only too glad to believe the legend that the "Jewified" management had held a protecting hand over Jewish employees when reducing the staff.[55] The fact that dismissed employees were preferably replaced by "Party veterans" was also explained by the particular disadvantages which employees who openly supported National Socialism had supposedly suffered under the "Jewified" executive of the Weimar "system period."

This association of an anti-Semitic "attitudinal climate" and professional logic proved to be a really robust combination, which was strengthened by particular structural conditions. The major motivating force of all the managing boards of the great banks from spring 1933 at least until the SA and the NSBO were deprived of power in the middle of 1934 was the maintenance of their company's room for maneuver. The crude politico-economic ideas to be found in the early programmatic statements of the NSDAP, which continued to be pursued by influential personalities in the Party, were well-known to the executives.[56] They could be quite sure that Göring, Schmitt, Schacht, or probably even Hitler might not dare to experiment with the structure of the banking system. Up to the middle of 1934 it was not clear, however, whether or not the pragmatists in the party and the government would prevail against the ideologists. It is not surprising, therefore, that the executives hoped to take the wind out of the sails of the radical elements by practicing "obedience in advance."

The forced resignation of the two practicing Jewish members of the managing board of the Deutsche Bank on the "recommendation" of the President of the Reichsbank in May 1933 has already been mentioned. The threat is even clearer in the case of the Dresdner Bank. There an occupation of the bank by the SA and NSBO in early May 1933 was only warded off by a personal intervention of Göring. There are clear indications that, as a concession to the factory cell, the bank consented to the immediate implementation of the Professional Civil Service Law, but was in return able to prevent the fulfillment of the factory cell's proposal for the occupation of the vacant post of head of the personnel department. The demand of a self-appointed "commissar" to become a member of the managing board contradicted the directives of the Ministry of the Interior and the Economics Ministry anyway. It was not only possible to dismiss the "commissar." As a warning for all hotheads in the factory cell he was thrown out of the party as well. In this way the immediate danger of a "hostile takeover" by the party was banned. But the government commission of inquiry into banking affairs convened a few months later made the persistent threat to the existing structures clear once again. In the commission the representatives of the great banks were confronted by an admittedly disunited front consisting of National Socialist ideologists, National Socialist private bankers and National Socialist officials of the savings banks, who all spoke of breaking up or at least decentralizing the great banks.[57] The most important ally of the great banks, however, was the very man who, a few months earlier, had urged the Deutsche Bank to dismiss the Jewish members of their executives "voluntarily." It is quite conceivable that Schacht threatened to terminate the old agreement between the Deutsche Bank and the subsidiary of the Reichsbank, the Golddiskontbank, whereupon the latter withdrew its abandonment of sending a representative to the supervisory board of the Deutsche Bank if the bank did not for its part make concessions to the new government in the "Jewish question." If one attributes the "robust motives" described above to the non-Jewish executives of the great banks, the dismissal of 1,000 Jewish employees will not, from their point of view, have been too high a price to pay for their ultimately successful defensive struggle.

The members of the staff of great big banks possibly saw this threat to the independent existence of their employers as a threat to their own jobs. But it is very doubtful whether they recognized the connection between "dejewification" and the structural status quo. At all events this threat to the overall structure of the banks does not explain why the banking organism functioned so smoothly during the "dejewification." A further structural factor plays its part here, which will be explained in what follows by taking the Dresdner Bank as an example, but which probably applies in a similar fashion to the Commerzbank and possibly even to the Deutsche Bank.[58]

After the reduction of staff following the merger of the Dresdner Bank and the Danat Bank, the channels of promotion within the Dresdner Bank became extraordinarily narrow on account of the age structure after the implementation of the merger and the reduction in staff. In view of the large number of senior posts lost in the process of restructuring the personnel, very few competent, young and ambitious employees could reasonably hope to climb the professional ladder in the foreseeable future. From the point of view of this group the Professional Civil Service Law created a completely new situation. Due to the above average share of senior staff among those affected by the Civil Service Law, non-Jewish employees could suddenly reckon on much swifter promotion.

A well documented and at the same time particularly striking example of this is the management level itself. A "new generation" of deputy executives owed their appointment primarily to the departure of those members of the management who were Jews. Between the fall of 1933 and the fall of 1934 two members of the managing board and five "A-directors" or general agents left the bank. Within a few months Hermann Richter (born 1900), Alfred Busch (born 1893), Emil Meyer (born 1886), and Hugo Zinßer (born 1900) all joined the management. With the exception of Emil Meyer they were all professional experts who would possibly have achieved such positions without the expulsion of the Jews. But because of the blocked channels of promotion it would certainly not have been in the 1930s.

This bundle of structures and motives—protection of the freedom of action of the great banks as economic subjects within an economy controlled by the National Socialists, the professional logic of the "Aryanization business" (coupled with the longstanding experience of the threat of unemployment), the anti-Semitic reservations in society in general and among banking employees in particular, the constitutional camouflage of the first anti-Jewish laws and, finally, the advantages that the expulsion of the Jews brought to many non-Jewish employees within the banking organism—seems to have been sufficiently robust to explain a fact that is so surprising from the perspective of the present, the astoundingly conflict-free participation of the great banks in the measures of economic persecution of the National Socialist regime.

Notes

1. The recommendation of the OMGUS Finance Division, Financial Investigation Section, in the case of the Deutsche Bank and Dresdner Bank was to liquidate the banks, to prosecute the managers responsible as war criminals, and to exclude them in future from important or responsible positions in economic and political life. On this point see *Ermittlungen gegen die Deutsche Bank–1946/47* (ed. Hamburger Stiftung f. Sozialgeschichte des 20. Jahrhunderts—Nördlingen, 1985) and *Ermittlungen gegen die Dresdner Bank–1946* (ed. Hamburger Stiftung f. Sozialgeschichte des 20. Jahrhunderts—Nördlingen, 1986).
2. On this point see, for example, the statement of defense of the Dresdner Bank of the year 1947, Historisches Archiv der Dresdner Bank, Bestand 125, 13761–2000 and the interrogation of Karl Rasche, BAB 99 US 7, Nr. 161.
3. Nathan Stoltzfus, "Third Reich History as if the People Mattered," *Geschichte und Gesellschaft* 26 (2000): 683.
4. Frank Bajohr, "Verfolgung aus gesellschaftsgeschichtlicher Perspektive. Die wirtschaftliche Existenzvernichtung der Juden und die deutsche Gesellschaft," *Geschichte und Gesellschaft* 26 (2000): 629.
5. Daniel Goldhagen, *Hitlers willige Vollstrecker. Ganz gewöhnliche Deutsche und der Holocaust* (Berlin, 1996), p. 8 (preface to the German edition) idem, *Hitler's Willing Executioners: Ordinary Germans and the Holocaust* (New York, 1996), p. 14 (emphasis in the original).

6. On the following see Wolfgang Seibel, "A Market for Mass Crime? Inter-Institutional Competition and the Initiation of the Holocaust in France, 1940–1942," *Journal of Organization Theory and Behavior* 5 (2002): 219–257.
7. See Hans Mommsen, "Die Realisierung des Utopischen: Die 'Endlösung der Judenfrage' im Dritten Reich," *Geschichte und Gesellschaft* 9 (1983): 381–420.
8. Christopher Kopper, *Zwischen Marktwirtschaft und Dirigismus. Bankenpolitik im "Dritten Reich" 1933–1939* (Bonn, 1995), especially chap. IV, pp. 126–155 and chap. VI, pp. 220–291.
9. Harold James, "Die Deutsche Bank und die Diktatur 1933–1945," in Lothar Gall, Gerald Feldman, Harold James, eds., *Die Deutsche Bank 1870–1995* (Munich, 1995), pp. 334–351.
10. Harold James, *The Deutsche Bank and the Nazi Economic War Against the Jews* (Cambridge, 2001).
11. Bernhard Lorentz, "Die Commerzbank und die 'Arisierung' im Altreich," Vergleichende Studien über Netzwerkstrukturen, Handlungsspielräume und Wettbewerb von Großbanken in der NS-Zeit, vierteljahrshefte Jür Zeitgeschichte 50 (2002), pp 237–268.
12. Dieter Ziegler, "Die Verdrängung der Juden aus der Dresdner Bank 1933–1938," *Vierteljahrshefte für Zeitgeschichte* 47 (1999): 187–216.
13. Not even a contemporary commentary on the legislation against the Jews defines the concepts of "dejewification" and "Aryanization": Alfred Krüger, *Die Lösung der Judenfrage in der deutschen Wirtschaft* (Berlin, 1940). On the concepts in general see Frank Bajohr, "'Arisierung' als gesellschaftlicher Prozess. Verhalten, Strategien und Handlungsspielräume jüdischer Eigentümer und , 'arischer' Erwerber," in Fritz Bauer Institut, ed., *"Arisierung" im Nationalsozialismus* (Frankfurt on Main, 2000), pp. 15–16.
14. See Dorothee Mußgnug, *Die Reichsfluchtsteuer 1931–1953* (Berlin, 1993), chap. 2, pp. 30–62.
15. See the contemporary studies: Alfred Marcus, "Die Juden im deutschen Bankwesen," *Jüdische Wohlfahrtspflege u. Sozialpolitik* N.F. 1 (1930): 339–351; Jacob Lestschinsky, *Das wirtschaftliche Schicksal des deutschen Judentums* (Berlin, 1933); see also Rolf Walter, "Jüdische Bankiers in Deutschland bis 1932," in Werner Mosse and Hans Pohl, eds., *Jüdische Unternehmer in Deutschland im 19. und 20. Jahrhundert* (Stuttgart, 1992), pp. 78–99.
16. On the circumstances under which Quaatz was appointed see Hermann Weiß and Peter Hoser, eds., *Die Deutschnationalen und die Zerstörung der Weimarer Republik. Aus den Tagebüchern von Reinhold Quaatz 1928–1933* (Munich, 1989), p. 242f.
17. The understanding of the structure of NS rule on which this interpretation is based follows Ludolf Herbst, *Das nationalsozialistische Deutschland 1933–1945* (Frankfurt on Main, 1996), pp. 9–24, 73–79.
18. On this point see Peter Hayes, "Big Business and 'Aryanization' in Germany," *Jahrbuch für Antisemitismusforschung* 3 (1994): 254–281; Albert Fischer, *Hjalmar Schacht und Deutschlands "Judenfrage"* (Cologne, 1995). The affinity between the early NS measures on "Jewish policy" and the conservatism of the German elite is particularly emphasized by Saul Friedländer, *Das Dritte Reich und die Juden*, vol. 1 (Munich, 1998), p. 49.
19. Apart from the well-known National Socialist sympathizer Friedrich Reinhart, three members of the managing board joined the NSDAP as so-called "Märzgefallene" in spring 1933. Moreover, the longstanding member of the supervisory board Witthoeft was a member of the so-called Keppler Circle. At the Deutsche Bank the only member of the executive to have close connections with the National Socialists, Georg Emil von Stauß, was deprived of his office shortly before the seizure of power and put on the shelf in the supervisory board. At the Dresdner Bank there was no one closely associated with the National Socialists in spring 1933. Kleemann's successor, Reinhold Quaatz, although he was a "half-Jew," was even appointed to the managing board as he enjoyed the confidence of Hugenberg.
20. Erste Verordnung zur Durchführung des Gesetzes zur Wiederherstellung des Berufsbeamtentums vom 11. April 1933, RGBl. I (1933), p. 195. On the significance of the Aryan clause as a "necessary precondition for all forms of persecution" see Friedländer, *Das Dritte Reich*, p. 40. On the professional Civil Service Law in general see Hans Mommsen,

Beamtentum im Dritten Reich (Stuttgart, 1966); Sigrun Mühl-Benninghaus, *Das Beamtentum in der NS-Diktatur bis zum Ausbruch des Zweiten Weltkrieges* (Düsseldorf, 1996).
21. Zweite Verordnung zur Durchführung des Gesetzes zur Wiederherstellung des Berufsbeamtentums vom 4. May 1933 (§1), RGBl. I (1933), p. 233.
22. Ziegler, "Verdrängung," p. 204.
23. James, *The Deutsche Bank and the Nazi Economic War*, p. 56.
24. James, "Die Deutsche Bank und die Diktatur," p. 339.
25. Reichsbürgergesetz vom 15. September 1935, RGBl. I (1935), p. 1146; Erste Verordnung zum Reichsbürgergesetz vom 14. November 1935, §4 Abs. 1, RGBl. I (1933), p. 1333. See also in general Lothar Gruchmann, *Justiz im Dritten Reich 1933–1940. Anpassung und Unterwerfung in der Ära Gürtner* (Munich, 1988), p. 169f.
26. Ziegler, "Verdrängung," p. 204.
27. Ziegler, "Verdrängung," p. 206.
28. On this point see Martin Fiedler, "Die 'Arisierung' der Wirtschaftselite," in Fritz Bauer Institut, *"Arisierung" im Nationalsozialismus*, p. 72f.
29. Fundamental for this interpretation is Avraham Barkai, *Vom Boykott zur "Entjudung". Der wirtschaftliche Existenzkampf der Juden im Dritten Reich* (Frankfurt on Main, 1987), p. 26f.
30. Bajohr, "'Arisierung' als gesellschaftlicher Prozess," p. 25f.; see also Avraham Barkai, "'Die stillen Teilhaber' des NS-Regimes," in Lothar Gall and Manfred Pohl, eds., *Unternehmer im Nationalsozialismus* (Munich, 1998), pp. 117–120.
31. See Gerhard Kratzsch, *Der Gauwirtschaftsapparat der NSDAP. Menschenführung—"Arisierung"—Wehrwirtschaft im Gau Westfalen-Süd* (Münster, 1989); Dirk van Laak, "Die Mitwirkenden bei der 'Arisierung'. Dargestellt am Beispiel der rheinisch-westfälischen Industrieregion 1933–1940," in Ursula Büttner, ed., *Die Deutschen und die Judenverfolgung im Dritten Reich* (Hamburg, 1992), pp. 231–257.
32. I owe this information to Mr. Ingo Köhler, who calculated the figures from information provided by the Centralverband des Deutschen Bank- und Bankiergewerbes.
33. See Kopper, *Marktwirtschaft*, chap. VI, pp. 220–291; Albert Fischer, "Jüdische Privatbanken im 'Dritten Reich,'" *Scripta Mercaturae* 28 (1994): 1–54; Harald Wixforth and Dieter Ziegler, "Deutsche Privatbanken und Privatbankiers im 20. Jahrhundert," *Geschichte und Gesellschaft* 23 (1997): 205–235.
34. I owe this information to Mr. Köhler.
35. Lorentz, "Beteilugung der Commerzbank." p. 244.
36. See James, *The Deutsche Bank and the Nazi Economic War*, pp. 70–77. The older treatments by Wilhelm Treue, "Das Bankhaus Mendelssohn als Beispiel einer Privatbank im 19. und 20. Jahrhundert," *Mendelssohn Studien* 1 (1972): 27–80 and James, "Die Deutsche Bank und die Diktatur," p. 249, are similar in tendency. For a more critical recent approach see Julius H. Schoeps, "Wie die Deutsche Bank Mendelssohn & Co. schluckte. Berlin, Herbst 1938: Ungereimtheiten bei der Liquidation bzw. 'Arisierung' des renommierten Privatbankhauses," *Frankfurter Rundschau*, 27 November 1998.
37. The following treatment is based mainly on the above-mentioned manuscript of Ingo Köhler and the research of Simone Lässig, "Nationalsozialistische 'Judenpolitik' und jüdische Selbstbehauptung vor dem Novemberpogrom: Das Beispiel der Dresdner Bankiersfamilie Arnhold," in Rainer Pommerin, ed., *Dresden unterm Hakenkreuz* (Cologne, 1998), pp. 129–191; see also the OMGUS treatment in *Ermittlungen gegen die Dresdner Bank*, pp. 79–81.
38. The accusation of race defilement ("Blutschande") was very common, as in the case of one of the owners of the Nuremberg banking house A. Kohn: see Maren Janetzko, *Haben Sie nicht das Bankhaus Kohn gesehen? Ein jüdisches Familienschicksal in Nürnberg 1850–1950* (Nuremberg, 1998). Occasionally the accusation of homosexuality is also made, as in the case of the non-Jewish but politically undesirable chairman of the managing board of the Dessauer Gas Company: see Martin Fiedler, "Netzwerke des Vertrauens: Zwei Fallbeispiele aus der deutschen Wirtschaftselite," in Dieter Ziegler, ed., *Großbürger und Unternehmer. Die deutsche Wirtschaftselite im 20. Jahrhundert* (Göttingen, 2000), pp. 106–113.

39. Lorentz, "Commerzbank." p. 246.
40. James, *The Deutsche Bank and the Nazi Economic War*.
41. Ibid., *The Deutsche Bank and the Nazi Economic War*, p. 113.
42. Lorentz, "Commerzbank"; James, *The Deutsche Bank and the Nazi Economic War*.
43. James, *The Deutsche Bank and the Nazi Economic War*, p. 50.
44. On the part played by Giebel in the "Aryanization" of the Engelhardt Group see Johannes Ludwig, *Boykott, Enteignung, Mord. Die Entjudung der deutschen Wirtschaft* (Munich, 1992), chap. 1, pp. 15–86. Ludwig evaluates the statements of the participants in a very one-sided manner and fails to provide detailed references on his sources.
45. This definitely seems to have been the original motive for driving the general manager of Engelhardt breweries, Ignatz Nacher, out of the company. Nacher had repeatedly fallen out with the chairman of the supervisory board appointed by the Dresdner Bank, who (before the "seizure of power") had no option but to resign. The creditor bank was too weak to take any stronger measures. The "seizure of power," however, opened up new opportunities.
46. Until the reform of company law in 1937 it was possible to stipulate in the general business conditions that the bank was entitled to vote for the customer if he did not exercise his right himself. The reform restricted the rights of the banks to some extent by requiring that a bank must have a written authorization from a customer, which was, moreover, to be limited in time. But this did not lead to any fundamental change. On the reform of company law in 1937 see Kopper, *Marktwirtschaft*, p. 194f.
47. On this point see Kopper, *Marktwirtschaft*, p. 130f.
48. James, *The Deutsche Bank and the Nazi Economic War*, p. 28.
49. Ziegler, "Verdrängung," pp. 210–216.
50. I owe this information to Dr. Thomas Weike.
51. Mommsen, *Beamtentum*, p. 49. On this point see also the personal testimony of one of the authors of the State Citizenship Law, which is very informative in spite of its essentially self-excusing tone: Bernhard Lösener, "Als Rassereferent im Reichsministerium des Inneren," *Vierteljahrshefte für Zeitgeschichte* 9 (1961): 264–313.
52. Ziegler, "Verdrängung," p. 200.
53. Lorentz, "Beteiligung der Commerzbank." p. 268.
54. Quoted from Gerald Feldman, "Politische Kultur und Wirtschaft in der Weimarer Zeit," *Zeitschrift für Unternehmensgeschichte* 43 (1998): 17.
55. This claim, which I have dismissed as a legend after failing to find any substantiation in the available documents of the personnel department, was still in circulation in the former Dresdner Bank after the war. I owe this information to a former manager of the Bremen branch of the Dresdner Bank who was a junior clerk at the Lübeck branch of the Dresdner Bank, at the end of the 1940s and was correspondingly "instructed" in the matter at this time by his older colleagues.
56. For a detailed treatment see Kopper, *Marktwirtschaft*, pp. 86–92.
57. Ibid., pp. 93–112.
58. In this context it should be pointed out that the structural preconditions in the Commerzbank and the Deutsche Bank were very similar in as far as the Commerzbank merged with the Barmer Bankverein at about the same time as the Dresdner Bank merged with the Danat Bank. The Deutsche Bank had also had "severe digestive problems" a few years before with the incorporation of the Disconto-Gesellschaft. In both cases the crisis led to a reduction of staff. The circumstances under which the reduction was carried out at the Deutsche Bank seem very similar to those described here, except that the number involved was smaller. On this point see Gerald Feldman, "Die Deutsche Bank vom Ersten Weltkrieg bis zur Weltwirtschaftskrise 1914–1933," in Gall et al., *Deutsche Bank*, p. 285f.

CHAPTER 4

THE LOOTING OF JEWISH PROPERTY AND FRANCO-GERMAN RIVALRY, 1940–1944

Philippe Verheyde

The exclusion of the Jews from French economic life was a complex phenomenon veiled by a façade of legal acts and administrative routines. Although the anti-Semitic concerns of the new government in Vichy corresponded closely to a long confirmed German will, the objectives and modalities were indeed very different. Keeping the Jews out of economic life did not pose a moral dilemma for the French, as long as the property remained French. But certain Germans tended to make the most of the "Aryanization" process in order to derive economic and financial benefits. The rivalries that can sometimes be found did not rest on the treatment inflicted on the Jews, but rather on the economic stakes. To analyze these relationships (rivalry, but also sometimes complementarity), one must begin by identifying the networks that organized the economic "Aryanization" in France and analyzing how it was carried out in the occupied zone.

The State Networks of Economic "Aryanization"

The elaboration and dissemination of anti-Semitic measures gave rise to much to-ing and fro-ing between the French and German authorities. As early as the summer of 1940, the French government took measures to limit access to certain medical professions (doctors, dentists, chemists) and to jobs in the civil service or the legal system. These laws mainly concerned the Jews who were, de facto, subjected to a *numerus clausus*. Finally, the French law of 3 October 1940 clearly defined the status of the Jews and recapitulated the professions from which they were banned, especially in administration. In the meantime, the Germans enacted their first decree on the Jews, which stipulated that they could not return to the occupied zone and, above all, that they had to place a yellow sticker on the shops they owned. But it is especially the second decree—that of 18 October 1940—that launched the "Aryanization" process. Three logical operations were specified: the definition of a Jewish firm,[1] the inventory of these firms in the occupied zone and the nomination and installment of provisional administrators (Komissarische Verwalter) by the Occupation authorities. The role of the provisional administrators as defined by the administrative general staff on 12 November 1940 was clear: "the main task of the provisional administrators of Jewish firms is to eradicate the Jewish influence on the French economy... [and] they are not responsible to the former owners."[2] Franco-German cooperation rapidly materialized on the basis of these three logical operations. The Paris police headquarters and the prefectures in the departments of the occupied zone carried out the inventory ordered by the German authorities. The representative of the French government in the occupied zone, General de La Laurencie, asked his functionaries to carry out the inventory as diligently, thoroughly, and rapidly as possible. He invited them to use all the means at their disposal to control and ensure that "nothing is left out of the inventory."[3] Because the task was enormous, the German authorities authorized the prefectures to nominate provisional administrators for the Jewish firms as from early December 1940. Consequently, from the summer and fall of 1940 on, the "Aryanization" of the economy was shared between the French and the Germans. It was the occupying forces that defined the actions and launched them, but it was the French agencies that implemented them. In this division of tasks, the one took the initiative and the other put it into practice. Later, the Germans first prohibited the transfer of the proceeds of "Aryanization" to the Jewish owners (26 April 1941) and then went on to block all the Jewish accounts and to forbid the transfer of capital (28 May 1941). But up to the summer of 1941 all of these measures, whether they were of German or purely French inspiration, only applied to the occupied zone. It was the French law of 22 July 1941 that officially extended the measures concerning the "Aryanization" of the economy to all the territories under the Vichy Government. This to-ing and fro-ing between the German decrees and the French laws and the division of tasks that seems to have been established between the occupying forces and the occupied—the expression of a form of competition and cooperation—can be found in the administrative structures set up from the summer of 1940.

Both the German and the French authorities were responsible for the many administrative tasks related to the process of "Aryanization." The control of the operations was in the hands of the Germans. The Military Command (Militärbefehlshaber in Frankreich—MBF), created in June 1940, included the general military staff and the administrative staff. Its numbers were increased and the areas of competence clarified following the signing of the armistice. Installed in rooms of the Hôtel Majestic, the administration comprised three departments, including the economic department (Wirtschaftsabteilung or Wi), which was headed by Elmar Michel and itself divided into seven sections dealing with all economic issues. The first section—Wi 1—was responsible for the "Aryanization" of the economy.

The German functionaries who were atttached to the French organizations to control their activities were responsible to this section. Except for the promotion of Elmar Michel to the post of head of the administrative staff, this structure—a model of German organization—remained in operation throughout the Occupation.[4]

On the French side, an organization dealing specifically with "Aryanization" was created in early December 1940 in order to meet the need for an administration capable of controlling the work of the thousands of provisional administrators appointed or about to be appointed to the Jewish firms. Its name was very explicit: Service du Contrôle des Administrateurs Provisoires (SCAP). From its creation (9 December 1940), it was attached to the Ministry of Industrial Production, and Pierre Fournier, a top civil servant and former governor of the Banque de France and Director-General of the French Railways, was appointed as its head. The SCAP was divided into sections (IA to IX) and responsibilities shared out according to the sector of activities. We have little information about the principles that guided the formation of the sections. It could have been an imitation of what the Germans had already set up in Germany several years before. To these sections were added all the services that go with a true administration: a general secretariat, mail, archives, translations, files. But this organization did not seem to suffice, especially in the eyes of the Germans, for whom the very name SCAP failed to express the will to solve the Jewish problem. After bitter debates between the German authorities, represented by Helmut Knochen, and the Vichy Government, the latter created the Commissariat Général aux Questions Juives (CGQJ) on 29 May 1941, which can rightly be termed a Ministry of Anti-Semitism. Its establishment was an answer to the observation of the head of the German police in France, Helmut Knochen, that "anti-Jewish feelings cannot really develop amongst the French at the ideological level, but, when there are economic advantages, approval for the struggle against the Jews can be more readily obtained."[5] But it also met the double wish of the French to control the process, whilst at the same time developing their own concept of anti-Semitism. Xavier Vallat was appointed head of the CGQJ, was Xavier Vallat a convinced anti-Semite, famous for having said about Leon Blum at the National Assembly in 1936 that "for the first time, this ancient Gallo-Roman country will be governed by a Jew."[6] From the outset, the Commissariat had a precise objective: to replace the German decrees by purely French legislation. Indeed, it took less than four months for this to be fully achieved. On 22 July 1941 the French state promulgated its own law on economic "Aryanization." It extended the legal texts and decrees that formerly applied only to the occupied zone to all the territories under its jurisdiction. But the activities of the CGQJ now focused on economic "Aryanization" and, in June 1941, it integrated the departments of the SCAP, which henceforth constituted its backbone. The various departments developed and expanded rapidly, and by 1944 there were over 1,000 employees, who formed a real administration specialized in questions of "Aryanization" and spoliation.

One must therefore ask oneself whether the two sets of legislation and the two administrations were complementary. In other words, did they promote certain goals that were common to the Germans and the French? It is well known that anti-Semitism was one of the favorite themes of the initiators of the national revolution. The fanatical anti-Judaism of the monarchist Charles Maurras, of Raphaël Alibert, the Minister of Justice under Marshal Pétain in July 1940, or of Xavier Vallat owed nothing to German pressure alone. The convictions expressed by the first General Commissioner for Jewish Questions clearly show the nature of French anti-Semitism. He declared, a posteriori, that it was because "the Jewish influence in France had become too strong not to constitute a political and social threat, as well as an economic threat, that the government of Marshal Pétain decided to contain this influence by promulgating a law that created a special status for the Jews."[7] The type of anti-Semitism expressed by Xavier Vallat is representative of the ideology that reigned not only in the Vichy government but also among a fairly large sector of the French population. French anti-Semitism was less strong than German anti-Semitism, although this statement needs to be qualified in view of the development of certain French movements that were directly influenced by the Nazis. Yet for the government and for the heads of the SCAP and the CGQJ such racist excesses did not really reflect their concerns. The main objectives of the leaders of the Vichy regime were to exclude, expropriate, and isolate, on the one hand, and to deprive, impoverish, and despoil, on the other. But extermination was not part of their doctrine. Hence, it was on the issue of economic "Aryanization" that both parties agreed. This was expressed by one of the heads of the SCAP, writing in 1943: "essentially a political formula, 'Aryanization' in France has found its widest application in the economic sphere, since this is where the Jewish race concentrates its efforts. Hence, the task entrusted to the CGQJ in the public interest is reflected in the extent of its policy of economic 'Aryanization.' A real government program is being established."[8] Figure 4.1 presents the administrative networks of this government program.

How was the "Aryanization" of Jewish property carried out in occupied France? Once the property had been defined and classified, a provisional administrator was appointed to the Jewish firms and the legal owners were dispossessed. From then on, the actions, the fates and the course events took differed according to complex variables. But there were three main procedures under which all of the methods applied can be grouped, depending on the nature of the cases. First, the legal status of the Jewish firm could be changed. This mainly concerned the small firms dealing in skins and furs (furriers, glovers, traders in leather goods) whose production interested the Germans. As a first step, the French envisaged transforming these firms into handicraft businesses. But the Germans categorically refused, justifying their decision by stating that "even if they start as craftsmen, the Jews could climb the social ladder through their ingenuity."[9] The hybrid profession of craftsman-workman-outworker was born of this contradiction. The main aim of this status was to put a strict limit on the activities of those included in it. It

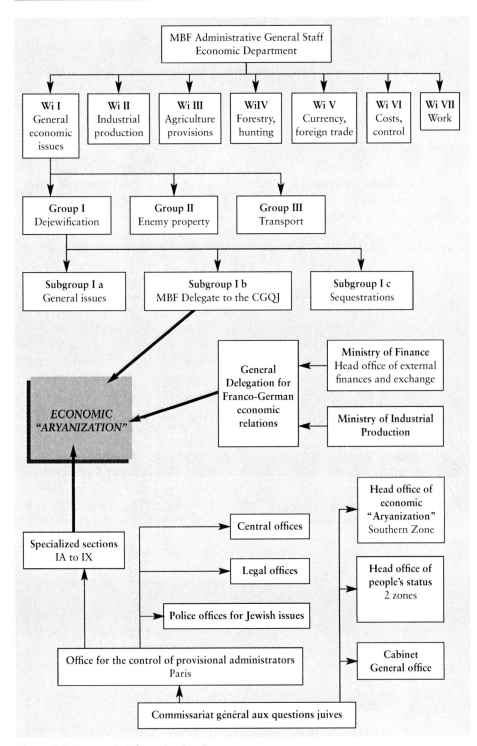

Figure 4.1 Economic "Aryanization."

was only open to those who had no contact with the customers, no shop, no stock, who worked alone or as a family, and who were registered at the police headquarters. This was a very purposeful technique by means of which benefits could be accrued from the competence of a workforce without granting it any rights. The measures affected 98 percent of the those engaged in the textile and leather trades. Indeed, except for this very special procedure, most firms could only choose between sale and liquidation. The liquidation could be pronounced with or without the consent of the legal owner. The procedure was extremely clearly defined and consisted in a certain number of actions, ranging from an inventory of the property to expulsion from the Chamber of Commerce or Industry. Liquidations, i.e., closures, mostly concerned small firms with a low turnover. Over 97 percent of the firms with a turnover of less than 200,000 francs were affected by these measures. In addition to the closing down of many small Jewish firms, liquidation offered the advantage of rationalizing certain sectors of activity. This was clearly expressed by Stülpnagel, who stated that "it is pointless to propose an administrator for firms that do not meet an urgent need of the French economy. A general fidei-commissary is to be nominated for these firms in order to guarantee a uniform and equitable use of the stocks."[10] But liquidating smaller firms on a massive scale also corresponded to the wish of the French authorities to rationalize and modernize commercial circuits and certain industrial activities that did not seem to meet the criteria of the modern economy. Finally, sales or liquidations could also be carried out with or without the consent of the legal owners. In French, the term *"Aryanisation"*—which did not exist etymologically[11]—meant both the exclusion of the Jews from economic life and the sale of Jewish property to Aryan buyers. Hence, the same word was used to express two closely related but different concepts. The provisional administrator found buyers, verified that these or their capital were of Aryan origin, established the value of the property and "the normal character of the price of transfer under the given present circumstances."[12] All of this information had be included in a report that was submitted to the appropriate department of the SCAP, which gave or withheld its consent for the operations that had been executed. Once this was acquired, the bill of sale of the property was drawn up; it had to include a suspensive clause, since the sale depended on the official confirmation of the German administrative authorities, which, after having studied the dossier presented by the SCAP, approved or disapproved the terms of the sales contract. Once confirmation had been obtained, the provisional administrator contacted the buyer and the notary in order to waive the suspensive clause. Finally, the PA had to submit his final report to SCAP, accompanied by a statement of account, after transferring the funds and depositing them at the Caisse des Dépôts.

These legal texts and the administratitive measures adopted in regard to economic "Aryanization" were characterized by the joint involvement of the German and French agencies. Yet, although the inspiration was German, the concretization was almost entirely French. It seems paradoxical that it was on the issue of economic "Aryanization," inspired and launched by the occupying forces, that the French employed the greatest technical and financial means. But, beyond the legal and administrative structure, one must reflect upon the type and level of Franco-German relations in matters of "Aryanization."

Franco-German Industrial and Commercial Relations in the Process of Economic "Aryanization"

One must specify from the outset that the analysis of the industrial and commercial relations concerns only the large firms. We shall not make an artificial distinction between small and large firms, but rather analyze an objective reality. The "Aryanization" of the small firms did not entail economic stakes that required Franco-German cooperation. But the large firms, in view of their size, their financial resources, and production, that was more or less vital for the war effort of the Reich, were at the centre of many interests.

Figures 4.2 and 4.3 help to visualize the difference between small and large firms.

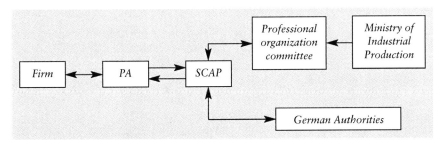

Figure 4.2 Patterns of intervention in small firms.

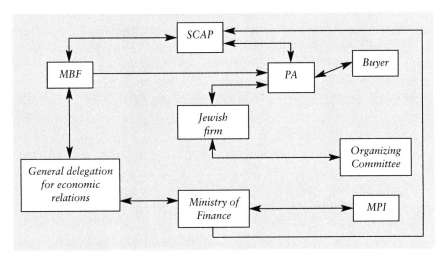

Figure 4.3 Patterns of intervention in large firms.

Franco-German relations revolved around one basic question in matters of economic "Aryanization": would the Germans benefit from the transfer of firms that belonged to French Jews? This was a crucial issue for the French, a real fear that partly motivated their wish to carry out the "Aryanization" process themselves. But the relations between businessmen and merchants on either side of the Rhine were also—despite the political context—business relations. The study of a significant number of dossiers of Jewish firms—175 in the textile, leather, furniture, retail, metallurgical, chemical, and mechanical industries—shows that there was often a German interest. One finds German interference in forty-one, i.e. 23 percent, of the 175 dossiers. Can one extrapolate from this percentage and claim that the Germans interfered in one case out of four? Considering the composition and structure of the sample of firms, this percentage seems exaggerated in relation to the "Aryanization" process, which mainly concerned small firms. Rather, German interest was proportionate to the value of the firms. But there were many reasons for German interference and different or even sometimes contradictory objectives, which can be classified according to a double criterion: was there a wish to seize the whole or even part of the capital of the Aryanized firms or not?

Of the forty-one cases, twenty-five involved some form of effective interference in the capital, but the other sixteen do not reveal a strong wish for Germanization. The latter can also be divided according to the type of relationship: support for a French buyer, commercial contracts or arbitration.

Support for a French buyer played a part in nine cases, but not necessarily on the initiative of the the occupying forces. It could arise from the French buyer's wish to benefit from the support of influential Germans in order to accelerate the process or obtain a decision to his advantage. The "Aryanization" of the Paris-France group[13] illustrates this wish. The Jewish shareholders commercial holding of sixty-six shops of the group began by accepting the sale of part of their shares to the Nouvelles Galeries group, which had the support of the German authorities. A first transaction, involving 13,800 shares, took place on 15 July 1941 in the offices of the German General Administrative Staff, which, despite the date, consented to the transfer of the funds, which were in the hands of the legal owners in the Southern zone. But the Ministry of Industrial Production feared a connivance between the Nouvelles Galeries and the Germans and even wondered whether the Germans perhaps had a share in the Nouvelles Galeries, since they "show extreme good will in carrying out the 'Aryanization' process by accepting that the funds be transferred to the non-occupied zone."[14] From then on, the MPI functionaries pressed for a second buyer to be associated with the Nouvelles Galeries. This was accepted and the Nouvelles Galeries group and La Samaritaine ended up sharing the spoils of Paris-France. One can see here that German support only helped the potential buyer during the first stage, since the business was shared with one of its rivals.

The second type of relationship was based on a commercial or industrial contract. The most significant case was the Sciaky group. It was made up of two closely associated businesses: the Sciaky group itself, which was one of the three or four French firms that specialized in the manufacture of a new type of electrical welding machine and the metallurgical company de l'Aisne, which made steel tubes using the new Sciaky technique, thus saving considerably on raw material. The former sales manager, who became president in November 1940, was appointed PA of the firm in March 1941. As early as February 1941 he had established a draft agreement with the Paul Knopp house in Berlin-Tempelhof. Without going into details, it can be said that the terms of the contract seem odd, since they do not appear to be based on reciprocity. In fact, the main beneficiary seems to be the Paul Knopp firm, for, even though it agreed to suspend the manufacture of its goods (which were not as good as Sciaky's), it derived a triple advantage: technical skills, the German market, and, in the long run, an interest in the capital of the firm. But, although this was not stipulated, it seems, in view of the developments, that the Knopp firm committed itslf to preventing the dismantlement of the French firm by protecting to a certain degree the permanence of the new president's management. The Paul Knopp firm informed the German authorities on several occasions that the Sciaky firm "has received large orders from our company and, as a result, has been placed under the control of our armaments inspection, Paris, aviation sector."[15] Moreover, it is explicity stated that it was out of the question to liquidate this firm, which contributed to "the reputation of French welding machines abroad."[16] This point is stressed a little later by the affirmation that "it is in the interest of the arms industry and of the economy in general that the firm should not be dismantled so that production can go on as usual."[17] In one of his last reports, the PA noted that the firm enjoyed great credit with the armaments inspection board (*Rüstungsinspektion*), which hoped that its "Aryanization" would in no way prejudice the production for the German army and proposed that it continue "to work *without interruption.*"[18] The fate of this firm, which was in the process of "Aryanization," showed that a judiciously negotiated industrial and commercial contract could help to save a firm, especially when its production was of interest to the German arms industry.

The last method can be compared to a mediation or technical assistance on the part of the Germans when there was a conflict between various French organizations. The "Aryanization" of the Galeries Barbès is a good example. In 1940, it was the most important furniture firm in France. It had already established a reputation for itself in the 1930s on account of its industrial structure, commercial methods, and massive advertising. But it was also envied by other members of the trade, who reproached it for its excessive activism and its predominance in the sector. The members of the Groupement National de l'Ameublement, which grew out of the Comité d'Organisation des Industries du Bois, insisted on the liquidation of a firm whose methods, "which are intrinsically Jewish, are incompatible with the reconstruction and reorganisation."[19] of the trade. But the CGQJ, which tended to privilege sales rather than liquidations, refused to liquidate a firm for which buyers had already declared their interest and committed themselves financially. By favoring sales, CGQJ wanted to involve a large number of French people in its anti-Semitic crusade. The spokesmen of the furniture trade maintained their standpoint and were backed by the Ministry of Industrial Production This led to conflict with the CGQJ. Since both administrations refused to yield, a decision was taken to consult the German authorities. The situation was rather surrealistic, as the occupying forces were in a certain sense required to mediate in a conflict between two French agencies. Out of either caution or pragmatism, the MBF recommended that part of the shares of the group be liquidated and the rest sold, thus satisfying both French administrations, which agreed to this solution. In the events we have just described, the positions adopted and the interventions undertaken could raise a smile if they did not express reality. Every attempt was made to keep the Germans out of the "Aryanization" process, fearing their interference in the capital of the French firms. Yet one did not hesitate to call on their judgment to clarify a situation that was blocked by the contradictory arguments of the two French administrations. In this case it is clear that the occupying forces did not seem interested in obtaining economic and financial benefits.

These three cases may seem curious, since there was no coercion. The operations might just as well have been carried out outside the political and military context of the Occupation. But other procedures clearly show who the occupying force was and who was being occupied.

"Aryanization" and Germanization

Of our forty-one cases, twenty-five, i.e., 15 percent of the total sample, were the object of a German attempt at interfering in the capital. But, here too, the course of events enables one to distinguish between several types of behaviour and to attempt a typology. One can distinguish operations that resembled looting or requisitioning from those that consisted in acquiring a share in the capital of the firms to be Aryanized, participation in regard to possessions in France or abroad or with the help of businessmen who were working for the Germans.

The most efficient, simple and radical way of obtaining economic benefits in Aryanized firms was to loot them or requisition their goods. When the units of Major Schu came to dismantle the metal superstructures of the Ulmo ironworks in Rimaucourt (Haute Marne)[20] in the second half of 1943, it was perhaps because the firm was considered not sufficiently or badly "Aryanized." Despite the French protests delivered by de Boisanger, the French economics delegate at the Armistice Commission, to his German counterpart, Hemmen, the requisitioning continued, but without the usual declarations. The five mill trains that existed at the beginning of the war and the metal frameworks of the buildings were dismantled and the metal was recovered and sent to the furnaces in Antwerp. After the war, the owners informed the restitution authorities that all the factories at Rimaucourt and Doulaincourt had been destroyed by the Germans.

A much more subtle way of seizing part of the capital of the French Jewish firms was to call upon a straw man. Four dossiers are relevant here, in which the nationality of the buyer—who could on no account be German—is the indispensable common denominator. The most well-known case is the Galeries Lafayette. Most of its capital was handed over to an obscure French industrialist associated with a Swiss businessman, who probably had the support of influential Germans. Soon afterwards, they sold a large part of their shares to a German organization, the Treuhandverwaltung für das Deutsch-Niederländische Finanzabkommen, represented by its deputy administrator, Alexandre Kreuter. Although less well known, the case of the Papeteries Braunstein is just as revealing. One of the world leaders in the manufacture of cigarette paper (Zig-Zag)—in which 80 percent of the turnover was for export and especially for the American market—its "Aryanization" was at first directly arranged by the PA and the MBF, which wanted to keep 30 percent of the capital for the German syndicate of cigarette-paper users. Faced with the categorical refusal of the Ministry of Finance, which "believes that nothing justifies a participation of this kind and (is) not ready to grant the dispensation required for its realization,"[21] the MBF yielded. A little later, the Papeteries Braunstein was approached by the Papeteries de la Chapelle group, most of whose capital was in Swiss hands; it was represented by its president Carl Thiel, whose position was backed by the Wirtschaftsministerium in Berlin. CGQJ, the Ministry of Finance, and the Ministry of Industrial Production were in complete agreement on the matter and rejected the offer because the shareholders were foreign. The French were about to complete its "Aryanization" when Pierre Cathala, the new French Minister of Finance, who was very close to Pierre Laval, ordered one of his functionaries to inform MBF that "he is no longer opposed to the acquisition of Braunstein shares by the Papeteries de la Chapelle ... and is glad to make a gesture of reconciliation that is agreeable to the MBF."[22] Since the Papeteries de la Chapelle was on French territory, the functionaries of the Ministry of Finance could not question the nationality of its president and were obliged to follow the Minister's recommendations. One can legitimately suppose that a few weeks after his return to power, Pierre Laval wanted to show his good will and indicate by this gesture that he intended to pursue and intensify Franco-German collaboration.

The last way of integrating the capital of Jewish firms was simply to acquire directly all or part of the shares of the firms that were put up for sale. Of our sample of 175 large firms, fourteen were the object of such methods. Cases include a proposal of the Bremen shipyards, which wanted to acquire 26,000 shares of the Ateliers et Chantiers de Saint Nazaire Penhoët. This would have offered it a blocking minority in one of the leading French shipbuilding groups. Another is the proposal by Freudenberg, who represented a large German shoe firm which wanted to obtain 20 percent to 30 percent of the capital of the Chaussures André group—the French leader in this sector. Another is the German decision to confirm its approval of the "Aryanization" of the Société Cotonnière du Nord et de l'Est in return for a transfer to the benefit of German industrialists. The Gillet-Thaon firm, which owned the Koechlin, Baumgartner, and Cie factory in Lörrach in Baden, was asked to sell it if it wished to see the agreement reached with the Schwob d'Héricourt family to buy its textile firms successfully concluded. The Administrative Board of the Gillet-Thaon firm then made it known in diplomatic terms that "although it recognises the benefit that the 'Aryanization' of the Société cotonnière du Nord et de l'Est, in which our firm is participating, may represent for us, and taking into account the liaison established by your Government—according to which this 'Aryanization' cannot be achieved to our advantage without a simultaneous transfer of our interests in the Manufacture Koechlin, Baumgartner et Cie—it believes it cannot fulfill the wishes of your Minister of the Economy and envisage this transfer, given all the interests which it represents (bond holders, shareholders, billholders), for less than 10 million marks."[23] No doubt impressed by such a sum—which was probably an overestimation—the potential buyer did not follow up the proposal. Another case is the purchase of the assets of the perfume company and beauty parlour held by Helena Rubinstein by a German-Argentinian industrial chemist (Carlos Wetzell), against the advice of the Minister of Finance. One can also mention the acquisitions of capital that were carried out directly either for property abroad or for foreigners who had assets in France. The most illuminating case is no doubt the "Aryanization" of the firms owned by a Dutch citizen, Bernard Van Leer, who lived in Amsterdam and owned the factories that bore his name. Established in Germany, The Netherlands, Belgium, and France, they produced, maintained, and commercialized all types of metal packaging (barrels, kegs). The global value of the group was estimated at between 300 and 500 million francs, but the French branch of the group seemed fairly modest (evaluated at between 7 and 8 million francs). However, at the French level, the four Van Leer factories represented 8 percent of the national production and were seventh of the twelve French firms in this sector, which is far from negligible. The French tried to "Aryanize" the factories with the help of experts in the branch, but in vain. Indeed, in the meantime, the Germans had negotiated directly with Bernard Van Leer in Amsterdam. He was willing to sell all his property to the Mannesmann Röhren Werke in Düsseldorf and received permission to retire in the United States.[24] The agreement, which was submitted to the German government for approval, was signed in May 1941. The French, who seem to have been left out in the cold, tried to acquire a share in the capital of the new firm that Mannesmann wished to create in order to exploit the French factories. The irony is that it was the French who asked the Germans for a share in the firm "in order to show public opinion a positive effect of Franco-German collaboration."[25] One can observe here the degree to which anti-Semitic legislation was fully integrated and understood by the functionaries of the French State. Indeed, the officials of the Ministry of Finance, following the logic of opposition to German claims to French capital, declared that "M. Van Leer, an Israelite industrialist, whose rights have been abrogated and transferred to a PA, cannot dispose of his property."[26] The many methods described above are synthesized in Figure 4.4.

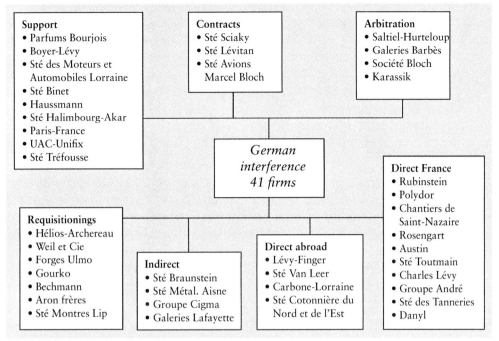

Figure 4.4 German interference in forty-one firms.

But, in the final analysis, what helps one to understand, explain, and interpret Franco-German economic relations in the context of the "Aryanization" of Jewish firms largely depends on the effective outcome of the interference of German capital.

"Aryanization" and Collaboration

It is a very delicate—not to say difficult—matter to acquire a clear idea of the status reserved for the "Aryanization" of Jewish property in the context of Franco-German collaboration. One must no doubt take into account not only German intentions and French opposition,[27] but also the contribution of economic reflection on the development of industrial and commercial relations in continental Europe.

We have seen that, of the 175 dossiers, forty-one reveal a German attempt at interference. It has been shown in great detail how only twenty-five out of these forty-one dossiers indicate a clear wish on the part of the Germans to acquire shares. In eighteen of these twenty-five dossiers, i.e., about 10 percent of the total sample, there is an attempt to acquire a fairly large share of the capital. But what helps us to see the degree of resistance of the French administrations is an analysis of the final outcome of this interference. Of the eighteen "Aryanized" Jewish firms that interested the

Germans, only 7 ended the war with foreign capital.[28] Hence, there was a penetration of capital of some 4 percent, which may seem rather little, given the fears expressed by a certain percentage of the French population. Indeed, as early as fall 1940, Jean Bichelonne, the then Secretary-General for Commerce and Industry, "had been warned through the contacts he had with the occupying forces at the Majestic that the latter intended to lay hands on *every* firm that belonged to Jews. He saw the risk that this might lead to a massive penetration of German interests in the French industrial and commercial heritage."[29] To try to counterbalance this economic invasion, the Ministry of Finance began by restructuring its administration and created the Direction des Finances Extérieures, to which the Office des Changes was attached. The latter was divided into four departments: the administrative section, the exchange section, the foreign section and the Franco-German section. The latter was created specially to follow up the German attempts at interference and to limit the claims of the occupying forces. It was entrusted to a young councillor at the Cour des Comptes, Jacques Berthoud, who was also the son-in-law of the pastor Marc Boegner, head of the Protestant Federation of France. Then, the Ministry promulgated on 10 October 1940 a decree that modified the exchange regulations and submitted to the approval of the Direction des Finances Extérieures the transfer of all securities and property to foreigners. The Germans were the main target of this step, although they were not specifically named. This technical measure, which Jacques Berthoud called a "very fragile measure,"[30] was aimed at "blocking German proposals."[31] He concluded by saying that "all in all, the outcome of this defensive war can be considered satisfactory, since the German penetration of the French economy is very limited."[32] But, a little later, he added that the resistance organized by his departments "did not obtain such satisfactory results with French interests in Central Europe, which is totally under German hegemony."[33] Our findings confirm this and we may add that the safeguarding of French interests abroad—and not only in Central Europe—turned out to be well-nigh impossible. Of the seven firms that ended the war with German capital, two were not French (Bernard Van Leer and Helena Rubinstein), two were infiltrated through foreign branches (the Belgian branch of Lévy-Finger Paint Company and the German branch of Carbone-Lorraine), and a further two cases were the result of the clearly expressed wish of the Minister of Finance, i.e., of a political and not an administrative agreement (Galeries Lafayette and Papeteries Braunstein).

For the French functionaries, whether they were part of the Ministry of Finance or the Ministry of Industrial Production or even of other administrations, defending the integrity of French capital was vital. The Jewish nature of these firms was not obvious, if one considers that, once they had lost their Jewish directors and were managed by PA, they remained French, unlike people who were no longer considered ordinary citizens. The anti-Semitic atmosphere in these administrations was probably not very strong. But all measures were applied without a qualm, using the anti-Semitic legislation if necessary to reach the goals set. At the political level, the Jewish issue and "Aryanization" in general seem to have been a card to be played in the important negotiations with the Germans. This is probably why the SCAP and the CGQJ declared that "it is impossible to say where these funds will end up, as long as the status of the Jews in France and the types of activity they can carry out have not been clearly established, once *peace is achieved*."[34] This is also perhaps what justified the position of the Minister of Finance, Pierre Cathala, who was close to Pierre Laval, when, despite the oft repeated opinion of his services, he agreed to the transactions concerning the Galeries Lafayette and the Papeteries Braunstein. Maybe one should see here a token of good will on the part of Pierre Laval, whose desire for and commitment to the signing of a definitive peace treaty with Germany is well known. By using the fate of the Jews and their property, the France of Vichy no doubt thought that it held a bargaining chip in the future negotiations it hoped would take place. The note of 20 May 1942 from the CGQJ to the Head of Government confirms this interpretation. It indicates that the measures put forward by the Vichy Government that led to "a limitation of Jewish activity especially in the economic sectors"[35] could attract "the attention of the German authorities ... during the negotiations it would carry out with them."[36]

The position of the occupying authorities fluctuated. It evolved not only in relation to the date at which it was expressed, but also in relation to the status of the actors. For many Germans, the equation was simple: the French have been conquered, they must pay. In the summer of 1940, Reichsmarschal Göring, who was responsible for the Four Year Plan, clearly stated that "increasing German influence in foreign firms is one of the goals of the German economic policy."[37] Following suit, others, such as an officer of the Propaganda Staffel, stated just as bluntly that "the Germans, having won the war, had lasting designs on some large French firms."[38] Or, again, there was the Southern German delegate of the dye factories who stressed the advantages of his offer to buy the Saint Nazaire shipyards "since the peace treaty would foresee the compulsory participation of German interests in the large French firms [and hence these would benefit] from accepting the introduction of such participation on a commercial basis with compensation, rather than waiting for it be imposed on them."[39] Then, very rapidly, the position became less pressing. The lucidity and pragmatism of the MBF seem to have prevailed over Göring's will for domination and hegemony. If the objective was more or less the same, the means were not assessed in the same way. This is the meaning of the metaphor used by Otto von Stülpnagel, the head of the MBF: "if one wants a cow to give milk, one must feed it."[40] Moreover, the social background of the members of the general administrative staff, which was characterized by "the grey of the Army rather than the brown of the Party"[41] (65 percent came from the German administration, 20 percent from economic organizations and 15 percent from the private sector), no doubt partially explains the easing of pressure. And all the more so as Göring's demands carried less weight after his defeat in the Battle of Britain. There was an evolution from a policy that encouraged more or less accentuated kinds of looting to one of buying, contracts, and orders, on the one hand, and dialogue, exchanges, and negotiations, on the other, which did not, however, prevent the confrontation of diverging interests. This is how one must understand the note of October 1942 which said that "the German authorities have made it known verbally on several occasions, and even in writing at least once, that "Aryanization" does not mean Germanization."[42] Jacques Berthoud also encapsulated this complex situation as follows: "several weeks after the signing of the Armistice, German industry had made many contacts with the heads of French firms. In the framework of the new Europe, they were invited to create new outlets constituted by the greater Europe, allowing for German influence in their businesses in return for which French industry would participate in the remarkable German technical advances and would benefit from the long era of peace and prosperity that the German victory would bring."[43] But, showing perceptiveness as to the evolution of the military and political situation, he confirmed that "as from 1942 the interest shown by the German leaders for French issues had changed. Following the Armistice, the Reich saw itself as having won a definitive victory and concentrated its efforts on the organisation of Europe."[44]

This difference in behaviour according to the perception of the way military operations developed no doubt explains many of the attitudes adopted, as, for example, when Carlos Wetzell, who had won his case in the struggle for the acquisition of Helena Rubinstein, abandoned the project and withdrew in favor of a cosmetics manufacturer in Frankfurt. One can easily imagine that the date of 22 February 1944 played a part in his decision. One finds similar reactions among French buyers of Jewish property who withdrew in 1944 from businesses for which they had shown great interest before. But, for others, apart from considerations based on a short term anti-Semitic policy, there was a true wish to build long term economic and financial relations. As René Norguet, head of mechanical and electrical production at the Ministry of Industrial Production, put it: "some Germans who are seeking agreements or participation with French businesses do not always wish for hegemony or domination, but on the contrary are trying to protect themselves against all risk. Indeed, some question the German victory and the survival of the Nazi regime, or act as bourgeois seeking to associate with foreign bourgeois."[45] The most illuminating example is the "Aryanization" of the Chaussures André group. As from early 1942, a German manufacturer represented by a certain Freudenberg[46] tried to obtain a stake in the leading French group in the shoe industry. Later, he reiterated his request, adding that "a Freudenberg–Chaussures André alliance would help to counteract positively the Bata influence and re-establish a balance in the European shoe industry."[47] He did not hesitate to add that he "is ready to face the risks of the future, including the risk of seeing his capital confiscated if the Germans are defeated, for he does not doubt that the superiority and advantages of this alliance are such that he can in no way be excluded from the deal, whatever happens."[48] Hence, certain Germans and also certain French people had a long-term vision of Franco-German relations, especially in economic, industrial, commercial, or financial matters. The reasons that have been briefly outlined here may explain the relative weakness of the penetration of German capital in the large "Aryanized" firms. It is also possible that, as Patrick Fridenson suggests, the European industrial firms that were under German domination (automobiles, dyes, synthetic fibers) "aim to prepare a non-American Europe and create a synergy of the technologies and management methods between European firms in order to build a European economic area that is oriented towards growth and complementarity between these firms."[49] Clearly, these hypotheses need to be studied in depth and elaborated in order to confirm or refute them. They would need to be put into perspective at the Western European level in order to observe certain convergences. Our work has enabled us to show how economic "Aryanization" in France was an opportunity to restructure certain sectors of business activity. In addition to the closing down of many small firms, one also sees an economic concentration and modernization in larger firms, especially in the textile industry and commercial companies (department stores, shops with many branches) to the degree that, for some, the positions acquired under the Occupation continued after the war. It would be interesting to be able to compare these facts with those for other countries, on the one hand, and to determine the exact level and quality of the networks and relations that existed between France and Germany in all of these issues, on the other.

By Way of a Conclusion

It is always a delicate and difficult matter to reach conclusions on a subject that historical research has not studied in detail. New issues, unexplored archives, the comparison of studies at the European or even international level, such as those in the various contributions to this book, will no doubt throw new light on the question of Franco-German economic relations in the context of economic "Aryanization."

But one can already stress two important points. First, the economic "Aryanization" introduced by the occupying forces in the autumn of 1940 was carried out entirely by French organizations. Without the help of the administration and the agencies of the Vichy Government, the Germans would probably not have been able to implement the process themselves. In this sense, the France of Vichy was a precious help to Hitler's Germany. By relieving the occupying forces of a laborious task and by weakening the social and financial situation of the Jews, the French state aided and supported the operations of the Nazi regime, whilst developing its own anti-Semitic concerns. Secondly, one can observe that, despite the commonly held opinion in France of a total takeover of the French economy by the Reich and a massive penetration of German capital[I] in French firms, the sample of 171 large firms we have studied indicates a level of only 4 percent. This finding hardly corresponds with the fears expressed by the highest administrative authorities. It must be seen not only as the result of French resistance, but also of a sort of self-limitation of German greed, which was crucial for the French. Franco-German relations oscillated between collaboration or cooperation and rivalry, depending on the circumstances and especially on the degree of economic interference by the victor.

Notes

1. Those firms were considered Jewish in which over a third of the capital belonged to Jewish shareholders and those whose president of the administrative board or over a third of the administrators were Jews. One must note that this definition *sensu stricto* seems more favourable than that which was the law in Germany, where 25 percent of the capital and one Jewish administrator were enough for a firm to be declared Jewish.
2. Archives du Centre de Documentation Juive Contemporaine (CDJC), XXXIX–2, in Joseph Billig, *Le Commissariat général aux Questions juives 1941–1944*, 3 vols. (Paris, 1955–1960), vol. 1, p. 35.
3. Archives Nationales (AN), F1a 3645, note from General de La Laurencie of 27 October 1940 to the prefects following and applying the German decree of 18 October 1940.
4. See the general schematic organigram of the administrative networks in Figure 4.1.
5. CDJC V–63 in Billig, *Le Commissariat*, vol. 1, p. 50.
6. Quoted by Richard Millman, *La Question juive entre les deux guerres—ligues de droite et antisémitisme français* (Paris, 1992), p. 285.
7. Xavier Vallat, *Le Nez de Cléopâtre, souvenirs d'un homme de droite 1918–1945* (Paris, 1957), p. 226.
8. AN AJ38 330, personal correspondence of Lucien Boué, letter addressed to M. Combalat, administrator-director of the Cahier Jaune of 15 February 1943.
9. Billig, *Le Commissariat*, vol. 3, p. 56.
10. AN F60 1548, note of 12 November 1940 from MBF, Economic Department, to the district heads of the military administration.
11. The neologism "*Aryanisation*" comes from the translation from the German *Arisierung*, which means to render "Aryan."
12. General instructions and memento for the provisional administrators, 2nd edition, 1942, published by the CGQJ–SCAP.
13. AN AJ38 1539 to 1542, 11 dossiers, 2835 documents.
14. F37 38, archives of the Délégation générale aux Relations économiques franco-allemandes (DGREFA), Jewish affairs, Paris-France dossier.
15. AN AJ38 2911, dossier 2207, telegramme from Paul-Knopp of 5 March 1941, document 14.
16. Ibid., report of the PA of 3 July 1941, documents 121 to 206.
17. Ibid., letter of the MBF to SCAP of 4 February 1942.
18. Ibid., report by Vopel to SCAP of 22 June 1942, emphasis in the text.
19. AN AJ38 2794, dossier 16, 611 documents, letter from the PA to SCAP of 27 May 1941, document 304.
20. AN AJ38 4667, Société des forges Ulmo Fils et Cie, dossier 1087.
21. AN AJ 38 2297, dossier 86, 326 documents, letter from the Ministry of Finance signed by Maurice Couve de Murville, 29 July 1941, document 180.
22. AN F 37 38, dossier quoted. Jacques Berthoud bore witness that Blanke received this information with his usual politeness.
23. AN AJ 40 612, letter of 2 November 1943 from the Director-General of Gillet-Thaon to Doctor Blanke (*Kriegverwaltungsrat*), document 258. One must remember that one mark is worth 20 F (rate imposed by the Germans), which brings the cost of the transaction to 200,000,000 F. In 1936, the capital of the firm Koechlin, Baumgartner et Cie amounted to 5.5 million Reichmarks (Archives of the Crédit Lyonnais, direction des études économiques et financières, dossier 50.682).

24. AN AJ38 4966, dossier 457.
25. Ibid., report of 14 June 1941 from the PA to the préfet.
26. Ibid., letter no. 4885 of 19 July 1941 from the Ministry of Finance to the general comptroller.
27. The term resistance here must not be confused with the Resistance. These are two concepts whose meaning is very different, just like the concepts of *Resistenz* and *Widerstand* developed by German historians.
28. This concerns the Lévy-Finger firm, the Etablissements Braunstein, the Austin firm, the French businesses of Bernard Van Leer, and the German branches of Carbone-Lorraine, of the Galeries Lafayette and of the Helena Rubinstein perfume firm (list to be compared with the diagram in Figure 4.4.
29. François Bloch-Lainé and Claude Gruson, *Hauts fonctionnaires sous l'occupation* (Paris, 1996), p. 41. The emphasis is ours.
30. Service des Archives économiques et financières (SAEF), B33 590, general dossier, article written at the time of the Libération (16 September 1944) for an American journal (7 typed pages): La défense de l'Industrie française contre l'emprise allemande.
31. Ibid.
32. Ibid.
33. Ibid.
34. Xavier Vallat, *Le nez*, p. 250, quoted in Henry Rousso, "L'aryanisation économique: Vichy, l'occupant et la spoliation des Juifs," *Yod*, special issue, *Les Juifs de France et d'Algérie pendant la Deuxième Guerre mondiale* (1982): 15–16. The emphasis is ours.
35. AN AJ38 64, dossiers by sector of activity of the Cabinet du Commissariat, dossier M 78, Présidence du Conseil, note of 20 May 1942 from the CGQJ to the Head of Government.
36. Idem.
37. SAEF B 631, Office of financial investigations in Berlin, letter by Göring of 2 August 1940.
38. AN AJ38 2898, Hélios-Archereau dossier.
39. SAEF B33 592, Chantiers et Ateliers de Saint-Nazaire dossier.
40. Eberhard Jäckel, *La France dans l'europe de Hitler* (Paris, 1986), p. 139.
41. Ibid., p. 98.
42. AN F37 38, document quoted.
43. SAEF B33 590, document quoted.
44. Ibid.
45. AN F37 27, Papiers Barnaud, German shares in French businesses, dossier "Aide apportée par l'Allemagne à l'Economie française," note by the head of mechanical and electrical industries René Norguet of 7 December 1941, 7 pages, confidential.
46. I did not find much information on the group he represented. During a journey to Germany, the head of the leather CO was approached to grant 51 percent of the capital of the Chaussures André to the Salamander group. This may explain how and why Elmar Michel became one of the heads of the Salamander group after the war.
47. AN AJ38 2045, document 1497, between May and November 1942.
48. Ibid.
49. Patrick Fridenson, "Vichy entre archaïsme et modernité," in Jean-Pierre Azéma and François Bédarida, eds., *Vichy et les Français* (Paris, 1992), p. 362.
50. Pierre Arnoult, *Les Finances de la France et l'occupation allemande (1940–1944)* (Paris, 1951).

CHAPTER 5

SEIZURE OF JEWISH PROPERTY AND INTER-AGENCY RIVALRY IN THE REICH AND IN THE OCCUPIED SOVIET TERRITORIES

Martin C. Dean

The thesis of "institutional Darwinism" or "polycracy," which argues that Hitler encouraged rival agencies with unclear jurisdictional boundaries to compete for the implementation of key ideological tasks, has proved to be one of the most insightful interpretations of the Nazi regime.[1] Clearly it would be misleading to depict bureaucratic wrangling over jurisdiction as always leading to the swift implementation of the most extreme solution. Nevertheless, the active competition between agencies for control of both resources and policy on many occasions led to a progressive radicalization in pursuit of these goals. Wolfgang Seibel has recently identified examples of this type of radicalization involving both German and French agencies in the development of Jewish policy in France in the period 1940–1942.[2]

In regard to the seizure of Jewish property, careful distinctions have to be made between active competition for control over policy, over its implementation, and especially over the most lucrative parts of the spoils, as against the understandable reluctance of institutions to take on extra administrative burdens. An analysis of the inter-agency correspondence regarding property confiscation demonstrates that concerns to expand institutional competence had to be balanced against available resources and the likely advantages to be gained.

Both within the Reich and in the occupied eastern territories, the rough division of labour was primarily a combination of the technical expertise of the financial administration with the executive authority of the Gestapo. Whilst the classic study of Hans Adler rightly stresses the many conflicts between different branches of the bureaucracy over property issues within the Reich, a comparison with events in Reichskommissariat Ostland proves to be instructive in helping to put this fully into its correct perspective.[3]

The most striking difference between the implementation of the Holocaust in the Reich and the occupied Soviet territories was the method of open and direct killing, mainly by mass shooting, in the East. This can be contrasted with the deportations from the Reich that intentionally removed the killing from public sight. In more general terms this also reflected a "wild East" mentality: the civil administration and police authorities exerted almost unrestrained power in the occupied Soviet territories. Inside the Reich, the firmly established and complex social and bureaucratic structures demanded a more circumscribed and "rational" path to the same terrible goal of destruction.[4]

Due to the complex nature of the dual comparison undertaken in this chapter, it has not been possible to conduct a comprehensive analysis of all issues concerning "competition and rivalry" in the seizure of Jewish property. Instead the approach has been to look for a few well-documented examples of competition (and cooperation) that can be found in the official correspondence. Detailed examination of these case studies within the overall context of Nazi confiscation policy permits the analysis of some of the motivations that affected inter-agency relations. At the same time these examples offer certain valuable insights into the role of inter-agency relations in the development of Nazi confiscation policies.

Case Study 1: Relations between the Civil Administration and the German Police Regarding the Seizure of Jewish property in Reichskommissariat Ostland and Ukraine, 1941–1944

The two main German agencies involved in the seizure of Jewish property in the occupied Soviet territories were the civil administration and the police. The ambiguous relationship between these two organisations at the local level ensured a high degree of jurisdictional conflict between them. As one official from the Zhitomir Generalkommissariat complained: "There is simply no question of a unified command structure from the centre down to the local agencies. In fact two Reich departments rule alongside one another quite independently, breaking the horizontal links which the Führer ordered."[5] At the same time more recent historiography has demonstrated a broad consensus among senior officers in both organizations in regard to many aspects of occupation and Jewish policy.[6]

Nazi seizures of Jewish property in the occupied Soviet Union were closely linked to the extermination program from the start. Evidence discovered recently in the records of the Reichshauptkasse Beutestelle (the War Booty Office of the Reich Treasury) demonstrates that the Einsatzgruppen and other mobile killing units sent collections of valuables to Berlin in the wake of the first anti-Jewish actions in the summer of 1941. Valuables were routinely collected from victims just prior to the mass shootings and were treated initially in a similar fashion to "war booty." Transcriptions prepared by officials of the Finance Ministry indicate that they had no illusions as to the means by which these items were acquired.[7]

The Wehrmacht was also involved in large-scale collections of silverware and valuables from local Jewish communities, sometimes in conjunction with the mass shooting of Jews, as can be seen in documents from Volhynia and Mir in Belarus.[8] The degree of Wehrmacht participation varied widely, depending partly upon the local duration of the military administration. Jewish contributions levied in some towns were used to bolster the finances of the local administration; in Glebokie (Glubokoye) the District Commissar (Gebietskommissar) complained of some Jewish property having been removed by units of the military administration as they passed through.[9]

Available records indicate that initially several competing channels were used for sending valuables to Berlin. Some items were also placed into safe keeping locally. In Latvia it was not uncommon for specific items of Jewish property, including livestock, to be distributed among members of the local population or German offices for their own use: for example, the local police and Order Police units received numerous items of furniture.[10] The disorganized nature of some of these early confiscations conducted under the military administration created certain problems for the civil administration that followed.

The establishment of a civil administration in the western districts of the occupied Soviet Union in the summer and fall of 1941 created the infrastructure for the more orderly registration, administration, and sale of Jewish property. Reichskommissar Lohse in Ostland proclaimed in October that he would confiscate, administer, and take over all Jewish property. He also instructed private persons to register Jewish property that was in their possession.[11] The processing of Jewish property kept part of the civil administration busy throughout the occupation.[12] Detailed instructions were issued for valuables to be sent back to Berlin for processing, whilst local currency and less valuable items were to be utilized directly in the occupied territories. The proceeds realized from the sale of valuables forwarded to Berlin were subsequently to be booked to the budget of the Reichskommissar.[13]

Despite the official transfer of responsibility for Jewish property to the civil administration in the summer and fall of 1941, the executive forces of the police continued to play an important role in its collection. As the agents primarily responsible for the murder of the Jews, they were on the spot and also had the available manpower for the collection of Jewish valuables at the sites of mass killings. Some property remained in their safe keeping from earlier actions and not all property was swiftly handed over to the civil administration once acquired. Thus there remained continuing friction between civil and police agencies over the administration of Jewish property.

One of the first conflicts over Jewish property emerged in the district of Siaulai in Lithuania. Following complaints at the local level, *Reichskommissar* Lohse wrote to the Higher SS and Police Leader (HSSPF), Hans-Adolf Prützmann, on 25 September 1941 requesting that the police hand over confiscated Jewish property to the relevant District Commissars.[14] This dispute takes on some added significance in the light of recently discovered "Beutestelle" records, which indicate large collections of valuables arriving in Berlin from Einsatzgruppe A in the Baltic States in early 1942.[15]

Criticism of the police by the civil administration culminated in a letter from Rosenberg to Lammers in October 1941, in which he complained vigorously that the police leaders in the East were not adhering to the Führer decree of 17 July regarding jurisdiction. Instead they were accused of referring to "secret orders unavailable to the civil administration." He protested especially that the SS (Schutzstaffel) had removed large amounts of silver and gold.[16]

Probably in response to these and other complaints, Himmler issued clear instructions to the Higher SS and Police Leaders in the East (I/1630/41). This new order, distributed in January 1942, stipulated that gold and silver items were to be collected and administered by the Senior Security Police Commanders. These confiscated valuables were then to be transferred to the finance departments of the relevant Reich Commissars. In exceptional cases permission could be requested from the Reich Commissar for specific confiscated sums to be retained for SS and Police requirements in that region.[17]

The example of the mass shooting of Jews in Riga demonstrates that in spite of the clear jurisdiction of the District Commissar in Jewish property matters, the executive authority of the Police still took precedence. Officials subordinate to the District Commissar complained bitterly of their inability to influence the actions of the SS.[18] The Police had carried out the murder of the Jews at short notice without prior consultation. This wrecked the existing plans for an orderly collection of Jewish property, rendering any effective accounting for Jewish property by the District Commissar impossible.[19] The response of the District Commissar under these circumstances demonstrated that the defense of his competence was less important to him than covering his back against any criticism.

Nonetheless, the police instructions to transfer secured items to the civil administration were partially implemented over the following months. The clarity of the initial Himmler order (I/1630/41) was subsequently superseded by a secret order issued on 12 August 1942. This stipulated that all quantities of "old gold," silver, other precious metals and valuables were to be delivered without exception to the SS Economic Administration Main Office (SS-WVHA) in Berlin, which would then transfer them to the relevant offices.

Himmler's strategy was to avoid carefully any accusation that the SS was exploiting Jewish valuables directly for its own purposes without permission. Instead he sought to centralize all deliveries of valuables from the East in the hands of the SS-WVHA, in order to maximize the size and impact of these deliveries. Oswald Pohl would then report to the Finance Ministry that a certain sum from the "Jewish evacuations" (*Judenumsiedlungen*) had been delivered to the Reichsbank without a single penny being held back by the SS: "In this manner, it will be easier to obtain the corresponding funds correctly from the Finance Ministry."[20]

This was the modest strategy developed by Himmler in mid August of 1942 that resulted in the Melmer deliveries to the Reichsbank.[21] Far from being a "top secret" operation unknown to the Reich leadership, it was intended to convince them of the squeaky-clean efficiency of the SS, to strengthen the position of the SS in regard to budget negotiations.

Even prior to the August 1942 order, there was a tendency for the police administration to hang on to valuables they had collected. The District Commissar in Vileyka complained that only on one occasion had he been able to extract a large monetary sum and valuables, including minted coins, from the SD (Security Service of the SS) during the previous year.[22] As a result of such protests, during 1943 the SS-WVHA and the Reich Security Main Office (RSHA) instructed subordinate police offices in Ostland to hand over all money, property, and valuables to the civil administration.[23]

How is one to interpret this gradual and apparently reluctant transfer of funds from Jewish property by the police? Part of the problem was clearly the very existence of competing jurisdictions and the reliance of the civil administration upon the police for the implementation of certain aspects of policy. Analysis of the available correspondence suggests that the temporary withholding of large sums from confiscated Jewish property by the police may have been connected to ongoing negotiations over the hard-pressed budget for the occupied eastern territories. By 1943 plans existed for some of the costs of policing to be transferred to the overall budget for the Reichskommissariat Ostland.

On paper at least, the civil administration won most of the jurisdictional battles over responsibility for Jewish property. The Security and Order Police, however, fought a prolonged rearguard action, based mainly on their direct executive powers and ability to issue "secret orders" within their own vertical chain of command. This was viewed by the civil administration as undermining their authority in these matters. However, evidence from later in the occupation indicates that the "wild" nature of the initial destruction and expropriation process was gradually tamed by bureaucracy even here.

Case Study 2: Relations between the Security Police and the Financial Administration Regarding Confiscated Jewish Assets within the Reich, 1933–1945

A significant aspect of the confiscation process in the Reich that has been underestimated hitherto is the extent to which it relied on close cooperation between the Gestapo and the financial administration. This is particularly well illustrated by Nazi denaturalization policies toward Jewish emigrants. The implementing decree of 26 July 1933 regarding the repeal of naturalizations and the adjudication of German citizenship assigned responsibility for the sequestration of property to the Finance Offices (Finanzämter—FA).[24]

In January 1934 the Gestapo wrote to the Finance Ministry requesting the tax records of a number of persons who were being denaturalized. The list included socialists and writers who had emigrated in 1933, such as Berthold Brecht, Max Brod, Arnold Zweig, and Else Lasker-Schuler. Detailed replies from the relevant Finance Offices included tax details. For example the *FA* Wilmersdorf South handed over the tax file of Arnold Zweig to the Gestapo on 2 February 1934.[25]

Arnold Zweig's lawyer put up a spirited defense against the confiscation of Zweig's property. The notification letter of the Gestapo made reference to the recent laws for the "confiscation of Communist property" and of "the property of enemies of the people and the state." Zweig's lawyer replied that "the confiscated items do not belong to a Marxist party, but are the private items of Mr. Zweig. Therefore they cannot be confiscated according to the laws mentioned above. The apartment furnishings as well as the carpets and rugs [*Läufer*] certainly do not serve the furtherance of Marxist purposes."[26] Despite Zweig's protestations, these were in fact the laws under which the property of many Jews was subsequently seized.[27]

Additional examples demonstrate the extent to which different arms of the bureaucracy interlocked to ensure the efficient seizure of Jewish assets. For example, by September 1935 a Central Information Office had been created at the Landesfinanzamt (Finance Office) Berlin to coordinate information with regard to nonpayment of taxes, capital flight, and property transfer. This was directed primarily against Jewish emigrants. In October 1935 the Gestapo urged that local Finance Offices and Customs Investigation Offices give immediate notice regarding any cases of Jews, especially Jewish businessmen, who were planning to leave the country.[28]

The financial incentives involved also meant that sometimes local officials took the initiative in introducing new anti-Semitic measures. In Mannheim a central office for the region was established in October 1935 by the Finanzamt to register emigration intentions as quickly as possible. Jews were specifically targeted and 600 Jews with assets of RM 20,000 or more were placed on a watch list, in case they should show any signs of intending to emigrate. The experiences gained in Mannheim also included recommendations that insurance companies and banks should be instructed to notify the relevant FA of any repurchased policies or liquidated accounts as indications of the intention to emigrate. Since the Gestapo lacked sufficient personnel to interview all Jews eligible to pay the Flight Tax, an internal report within the financial administration proposed that random persons from the list should be subjected to telephone and postal observation. The report also suggested that those who had come to the attention of the *FA* or had been reported by other institutions should also be watched. The Finanzamt reported that cooperation with the Gestapo so far had produced "very good financial results." In January of 1936 the President of the Landesfinanzamt in Berlin brought the centralization of work on Flight Tax cases practised in Mannheim to the attention of other Finance Offices in his region. However, in most areas the lack of sufficient personnel prevented the adoption of all aspects of the "Mannheim model" throughout Germany.[29]

The practical consequences of the fiscal bureaucracy registering suspected emigration plans can be seen from the case of the family of Dr. M.S. and his wife.[30] The family returned from their holiday abroad on 8 August 1937 to find their furniture had been confiscated in their absence. They only managed to remove the confiscation order and recover their furniture once a considerable security deposit for the *Reichsfluchtsteuer* (Flight Tax) had been set up in government bonds. This example provides a vivid demonstration of the power financial officials could exert over Jewish property even prior to *Kristallnacht*.[31]

As the 1930s progressed the closely-knit web of decrees, guidelines and institutions closed ever more tightly around remaining Jewish property. In April 1937 Heydrich issued new guidelines to the Gestapo-Leitstellen with respect to denaturalization cases. Specific reports were to be written on the economic activity of emigrant Jews before and after the National Socialist uprising and any debts or unpaid taxes they had left behind. Precise details were to be provided about any typically Jewish crimes.[32] In a preceding decree, Himmler had specifically identified the economic activities of Jewish emigrants, such as the transfer of capital abroad and the non-payment of central and regional taxes as activities that demonstrated their hostile attitude to the "state and the people."[33]

In December 1938 Himmler proposed that the relevant Finance Offices be made responsible for the administration of secured property prior to denaturalization, as the police did not have sufficient skilled personnel to deal with these complex property cases.[34] The response of the financial bureaucracy to this proposal that they expand their competence is quite revealing of what could be described as a "bureaucratic response." The proposal was treated skeptically on practical grounds, as the *FA* Moabit-West would also require further staff in order to cope with the increased workload. In addition it was argued that only the Security Police had sufficiently wide-ranging powers under the decree of 28 February 1933 and the operational flexibility to carry out the securing of property in advance of denaturalization.[35]

At a meeting with representatives of the Oberfinanzpräsident (OFP) Berlin, the Reich Finance Ministry (RFM) decided that, for "tactical reasons," it was not desirable to reject the expansion of competence of the Finance Offices proposed by the RFSS. The *FA* Moabit-West stressed again its urgent need for more qualified staff to deal with the increasing workload. The Finance Ministry proposed negotiating with the Reichsführer SS (RFSS) for an earlier handover of property administration matters from the Gestapo to the *FA* Moabit-West. However, the Gestapo would remain responsible for the executive measures required for securing the property.[36]

The available documentation demonstrates that the selection of emigrant Jews for the removal of citizenship was increasingly conducted according to whether they still owned property in Germany that could be seized. For this purpose the *Judenvermögensabgabe* (Punitive Tax) files of Jews living overseas were passed on from the FA Moabit-West to the Security Police, in order to determine whether any property was known to exist in the Reich. This close cooperation is documented clearly in both individual case files and the few general files preserved by the financial administration in Berlin.

On 17 May 1940 Heinrich Himmler issued a decree stating that the denaturalization of Jewish emigrants with considerable property in Germany should be accelerated as a key war task. He warned that any delay might enable such persons to obtain the citizenship of another country, which would cause these sums to be lost to the Reich.[37]

The implementation of property confiscation under the Eleventh Decree, following the deportation of German Jews, relied very heavily on a system of mutual notification, derived from the procedures developed for the removal of citizenship. The deportation lists prepared by the Gestapo[38] took the place of the lists of persons proposed for denaturalization published in official gazettes.[39] The system developed for the phase of emigration was adapted for the confiscation of property from those Jews destined for destruction.

This outcome was the result of detailed negotiations between the Security Police and the Finance Ministry, as well as other ministries involved. From the perspective of the OFP Berlin, the original purpose of the Eleventh Decree was to simplify the seizure of property from Jews who had emigrated abroad, as there were many thousands of cases still to be completed.[40] Following a meeting in March 1941 the RFM agreed to renounce the previous procedure of publishing all the names in return for a concession by the RSHA that they would drop their claim to all of the real estate. Importantly, it was agreed that the application of derived funds for the "solution of all Jewish problems" would not be binding on either the RFM or the RSHA.[41] The assignment of responsibility for establishing if the "forfeit of property to the Reich" had occurred to the Head of the Security Police and SD was welcomed by the RFM in a memo dated March 1941 as relieving some of the increased burden of work arising from the sudden seizure of property of thousands of individuals in one fell swoop.[42] However, the Property Realization Office (Vermögensverwertung-Aussenstelle) of the OFP Berlin-Brandenburg (successor institution to the FA Moabit-West) complained in February of 1942 that the transport lists of the Security Police were inadequate, as they were not organized alphabetically.[43]

Despite Hitler's expressed desire to reduce the bureaucratic efforts involved in property confiscation,[44] individual property files were opened for each Jewish victim, as creditors were only to be paid up to the level of remaining property collected, although hardship payments could be made in special cases.[45] Each file usually contained a property declaration filled out by the deportee just prior to departure and forwarded to the OFP by the Gestapo. This is followed in many files by a notification of the seizure of the property according to the laws for the confiscation of the property of Communists and enemies of the "people and the state." The file also records the receipt of this notification (*Zustellungsurkunde*) by the deportee prior to departure. Further documentation then concerns the collection of outstanding sums from bank accounts, the sale of property, security deposits, and the like, together with the payment of claims made by legitimate creditors.[46]

This detailed analysis of the historical development of the interactive property confiscation process helps to put Hans Adler's critical analysis of relations between the Finance Ministry and the Security Police into full perspective. Hans Adler himself describes in detail the degree of co-operation involved in the deportation process and comes to the following conclusion:

> In connection with the Eleventh Decree to the Reich Citizenship Law a remarkable perfection of the cooperation between the RSHA and the Finance Ministry developed, initially with regard to these central offices, but then also for the Gestapo as well as the OFPs and Finance Offices as the executing agencies. The Finance Ministry intervened in this game so resolutely and unscrupulously, that solely on account of this its participation in the deportations becomes one of considerable shared responsibility for the "final solution."[47]

A key principle that was developed during the 1930s was the concept that the anti-Jewish measures leading to the removal of the Jews should be self-financing. Reference is made to this in a number of key documents, including the Eleventh Decree itself, which states that "the forfeited property is to be used to promote all aims connected to the solution of the Jewish question."[48] In regard to the deportation of the Jews from the Palatinate and Baden, the office of the RFSS ordered that 10 percent of the cash sums collected were to be paid into a special account to cover the costs of the deportations.[49] The Security Police conducted the confiscations accompanying the deportations in 1940 on their own authority in conjunction with the regional governments. At a meeting held on 4 December, 1941 between the representatives of the Gestapo and the Finance Ministry, responsibility for this property was transferred from the Plenipotentiary of the RFSS to the relevant Oberfinanzpräsidenten (director of a regional tax office).[50]

The main area of conflict between the Security Police and the Finance Ministry is summarized in the comments of Dr. Mädel in a memorandum from December 1942. He complained about Himmler's management of the considerable funds collected through the "Reichsvereinigung" (RV) by the SS: "The RFSS expresses on the one hand the opinion that all Jewish property must go to the Reich. On the other hand he has the intention to dispose of funds extracted from this mass of assets freely, without reference to budgetary controls. This shows once again the effort, where possible, to finance operations outside the regular control of funds through the budgetary process, with only net returns appearing in the official accounts."[51]

The executive authority of the Security Police in organizing the deportations and their control over the Reichsvereinigung der Juden[52] enabled them to divert considerable sums from the remaining property of Jews being deported. They issued instructions for Jews to pay at least 25 percent of remaining property into Special Account W, as well as paying all outstanding contributions to the Reichsvereinigung. These sums were ostensibly to cover various costs of the deportations.[53] The Security Police put further amounts beyond the reach of the Finance Ministry through the so-called *Heimeinkaufverträge* (literally "home purchase") contracts, which promised to cover the living expenses of those Jews deported to Theresienstadt.[54] The available accounts of the RV from 1942 to 1943 make reference to regular payments of 8 million RM to Theresienstadt.[55]

In the absence of detailed accounts of the actual expenditure of the sums collected from the Jews by the Security Police it is difficult to assess the significance of these diversions of property for the Reich budget. A postwar report prepared by the archive of the former Reich Finance Ministry noted that the RFM took over the administration of the property of the Reichsvereinigung according to a decree issued on 3 August 1943 (O 5210—350 VI).[56] The criticism of the Finance Ministry stopped short of accusing the Security Police of using funds from Jewish property for "illegitimate" purposes.[57]

The management of this dispute is in itself revealing. Far from provoking an open conflict with the Security Police, most Finance Ministry criticism was confined to internal memoranda. Patzer of the General Office wrote to Maedel on 24 December 1942 listing several examples of diversions of funds in favour of the Reichsvereinigung and requesting that clarity be established.[58]

The outcome was that transfers in favour of the Reichsvereinigung were recognized, provided that they took place prior to the moment when the deportee left the borders of the Reich. According to the Eleventh Decree, Jewish property fell to the Reich and was legally transferred at precisely this instant. The main concern of the Finance Ministry was that "Aryan" creditors might be disadvantaged as a result.[59]

Thus a compromise was reached that recognized de facto the diversions in favour of the Gestapo, provided they occurred within the framework of existing laws. This system of apparent "honour" among murderers and thieves must be contrasted with the even more acrimonious tone of similar negotiations in the East.

Conclusions

In the initial chaos that accompanied "experimental" mass murder and the creation of a civil administration from scratch, there was a greater intensity of jurisdictional disputes over Jewish property in the East than within the Reich. In the absence of clearly established structures and procedures, conflicting orders were issued by the competing authorities; both the civil administration and the police were eager to carve out their own jurisdiction without external interference. There was a certain "wild East" mentality: this led not only to the brutalization of officials, but also to some confusion and disorganization.

By contrast the handling of Jewish property within the Reich was characterized by a close degree of interdependence between the police and financial bureaucracies from the start. A combination of the "special powers" of the police and the practical expertise of the Finance Offices was required to achieve the most efficient expropriation.[60] This does not mean that there was not a certain duplication of effort or rivalry over the spoils. Rather these conflicts took place largely within the established procedures and channels with a greater degree of consultation.

The disputes over sums diverted from the Finance Ministry by the Security Police have rightly attracted the attention of historians. Nevertheless, these should be seen in the overall context of the greater part of the revenue being carefully paid into the accounts of the Reich with the active cooperation of the Security Police.[61] The Security Police successfully diverted certain funds for their own operations. They thereby exploited the official rhetoric developed during the 1930s that anti-Jewish measures should be self-financing, confronting Finance Ministry officials with a *fait accompli* based on their executive powers.

Within the Reich the outstanding conflicts arising from these dual confiscation systems were resolved largely by mutual consultations between the officials concerned. The exploitation process there was based on a complex network that also incorporated even private institutions such as banks and insurance companies. This was calculated to achieve the most complete exploitation of Jewish property by enforcing "legal confiscation" under the Eleventh Decree as an extension of previous denaturalization policy. This networking strategy served to slow down actual implementation through the bureaucratic effort involved. But it was less open to the corruption and confusion that characterized the looting of Jewish property in the East.[62]

The direct method of murder by shooting, by contrast, left little time for the establishment of sophisticated systems of economic exploitation. The conflict over Jewish property was an institutional battle for control over resources and independence of action. Here the strong executive powers of the police were pitted against the traditional strengths of the Finance Ministry, which acted as the arbiter of jurisdictional conflicts through control over budgetary funds.

The murder of Europe's Jews was carried out for racial and not financial reasons. Nevertheless, there was a financial subplot that helped shape the course of events. Many historians have chosen to describe the seizure of Jewish property primarily as a direct competition between the Finance and Police administrations over the proceeds.[63] Concentration on this aspect of competition, however, threatens to overlook, or at least underestimate, the high degree of cooperation that was necessary to carry out this task effectively.

The analysis of examples from the East demonstrates that "polycracy" there could also lead to waste and the hoarding of resources due to unbridled competition. Inside the Reich the methods developed earlier, based on close cooperation between the Security Police and the financial administration over denaturalization, were subsequently adapted for the collection of property arising from the process of destruction. Continuing rivalry still produced new initiatives, such as the *Heimeinkaufverträge*, whereby deportees legally signed over much of their property to the Gestapo prior to deportation. The perspective offered by direct comparison with events in the East demonstrates, however, that the extent of mutual cooperation was far more refined within the complex structures in the Reich than was possible during the fierce struggles for power that developed in the newly occupied East.

Notes

1. Karl Dietrich Bracher, *The German Dictatorship: The Origins, Structure, and Effects of National Socialism* (New York, 1970), p. 332 attributes the term "institutional Darwinism" to David Schoenbaum; Martin Broszat, *The Hitler State: The Foundation and Development of the Internal Structure of the Third Reich* (London, 1981) (translated from the German edition of 1969), p. 294, uses the term "departmental polyocracy" for one of his chapter headings.
2. Wolfgang Seibel, "Perpetrator Networks and the Holocaust: Resuming the 'Functionalism' versus 'Intentionalism' Debate," Paper delivered at the 2000 Annual Meeting of the American Political Science Association in Washington, DC, 31 August–3 September 2000, pp. 25–32. See also the contributions of Marc-Olivier Baruch and Philippe Verheyde in this volume.
3. See, for example, H.G. Adler, *Der verwaltete Mensch* (Tübingen, 1974), 562–571, 601–603, 629–633.
4. Christopher Browning makes a similar point in his recent book, arguing that the brutalization of the police proceeded far more rapidly in the occupied territories than within the Reich: see Christopher Browning, *Nazi Policy, Jewish Workers, German Killers* (Cambridge, 2000), p. 150; Jonathan Steinberg, "The Third Reich Reflected: German Civil Administration in the Occupied Soviet Union 1941–44," *English Historical Review*, 110, no. 437 (June 1995): 632; Broszat, *The Hitler State*, p. 319, was amongst the first to note that it was easier for Himmler to expand his power in the newly occupied eastern territories than within the Reich.
5. On the jurisdictional conflict between the civil administration and the police, see Steinberg, "The Third Reich Reflected," pp. 641–642; the document referred to as KO 76B can be found in BAB R 19/333, p. 50.
6. On the relationship between civil and police authorities in the East see Christian Gerlach, *Kalkulierte Morde: Die deutsche Wirtschafts- und Vernichtungspolitik in Weissrussland 1941 bis 1944* (Hamburg, 1999), pp. 194–196; for a survey of some of the recent German scholarship that stresses "the importance of local initiatives, and the unspoken consensus among and the broad participation of the entire occupation apparatus in the killing process," see Browning, *Nazi Policy*, p. 117, fn.4.
7. See Martin Dean, "Jewish Property Seized in the Occupied Soviet Union in 1941 and 1942: The Records of the Reichshauptkasse Beutestelle," *Holocaust and Genocide Studies* 14, no. 1 (Spring 2000): 83–101. On the actual distinction between "war booty" and Jewish property, see Oberfinanzdirektion Berlin (henceforth OFD), *Archiv (Fasanenstr.) Div. Ordner* I (*Ausarbeitungen des Archivs des ehem. RFM—Handakte* Scheerans), p. 310, *Referent* Eckhardt Y 5205/1—243 V, 29 October 1942.
8. Ibid., pp. 87–89.
9. Martin Dean, "Die Enteignung 'jüdischen Eigentums' im Reichskommisariat Ostland 1941–1944," in Fritz Bauer Institut, ed., *"Arisierung" im Nationalsozialismus: Volksgemeinschaft, Raub und Gedächtnis* (Frankfurt on Main, 2000), pp. 204 and 208; V.I. Adamushko, G.D. Knatko and N.A. Redkozubova, *'Nazi Gold' from Belarus: Documents and Materials* (Minsk, 1998), pp. 66–67, Gebietskommissar Glebokie Abt. IIa an GK Weissruthenien, 22 June 1942.
10. See Martin C. Dean, "Seizure, Registration, Rental and Sale: The Strange Case of the German Administration of Jewish Moveable Property in Latvia, 1941–44," in Andris Caune, Daina Klavina and Inesis Feldmanis, eds., *Latvia in World War II: Materials of an International Conference 14–15 June 1999, Riga* (Riga, 2000), pp. 372–378.

11. V.I. Adamushko et al., 'Nazi Gold', pp. 28–29, Verkündungsblatt des Reichskommissars für das Ostland, 24 October 1941; NARA T-459, roll 21, Anordnung über die Anmeldung jüdischen Vermögens, 11 October 1941.
12. See Dean, "Seizure, Registration, Rental and Sale," p. 373.
13. V.I. Adamushko et al, 'Nazi Gold', pp. 110–113, Reichsminister für die besetzten Ostgebiete an RKO u. RKU, 7 September 1942; see also NARA T-459, roll 3, fr. 731, Städt. Pfandleihanstalt Berlin an RKO, 4 August 1942.
14. USHMM 1996.A.0169 reel 5 (Yad Vashem) M41/307 (Belarus National Archives, Minsk) 391-1-39, RKO an HSSPF, 25 September 1941; see also Raul Hilberg, *Die Vernichtung der europäischen Juden* (Frankfurt on Main, 1990), pp. 380–381 and Nuremberg Document 3661-PS, see International Military Tribunal (Blue Series) (Nuremberg, 1947), vol. XXXXII, pp. 434–435, Gebietskommissar in Schaulen an RKO, 8 September 1941.
15. See Dean, "Jewish Property," p. 85.
16. NARA T-1139, roll 21 NG-1683, Reich Minister for the occupied eastern territories (RmfdbO) Rosenberg an Chef der Reichskanzlei Lammers, 14 October 1941. The Führer decree on "Police and Security in the newly occupied eastern territories" can be found in BAB R 43II/686a.
17. USHMM RG 18.002M reel 5 (Latvian State Historical Archive, Riga (LSHA)) 70-5-24, p. 8, RFSS an HSSPFs Ostland, Ukraine & Center n.d. (copy of a copy)—on the distribution of this order in January and March 1942, see (LSHA) 70-5-24, p. 37, RSHA an BdS Riga und Kiew sowie die Chefs der Einsatzgruppen B und D, 26 November 1942. For example, HSSPF Ostland requested 40 grammes of gold from the Treuhandverwaltung in February 1942 for the restoration of the "chewing ability" (teeth) of SS-Hauptsturmführer Witte, see NARA T-459, roll 3, fr. 110–111.
18. NARA T-459, roll 21, fr. 158–159, Riga, 8 December 1941.
19. Ibid., fr. 145–146, Gebietskommissar an HSSPF, 13 December 1941; fr. 147, Gebietskommissar an HSSPF, 11 December 1941; fr. 149–150, Vermerk Riga, 11 December 1941; fr. 163, An den Reichskommissar, 4 December 1941.
20. NARA T-175, roll 54, fr. 2568620, RFSS Pers. Stab an Chef des Stabsamtes SS Gruppenführer Greifelt, 14 August 1942.
21. *U.S. and Allied Efforts to Recover and Restore Gold and Other Assets Stolen or Hidden by Germany During World War II: Preliminary Study,* coordinated by Stuart E. Eizenstat (Washington, DC, 1997), see Chapter IX: "Disposal by the U.S. of Captured Gold Looted by Germany from Individual Victims of Nazi Persecution and from European Central Banks."
22. USHMM RG 18.002M reel 5 (LSHA) 70-5-24, p. 34, Gebietskommissar Wilejka an den Generalkommissar in Minsk, 12 February 1943.
23. Ibid., p. 42, SS-WVHA an HSSPF Ostland, 22 June 1943 and p. 46, BdS Ostland an Reichskommissar, 23 October 1943.
24. *Nazi Conspiracy and Aggression* (Red Series) 5: (Washington: USGPO, 1946): 530–532, 2870-PS; on the role of the Interior Ministry in introducing the property confiscation clauses, see Uwe Adam, *Judenpolitik im Dritten Reich* (Düsseldorf, 1972), p. 80.
25. LAB 092/54592 Versendung von Steuerakten an das Gestapo, 1934.
26. Geheimes Staatsarchiv Preussischer Kulturbesitz, Dahlem, Rep. 151 Nr. 8074 (Arnold Zweig) Beschwerde, 29 December 1933.
27. Surprisingly *Einziehungsverfügungen* referring specifically to these laws continued to be issued by the Gestapo to many Jews even following the publication of the Eleventh Decree on 25 November 1941: see for example LAB A Rep. 092 1152 & 3235 both containing *Einziehungsverfügungen* from fall 1942.
28. USHMM RG 14.106M (BAB) R 58/276, pp. 27–28, Polit. Polizeikommandeur der Länder B. Nr. II 1 E -2746/35, 11 September 1935 & 38662/35 II 1 E -2746/35, 10 October 1935. The work of Gisela Möllenhoff and Rita Schlaitmann-Overmeyer, *Jüdische Familien in Münster 1918–1945: Biographisches Lexikon* (Münster, 1995), p. 22, based on the experiences of Jewish victims as well as the records of the Oberfinanzdirektion Münster, is one of the few to note the importance of the sharpened implementation of existing laws in specifically anti-Jewish ways in this period prior to *Kristallnacht*.

29. BAB R 2/5973, pp. 58–96.
30. The names of the persons concerned have been anonymized as required by the Oberfinanzdirektion as a condition of gaining access to these records, which are still covered by German data protection laws.
31. OFD Reichsfluchtsteuer file of FA Charlottenburg Ost, Reg. Bez. 138, 361-end, File of Dr. M.S. & Frau C.S.
32. USHMM RG 14.106M (BAB) R 58/62, Heydrich to Gestapo-Leitstellen, 12 April 1937.
33. Ibid., RFSS an Gestapa, 30 March 1937.
34. LAB A Rep. 092/54564, RFSS B. NR. S-PP (II B) *Nr.* 4575/37, 28 December 1938.
35. LAB A Rep. 092/54564, FA Moabit-West an OFP O.1300 – 2/39, 3 February 1939 & OFP Memo., 8 March 1939.
36. LAB A Rep. 092/54564, *Vermerk* OFP Berlin, 9 May 1939.
37. LAB A Rep. 092 Acc. 3924 Nr. 769, Generalia—Judenvermögensverwertung, Handakte Moser, RFSS, 17 May 1940 Nr. S I A 11 Allgem. 1427, *Betr.: Vermögensbeschlagnahme von jüd. Emigranten*; for the internal RSHA instructions regarding this policy, which stressed the need to prioritize work due to the war, see USHMM RG 14.106M (BAB) R 58/62, RSHA an Stapo(leit)stellen, 8 May 1940.
38. See, for example, USHMM 1996.A.0342 for examples of deportation lists for Berlin.
39. For examples of the lists of those proposed for denaturalization, see LAB A Rep. 092/50480, 50482, 54544, 54553, 54597; the published lists can be found in Michael Hepp, ed., *Die Ausbürgerung deutscher Staatsangehöriger 1933–45 nach den im Reichsanzeiger veröffentlichten Listen* (Munich, New York, London, Paris, 1985), 2 vols.
40. BAB R 2/5980, Oberfinanzpräsident Berlin, 28 Febrary 1941 claimed that more than 20,000 propertied Jews from the *Ostmark* (Austria) remained to be denaturalized.
41. Ibid., p. 52+ Note of a meeting on 15 March 1941.
42. Ibid., pp. 59–60, RFM O 1300 – 6012 III R, March 1941 (undated Vermerk summarizing correspondence with the Interior Ministry).
43. LAB A Rep. 092 Acc. 3924 Nr. 769 Generalia—Judenvermögensverwertung, Handakte Moser, OFP Berlin Verv-Auss. O 5205–Allgemein–P II Verv., 9 February 1942.
44. Cornelia Essner, "Das System der 'Nürnberger Gesetze' (1933–1945) oder der verwaltete Rassismus" (Ph.D. Berlin, 1999), p. 376. I am indebted to Prof. Hans Mommsen for making a copy of this recent thesis available to me.
45. S. Mehl, *Das Reichsfinanzministerium und die Verfolgung der deutschen Juden* (Berlin, 1990), p. 93.
46. See, for example, LAB Rep. A 092/1152 & 3235; for further examples see Inka Bertz, Ein Karteiblatt für jeden abgeschobenen Juden erleichtert die Übersicht", in Dorothea Kolland, ed., *Zehn Brüder sind wir gewesen…Spuren jüdischen Lebens in Neukölln* (Berlin, 1988), pp. 372–386.
47. Adler, *Der verwaltete Mensch*, p. 506.
48. Elfte Verordnung zum Reichsbürgergesetz. Vom 25. November 1941, RGBl. I, Nr. 133, 26 November 1941, pp. 722–724, published in facsimile in *Behandlung der vermögensrechtlichen Ansprüche der NS-Verfolgten. Schriftenreihe des Bundesamtes zur Regelung offener Vermögensfragen* (Berlin, 1994), pp. 227–229.
49. BAB R 2/12222, RFSS S–IV A 5 b – 802/40, Richtlinien für die Erfassung, Verwaltung und Verwertung der zurückgelassenen Vermögenswerte, 9 November 1940; see also R 58/276, pp. 267–271, RFSS, Ergänzende Richtlinien, 25 March 1941.
50. NARA T-1139, roll 53 NG-5373, RFM O 5210–1724 VI, 8 December 1941, Niederschrift über eine Besprechung am 4. Dez. 1941.
51. BAB R 2/12222, pp. 226–229, Referat Maedel 'Finanzierung der Massnahmen zur Lösung der Judenfrage,' 14 December 1942; see also Adler, *Der verwaltete Mensch*, p. 571.
52. The compulsory association of German Jews made directly accountable to the Gestapo.
53. Adler, *Der verwaltete Mensch*, pp. 562–569.
54. Ibid., pp. 569–570; these sums were paid into "special account H"; for examples of *Heimeinkaufsverträge*, see USHMM RG14.003M (Reichsvereinigung der Juden) file nos 501–584.

55. For example, USHMM RG14.003M no. 65 RV Ausgaben u. Einnahmen, Dez. 1942 includes payment V to Theresienstadt of 8 million RM; no. 66 RV Ausgaben u. Einnahmen, Feb. 1943 includes payment VII to Theresienstadt of 8 million RM. Further research is required to determine the actual use of these funds.
56. OFD, Div. Ordner I (RFM Handakte Scheerans) 'Die Massnahmen gegen die jüdische Bevölkerung und ihre Einrichtungen seit 1933' (Ausarbeitung des Archivs des ehem. RFM Febr. 1949), pp. 165–168; see also Mario Offenburg, ed., Adass Jisroel: Die Jüdische Gemeinde in Berlin (1869–1942)—Vernichtet und Vergessen (Berlin, 1986), p. 269.
57. On the avowed intent of the RSHA, Bormann and Heydrich to use the funds of the Reichsvereinigung to finance the deportations, see Wolf Gruner, "Die Grundstücke der 'Reichsfeinde': Zur 'Arisierung' von Immobilien durch Städte und Gemeinden 1938–1945", in Fritz Bauer Institut, ed., *"Arisierung"*, p. 142.
58. NARA RG 238 T-1139, roll 47 NG-4584, Generalbüro an Abt. VI (Ref. Dr. Maedel), 24 December 1942.
59. NARA RG 238 T-1139, roll 47 NG-4583, RMF O 5205: 495/42 VI g, Betr. Beschaffung der Mittel für die Abschiebung der Juden, 17 March 1943; see also Cornelia Essner, *Das System*, p. 397.
60. Mehl, *Das Reichsfinanzministerium*, p. 91, argues that the SS willingly handed responsibility for the subsequent accounting arising from the deportations over to the RFM in order to be able to concentrate on their executive tasks.
61. Mehl, *Das Reichsfinanzministerium*, p. 97, makes this point, citing the considerable income for the Reich arising from the Eleventh Decree.
62. On the issue of corruption see the contribution by Frank Bajohr in this volume.
63. See, for example, Avraham Barkai, *Vom Boykott zur 'Entjudung': Der wirtschaftliche Existenzkampf der Juden im Dritten Reich 1933–1943* (Frankfurt on Main, 1988), pp. 189–203.

CHAPTER 6

THE POLYCRATIC NATURE OF ART LOOTING: THE DYNAMIC BALANCE OF THE THIRD REICH

Jonathan Petropoulos

The National Socialist (NS) regime executed the most elaborate and prodigious art-looting program in history, outpacing even Napoleon.[1] Art looting was part of a much larger expropriation project that included residences and businesses, furniture and other cultural property, valuable metals and jewels, and of course, cash. While the seized art was sometimes precious and unique, the vast majority of works were not of museum quality, and shared much in common with the more anonymous assets noted above. Moreover, the way in which art was secured was representative of much that transpired during the Third Reich. Perhaps most fundamentally, art looting was a division-of-labor-based crime grounded in a polycratic administrative structure. This gave the Nazi leaders—and Hitler in particular—a range of options in terms of the spoliation of enemies' assets and maximized the chances for the leaders' personal enrichment. Most scholars would agree that there was a great deal of bureaucratic redundancy in the Third Reich; and, indeed, nearly all of the policy spheres in the National Socialist state have been analyzed structurally.[2] This is also to a large extent true for the art-plundering bureaucracy. But it is nonetheless useful to raise certain questions in connection with art looting – questions that are central to the nature and operation of the Nazi dictatorship.

The first concerns the extent to which policy was made from above (e.g., by Hitler, Himmler, Goebbels, and others) rather than coming from below. Were the hands-on art plunderers just following orders, or did they initiate measures on their own? The second question pertains to rivalry and the way that competition spurred on the plunderers. Did the race for spoils contribute to a more radical and oppressive plundering program? And, thirdly, yet in a somewhat countervailing way, to what extent did the polycratic art-looting administration rely upon cooperation and networking? The common element in the answers to these three questions is balance: it was the duality of rivalry and cooperation, like the tension between orders from above and initiatives from below, that gave the Third Reich its unique but dynamic political culture.

As suggested above, the National Socialists' program for seizing cultural property from its enemies is inextricably linked with the Holocaust more generally. There was always a cultural component to the Nazis' racialistic ideology, going back to the crude notion of "Aryans" as upholders of culture ("Kulturträger") versus Jews as cultural parasites and profiteers.[3] In a more material sense, the forced sales of Jewish property in the years immediately after 1933 represented an important and feasible early step in the gradually more radical Jewish policy of the regime. As Jews began to lose their cultural property—amidst their property more generally—they appeared less affluent, less civilized than their Christian counterparts. Expropriation often preceded or accompanied deportation; and taking individuals' cultural property, because of its often personal and sentimental value, made it a particularly aggressive act – an act consciously directed toward the dehumanization of victims.[4] Indeed, the other frequently used Nazi phrase for expropriation besides "Aryanization" was "dejewification" (adopted in 1939 by the Reich Economics Ministry), which suggests a more direct link between dispossession and genocide.[5] The men who carried out the plundering were very much like the "ordinary men" or "willing executioners" who have been examined in recent works on the hands-on murderers. They were the labor force of a gargantuan undertaking, and the murder of millions brought with it almost inconceivable quantities of property that required administrative processing.

An Overview of the Art-Plundering Bureaucracy

In order to understand the National Socialist leaders' polycratic plundering program, and answer the questions raised above, it is useful to consider an overview of the various organizations. Those discussed below were the most important in the Third Reich, but this survey is by no means exhaustive.

The Sicherheitsdienst (SD), including the Gestapo and Vugesta

Himmler and Heydrich controlled the first of the agencies to expropriate declared enemies' property. We still do not know a great deal about the early confiscations and forced sales involving art, including the so-called *Judenauktionen* (Jewish auctions). Much of the evidence is fragmentary—a catalog here, a report there: the cases of the Breslau collections of the Littmanns and the Silberbergs offer two recently researched examples.[6] And, of course, victims were not exclusively Jewish, but included others whom the regime opposed, including Sinti and Roma and the "asocial."[7] Most of the property confiscated by the Gestapo or other police organs was "liquidated" through the Reich Finance Ministry—and many of these files in the various Finanzdirektionen (Finance offices) were closed for many years because of the Federal Archive Law and the provisions for tax files. But there have been recent court rulings that make files concerning confiscation and restitution available to family members and qualified researchers (for example, in Munich in 1999).[8] Because the agencies headed by Himmler and Heydrich looted during all phases and in nearly every geographic area encompassed by the Third Reich, there is much to research. These regions extended progressively from the Altreich to the "Ostmark" (Austria), after the Anschluss, to the other conquered lands, and entailed an expanding array of agencies: e.g., in former Austria after 1938, the Zentralstelle für Jüdische Auswanderung (Central Office for Jewish Emigration) and the Vugesta—an acronym for Vermögensumzugsgut Gestapo (Office for the Sale of Jewish Removal Goods)—took over the property in many Jewish homes, including some works of art.[9]

The official ethos stressed the idea of no self-enrichment: Himmler said as much in his speeches, including the famous ones in Posen in October 1943, and high-profile violators were punished severely on charges of embezzlement (most famously Karl Lasch in Poland, who was executed in 1942 in Wrocclaw/Breslau).[10] But there were theft and self-enrichment throughout the Schutzstaffel (SS) empire: Amon Goeth and his grandiose appetites in *Schindler's List* is not pure fiction; indeed, his villa, horses, and wine consumption would be considered modest compared to the lifestyles of thousands of others, many of whom would have ranked above him. The case of Karl Lasch shows how carefully even SS officials needed to tread. The SS itself was polycratic and featured a great deal of internal competition: the Gestapo, for example, was often at odds with the Waffen-SS, the Kripo, the intelligence agencies (Abteilung VI of the Reich Security Main Office (RSHA)), the Personal Staff of the Reichsführer-SS (including das Ahnenerbe—Ancestral Heritage Society), the Feldpolizei ("Plain Clothes" Military Police), and so on. Between these various agencies there were personnel with all the necessary skills: from art historians (Peter Paulsen) and art dealers (Wilhelm Vahrenkamp) and conservation experts (Richard Teichler) to warehouse experts and transportation specialists.

The Dienststelle Mühlmann in Poland

Kajetan Mühlmann "trained" as a plunderer in Vienna after the Anschluss. As the cultural commissioner (Kulturbeauftragter) for the newest Gau, he played an important role after March 1938 in determining which organizations received money, but he also oversaw the "Aryanization" of much property and art in particular. There were a number of Viennese Jews with remarkable art collections: the Rothschilds, Bondys, and Bloch-Bauer families are examples.[11] Mühlmann himself received an "Aryanized" apartment in Vienna (and a villa in Salzburg-Anif where he installed his first wife); he also had a remarkable art collection and some fine furniture.[12] Although Mühlmann lost his position in "*ostmärkische*" cultural administration because he wanted to keep the confiscated art in Vienna—the problems of those with "Austrian tendencies" have been well documented[13]—he moved on to conquered Poland in October 1939 and led the organization that cleaned out the museums, the churches, and the finer private collections. He continued to work as an art historian—for example, publishing a book with fellow plunderer Gustav Bartel on the German cultural roots of Cracow—but his "scholarly" work was more likely to concern inventories of art that he secured in his official capacity.[14]

The Einsatzstab Reichsleiter Rosenberg (ERR) and ERR-Ost

This Nazi Party agency, which had branches in both the occupied West and the conquered territories of the East, stands out as an infamous organization because it was the largest one whose sole function was to seize property. The ERR (Reich Leader Rosenberg's Special Task Force) originated out of a project that sounded more innocuous: the creation of the Hohe Schule, or the series of centers for higher education planned by the Nazis.[15] Its founder, the philosophically inclined Reichsleiter Alfred Rosenberg, planned institutes for the study of National Socialism's enemies; with the onset of the war came the opportunity to capture these enemies' libraries and archives. Rosenberg induced Hitler to support the creation of an agency in France and the ERR was born. He was subsequently able to prevail in a turf war with the Army's Kunstschutz (Art Protection) unit, and the Foreign Office's Special Commando led by Eberhard Baron von Künsberg, among others.[16] That Alfred Rosenberg prevailed in France is surprising, but it was due to two main factors: the first was the support of Hermann Göring, who defended the ERR from attack, put resources at its disposal (from his Devisenschutzkommando (Currency Protection Commando) to Airforce trains), and thoroughly coopted the agency for his own collecting purposes. The second factor was Hitler, who favored the somewhat hapless Rosenberg because he represented the smallest threat and was the most controllable. To give the dominant plundering agency to the more competent and powerful Goebbels or Himmler would have strengthened the position of the latter and endangered the balance of power. It might have made it difficult for Hitler to exercise his prerogative over art.

The Dienststelle Mühlmann in the Low Countries[17]

Attached to the office of Reichskommissar for the Occupied Netherlands Arthur Seyss-Inquart, this agency liquidated the art seized by the various Nazi agencies in The Netherlands and the northern part of Belgium. Mühlmann employed a team of art historians who identified works seized by the SD or the Enemy Property Control Administration (among other agencies), and also scoured the Dutch market for works. The Dienststelle

Mühlmann (Mühlmann Department) functioned as a kind of art dealer: although Hitler and Göring had first choice of the works, they paid for them, and the rest were sold to other Nazi leaders and their friends (including cultural luminaries like film-maker Luis Trenker).[18] The two decrees of 1941 and 1942, which required Jews to deposit property at the "Aryanized" firm, the Bankhaus Lippmann, Rosenthal & Co., provided another source of art to the Dienststelle Mühlmann.[19] Much of the property liquidated by Mülhmann's agency was seized by others in the occupation bureaucracy, making The Netherlands a place where the plundering network was particularly strong.

Göring's Realm

Reichsmarschall Hermann Göring not only possessed an inordinate number of titles, but also controlled a number of organizations whose main purpose was to plunder; e.g., the Haupttreuhandstelle Ost and the Devisenschutzkommando within the Vierjahresplan agency. In addition to his influence over the ERR, which permitted him to acquire over 700 works from the agency without payment, his other primary means of acquiring art was through his personal art director, Walter Andreas Hofer, and the staff that assisted him. Although Hofer was an established independent art dealer, by 1939 he was using the title Direktor der Kunstsammlung des Reichsmarschalls (and had high-quality stationery to advertise his position). His aides included Dr. Bruno Lohse, an art historian from Berlin who was stationed in Paris during the war, and Gisela Limberger, the registrar who lived at Carinhall.[20] Hofer and his team pursued the best pieces via both the market and the storage depots: they had resort to Göring's considerable financial resources and purchased in Paris, Brussels and other Western European cities, but they also turned to the various plundering agencies over which the Reichsmarschall had more direct control.

Sonderauftrag Linz (The Linz Special Assignment)

The project to create the Führermuseum had its own staff and budget (mostly derived from the special postal stamps). The staff was headed by Dr. Hans Posse until his death in December 1942, and thereafter by Dr. Hermann Voss, and included directors for specific collections (e.g., armor, the library, and coins), as well as an array of official and semi-official agents. Posse turned to plunder to augment the collection from the outset: shortly after receiving his commission in 1939, he earmarked pieces seized in Vienna for the Führermuseum. Similar steps occurred in Poland with the Dienststelle Mühlmann and in France with the ERR. The political maelstrom of post-Anschluss Vienna had induced Hitler to issue the "*Führervorbehalt* (Führer's Prerogative)" with respect to art: he and his agents had first choice of the spoils (and most was destined for Linz). Posse and Voss not only had extraordinary political clout, but also almost unlimited financial resources.

They spent over RM 163 million, much of it in the occupied West, where they engaged in what is now called "technical looting" (due to the prejudicial exchange rates and the enormous financial advantages that resulted for the Germans).[21]

The discussion above provides an overview of only the most important art-plundering agencies. Others, like the Sonderkommando (Special Commando) Künsberg, which started in France but moved on to help ravage the Soviet Union, or the Sonderkommando Ribbentrop, which operated on the Eastern Front as well (gaining renown for seizing a prodigious number of books), also deserve mention.[22] The array of plundering agencies in operation during the Third Reich is truly stunning. And, as noted above with respect to the connection to the Holocaust, the number of participants—or perpetrators—is almost as remarkable. It is difficult, if not impossible, to arrive at a precise number of art looters. It partly depends on whom one counts: there were probably several hundred to a thousand art historians, art dealers, conservation specialists, and museum directors who were engaged by the plundering agencies. But they were supported by thousands of research assistants, secretaries, packers, and drivers. The remainder of this chapter, however, will concentrate on the art experts, who formed an elite among the plunderers and ranked just below the Nazi leaders in the plundering bureaucracy.

Orders from Above and Initiatives from Below

The "Nuremberg defense" has gained a foothold in popular parlance, signified by the phrase "I was just following orders." Despite this crude characterization of the accused leaders' defense strategies, the phrase refers to one of the key questions of the Nazi dictatorship: to what extent were the perpetrators and functionaries compelled and coerced from above and to what extent did they initiate acts of persecution? This is a question, of course, raised by Daniel Goldhagen's controversial study *Hitler's Willing Executioners* and the Wehrmacht exhibition organized by the Institut für Sozialforschung in Hamburg.[23] In short, it has become increasingly evident that the Nazi state operated according to a combination of initiative from below and orders from above. But it was the former that was ignored for so long and now seems to hold the greatest fascination. And, while this question has been raised with respect to the Holocaust and other murderous activities during the war, it has not been explored with respect to plundering.

Although the Nazis were long perceived as rowdy bullies who were inclined to take things (Frank Bajohr's recent study on corruption makes it clear that theft commenced directly after the seizure of power), the tenor or public appearance of the dispossession nonetheless changed significantly, if temporarily, after 1934.[24] Coinciding to some extent with the Röhm purge, the state discouraged violent and unregulated activities (the exception being

Austria, where the illegal activists were surreptitiously encouraged to act lawlessly and sabotage the Schuschnigg regime). This veneer of orderliness masked the increasingly systematic pursuit of the assets of Germany's Jews. As Martin Fiedler wrote, "All proprietors or associates in partnerships, as well as members of corporate boards and advisory councils, who qualified as Jews according to the racial criteria of the NS state, had to cede their interests and give up their offices by the second half of 1938 at the least."[25] There is no doubt that *Schreibtischtäter* (desk murderers) never ceased to exercise initiative, as individuals in agencies like the Reich Finance Ministry, the Gauleiter's office, and the Security Service, and also in the private sphere continually took action in an attempt to dispossess victims. But there was a period after 1934 when the pressure from below was more carefully regulated by higher-ranking state authorities in the interest of stability and control.

Hitler and his top leaders permitted a release of this pressure in 1938, especially with the "wild Aryanizations" that accompanied the Anschluss. Even at the time, it was widely known that non-Jewish Viennese were acting on their own initiative during the first stage of the Anschluss, and simply taking Jews' property. This was more common among Party members, who had the connections and were therefore not challenged from above. Bruce Pauley captured a sense of this initiative from below when he wrote:

> With the blessings of the new Nazi government, anti-Semitism now became a patriotic virtue.... Now gangs of Nazis invaded Jewish department stores, humble Jewish shops in the Leopoldstadt, the homes of Jewish bankers, as well as the apartments of middle-class Jews, and stole money, art treasures, furs, jewelry, and even furniture.... Even after this initial looting rampage subsided, about a week after the Anschluss, bargain hunters could buy Jewish possessions at nominal prices when word got around that a particular Jewish family was desperate for money.[26]

Because many Viennese Jews possessed a relatively great amount of art and cultural property, this was indeed a significant category of plunder; while most of the museum-quality art went to the Neue Burg and the confiscated Rothschild Schloss Wildhof, much that was valuable was never processed in an official repository.[27]

Even though authorities in Berlin asserted themselves in Vienna and restrained the locals from acting alone, the punishments meted out to thieves was minimal. The "Viennese model," which was emulated in the Altreich, included the notion of individual initiative, especially in the aftermath of *Reichskristallnacht*. Although part of the lesson drawn from Vienna involved circumspection—it was best to establish a veneer of legality when operating in the Reich and later the occupied West—it had become clear to a wide range of people that they could profit personally if they could locate Jewish property and seize it themselves. And, indeed, it appears that the majority of the "Aryanizations" of Jewish art dealerships and confiscations of Jewish art collections took place in 1938 or later—after the "lessons" of the preceding years. Ernst Buchner, the Generaldirektor der Bayerischen

Staatsgemäldesammlungen, was charged after the war by Else and Hugo Marx with coming to them in 1938 and urging them to sell works below market price, lest the Gestapo come and simply confiscate the art.[28] While Buchner was acquiring art for his museum (and not his own collection), in a more general sense personal enrichment was a by-product of the persecution of the Jews. There is much truth in the phrase "Arisierung als Zentrum der Korruption" (Aryanization as a centre for corruption).

Two points need to be stressed with respect to the "Aryanization" process. The first, suggested above, is that liquidation of property involved many people. As Frank Bajohr has written, "'Aryanization' as a political-social process would not have been possible without the direct and indirect participation of millions of Germans."[29] The dispossession of Jews was a mass phenomenon founded upon plebiscitary support, and the Nazi leaders tapped this wellspring of popular enthusiasm. The second point involves controlling this enthusiasm. After the lawlessness and destruction of the "wild Aryanizations" and the pogrom of *Reichskristallnacht* in 1938, the Nazi leaders reasserted themselves and imposed greater limits with regard to expropriation within the Reich and the occupied West, as compared to the East.[30] For example, over 21,000 cultural objects were secured by the ERR in France and stored at Schloss Neuschwanstein, which speaks for official control (as compared to the self-enrichment of individuals), whereas there was much more individual plundering and willful destruction in the East, as Martin Dean, Wolfgang Eichwede, Ulrike Hartung, and Anja Heuss have shown.[31] This said, there were still great opportunities for personal enrichment in the Reich and the West, and the Nazi leaders to a certain extent tolerated this corruption. They viewed it as a kind of incentive—a means of increasing motivation and activism among subordinates. The Nazi leaders were always concerned about stagnation within the bureaucracy and therefore afforded subordinates both *Handlungsspielraum* (room for maneuver) and some opportunities for personal (including professional) gain.[32]

It is instructive to refer to several specific examples to understand this balance. To return to Ernst Buchner, whose career I examined in great detail in *The Faustian Bargain*: the museum director is most notorious for his role in securing two altar pieces that had panels removed from Germany and given to Belgium as part of the Treaty of Versailles. Sections of the Van Eyck brothers' *The Mystic Lamb* and Dirk Bouts's *The Last Supper* had been handed over in accordance with article 247 of the Treaty as compensation for the Belgians' loss of cultural property (e.g., the willful destruction of the library at Louvain). Most Nazis, including Buchner, wanted them back. In the case of the former, Buchner received orders from Hitler (via the Reich Chancellery) in June 1942 to travel to Pau, France, and seize the Van Eycks' masterpiece.[33] Accordingly, Buchner and his chief conservator accompanied an armed detachment and carried out the mission. But, at the same time, Buchner himself seized the initiative and wrote to the Reich Chancellery suggesting that he go after the Bouts altar piece: he wrote to Ministerialdirigent Walter Hanssen in Munich on 7 July 1942 and proposed that "the four panels be returned."³⁴ Hitler gave his approval for this second undertaking and Buchner went to Louvain in August 1942 to capture this prize. Hitler rewarded the museum director with a dotation of RM 30,000. Here, one can see the combination mentioned above: the seizure of the Van Eycks' altarpiece resulted from an order from above and that of Bouts from the initiative of a hands-on plunderer. The result was mutually advantageous. One sees this pattern time and again—for example, with the "Aryanization" of the Goudstikker art dealership in The Netherlands, where the dealer, Alois Miedl, approached Göring with a proposal. The Reichsmarschall provided the bulk of the capital for the purchase from the dealer's widow (2 million guilders versus 500,000 from Miedl), and received 600 of the best works.³⁵ Of course, Miedl also made a handsome profit. But there it was: initiative from below and a response that protected the interests of the Nazi leaders.

Every act of theft featured its own unique balance between centralization and "entrepeneurship" and the norm was somewhere in the middle. In terms of centralization, most looters would have had an organizational affiliation and been cognizant of a system of organized plunder that delivered the art to the Nazi leaders—starting with Hitler and his *Führervorbehalt*. But on the other hand, these orders, even the *Führervorbehalt*, were not always followed or enforced, and there was a degree of initiative and volition on the part of the thieves.³⁶ There were no reported cases of someone being forced to plunder at gunpoint (as with the actual killers in the Holocaust). The plunderers themselves made the decision to participate in the seizure of property.

Rivalry and Competition

Because art-plundering was potentially so lucrative and because it was intertwined with issues of power and prestige, it was naturally the source of great rivalry. The mutually beneficial arrangement that developed between Hitler and Buchner or Göring and Miedl should not obscure the fact that competition was at the heart of this polycratic looting bureaucracy. In every land controlled by the Nazi regime, there were fierce struggles between the competing agencies outlined above. These rivalries usually involved complex and lengthy struggles. It is not surprising that recent scholarship on looting has often tackled one or several specific regions, such as Anja Heuss's nuanced book examining the plundering bureaucracies in France and the Soviet Union.³⁷ In general terms, one can talk about three geographic sectors where these rivalries were played out: the Reich, the occupied West, and the occupied East (including the Eastern Front). Within a given sector, there tended to be not only specific Nazi leaders but also specific hands-on plunderers who were predominant. Hitler and, to a lesser extent, the forces of Himmler and Heydrich were the exceptions, as their influence extended to all three sectors. Alfred Rosenberg is a more typical case: he prevailed against all odds in France, but was weak in the Reich and in the East, despite the fact that there was an ERR-Ost and he held the position of Reichskommissar für die besetzten Ostgebiete (Reich Commissioner for the Occupied Eastern Territories). This weakness in the Reich and the East also applied to his staff of plunderers, such as Robert Scholz, who headed the Sonderstab Bildende Kunst (Special Staff for the Visual Arts) within the ERR in France, but claimed after the war not even to have visited the occupied East.

Despite the emergence of relatively dominant agencies and individuals in specific spheres, the unending competition made the plunderers more industrious and more radical. This was clearly evident in Vienna, the first city whose Jewish population endured unbridled looting. With the agents of Hitler, Göring, Goebbels, Arthur Seyss-Inquart, Josef Bürckel, Odilo Globocnik, Himmler, and Heydrich all striving to gain an advantage, there was scarcely a Jewish collection that remained untouched. It is no wonder that art dealer Karl Haberstock, who was sent to Vienna in mid 1938 to help organize the plunder, wrote letters to Hans Lammers and Martin Bormann saying that he was receiving no cooperation and could not carry out his tasks. He ultimately retreated back to Berlin and returned to his art-dealing business. This competitive scenario was played out repeatedly. One can write a history of the looting of Munich art galleries after *Reichskristallnacht* that is very similar. Gauleiter Adolf Wagner marshaled his forces and tried to take the art for his own offices, while the Reich Finance Ministry struggled to implement the liquidation policies as they understood them. Meanwhile, Hans Posse attempted to exercise the *Führervorbehalt* and obtain the best pieces for Linz.[38] In Munich, as in Vienna and most other locales, there was enough art and cultural property to reward most of those who demonstrated initiative. It seems that everyone got something. Historians are just now gaining a precise understanding of self-enrichment during the Third Reich: the useful chart in Frank Bajohr's *Parvenüs und Profiteure*, for example, shows an average annual sum of RM 1,856 in 1937 for the Reich as a whole, with Reichminister earning much larger amounts (Goebbels in 1943 earned RM 424,317).[39] The art experts/plunderers also did very well for themselves, and it was common to see annual incomes above RM 50,000. In this Darwinian environment, those who survived reaped great material rewards.

Cooperation and Networks

One should not construe the liquidation of victims' property as entirely adversarial; indeed, the plundering polycracy involved a series of agencies and businesses that often worked together. Inter-agency alliances, such as the cooperation between the ERR and Göring's Devisenschutzkommando (Currency Protection Commando), offer a prime example. More recently, scholars have begun to appreciate fully the role of those in the private sector in this liquidation process. For example, auction houses, such as Adolf Weinmüller in Munich, the Dorotheum in Vienna, and Hans Lange in Berlin, were instrumental in the processing of seized artworks.[40] They worked closely with the Reich Finance Ministry in selling the booty. But they also had extensive contact with more brutal agencies like the Gestapo, as revealed in the postwar testimony of the director of the firm during the Third Reich, Dr. Eberhard von Crannach-Sichart:

> In default of all documents, which burnt, we wanted to state by heart with the following, what kind of connection existed between the Gestapo Prague and the art-dealer firm Weinmüller. During the course of the year 1941 a shipment of the Gestapo Prague arrived by truck with the order to sell the contents by auction. They mostly were paintings by old and modern painters, some graphic maps [albums] and some Persian rugs. Not a single object of international value or of higher quality was among these items. They rather had a generally medium rank, so that it was not worth while to have a special auction for them.... We are no more in a position to give specific instructions on number or details. We were not told from where the objects originated. There were no further orders. The objects were sold during the following auction. Because of the above mentioned reason, we are no more able to state to which owner they went.[41]

In short, there were a series of alliances that extended both vertically and horizontally and made the art-theft program as effective as it was. The cooperation transcended the boundaries of official and nonofficial. Indeed, the questions posed by categorization are difficult: where, for example, does one place a dealer like Karl Haberstock, who maintained his high-profile private gallery in Berlin, but served as an advisor to Hitler, Goebbels, and others in actions varying from the liquidation of modern art in state collections to the disposition of Viennese collections and the seizure of Jewish art in France?

The key points to be emphasized here concern not only the fluidity of distinctions among the art plunderers, but also the extensiveness of the networks. Again, one is talking here about those at the "elite" level of art experts. Yet the contact between them is nonetheless striking. The Art Looting Investigation Unit, the American-led group of art historians who interrogated the most important art experts and drafted important reports, appreciated this network. Indeed, their reports invariably included lists of individuals who collaborated with the chief plunderers (e.g., dealers in France) and the *Final Report* featured a lengthy list of individuals implicated in the looting.[42] Interviews with those who were part of this network confirm its existence. Göring's agent Bruno Lohse has discussed his associations with the author on numerous occasions, and he was almost invariably familiar with every other elite plunderer. Oftentimes, his opinion of the person was negative (his favorite adjective is "widerlich" [revolting]). But he almost always knew who they were and could offer some details about the individual's actions and personality. Many of these ties between members of the plundering bureaucracy were sufficiently strong to continue into the postwar period. In Lohse's case, he continued his business and social relations with Haberstock, Mühlmann, Walter Andreas Hofer, Maria Almas Dietrich (a Munich art dealer and favorite of Hitler), Gustav Rochlitz (who arranged trading between the ERR and Swiss dealer Theodor Fischer), and Alois Miedl, among many others. Lohse seems to have maintained contact with every important art dealer who survived the Third Reich. This contact offered a means of rehabilitating his and others' careers and generating considerable income (Lohse's own art collection in his Munich apartment currently includes works by Nolde and other German Expressionists, as well as Dutch Old Masters).

Conclusion

The key to the National Socialist art-plundering program—the reason it was so relentless and exhaustive—lies in its myriad tensions. The two most important of these tensions have been discussed above. The first grew out of the vertical or hierarchical relations, where there were not only orders from above but also initiatives from below. The plunderers would not have undertaken the expropriation measures without orders from above. Note in this respect that much art-plundering in the Third Reich was therefore not "illegal" or "criminal" in that it took place in accordance with German laws and decrees. But this impetus was augmented by the desire of subordinates to participate in the looting. Their motivations varied, including a sincere belief in the ideological project, the wish for promotion, some professional ambition (such as expanding a museum collection), and, of course, the pursuit of wealth. All of this was contained in this vertical dynamic. The second, horizontal tension involved competition and rivalry. Inter-agency rivalry was a spur to more radical and industrious undertakings by the competing organizations. The Nazi leaders and their agents were constantly looking for an advantage—whether it be another victim, a new collaborator, or an untapped region to exploit. Creating a competitive environment with bureaucratic redundancy was the best way to exploit the situation. Complicating this picture, and yet underscoring the theme of balance, were the networks that existed. Therefore, both in a vertical and horizontal sense, there were "creative" tensions that contributed to the effectiveness of the plundering program. It is the unique balance of these diverse forces—of control versus initiative and rivalry versus cooperation— that is the key to the greatest looting program of all time.

Notes

1. See Susanne Anderson-Riedel, "Dominique-Vivant Denon (1747–1825), Napoleons 'Directeur des Arts,'" *Kunstchronik* 54 (2001): 15–20. Also Russell Chamberlain, *Loot: The Heritage of Plunder* (New York, 1983); Jeanette Greenfield, "The Spoils of War," in Elizabeth Simpson, ed., *The Spoils of War: World War II and Its Aftermath* (New York, 1997), pp. 34–39.
2. One of the first scholars to examine the "multiplication of offices" was Hannah Arendt, *Origins of Totalitarianism* (San Diego, 1951). But other scholars, such as Hans Mommsen, have also done a great deal to enhance our understanding of polycracy.

3. This cultural-racial argument is reflected in many documents in the Third Reich, perhaps most vividly in the catalog to the "Entartete Kunst Ausstellung" of 1937, which is reproduced in Stephanie Barron, ed., *Degenerate Art: The Fate of the Avant-Garde in Nazi Germany* (New York, 1991). Also Sander Gilman, "The Mad Man as Artist: Medicine, History, and Degenerate Art," *Journal of Contemporary History* 20 (1985): 575–597; Otto Karl Werckmeister, "Hitler the Artist," *Critical Inquiry* 23 (Winter 1997): 270–297.
4. Avraham Barkai, *From Boycott to Annihilation: The Economic Struggle of German Jews, 1933–1943* (Hanover, N.H. 1989). Also see Terence des Pres, *The Survivor: Anatomy of Life in the Death Camps* (Oxford, 1980).
5. Frank Bajohr, "'Arisierung' als gesellschaftlicher Prozess: Verhalten, Strategien und Handlungsspielräume jüdischer Eigentümer und 'arischer' Erwerber," in Fritz Bauer Institut, ed., *"Arisierung" im Nationalsozialismus: Volksgemeinschaft, Raub und Gedächtnis* (Frankfurt on Main, 2000), p. 15.
6. See, for example, Anja Heuss, "Die Vernichtung jüdischer Sammlungen in Berlin," *Neue Zürcher Zeitung*, 25 February 1997.
7. For a treatment of other victims, see Robert Gellately and Nathan Stolzfuss, eds., *Social Outsiders in Nazi Germany* (Princeton, 2001). For an example of the confiscation of the art of a non-Jewish victim, see the case involving feminist and pacifist Anita Augspurg in Jonathan Petropoulos, *The Faustian Bargain: The Art World in Nazi Germany* (Oxford, 2000), p. 27.
8. Jim Tobias, "Forscher erhalten Einblick in NS-Akten: Generaldirektion der Staatlichen Archive in München spricht ein Machtwort," *Süddeutsche Zeitung* 205 (6 September 1999): L6.
9. Herbert Posch, "Inventarisiert: Raub und Verwertung—'arisierte' Wohnungseinrichtungen im Mobiliendepot," in *Inventarisiert* (Vienna, 2000).
10. Frank Bajohr, *Parvenüs und Profiteure. Korruption in der NS-Zeit* (Frankfurt on Main, 2001), pp. 137–177, where he explores "die Bekämpfung der Korruption und ihre Grenzen" (the fight against corruption and ist limits).
11. See, for example, Hubertus Czernin, *Die Fälschung: Der Fall Bloch-Bauer*, 2 vols. (Vienna, 1999).
12. Jean Vlug, *Report on Objects Removed to Germany from Holland, Belgium, and France during the German Occupation on the Countries* (Report of Stichting Nederlands Kunstbesitz, Amsterdam, 1945).
13. Oliver Rathkolb, "Nationalsozialistische (Un-) Kulturpolitik in Wien, 1938–1945," and Jan Tabor, "Die Gaben der Ostmark: Österreichische Kunst und Künstler in der nationalsozialistischer Zeit," in Hans Seiger/ Sabine Plakolm-Forsthuber, ed., *Im Reich der Kunst. Die Wiener Akademie der bildenden Künste und die faschistische Kunstpolitik* (Vienna, 1990), pp. 247–296.
14. Kajetan Mühlmann and Gustav Barthel, *Krakau: Hauptstadt des deutschen Generalgouvernements Polen. Gestalt und künstlerische Leistung einer deutschen Stadt im Osten* (Breslau, 1940); Kajetan Mühlmann, *Sichergestellte Kunstwerke im Generalgouvernement* (Cracow, 1941); ibid., *Sichergestellte Kunstwerke in den Besetzten niederländischen Gebieten* (The Hague, 1943). Mühlmann also produced the catalogue for the Mannheimer collection, which was acquired by German authorities through Arthur Seyss-Inquart.
15. See Reinhard Bollmus, *Das Amt Rosenberg und seine Gegner: Studien zum Machtkampf im nationalsozialistischen Herrschaftssystem* (Stuttgart, 1970); James Plaut, *Consolidated Interrogation Report Number 1: Activity of the Einsatzstab Reichsleiter Rosenberg* (Washington, D.C., 1945).
16. Wilhelm Treue, "Zum nationalsozialistischen Kunstraub in Frankreich. Der 'Bargatzky Bericht,'" *Vierteljahrshefte für Zeitgeschichte* 13 no. 3 (July 1965): 285–337. See also Willem de Vries, *Sonderstab Musik: Organisierte Plünderungen in Westeuropa, 1940–1945* (Cologne, 1998).
17. See also contribution by Gerard Aalders in this volume.

18. Vlug, *Report on Objects Removed to Germany from Holland, Belgium, and France*; Gerard Aalders, *Geraubt! Die Enteignung jüdischen Besitzes im Zweiten Weltkrieg* (Cologne, 2000); Adrian Venema, *Kunsthandel in Nederland, 1940–1945* (Amsterdam, 1986); Stephan Lindner, *Das Reichskommissariat für die Behandlung feindlichen Vermögens im Zweiten Weltkrieg. Eine Studie zur Verwaltungs-, Rechts-, und Wirtschaftsgeschichte des nationalsozialistische Deutschlands* (Stuttgart, 1991).
19. For the "Liro-Verordnungen," see Aalders, *Geraubt!*, p. 72. See also A.J. van der Leeuw, "Entziehung und Verbringung nach Deutschland der beim Bankhause Lippmann, Rosenthal & Co. Sarphatistraat abgelieferten Vermögensgegenstände," in Institut für Zeitgeschichte, Munich (IfZ), MS-112/3.
20. James Plaut, *Detailed Interrogation Report No. 6: Bruno Lohse* (Washington, D.C., 1945); Theodore Rousseau, *Detailed Interrogation Report No. 7: Gisela Limburger* (Washington, DC, 1945); idem, *Detailed Interrogation Report No. 9: Walter Andreas Hofer* (Washington, 1945).
21. S. Lane Faison, *Consolidated Interrogation Report No. 4: Linz. Hitler's Museum and Library* (Washington, 1945), p. 18. For "technical looting," see Gerard Aalders, "By Diplomatic Pouch: Art Smuggling by the Nazis," *The Spoils of War International Newsletter* 3 (December 1996).
22. See Ulrike Hartung, *Raubzüge in der Sowjetunion. Das Sonderkommando Künsberg, 1941–1943* (Bremen, 1997); Anja Heuss, "Das Sonderkommando Künsberg und der Kulturgutraub in der Sowjetunion," *Vierteljahrshefte für Zeitgeschichte* 4 (1997).
23. Daniel Goldhagen, *Hitler's Willing Executioners: Ordinary Germans and the Holocaust* (New York, 1996). See also Hamburger Institut für Sozialforschung, ed., *Vernichtungskrieg. Verbrechen der Wehrmacht 1941 bis 1944* (Hamburg, 1996); Landeshauptstadt München ,ed., *Bilanz einer Ausstellung. Dokumentation der Kontroverse um die Ausstellung "Vernichtungskrieg. Verbrechen der Wehrmacht 1941 bis 1944" in München* (Munich, 1998).
24. Bajohr, *Parvenüs und Profiteure*, pp. 17–34.
25. Martin Fiedler, "Die Arisierung der Wirtschaftselite," in Fritz Bauer Institut, ed., *"Arisierung" im Nationalsozialismus*, p. 60.
26. Bruce Pauley, *A History of Austrian Antisemitism* (Chapel Hill, 1992), pp. 280–281. See also Gerhard Botz, *Wien vom "Anschluss" zum Krieg: Nationalsozialistische Machtübernahme und politisch-soziale Umgestaltung am Beispiel der Stadt Wien 1938/39* (Vienna, 1978).
27. Herbert Haupt, *Jahre der Gefährdung: das Kunsthistorisches Museum 1938–1945* (Vienna, 1995).
28. BHSA MK 44778, Statement of Otto Marx, 13 September 1945.
29. Bajohr, "'Arisierung' als gesellschaftlicher Prozess," p. 17.
30. See Frank Bajohr in the present volume.
31. Martin Dean, *Collaboration in the Holocaust: Crimes of the Local Police in Belorussia and Ukraine, 1941–1944* (New York, 2000); Wolfgang Eichwede and Ulrike Hartung ,eds., *"Betr. Sicherstellung": N.S.-Kunstraub in der Sowjetunion* (Bremen, 1998); Hartung, *Raubzüge in der Sowjetunion*; Anja Heuss, *Kunst- und Kulturgüterraub: eine vergleichende Studie zur Besatzungspolitik der Nationalsozialisten in Frankreich und der Sowjetunion* (Heidelberg, 2000). The lawlessness of the East is confirmed by countless specific examples, e.g., see the report in IfZ, "Plünderungen der Radziwill Sammlung durch deutschen Soldaten. Gemälde, Möbel, usw. im Besitz Gauleiter Kube," 20 April 1943.
32. For "Handlungsspielraum," see Dieter Ziegler in this volume. For concerns about "stagnation" in the bureaucracy, see Marnix Croes, "Sicherheitspolizei and Sicherheitsdienst in the Netherlands: Limits of Hierarchical Control," prepared for delivery at the International Conference: "Networks of Persecution: The Holocaust as Division-of-Labor Based Crime," Konstanz University, 24–26 September 2000.
33. Petropoulos, *The Faustian Bargain*, pp. 33–36.
34. Buchner to Hanssen is reproduced in Hildegard Brenner, *Kunstpolitik des Nationalsozialismus* (Reinbek bei Hamburg, 1963), pp. 226–227.

35. Nancy Yeide, Amy Walsh, and Konstantin Akinsha, *The AAM Guide to Provenance Research* (Washington, DC, 2001), p. 135.
36. For the *Führervorbehalt* and its progressive extension to the occupied territories, see Bundesarchiv Lichterfelde, R43II/1269a, Bl. 53–54, Lammers' Vermerk, 7 November 1942.
37. Heuss, *Kunst- und Kulturgüterraub*.
38. For the rivalry in plundering art in Munich, see BAL R2/31098, where Munich Oberfinanzpräsident Wiesensee, Gauleiter Wagner, Hans Posse, and others compete for the spoils. See also Münchener Stadtmuseum, ed., *"Hauptstadt der Bewegung": Bayerns Metropole und der Nationalsozialismus* (Munich, 1993).
39. Bajor, *Parvenüs und Profiteure*, p. 235.
40. Anja Heuss, "Die Reichskulturkammer und die Steuerung des Kunsthandels im Dritten Reich," *Sediment* (Bonn, Zentralarchiv des Deutschen und Internationalen Kunsthandels) 3 (1998): 49–61. Also see Monika Kingreen on Frankfurt museum director Ernst Holzinger, "Wie sich Museen Kunst aus jüdischem Besitz aneigneten," *Frankfurter Rundschau*, 9 May 2000.
41. Testimony of Crannach-Sichart in 1947 in NARA RG 260, Ardelia Hall collection, box 373, Office of Military Government for Bavaria, "Monthly Consolidated Field Report," March 1948, item 33.
42. Art looting Investigation Unit, *Art Looting Investigation Unit Final Report* (Washington, D.C., 1946). Note that this report can be found at http://docproj.loyola.edu.

CHAPTER 7

THE HOLOCAUST AND CORRUPTION

Frank Bajohr

Political corruption was one of the central structural problems of National Socialist (NS) rule.[1] The decisive factor underlying its pervasiveness was that in abolishing the separation of powers, National Socialism eliminated practically all the potential supervisory bodies. Consequently, after 1933, there was no critical, independent press in Germany. The dissolution of parliaments or their transformation into mere rubber-stamp organs destroyed the system of parliamentary control, which included budget-control rights and public debate on abuses or the possibility of critical questioning. Beyond this, the NS dictatorship politicized and controlled the judicial system and limited the competence of traditional institutions of control, such as auditing offices.

The structure of the National Socialist movement also contributed to the spread of corruption. In this connection two aspects played particular roles. First, the institutional rivalry typical of the NS system was not limited to the struggle for political influence, but also extended to the control of material resources. The widespread competition for enrichment through the "Aryanization" of Jewish assets was a typical example of how polycratic institutional rivalry contributed to the spread of corruption. Secondly, the formation of cliques and camaraderie typical of the National Socialist movement encouraged corruption. Since the position of the individual functionary in the authoritarian "Führer" -party was not legitimated by elections, it depended primarily on the integration of the respective leader into party-internal old-boy and personnel networks. These extended horizontally through the entire party and were subject to no limitations on power and no pressure for accountability. The patronage-oriented political conception of the Nationals zialistische Deutsche Arbeiterpartei (NSDAP) had its roots here. It was additionally encouraged by the fact that many National Socialists defined themselves as "victims" of a "Weimar system" personified by Jews and Social Democrats and after 1933 vehemently called for "compensation." From a social-psychological viewpoint one could call the NSDAP a party of organized self-pity. Systematic nepotism in favor of party members, especially of "old fighters" (party veterans), was one of the central characteristics of political corruption in the Third Reich. The clientele-oriented substructure of the NSDAP often regulated the relationships of the National Socialists to one another much more strongly than formal organizational membership and hierarchies. In this way a Gauleiter's chauffeur could have greater chances of self-enrichment than a functionary positioned much higher in the official hierarchy.

In many respects National Socialist ideology also contributed to the growth of corrruption; in the occupied territories of Eeastern Europe, for example, corruption can be traced to racist hierarchical concepts and an internalized "master race attitude" held by many members of the occupation machinery.

Political corruption is generally defined as the "misuse of public offices for private ends," i.e., it is not limited to a conventional understanding that associates corruption first of all with bribery and corruptibility, but extends beyond this to behaviors such as improper use of office, fraud, embezzlement, nepotism, patronage, etc. But even this classical definition only partially grasps the diverse forms of political corruption characterizing the Third Reich. A major contributor to this variety was the fact that, while the National Socialists officially condemned corruption, in actual practice they failed to observe their own condemnations. If we take as a standard the way NS rulers dealt with corruption, three basic variants can be identified: The first comprises corrupt practices officially encouraged and implemented by the state and the NS movement, which were not based on the individual misuse of offices but represented an organized system of power abuse. This, furthermore, not only served private ends but also contributed to the functional stabilization of the system. This institutionalized corruption included, for example, organized forms, e.g., privileging party members, especially party veterans, through special Employment Office measures, or the opulent gifts and endowments provided by Hitler for the members of the military, political, scientific, or cultural elites. To be distinguished from this type is tolerated corruption, which, due to structural weaknesses in the agencies responsible for fighting corruption under the Third Reich, spread in a particular manner and was tolerated either knowingly or out of necessity. The toleration of corruption included, for example, black- market transactions, especially in the occupied territories, which were accepted, just as were the creeping replacement of public budgets by special funds and illegal bank accounts and foundations, above all by the Gauleiter, who were subject to no effective control of their power or finances. Thirdly, there was also a type of corruption under National Socialist rule that was combated, i.e., behaviors that were prosecuted on the basis of existing normative principles. Above all, this included the broad area of corruption at the expense of the NSDAP and its organizations, e.g., the widespread embezzlement of membership dues and contributions.

The boundary lines separating the three forms of corruption were, of course, not impermeable, but fluid and easily blurred. For example, a corrupt practice for which a subordinate official might be severely punished was often tolerated when committed by a higher NS functionary. Some corrupt practices, such as black-market transactions, were differently treated at different times—sometimes officially encouraged, sometimes only tolerated, or perhaps even combated. These fluid boundaries were the typical identifying features of a system of rule that had tended to cut itself off from normative constraints, i.e., that enjoyed the absolute power to decide, in accordance with the opportunities presented and the position of and benefits for a functionary, in which cases normative principles would be followed and in which the culprit would go unpunished.

This multiplicity of forms and the fluid boundaries of corruption in the Third Reich also characterized the creeping loss of rights by Jews, their financial and economic ruin, their forced expulsion, and finally their deportation and murder. In this process the state's claim to dispose of Jewish property could only be partially established. There was rather a latent tension between the financial and foreign-exchange policy interests of the Reich and the desire for personal enrichment or the promotion of the interests of the party and its representatives. On the one hand, the right to dispose of Jewish property was always linked with questions of power and institutional influence, which above all touched on the relationship of party and state. On the other hand, anti-Semitic activists—above all in the NSDAP and its organizations—were unwilling to subordinate their individual "claims" to the Reich's sole right of disposition. Pointing to their alleged "sacrifices" in the "time of struggle" (*Kampfzeit*), they demanded their personal share of the expected booty and emphasized this with a multiplicity of individual activities, through which they began to assert their claims immediately after the National Socialist seizure of power.

Anti-Semitic Violence and Individual Enrichment

The anti-Semitic terror of the period in which the National Socialists seized power (*Machtergreifungsphase*) was characterized not merely by violent attacks on Jews: it was from the start directed at their material assets, which National Socialist propaganda did not respect as personal property, defining it instead ideologically as "fraudulently acquired" or "stolen assets of the people."[2]

Many NS activists launched their "hunt for booty" as early as 1933. In Hamburg, Sturmabteilung (SA) troops made sham searches of Jewish homes, seizing jewelry and cash and abusing the representatives of the Jewish community, who were peremptorily called upon to turn over the keys to safes.[3] In Munich, Schutzstaffel (SS) storm-troop units distinguished themselves above all in robbing Jews, some of their members even exploiting the opportunity to commit private acts of revenge. In one case, a dismissed employee attacked his former Jewish employer and forced him to turn over a large sum of money from the safe of the firm.[4] In Berlin, SA members kidnapped and robbed the Jewish director of a knitted-fabrics factory from Zschopau, then held him captive and tortured him for days in their "Storm

Headquarters" in order to extort a large ransom.⁵ Officials of the National Socialist People's Welfare Organization (Volkswohlfahrt—NSV) in Berlin practiced an especially perfidious method of personal fund-raising: they admitted Jews to the NSV, knowing full well their Jewish descent, and then subpoenammoned them for "sneaking into the NSV" as a pretext for extorting money from them.⁶ In Pillau and Elbing, members of the SS Security Service obtained an identification card with a facsimile signature of the East Prussian Gauleiter, visited the homes of wealthy Jews, and extorted increasing sums of money with threats each time they came.⁷ In Breslau, an SA Obersturmbahnführer (lieutenant colonel) forced the owners of a Jewish department store to turn over a "donation" of RM 15,000, most of which he deposited in his wife's savings account.⁸ Similarly, in Breslau, members of the intelligence service office of the NSDAP District Headquarters (Kreisleitung) specialized in blackmailing Jews, who were summoned subpoenaed and forced with threats and violence to turn over funds.⁹ This procedure was characterized as "excessive National Socialist zeal" by the investigating Public Prosecutor (Oberstaatsanwalt) at the District Court of Breslau and the criminal acts were pardoned on the basis of the Amnesty Law of August 1934¹⁰—a common practice in sentencing persons guilty of anti-Semitic theft and violence. Such activities gradually declined after mid 1934, but, in the wake of rowdy anti-Semitic actions by the party in the summer of 1935, they broke out again, reaching a sad peak with the "annexation" of Austria in spring 1938.

During the pogrom-like attacks in Austria about 25,000 self-appointed "commissars" had, furthermore, occupied Jewish businesses and greedily satisfied their material needs without restraint after the removal of the Jewish owners.¹¹ Josef Bürckel, Commissioner for the Reunification of Austria with the German Reich, sarcastically commented that many of these commissars had "gotten 'mine' and 'thine' confused."¹² The violent confiscation of such vast amounts of property was not repeated even in the 'Old Reich" during the excesses of the November pogrom of 1938, when similar "wild" confiscation¹³ and plundering occurred. In the South Hanover-Braunschweig Gau, for example, the SS forced its way into businesses and homes, confiscated money, valuables, typewriters, and automobiles. The NSDAP Reich Treasurer reported on similar incidents in Stettin: "A few party comrades from District Headquarters went to the Jews and first cut their telephone lines. Then they presented the Jews with 'deeds of gift' prepared by a notary informing them that they were being given an opportunity to make a donation. Occasional bold replies were answered with threats of shooting."¹⁴ The NSDAP Gau leadership in Berlin combined pogroms and enrichment in a particularly cynical manner. Thus the Gau Head of Propaganda Chief Wächter compelled leading representatives of the Berlin Jews, among others Leo Baeck, to make a "voluntary contribution" amounting to RM 5 million as "reparations" for the damages caused.¹⁵ Among other things, the "state funeral of Party comrade vom Rath" was financed at a cost of RM 300,000 from these so-called "debris funds" (*Scherbenfonds*), while the Berlin party organization received RM 200,000, and the SA and SS RM 70,000 "for daylong service, including night duty." NSDAP political leaders who had torn their shirts and coats during the nightly plundering and destruction were likewise compensated from the "debris funds," as was the widow of an SA Obersturmführer, whose sudden death was attributed to his "superhuman exertions" in arranging the state funeral.[16]

"Aryanization" as a Focus of Corruption

Robbery and "wild" confiscation of Jewish property reflected not only the precarious legal status of the Jews in National Socialist Germany, but also the pressure exerted by National Socialist activists, who above all expected the NSDAP to redistribute Jewish assets to them personally and therefore vehemently rejected the state's claim to dispose of them. This basic attitude was symptomatically expressed by the deputy leader of the Weser-Ems Gau, who in a letter to the Führer's Deputy voiced the fear that "Jewish assets will accrue to the state" and party comrades could "go away empty-handed." Therefore it was necessary "that the Party assert its claims."[17] Thinking along similar lines, for example, Christian Weber, who with the "Bureau for the 8th/9th of November" represented the interests of those in the NSDAP who had earned the "Blood Order" (*Blutordensträger*), demanded that proceeds from the "Jewish wealth levy" (*Judenvermögensabgabe*) which was imposed in November 1938, be allocated to benefit party veterans. RM 10 million of the proceeds should in his view be diverted to help *"Blutordensträger"* who wished to buy "Aryanized" Jewish property.[18] The greatest expectations of the National Socialists were centered on the forced "Aryanization" of Jewish property, which proceeded gradually after 1933 and was legally enforced after 1938. The NSDAP arrogated a key position in this process for itself, insofar as after 1936/37 purchase contracts between Jewish owners and "Aryan" buyers had to be submitted to NSDAP Gau Economic Advisors for authorization, and many Gauleiter and high NSDAP functionaries in any case also exercised a crucial influence on state authorization organs.[19]

NSDAP members thus zealously exploited the enrichment opportunities offered by their key positions in the process of "Aryanization." Many Gau headquarters (Gauleitungen) and regional party organizations used "Aryanization" to set up unauthorized, concealed funds outside party budgets and also outside the public budget, which they could dispose of as they saw fit without accountability. The funds stemmed mostly from forced "contributions" extorted from former Jewish owners and partially also from "Aryan" buyers as a condition for authorizing "Aryanization" contracts. In the Saar-Pfalz Gau, NSDAP Gauleiter Bürckel founded the Saarpfälzische Vermögensgesellschaft (Saar-Pfalz Property Company) for this purpose. It forced Jewish owners, some of whom had already been deported to concentration camps, to endorse powers of attorney which commissioned the Property Company to "Aryanize" their property and 40 percent of the sales proceeds were deposited in a special account of the Gau Headquarters.[20] In comparison, the demands of the Franconian NSDAP Gauleitung (Gau Headquarters) appear quite modest, as they required buyers to make a contribution of only 1.5–3 percent of the purchase price. This was first deposited in a special account of the Stürmer Publishing House at the Bank der Deutschen Arbeit and then transferred to the account of the Gau Treasury (Gauschatzamt), where ca. RM 350,000 accumulated.[21]

In Hamburg, the Hamburger Grundstücks-Verwaltungsgesellschaft von 1938 GmbH (Hamburg Real Estate Management Society of 1938, Ltd.) was active in acquiring "Aryanization donations" for NSDAP Gauleiter Kaufmann, to whom it transferred at least RM 854,000 in compulsory "donations."[22] In the Württemberg-Hohenzollern Gau, Gauleiter Murr deposited the requisitioned donations in a special fund referred to as "financial thanks" (*Wirtschaftsdank*). The money in the fund was employed among other things to acquire formerly Jewish businesses.[23] In Thuringia, the NSDAP Gau Economic Advisor collected 10 percent of the purchasing price from "Aryanizations" and declared the compulsory contributions to be necessary compensation to financially offset alleged "expenses."[24] He then transferred the money to a special account of the Gau Administration. Originally this was supposed to finance old-age benefits for "party veterans." A large share of the money collected was, however, distributed to Party members as "loans," enabling them to acquire Jewish firms which were to be "Aryanized."[25] This procedure was also practiced in other Gaus, for example in East Prussia, where the SS Security Service noted in an Annual Report that "the NSDAP had helped many party members achieve economic security by providing loans from its funds."[26]

Through an organized system of patronage the state-imposed expropriation of the Jews was utilized to satisfy the material claims of party comrades. As a justification they insisted on the standard empty platitude of "economic hardships" suffered during the "time of struggle."[27] The practice of institutionally privileging party comrades reached its zenith in 1938/39, when Jewish owners had lost all room for maneuver in the course of forcibly imposed "Aryanization" and the party's influence was so comprehensive that, above all, the "Aryanization" of the retail trade could be openly exploited as a full-blown benefit program for NSDAP members. That "old and meritorious party comrades who suffered hardships during the time of struggle should be at the head of the line" was accordingly maintained in a comprehensive report on the "dejewification" (*Entjudung*) of the Berlin retail trade.[28] Beyond this, preferential loans from city banks and savings and loan associations were available to these—as they were officially called—"valuable applicants," to facilitate the acquisition of Jewish assets. The second privileged category included "party comrades who wanted to become independent, who, however, must have business experience"[29]—a criterion which was obviously not imposed on "old and meritorious party comrades." In reality, "Aryanization" developed into an enrichment market in which all categories of party comrades—from the block warden to the Gauleiter —became equally active.[30]

NSDAP comrades by no means constituted the only group which was systematically favored in the process of "Aryanization" and profited from this public, institutionalized form of corruption. The bourgeoisie, the younger professional generation, or former employees of Jewish businesses also belong to the category of buyers recognized as being worthy of support.[31] Furthermore, "Aryanization" would not have been possible without contributions by the most varied professional groups, who assumed important intermediary functions—among them lawyers, brokers, appraisers, assessors, trustees, and liquidators, who had numerous opportunities for enrichment.[32] This "intermediary branch" was characterized, on the one hand, by an often extreme degree of specialization—thus there were brokers primarily specialized in the sale of Jewish pharmacies—and, on the other, by fluid transitions to a criminal milieu of con men and shysters who enticed Jewish businessmen with false promises and often ruthlessly exploited their desperate situation to personal advantage. A Jewish businessman compared some of the intermediaries to "vultures circling above a dying man."[33] When numerous Jewish businessmen were arrested and sent to concentration camps after the November pogrom of 1938, thousands of trustees and liquidators took over the management of their businesses. These were all "trustworthy" people from commerce, trade, and industry, who almost without exception held a NSDAP membership card and commanded princely fees for their services.[34]

This authorization practice enabled not only a variety of party institutions and NSDAP functionaries to enrich themselves from Jewish property, but also the cities and communities, which were in part active as Reich trustees in the context of anti-Jewish expropriation policy. Thus, in the wake of the 3 December 1938 Ordinance on the Disposition of Jewish Assets, all Jews were required to hand over jewelry, jewels, and art objects containing gold, platinum, and silver, and the municipal pawnbroking offices were elevated to the status of Reich collecting and purchasing offices.[35] The pawnbroking offices reimbursed Jewish owners with at most a sixth of the actual value of their jewels, jewelry and art objects and were also authorized to acquire for themselves items worth up to RM 1,000 (later reduced to RM 300 and 150)). This amounted to a covert invitation to reduce the reimbursement rates and dispose of the assets acquired at a low price to the advantage of community budgets. As a result of events in Nuremberg, the Court of Restitution Affairs in the American occupation zone reached the conclusion after 1945 that the municipal pawnbroking offices "had succeeded in embezzling a large part of the acquired assets or in stealing them from the Reich. Low assessments, partial assessments, unreported sales to Party favorites, always under the RM 1,000, 300 and 150 RM maximum limits, appear to have been standard practice at the pawnbroking offices."[36] The opportunities for enrichment were so great that the Reich's promulgated claim to dispose of the assets was never understood by its protagonists as a monopoly of disposition, but rather the enrichment of others was included from the start. Therefore the dispossession plans—according to the Court of Restitution Affairs—were conceived with the clear intention of giving not only the Reich itself, but also local communities the opportunity to profit from expropriated Jewish assets.[37]

Hence "Aryanization" as a whole developed into an enrichment competition, in which favoritism and corruption were the order of the day and from which numerous institutions and persons, indeed, growing segments of German society, profited: cities and communities, the NSDAP, party members, and a large number of persons and professional groups outside the party.

Two aspects are essential to an understanding of the overall function of corruption in connection with the "Aryanization policy." First, corruption, above all in its "official" form of protection and support payments, bound its beneficiaries directly to the National Socialist system of rule, even if the patronage was not usually justified as a means of ensuring future loyalty but rather declared to be "compensation" for material "sacrifices" in the past.[38] The connection between the alleged "sacrifices" of the "time of struggle" and their "compensation" after 1933 thereby formed a central social-psychological element of the "redemptive anti-Semitism" which Saul Friedländer characterizes as a specifically German or National Socialist variant of anti-Semitism.[39] Secondly, enrichment with Jewish property had a radicalizing effect on anti-Jewish policy as a whole, because robbing the Jews created a steadily growing circle of beneficiaries with a strong personal interest in never becoming liable to recourse. The beneficiaries had crossed a moral Rubicon, which encouraged further radical steps forward, because the road back could not be taken without admitting guilt and the legitimacy of material restitution.

Corruption and Extermination Policy

With the transition from "Aryanization" to forced emigration, deportation, and mass murder, the responsibility for and the structures of National Socialist "Jewish policy" also changed. Whereas "Aryanization" was still characterized by a multiplicity of regional institutions and decision-makers, after 1939 many competencies were centralized at the national level, for example in the Reich Security Main Office (RSHA). However, these structural changes by no means destroyed the basis for corruption. In all its aspects, it permeated even extermination policy, increasing with the progressive disenfranchisement of the Jews. Many of those participating in Jewish deportation and extermination thought they were personally entitled to dispose of their victims' remaining possessions.

This was clearly mirrored, for example, in everyday Gestapo practices centered on personal enrichment with Jewish property. Max Plaut, appointed by the Gestapo in late 1938 to the post of North-West German District Director of the "Reich Association of Jews in Germany," recalled in his memoirs sham "house searches whose sole purpose was to supply Gestapo members with all kinds of goods."[40] In East Frisia and Oldenburg, Kirchmeyer, the responsible head of the Jewish Department (Judenreferent), was particularly active in paying "visits" to prosperous Jews, using the opportunity for extensive plundering. In Lübeck, Wilhelm Düwel, the local head of the Jewish Department, distinguished himself through such actions and afterward pressed for the accelerated deportation of the Jewish owners as a means of eliminating inconvenient witnesses as quickly as possible.[41]

A special form of "house search" was practiced by Willibald Schallert, director of the Labor Deployment of Jews and Gypsies Department of the Hamburg Labor Office.[42] When visiting the Jews under his jurisdiction, he not only arranged to receive numerous "gifts," but used the opportunity to extort sexual favors from women. He granted—presupposing cooperative behavior—favors and alleviation, often behaved sympathetically and charmingly, but, on the other hand, ruthlessly added the names of those who incurred his displeasure to deportation lists. For this type of perpetrator, it was not merely a question of satisfying material and nonmaterial needs; he first of all paraded his personal might before his victims, whom he could manipulate, replace, or remove as he pleased.[43] Without the backing of the Gestapo and the responsible head of the Jewish Department, Claus Göttsche, this would hardly have been possible. Göttsche himself was, moreover, corrupt and enriched himself by diverting over RM 237,000 for personal purposes from a Gestapo account in which the proceeds of auctioned Jewish property had been deposited.[44] Similarly corrupt practices prevailed at the Berlin Gestapo headquarters, where the head of the Jewish Department, Gerhard Stübs, and his deputy, Franz Prüfer, exploited chaotic cash accounts and budget management practices for personal enrichment. In December 1941, the Reich Accounting Office determined in an audit "that the Berlin State Police Headquarters had neither rendered account nor kept account books on the evacuation transports of Jews. Furthermore, money, valuables and savings account books were not correctly recorded, the receipts were incomplete or simply lacking."[45] In this chaotic situation, Gestapo officials passed Jewish assets back and forth among themselves, a practice the Accounting Office referred to as "great irregularities." The head of the Jewish Department, Gerhard Stübs, committed suicide shortly before his arrest, while Prüfer died in a bombing raid during pre-trial detention.[46]

An Accounting Office review revealed that there were also a great number of "irregularities" at the Reich Security Main Office.[47] Thus it was found that, among other things, SS officers had charged the costs of installation work in their rented housing, paid bills for clothing, and approved unbudgeted additional salaries for themselves at the expense of the Main Office. After the Reich Security Main Office had settled the accounts of the first ten so-called "Transports of Jews" (*Judentransporte*), over RM 100,000 had not been collected or could not be accounted for. In one special account of the Reich Association of Jews in Germany, there was a deficit of RM 340,000.

An important starting point for corruption was the payments which prosperous Jews were often called upon to make in 1938/39 to compensate for the budget deficits of pauperized Jewish communities which had lost many financially well-situated taxpayers through emigration. That the compulsory contributions were in each case used for the intended purpose is greatly to be doubted. There are various reasons for suspecting that they were diverted to private accounts. Berlin Polizeipräsident (Chief Constable) Graf Helldorff, a man-about-town notorious for his lack of cash, extorted money from prosperous Jews, which he—it appears—also used as personal "lucrative sources of income."[48] He imposed a ban on the issue of passports to all Jews with assets in excess of 300,000 RM. A permit to leave the country could only be obtained in exchange for a forced contribution, also termed a "Helldorff contribution" by the victims, often amounting to several hundred thousand Reich marks.[49] Helldorff extorted a total of RM 1.15 million from two cigarette manufacturers, Moritz and Eugen Garbaty, alone.[50]

The Munich "Aryanization Office," active until 1943, squeezed large "contributions" from prosperous Jews with the assurance that they would be protected from deportations to the East.[51] In reality, almost all of them were deported shortly after paying the "contribution." As in the case of Gestapo "house searches," corruption accelerated the praxis of deportation and extermination by means of which perpetrators disposed of unwanted-inconvenient witnesses.

While enrichment and corruption were an important side-effect of the extermination policy in the "Old Reich," they were even more widespread in the occupied territories of (Eastern) Europe, where there were few mechanisms of bureaucratic control. Retrospectively, at least five forms of appropriating Jewish assets can be identified in the occupied countries.

The first category included plundering, "wild" confiscation, and enrichment from Jewish assets, which usually occurred from the start of the occupation and, furthermore, accompanied the operations of the mobile killing squads (Einsatzgruppen). Members of the Wehrmacht, the police, and the occupation apparatus, as well as the populations of the occupied areas, took part in the plundering.[52] Members of the Order Police, for example, took advantage of being quartered in the Villa Bondy in Prague in 1939 to boldly and openly appropriate cash, jewels, stocks, art objects, etc.[53] "Wild" enrichment in occupied territories was encouraged by the fact that the systematic recording of Jewish assets proved to be a "political and organizational impossibility," as Erich Koch, the Reich Commissar for the Ukraine, stated.[54] Members of the German occupation apparatus who had seized Jewish assets and were obligated to report them could ignore the official requirements with relative impunity because even proven violations were seldom prosecuted.

In the course of killing operations against the Jewish population in the occupied territories, some Jewish wealth disappeared into the pockets of the murderers and others indirectly involved, and did not even appear in the official statistical records. In an auditing report, the Reich Accounting Office pointed out in this connection:

> The sums of money and jewels collected were in many cases not officially registered, so that it can never be determined whether and how much of the confiscated wealth has already disappeared. In the GG [General gouvernement], large-scale transfers of confiscated jewels were made to the SS-Einsatzstab Reinhard and the SS- and Police Chief of Lublin without an itemized list or registration by the task force responsible [*Erfassungskommando*]. A particularly crass incident occurred at the Stanislau branch office in Galicia. Here large amounts of confiscated money and jewels were retained. During a local audit in the offices of the responsible administrative official, Pol. Secr. Block, Accounting Office examiners found stashed in all the available chests and containers, desks, etc., great quantities of money, gold coins, all conceivable currencies—among others $6,000 alone—stashed in all the available chests and containers, desks, etc., as well as whole crates of the most valuable jewels, none of which had been either officially collected or registered.[55]

A special form of "wild" enrichment consisted of the bribes and "gifts" which members of the occupation administration, Gestapo authorities, and police received from the Jewish Councils (Judenräte) in the ghettos or extorted in the form of "contributions." Christian Gerlach has pointed out that "enormous sums" were diverted past the main Reich treasury by "thoroughly corrupt functionaries in the civilian administration and police," who put them into their own pockets.[56] Some Jewish Councils had adapted so completely to the venality and corruption of the German officeholders that they set up extensive storehouses of gold, jewelry, alcohol, and valuable scarce items.[57] The chairman of the Zamosc Jewish Council estimated the monthly "bribery requirement" at 150,000–200,000 zloty. In this manner, individual favors could be bought; in some cases deportations were even stopped after they had begun. In a medium-term perspective, however, such strategies proved not only ineffective, but in some cases even counterproductive, as the donors were not spared, but instead deported as rapidly as possible in order to eliminate witnesses.[58] Isaiah Trunk correctly called the bribes and gifts "another form of spoliation of Jewish property by the Nazis."[59]

To be distinguished from forms of "wild" enrichment by individuals is the unauthorized confiscation of Jewish property practiced by various organizations and institutions, and also by higher officeholders. Without authorization they acquired Jewish property and deposited it in "special funds" and illegal concealed accounts, where it was exempt from any sort of control and contributed to both personal and institutional enrichment. Thus, for example, during their killing operations Einsatzgruppen requisitioned "Jewish money," which in part was not even counted but simply turned over to the responsible commanders of the Security Police "by the sack" and later deposited in special funds. Accounting Office audits found such funds held by the commanders of the Security Police in Lemberg, Cracow, Warsaw, Biala-Podlaska, and the Stapo- Leitstelle (State Police Regional Headquarters) in Kattowitz.⁶⁰ In most cases neither the amounts nor the purpose of the funds could be determined. Accounting Office requests for explanations always went unanswered. In some cases it could be determined that the funds, which the Accounting Office estimated at several hundred thousand RM each, were being employed to meet private expenses of members of the Security Police and to finance building and installation work for the SS, including among other things housing for SS leaders, SS casinos, and SS theaters.⁶¹ At the Deutsche Bank in Kattowitz, the local Stapo office (Stapostelle) had a special account containing payments extorted from Jewish communities to finance deportations. In part, police officials were paid advances or sums of money for "special purposes" from this source without formal clearing.⁶²

In the annexed Eastern territories the NSDAP also took part in setting up illegal funds and the "wild" confiscation of Polish and Jewish property. Thus the NSDAP District Administration (Kreisleitung) in Bromberg set up "reimbursement funds" amounting to RM 750,000 from the proceeds of selling confiscated Jewish property⁶³—a procedure also practiced by other NSDAP district administrations and local branches (Ortsgruppe). Arthur Greiser, NSDAP – Gauleiter and Reichsstatthalter (governor) of the newly formed Reichsgau Wartheland, for example, set up a "deposit account" at the Bank for Commerce and Industry in Poznan "for money confiscated from Jews and enemies of the Reich," from which he alone was authorized to make withdrawals.⁶⁴

Jewish property was confiscated and the proceeds placed in special accounts not only in the East, but also in Western and Northern Europe, thereby bypassing Reich revenue authorities. Thus the Military Commander for Belgium and Northern France established a special fund amounting to RM 2.5 million, fattened with the profits from sales of plundered diamond stocks.⁶⁵ Gauleiter Josef Terboven, Reich Commissar for the occupied Norwegian territories, set up a foundation called the German Relief Organization (Deutsches Hilfswerk) in Oslo using the assets of persons "hostile to the Reich." This foundation was merely a front for the Gauleiter's personal discretionary fund (*Verfügungsfonds*), with which he financed expensive gifts for favorites, influential patrons, and persons in positions of power. In this connection, Hermann Göring, Commissioner for the Four Year Plan, received a consignment of 102 kg of salmon and lobster and his wife two platinum fox furs.⁶⁶ Thirty-six fur coats in Terboven's "gift stock" were worth over RM 100,000 alone. The Wehrmacht was also generously provided for by the Reich Commissar. Thus, among other things, he gave 337 gold watches taken from confiscated Jewish property to Wehrmacht commanders in Norway.⁶⁷

Terboven's generous gifts characterized a third form of appropriation of Jewish property, namely uncontrolled, decentralized distribution of assets, even squandering by institutions that had already confiscated them in the interest of the German Reich. In Serbia, for example, the Wehrmacht systematically sold off Jewish property. After the occupation of Belgrade, Field

Command Office 599 confiscated the stocks of Jewish businesses and sold them at dumping prices to Wehrmacht members, who in part used this opportunity to literally make bulk purchases. Thus a military administration officer bought 166 meters, a first lieutenant 217 meters, and a military administration inspector over 500 meters of various fabrics.[68] The proceeds from this dumping were deposited in a special account. Jewish jewelry and valuables were sold by the property administration of the General Director for the Economy (Generalbevollmächtigter für die Wirtschaft) at a "frozen price" to members of the occupation administration.[69] "Jewish real estate" could likewise be acquired at preferential prices. Thus the wife of a Reich bank director transferred to Belgrade purchased the Villa Eisenschreiber for ca. one million dinars in October 1941 and resold it in March 1942 for three times the purchase price.[70]

In Lower Styria the regional office of the Reich Commissioner for the strengthening of Germandom (Reichskommissar für die Festigung deutschen Volktums) proved downright generous when dealing with the property of—to use official terminology—"evacuated Jews."[71] The stocks of Jewish businesses were handed over to their competitors without a fair appraisal. The employees of the office helped each other to acquire furniture and furnishings, gold, silver, jewelry and diamonds. In one case over 20 kg of silver where "disposed of" to a jeweler free of charge. In another case the goods were paid for, but the buyer—a Graz silversmith—was permitted to name his price. Usually there were no statements of assets and liabilities or itemized statements of resources and their application. The total extent of illicitly sold and dumped property could therefore not be determined, especially since several hundred so-called "loan authorizations" (*Ausleihbescheinigung*) were allegedly "mislaid."[72]

The participation of many people in the uncontrolled distribution of property belonging to deported and murdered Jews served—as in the above case of "Aryanization"—in a particular manner to "grease palms" in the complex network of National Socialist ruling cliques, which were stabilized through the mutual exchange of material "favors." Desiring to please the Führer, for example, the Reich Commissioner for the occupied Dutch territories, Seyss-Inquart, purchased an art collection for over RM 8 million, which he donated to the Führermuseum in Linz. He obtained the money without authorization from the Reich Finance Ministry from confiscated "Jewish assets."[73] Henriette von Schirach, wife of Baldur von Schirach, Vienna Gauleiter and former Reich Youth Leader, reported in her memoirs that during a stay in the Netherlands explicit, open enrichment offers were made to her personally. An SS officer showed her huge piles of wedding rings and precious gems and proposed: "'You can buy diamonds for ridiculous prices. Would you like to? Flawless gems carefully broken out of their settings by experts; I don't have to explain to you whom they belonged to.' ... Naturally they thought that I would have the instincts of a grave robber, because the price was probably the least important matter in this transaction; the only important thing was only that I was one of the powerful who could not be called to account for what they saw and did."[74]

Besides "wild" enrichment, unauthorized confiscation, and unsupervised distribution, there were two forms of organized appropriation of Jewish property:, namely, first, administration and utilization by trustees and, secondly, organized distribution. These forms were likewise not free of enrichment and corruption, if we bear in mind the procedures of the trustee offices in the General Government or the activities of the Main Trustee Office for the East (Haupttreuhandstelle Ost—HTO). The HTO managed the confiscated property of Poles and Jews in the Eastern Territories of Danzig-West Prussia, Wartheland, and Upper Silesia, which were "annexed" in 1939. The mutual assistance of employees in corruption was proverbial (e.g., "Eine Treuhand wäscht die andere"). The HTO not only granted its employees opulent trustee fees,[75] but also gave them an opportunity to acquire businesses at preferential prices for themselves. Thus the Director of the HTO in Kattowitz, NSDAP Gau Economic Advisor Dr. Artur Jakob, purchased the Sosnowitz Pipe and Iron Works on the basis of a price evaluation that included only 60 percent of its business value and did not even take account of the firm's land.[76] Leading HTO officials, among them Dr. Walter Lorenz, chief department head (Hauptreferent) in the Danzig-West Prussia Gau, for years passed textile fiber and textiles on to one another without allotment authorizations.[77] HTO accounts served as a welcome source of financing for the most varied organizations and persons. The renovation of an apartment belonging to Dr. Walter Moser, government vice president (Regierungsvizepräsident) in Litzmannstadt (Łódź), was financed with RM 312,000 from trustee office funds.[78] The Higher SS and Police Commander of Poznan arranged for the alleged "services of the SS" to be reimbursed with a sum of RM 300,000. The Gestapo in Kattowitz received RM 100,000 without having to submit a statement of application.[79] The NSDAP Gauleiter of Danzig-West Prussia, Albert Forster, was privileged to receive the same amount—as a reimbursement "for securing Polish property before the HTO began its operations."[80]

Heinrich Himmler, the SS Reichsführer-SS, who simultaneously functioned as the Reich Commissioner for the strengthening of Germandom, was responsible for the organized distribution of wealth accruing from murdered Jews' property;. He was highly active in this role, distributing goods from the estates of murdered victims within his personal sphere of power: SS businesses received machinery from the Jewish ghettos[81] and millions from the so-called "Reinhardt Fund."[82] For his higher-ranking officers he hoarded a large number of "Jewish properties" as official apartments.[83] Waffen-SS members and concentration camp personnel were given furs and watches,[84] SS families received children's clothing,[85] and the ethnic German settlers under his care were issued great quantities of clothing and household furnishings.[86] In order to morally justify this sort of patronage, so typical of National Socialist rule, the property of murdered Jews was frequently redefined in official documents as "goods in the possession of Jewish fences and thieves."[87]

Even ordinary "national comrades" profited from the organized distribution of murdered Jews' property. As early as 1939 confiscated "Jewish silver" was offered for sale at public auctions.[88] In the war years, Jewish property seized throughout Europe was transported to the Reich territory and auctioned off to the general public.[89] In Hamburg and its immediate North German vicinity alone probably over 100,000 persons acquired items of Jewish property after 1941; the buyers—due to the absence of many men—were predominantly women, who exploited these enrichment opportunities as unscrupulously as their male counterparts. So much loot was transported to Cologne that the responsible head of the regional finance office (Oberfinanzpräsident) announced in July 1942 that available storage capacity was exhausted.[90] In rural villages with Jewish communities the assets of deported Jews were auctioned off in the streets.[91]

Among the NS rulers such operations were always accompanied by calculations as to the resulting moral corruption. They assumed that Germans would identify more strongly with National Socialist rule and would fight more "fanatically" for the "final victory" the more completely they had burnt their moral bridges behind them. Propaganda Minister Goebbels noted in his diary: "Above all in the Jewish question we are so deeply involved that there is absolutely no escape for us. And that is a good thing. A movement and a people which has burned its bridges behind it will fight, as experience shows, much more unconditionally than those that still have a means of retreat."[92] Therefore it is not surprising that a Jewish merchant from Hamburg, who survived NS rule in a "privileged mixed marriage," noted in early 1945 in his private records that a part of the population anticipated the coming victory of the Allies with great apprehension. He commented "that many who had taken over Jewish apartments and Jewish possessions have the greatest fear today that the Jews could return, demand their property back and also bring charges against them for robbery and theft."[93]

When we survey the overall extent of plundering, "wild" enrichment, unauthorized confiscation and unsupervised distribution and squandering of Jewish property that accompanied the National Socialist extermination policy, it becomes clear that corruption was not an isolated marginal occurrence, but rather a mass phenomenon immanent in the system—one could even say a constitutive element of NS rule. This fact serves to modify the image of a precisely functioning, mechanistic, bureaucratic clockwork that historians, sociologists, and philosophers have in the meantime adopted to describe the Holocaust. Thus Hannah Arendt spoke of "administrative massacres,"[94] Raul Hilberg attributed to the bureaucracy an incorruptible thoroughness in planning and administration,[95] and Zygmunt Bauman has described the destructive machinery of the Holocaust as a gigantic, rational-bureaucratic apparatus, as though the participating institutions were bureaucracies in Max Weber's sense.[96] He thereby fails to recognize not only the extent of personal and institutional enrichment, but also the significance of the uncontrolled exercise of power and the motivating force of ideology in, for example, the institutions under the RSHA or the administration in the occupied territories, whose structures and behavior can hardly be described adequately using Weber's categories for the concept of bureaucracy. Above all in occupied Eastern Europe, the dominant type was a "totalitarian colonial administration," [97] characterized by "de-bureaucratization," suggestive of a ruling clique whose representatives often conducted their administrative activities as a personal regime and did not administer, but rather dominated. Bureaucratically undifferentiated, lacking normative ties, the occupation administration acted mainly informally and had to fear possible controls even less than the administration in the "Old Reich." As the Security Police in the General Government complained, Reich Germans in the most varied institutions—such as the Wehrmacht, the occupation administration, the economy, and the legal system—had developed a network of corrupt relationships that were largely insulated against external influences, so that "the total lack of the necessary controls gave corruption full possibilities for development," [98] whereas the criminal investigation department of the police was not "strong enough to master the extraordinarily corrupt situation." [99]

In summary, it can be said that the mass murder of the European Jews would not have been possible in its vast dimensions without the institutions of a modern bureaucratic state. To describe the actions of these institutions under the rubric of classical "bureaucratic" behavior, however, conceals the actual character of many of the participating institutions, whose substructure was characterized by a network of personal relationships and clique-like structures. In this context, personal and institutional enrichment was clearly not the cause of mass murder, but merely an attendant phenomenon. However, it provided a motivational basis for many of those involved which should not be underestimated. "Base motives" such as greed also contributed to the Holocaust.

Enrichment influenced the praxis of mass murder in three ways: as a concomitant "secondary phenomenon" that did not directly influence the murders, as an accelerating factor if the perpetrators felt an urgent interest in eliminating the witnesses to their corruption by disposing of their victims, and in certain cases also as an inhibiting or retarding factor if, by bribing officeholders,[100] the victims managed to save their lives or, at least temporarily, to improve their situation. The leadership of the NS regime viewed the corruption typical of "Aryanization" and the subsequent extermination policy ambivalently. On the one hand, it was compatible with the regime's aims, because it motivated the actors involved in "Jewish policy" and mass murder, simultaneously entangling them in a specific way in the Holocaust and thereby binding them to NS rule. Without these—from the regime's viewpoint—desirable effects, corruption would probably not have become so widespread.

On the other hand, the regime's leadership, above all SS Reichsführer-SS Heinrich Himmler, had a manifest interest in drawing a clear line between mass executions as part of the extermination policy and common murder for personal gain, in order to uphold an ideologically-based "morality." Himmler's claim to have "remained decent" while committing mass murder was after all based on the alleged selfless detachment with which mass murder was conceptualized and executed as an impersonal ideological task.[101] Corruption was incompatible with this required "attitude" and cast doubt on the perverse morality with which Himmler, above all, sought to justify the killings. For this reason the norms of the criminal code continued to apply unchanged to the treatment of Jews: anyone who killed Jews exclusively out of greed and did not thereby act on institutional orders was officially regarded, even in the Third Reich, as a murderer. Thus, for example, a Berlin railway employee who in late 1943 murdered a Jewish woman and her "half-Jewish" daughter with the intent to steal their jewelry, was sentenced to death for double murder and duly executed in March 1944.[102]

Flourishing corruption, of course, counteracted the ideologically based distinction according to which, depending on the motive, killing Jews was treated as either murder or a "never written and never to be written page of glory." Anyone who kept within the safe area of an institutional assignment or institutional jurisdiction could *de facto* also enrich himself through the murder of Jews without being prosecuted. The "base motives" constitutive of the definition of murder—such as greed, sadism, malice—were of course not officially condoned, but were unofficially widely tolerated because they could be were functionally instrumentalized to implement the Holocaust. Only those who pursued exclusively personal motives and acted outside an institutional context could expect to be classified and treated as murderers.

Notes

1. Cf. on this my study: Frank Bajohr, *Parvenüs und Profiteure. Korruption in der NS-Zeit* (Frankfurt,, 2001); Richard Grunberger, *A Social History of the Third Reich* (London, 1971), pp. 90–107.
2. Symptomatic of this "conception of the law" was the position taken by the Director of the Munich "Aryanization Office," who asserted in a report: "The assets held by Jews represent, from the National Socialist viewpoint, a part of the German people's heritage which in the course of time was largely stolen from members of the German people even if with the appearance of legality." Cited according to the Final Report on the Activity of the Munich Assessors Office (Vermögensverwertung) GmbH of 25 January 1939, Archive of the Institut fü Zeit-geschicht in Munich (IfZ), Gm 07.94/8, vol. 1, Sh. 2.
3. See Frank Bajohr, *"Arisierung" in Hamburg* (Hamburg, 1997), p. 29. An English translation was published by Berghahn Books in fall 2002: 'Aryanisation' in Hamburg. The economic exclusion of Jews and the confiscation of their property in Nazi Germany (Oxford/New York, 2002).
4. See the judgment of the Third Criminal Chamber of the Regional Court (Landgericht) Munich I of 1 June 1954, Archive of the IfZ, Gm 07.94/9, Sh. 2–5.
5. The kidnapping was finally ended by police intervention. See the Berlin Special Court decision of 9 March 1934, Archive of the IfZ, F-92, Sh. 36–68.
6. Bundesarchiv Berlin (BAB), R 22/946, Sh. 117f.
7. Files of the NSDAP Party Chancellery (Akten der Partei-Kanzlei der NSDAP), part I, Sh. 12402148-52.
8. BAB, R 22/131, Sh. 47.
9. BAB R 22/1088, Sh. 88f.

10. Ibid., Sh. 90.
11. Hans Witek, "'Arisierungen' in Wien," in: Emmerich Talos et al., eds., *NS-Herrschaft in Österreich 1938–1945* (Vienna, 1988), pp. 199–216, here p. 204.
12. Cited from ibid.
13. In the area of the North Sea SA group alone almost RM 200,000 in cash was "collected" during the pogrom. See Aktenvermerk des Hauptamtes I des Reichsschatzmeisters der NSDAP vom 21.10.1939 betr. "unerledigte Arisierungsvorgänge bei SS und SA" (memorandum of Main Office I of the NSDAP Reich Treasurer of 21 October 1939 concerning "incomplete Aryanization proceedings in the SS and SA"), BAB, NS 1/430.
14. Reichsschatzmeister Schwarz an den Stabsleiter StdF, Reich Treasurer Schwarz to the Stabsleiter (Headquarters director) StdF of 2 December 1938, BAB, NS 1/430.
15. On the following see Hans-Erich Fabian, "Der Berliner Scherbenfonds." *Der Weg. Zeitschrift für Fragen des Judentums* 1, No. 37, (8 November 1946).
16. Ibid.
17. Correspondence of 19 November 1938, BAB, NS 1/2520, Sh. 1.
18. NSDAP-Reichsschatzmeister Schwarz an den Beauftragten für den Vierjahresplan, NSDAP Reich Treasurer Schwarz to the Officer for the Four Year Plan of 22 May 1939, Archive of the IfZ, Fa-74, Sh. 46f.
19. See Bajohr, *"Arisierung" in Hamburg*.
20. Schreiben des Reichsschatzmeisters der NSDAP an den Stabsleiter des StdF, Memorandum of the NSDAP, Treasurer to the StdF chief of staff of 2 December 1938, BAB, NS 1/430.
21. Der Prozeß gegen die Hauptkriegsverbrecher vor dem Internationalen Militärgerichtshof (Nuremberg 1947–1949), The trial against the chief war criminals before the International Military Court (Nuremberg, 1947–1949), Document 1757-PS, vol.Bd. XXVII, 129f.
22. On the following see Bajohr, *"Arisierung" in Hamburg*, pp. 290f., 380ff.
23. Schreiben des NSDAP-Reichsschatzmeisters Schwarz an den Leiter der Partei-Kanzlei, Memorandum from NSDAP Reich Treasurer Schwarz to the director of the Party Chancellery of 15 November 1943, *Akten der Partei-Kanzlei der NSDAP*, Teil I, Sh. 30705184–89.
24. Schreiben des NSDAP-Gauschatzmeisters Thüringen an Reichsschatzmeister Schwarz, Memorandum from NSDAP Thuringia Gau treasurer to Reich Treasurer Schwarz of 22 July 1938, BAB, NS 1/554.
25. Thus, among others, "Pg. Ulrich Klug" received RM 75,000 to start operations in the Portland cement work in Bad Berka, and "Pg. Ignaz Idinger" received RM 25,000 for the "Aryanization" of Hotel Blum in Oberhof. See BAB, NS 1/1120.
26. Cited from the *Jahreslagebericht 1938 des SD-Oberabschnittes Nord-Ost 1938, Ref. II 1121938* Annual Report of SD North-East Higher Section, Ref. II 112, Archiv FZH, 93121, Sh. 3.
27. Anordnung Nr. 89/38 des StdF, Decree No. 89/38 des StdF of 2 August 1938. I am grateful to Armin Nolzen for the reference.
28. Sonderbericht des Stadtpräsidenten der Reichshauptstadt Berlin über die Entjudung des Einzelhandels in Berlin, Special report of the city president of the Reich Capital City of Berlin on the de-Judaization of the retail trade in Berlin of 5 January 1939, BA/MA, RW 19, 2376, Sh. 2–22, cited Sh. 7.
29. Ibid.
30. On the institutionalized enrichment of party members see Bajohr, *"Arisierung" in Hamburg*, p. 312ff.; Britta Bopf, "Zur 'Arisierung' und den Versuchen der 'Wiedergutmachung' in Köln," in: Horst Matzerath et al., eds., *Versteckte Vergangenheit* (Cologne, 1994), p. 178; Wolfram Selig, "Vom Boykott zur Arisierung," in: Björn Mensing and Friedrich Prinz, eds., *Irrlicht im leuchtenden München?* (Regensburg 1991), p. 197f.; Arno Weckbecker, *Die Judenverfolgung in Heidelberg 1933–1945* (Heidelberg, 1985), p. 124f.; Gerhard Kratzsch, *Der Gauwirtschaftsapparat der NSDAP* (Münster, 1989), pp. 237–244.

31. See Bajohr, *"Arisierung" in Hamburg*, p. 241ff.; Sonderbericht des Stadtpräsidenten der Reichshauptstadt Berlin über die Entjudung des Einzelhandels in Berlin, Special Report of the City President of the Reich Capital of Berlin on the de-Judaization of the retail trade in Berlin of 5 January 1939, BA/MA, RW 19, 2376, Sh. 2–22.
32. Kratzsch, *Gauwirtschaftsapparat*, p. 240ff.; Dirk van Laak, "Die Mitwirkenden bei der 'Arisierung,'" in: Ursula Büttner (ed.), *Die Deutschen und die Judenverfolgung im Dritten Reich* (Hamburg, 1992), p. 244f.; Bajohr, *"Arisierung" in Hamburg*, pp. 320–323; on the activities of real estate and trusteeship societies see also Monika Schmidt, "Arisierungspolitik des Bezirksamtes," in: Karl-Heinz Metzger et al. (eds.), *Kommunalverwaltung unterm Hakenkreuz* (Berlin, 1992), pp. 169–228, here p. 204f.
33. Cited from Fritz Vincenz Grünfeld, *Das Leinenhaus Grünfeld* (Berlin, 1967), p. 125.
34. On liquidators see among others Kratzsch, *Gauwirtschaftsapparat*, p. 242f., Angela Verse-Herrmann, *"Arisierungen" in der Land- und Forstwirtschaft* (Stuttgart, 1997), p. 92.
35. Authoritative in this connection were the *Verordnung zur Durchführung der Verordnung über den Einsatz des jüdischen Vermögens vom 16. Januar 1939* and *die dritte Anordnung über die Anmeldung des Vermögens von Juden vom 21. Februar 1939*, Decree pertaining to the implementation of the Ordinance on the Utilization of Jewish Assets of 16 January 1939 and the Third Ordinance on the Reporting of Jewish Assets of 21 February 1939, RGBl. 1939, Teil I, 37, 282.
36. Cited from the *Court of Restitution Appeals Reports*, Vol. I (Mehlem, 1951), p. 262. I am grateful to Jürgen Lillteicher for this reference.
37. Ibid.
38. The populations of the occupied countries were also to be bound to National Socialist rule through "Aryanization." This was stated in a report on the "dejewification of the French economy," among other things: "The numerous acquirers of Jewish businesses have an economic stake in German successes and have thereby been inwardly drawn to the German side." Cited from a report of Abt. Wirtschaft Wi 1/1 of the Military Commander in France, BA/MA, RW 35/255, p. 33.
39. Saul Friedländer, *Nazi Germany and the Jews*, vol. I (New York, 1997), p. 73ff.
40. Max Plaut, "Aufzeichnungen über die Zeit nach 1939" ("Records of the period after 1939"), p. 8, Archive of the Institute for the History of the German Jews, 14.001.1.
41. Max Plaut, "Die jüdische Gemeinde in Hamburg 1933–1945" ("The Jewish community in Hamburg 1933–1945"). Transcript of a tape-recorded interview by Christel Riecke 1973, p. 4., ibid., 14.001.2 8).
42. On Schallert, see Beate Meyer, *"Jüdische Mischlinge". Rassenpolitik und Verfolgungserfahrung 1933–1945* (Hamburg, 1999), pp. 62–67.
43. Ibid., p. 67.
44. Memorandum of the Norddeutsche Bank to the Hamburg Oberfinanzpräsident (head of the regional finance office) of 26 January 1950, Staatsarchiv Hamburg, Oberfinanzpräsident, 47 UA 13.
45. Cited from "Erinnerungen des Prüfungsgebietes VI 6 aus dem letzten Jahre, die sich gegen Eigennutz, Verschwendung usw. richten" (Reminders of the VI 6 auditing section for the last year which are directed against self-serving actions, waste, etc.", BAB, 23.01/2073/2, Sh. 99.
46. See Raul Hilberg, *Die Vernichtung der europäischen Juden* (*The Destruction of the European Jews*) (Frankfurt, 1990), p. 484. The Reich Accounting Office (Rechnungshof) reported that "numerous members of the administrative office had received severe punishment," BAB, 23.01/2073/2, Sh. 99.
47. On the following see BAB, 23.01/2072/2, Sh. 99–101.
48. See Ted Harrison, "'Alter Kämpfer' im Widerstand," *Vierteljahrshefte für Zeitgeschichte* 45 (1997): 385–422, esp. 406–409.
49. See Hans Reichmann, *Deutscher Bürger und verfolgter Jude* (Munich, 1998), p. 103f.
50. *Der Prozeß gegen die Hauptkriegsverbrecher* (1947–1949), Bd. XXVIII, Dok. 1759-PS, 234–254, Affidavit of Raymond H. Geist of 28 August 1945, to Helldorff, p. 251; Affirmation on oath of notary Dr. Georg State of 30 October 1948 (private possession); Moritz

Garbaty had to pay Helldorff RM 500,000 on 19 November 1938 and on 9 February 1939 RM 300,000, Eugen Garbaty RM 350,000 on 19 November 1938.
51. See the decision of the Third Criminal Court of the Regional Court of Munich I of 11 July against Hans Wegner, Ludwig Schrott, and Franz Mugler for criminal extortion, Archive of the IfZ, Gm 07.94/8, Bd. 2.
52. See Hilberg, *Vernichtung*, p. 378ff.
53. Schreiben des Rechnungshofs des Deutschen Reiches an den Reichsprotektor in Böhmen und Mähren, Memorandum of the Accounting Office of the German Reich to the Reich Protector of Bohemia and Moravia of 21 June 1941, BAB, 23.01/5758.
54. Cited from Hilberg, *Vernichtung*, p. 383.
55. BAB, 23.01/2073/2, Sh. 86f.
56. Christian Gerlach, *Kalkulierte Morde. Die deutsche Wirtschafts- und Vernichtungspolitik in Weißrußland 1941 bis 1944* (Hamburg, 1999), p. 681.
57. See Isaiah Trunk, *Judenrat. The Jewish Councils in Eastern Europe under Nazi Occupation*, (New York, 1972), pp. 394–400.
58. See ibid., p. 400. Marcel Reich-Ranicki also states in his memoirs that certain Jewish smugglers from the Warsaw ghetto were liquidated by their German business partners as inconvenient witnesses. Reich-Ranicki, *Mein Leben* (Stuttgart, 1999), p. 211.
59. Trunk, *Judenrat*, p. 400.
60. BAB, 23.01/2073/9, Sh. 14f.
61. BAB., 23.01/2073/2, Sh. 82ff.
62. Ibid., Sh. 87.
63. Ibid., Sh. 569ff.
64. BAB., 23.01/5993, Sh. 11–20.
65. BAB., 23.01/2073/2, Sh. 401.
66. Ibid., 23.01/2073/3, Sh. 34.
67. BAB., 23.01/2073/2, Sh. 420.
68. Ibid., Sh. 406ff.
69. Ibid., Sh. 409. Expressly named were Güterdirektor (Resources Director) Schwarzenbrunner and Militärverwaltungsoberrat (Military Administration Senior Councilor) Dürrigl.
70. Ibid., Sh. 408.
71. On the following see BAB., 23.01/2073/2, Sh. 46–51, here Sh. 50f.
72. Ibid., Sh. 51.
73. Ibid., Sh. 423f.
74. Henriette von Schirach, *Der Preis der Herrlichkeit* (Munich, 1975), p. 214.
75. Thus, for example, international businessman Kurt Lindener, who in 1941/42 administered businesses in Litzmannstadt and Dombrowa, received a total remuneration of RM 23,950 for his year's work, which SS-Gruppenführer Greifelt, Staff Main Office Director (Stabshauptamtleiter) of the Reichskommissar für die Festigung deutschen Volkstums (Reich for the Strengthening of the Commissioner Germandom), Reich Commissioner for the strengthening of Germandom, did "not regard as justified," but which was nevertheless paid by the HTO. See findings concerning the appointment of supervisors by large enterprises managed by trustees subject to the administration and utilization of the HTO in Berlin on the basis of special department documents of the HTO (Feststellungen betr. die Bestellung von Aufsichtspersonen über die Verwaltung und Verwertung der HTO in Berlin unterstehenden treuhänderisch verwalteten Großbetriebe an Hand der Fachakten der HTO), Anlage 2, BAB, R 2301, 5991, Sh. 12–14.
76. BAB, R 23.01, 2073/2, Sh. 12.
77. BAB, R 22/4331, Sh. 22, 27.
78. BAB, R 23.01, 2073/2, Sh. 13.
79. Ibid., Sh. 565f.
80. Ibid., Sh. 567.

81. Correspondence of SS-Obergruppenführer (Lieutenant General) Pohl "concerning machinery and goods in the Jewish ghettos" to the RFSS of 2 December 1942, BAB, NS 19/1612.
82. Archive of the IfZ, NO-2190, memorandum of 26 May 1943 concerning capital increases of the daughter societies of the DWB from the assets of the Reinhardt Fund; Archiv IfZ NO-554, Memo of the German Commercial Enterprises to SS-Gruppenführer (Major General) Frank of 7 June 1943 concerning loans by the Reinhardt Fund.
83. See among other things the note by Wolff of 17 November 1941 that the future Chief of the SS Personnel Main Office von Herff should be assigned a "Jewish object"(Juden-Objekt) as an official apartment, BAB, NS 19/803, Sh. 34.
84. Ibid., NS 19/1918, Sh. 39–42; NS 19/1612, Sh. 1.
85. Archive of the IfZ, NO-2558, Memorandum of the RFSS to the Chief of the Race and Resettlement Main Office (Rasse- und Siedlungshauptamt) of 28 October 1942.
86. BAB, NS 19/1801, Sh. 4; BAB., NS 19/225, Sh. 18.
87. Memorandum to the RFSS of 13 May 1943 concerning the "Utilization of goods in the possession of Jewish fences and thieves" (Verwertung des jüdischen Hehler- und Diebesguts), BAB NS 19/1918, Sh. 1f.
88. See Ralf Banken, "Der Edelmetallsektor und die Verwertung konfiszierten jüdischen Vermögens im 'Dritten Reich,'" *Jahrbuch für Wirtschaftsgeschichte* 1 (1999), p. 146f.
89. Wolfgang Dreßen, *Betrifft: "Aktion 3". Deutsche verwerten jüdische Nachbarn* (Berlin, 1998); Bajohr, *"Arisierung" in Hamburg*, pp. 331–338.
90. Bopf, "'Arisierung,'" pp. 178, 191.
91. Franziska Becker, *Gewalt und Gedächtnis. Erinnerungen an die Verfolgung einer Jüdischen Landgemeinde* (Göttingen, 1994), pp. 77–140.
92. Cited from *Die Tagebücher von Joseph Goebbels* (1993), Teil part II, vol. 7, p. 454, entry of 2 March 1943. Already in June 1941 Goebbels had expressed this attitude with the words: "We already have so much to answer for that we must triumph." Cited from ibid part I, vol. 9 (1998), p. 379, entry of 16 June 1941.
93. Cited from notes of Edgar Eichholz (1944/45), in private possession, Sh. 43. In a similar manner a young businessman commented in late 1944 to American officer Saul K. Padover: "At least eighty percent of the Germans have sinned against the Jews, not out of conviction, but rather out of self-serving motives, the worst sin. Now their conscience is plaguing them, and they are afraid." Cited from Saul K. Padover, *Lügendetektor. Vernehmungen im besiegten Deutschland 1944/45* (Frankfurt on Main, 1999), p. 55.
94. Hannah Arendt, *Eichmann in Jerusalem. A Report on the Banality of Evil* (New York, 1965), pp. 288, 294.
95. Hilberg, *Vernichtung*, p. 60. At the same time Hilberg cites a wealth of examples of corruption in the context of the Holocaust.
96. Zygmunt Bauman, *Dialektik der Ordnung. Die Moderne und der Holocaust* (Hamburg, 1992), pp. 24, 120.
97. See Dieter Pohl, *Nationalsozialistische Judenverfolgung in Ostgalizien* (Munich, 1996), p. 94; Bogdan Musial, *Deutsche Zivilverwaltung und Judenverfolgung im Generalgouvernement. Eine Fallstudie zum Distrikt Lublin 1939–1944* (Wiesbaden, 1999), p. 80f; See also Gerlach, *Kalkulierte Morde*, p. 222ff.; on German occupation policy in general: Hans Umbreit, "Die Deutsche Herrschaft in den besetzten Gebieten 1942–1945," in Militärgeschichtliches Forschungsamt, ed., *Das Deutsche Reich und der Zweite Weltkrieg*, vol. 5/2, (Stuttgart, 1999).
98. Cited from a Report of the Commander of the Security Police and the SD for the District of Galicia of 26 June 1943 concerning the behavior of Reich Germans in the occupied territories, BAB, R 58/1002, Sh. 107–206, here Sh. 120.
99. Ibid., Sh. 191.
100. Thus Hilberg, *Vernichtung*, p. 664, refers to the escape of hundreds of Jews from the French internment camps, made possible by bribing camp personnel.
101. See the notorious speech by Himmler on 4 October 1943 in Poznan, *Der Prozeß gegen die Hauptkriegsverbrecher*, vol. XXIX, Document 1919-PS, p. 145.
102. Heinz Felfe, "Der Mord an Vera 'Sara' Korn,", *Kriminalistik* 3 (1992), pp. 153–173.

Part II

"Smooth Cooperation"

CHAPTER 8

INTRODUCTION: COOPERATION AND COLLABORATION

Gerhard Hirschfeld and Wolfgang Seibel

Division of labor in complex organizations appears in a horizontal and a vertical dimension. The vertical axis is organized along hierarchical lines while the horizontal axis is based on cooperation. This distinction remains blurry, however, as is obvious when subordinate individuals or units do not cooperate and enforcement of cooperation by hierarchal means is counterproductive. By the same token, cooperation is rarely non-hierarchical in the pure sense since working together may be stimulated by hidden hierarchies and competition for relative gains in terms of resources and power.

The chapters in the present section are devoted to the very gray zone of hierarchical cooperation and cooperative hierarchy in the persecution of the Jews. While the previous section focuses on division of labor and interorganizational networks as loosely coupled arrangements in which the radicalization of persecution was stimulated by rivalry and competition, the subject of the chapters in the present section is a more tightly coupled organizational setting in which *reibungslose Zusammenarbeit* (smooth cooperation) prevailed (see contribution by Wendy Lower). From the very beginning, cooperation within formal organizational settings was a consequence of the core group of persecutors' resource dependency. Gestapo and SS were dependent on third-party support, starting with the registration of Jews by municipal agencies and ending up with the confiscation of Jewish property by the fiscal administration. The basic pattern had been established in Germany proper between 1933 and 1939 and was then extended to German-occupied Europe.

Alfons Kenkmann sheds new light on the relationship between the Gestapo and the German fiscal administration whose radicalizing effect has been explained, in previous research,[1] by rivalry rather than by conventional cooperation. Rivalry might have been overstated by research focusing on the national level of legislation and struggle for general jurisdiction. At the local level, however, cooperation between Gestapo and fiscal administration functioned without major frictions. What is more, fiscal authorities very actively implemented anti-Jewish tax law and various tax surcharges without any SS or Gestapo initiative. Kenkmann gives a richly illustrated account of the participation of ordinary, non-Nazi civil servants of local fiscal administration in the persecution as well as of the fate of their Jewish victims. Moreover, the chapter highlights the uninterrupted career of those civil servants after 1945. None of them had to stand trial for the involvement in the destruction of the civil existence of their Jewish fellow citizens but, due to their undisputable "expertise," some were in charge of restituting the property of the very few survivors.

Inter-agency cooperation in Germany proper delivered the blueprint for cooperation in the occupied territories. However, occupation regimes differed substantially in terms of both legal status and availability of human and organizational resources. Although no coherent determinants of institutional choice can be identified, long-term German goals in terms of political relationship and short-term economic requirements were crucial in shaping the overall administrative structure. Administrative regimes in Eastern Europe were adjusted to the colonial status that Nazi Germany had assigned to the respective regions, while administration in Western Europe was designed to mobilize industrial resources for the German war effort. German rule in Western and Northern Europe was administered through just a thin overlay of agencies supervising native institutions that had been left more or less intact. By contrast, German rule in Eastern Europe—with Poland and the Soviet Union as the most important cases—not only destroyed legal statehood but also replaced native administrative structures almost entirely, with the main branches of German authorities reaching down to the local level.

Accordingly, the organizational substructure of the Holocaust in Eastern Europe was similar and dissimilar to regular German administration at the same time. On the one hand, the newly created administration was poorly staffed and anything but efficient. On the other hand, administrative skills along with racist ideology and the will to rule ruthlessly in the name of German superiority largely compensated for those deficiencies. It is here that the chapters by Isabel Heinemann and Wendy Lower set their respective focus.

The agencies for "ethnic resettlement" in Western Poland analyzed by Heinemann were part of the SS Rasse- und Siedlungshauptamt (RuSHA) (Race and Resettlement Main Office) and, thus, belonged to the realm of Heinrich Himmler in his capacity as Reichskommissar für die Festigung Deutschen Volkstums (RKF) (Reich Commissioner for the Strengthening of Germanidom). Their task was to settle ethnic Germans from outside Germany in the annexed Reichsgau Wartheland in Western Poland, to select Poles to be exempted from expulsion to what was then the "General Government" according to racial criteria, and to support actively the deportation of all Jews, initially to the ghettos in the General Government and, later on, to the annihilation camps. At the administrative level, the resettlement measures were incompatible with the overall goal to establish efficient German rule in the newly conquered territories. Even the infamous Gauleiter Arthur Greiser, a hard-boiled racist and chiefly responsible for the "final solution" in Western Poland, at some point complained to Himmler about the detrimental effects of the resettlement agencies for political stability and economic exploitation. Finally, however, it was the racist ideology that, time and again, was successfully used as an efficient mechanism to overcome those frictions. The overall goal of colonizing the East and related ethnic resettlement was strong enough an appeal to coordinate the divergent interests of heterogeneous agencies and to mitigate the tensions among their rival representatives.

While the Germans hastened to establish full-scale administration in the conquered regions of Western Poland—large parts of which had belonged to the Reich until 1919—administrative conditions in the occupied parts of the Soviet Union remained much more improvised and unstable due to the ongoing war on Soviet territory. Moreover, there were different kinds of occupation regimes with either civilian or military status. The Germans created two territorial units under civilian administration (Reichskommissariat Ostland, Reichskommissariat Ukraine), while a strip of some 100 miles in the rear area of the Eastern front remained under military administration with the army headquarters as regional governing units. Local and regional autonomy of both civilian and military occupation administration was considerable. Wendy Lower, comparing German civilian and military administration in the Ukraine, describes how local autonomy and improvised administration did not hinder the effective implementation of the Holocaust. Rather, not only police units but all kinds of technical and administrative staff—construction squads of the Organisation *Todt* (OT), postal employees, railroad workers, foresters—actively hunted Jews, killing them on the spot or handing them over to the SD for *Sonderbehandlung* (special treatment), i.e. murder, while the welfare, medical, and nutrition administration supported the *Vernichtung durch Arbeit* (annihilation through labor) to which the remaining Jews were subjected. As is well known, Wehrmacht and SS units cooperated smoothly. But no significant difference between military and civilian administration can be recognized either when it comes to the cooperative persecution of the Jews on a large division-of-labor-based scale. And, again, there is no evidence that participation in mass crime was a matter of material incentives or pragmatic tactics. Rather, deep-rooted anti-Semitism was clearly the source of both the initiation and coordination of persecution and mass murder.

By contrast to the conditions in Eastern Europe where the Germans destroyed the administrative infrastructure almost entirely, the vertical axis of division of labor between the occupying power and operational native institutions remained crucial in Western and Northern Europe. The contributions by Gerard Aalders and Marc-Olivier Baruch, focusing on the spoliation of Jewish assets in the Netherlands and in France, describe two different variants of this general pattern.

The civilian Reichskommissariat in the Netherlands enabled the Germans to exert a much tighter control over native actors than did the fragile relationship between the German military administration and the French government in Vichy. The Germans preferred to rely on Dutch institutions in general but they did establish German agencies in crucial areas of occupation policy. This applied both to the economic exploitation of the Netherlands and to the persecution of the Jews. After initial rivalry between the SS and Gestapo and the regular Reichskommissariat administration, the latter maintained jurisdiction over the economic side of persecution. German authorities founded or renamed a broad variety of agencies in charge of organized looting, most of which were run by German officials and staffed by Dutch clerks and civil servants. However, the complexity of institutional arrangements and latent frictions between the SS and regular German authorities did not affect the firm integration of the spoliation of Jewish property into the persecution machinery, whose logic was built on the destruction of the civil existence of the Jews prior to their physical elimination. While coherence among German tactics and actors was based on ideological commitment to the anti-Jewish cause, Dutch collaboration was facilitated by the formal legalism through which the looting of Jewish property was carried out.

The French case as analyzed by Marc-Olivier Baruch reveals a still more complex pattern of cooperation and collaboration. In German-controlled Europe during World War II, the case of occupied France was unique since the occupation regime was based on a formal armistice granting the French a full-fledged government ultimately to be located in the spa town of Vichy. The use of German agencies for administrative purposes was thus restricted and, while Vichy initiated anti-Jewish measures without German interference as early as the late summer and fall of 1940, the Germans had to negotiate for any further step towards what for them was the "final solution of the Jewish question" in terms of both legislation and institution-building, the crucial result of which was the erection of a central French authority of anti-Jewish policy, the Commissariat générale aux questions juives, in March 1941. Moreover, French military defeat had led to the collapse of the constitutional order of the Third Republic and the creation of an authoritarian regime, which spurred an elite exchange unparalleled in Western Europe under German occupation. It was a cohort of young technocrats who, in the absence of democratic control, formed the backbone of administrative collaboration. French professionals from both the administrative and the business world used what they perceived as a transitional order in an ongoing war for strengthening their respective positions both within domestic politics and vis-à-vis the Germans. Demonstrating administrative effectiveness in order to prevent the Germans from direct interference was part and parcel of that strategy. While Philippe Verheyde, in his contribution (see section "Competition and Rivalry"), points to inter-agency competition as a driving force behind the radicalization of anti-Jewish measures in the economic field, Marc-Olivier Baruch describes the variants of professional orientations and political illusions as the basis of collaboration of French elites in the economic persecution of their Jewish fellow citizens.

What conventional terminology terms collaboration is a classic case of hierarchical cooperation in the sense of native individuals or institutions cooperating with the occupying power.[2] During World War II, collaboration with the German occupants occurred in a broad variety of fields,[3] with the prospects and limits of accommodation and collaboration remaining, needless to say, subordinated to the interests of the occupying power.[4] Occupation policy varied across regions and countries in accordance with strategic German perspectives and so did the attitude of key representatives of the occupied territories themselves. Under the impact of German military successes during the initial *Blitzkrieg* era, the prevailing attitude in most Western and Northern European countries hovered between a cautious waiting approach, a mode of playing for time (*attentisme*), and a growing willingness to accommodate the supposedly victorious power. While espousing the idea of German supremacy in Europe, the majority of occupied nations clearly sought some kind of peaceful arrangement with the occupiers in the interest of maintaining law and order[5] according to a *politique du moindre mal* (the policy of accepting the lesser evil).

However, short-term tactics of accommodation were eclipsed by long-term strategies of positioning one's own country in a Europe under presumed German hegemony. The prospects of a "New Economic Order" was debated among Dutch, Belgian, and French industrialists and high-ranking civil servants, a discourse dominated by fear of economic and social chaos and concern for the maintenance of an industrial basis of production and employment.[6]

So both entrepreneurial and general economic reasons ensured economic cooperation with Germany, which included an interest in maintaining companies as viable entities, a desire to safeguard invested capital and its proceeds in the future from possible seizure by the occupying power and the aim of preventing the penetration of the national economies by German big business.[7] Last but not least, economic collaboration yielded profits and a chance of entrepreneurial survival and even innovation in difficult times.[8] The Germans were well aware of those concerns and soberly took them into account in the pursuit of the "final solution of the Jewish question." To French administrative and economic elites, as one may conclude from the contribution by Marc-Olivier Baruch, the German threat to intervene in national economic affairs was at least as important in stimulating compliance with the economic persecution of the Jews as was ideological commitment in terms of traditional French anti-Semitism.

The fate of the Jewish communities in the respective countries clearly defies the justification of collaboration as a variant of a *moindre mal* policy. As the contribution by Gerard Aalders underlines, the administrative compliance of the Dutch civil service decisively contributed to the effectiveness with which German and some units of Dutch police carried out the roundups and deportations of Jews.[9] With only a few exceptions, all sectors of the state and municipal administrations followed the example of the Secretaries-General, the heads of the governmental departments, whose formalistic and mediating approach to the ill-famed "Aryan Declarations" led to the suspension and, ultimately, to the dismissal of Jewish civil servants and clerical workers. Another lamentable example is the role played by the Netherlands' Central Registration Office, run by a skillful non-Nazi civil servant, which effectively organized the registration and separation of Dutch Jews from the residents' registers.

The chapters presented in this section illustrate the smooth cooperation between German and collaborating institutions in occupied countries preceding and accompanying the processes of Jewish defamation, segregation, and, ultimately, destruction. The looting of Jewish property remains a particularly illuminating case. Philippe Burrin refers to a number of "at least 10,000 Frenchmen" who acted "as temporary managers of some 40,000 despoiled Jewish businesses." When, in May 1944, "Aryanization" had been almost completed, there were still 5,522 French "managers" working alongside 110 German commissioners,[10] while German involvement in the capital of French "Aryanized" businesses amounted to just 4 percent.[11] In the Netherlands, too, native banks, traders, museums, and even the Amsterdam stock exchange, with the assistance of the former Jewish bank and trading company Lippmann, Rosenthal & Co., hugely benefited from the sale of Jewish properties, valuables, and financial securities at dumping prices.[12] Ironically, most of the Dutch non-Nazi profiteers continued to enjoy a moral satisfaction in the sense that by keeping Jewish properties and assets in native hands they even exercised some sort of damage control. A similar pattern of justification and self-deception had occurred in Germany proper, where, throughout the years 1937 and 1938, the then enforced sale of Jewish firms and enterprises provided attractive bargains for non-Jewish investors.[13] While most of these beneficiaries were apolitical businessmen, presumably resembling the majority of Dutch civil servants, their economic and financial efforts nevertheless contributed decisively to the ongoing process of Jewish impoverishment and, ultimately, the destruction of their civil existence.

Notes

1. See Hans Adler, *Der verwaltete Mensch. Studien zur Deportation der Juden aus Deutschland* (Tübingen, 1974).
2. Cornelis J. Lammers, "The Interorganizational Control of an Occupied Country," *Administrative Science Quarterly* 33 (1988): 438–457.
3. See Werner Röhr, ed., *Okkupation und Kollaboration (1938–1945). Beiträge zu Konzepten und Praxis der Kollaboration in der deutschen Okkupationspolitik* (Berlin/Heidelberg, 1994).
4. See Hagen Fleischer, "Nationalsozialistische Besatzungsherrschaft im Vergleich: Versuch einer Synopse," in Wolfgang Benz, Johannes Houwink Ten Cate, Gerhard Otto, eds., *Anpassung, Kollaboration, Widerstand* (Berlin, 1996), pp. 257–302; Gerhard Hirschfeld, "German occupation of Europe, the Axis 'New Order' and Collaboration," in Loyd E. Lee,

ed., *World War II in Europe, Africa and the Americas, with General Sources. A Handbook of Literature and Research* (Westport/London, 1997), pp. 267–284.
5. See Gerhard Hirschfeld, "Collaboration and attentisme in the Netherlands 1940–41," *Journal of Contemporary History* 16 (1981): 467–486.
6. See Gerhard Hirschfeld, "Collaboration in Nazi-occupied France: Some introductory remarks," in Gerhard Hirschfeld and Patrick Marsh, eds., *Collaboration in France. Politics and Culture during the Nazi Occupation, 1940–1944* (Oxford/New York, 1989), pp. 1–14.
7. Philippe Burrin, *Living with Defeat. France under the German Occupation, 1940–1944* (London/Sydney/Auckland, 1996), p. 245; see also Stefan Martens and Maurice Vaisse, eds., *Frankreich und Deutschland im Krieg (November 1942 – Herbst 1944): Okkupation, Kollaboration, Résistance* (Bonn, 2000), pp. 269–395.
8. See Peter F. Klemm, "La Production aéronautique française de 1940 à 1942," *Revue d'Histoire de la Deuxième Guerre Mondiale* 107 (1977): 53–74; Patrick Facon and Francoise de Ruffray, "Aperçus sur la collaboration aéronautique franco-allemande (1940–1943)," *Revue d'Histoire de la Deuxième Guerre Mondiale* 107 (1977): 85–102.
9. See Bob Moore, *Victims and Survivors. The Nazi Persecution of the Jews in the Netherlands 1940–1945* (London/New York/Sydney/Auckland, 1997), pp. 194–199.
10. Burrin, *Living with Defeat*, p. 282.
11. Philippe Verheyde, *Les Mauvais Comptes de Vichy. L'aryanisation des entreprises juives* (Paris, 1999).
12. See Gerald Aalders, *Roof. De ont-vremding van joods bezit tijdens de Tweede wereldoorlog* (The Hague, 1999).
13. See Avraham Barkai, *From Boycott to Annihilation. The Economic Struggle of German Jews 1933–1943* (Hanover, 1989).

CHAPTER 9

THE LOOTING OF JEWISH PROPERTY AND THE GERMAN FINANCIAL ADMINISTRATION

Alfons Kenkmann

We do not want to see any fossilized, arrogant bureaucrats among us! Our profession demands economic understanding, vigorous treatment of the efficient producer, and a warm heart for the weak. Our laws must be administered in the spirit of the movement to which we have dedicated ourselves and of the people to which we belong.[1]

These are the words of the director of a regional tax office (Oberfinanzpräsident) addressing members of the "Aryan" ethnic community in March 1939. For the Third Reich and its administrative institutions—among them in a prominent position the fiscal authorities—were preparing an inferno for the Jews and "gypsies" (Sinti and Roma). This chapter focuses on how remarkably smoothly the cooperation among different agencies and officials functioned in plundering the Jews and how successfully and smoothly a division of labor was used in its implementation. The "efficiency" of the bureaucratic machinery is presented in structural terms, using the example of the regional financial administration of the Reich in Westphalia (later the Westphalian Director of Finance (Oberfinanzpräsident))[2] and in biographical terms on the basis of two life histories—those of a high-ranking financial officer and a German-Jewish woman. In this way the tableau of social reality and the actors' fields of action in the years from 1933 to 1945 become more clearly visible.

Financial Administration and the Holocaust as Topics of Historical Research

During the 1950s the role played by financial officials in Third Reich Jewish and racial policy was lost sight of in the intoxication of the postwar West German "economic miracle" and received no attention in the few publications by former financial officials.[3] In the intensity of their repression of the past, financial administration officials differed in no regard from the officials of other administrative organizations, such as the judicial system and police.[4] Only in the past decade has the involvement of financial authorities in the coercion and plundering of the Jews come to light through the intensive research of various scholars. At first only very limited attention was paid to this topic, as in a detailed 1993 monograph on the history of the Cologne Regional Tax Office, which, in a text of twenty-two pages on the NS period, termed the plundering of the Jews a "forecourt of horror," but nevertheless devoted a mere three-quarters of a page to this topic.[5]

In the second half of the 1990s, with two extensive articles on "Financial administration in the Third Reich" and "The customs administration and the foreign-exchange office in the Third Reich," the first notable historical self-examination was begun on financial officials and their role in National Socialism.[6] Regional studies that also devoted major sections to the involvement of fiscal authorities, were published in Hamburg and Göttingen in 1997.[7] In 1998/99 the Düsseldorf Municipal Museum presented an exhibition entitled "Concerning: 'Action 3'" on the participation of the Cologne Regional Tax Office in the plundering of "Jewish neighbors."[8] In December 1999, the touring exhibition "Persecution and Administration. The Economic Plundering of the Jews and the Westphalian Fiscal Authorities" offered the first didactically conceived historical presentation of the topic, which, due to widespread interest throughout the Federal Republic, is booked up until at least early 2004.[9]

Since then—motivated not least by the successful Westphalian cooperative exhibition project—a series of further research projects have been started in the Federal Republic of Germany on the participation of financial administrations in the control and plundering of the Jews,[10] and further studies have also been published.[11]

Structure and Officials of the Financial Bureaucracy

First we will consider the organizational structures of Third Reich financial administration. After the Erzberg reforms and the coming into effect of the Law of 10 September 1919 on Reich Financial Administration, it had three levels. As the highest authority, the Reich Ministry of Finance had jurisdiction over the regional tax offices and, after 1937, over the director of the regional tax offices (Oberfinanzpräsident) as intermediate authorities and the tax and customs offices as local authorities.[12] In 1928 there were

26 regional tax offices (Landesfinanzämter), with 990 local tax offices (Finanzämter) and 237 main customs offices (Hauptzollämter).[13]

How did the seizure of power by the National Socialists and the Law for the Restoration of the Professional Civil Service affect a part of the state administration which to a high degree endeavored to achieve "high technical quality and most strongly embodied the continuity of the civil service"? If one considers that at the time of the seizure of power the organizational structure of the Reich financial administration was little more than a decade old,

> it is noteworthy that specific cases of political dismissal were rare. Of a total of 2,593 pending cases, of which 1,552 were settled in December 1933 and a further 457 were still pending, five cases fell under §§ 2 and 2a (dismissal due to Communist activities), 40 cases under § 3 (Jewish ancestry), whereby in ten cases exceptions were made according to Paragraph 2 (exemptions for former front-line soldiers), and 253 under § 4 (political unreliability); apart from 32 still pending cases, dismissals or compulsory retirement were decreed in only 49 cases; in 172 cases no measures were taken based on the law, since, in itself, belonging to the SPD, the State Party [Staatspartei] and the Center Party [Zentrum], the Reichsbanner party and the Republican Union [Republikanische Vereinigung] did not as such suffice as grounds for dismissal.[14]

This very low number of political cases was due to the conservative makeup of the civil service, a bureaucracy first built up in the Weimar Republic, and, additionally, to the very restrained application of the Law for the Restoration of the Professional Civil Service.

The number of transfers and compulsory retirements without political and racial motivation was, on the contrary, considerably greater. Around 2,000 persons were pensioned off or in individual cases dismissed or transferred to less responsible positions. These cases were often connected with the closing of tax offices and the simplification of administration. Hans Mommsen drew the conclusion from this "that the administration used the 'Law for the Restoration of the Professional Civil Service'" to a great extent "not for political, but rather for technical administrative reasons."[15]

Like the majority of the German population, in the period from 1933 until the defeat at Stalingrad and the escalating Allied air raids, which brought the war home to Germany, the majority of financial officials saw little reason to mourn the passing of the Weimar Republic. Within the civil service, the attitude toward the first Republic on German soil had been reserved, and there was little sympathy for the multi-party state.[16] But it would be false to infer from this attitude that there was necessarily a propensity for racist world views. This will be shown by the personal and professional biography of a senior financial official of the Westphalian financial administration who participated in the coercion and financial plundering of Jews in a prominent position.

The Westphalian Regional Tax Office, where this senior executive officer, Oberregierungsrat Heinrich Heising, served, was responsible for a region in north-west Germany with the medium-sized cities of Siegen in the south and

Detmold in the north, Ahaus in the west and Gelsenkirchen in the east. The headquarters of the Regional Tax Office was Münster, the state capital—often also referred to as the "desk of Westphalia" (*Schreibtisch Westfalens*)[17]—because of the numerous intermediate administrative authorities and officials located there. United under the Westphalian Director of Finance were forty-nine tax offices and nine main customs offices, as well as six border and forty-four tax commissions and sixty-four customs offices.[18] In addition, he presided over a customs investigation office in Dortmund, which monitored compliance with import, export, and transit restrictions and was employed to combat smuggling.

All the offices subordinate to the regional authority in Münster participated in implementing National Socialist Jewish policy. Financial officials collected a tax on emigrants, the so-called Reich Flight Tax (*Reichsfluchtsteuer*), the Jewish Wealth Levy (*Judenvermögensabgabe*) and fees for emigrants' hand luggage and forwarded luggage. They froze bank accounts, monitored observation of export and foreign-exchange regulations, opened proceedings on foreign-exchange violations and, after the deportation of German Jews, confiscated their few remaining assets and abandoned household goods. This is the context of Oberregierungsrat Heinrich Heising's duties in the Westphalian financial administration (Figure 9.1).

Born in Berlin on 25 January 1885, Heinrich Heising received his legal training in the German Empire. He studied at universities in Lausanne, Munich, Kiel, and Münster and completed his legal studies with a grade of "satisfactory." He returned from World War I decorated with the Iron Cross first and second class.[19]

Figure 9.1 Oberregierungsrat Heinrich Heising.

For over a quarter of a century Heising was active in the tax office, from 1920 until 1948. and during the period from 1931 to 1947 he continuously held the position of Oberregierungsrat.

Heinrich Heising, before 1933 a Center Party voter and member of the Lawyers Association (Juristenbund), which was dissolved after the seizure of power, was never a NSDAP member, but merely an ordinary member of a professional organization, the Reich Association of German Civil Servants (Reichsbund der Deutschen Beamten).[20] He was therefore among the one-third of all civil servants in the Westphalian financial administration who were not NSDAP members. For, of the 4,657 officials who served in the financial bureaucracy of the Westphalian regional financial district in 1939, 68.9 percent (3,209 officials) were NSDAP members.[21] The level of NSDAP membership in the financial administrative area was accordingly almost 6 percent higher than for all officials on non-Prussian Reich territory.[22] Like millions of others—from pastors to laborers—Heising belonged to the National Socialist People's Welfare Organization (NSV). To be sure, he also belonged to the National Socialist Lawyers Association (Rechtswahrerbund), an essential precondition for successful career advancement. In the social world of his profession, Heising was one of Münster's established local dignitaries. In 1932 he joined the renowned Two Lions Club,[23] to which he belonged until 1945.[24]

Numerous letters and inquiries from the group of around 21,500 Westphalian Jews[25] were addressed to the various branches of the financial administration in Münster—the Property and Property Transfer Tax Department with the local tax offices, the Customs and Excise Tax Department with the Customs Investigation Office (Zollfahndungsbehörde), and also a subsidiary office of the Reich Ministry of Economic Affairs, the Foreign-exchange Office (Devisenstelle) with its enforcement and auditing division, which Heinrich Heising directed.[26] A certain Jewish family, the Baers (Figure 9.2), was among those whose letters reached Heising's office.[27]

Richard Baer resided in Bielefeld, together with his wife Irmgard (b. 1910) and their son Heinz (b. 1934). Both elder Baers worked for Irmgard Baer's father, Louis Ostwald, who operated a basic commodities business in Bielefeld.[28] Like other Jews, the Baers suffered under the increasingly draconian measures directed against Jewish citizens by NS officials. In Bielefeld this included the November 1936 independent initiative of the local fiscal investigation office, which called on tax offices to register all non-"Aryans" who disposed of incomes over RM 20,000 and assets valued at over RM 50,000. The names of the affected persons were sent on to the local police departments – with orders to confiscate their passports. New passports were to be issued only upon receipt of a security deposit equal to 25 percent of their assets.[29] "No week, no day" passed, the German literary critic Marcel Reich-Ranicki recalls, "without new regulations and ordinances, and that meant without new chicanery and humiliation of the most varied sorts."[30] The pressure became so great that in 1938 the Baer family resolved to leave Germany.

Figure 9.2 Richard Baer (standing), Irmgard Baer (second person from left, seated) and Heinz Baer (child next to her).

The family's desired destination was Australia, regarded by potential emigrants as a suitable refuge, as it had liberalized its immigration policy in the mid-1930s.[31] However, before reaching a safe haven—as historian and eyewitness Peter Gay of Yale University recalls in his memoirs—the would-be refugee had "to run the gauntlet of the bureaucracy."[32]

Persecution and Exclusion of the Jews by Means of the "Reich Flight Tax" and Foreign-Exchange Controls

Among the tangled web of decrees and laws that threatened to strangle the Baer family, like all Jews in the Third Reich, were the Reich Flight Tax and other specific measures that arose from foreign-exchange control. In the first year after the seizure of power, 37,000 of the 560,000 Germans of Jewish origin had already fled from the territory of the German Reich. They saw the implications of an overall social climate that worsened daily. If they possessed an income of over RM 20,000 or assets exceeding RM 200,000, they had to pay the Reich Flight Tax.

The legal basis for collecting this special tax was the "Fourth Ordinance of the Reich President for the Security of the Economy and Finances and for the Protection of Internal Peace," already decreed by the Brüning government on 8 December 1931 (*Vierte Verordnung des Reichspräsidenten zur Sicherung von Wirtschaft und Finanzen und zum Schutze des inneren*

Friedens). Every German citizen who moved abroad after 1 April 1931 was expected to pay this contribution. The purpose of this requirement was to discourage the flight of capital abroad, as it further reduced the tax revenues of an economy that was already in a catastrophic state. This tax, collected by local tax offices, amounted to 25 percent of taxable assets. If the potential emigrant chose not to pay the special contribution, he was subject to imprisonment for tax evasion and the confiscation of his property.[33]

Due to the low emigration rates up to 1933, the Reich Flight Tax at first brought the German Reich little tax revenue. The situation changed with the National Socialist seizure of power. Within a single year, between April 1933 and March 1934, the income from this special tax rose to RM 17.5 million. One year later the Reich Ministry of Finance had already collected RM 38.1 million. The increased income can be explained by the fact that after the enactment of an ordinance of 18 May 1934 the number of persons subject to the Reich Flight Tax had increased considerably. According to the new law, assets of RM 50,000 and income of RM 10,000 were subject to taxation. Additionally, the new requirements authorized tax officials to demand a security deposit equal to the foreseeable Reich Flight Tax if intent to emigrate was suspected. In order to secure prompt payment of the tax, the tax offices cooperated after 1935 with customs and other authorities to control the emigration of Jewish citizens more rigorously and to monitor their activities more systematically. New legal stipulations facilitated this surveillance.

Starting in 1935, tax revenues from the Reich Flight Tax increased steadily: in the fiscal year 1935/36 (April 1935–March 1936) to RM 45.3 million, in the following year to RM 69.9 million and in 1937/38 to RM 81 million. The Reich collected the largest amounts, some RM 342.6 million, in 1938/39.[34] Increasing harassment and the terror of *Kristallnacht* had confronted the Jews with tangible evidence of how desperate their situation was becoming; the pressure on those unwilling to emigrate increased further. Jews imprisoned in concentration camps immediately after 9 November 1938 were only released on the condition that they leave Germany immediately.

Between April 1939 and March 1940 the National Socialist state squeezed the unheard of sum of RM 216.1 million out of Jews anxious to emigrate. In the following twelve months these revenues fell to RM 47.7 million, since very few Jews managed to emigrate in this period.[35] Overall, RM 900,000,000 was extorted from "emigrating Reich citizens" by the Reich financial administration.[36]

The tax office issued "tax-evasion warrants" (*Steuersteckbrief*) against persons who emigrated abroad without paying the Reich Flight Tax and published them for all state agencies in the Reich and State Gazette, Reich Financial Gazette, German Police Newspaper, and the German Register of Warrants of Arrest. The warrants listed names, old and new foreign addresses and the amounts of unpaid flight taxes. On the strength of such a warrant the emigrant could be taken into temporary custody by officials of the Police and Security Service as well as the Tax and Customs Offices.[37]

In order to continue their lives after emigrating, it was important for potential refugees, besides taking personal effects, to transfer funds abroad. A Jewish emigrant could not, however, personally take his remaining assets abroad without further restrictions, even after paying the Reich Flight Tax. The acquisition and use of foreign currency and the export of Reich currency were forbidden; funds could subsequently be transferred or carried abroad only with a foreign-exchange authorization.[38] At the regional tax offices the extortion strategy necessitated the establishment of a new department, the Foreign-exchange Office, whose chief activity consisted in issuing authorizations to export foreign currency.

The scope of the activities and the personnel of this office grew subsequently, because foreign-exchange controls were steadily expanded and continually sharpened. In particular, the tax-free amount for business requiring authorization, initially set at RM 3,000 per person, was gradually reduced: on 31 August 1931 to RM 1000 and on 3 October 1931 to RM 200. The tax-free amount was further reduced in April and September 1934 to RM 50 and ultimately to RM 10.[39]

The flood of printed forms and applications alone that would-be emigrants had to deal with and their correspondence with intended countries of destination were used by the National Socialist persecutors to expand the control network. In accordance with the foreign-exchange controls, foreign currency could not be imported or German currency exported without controls. The basis for this was the above-mentioned foreign-exchange control ordinance introduced on 1 August 1931, which also affected the Baer family's plan to settle in Australia. On 28 June 1938 family head Richard Baer applied to the director of the Münster Regional Tax Office for authorization to export the sum of one English pound, the reason being that the Australian immigration office required this sum as a fee for returning the health certificates and police certificates of good conduct that Richard Baer had submitted. The matter was promptly dealt with by a member of the Foreign-exchange Office of the Münster Regional Tax Office. On 1 July 1938 the administrative department responsible authorized the acquisition of the English banknote, citing § 13 Paragraph 1 of the Foreign-exchange Law of 4 February 1935.[40] Jewish emigration was still being encouraged by the National Socialists.

Emigration Control

By submitting this application, Richard Baer made himself a permanent target of the National Socialist persecution network. Nine days later, on 7 July 1938, Heising's department, the Foreign-exchange Office, informed other authorities of the persecution network—the Customs Investigation Office in Dortmund and the dependencies of the local tax office, the state police, the municipal administration, and the Reichsbank office in Bielefeld—of its suspicion that the Baer family was undertaking "preliminary measures to transfer its place of residence abroad."⁴¹ Cooperation between the regional financial administration and the Gestapo became customary practice after November 1935 and underlined the general suspicion harbored by financial officials about Jews wishing to emigrate: every emigrant was a potential smuggler of capital.

After late 1936 the control network tightened considerably. The most severely affected were Jews wishing to emigrate. In December, the Reich Minister of Finance circulated to his administrative offices a Gestapo directive concerning "cooperation with the tax offices in cases of preparations to emigrate," in which the reporting procedure introduced a year previously was further expanded. After that, all suspected emigration plans were to be reported on a two-page form to, among others, the tax office of residence, the customs investigation office, and the foreign exchange office. As grounds for suspicion of intent to move abroad the form named, among other things, passport application, sale of a business or residence, sale of real estate or stockholdings, etc. The Gestapo's directive was increasingly followed after early 1937. Consequently, emigration reports, usually prompted by the Gestapo or the tax and customs offices, with which the authorities continually notified each other of suspected emigration plans, were submitted in increasing numbers in 1937/38 and helped perfect the surveillance praxis.

Private businesses and additional government authorities were also integrated into the surveillance system for potential Jewish emigrants. The Reich Post Office was expected to inform the financial administration automatically about requests for forwarding mail, and the German National Railroad was required to report suspicious safe-deposit luggage to customs investigation offices.⁴² Shipping firms were also required to report all suspicious property shipments.

Plundering after *Kristallnacht* – "Atonement" through "Jewish Wealth Levies"

The Baer family's dream of departing for Australia was ultimately frustrated, not because of the National Socialist control network, but rather due to the outrages of *Kristallnacht* in 1938. That night, family head Richard Baer was arrested and, like 27,000 other Jewish men, transported to a concentration camp.⁴³ In Richard Baer's case this was Buchenwald, where he was obviously so brutally maltreated that he died, as did some 200 other victims.⁴⁴ His family was not permitted to open his coffin when it was returned to Bielefeld.⁴⁵

After *Kristallnacht*, the Decree on an Atonement Fine for all Jews who are German Subjects (*Verordnung über eine Sühneleistung der Juden deutscher Staatsangehörigkeit*) of 12 November 1938 imposed a special tax on Jews, the so-called Jewish Wealth Levy (*"Judenvermögensabgabe"*) for damages to their property. Peter Gay recalls that "as if to prove the extent of their cynicism, they decided that Jewish victims of the pogrom should not only be forbidden to apply for insurance compensation, but should also be forced to pay for and clean up the devastation caused by Nazi marauders."[46] The special levy was justified by Hermann Göring by the assassination of the German diplomat Ernst vom Rath in Paris and treated as an "atonement fine," which was decreed "because of the hostile attitude toward the German people and Reich of Jewry, which does not even shrink from cowardly murder." The registration, control, and robbery began to assume new dimensions. Tax and customs offices worked closely together with, among others, banks and insurance companies to deprive the Jews of their last financial loopholes.

Overall, the Jewish Wealth Levy on German Jews whose annual income exceeded RM 5,000 was meant to raise a total of one billion Reichsmarks. The levy, with which National Socialist authorities for the first time imposed a charge solely on Jews, was initially set at 20 percent of assets and, according to the implementation decree of 21 November 1938, had to be paid in four installments on or before 15 November 1938, 15 February, 15 May, and 15 August 1939.[47]

The local tax office of residence was responsible for determining and collecting the levy and informed the affected persons of the amounts in a "Notification on the Jewish Wealth Levy" (*Bescheid über die Judenvermögensabgabe*). When it became clear in August 1939 that one billion marks had still not been collected, a fifth installment was scheduled in the second implementation ordinance of 19 October 1939. It was due on or before 15 November 1939; at the same time, the rate of taxation was raised to 25 percent of taxable assets.[48] The tax offices then demanded the fifth installment in a new "Notification on a further contribution to the Jewish Wealth Levy." After collecting this final installment, they had extorted from the Jews required to pay the tax throughout the Reich—according to the meticulous accounting of the Reich Ministry of Finance—a total of exactly RM 1,126,612,495.48.[49]

Surveillance of Accounts and Monitoring of Wealth

To prevent emigrating Jews from transferring property abroad more effectively, the tax and customs offices devised additional measures and controls. The blanket suspicion was expressed that those desiring to emigrate were attempting by moving to take princely sums out of the country. Therefore after May 1938 the possibility of moving goods was strongly limited, and notification of the regional foreign-exchange offices at least fourteen days before packing and sending goods was required. The value and date of acquisition of the property to be transferred had to be reported on an additional list. Furthermore, authorization to export goods acquired after 1 January 1933 (so-called "new property") was contingent on the payment of a fitting tax to the Deutsche Golddiskontbank (Dego). According to a decree of the Reich Ministry of Finance of 23 May 1938, the regional foreign-exchange office was to decide in close cooperation with the customs investigation offices what could be taken abroad. The customs investigators were to carry out a check on the suspect's dwelling if "the personality of the individual desiring to emigrate (e.g. especially favorable financial situation), large quantities of items, or the inclusion of particularly valuable articles, or other circumstances arouse the suspicion of capital flight."[50] Customs officials were additionally to check the packing and loading of the goods to be moved so that only property authorized by the foreign-exchange office would be shipped.

Richard Baer's widow, who was now in the final months of pregnancy, continued to prepare for emigration with her three-year-old son in the months following her husband's death, now hoping to move via Great Britain to the U.S.A. But she fell victim to the new differentiated control practice. To obtain permission to emigrate at all, she first had to fill out a "Questionnaire for Emigrants" at the Foreign-exchange Office of the Münster Regional Tax Office, which inquired as to family situation, emigration goal, date of departure, and also income, property, and assets (cash, bank accounts, real estate, business assets, mortgages, loans, and insurance policies). Along with this questionnaire, she also submitted a list of the household effects she wished to take with her to the Foreign-exchange Office on 27 December 1938.[51] The Law on Foreign-exchange Control of 12 December 1938 had once again considerably limited the amount of property that could be taken out of the country.[52] Only indispensable personal effects could be removed, whereby a distinction was made between household effects and hand luggage. Jewelry and precious metals, pearls, etc. could not be exported at all. To enforce these strict regulations, goods to be moved abroad were to be examined by foreign-exchange office officials.[53]

Heising's subordinates checked the lists of goods to be forwarded, set the tax for the family's "new acquisitions" at RM 575 and then sent the files on to the Customs Investigation Office in Dortmund with a request for its opinion.[54] Customs investigators also estimated the value of movable goods in people's homes and decided which items could be taken along and what sums were to be paid to the Deutsche Golddiskontbank. In the Baer case the Customs Investigation Office in Dortmund declared on 6 January 1939 that it had "no objections to the removal of the goods ... after the payment of the fees for newly acquired articles."[55] Ten days later Frau Baer paid the required tax to the Golddiskontbank and submitted the receipt to the Foreign-exchange Office in Münster to obtain authorization to move her possessions abroad.

In response to the widow's application, the Municipal Tax Department in Bielefeld also announced that it had no "tax-related objection" to her emigration. According to the certification of the Bielefeld Tax Office of 6 January 1939, the Reich Flight Tax and Jewish Wealth Levy could "not be collected" from the virtually penniless widow.[56] The Municipal Tax Department also confirmed that she was not in arrears with her Reich taxes. The valuation of the family jewelry by an "Aryan" jeweler also revealed no cause for complaint.[57]

After the birth of her second child, Ruben, on 5 March 1939 and continued preparations for emigration, the widow submitted a list of possessions intended as luggage for herself and her two sons to the Foreign Exchange Office of the Regional Tax Office on 10 July (Figure 9.3).[58] Even the list for her four-month-old infant was meticulously examined to determine whether it contained anything that by law could not be taken abroad. The purchasing prices of clothing were also checked for accuracy. To take along "newly acquired" items, i.e. goods purchased after 1933, a charge had to be paid—thus, for example, for a heating pad the widow had purchased to make the trip easier for the four-month-old Ruben.

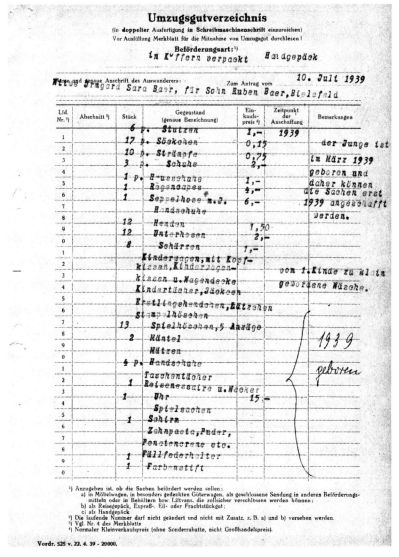

Figure 9.3 Control of possessions.

Finally, on 31 August 1939, Irmgard Baer received a stamp from the Foreign Exchange Office authorizing her to "transfer" her luggage abroad[59]—the day before the outbreak of World War II. The next morning, radio broadcasts announced that Germany had "returned fire." The entry of England into the war prevented the departure. This did not, however, end the control of Irmgard Baer's few remaining resources, as the further administrative proceedings show.

With the aim of relieving the foreign-exchange offices of the previously practiced time-consuming procedures for controlling individual accounts, the Reich Ministry of Economic Affairs ordered that in the future new security accounts (*Sicherungskonten*) could only be opened after a printed form had been filled in and that only a monthly "allowance" (*Freibetrag*) could be withdrawn from the account. After October 1939, two officers of the Foreign-exchange Office of the Regional Tax Office mailed out the now standardized security orders. By March 1940 the two officials had issued 4,162 security orders to the remaining Jews of Westphalia—Irmgard Baer also received one. The recipient had no means of withdrawing additional funds from her account other than the allowance, which usually amounted to between RM 150 and 300 a month. With § 37a of the Foreign-exchange Law, later § 59, the right of Jews to dispose of personal property was abolished, although they formally continued to own their assets. "Irmgard Sarah Baer" received the official notification in which it was specified that she would receive the low standard allowance (*Regelfreibetrag*) of RM 150 per month.[60]

Irmgard Baer and her two sons survived two-and-a-half years under these circumstances in Bielefeld. Then, on 31 July 1942, the thirty-two-year-old widow, along with Ruben, by then two years old, and the seven-year-old Heinz, were deported, first to Theresienstadt and, on 12 October 1944 to Auschwitz, where they were put to death.[61]

Utilization of Property after Deportation

In October 1941, the first mass deportations of Jewish citizens from the German Reich began. This initiated the final phase of National Socialist Jewish policy. With the deportations—which meant crossing the borders of the Old Reich—the Jews automatically lost their German citizenship and thereby forfeited their assets to the Reich.[62] The collection, administration, and exploitation of the assets and possessions of deported Jews were the responsibility of the Reich Minister of Finance and the Director of the Tax Office in Berlin, who assigned "the fulfillment of these tasks"[63] to the directors of the regional tax offices. In the "Aryanization" and liquidation of Jewish businesses, the state had scarcely made its presence felt and had concentrated on siphoning off profits from the taxation of assets. But, in contrast, it profited directly from the confiscation of real estate, which was only partly "Aryanized" by private parties, the lion's share being transferred to the state for disposal.[64]

On 4 November 1941 the Reich Ministry of Finance notified the directors of the regional tax offices of the impending deportations and its intention to collect the assets of the deported Jews for the Reich. Financial officials were to receive authorizations to collect and register assets from the Gestapo and to acquire control of "vacated dwellings." At the same time, it was decreed that the regional tax offices should set up an additional office for the new tasks that had arisen, which would conduct its business under the name Office for the Collection of Assets (Dienststelle für die Einziehung von Vermögenswerten). This newly created institution was virtually necessitated by the beginning of the deportations – the surveillance departments of the foreign-exchange offices lacked the requisite manpower. What remained were household inventories, bank balances, and immovable property. In this situation Heinrich Heising was now promoted to director of the Office for the Collection of Assets. The work in this bureau offered the employees and officials assigned to it an additional benefit, the improved chance of avoiding transfer to occupied Eastern Europe.

In order to implement the deportation of the Westphalian Jews as smoothly as possible and to benefit from experience with the deportation of the Rhine Jews, a meeting was held on 19 November 1941 in the office of the Mayor of Münster, which was treated as "extremely confidential"—a sort of "little Wannsee Conference." Besides the Deputy Gauleiter, Police Chief Heider, and Dr. Busse from the Münster Gestapo headquarters, Heinrich Heising also participated in his new capacity. At this "little Wannsee Conference" problems were anticipated, half-way solutions rejected, previous experience evaluated, and procedures harmonized. Oberregierungsrat Heising requested twenty liters of gasoline for personal use on "Day X," the day of the deportation, so that he could personally examine all the dwellings that would be vacated and the effects left behind.[65]

With the decree of 8 December 1941, the Director of the Westphalian Tax Office informed his financial officials of the precise date of the deportation—13 December 1941. Immediately after the deportation, the financial bureaucrats under Heising's direction began to collect the forfeited property. They proceeded in the same manner after subsequent deportations. Shortly after the police had removed the Jewish owners, the contents of the dwellings were carted away by tax office officials. If they were not needed by the financial administration or other state offices, they were auctioned off in numerous Westphalian communities and towns to members of the German community. Goods otherwise difficult to obtain and replace under conditions of economic scarcity on the "home front" and due to air raids could often be purchased at these public auctions. The sales proceeds went to the revenue department of the tax office. Funds remaining in the bank accounts of deportees were transferred by the banks to the Regional Revenue Office in Münster.[66]

The immovable property of the victims was also confiscated, to the benefit of the Reich. Under Heising's jurisdiction there were 564 houses, 254 undeveloped plots of land, and even fifty cemeteries. On the basis of the

Eleventh Decree regarding the Reich Citizenship Law, it was no longer necessary after December 1941 for the financial authorities to issue confiscation authorizations for its measures.[67] In the German Reich as a whole the total income collected on the basis of this decree amounted to Rm 777.7 million.[68]

When they expropriated the property of the "gypsies," the financial authorities drew on the experience gained during the confiscation of Jewish assets.[69] The sales proceeds were deposited in "summary accounts for gypsies" (*Zigeuner-Sammelkonten*) especially set up for this purpose.[70]

After May 1945 Heinrich Heising continued to occupy a prominent position at the Münster Regional Tax Office. He was appointed to deal with issues of restitution. The man who had played a leading part in the administration and exploitation of the assets of Jews in Westphalia was now expected to reimburse the victims. He successfully adopted a strategy of concealing the financial bureaucracy's role in the confiscation process. In 1947 Heising was promoted to Government Executive Officer (Regierungsdirektor) and, in 1949, he became the President of the Düsseldorf Financial Court (Finanzgerichtspräsident) in the very young Federal Republic.[71] His likeness can be viewed there today in the "ancestors gallery" of former presidents. Administrative experts are always needed.[72]

Summary

According to Max Weber, "bureaucracy [has a] 'rational' character: rules, ends, means, 'objective' impersonality dominate its behavior."

Heinrich Heising's professional biography underlines the central role in the financial plundering of the Jews played by representatives of the traditional specialized bureaucracy, who years before the National Socialist seizure of power were already active in administrative service. In order to implement the financial plundering of the Jews, the financial administration did not need the help of racist ideologists, but merely of traditional representatives of the "core group of the government civil service."[73] In strong contrast to the radical caesuras of 1933 and 1945, a clear continuity of personnel can be ascertained. The knowledge and skills needed for traditional administration made possible the implementation of NS ideological goals. Heinrich Heising's professional qualities – competent fulfillment of administrative leadership functions, planning and organization of problem-solving processes within the bureaucratic system – made a major contribution to the successful plundering of the Jews.

Financial officials were deployed at the interfaces of the normative and regulative state. Their specialty was "legal" "plundering with printed forms." Thus, in the deprivation of the Jews of their rights, financial regulations from the Weimar period—e.g., the collection of the Reich Flight Tax, which had been in effect since 1931—were combined with elements of the National Socialist regulatory state.

With a combination of the civil servant's duty to obedience, the splitting up of the persecution process into small parts, and its transformation into routine administrative procedures, the segmental tasks involved in plundering the Jews assigned to the financial administration could be smoothly worked through and implemented. In the area of the control and exploitation of Jewish property and assets, and despite any polycratic difficulties and party and bureaucratic competition, the financial administration displayed at all levels—from the small local tax office to the ministry in Berlin—the "efficiency feared throughout Europe"[74] of the German bureaucratic apparatus.

But, even where there was institutional friction and conflict, it was precisely the dualism of the division of labor and polycracy that furthered the implementation of persecution and extermination measures, because they created structures enabling selective perceptions and selective incentives and thereby obscured the overall context of "persecution and murder."[75] The persecution network that participated in the plundering of the Jews led not only to competition among administrative offices, but also to effective cooperation in setting up the surveillance network. Both—competition and cooperation—increased the overwhelming efficiency of the persecution apparatus.

For Raul Hilberg, "the bureaucratic apparatus of an entire nation" was integrated into the process of excluding and exterminating the Jews, and "its efficiency was also increased by an atmosphere promoted by the individual initiatives of officials and departments on all levels."[76] With the aid of its customs inspections, the financial administration kept the borders under surveillance; it participated in confiscation, collected information, and realized the profits from the property taken from Jews and "gypsies." None of these extortion and exploitation operations occurred without the participation of the financial administration.

The only surprising thing is how long Irmgard Baer and others like her nevertheless persisted in trying to wring an option for the future for her children and herself from the bureaucratic apparatus, in spite of the overwhelming power of the state and the profound sense of being abandoned which, as Hannah Arendt states, constituted life under National Socialist totalitarian rule.[77]

Notes

1. Kölner Finanzpräsident Kühne (head of the Cologne Regional Tax Office), cited from Bernd-A. Rusiuck, "'Arisierung' als bürokratischer Prozeß." Address held at a symposium in Recklinghausen organized by the Villa ten Hompel Memorial Research and Historical-Political Educational Facility and the Justice Academy of the State of North-Rhine Westphalia, entitled "Between Writing Desk and Judicial Bench – Administration as a Locus of Decision-Making in the 'Third Reich' and Post-War Germany" (Recklinghausen, 23–24 August 2000).
2. In portraying the participation of Westphalian tax and customs officials in the economic plundering of the Jews, I draw on findings published in connection with an exhibition project, *Persecution and Administration. The economic plundering of the Jews and the Westphalian Financial Authorities*, which appeared as an exhibition catalogue. In particular,

I follow the contribution by Gerd Blumberg, "Etappen der Verfolgung und Ausraubung und ihre bürokratische Apparatur," in Alfons Kenkmann and Bernd A. Rusinek , eds., *Verfolgung und Verwaltung. Die wirtschaftliche Ausplünderung der Juden und die westfälischen Finanzbehörden* [Catalogue of the touring exhibition] (Münster, 1999), pp. 15–40.

3. Jakob Kau, "Verwaltung unter Diktatur und Terror. Das Landesfinanzamt 1933–1944," *Die Heimat* 13 (1962): 18–22, 51–55, 75–79, 102–105.
4. See, for example, the tendentious and historically misleading memoirs of former commanders of the National Socialist Regular Police; Heinrich Bernhard Lankenau, *Polizei im Einsatz während des Krieges 1939/1945 in Nordrhein-Westfalen* (Bremen, 1957); Paul Riege, *Kleine Polizei-Geschichte*, 3rd ed. (Lübeck, 1966, 1st ed. Lübeck, 1954).
5. Michael Alfred Kanther, *Finanzverwaltung zwischen Staat und Gesellschaft. Die Geschichte der Oberfinanzdirektion Köln und ihrer Vorgängerbehörden 1824–1992* (Cologne, 1993), pp. 169–170; Franziska Becker, *Gewalt und Gedächtnis. Erinnerungen an die nationalsozialistische Verfolgung einer jüdischen Landgemeinde* (Göttingen, 1994). On Austria see Irene Etzersdorfer, *Arisiert. Eine Spurensicherung im gesellschaftlichen Untergrund der Republik* (Vienna, 1995).
6. Ilse Birkwald, "Die Steuerverwaltung im Dritten Reich," in Wolfgang Leesch, Ilse Birkwald and Gerd Blumberg, eds., *Geschichte der Finanzverfassung und -verwaltung in Westfalen seit 1815* (Münster, 1998), pp. 239–286; Gerd Blumberg, "Die Zollverwaltung und die Devisenstelle im Dritten Reich," in Leesch et al., *Geschichte*, pp. 289–356.
7. Frank Bajohr, *"Arisierung" in Hamburg. Die Verdrängung der jüdischen Unternehmer 1933–45* (Hamburg, 1997); Alex Bruns-Wüstefeld, *Lohnende Geschäfte. Die "Entjudung" der Wirtschaft am Beispiel Göttingens* (Göttingen, 1997).
8. Wolfgang Dreßen, *Betrifft "Aktion 3". Deutsche verwerten jüdische Nachbarn. Dokumente zur Arisierung* (Berlin, 1998).
9. Kenkmann and Rusinek , *Verfolgung*.
10. For example in the states of Lower Saxony, Hesse, Rhineland Palatinate and Bavaria. See, for example, Hans Günther Hockerts, Christiane Kuller and Winfried Süß, *Exposé: Die Finanzverwaltung und die Verfolgung der Juden in Bayern. Ein Forschungsprojekt des Historischen Seminars der Ludwig-Maximilians-Universität München, Abteilung Neueste Geschichte und Zeitgeschichte im Auftrag des Bayerischen Staatsministers für Finanzen* (Munich, 2000); Fritz Bauer Institute of Frankfurt on Main in cooperation with the Hessian Hauptstaatsarchiv Wiesbaden, eds., *Exposé: Die fiskalische Entrechtung und Ausplünderung der Juden 1933–1945 in Hessen. Dokumentations- und Forschungsprojekt* (Frankfurt o.M./ Wiesbaden, 2000); Landeshauptarchiv Koblenz, "Enteignung, Verwaltung und Rückerstattung jüdischen Besitzes im Gebiet des Bundeslandes Rheinland-Pfalz 1933–1945. Ein Projekt zur Information über die geschichtlichen Sachverhalte und die archivarische Überlieferung (manuscript – Koblenz, 2000). On the Lower Saxony project see the following Internet site: http://www.staatsarchive.niedersachsen.de/Projekte/finanzverwaltung_und_judenverfol.htm.
11. See the contributions in "Arisierung im Nationalsozialismus. Volksgemeinschaft, Raub und Gedächtnis," (published as Irmtraud Wojak and Peter Hayes, eds., *Jahrbuch 2000 zur Geschichte und Wirkung des Holocaust* (Darmstadt, 2000); Ilsebill Barta-Fliedl and Herbert Posch, *Inventarisiert. Enteignung von Möbeln aus jüdischem Besitz*, with photographs by Arno Gisinger and a contribution by Monika Schwärzler (Vienna, 2000); Hans-Dieter Schmid, "'Finanztod'. Die Zusammenarbeit von Gestapo und Finanzverwaltung bei der Ausplünderung der Juden in Deutschland," in Gerhard Paul and Klaus-Michael Mallmann, eds., *Die Gestapo im Zweiten Weltkrieg. 'Heimatfront' und besetztes Europa* (Darmstadt, 2000), pp. 141–154, Marian Rapp, "Arisierungen in München. Die Verdrängung der jüdischen Gewerbetreibenden aus dem Wirtschaftsleben der Stadt 1933 bis 1939," *Zeitschrift für Bayerische Landesgeschichte* 63 (2000), p.123–184.
12. Horst Bathe and Dr. Johann Heinrich Kumpf , eds., *Die Mittelbehörden der Reichsfinanzverwaltung und ihre Präsidenten 1919–1945. Eine Dokumentation* (Brühl, 1999), p. 7.
13. Bill Drews and Franz Hoffmann , eds., *Von Bitter, Handwörterbuch der Preußischen Staatsverwaltung* (Berlin/Leipzig, 1928), vol. 2, p. 428ff. In the latest historical research the

regional character of the financial bureaucracy either is not recognized or is mistakenly viewed as local; see Yaacov Lozowick, *Hitlers Bürokraten, Eichmann, seine willigen Vollstrecker und die Banalität des Bösen* (Zürich/Munich, 2000), p. 66.

14. Hans Mommsen, *Beamtentum im Dritten Reich. Mit ausgewählten Quellen zur nationalsozialistischen Beamtenpolitik* (Stuttgart, 1966), p. 54. In another passage he confirms a "modes... 'purge.' 100 dismissals and over 1000 transfers"; see Werner Hagedorn, ed., *Das Finanzpersonal im Spiegel der Geschichte. Fünftausend Jahre Finanzdienst. Verfaßt von Dr. Alfons Pausch und Jutta Pausch* (Bonn, 2nd ed. 1987), p. 68.
15. See Mommsen, *Beamtentum*, p. 55.
16. See Karin Werum, "Die Entnazifizierung der Verwaltungsbeamten. Ein Beitrag zur Kontinuität der Bürokratie nach dem Ende des Dritten Reiches," *Demokratie und Recht* 4 (1989): 422–434, here p.423; Bernd A. Rusinek, "Nationalsozialismus, Judenverfolgung und Bürokratie," in Kenkmann and Rusinek , eds., *Verfolgung*, pp. 138–150, here p. 148.
17. Thomas Kleinknecht, "Sammelrezension von Neuerscheinungen zur Polizeigeschichte," *Westfälische Forschungen* 47 (1997): 922–927, here p. 926.
18. See Gerd Blumberg, "Flucht über die Grenze. Die Hollandflucht im Dritten Reich über die niederländisch-westfälische Grenze und Kontrollmaßnahmen der Steuer- und Zollbehörden," *Unser Bocholt* 46 (1995): 3–19, here p. 5. In the area of border customs surveillance (*Zollgrenzschutz*) there were constant jurisdictional disputes between the Reich Ministry of Finance and the RFSS; see Thomas Sandkühler, "Von der 'Gegnerabwehr' zum Judenmord. Grenzpolizei und Zollgrenzschutz im NS-Staat," *'Durchschnittstäter' . Handeln und Motivation* 16 (2000) (= *Beiträge zur Geschichte des Nationalsozialismus* 16-2000): 95–154, here pp. 99–103.
19. My reconstruction of this financial official's life history is based on documents of the denazification files in: Nordrheinwestfälisches Hauptstaatsarchiv Düsseldorf (NWHStAD), Bestand Entnazifizierungsakten (NW 1039), Bd. H 297 and the "main file" (*Stockakte*) on Heinrich Heising preserved in the Münster Regional Tax Office.
20. NWHStAD, Bestand Entnazifizierungsakten (NW 1039), Bd. H 297.
21. Birkwald, "Die Steuerverwaltung," pp. 239–286, here pp. 247–248. A substantially lower degree of organization is found among salaried employees: of the 1,523 salaried employees only 789 and of the 505 workers only 68 were members of the NSDAP.
22. In 1937, 86 percent of all Prussian civil servants were members of the NSDAP, in the remaining Reich territory only 63 percent; see Wolfgang Reinhard, *Geschichte der Staatsgewalt. Eine vergleichende Verfassungsgeschichte von den Anfängen bis zur Gegenwart* (Munich, 1999), p. 472.
23. See Bernd Haunfelder, *1796–1996. Zweihundert Jahre Zwei-Löwen-Klub zu Münster* (Münster, 1996).
24. See NWHStAD, NW 1039/H-279.
25. See Arno Herzig, Karl Teppe and Andreas Determann , eds., *Verdrängung und Vernichtung der Juden in Westfalen* (Münster, 1994), pp. 10–13. Statistics of the Director of the Westphalian Tax Office of April 1939 indicate that in Westphalia 2,533 Jews were liable for taxes under the Jewish Wealth Levy (*Judenvermögensabgabe*); See Stefan Mehl, *Das Reichsfinanzministerium und die Verfolgung der deutschen Juden 1933–1944* (Berlin, 1990), p. 70ff.
26. See Bajohr, *"Arisierung" in Hamburg*, p. 189.
27. The history of the Baer family's suffering was reconstructed from surviving foreign-exchange records in the archives of the Oberfinanzdirektion Münster, D-107B-373/58-Z III-62, and the compensation records of the Düsseldorf District Government, Abteilung Wiedergutmachung, BZK Nr. 60826, 60894a, 60895a, 60897, and 60897a. I am grateful to Frau Julia Volmer of Münster for information on compensation records (*Entschädigungsüberlieferung*).
28. District government of Dusseldorf, Abteilung Wiedergutmachung, BZK Nr. 60896a.
29. See Blumberg, "Etappen," p. 23.
30. Marcel Reich-Ranicki, *Mein Leben* (Stuttgart, 1999), p. 53.

31. See Eberhard Jäckel, Peter Longerich and Julius Schoeps, eds., *Enzyklopädie des Holocaust. Die Verfolgung der europäischen Juden*, vol. I, 2nd ed. (Munich/Zürich, 1998), p. 134.
32. Peter Gay, *Meine deutsche Frage. Jugend in Berlin 1933–1939*, 2nd ed. (Munich, 1999), p. 164.
33. See Dorothee Mußgnug, *Die Reichsfluchtsteuer 1931–1953* (Berlin, 1993).
34. See Blumberg, "*Etappen,*" p. 29ff.
35. See Mehl, *Das Reichsfinanzministerium*, p. 44.
36. Raul Hilberg, *Die Vernichtung der europäischen Juden*, vol. 1 (Frankfurt on Main, 1990), p. 145.
37. See Blumberg, "Flucht über die Grenze," pp. 5–6.
38. See Bajohr, *"Arisierung" in Hamburg*, p. 189ff.
39. See Blumberg, "Etappen," p. 18.
40. See Genehmigungsbescheid des Oberfinanzpräsidenten Westfalen, Devisenstelle, 1 July 1938, in Oberfinanzdirektion (OFD) Münster, Gruppe Devisenüberwachung, D 1017B-373/58-Z III-62, not paginated.
41. See the filled-out printed form of Oberfinanzpräsident Westfalen in Münster, Devisenstelle, 7 July 1938, ibid. not paginated.
42. See Wolfgang Lotz, *Die Deutsche Reichspost 1933–1945. Eine politische Verwaltungsgeschichte*, vol. I: *1933–1939* (Berlin, 1999), p. 172ff.
43. Communication of Irmgard Baer to the Devisenstelle beim Oberfinanzpräsidenten Westfalen, 27 December 1938 in OFD Münster, D 1017B-373/58-ZIII-62, not paginated.
44. Dieter Pohl, "'Rassenpolitik', Judenverfolgung und Völkermord," in Horst Möller, Volker Dahm and Hartmut Mehringer, eds., *Die tödliche Utopie. Bilder, Texte, Dokumente, Daten zum Dritten Reich*, 2nd ed. (Munich, 2000), pp. 202–261, here p. 206.
45. Information from the contemporary witness H., Detmold.
46. Gay, *Meine deutsche Frage*, p. 156.
47. See Birkwald, "Die Steuerverwaltung," p. 266; Susanne Freund, "*'Arisierung' in Münster – dargestellt anhand lebensgeschichtlicher Zeugnisse,*" in Kenkmann and Rusinek, *Verfolgung*, pp. 41–56, here p. 43.
48. Avraham Barkai, *Vom Boykott zur "Entjudung". Der wirtschaftliche Existenzkampf der Juden im Dritten Reich 1933–1943* (Frankfurt on Main, 1988), p. 150f.
49. ibid., p. 267.
50. Blumberg, "Etappen," p. 26.
51. See the procedures in OFD Münster, D 1017B-373/58-ZIII-62, not paginated.
52. See Blumberg, "Etappen," pp. 26–27.
53. See ibid., p. 32.
54. Genehmigungsbescheid des Oberfinanzpräsidenten Westfalen, Devisenstelle, 9 January 1938 [mistakenly dated incorrectly—it should be 9 January 1939: A.K.], OFD Münster, D 1017B-373/58-ZIII-62, not paginated; Bescheinigung des Oberstadtdirektors Bielefeld—Vertriebenenamt und Amt für Wiedergutmachung, 21 September 1960, Düsseldorf District Government (Bezirksregierung Düsseldorf), Abteilung Wiedergutmachung, BZK No. 60896a.
55. Schreiben der Zollfahndungsstelle Dortmund an den Oberfinanzpräsidenten Westfalen—Devisenstelle, 6 January 1939, OFD Münster, D 1017B-373/58-ZIII-62, not paginated.
56. See Bescheinigung des Finanzamtes Bielefeld, 6 January 1939 in ibid., not paginated.
57. See letter from Irmgard Baer to the Finanzoberpräsident Westfalen of 3 January 1939 in ibid., not paginated.
58. The hand-luggage list is printed in facsimile form in Kenkmann and Rusinek, *Verfolgung*, ill. 13.
59. Drawing on § 57 of the Law on Foreign-exchange Control of 12 December 1933. See ibid.
60. Bescheid des Oberfinanzpräsidenten Westfalen in Münster (Devisenstelle-Überwachungsabteilung) an Irmgard Sarah Baer, 9 March 1940, OFD Münster, D 1017B-373/58-ZIII-62, no pagination.

61. See Monika Minninger, Joachim Meynert and Friedhelm Schäffer, *Antisemitisch Verfolgte. Registriert in Bielefeld 1933–45. Eine Dokumentation jüdischer Einzelschicksale* (= Bielefelder Beiträge zur Stadt- und Regionalgeschichte, vol. 4 (Bielefeld, 1985), no. 25, p. 15.
62. Peter Longerich, *Politik der Vernichtung. Eine Gesamtdarstellung der nationalsozialistischen Judenverfolgung* (Munich/Zürich, 1998), p. 446.
63. See I. Arndt, "Entziehung und Verbringung jüdischen Vermögens (Ausland und Deutschland)," *Gutachten des Instituts für Zeitgeschichte*, II (1963):92–125, here p. 122.
64. See Bajohr, "*Arisierung*," in *Hamburg*, p. 296.
65. See the printed protocol excerpts of the discussion in Birkwald, *Die Steuerverwaltung*, p. 276ff.
66. See as an exemplary case the confiscation of property belonging to Albert Samson, Bielefeld, in the North Rhine-Westphalian Archive in Detmold, D 26, No. 4774, not paginated.
67. The Eleventh Decree regarding the Reich Citizenship Law (*11. Verordnung zum Reichsbürgergesetz*) of 25 November 1941 stipulated in § 2 the loss of German citizenship if a Jew's permanent residence was located abroad, whereby the Generalgouvernement and other occupied territories also counted as "abroad" and, in § 3, required the automatic forfeiture of Jewish property to the Reich.
68. Mehl, *Das Reichsfinanzministerium*, p. 97.
69. See Ulrich Friedrich Opfermann, "Zigeunerverfolgung, Enteignung, Umverteilung. Das Beispiel der Wittgensteiner Kreisstadt Berleburg," in Kenkmann and Rusinek, *Verfolgung*, pp. 67–86.
70. See, for example, OFD Münster, Finanzamt Siegen, Titelbuch 1943/44, not paginated.
71. See Oberfinanzdirektion Münster, Stockakte Heinrich Heising.
72. Bernd-A. Rusinek, "Deutsche Eliten im 20. Jahrhundert," Tilman Spengler, ed., *Die neuen Eliten* (= Kursbuch 139 [Berlin, 2000]), pp. 31–44, here p. 41.
73. Otto Hintze, "Der Beamtenstand," in Kersten Krüger , ed., *Otto Hintze, Beamtentum und Bürokratie* (Göttingen, 1981), pp. 16–77, here p. 19.
74. Michael Ruck, "Die deutsche Verwaltung im totalitären Führerstaat 1933–1945," *Jahrbuch für Europäische Verwaltungsgeschichte* 10 (1998): 1–48, 35.
75. Wolfgang Seibel, "Market for Mass Crime? Inter-Institutional Competition and the Initiation of the Holocaust in France, 1940–1942, " *Journal of Organization Theory and Behavior* 5(2002), 219–257.
76. Cited according to Götz Aly, "*Endlösung.*" *Völkerverschiebung und der Mord an den europäischen Juden* (Frankfurt on Main, 1995), p. 385. Zygmunt Bauman attributes an "unheard of efficiency" to German bureaucracy in implementing the order to cleanse the Reich of Jews (*judenrein*), see Zygmunt Bauman, *Dialektik der Ordnung. Die Moderne und der Holocaust* (Hamburg, 1992), p. 119.
77. See Hannah Arendt, *Elemente totalitärer Herrschaft* (Frankfurt on Main, 1958), p. 277; see also Claudia Althaus, *Erfahrung denken. Hannah Arendts Weg von der Zeitgeschichte zur politischen Theorie* (Göttingen, 2000).

CHAPTER 10

ORGANIZED LOOTING: THE NAZI SEIZURE OF JEWISH PROPERTY IN THE NETHERLANDS, 1940–1945

Gerard Aalders

Introduction

During the Second World War, the Nazi occupiers in the Netherlands carried out a thorough and almost perfectly organized program in which 135,000 Dutch Jews were robbed of their possessions. The confiscation of Dutch Jewish property was carried out in an extremely systematic way. Expropriations were generally based on decrees (*Verordnungen*) which had the force of statute law, but in addition, the occupying forces sometimes made use of "measures," "ordinances," or "orders" issued by the Sicherheitsdienst (SD), the German security police. These were usually used to sanction the theft of everyday items, such as bicycles, radios and small household effects. According to my calculations, in total the Nazis stole at least NLG 1 billion in assets from the Dutch Jews.[1] This is the equivalent of about NLG 14 billion today (or more than $6 billion).

Of approximately 107,000 people deported from the Netherlands to the extermination camps only some 5,200 returned, a mortality rate of 84 percent. This was one of the highest in Europe, being much higher than other Western European states such as Belgium (38 percent), France (29 percent), Denmark (1.4 percent), Norway (42 percent) and Italy (18 percent) and more in line with rates experienced in Eastern Europe, such as Poland (93 percent) or Yugoslavia (83 percent)[2] While the debate on the precise reasons for the disproportionate level of deportations and mortality of Jews from the Netherlands continues,[3] the purpose of this chapter is to explain how the expropriation of Jewish property in the Netherlands was carried out and the context and circumstances in which it took place.

Civil Government during the Occupation

The German attack on the Netherlands took place early in the morning of 10 May 1940. Five days later, all Dutch forces had surrendered and the German occupation, which was to last until 5 May 1945, began. The country remained under military control until 29 May 1940, when a German civil government was introduced, headed by the Austrian-born Dr. Arthur Seyss-Inquart, who was appointed by Hitler as Reichskommissar (Reich Commissioner) to lead the Dutch administrative apparatus. The Dutch government had fled into exile in London, but had instructed the secretaries-general (the chief civil servants in the ministries) to stay at their posts and to continue their work, provided that it remained within the terms of the existing laws and constitution. In effect, the occupier took over a fully operational administrative system. The secretaries-general were placed under the supervision of four German General Commissioners (Generalkommissare): Hans Fischböck (Financial and Economic Affairs), Friedrich Wimmer (Justice and Administration), Hanns Albin Rauter (Higher SS and Police Leader) and Fritz Schmidt (Party and Special Affairs). Fischböck and Wimmer had been nominated by Reichskommissar Seyss-Inquart but Schmidt and Rauter were the personal appointees of the Führer.[4] Hitler's choices placed Seyss-Inquart at a serious disadvantage, because they restricted his personal control in both political and police matters. Schmidt's appointment created an additional problem for Seyss-Inquart in that, through him, influential members of the National Socialist German Workers Party (NSDAP) were able to exert considerable influence on governmental matters in the Netherlands. Likewise, the appointment of Rauter provided SS-leader Heinrich Himmler with a guarantee of influence in the Netherlands, as it had been Himmler who had originally brought Rauter to the attention of Hitler for the post of General Commissioner of SS and police matters. Furthermore, Seyss-Inquart was already indebted to Himmler because the SS Chief had recommended him to Hitler for the post of Reichskommissar. Seyss-Inquart himself was a moderate National Socialist with little or no power base in the party.[5]

Thus it is evident that, through the appointment of General Commissioners Rauter and Schmidt, leading Nazis in Berlin had assured themselves of considerable influence in the Netherlands. In practice, it meant that the ideological aims of the regime in Berlin could be carried out more easily and effectively than if the country had remained under military administration. Himmler, for instance, could give orders directly through Hanns Rauter, while in the rest of occupied Europe he had to communicate through the military authorities. The effect of having the right man in the right place was to create a better, more thorough, and smoother-working organization, something that was reflected in the speed with which anti-Jewish measures in the Netherlands were introduced. If one compares the Netherlands with Belgium (the latter having a military regime similar to that in most occupied European countries), the conclusion must be that, although the deportations in both countries started in the same week, the authorities in Holland were better and more thoroughly prepared than the functionaries in Brussels. The historian Bob Moore has observed that the competition between organizations and individuals within the German governmental structures in the Netherlands may also have contributed to the speed with which the system of persecution and deportation machinery was developed. However, as Moore has also observed, "If the 'system' was driven initially by internal conflicts and the wishes of German functionaries inside the Netherlands, by the summer of 1942 their leadership had been superseded by the demands being made from Berlin."

The quotas for deportation were dictated from Berlin by Adolf Eichmann's Referat IVB4, a subdivision of the Gestapo (Secret State Police) and thus of the Reichssicherheitshauptamt (RSHA), the Reich Security Main Office. The RSHA, under the overall command of SS-leader Heinrich Himmler was run under the supervision of both the SS and state agencies, and controlled offices responsible for security, police matters and intelligence, including the Gestapo and the Sicherheitsdienst, the security and intelligence service of the SS.[6] However, the increasing SS influence in the Netherlands was seen mainly in relation to the deportation program. Its influence on the looting of Jewish assets was limited, leaving it much more firmly in the hands of Seyss-Inquart and his confidants, the General Commissioners Fischböck (Finance) and Wimmer (Justice).

After Seyss-Inquart's inauguration in May 1940, no immediate steps were taken against Jewish property. The installation of the new regime took some time and the war against France, which had begun on the same day as the attack on the Low Countries, was still going on. At this early stage the Germans did not want trouble and they took great pains to avoid civil disturbances or unrest. Hitler had much better uses for his troops in France. This deliberate avoidance of unrest and disturbance remained a remarkable constant in the German policy vis-à-vis the Jews, as we shall observe later. This initial attitude also probably served to lull the Dutch Jews into a false sense of security. They were undoubtedly aware of what was happening to their German coreligionists a mere 150 kilometers east of Amsterdam across the border, but it remains to be seen if they fully realized the seriousness of the situation. The Dutch (Jewish) historian, Jacob Presser, describes a conversation of his father with a non-Jewish friend on the day of the invasion. When asked what he was going to do now with the Germans all over Holland, Presser Sr. answered: "We are doing nothing. Why should we?"[7] In fact, the Germans did not expect to encounter much trouble in the Netherlands. The Dutch were considered to be fellow "Aryans" who might be induced to accept National Socialist ideology and, in due course, become an integrated part of the Third Reich. The Dutch were, with a "firm but very gentle hand," to be brought back into the "Germanic community."

Reich Commissioner Josef Terboven of Norway (which had been occupied in April 1940) had provided Berlin's blueprint on how to deal with conquered nations that from a racial perspective resembled the German people.

The installation of a civil government had important political and psychological advantages, not least in going some way to quelling fears that the country might be annexed.[8] This undoubtedly contributed to keeping the population quiet, and thereby meant that a relatively small occupation force was needed to control the country.

The Hague Convention on Land Warfare

With hindsight, it seems quite remarkable that the Nazi regime tried to keep up an appearance of adhering to international law. The Germans often sought to justify their (looting) actions by reference to the Hague Convention on Land Warfare (1907), to which Imperial Germany had been a signatory, and the Hitler regime was always at great pains to take account of the Hague Convention and abided by its terms while carrying out the process of expropriating assets in conquered countries.[9] When Seyss-Inquart issued his decrees to seize property from the Dutch Jews, he always referred to the Führer Decree (*Erlass des Führers*) of 18 May, 1940. According to this decree Seyss-Inquart was directly subordinate to Hitler as head of the German state, and derived his authority as supreme representative of the occupying power from the Führer, in line with the Hague Convention. Section 1 of the Führer Decree read: "Should the interests of the Greater German Reich ... render it necessary, the Reichskommissar may take the necessary measures, including those of a legislative nature. These decrees by the Reichskommissar have the force of law."[10] German interests took precedence, but Dutch laws "hitherto valid" would remain in force, at least insofar as they were "compatible with the occupation" and as long as they were not contrary to the provisions contained in the Führer Decree of 18 May 1940. It is evident that Hitler's line on respecting the laws of the occupied Netherlands if "compatible with the occupation" was markedly different from the phrasing in article 43 of the Hague Convention where the laws were to be respected "unless absolutely prevented," and provided him with ample space to maneuver as he wished.

Decree 3 of 29 May 1940 made the secretaries-general of the Netherlands ministries responsible to Seyss-Inquart for the proper conduct of their offices "within the limits of their jurisdiction." The Decree also made the rest of the Dutch governmental structure and civil service absolutely subordinate to the occupier. The highest legislative and executive power was vested in the Reichskommissar. The result of this power concentration was that, behind a façade of legality, Berlin could easily and effectively carry out all the measures in the Netherlands it wanted, including looting. It produced a new phenomenon: looting by decree instead of at gunpoint. The gun had been replaced by the pen of the legislator.

For the population in general and for the Jews in particular, the Nazi civil administration in the Netherlands was particularly detrimental because it was more concerned with implementing the (looting) directives from Berlin than its military counterparts in the other Western European occupied countries. As a result of the experience gained in the Third Reich from 1933 onwards (and subsequently in Hitler's native country Austria after the Anschluss), the Nazis were able to set up an efficient machinery for expropriation in a very short time. Military administrations lacked this experience, which meant that organized looting in their jurisdictions took more time to become effective. However, it is likely that this only delayed the process and made little difference to the overall quantity of property seized in each country. Nevertheless, speed and time were important factors because Nazi Germany was in increasing, desperate need for foreign exchange to support its war effort, and the wealth of the European Jews could undoubtedly be of substantial help to meet this need. We must bear in mind that certain strategic materials that were crucial for the conduct of war could only be purchased with hard currency in the world market, where Reichsmarks were not welcome.

Finally, it can be argued that the presence of Reichskommissar Seyss-Inquart and his General Commissioner for Finance, Hans Fischböck, in the Netherlands was seriously detrimental to the Jews because both had gained experience in removing the Jews from the Austrian economy. Both men were professionals in matters of looting. Thus, while it is difficult to quantify their role precisely, there is no doubt that all these factors contributed to the establishment of an effective machinery for looting in the Netherlands.

One crucial question is the role played by the Dutch secretaries-general in the looting process. Did they try to halt, or at least protest against the expropriation measures that were taken against their Jewish fellow countrymen? Under the circumstances, stopping the process would have been impossible, but protests were certainly an option, and yet seldom employed. The secretaries-general did mount protests on one or two occasions but these were neither convincing nor sustained. They could have resigned but only a few chose this course of action. Soon they adopted a far-reaching accommodation with the new regime and the attitude of these men undoubtedly had a negative influence on their subordinates at all levels of the civil service, including the Dutch police forces. A broadcast from the Dutch government-in-exile in October 1943 described the attitude of the majority of the civil servants as follows: "They [the civil servants] had spent their whole lives accustomed to obey, they were always—and rightly—so proud of the impeccable execution of their tasks and conscientious fulfilment of their duties, that they brought the same conscientiousness and the same fulfilment of duty to the scrupulous organisation of the plunder of our country, to the advantage of the enemy."[11]

Dutch society was heavily imbued with a spirit of *gezagsgetrouwheid*—law-abiding, compliant, and docile people with a deep respect for authority. In this respect, civil servants and Jews were no exception. This culture of deference makes the activities of those who did engage in resistance or who risked their lives by hiding the 25,000–30,000 Jews who tried to escape deportation all the more admirable. It was mainly student groups that saved 4,000 Jewish children by rescuing them from the hands of the Germans and then distributing them to foster families in different parts of the country.[12] Yet, although around 16,000 Jewish adults and children were saved by going into hiding, they did not escape the German expropriation measures. When they returned to their homes after the war, they appeared to have been as thoroughly robbed as the other victims of Nazi racial hatred.

Before turning to the methods of looting used by the Germans in the Netherlands, it is worth examining the methods employed in the Reich to provide a comparison for those applied subsequently in the Low Countries.

The Looting of Jews in Germany and Austria

Governmental sources that might provide an insight into the plans to expropriate Jewish property in Germany are poor. While discriminatory measures began soon after Hitler became Chancellor in January 1933, they fall outside the scope of this chapter, but it is possible to chart the process in the Third Reich from the policies adopted by the regime toward the Jews. An attack on Jewish property was a natural consequence of the Nazis' ideological perception of Jews and the contemptible role they were judged to have played in German history. In the view of the National Socialists, the Jews had swindled, deceived, and bled the German people. They were seen as the parasites of the unsuspecting, innocent Germans and for that reason they deserved to be dispossessed of what they had taken from the "Aryans."

It is not known exactly when Hitler gave orders to start the removal of Jews or "Aryanization" of the German economy as the first stage on the way to total expropriation, but we do know that on 22 April 1938 plans were discussed for the "Aryanization" of Jewish capital. At this meeting, under the chairmanship of Reichsmarshall Hermann Göring, it was decided that Jews should have their capital registered as a first step on the road to complete sequestration. As a result, a decree for the registration of Jewish firms was issued on 30 June 1938. A week after this meeting (29 April 1938) a gathering of ministers, including Göring, decided that Jews should be totally removed from the German economy. However, while the idea had been discussed, its realization was going to be a rather slow process, complicated by, among other things, detailed discussions with the Foreign Ministry about what to do with foreign Jews living in Germany. While it can be argued that this debate impeded the process, it undoubtedly did not stop it. The seizure of foreign securities was the next phase in the material warfare against the Jews, a decision taken in November 1938. This began with compulsory registration, followed by the actual surrender of the securities themselves. However these were not resold until 1941, as it was feared that a huge influx of Jewish-owned securities might disturb the stock market. The proceeds, as in all the looting procedures, went to the Reich. The plunder of the Jews continued with the issuing of further new decrees: new ordinances for new targets. At the beginning of 1939, the Jews were forced by decree to offer their precious metals and jewelry to the municipal pawnbrokers, who paid minimal rates, in most cases not exceeding 10 percent of the real value.

The last phase of this process began with the mass deportations to the East in October 1941. Jewish possessions that had not already been transferred to the state were confiscated on the basis of Decree 11 *(Verordnung zum Reichsbürgergesetz,* 25 November 1941), which ordained that the assets of all Jews who had their domicile abroad—either voluntarily or involuntarily—should be turned over to the Nazi regime. This measure provided Hitler with the "legal" basis to confiscate the belongings of Jews who had been deported to the extermination camps: they had their involuntary domicile abroad.[13] A striking example of Nazi logic! In summary: from the summer of 1938, the Reich gradually and systematically confiscated the wealth of its Jewish citizens using a series of legal decrees. Returning to the Netherlands, it is possible to compare these methods with those employed in an occupied country.

Types and Dimensions of Looting

According to international law, an occupying power has certain rights to issue laws in the occupied country. In the Netherlands, the Germans sanctioned their plundering through the use of *Verordnungen* (decrees) that had the force of law. Dutch citizens were required, by law, to declare their possessions to the occupiers. There was one major difference in the treatment of Jews and non-Jews: the former were required to declare all their assets, while the latter were forced to declare only certain types of goods. When compared with the Jewish population, the non-Jews were treated rather "mildly." The Jews were systematically robbed of all their belongings while non-Jews were forced at certain stages of the war to hand in certain goods, mostly in fixed quantities.

In surveying the methods of plundering used in the Netherlands, various forms of pillaging can be identified, such as looting "by purchase," "indirect looting," "compulsory charity," confiscation, enforced surrender, and impositions of collective fines. Robbery of Jews (at the beginning of the occupation before the looting decrees were issued) and non-Jews "by purchase" or "indirect looting" was popular with the German authorities as it gave the appearance of honest trading. Looting by purchase (often referred to as "indirect looting" or "technical looting") came about when citizens were forced by the occupiers to sell their goods (including works of art) under duress, usually at unreasonably low prices. The Allied Powers were aware of these processes from an early date and warned the Nazis in a Declaration of 3 January 1943:

> The Allies reserve all their rights to declare invalid any transfers of, or dealings with, property, rights and interests of any description whatsoever which are, or have been, situated in the territories which have come under the occupation or

control, direct or indirect, of the governments with which they are at war or which belong or have belonged, to persons, including juridical persons, resident in such territories. This warning applies whether such transfers or dealings have taken the form of open looting or plunder, or of transactions apparently legal in form, even when they purport to be voluntarily effected.[14]

At that time, the Allies' main worry was that Germany would use the confiscated hard currency, gold, silver, jewels, etc. to purchase strategic raw materials and goods on the world market. It had little to do with ethics and Christian virtues such as "Thou shalt not steal."

Few dared to oppose any of the forms of looting, as the possibility of a German on the doorstep threatening prison or incarceration in a camp was very persuasive. Sometimes individuals were "advised" to sell and told that, if they refused, their property would be confiscated. In that case they would receive nothing at all. This form of indirect looting was not regulated by decrees, unlike the plunder of the Jews, and any citizen could fall victim to it. Art collectors in particular became familiar with this type of theft.

Indirect Looting

The (indirect) looting of art started almost immediately after the occupation in May 1940. However, the Dutch national museums did not suffer from this form of German greed and were excluded from the process. The reason for this was a logical one: simply that, if the Netherlands was to be integrated in the Reich as a more or less autonomous province, it did not matter very much if works of art were on exhibition in Amsterdam or in Berlin.

Private collections were a different matter. Art collections owned by Jews were subject to the Nazi plunder laws (according to the so-called Second Liro Decree), but, even before its promulgation in May 1942, the Germans had succeeded in obtaining a substantial proportion of Jewish cultural riches. The Germans invariably paid in guilders, which created a financial problem because these were Reichsmarks that had been converted into Dutch guilders. The Reichsbank in Berlin refused to take back its own currency and thus it remained with the Dutch Central Bank, The Nederlandsche Bank. As a consequence, after the war the Nederlandsche Bank was saddled with about 4.5 billion Reichsmarks, which had become worthless when the German state collapsed in May 1945.

One of the most active "buying organizations" for art was the Dienststelle Mühlmann (Mühlmann Department), named after its leader Dr. Kajetan Mühlmann, a friend of Seyss-Inquart. Many thousands of paintings and other artworks found their way to Germany through the offices of his Dienststelle. The "regular customers" included Hitler and Göring but Seyss-Inquart always made sure that Hitler had the first choice. Both top Nazis also had their own special agents, who roamed the art markets in occupied Western Europe on their behalf. The items earmarked for Hitler went to the Führermuseum in Linz, the Austrian town where the Führer had spent his youth. The museum, which was never built, was intended to be the biggest in the world. Göring had a huge estate, Karin Hall, filled with (partly stolen) art, close to Berlin. Art that did not satisfy their quality criteria was left to other high-ranking Nazis and German museums, galleries, and art dealers.

The plundering of art collections, books, and archives forms a separate chapter in history's greatest example of banditry. Hitler had created a special unit for this type of theft, the Einsatzstab Reichsleiter Rosenberg [ERR]), which arrived directly behind the victorious German troops. The staff of the ERR (Reich Leader Rosenberg's Special Task Force) included (art) historians, linguists, literature experts, musicologists, and archivists: specialists for specialist theft. The ERR had its sights set chiefly on the book and art collections of Jews and Freemasons "and the ideological opponents of National Socialism related to these groups who are the instigators of the war conducted against the Reich." In order to understand the hostile thoughts of these opponents it was deemed necessary to confiscate their books, art collections, and archives, because only in this way could their "perfidious" trains of thought be analyzed and combated. In the Netherlands, the ERR was not very active in the art sector because that was left to Mühlmann and the special art agents of Hitler (Hans Posse and, after his death, Hermann Voss) and Göring (Walter Andreas Hofer).

Direct looting, at gunpoint so to speak, did take place, but remained rather unusual until the autumn of 1944, the eve of Germany's defeat. Private looting by soldiers was strictly forbidden, mainly because—in the Nazi view—all Jewish property was deemed to belong to the Reich. "Looting by decree" took absolute precedence. It was mainly Jews who suffered from this method of dispossession and it was carried out in three consecutive phases: first definition of the victim, then registration, and finally the foundation of an institution where the assets were deposited and the proceeds administered. In the Netherlands the "Gypsies" and Jews were the main victims of this process. There is hardly any information available about the seizure of "Gypsy" possessions and discussion here is therefore restricted to the Jewish case.

Definition of Jew

The German expropriation of Jewish assets included expropriation of non profit associations and foundations, companies, and individuals. Before the victim was robbed he had to be defined. A "Jew" was defined in decree VO189/1940 (article 4) as:

> (1) ... a person with at least three grandparents who are full-blooded Jews by race.
> (2) A Jew is also a person with at least two grandparents who are full-blooded Jews and who 1) was either a member of the Jewish religious community on May 9, 1940 or who subsequently became a member or 2) was married to a Jew on May 9, 1940 or subsequently married a Jew.
> (3) A grandparent shall be a full-blooded Jew if he or she was a member of the Jewish religious community.

This decree, promulgated on 22 October 1940, ordered the registration of Jewish companies as the first stage toward confiscation. This conformed to the pattern established in Germany. The definition of "Jew" may seem quite precise, but it still created many borderline cases. For instance, adopted children and (in particular) so-called mixed marriages between Jews and non-Jews *(Mischehen)* caused many administrative problems which could only be resolved by a deluge of provisions, exemptions and individual measures.[15] The Nazis were always eager to keep up the appearances of (sham) justice.

Registration

After the definition of a Jew, the logical second step followed: registration in writing. Decree VO6/1941 of 10 January 1941 ordered the registration of all Jews. Both Dutch and foreign Jews were forced to complete a questionnaire. Seyss-Inquart wanted to know where they lived, the structure of their families, their addresses, and their professions. For that purpose, Dutch local authorities set up offices in every community. The registering process started almost immediately after the decree's promulgation and was completed in only a few months. The response was overwhelming and leaves the impression that hardly anyone attempted to evade registration. On 22 August 1941 160,820 registration forms had been submitted and 140,522 Jews had, on the basis of their own data, been labelled as "full-blooded" Jews. This total comprised 68,388 "full-blooded" Jewish males and 72,164 "full-blooded" Jewish females. Amsterdam, the capital of the Netherlands, had by far the largest municipal Jewish population: 79,140 souls. In addition, 22,252 Jews were registered as foreign nationals, 14,652 of them Germans who had left Hitler's Reich and settled in the Netherlands before the outbreak of war in the hope of finding a safe place to live.[16]

Explaining the amazing docility and compliance of the Jews is difficult, as is explaining their compliance with the registration process. Dutch Jews appeared to be credulous and unsuspecting. Holland had not been at war since the days of Napoleon in the early nineteenth century and pogroms were an unknown phenomenon in the Low Countries.[17] They were not used to being discriminated against by the Dutch state on account of their Jewish identity. Anti-Semitism within the Dutch population was, although not absent, certainly not fierce. Jews were rather well integrated into Dutch society, but the Netherlands at that time was a society subdivided into pillars based on political ideology and religion. The Jewish community had its own organizations and structures, like for instance the Catholics, the Protestants and the Social Democrats. The groups in this pillarized society did not mix easily and, in general, the Jewish community showed no great inclination toward mixing, thus remaining a more or less isolated minority group, separate from any of the main pillars. Furthermore, the Jews in the Netherlands refused to believe that what had happened to Jews in Germany could also happen to them: after all Holland was not Germany. Nonregistration carried a maximum prison sentence of five years but that seems to have been of minor importance: the law (i.e. decree VO6/1941) ordered registration and the Dutch (the Jews being no exceptions) followed their traditional deference to authority and respect for the rule of law. Obedience to the law, not the possible five years imprisonment, was the main incentive for Jews to fill in the registration questionnaire. They were not lawbreakers, least of all if disobedience might result in a long imprisonment. It was also reasoned that avoidance was no use because their names and addresses could already easily be found in the up-to-date local population registers, or otherwise—for the religious Jews—in the records of the synagogues to which they belonged.[18]

Foundation of the Administrative Apparatus for Looting

Having defined the target group and gathered information about their personal circumstances, the Germans were in a position to begin the actual looting process. Nevertheless, the physical seizure of the assets concerned still required thorough preparations. What Seyss-Inquart needed was an apparatus for the administration of the process, and storage facilities for the movable goods.

On 31 May 1941, the Reichskommissar founded the Vermögensverwaltungs- und Rentenanstalt (VVRA), the Property Management and Interest Institute. The enormous proceeds of the "Aryanization" and the sequestration of noncommercial associations and foundations were processed at this Institute, with an initial capital of just 100 guilders.

The most infamous institution for looting was founded in Amsterdam in July 1941. To the outside world it looked exactly like a bank and it went under the name of Lippmann, Rosenthal & Co., usually abbreviated to Liro. There were two concerns that bore the name Lippmann, Rosenthal & Co. distinguished only by their addresses, Nieuwe Spiegelstraat and Sarphatistraat. The institution in the Sarphatistraat, disguised as a bank, was to acquire an evil reputation as the "robbery bank." Here the Jews were forced to open an account into which their money and securities were transferred. This false "bank" was under the supervision of Seyss-Inquart's representative at the Central Dutch Bank, Dr. Albert Bühler, who in turn reported to Generalkommissar Fischböck.

The name of the new "bank" was chosen intentionally, as the "other" Lippmann, Rosenthal & Co., with its offices at Nieuwe Spiegelstraat, was run by two Jewish bankers and had an outstanding reputation. The good name of the older bank was therefore used to allay any disquiet and possible panic that might result from the forced transfers. The mandatory depositors had no direct power to dispose of the assets and valuables they deposited. Use of their own accounts was severely restricted and invariably involved a mountain of paperwork. Of course, the Jews felt disappointed and were irritated about the way they were treated, but the fact that Liro was ostensibly a Jewish bank with an excellent name made them less suspicious and strengthened the false hope that the measures would be of a temporary nature.[19] Even the Jewish directors of Liro, Nieuwe Spiegelstraat, who were still in charge during the summer of 1941, albeit under the supervision of a custodian, advised their staff to go over to the "new branch" because their long-term prospects with the mother bank, under the dark clouds of the approaching "Aryanization" were bad. Their future seemed therefore to be more secure at the Sarphatistraat. Thus, with the foundation of VVRA and Liro all the preconditions for a successful looting operation had been established.

The orders for the expropriation of Jews came, not surprisingly, directly from Berlin. Seyss-Inquart himself, with his ample experience in looting matters, played a central role, but it was Fischböck who was the brain behind the execution of this complicated operation. These two men were able to counter successfully an attack on their authority in this sphere by Rauter and the Chief of the Security Police and SD, Dr. Wilhelm Harster, who also had designs on Jewish assets. For what was undoubtedly the main prize, namely Jewish businesses and assets, Fischböck had developed a plan to remove the Jews from the Dutch economy in phases until they were completely excluded. His plan was to concentrate Jewish assets in one single bank. This was a lesson he had drawn from his work in Austria and Germany, where the "Aryanization" and confiscation of Jewish assets had been accompanied by widespread corruption. Fischböck had discussed his plan with Göring, who had approved it. The plans of Rauter and Harster had been much vaguer and, with no higher sanction, their challenge evaporated.

The Sequestration of Jewish Foundations, Companies, and other Assets

The first move toward the liquidation of "non-commercial associations and foundations" was made as early as 20 September 1940. Decree VO145/40 ordered their registration. This measure did not apply exclusively to Jewish institutions. For instance, non-Jewish trade unions and football clubs were also affected. The reason was that the Germans wanted to keep all societies, clubs, associations, and unions under control because these were places and institutions where many people gathered. In the German occupiers' perception, such places were considered as potential centers for subversive actions and resistance. It was therefore a purely precautionary measure to keep them under control. The difference between Jewish and non-Jewish associations and foundations was that the former were all liquidated and their assets sold. The non-Jewish institutions escaped that fate.

In early 1941, the Jewish business community became the target. The basis for the compulsory sale of companies was laid with Decree VO48/1941 of 12 March 1941, which determined that Jewish enterprises had to be placed in trust. Registration had already taken place in October 1940 under decree VO189/1940, which, as was shown above, also contained the definition of a Jew.

All Jewish businesses were put under control of the Wirtschaftsprüfstelle (Bureau of Economic Investigation), which appointed an administrator (Verwalter or Treuhänder). These firms either were sold to Dutch collaborators or German customers or were wound up. In general, only the larger Jewish concerns were considered for preservation. Small, destitute companies were liquidated, usually by the Omnia Treuhand organization. Large companies proved difficult to sell owing to the risks attaching to them: if Hitler were to lose the war, the sale would be reversed. The Dutch government-in-exile had repeatedly broadcast warnings not to buy looted property through its mouthpiece in London, Radio Oranje.

Most of the medium-sized and larger firms continued to operate under an administrator or Verwalter. More prosperous smaller companies either got a custodian or were sold through the mediation of the Netherlands Company for the Liquidation of Enterprises (Niederländische Aktiengesellschaft für Abwicklung von Unternehmungen), which was established for the express purpose of determining the value of the expropriated enterprises and of finding a suitable buyer. There were two kinds of administrators: Liquidations-Treuhänder, who had orders to liquidate firms, and Verwaltungs-Treuhänder, whose task it was to administer a firm pending its sale. The proceeds of the sales were deposited with the VVRA. The VVRA was responsible for repaying the original Jewish owners in 100 quarterly installments, i.e., over 25 years, or at 4 percent per annum without interest. In practice, the length of the repayment term was immaterial because, when Seyss-Inquart established the VVRA in May 1941, there were already plans to deport the Dutch Jews. The repayment was a cosmetic move, entirely in keeping with the Germans' desire for a veneer of legality and their wish to avoid sowing panic or confusion among their victims.

The "Aryanization" of the Dutch economy was almost complete. About 2,000 companies were "dejewified" and a further 13,000-plus small ones were liquidated. It is virtually impossible to put a figure on their value. The purchase prices were almost always far lower than their true value (usually roughly one third of the market price) and no account was taken of good will. Moreover, the victims of these forced sales had no control over the money realized because the accounts into which the installments were paid were blocked. In any case, remittances from the VVRA generally stopped after one or two payments. Jews suffered the greatest financial losses in this area because they received virtually no compensation for their businesses, whereas other types of possessions were returned to their lawful owners after the war.[20]

Certain German firms took a great interest in the shares of some of the larger companies. Their sale provided an excellent opportunity to obtain total or partial control of important Dutch firms. However, the main buyers were Dutch stockbrokers, although it remains unclear how many of them acted as intermediaries for German businessmen. Share bonds and certificates of registered shares were sold mainly on the Amsterdam Stock Exchange, either through stockbrokers or directly by Liro. Both the liquidators and Liro ultimately deposited the proceeds of this enormous robbery (including that of the realized stock) with the VVRA.[21]

The "Aryanization" of the Dutch economy took place mainly in the following sectors: retail and wholesale trade, agencies, smaller banking agents, small food retailers, small clothing retailers, clothing industry, and some branches of the food industry. Four of the largest Jewish retail firms were taken over by compulsory purchase: the department stores of De Bijenkorf, Gebr. Gerzon, N.V. Hirsch & Co., and Maison de Bonneterie.[22] De Bijenkorf was "Aryanized" by the Handelstrust West (HTW), a branch of the Dresdner Bank.[23] In total, the Dutch Jews were relieved of assets of about 700 million guilders during the German occupation, based on amounts raised by the sales.[24] Jewish agricultural property, land, houses, and mortgage loans were also expropriated by means of decrees (March, May, and August 1941) and sold to German and Dutch citizens, usually collaborators.

The First Liro Decree

The decree of 8 August 1941 "concerning the handling of Jewish financial capital" compelled all Jews to open an account with Liro and to pay in or transfer all their cash, bank and giro (post office) accounts, securities, and checks. This so-called First Liro Decree was the first measure aimed at private Jewish capital. Bank and giro services were ordered to transfer the balances in the accounts of their Jewish customers to Liro. Whether a customer was Jewish was determined by means of a questionnaire that was sent to every account holder. The Jews lost virtually all control of their bank balances at Liro. Again, the most important sales channel for securities was the Amsterdam Stock Exchange.

The total value of Jewish shares amassed by Liro was about 350 million guilders, of which roughly 250 million were sold—about 150 million through the Amsterdam Stock Exchange either by Liro directly or through intermediaries. There is some disagreement about the final amount sold by the robbery bank: the figures vary from 213 to 250 million guilders. Roughly half a million securities were involved.[25] The management of Liro did its utmost to keep the books as accurate as possible but the booty was so overwhelming that the bookkeeping became a victim of its own success. The problems began when the records of Liro and VVRA became muddled. Enormous sums of money and packages of securities had been transferred from Liro to VVRA (and probably vice versa) without anybody being aware of the identities of the owner, or of the specific amounts. To make matters worse, virtually all deposits from 1 January 1943 onward were entered in a collective account, the so called *Sammelkonto*. The certainty that those deported would never return eliminated the need for individual accounts. After the war, it took four years to unravel the *Sammelkonto* and the closely interwoven administrations of the two looting institutions. However, this was an essential task in order to establish the true ownership of securities, money, and goods (the latter having been collected by order of the Second Liro Decree), because, otherwise, restitution to the rightful owners would have been virtually impossible.

The Second Liro Decree

The Second Liro Decree, VO58/1942, of May 1942 delivered the *coup de grâce* to private Jewish ownership. "Collections of whatever sort," insurance policies, pensions, gold, silver, platinum, works of art, precious stones, patent rights, copyrights, and concessions had to be surrendered. Article 12 stipulated that wedding rings and "dental fillings made of precious metals in personal use" were exempted from the order. "Until further notice" would have been a fitting addition, because the Wannsee Conference in January 1942 had already set in motion the physical annihilation of European Jewry and its culture. It was therefore only a matter of time before fillings, crowns, and wedding rings, in short the *Totengold*, would also fall into Nazi hands after their victims' deaths in the gas chambers. So it really was a case of "until further notice," even if that term was not included in the Second Liro Decree. Amounts receivable from third parties (including claims on foreigners) also had to be registered.

Horses, vehicles, and vessels underwent the same procedure. A total of 22,368 insurance policies were registered, most life insurance policies being redeemed by Liro with the companies concerned.

Deportation to Westerbork

The deportations to the East began in the summer of 1942. When the Jews, already stripped of practically all their possessions, arrived in the Westerbork transit camp, they were put through the Liro mangle one more time; the bank also had a "branch" inside the camp. Jewelry and money that deportees had smuggled in with them, and which, according to the authorities in Berlin, belonged to the German Reich, were taken from them in this antechamber of death. Directly after the victims' deportation to Westerbork, their houses were emptied from top to bottom. In Amsterdam this work was conducted by the Puls firm, which is why the plundering became known in Amsterdam as "pulsing." Crockery sets, household goods, and furniture, everything left behind was removed. Tables, chairs, and suchlike were mostly shipped to Germany to replace furniture that had been destroyed by Allied bombing.

A part of the capital surrendered to Liro was used to maintain and enlarge the transit camps of Westerbork and Vught, to cover the expenses of the removal of the household effects, and to pay "bounties" to people who betrayed Jews. In addition it went to cover the costs of the extensive Liro apparatus, which, at its height in 1942, employed no fewer than 400 people.

Stamps to Avoid Deportation

For Jews who had tried to retain money and valuables, a special method was devised to rob them of these "illegal" possessions before they were sent off to Westerbork and subsequently the extermination camps. In exchange for the surrender of gold, silver, and precious stones they received a stamp which exempted them from deportation "until further notice." In reality, this period was generally fairly short, being anything between half a day and three months. The stamp offered at best no more than a brief respite. Each exemption stamp was issued at a price of 300,000 guilders in precious stones or precious metals. The Germans were able to acquire a total of almost 100 million guilders (at today's values) of additional Jewish assets in this way.

Conclusion

The robbery of the Jews in the Netherlands was both thorough and systematic, and was carried out in a series of distinct phases. The procedures are very reminiscent of those followed in Germany but one notable difference was that in Holland the Germans tried very hard to forestall any unrest. The attitude of the Hitler regime vis-à-vis the Jews after January 1933 was manifest from the beginning. The Nazi regime spread hatred and the National Socialist Party wanted the Jews to be hated. The final expropriation of the victims of Nazi racial policy was probably the logical end and the consequence of a process that culminated in mass murder, although it is unlikely that genocide was the ultimate goal from the beginning. However, it was clear that Hitler wanted Germany to be free of Jews (*Judenrein*), even if this was achieved through emigration. That Jews should be forced to leave behind their riches was a consequence of the Nazi view that saw them as individuals who had robbed, exploited, and utilized their "host country" whenever they could. The Jews owed it to Germany to repay all that they had "stolen" before they left. At the same time, it was clear that the Nazis wanted all Jewish assets intact. *Kristallnacht*, the organized pogrom of 9–10 November 1938, had resulted in pointless and useless damage of Jewish property. In a decree issued on 10 December 1938, Göring ordered that this should not happen again. Henceforward nothing should be damaged or destroyed and the "Aryanization" of the German economy should be carried out according to the appropriate legal ordinances, while the proceeds should accrue to the Reich.[26]

Much the same pattern can be found in the Netherlands, where the lessons of *Kristallnacht* had been learned and the experience acquired was taken to heart. The Germans now took great pains to forestall disturbance because they realized that nothing was to be gained by unrest but trouble for themselves. Disorder would only have aroused Jewish suspicions and provoked attempts to hide assets and avoid confiscations. The Germans were always at pains to present their measures and actions under the guise of legality and normality because it was ultimately more profitable. The policy of avoiding panic was carried out until the bitter end. Even the gas chambers in Poland were disguised as showers.[27] Deception became an integral part of Nazi policy. It facilitated the German aim of carrying out their genocide unnoticed and with minimal disruption—not because they were ashamed of what they were doing but because it was the most effective and efficient way.

The German "civilized" way of plundering by decree had an additional advantage in the Netherlands, as the law-abiding population was far more likely to oppose the application of brute force than decrees with a veneer of legality. In effect, better results could be achieved by the use of the pen than at the point of a gun. Civil servants and other personnel who were involved in carrying out ordinances related to looting could almost convince themselves that they were doing nothing out of the ordinary. For example, the staff at Liro received packets containing securities, they wrote an acknowledgment of receipt, and then they administered the securities (and other goods). What they did felt like normal bookkeeping. It did not give them the impression of being part of a looting process because it was so impersonal.

The threatened Allied measures against looting were also a reason to hide the expropriations from the outside world. The Allied Declaration might not have had an overwhelming effect on the readiness of the neutral countries, such as Switzerland and Sweden, to abstain from buying looted Jewish property, but it did at least make them more careful, which produced a downward pressure on the selling prices of looted property. For the Nazis this was an unwanted development, as their need for hard currency for the purchase of strategic raw materials that they could not acquire in their own sphere of influence became increasingly urgent as the war progressed.

The existence of a civil government was probably detrimental to the victims of Nazi persecution because it worked more smoothly and more efficiently than a military regime could have done—and not only in regard to looting. A civil administration could make more efficient use of an existing civil service apparatus, which offered hardly any resistance to the measures against the Jews. However, a conclusive answer can only be given if we compare the situation in the Netherlands (and Norway) with that in countries with a military regime, but this necessitates taking into account the specific attitudes and cultures in the other occupied European countries. It is obvious that in Holland the widespread compliance and docility among civil servants and Jews facilitated the German efforts. It remains to be seen if this was also the case in other countries.

Looting in Amounts

This overview of the looting of Jewish assets in the Netherlands and the postwar legal rehabilitation refers exclusively to Jewish possessions confiscated by the Nazis. My estimate of at least NLG 1 billion for the value of the items looted by the occupying forces comprises only Jewish property seized in the Netherlands. The amounts listed in Table 10.1 in the different categories of Looting are the amounts confiscated. Particularly in relation to the theft of art, real estate, and "Aryanized" businesses, the sums are often a far cry from the actual economic value of the items concerned. The figures listed under Amount are in millions of guilders. They are approximate and are based on the amounts deposited with Liro and VVRA.

Both estimates in the table are certainly incomplete and far too low. Given the circumstances surrounding the "Aryanization" of businesses and other looting operations, the Nazis stole at least NLG 1 billion from the Dutch Jews.

Table 10.1 Looting in Amounts.

Looting	Amount
Securities	300–400
Bank and giro balances and cash	26–55
Insurance policies	25
Receivables	38
Mortgages	22
Properties	150
Agricultural properties	17
Businesses (liquidated)	6.5
Businesses ("Aryanized")	75
Art, gold etc.	6
Household effects	78
Exemption stamps and the like	10
Nonprofit associations/foundations	10
Confiscations by SD, Sicherheitspolizei and Devisenschutzkommandos (DSK)	10
Total of lowest estimate	NLG 774 (approximate)
Total of highest estimate	NLG 903 (approximate)

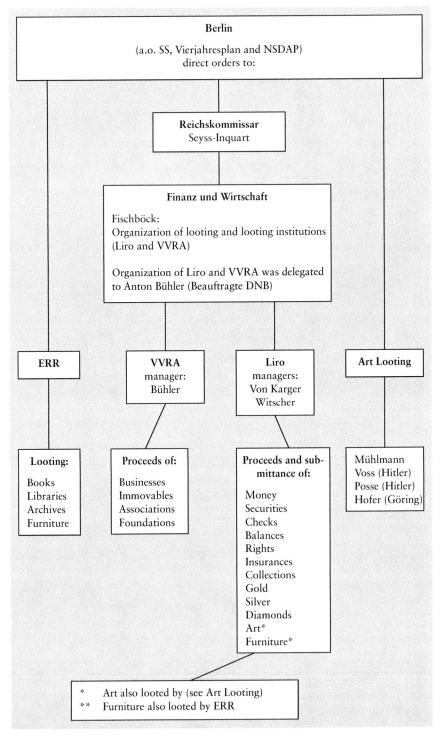

Figure 10.1 The Hierarchy of looting in the Netherlands.

Notes

1. Gerard Aalders, *Roof. De ontvreemding van joods bezit tijdens de Tweede Wereldoorlog* (The Hague, 1999, English translation forthcoming). Unless otherwise indicated the sources for this chapter are *Roof*.
2. See for the estimated percentages A.J. van der Leeuw, "Meer slachtoffers dan elders in West Europa," *Nieuw Israëlietisch Weekblad*, 15 November 1985. See also Wolfgang Benz, ed., *Dimension des Völkermords. Die Zahl der jüdischen Opfer des Nationalsozialismus* (Munich, 1991).
3. See, for instance, Pim Griffioen and Ron Zeller, "Jodenvervolging in Nederland en België tijdens de Tweede Wereldoorlog: een vergelijkende analyse," in Gerard Aalders, ed., *Oorlogsdocumentatie '40–'45. Achtste Jaarboek van het Rijksinstituut voor Oorlogsdocumentatie* (Zutphen, 1977); J.C.H. Blom, ed, *Geschiedenis van de joden in Nederland* (Amsterdam, 1995).
4. Gerhard Hirschfeld, *Nazi Rule and Dutch collaboration* (Oxford/ New York/ Hamburg, 1988), pp. 12–54.
5. Ibid., pp. 24–25, Netherlands Institute for War Documentation (NIOD), *Notities voor het Geschiedwerk*, no. 91, "Het ontstaan van het Duitse Rijkscommissariaat voor Nederland."
6. Bob Moore, *Victims and Survivors, The Nazi Persecution of the Jews in the Netherlands 1940–1945* (London, 1997), pp. 73–79, 254.
7. J. Presser, *Ondergang. De vervolging en verdelging van het Nederlandse jodendom, 1940–1945* (The Hagues, 1965), vol. 1, p. 10.
8. NIOD, *Notities voor het Geschiedwerk*, no. 91, "Het ontstaan van het Duitse Rijkscommissariaat voor Nederland," Moore, *Victims and Survivors*, p. 73.
9. Allan Bullock, *Hitler and Stalin. Parallel Lives* (London, 1993), p. 336; Michael Stolleis, *The Law under the Swastika. Studies on Legal History in Nazi Germany* (Chicago, 1998), p. 7.
10. *Reichsgesetzblatt*, Teil I, S. 778 (German State Gazette, part I, p. 778). Compare Article 43 of the Hague Convention (1907): "The authority of the legitimate power having in fact passed into the hands of the occupant, the latter shall take all the measures in his power to restore, and ensure, as far as possible, public order and safety, while respecting, unless absolutely prevented, the laws in force in the country."
11. Hirschfeld, *Nazi Rule*, pp. 132–154. The quote of the Dutch government, broadcast on 2 October 1943, is also taken from Hirschfeld (p. 154). For the role of the Dutch police: Guus Meershoek, *Dienaren van het Gezag: de Amsterdamse politie tijdens de bezettin* (Amsterdam, 1999).
12. Dick van Galen Last, "The Netherlands," in Bob Moore, ed., *Resistance in Western Europe* (Oxford, 2000).
13. NIOD, *Notities voor het Geschiedwerk*, no. 146. "Der Griff des Reiches nach dem Judenvermögen"; Joseph Walk, ed., *Das Sonderrecht für die Juden im NS-Staat. Eine Sammlung der gesetzlichen Maßnahmen und Richtlinien -Inhalt und Bedeutung* (Heidelberg/Karlsruhe, 1981); Bruno Blau, *Das Ausnahmerecht für die Juden in Deutschland, 1933–1945* (Düsseldorf, 1955); Wolfgang Benz, *Die Juden in Deutschland 1933–1945. Leben unter nationalsozialistischer Herrschaft* (Munich, 1988); Aalders, *Roof*, pp. 119–121.
14. Foreign Relations of the United States (FRUS), vol. I, 1943, *General* (Washington, 1968), p. 444.
15. See for this "deluge" of provisions, exemptions, and individual measures: NIOD, Doc II, Liro.
16. *Statistische gegevens van de joden in Nederland*, part I (The Hagues, 1942).
17. Dick van Galen Last and Rolf Wolfswinkel, *Anne Frank and After. Dutch Holocaust Literature in Historical Perspectives* (Amsterdam, 1996), p. 36.
18. Moore, *Victims and Survivors*, p. 64.
19. Aalders, *Roof*, pp. 149–169.
20. Gerard Aalders, *Bij Verordening. De roof van het Joodse vermogen in Nederland en het Naoorlogse Rechtsherstel* (The Hague, 2000).
21. L. de Jong, *Het Koninkrijk der Nederlanden in de Tweede Wereldoorlog*, vol. 7, (The Hagues,1976) pp. 419–434.

22. NIOD, HSSPF, 65 A, "Report of the Befehlshaber der Sicherheitspolizei und des SD für die Besetzten Niederländischen Gebiete to the Reichssicherheitshauptamt," April 1942; NIOD, Archief 266, BBT, Box 7, Map C, "Zusammengefasster Bericht über die Kapitalverflechtung mit Holland und Belgien seit der Besatzung im Mai 1940," not dated and NIOD, Archief 264, N. 85/3 Map 3, "Report on the economic penetration of Holland and Belgium by Germany since May 1940."
23. NIOD, Archief 266, N 157/1, Dresdner Bank. Extract from „Report on Dresdner Bank Investigation". The nominal capital of the Bijenkorf was 10 million guilders. At the beginning of the war 5% was in the hands of Westdeutsche Kaufhof A.G. (former *Leonhard Tietz*), Cologne: Algemeen Rijksarchief, Den Haag (ARA), NBI, 2.09.16, Invent. no. 520, Statisches Reichsamt Abteilung VI, Verzeichnis der niederländischen Gesellschaften bzw. die ganz oder teilweise in deutscher Hand sind. (List of Dutch companies totally or partly in Germans hands), undated but probably 1940. Gebr. Gerzon, Hirsch & Co., and De Bonnetterie are not mentioned on this list.
24. There is much confusion about these figures. For the 700 million guilders: Ministerie van Financiën, (Netherlands Ministry of Finance) Archief Bewindvoering, „Eindverslag van Beheerders-Vereffenaars betreffende Liquidatie van Verwaltung Sarphatistraat (L.V.V.S.) aan het Nederlandse Beheersinstituut te 's-Gravenhage' (1958) and "Eindverslag betreffende de taken van het Centraal Afwikkelingsbureau Duitse Schadeuitkeringen (C.A.D.S.U.). Uitgebracht door het Hoofd van het C.A.D.S.U." (1966).

    In a report of the Befehlshaber der Sicherheitspolizei und des SD the total worth of Jewish firms was estimated at between 700 million and 1 billion guilders. Altogether there were 21,000 Jewish firms (from a rag-and-bone business to industrial enterprises), of which only 1,000 to 1,500 were to be "dejewified" or "Aryanized"; the rest would be liquidated: RvO, "Zusammenfassende Darstellung der Entwicklung bezüglich Hortung des jüdischen Vermögens," 21 June 1941. Compare de Jong, *Koninkrijk*, vol. 5, pp. 586, 589, 591–601. De Jong writes that half of the Jewish businesses reported to the Wirtschaftsprüfstelle were included only because there was a matter of "Jewish influence," for example a Jewish director or supervisory director. These men could be replaced with the approval of the Wirtschaftsprüfstelle, although not free of "duty": as a rule the firm paid 1 percent of the stock for the approval. Roughly 2,000 enterprises were actually "Aryanized. In the spring of 1945, just before the end of the war, there were still about 1,000 cases waiting for decisions from the Wirtschaftsprüfstelle. Between 9,000 and 10,000 firms, mostly small ones, were liquidated. The average proceeds of these small firms was a little less than 500 guilders, which means a total sum of at most 5 million guilders in this category.

    In a letter from Seyss-Inquart to Reichskommissar Bormann of 27 January 1942 the former wrote that the "Aryanization" ordinances would generate about 1.5 billion guilders if every firm which, for example, had a Jewish supervisory director on the board was going to be involved [i.e., the above-mentioned "duty," G.A.]. Of the 2,000 firms that were indeed "Aryanized," about 1,000 had been dealt with in January 1942. Of these 400 were taken over by Dutchmen (total amount 60.5 million guilders), while 340 firms came into German hands (103 million guilders of capital). The remaining 260 firms were reserved for or given to war participants (*Kriegsteilnehmer*): NIOD, Archief 264, N. 90/1, Map B. It would seem that the Germans obtained firms that were about twice as big as those of their Dutch rivals.
25. The court that condemned Dr. Otto Rebholz, a banker and stockbroker who was regarded as one of the main Liro collaborators, mentioned "a low estimate" of 350 million guilders: Archives Ministerie van Justitie, Dossier A 55/0765 A Liquidatie vermogen Rebholz. "Vonnis inzake Erna A. Rebholz-Schröter, Otto Rebholz," 4 May 1955, and ibid. Letter from J.H. de Pont (Rebholz's attorney) to (attorney general) A.A.L.F. van Dullemen, 22 December 1950. De Pont writes that of the 350 million guilders, 100 million was used for the Jews (livelihood, paying debts, etc.), the rest (250 million) was sold. According to de Jong, *Koninkrijk*, vol. 5, p. 610, the total amount of sales was about 213 million guilders.
26. NIOD, *Notities voor het Geschiedwerk*, no. 146. "Der Griff des Reiches nach dem Judenvermögen."
27. Jaap Boas, "De misleidingstactieken van de nazi's bij de liquidatie van de Europese joden," in N.D.J. Barnouw, ed., *Oorlogsdocumentatie '40–'45. Vijfde Jaarboek van het Rijksinstituut voor Oorlogsdocumentatie* (Zutphen, 1994), pp. 69–96.

CHAPTER 11

PERPETRATOR NETWORKS AND THE HOLOCAUST: THE SPOLIATION OF JEWISH PROPERTY IN FRANCE, 1940–1944

Marc Olivier Baruch

The memory of the evils of anti-Semitism strongly marked France in the mid-1990s. Public observance of 100th anniversary of Captain Dreyfus' ordeal, culminated, by the end of the decade, in the centenary commemoration (1998) of the publication of Zola's *J'accuse*. The fate of the Jews living in France during World War II was, and still is, very much discussed and analyzed, so much so that some historians have come to see it as an obsession. The main shift in perceptions came from the state itself. On 22 July 1995, at the very place where Parisian Jews were detained in July 1942, the newly elected president Jacques Chirac acknowledged France's responsibility as an accomplice of the Nazi occupier in rounding up and deporting some 73,000 Jewish men, women, and children. Some two years later, an impressive ceremony of "repentance" was publicly held by the French Catholic Church in Drancy, from where most of the trains filled with human beings left France for Eastern Europe's extermination camps.

The question of compensation for the spoliation of Jewish property arose a short while later as both a symbolic and a material issue.[1] In March 1997, a "Study Task Force on the Spoliation of Jews in France" was officially set up. It was chaired by Jean Mattéoli, a member of the French Resistance and former Gaullist minister, and is hence referred to below as the "Mattéoli Commission"; it included historians and prominent members of the French Jewish community, and was set up "to study the conditions under which movable and immovable property belonging to the Jews of France was confiscated by fraudulent means, violence, or theft, both by the occupying forces and by the Vichy authorities between 1940 and 1944." Three years later, in April 2000, the commission presented its findings, i.e., an overall report along with seven specialized subreports (to which were added three further reports containing statistics and financial data), a guide to archival research, and a collection of official texts on both the spoliation and the restitution. This represented an impressive piece of work in terms of its volume and precision.[2] The general report gives a detailed view of the legal organization behind both the spoliation and the restitution processes. The main subreports deal with economic "Aryanization,"[3] the spoliation of financial assets,[4] and the looting of people arriving at the Drancy concentration camp.[5] A vast store of information and analyses was thus created by the Mattéoli Commission, which may help us evaluate the degree of cooperation between German and French state apparatuses in spoliating the Jews living in France. Since those apparatuses were made up, both on the French and on the German side, of numerous decentralized, occasionally antagonistic agencies and departments, it is necessary to describe them in some detail.

The first part of this contribution depicts the general setting of the occupation regime and the type of autonomy left to the theoretically independent French government. A masochistic view of the period, with which some of the media seem to comply, tends to forget that Germans occupied France and that they were the main perpetrators of genocide-related operations, viz., registration with the authorities, professional proscriptions, and plundering of Jews. This is not to suggest that the French government was only a passive accomplice in the "final solution"; the Vichy regime was indeed anti-Semitic. And yet anti-Semitism is not sufficient to explain the involvement of whole sections of the French civil service in the spoliation process, the escalation of which forms the core of the second part of this chapter. It will describe the main initiatives, instigators, and resulting laws before analyzing the way these were implemented by public and private institutions and whether these were already prominent in the French financial and administrative landscape at the time or specifically founded to carry out the anti-Semitic policy. Finally, in the third and main part of this chapter, I shall question the motives of both institutional and individual actors in the process, focusing on the different types of legitimacy involved.

The recent publication of the various texts making up the Mattéoli Report should not disguise the fact that from the end of World War II until the appearance of the report much had already been written about the fate of Jews in occupied Europe. There is little sense in trying to offer a historiographical summary of the Holocaust in Europe. Although it is also quite voluminous, the published literature devoted to the implementation of the "final solution" in France is less vast. We can distinguish three levels in the historical works. Shortly after the liberation of France, an effort was made from within the Jewish community – an undertaking that had actually begun during the war – to gather mostly public documentation related to the anti-Semitic policies undertaken in Marshal Pétain's France by both the occupying and French authorities. Thanks to the wealth of records conserved at the Centre de Documentation Juive Contemporaine (CDJC), Dr. Joseph Billig was able in the second half of the 1950s to write the history of the Commissariat Général aux Questions Juives (CGQJ), which has remained for two decades more or less the main history of the anti-Semitic policy followed by the French government.[6]

New sources of information and new historical studies appeared when Serge Klarsfeld published, from the mid-1980s on, a series of documents underscoring the importance, for the French authorities, of collaborating with the German superior police officials in France in their attempt to deport the Jews.[7] As for research, in 1981 Michael Marrus and Robert Paxton published *Vichy and the Jews*, a book that was almost immediately translated into French.[8] It gave rise to a new set of histories and papers, the most important of which were Renée Poznanski's study of daily Jewish life in Vichy France[9] and Richard Weisberg's analysis of Vichy's anti-Semitic policy.[10] Economic "Aryanization," moreover, has in fact been partly examined, but until recently the subject had never been the core of any historical study, except for a precursory but short study by Henry Rousso.[11] Newer aspects were brought to light by Philippe Verheyde in his doctoral thesis of 1997 on the "Aryanization" process in big business,[12] which benefited greatly from the easy access now given to public records once kept both by the German occupation apparatus and by the CGQJ,[13] many of which are dedicated to France's economic "Aryanization." A great deal of the work on this topic is also being carried out from within as it were, that is, by some of the very institutions involved in the spoliation, such as the Caisse des Dépôts et Consignations (CDC), or Deposits and Consignment Office. Since it played a very important part in the spoliation process, as we shall see, the CDC decided to start its own inquiry some four years before the Mattéoli Commission was created. It seems, therefore, that the right-wing journalist Henri Amouroux's wish to be rid of the study of Vichy[14] is fortunately not about to become a reality. It should be kept in mind, however, that, despite its importance, the fate of Jews living in France was not a crucial problem for the French authorities. As Renée Poznanski has put it, polarization around this issue today may be read as "a revenge of historiography on history."[15] It is especially important, in this regard, to refer to the approaches dealing with both the legal framework of the period,[16] and the overall attitude of the civil service during World War II.[17]

The General Setting of the Occupation Regime in France: 1940

In June 1940, the highly successful advance of German armies in France provoked a real panic within the population and split the French government. Ministers who wished to continue to prosecute the war by moving the government to French North Africa were forced to resign. With the immensely popular figure of Marshal Pétain at its head, a new cabinet was formed whose aim was to seek an armistice with the Germans. Hitler agreed to the proposal and the conditions of the occupation regime in France were settled by the Armistice Convention signed on 22 June 1940. The convention seems to have been acceptable to both parties; there were only a few instances of public dissent, and these all came from the then meager French forces that had fled to England to answer General de Gaulle's call for staunch opposition to the very idea of an armistice. Among such protestations was the philosopher Raymond Aron's denunciation of the clause that compelled Pétain's government to deliver up to the Nazis any German opponent of Hitler's regime who had earlier found refuge in republican France.

The terms of the Armistice recognized the sovereignty of the French government over the whole of France, including the zone occupied by German troops. Even in this Occupied Zone, French legislation was considered valid, although it might conflict with decrees promulgated by the German supreme commander in France, the Militärbefehlshaber in Frankreich, (MBF). According to the Hague Conventions, the scope of legal powers given to the occupying power is limited to matters dealing with the security of their troops. The very first weeks of the Occupation showed the helpless French authorities the highly selective reading Germany intended to make of the text it had just signed. The French had agreed to pay for their defeat at a very high price: Occupation fees amounted to a huge 400 million francs a day, and prisoners of war—there were more than a million and a half in the early summer of 1940—were to be held in Germany until a peace treaty was signed. These harsh conditions were nevertheless accepted by the new regime, which by then had chosen the small spa city of Vichy as its capital. The Armistice provided the regime with a formal legal framework, and the occupier's blessing, to launch its authoritarian and reactionary policy known as the *Révolution nationale*. France as a democracy was no more. On 10 July 1940, the French parliament handed over complete control to Marshal Pétain, who immediately suppressed the Republic by granting himself both executive and legislative powers. Pétain, head of the new *État français* that replaced the Republic—a highly symbolic change of names—and Laval, who seconded Pétain until 13 December 1940, now found themselves dealing with a complicated Occupation apparatus.

From the Nazi point of view, France was not racially pure enough to deserve a German Reichstatthalter, or Reich Governor, as "Germanic" Norway and the Netherlands had.[18] The military administration that was established was a highly centralized one, with corresponding local and departmental chiefs, namely, the *Kreiskommandanten* and *Feldkommandanten*. A high-ranking officer served as the head of the MBF; for a short time this was Alfred Streccius, then Otto von Stülpnagel, who in turn was succeeded by his cousin Karl-Heinrich in February 1942. In theory this officer was supposed to enjoy full hierarchical authority over all departments of the Occupation apparatus. Yet direct ties were forged and strongly maintained between Himmler's Reichssicherheitshauptamt (RSHA), the Reich Security Main Office, and the corresponding authority in France, Helmut Knochen. The same kind of hierarchic bypass functioned between Adolf Eichmann, head of the Referat IV-B-4 of the RSHA in charge of the Jewish Question, and Theodor Dannecker, who represented Eichmann in France. Direct contact was also organized by Ribbentrop, the Minister of Foreign

Affairs, through Otto Abetz, a former Nazi agent in prewar France who was appointed "ambassador" to France in August 1940. The extremely complicated and versatile German Occupation apparatus is a subject in itself.[19] One important step was taken in the spring of 1942 when the MBF lost its authority over the police force, which was put under the supervision of SS General Carl-Albrecht Oberg, seconded by Helmut Knochen as Beauftragter des Chefs der Sicherheitspolizei und des SD (BdS).

Far from being filled solely by professional administrators or military personnel (who were certainly not impervious to Nazi anti-Semitism, moreover), numerous positions of responsibility in the Occupation apparatus were entrusted to confirmed, long-standing supporters of the Nazi party. By this time such men had largely had the opportunity to show both their loyalty to the racial doctrine of the party and the National Socialist state and their capacity to translate that loyalty into concrete measures. We have mentioned Otto Abetz above, but we might also recall here Werner Best, a former jurist and member of the Gestapo, who was named chief of the administrative management staff (Verwaltungsstab) of the MBF.[20] One bureau especially, directed by Dr. Blanke and part of the economic section of the MBF, was commissioned to deal with general economic matters and the Jewish question in particular. From the organization of these departments it clearly follows that the elimination of Jewish influence, a policy that had been carried out in Germany since 1933,[21] was to be extended to France under German control.

However, at the start of the Occupation, this policy was introduced only indirectly. Immediately after the signing of the armistice, France's main concern was to substitute French authorities for the organizations and structures set up by the Germans to govern the lands they had conquered. If territorial control was inevitable, and made real by the presence of an army of occupation throughout much of the country, the Vichy regime was determined to avoid, or at least limit, political and economic domination by the Germans. Yet on 20 May 1940 the German commander-in-chief had already assumed, in the regions under his command, the power to name a provisional administrator (*kommissarische Verwalter*) to head any business that had been deprived of its directors. The risk of French businesses falling under German control was therefore considerable. The new Minister of Industrial Production (a portfolio created within the Vichy government to manage French businesses in the war economy and the penury that was then setting in) was naturally troubled by this possibility.

In keeping with a tactic that was to become generalized in the coming months, and in the name of French sovereignty, a law passed by the Vichy government regularized the German provision by extending it to all of France, occupied or not. The law, dating from 10 September 1940, gave Vichy the authority to appoint a provisional administrator (*administrateur provisoire*) to head any business deprived of its directors. Furthermore, to hinder the Germans from acting alone in matters concerning the provisional administrators in the Occupied Zone, a Service du Contrôle des Administrateurs Provisoires (SCAP), or Department of Management of Provisional Administrators, based in Paris, was created by Vichy on 9 December 1940. This department was instructed to interpret and administer German laws in a spirit that reflected as closely as possible the wishes of the French government, in particular by naming Frenchmen as provisional administrators. The department's first director was a senior official, Pierre-Eugène Fournier, an inspector general of finances, a former head of the Banque de France, and the president of the board of directors of the SNCF, the French national railroad system.

The SCAP dealt above all with businesses in which Jews owned all or the majority of the assets. An initial German ordinance regarding the Jews that dates from 27 September 1940, after providing a definition of Jews inspired by the Nazi Nuremberg laws,[22] prohibited those of the Occupied Zone from returning if they had already left; thus businesses belonging to Jews were de facto deprived of their directors. The same law, moreover, went on to stipulate that all Jews within the Occupied Zone had to register with the authorities. The files obtained at this time would later be put to terrible use when the police roundups began in 1942.

In the fall of 1940, however, things had not yet reached such a tragic point. At the time it was "only" a question of despoiling the Jewish segment of the population. An ordinance of 18 October set out the rules of what was soon to be officially called the "economic Aryanization." The principle was simple. A managing director was to be named to head any business that was deemed Jewish (i.e., if 33 percent or more of its capital belonged to Jews, or if its director, or more than a third of its board of directors, were Jewish); this managing director was instructed to sell off the business in question to a non-Jew or to liquidate it. The proceeds of this transaction were to be turned over to the Jewish owner, a practice that was to obtain only only a short while longer.[23] This decision ran counter to none of the principles espoused by the heads of the new French regime since they were themselves very much steeped in the current anti-Semitism of the 1930s.[24] As early as 12 July, the French state—born just two days earlier—had issued its first xenophobic laws, largely directed against Jews, although they were not named in the texts at this time. Not so with a later law, dating from 3 October 1940, touching on the legal status of Jews. As the regime saw it, because of the "preponderant, ingratiating, and ultimately disruptive" (*prépondérante, insinuante et finalement décomposante*) role of Jews in France, the law of 3 October was written to exclude them from any position of authority in the state, and entirely from the cinema and the press. As one senior French official wrote at the time, Vichy's anti-Jewish laws and those promulgated by the German occupier complemented one another, the latter stressing economic matters while Vichy proudly proclaimed that it was leaving Jewish property untouched.

Escalation of Anti-Semitic Persecution in the Economic Field

From being merely complementary the laws of the German occupier and the Vichy government were to become parallel when the French government made public a law of 22 July 1941 that aimed to "eliminate any and all Jewish influence in the national economy"—terms that could have been taken word for word from the Nazi's anti-Semitic vocabulary. Yet this was French law, hence applicable throughout all of France, including the so-called Free Zone, in which no German soldiers were stationed.

In the meantime, at the insistence of the German occupier, a new agency had appeared in the French administration in late March 1941, the Commissariat Général aux Questions Juives, the CGQJ. This agency was commissioned to conceive, propose, and carry out the official anti-Semitic policy of the French state of Vichy. The year 1941 thus marked a true hardening of such policy. Enemies of Nazi Germany, the Jews had now become enemies of the new French state as well. Instead of observing the rules of the *jus gentium* and protecting persons on French soil, be they French citizens or refugees who had believed in the haven offered by the land that had given the world the Declaration of the Rights of Man, the Vichy government was on the contrary poised to transform itself into their persecutors, before eventually becoming accomplices of their executioners.

Directed by Xavier Vallat, a severely wounded veteran of World War I and a deputy of the extreme right, the CGQJ began its mission by banning Jews from an ever-increasing number of professions. A new statute that went beyond the law of October 1940 in its severity was published in June 1941, although measures to exclude Jews from public office were nearly complete by this time. Implemented even before the creation of the CGQJ by the professional bureaucracy Vichy had inherited from the Third Republic, these measures had already affected more than 3,400 people by the start of 1941. Practically no one had taken advantage of the few possibilities of exemption granted by the law.

As for the Germans, the MBF continued to show a great interest in economic "Aryanization." A third ordinance dated 26 April 1941 banned Jews from practically every form of economic activity. Until this date the proceeds from the sale or liquidation of property had been turned over to the erstwhile owner. With this new ordinance, however, "the proceeds of any sales will remain frozen in the possession of the managing director. The despoiled retain the possibility of obtaining subsidies if that proves indispensable and the funds of the businesses in question permits such subsidies: two conditions that rarely coexist."[25] "Aryanization" had now indeed become spoliation.

Yet not all wealth was concentrated in businesses and the Nazis intended to deprive Jews of every resource. With their fourth ordinance against the Jews, made public the following 28 May, the occupier froze all bank accounts opened by Jews, whether in the name of individuals or businesses. While stressing once again economic spoliation (businesses without a provisional administrator were now prohibited from engaging in any commercial activity whatsoever), this new development implemented the financial spoliation on a vaster scale. Jews lost all control of their bank accounts, securities, loan certificates, and so on. They were only authorized to make withdrawals of no more than 15,000 francs per month for everyday expenses and personal upkeep, actually a rather high limit at the time. The complete control of the resources of Jews living in the Occupied Zone by the occupying forces and their French collaborators, the CGQJ, had now become a reality.

Faced with these developments, how did the men of Vichy react? They certainly did not, as they would claim after the war, seek to protect "the good French Jews of old stock" affected by the German ordinances, as the entire Jewish population in the Northern Zone was. On the contrary, in the name of its own conception of its sovereignty—and clearly through anti-Semitism—Vichy chose to extend the process of spoliation to the Southern Zone, that is, to the area free of all German presence. The turning point came with the law "relative to businesses, property and assets belonging to Jews" mentioned above, which was signed on 22 July 1941 and approved by the German occupier one month later. Significantly enough, Xavier Vallat had shown such eagerness to turn to the German laws for inspiration in drafting the CGQJ's own that even a few officials within the Finance Ministry expressed surprise at seeing the CGQJ exceed the Nazis' wishes. The principle adopted was simple. The CGQJ proposed, and the law decided, to generalize the appointment of provisional administrators to all Jewish businesses and property, except for bonds issued by the state or other public entities, on the one hand, and real estate constituting a principal residence, on the other. The provisional administrator answered to the CGQJ and, as in the German ordinances, was commissioned to manage a business during the period of its appraisal, prior to either its liquidation (this was the most common solution, especially for very small businesses, many of which were found in the garment industry) or its fair-price sale to a non-Jew.

Two other venerable departments of the French civil service were also directly implicated in this process. There was, first of all, the Service des Domaines. Part of the Finance Ministry, this agency managed the national property and assets. It became by law the provisional administrator of titles to property belonging to private individuals—titles belonging to businesses were managed by the appointed provisional administrator. Regardless of the original owner in question (business or private individual), the proceeds from these two processes were collected by a second state-related institution, the CDC. Founded in 1816 as a depository for funds managed by notaries or subject to litigation, the Caisse des Dépôts et Consignations opened an account for each expropriated Jewish owner into which 90 percent of the proceeds from the sale or liquidation of his or her property was deposited. The remaining 10 percent was assigned to the CGQJ to cover the costs of carrying out the economic "Aryanization." As in Germany, the victims themselves financed their own spoliation. For a time the Vichy government had considered creating a new ad hoc agency for handling the money raised by the "Aryanization" process.[26] In the end, however, Vichy preferred to turn to the CDC because of its reputation as a rigorous institution, proud of the independence that the law had entrusted it with and always prepared to defend that autonomy vis-à-vis the executive branch of the government. Recourse to the CDC served to stress publicly the "objective" character of the process, which was not presented as a discriminatory policy but rather as something dictated by the public interest.

In the Occupied Zone the legal situation was complex, which in terms of the law led to a confusion of responsibilities between the French government and the authorities of the occupying power. The existence of French laws, for instance, did not put an end to German ones, which the SCAP continued to enforce, even after it was merged with the CGQJ in June 1941. In fact, even though the German and French processes of spoliation could be superimposed on one another, each major step in the procedure—the naming of a provisional administrator, for example—continued to require approval by the MBF. To speed up the processing of day-to-day business, an agent of the MBF was present in the Paris offices of the CGQJ. To carry out the provisions of the law in the Unoccupied Zone, moreover, the CGQJ created a directorate for economic "Aryanization," which was organized along the lines of the SCAP, and with which the new department eventually merged. The agency that grew out of this union became by far the most important department in the CGQJ, employing by early 1944 two-thirds of the organization's one thousand or so agents.

The number of cases taken up by the authorities was considerable, some 50,000 (a figure that we might compare with the total Jewish population in France in 1940, estimated at 330,000 individuals), less than half of which would be completed by the end of the Occupation.[27] The total amount of the spoliation is no less staggering. Philippe Verheyde estimates the economic "Aryanization" alone to have reached 3.3 billion French francs.[28] The Mattéoli Commission calculated the total figure to be some 5 billion French francs.[29] which the commission arrived at by combining the amount advanced by Verheyde with the total for the financial spoliation, some 1.8 billion. This last figure notably includes the fine of 1 billion French francs that the MBF imposed on the Jewish population of the Occupied Zone on 14 December 1941 as a reprisal for "Judeo-Bolshevik" attacks committed against German soldiers. The Germans, it should be noted, rejected the French Treasury's proposal to advance this amount.[30] It was the Union Générale des Israélites de France (UGIF), or General Union of the Israelites of France, newly created under the aegis of the CGQJ to represent Jews in their dealings with the public authorities, that had to see to the payment of the fine. Here again, as in Germany and the rest of Europe occupied by the Nazis, Jews were forced to become the very agents of their own tragedy.

The Rationalities at Work: Convergences and/or Conflicts between Rationales

I would now like to try to shed some light on the different rationalities at work in the processes of the economic "Aryanization" and the financial spoliation. As the title of this study suggests, the focus here will be on those institutions, in particular those French institutions, that were active in these operations.

Thus, we shall hear little from the victims in this instance, since studies of the UGIF are highly fragmentary and caution dictates that I only mention the organization marginally. Readers, however, can break this nearly total silence (imposed by the nature of the subject treated here) by referring to several works devoted to the victims.[31] Yet this silence also takes on a metaphorical value in the light of the endless activity of the many different agencies that were incited to, and in some cases fiercely determined to, plunder these people. Institutionally, a good number of these agencies sought to explain, during the events or after the Liberation, their reasons for participating in this policy. In several rare instances it was the principal directors of such organizations who took it upon themselves to do so. Thus we have many accounts, given by the perpetrators, of their purpose in participating in the spoliation process. My analysis will therefore particularly focus on the strategies of the various actors, their connections, and the principles they imagined were at stake in the spoliation process. It is from that point of view that I shall try both to understand the rationales and legitimizations they developed, and to gauge the latitude enjoyed in acting or not acting. Thus light will mainly be shed on cooperation—whether smooth or not so smooth—between occupiers and occupied, whereas Philippe Verheyde's contribution to the present volume stresses the fierce competition between French and German negotiators when discussing possible participation of German capital in important French firms. It should be clearly understood that rivalry could coexist within the general setting defined by the official state collaboration policy.

To be pertinent, the analysis here should avoid simply throwing together an accumulation of dissimilar factors. Thus, although the present chapter may not explicitly state otherwise because of its tendency to synthesize disparate elements, we must bear in mind that the generality of the phenomenon of despoiling France's Jews masks a diversity in fact, specifically the diversity of the population in question. These thousands of individuals acquire a certain unity (artificial in part) from the mere fact of having been the victims of a comparable process. The same law, for instance, covered the "Aryanization" of both a large department store like the Galeries Lafayette and the workshop of a furrier in the eastern outskirts of Paris; it is easy to imagine that the conditions under which the law was applied were hardly comparable in the two cases. A few statistics are particularly eloquent in this regard : when the time came to make restitution after the war, 90 percent of the securities held by Jews that had been expropriated from their brokers were returned and only 10 percent remained unclaimed; the percentages are exactly the reverse for the belongings stolen from the internees held in the camp in Drancy...

Since this is a historical study, attention will also be paid to the impact of events that were liable to slow down or speed up the process, as it is understood that greater or lesser attunment to events and the difference in relationships relative to the passage of time are in themselves significant factors in the rationalities at work, as we shall see below. What are these rationalities then? Below I break them down into four categories classified according to their increasing degree of "altruism."[32] First, there were the strategies for profit, either collective or individual; secondly, those constructed upon the regard for professional qualities; thirdly, those founded on a political outlook; and, finally, those that we might attribute less to values—since it is certainly difficult to present anti-Semitism as a value, even while taking the usual methodological precautions—than to human passions.

Strategies of Individual or Collective Profit

First of all, we should not underestimate the fact that taking part in the "Aryanization" of a property could prove a good business deal. It was the opportunity for profit, more than any other reason, that motivated numerous provisional administrators.[33] Profit was indeed such a strong incentive that several of these administrators were dismissed from their posts by the CGQJ for unscrupulous behavior or fraud. A specialist in such questions, Theodor Dannecker, Knochen's right hand for "Jewish affairs," pointed out as early as 28 January 1941 that racist anti-Semitism worked poorly in France and that it was therefore judicious to hold out the possibility of profit in the process, to lend it a lucrative coloring.[34] For buyers, there was the opportunity to purchase a business at a price below its real market value, although the CGQJ, consumed by the notion of "honesty" in despoiling the Jewish population, usually prided itself on upholding the principle that prices were not to deviate too much from what was reasonable. Apart from these all-too-human motivations based upon money, there were other strategies that were founded on the collective benefits that might be reaped. Professions in which Jewish-owned businesses were numerous, for example, witnessed a decline in competition. A sector of the economy like retail sales, which had watched with alarm the development of chain stores before the war, was delighted by the disappearance of such chains owned by Jews. The anti-Semitic ideology of the government readily used every means available, criticizing both the growing numbers of small poor Jewish-owned businesses before the war and the appearance of a modern Jewish business sector that threatened the existence of the small French store, a symbol of honest work in the face of cosmopolitan speculation.[35]

One could offer comparable analyses of the other agencies associated with the spoliation. Although immediate financial interest was less significant, it is worth noting that the Commissaire Général of the CGQJ received the highest pay allowed to civil servants. At the other end of the administrative hierarchy presiding over the spoliation, the agents who worked for the Service des Domaines were partly remunerated in proportion to the amount of the securities sold off through their efforts. Finally, there existed rewards that were only semiofficial. When the less-than-honest Louis Darquier de Pellepoix was appointed to head the CGQJ, corruption began to develop rapidly throughout the department.

Far more widespread, if not frankly generalized, were attitudes vis-à-vis a collective benefit that one might best sum up as "bureaucratic," along with all that that word implies, especially in France, in terms of esprit de corps. The highest governmental bodies which were then on the rise within the state apparatus,[36] were associated with the spoliation process, at times quite directly so. The first head of the SCAP was, as we saw, a member of the Inspection des Finances, France's leading financial elite, while the Conseil d'État (grands corps) named two of its members to the CGQJ, one as the head of its legal section, the other as its general secretary. Appointed at the request of Werner Best, who was worried about Darquier de Pellepoix's lack of administrative experience, this general secretary was only to remain a short while in office. Although most of the agents employed by the CGQJ were not career bureaucrats, senior and mid-level civil servants, who had been trained at the appropriate administrative schools, did hold important positions there. Two general controllers from the army, for example, headed the SCAP in succession and the director of economic "Aryanization" came from the Seine prefecture, while one of his subordinates was an inspector from the Banque de France.

Bureaucratic maneuvering and factiousness also entered into the disputes over administrative limits and competence in cases where the spoliation of Jews was at issue.[37] In this respect, the SCAP's and the CGQJ's ministerial dependence changed many times in the short course of their existence. On a deeper level, quite different rationales for the objectives of the process drove two of the main supporters of the operations. Those who wished to modernize the regime, grouped around "technocrats" like the ministers of industry Pucheu and Bichelonne, and with the support of the *Comités d'organisation*,[38] pressed for a concentration within the framework of an organized economy. Hence the majority in this instance worked toward the liquidation of businesses rather than their takeover by "Aryan" owners. Placed under the authority of Minister Yves Bouthillier, himself an Inspector of Finances, the various departments of the Finance Ministry had a less ambitious vision. Their primary concern, which can be read in the Treasury Board's directives to the CDC,[39] was first and foremost to avoid throwing a fragile stock market into disequilibrium with the massive sales of securities. Attention was also paid to realizing cuts in the national budget, a natural part of the budget-conscious mentality that was never far from the ministry's preoccupations. Thus, rather than resort to the law of 17 December 1941 allowing for the closure of any business that proved of no benefit to the community, provided that just compensation was made, it was deemed appropriate to invoke the laws concerning economic "Aryanization"[40] whenever the business in question was "Jewish." Not only did this expedient cost nothing, but it even permitted the ministry to make the despoiled bear the costs of their own spoliation.

Valorization of Professional Abilities

For the civil servants who had to carry out the "Aryanization," as for a great number of the police officers who, from the summer of 1942 on, were called upon to arrest Jewish families singled out for deportation, the golden rule was to get the job done correctly. This professional obligation was given even greater weight in a regime that largely favored the call for competence in government. Vichy eagerly contrasted the aptitude and skill of professional experts, many of whom had become ministers, with the incompetence of earlier cabinets, composed of elected members of parliament. Governance, it was said and written, had to be placed in the hands of competent people— and clearly made off limits to those who were by nature incapable of reacting like trueborn citizens of French blood, that is, the Jews first and foremost. In this respect, Vichy proved to be a regime especially preoccupied both with competence and with incompetence—in the legal sense of the term.

The professions given the task of applying the law in cases involving this incompetence had first to prove their own competence and professional strengths. For civil servants (from the basic bureaucrat to the prefect), for those in the legal profession (from the judge to the notary public[41]), and, what may seem more surprising, for industrialists and financiers, obedience to the norm laid down by the state was the first of these strengths. Shielded by the impersonality and generality of the law, which was being regularly expanded in this domain, all these professionals benefited from such "innocence-generating mechanisms"[42] in fulfilling their professional duties. Usually they acted with total indifference to the fate of the people, who merged, in the eyes of these professionals, with the file opened in their name. This indifference is shocking today, although absolutely normal at the time.

Clearly, spoliation was in accordance with the law, a view shared by private businesses (banks), whose traditional mission was to safeguard their clients' assets, not to assist the government in plundering them. As Claire Andrieu points out, this class of professionals, ordinarily so quick to denounce the state's stranglehold over a sector of the economy that such professionals see as private by its very nature, namely financial property, in this instance unhesitatingly went along with the spoliation process, in some cases even exceeding the wishes of the French and German authorities.[43]

While the point of view of insurance companies is still relatively unknown, notaries public, on the other hand, were more suspicious and seem to have shown little enthusiasm for taking part in the spoliation process. With their professional regard for transactions that are both clear and easy to resolve, notaries public could not help but warn their clients, who might acquire assets formerly owned by Jews, about the uncertainty surrounding sales made under legal conditions that were without precedent and through intermediaries (provisional administrators) who were often viewed with suspicion by these practitioners of civil law. Moreover, the effect of different perceptions of time cannot be discounted. Notaries public, used to the long periods over which inheritances devolve for example, may not have doubted the permanence of the new regime any more than the rest of their fellow Frenchmen; as time passed, however, they were surely aware of the possibly temporary character of the exceptional legislation being introduced. The risk that such sales would be annulled, as already announced by the Gaullists on BBC radio in April 1941, was more sharply defined with the solemn declaration signed in London by the Allies and Gaullist Free France on 5 January 1943, and a later ordinance, dating from 12 November of the same year, which declared null and void by right all acts of spoliation committed by the enemy or under their control.

By that year civil servants, like the majority of the French, had concluded that Vichy stood a good chance of becoming a mere digression in the political and constitutional history of the country. Yet, if they persisted in serving the regime, which few of them actually opposed,[44] they did so because they considered it their duty to overcome their own scruples. Two significant examples will suffice in this regard. There were, first of all, France's legal experts and chief among them, Joseph Barthélemy, professor of public law, who became the Minister of Justice in January 1941. Although he deemed the terms of the law enacted on 22 July 1941 "contrary to the general regulations of French law," Barthélemy agreed to sign this piece of legislation "for reasons of overall policy."[45] Faced with such an example, why would simple professors of law show greater moderation—unless the passage of time played some part in the change? The legal experts commenting on the law in 1943 indeed proved less sure of their opinion than their predecessors of 1941. Nearly all of them describe, without raising an eyebrow or expressing a dissenting opinion, a law that "distrusts the prosperity of Jews ... [which] tends to disrupt to their advantage the economy's equilibrium," growing indignant only when the terms of the law lead to "an expropriation of Aryan associates which is unjustifiable."[46]

The attitude of the CDC offers a second striking example of an institution setting aside its principles, in this case principles that were the bedrock of the CDC since they concern deposits and consignations. In French law, a consignation is the freezing of a sum of money that is the object of a legal dispute. The law that founded the CDC formally prohibits any movement of this sum until the litigation is settled. By transferring from the consignation account opened in the name of the Service des Domaines to the UGIF's account the assets that were being generated by the sales of Jewish-held securities (funds that the UGIF was going to use to pay the one-billion-franc fine imposed by the occupier), the CDC openly violated the principle upon which its independence was established. Of course, one can justify this unprecedented behavior—indeed, the heads of this institution readily availed themselves of such an argument, notably at the war's end—by recalling the extraordinary pressure exerted by the German occupier. One would think that such pressure was brought to bear first and foremost on the Jewish community, which risked reprisals if it failed to show it was able to pay the fine. Yet it was not this risk that the CDC emphasized at the time. What the CDC found most troubling was the danger of seeing the German occupier seize, through its own authority, the securities needed to pay the fine and thus "to place under [ist] control businesses occupying an important place in the overall economy of the country."

Political Vision: Serving the Country

By way of this "patriotic" argument, the CDC, like many other parts of the French public administration, allowed itself to be transformed into a tool by France's political leaders in the name of its own apolitical character. It was neither the place nor the privilege of the administrative echelon, which represents the pure application of orders (as the regime liked to repeat endlessly), to set itself up in judgment over the nation's higher interests. It had been decided by the government of Marshal Pétain, a leader whose lucidity and self-sacrifice were also a constant theme in official propaganda, that these interests lay in a political and military collaboration with Nazi Germany. Going well beyond the notion of the "lesser of two evils," which the administration of occupied Belgium in particular would advance to justify its participation in the measures decided by the occupier,[47] the French form of collaboration was therefore a gamble at the price of a struggle. The gamble was that everything could be negotiated, including a reduction of the costs of the occupation and the degree of sovereignty conceded to the French government, and the outcome of the gamble was uncertain; the struggle, on the other hand, was quite certain, permanent and unequal. In the domain that concerns us here, several French agencies were involved. These included the CGQJ, of course, but only partially so since the main interests at stake, beyond the day-to-day management of the spoliation process, lay elsewhere.

The interests in question sprang from two interlocking objectives. First, there was the question of economic sovereignty. That objective implied an opposition to the predominance of German capital, which would have given the Reich mastery over businesses that were essential to the country's financial and industrial power. Secondly, there was the desire for political sovereignty, the overriding concern of the succeeding governments of the État français. The French government was indeed obsessed with affirming and regaining its sovereignty in every domain. The negotiations that were driven by this wish were marked by both successes and tribulations and, although they were quite challenging most of the time, we may not conclude that they amount to a form of "resistance." The term resistance must include the idea of subverting the order and organization that has been established between the occupier and the collaborating occupied[48]; were the opposite true, the men who served as high dignitaries under Vichy would not be mistaken in suggesting, as some of them did in fact hint in their memoirs, that Marshal Pétain was France's first and foremost Resistance fighter.[49]

Negotiations were twofold then. First, they were conducted by the French with the aim of countering the risk that French businesses important to the economy might fall under German financial control. To this end a new department had been created in late August 1940 within the Finance Ministry, the Direction des Finances Extérieures et des Changes (Exterior Finances and Exchanges Management). A young inspector of the Finance Ministry, Maurice Couve de Murville (a future prime minister under General de Gaulle in 1968–69), who was then thoroughly immersed in Vichy's patriotic rallying of the populace, was appointed to direct the new department. Couve de Murville was not driven by any anti-Semitic ideological passions and in fact sought to attenuate the severity of the laws freezing Jewish assets, notably those held in the Unoccupied Zone,[50] although he never reached the point of breaking with the Germans. It was essential in fact that negotiations continue, for Vichy greatly feared German domination of French capital.[51] What was of concern then was not the dispossession of legitimate owners resulting from the economic "Aryanization," but rather the property of businesses that once belonged to Jews, that is, the danger to the French economy springing from that dispossession. As Philippe Verheyde has made clear, the efforts of the Exterior Finances Management to oppose German takeovers were identical whether the business in question was Jewish or not. Thus, despite a show of opposition in a few case, which Claire Andrieu points out in her report, no true resistance to the economic "Aryanization" as such ever occurred.[52]

This dehumanized approach, doubtless the only one that a professional bureaucracy could adopt, was not limited to the economic "Aryanization." When the roundups began in the summer of 1942 with the assistance of the French police, the same cool dispassion that characterizes bureaucracy's normal handling of affairs was now applied to a more tragic situation—a question no longer of raw materials or restricted professions, but of men, women, and children, who were arrested because they were Jews and assembled in a few French internment camps from which they were to be deported from their homeland forever. Those who oversaw these operations—operations that fall outside the scope of this study[53]—in particular, the general secretary of police, René Bousquet,[54] and the head of the Vichy government, Pierre Laval, were wholeheartedly convinced that the job of arresting these people, however painful, was no less indispensable to the defense of French sovereignty. As they saw it, the fate of a few tens of thousands of Jews, who were, moreover, foreigners (xenophobia was an integral part of the Vichy regime), was not too high a price to pay to maintain the confidence of the Nazi occupiers and hopefully to continue to win from them a few crumbs of independence. In other words, for an uncertain outcome, they accepted becoming an accomplice to a criminal policy. Historians clearly see how from then on Vichy's hope—one of the regime's chief protagonists spoke of "illusions"[55]—was founded upon a grave overestimation of the Nazi leaders' willingness to make concessions, even if their local representatives proved more open to discussion.[56]

Thus the MBF opposed the creation of a "Jewish office." Conceived by the departments under Abetz's direction, this bureau would have been managed directly by the Germans and commissioned to administer the anti-Semitic ordinances that were applicable in the Occupied Zone. However, the formation of such an office was so clearly contrary to the clauses of the armistice that it was deemed not worth the trouble of provoking the French by defying their claim of sovereignty so openly. It was in neither partner's best interests to see the other lose face. Having become a participant in an endless negotiation by virtue of the collaboration at the national level, the enemy of yesterday was entitled to respect. To this we must add the specific function of law. It is well known that, in totalitarian regimes, a formal normative order was maintained even in the midst of the most extreme violence. Thus, when the process involved "only" property, not human lives, rules served all the more to limit the passions that might come into play.

Values and Passions

Passions, moreover, were certainly in need of restraint, for the process was indeed fraught with raw emotions. From the ideological passion of professional anti-Semites to the few extremely rare, cases of a morality based upon the very values that the Nazis intended to repudiate—here were the opposite ends of the spectrum; the area between these two extremes was usually occupied by the actions (already largely studied) of institutions that cherished the values of competence and reliability, which constituted their strength and their fame. These values, comprising a form of professional ethics, were able to accommodate the very principle of spoliation, and later deportation, in a way that may strike us today as shocking, but which deserves examination. Both the rules governing legal proceedings and the formal respect for the law played an essential part in the acceptance by the whole of French society (and initially by its elites, who were largely steeped in law) of the anti-Semitic policy jointly undertaken by the French and German authorities.[57]

By means of euphemization among law professionals and routinization among civil servants, each participant was able to persuade himself of the total honesty of his or her individual role in this collective theft. Excluding the payment of the one-billion-franc fine, a disturbing exception to be sure, the sums of money belonging to Jews that were frozen in their accounts were not taken from them, but merely held by the government, which pretended acting in the interests of the public. Jews who lost all control of their assets in this manner were not formally victims of plundering or even an expropriation; they were merely involved in a *dessaisissement* (a dispossession), a French legal procedure that could be read as relatively neutral, and had been used many times before.[58] Had it not frequently occurred in the past, this thinking went, that a particular interest had to yield to the overall interests of society which the law was obligated to defend?

The higher-ranking agents of the CGQJ were indeed anti-Semites, albeit "honest" ones. The French form of state anti-Semitism, furthermore, prided itself on its reasonable character. In the eyes of the presentable anti-Semites whom the Vichy government placed in positions of power at first, the violent nature of Nazi racism seemed in bad taste, even useless, when it could be established scientifically, as they were wont to boast, that the Jewish race would no more mix with the French than oil would with water. Hence there was no need for violence in plundering the Jews, still less so for dishonesty. One of the main tasks of the CGQJ in fact consisted of dismissing provisional administrators who played fast and loose with the terms of the law. This category included outright thieves and incompetent officials, as well as administrators who were willing to act as straw men by reaching an agreement with the former owners. This last-mentioned reproach was perhaps the most serious for an institution commissioned to "verify that the elimination of Jewish influence [was] effective and the price of sale ... normal."[59]

For all that, must we see in the behavior of these straw men a link with some type of Resistance? Only with a deeper understanding of who the provisional administrators were (our knowledge of the group remains sketchy at present) can historians try to distinguish in this type of attitude considerations of simple humanity from the desire to subvert the mechanisms of spoliation, or even a taking into account of considerations of opportunity and an appreciation of the circumstances. There were often multiple reasons for acting, and these motivations were probably more complex than those harbored by the civil servants caught up in the process. The culture of their professions was to weigh more heavily in the balance for a longer time. In many cases, although by no means all, we must wait until the second half of 1943 to see any change of behavior. The exceptional measures (in particular the anti-Semitic laws) may have inspired doubts in these civil servants, but it was only then that their reservations began to be translated into the search for a certain latitude, a margin of freedom in which to maneuver.[60] What is known at present about the process of economic "Aryanization" offers precious few examples of outright disobedience. Yet it is easy to imagine, if we are to judge from the well-known reactions of several civil servants vis-à-vis the status of Jews, that such examples existed—and that these reactions were graduated in all likelihood, running the gamut from those who deemed it necessary to withdraw from office rather than be associated with morally unacceptable measures to those who attempted to slow the process, realized their powerlessness to do so, and resigned themselves to the inevitable. This was so at least in terms of the economic "Aryanization"; attitudes changed when the roundups, a prelude to the deportations, began in the summer of 1942 in both zones by the French police under orders from the Germans. The stand taken by several high dignitaries in the Catholic and Protestant churches played a significant role here.[61]

Conclusion

It can be tempting to try to apply to the anti-Semitic measures taken by the French and the Germans the criteria that have been employed by the theoreticians and practitioners of public policy evaluation. The spoliation process in this instance was certainly public policy, implemented during a limited period of time, with objectives that were known, and whose results are beginning to become clear today. However, ratios alone give a singular view of the process. Arguments drawn from purely quantitative approaches indeed reach the conclusion, in the highly symbolic field of deportation for example, that the Vichy government actually protected Jews. The regime's erstwhile participants turned today's partisans never fail to compare the numbers of deportations in France, Belgium, and the Netherlands in order to underscore "objectively" to what extent Philippe Pétain, Pierre Laval, and René Bousquet, and even Xavier Vallat, in reality defended the Jews.

For over twenty years, however, research has shown that this approach is historically biased. One might likewise make similar inquiries in the field of evaluative research (which falls outside the bounds of the present study). With that approach, historians would focus less on the "effectiveness" of the anti-Semitic policy of the Nazi occupiers and their Vichy accomplices (the relationship between results and objectives) than on this policy's efficiency, by comparing the results with the means that were employed. At all events, the impossibility of reasoning from a position of "all things being equal elsewhere" would become obvious since a good deal of the parameters are actually variables here. Complex systems cannot be forced to get excessively simple models. The existence of an Unoccupied Zone did, of course, protect the populations in this zone, sparing them, at least for 28 months, direct contact with the occupier. At the same time, the steadfastness of a French government using its tolerated autonomy to launch a state-supported policy of anti-Semitism established the legitimacy of anti-Semitism, notably among the civil servants and legal professionals who were given the task of applying this policy. Similarly, through the particular play of forces in the collaboration with the Nazis, the involvement of the French authorities in the processes of exclusion, spoliation and eventually pillaging favored the acceptance of these processes by those who witnessed them, even by their victims.

By way of a conclusion, we might recall here the Nazis' initial objectives with regard to the Jews who were then in France. In a letter to the various *Feldkommandanten* dated 1 November 1940, Dr. Michel, the head of the MBF's economic division, summed up these objectives in the following terms: "We must do what is necessary so that the elimination of the Jews persists after the occupation. Furthermore, the Germans cannot mount an apparatus equal to the large number of Jewish businesses. These two considerations have led us to involve French authorities in the elimination of the Jews. The result is that the French public services share the responsibility and we have the French administrative apparatus at our disposal."[62]

The objectives were twofold then. There were final objectives concerning ends and intermediary objectives concerning means. The former were only partly realized. Despite the extent of the spoliation of Jews residing in France, the "complete elimination of Jewish influence in the French economy," an objective shared by the Nazis and the French, never became a reality. On the other hand, the latter objectives touching on the involvement of the French state apparatus in the process were achieved beyond the hopes even of those who favored the policy, given that 60 years later, and doubtless for a long time to come, the question of France's involvement in collaboration with the Nazis continues to fuel debate.

The question that lies at the heart of the present study, i.e., the influence of the multiplicity of institutional actors on the spoliation process, elicits fluctuating answers according to the period. Following a phase of mutual observation among the different partners, there was a tendency toward convergence between administrations with a strong ideological vocation, the CGQJ for instance, and those that were marked by their technical nature (i.e., their ability to respond efficiently to a given problem), such as the CDC. The workings of the former became increasingly routine, a fact that had paradoxical consequences: the bureaucrats working on the economic "Aryanization" took increasingly longer to process cases that were submitted to them, because of their fondness for a job well done. The initial aim of the "Aryanization" operation became secondary in comparison with the satisfaction of seeing one's work carried out competently and correctly. In the meantime, the latter agreed to participate in an ideological process in the name of obedience. Later, especially when the direction of CGQJ was transferred to a figure less socially acceptable than Xavier Vallat, the differences would be made more strikingly manifest in the light of the centrality of the anti-Semitic question to the institution. Increasingly clearer attempts to restrain the process would begin to appear in the higher echelons of the traditional administrations, whereas the CGQJ would continue its task of despoiling France's Jews to the very end. It is significant, and not a little ironic, that the departments given the task after the Liberation of returning stolen Jewish assets largely employed the same personnel of the CGQJ responsible for executing the agency's decisions: these employees were by far the most familiar with the legislation.[63]

The necessity of taking into account different temporalities also seems just as pertinent with respect to the four ideal-type behaviors defined above. Devotion to the professional norm and a certain regard for values that depend on an individual conception of natural law are rather indifferent to the evolution of a particular context and circumstances. On the other hand, attitudes involving monetary advantage or appreciation of the merits or validity of a political position prove quite attuned to events; obviously it is no accident that the two latter attitudes engender what one might call a dual allegiance after the fact, a capacity to run with the hares and hunt with the hounds when necessary that allowed these participants to pursue their activities after the war, generally without difficulty (except in the most flagrant cases).

Vichy's state-supported anti-Semitism, the constraints exercised by the Nazi occupier (both the real constraints and the actors' perceptions of them), and the burden of tradition in professional cultures are some factors that go to explain the easiness with which the French civil service participated in anti-Jewish politics. To process the "Aryanization" of a small home dressmaking shop that supported an entire poor family in the eastern suburbs of Paris as one would any file and as a pure bureaucrat (before other bureaucrats would "process" the deportation of the members of that family) is, of course, a form of anti-Semitism and anti-humanism. Yet there would be some bias in exaggerating the anti-Semitic intentionality of the actors; there rather existed a form of "functionalist intentionalism," which we might best define as indifference. Were only those defined by Hannah Arendt as "the few who were arrogant enough to trust only their own judgment …, the few who were still able to tell right from wrong [and who] went really only by their own judgments"[64] able to resist this indifference?

Among the "bridge hypotheses" built by W. Seibel to answer this question, protection from cognitive dissonance[65] seems of great interest, as applied to the long-time collaboration of the French higher civil service. The personal charisma of Marshal Pétain, routine, and legal-rationalistic legitimacy converged, for a long time, to make civil servants obey the Vichy regime.[66] Since this regime had defined state collaboration as the best possible policy, participating in its implementation—however unpleasant the consequences it may conjure up—was normal administrative work. There existed, for the bureaucrats working within the institutions dealing with the spoliation process, some degrees of latitude. These were used with some success, as Philippe Verheyde has shown, mainly to protect French industry from the risk of too high a penetration by German capital. Obedience and patriotism were thus solid justifications protecting civil servants from uncertainties about the moral legitimacy of their doings. As late as November 1942, high-ranking officials considered most of what was expected from them as the inevitable consequences of both the military defeat and the new political orientation. For the vast majority of them, collaboration appeared as the only sensible solution to the risks of "Polandization" of France: hence the ease with which it was accepted, in spite of everything it implied in terms of denial of French republican liberties. When he heard, in October 1940, about the first anti-Jewish law promulgated by the French government, left-wing writer Jean Guéhenno jotted down, in his diary: "The winner inoculates us with his diseases."[67] For a very long time, the French civil service did not even look for an antidote.

Notes

1. Shmuel Trigano, ed., *Réparation impossible, réparation nécessaire. À propos des spoliations* (Paris, 2000), pp. 4–8.
2. Jean Mattéoli, ed., *Mission d'études sur la spoliation des Juifs de France, Rapport général* (Paris, 2000). All the reports issued by the Mattéoli Commission can be found online at www.ladocfrancaise.gouv.fr.

3. Antoine Prost et al., *Mission d'études sur la spoliation des Juifs de France, Aryanisation économique et restitutions* (Paris, 2000).
4. Claire Andrieu, *Mission d'études sur la spoliation des Juifs de France, La Spoliation financière*, vols. 1 and 2 (annexes) (Paris, 2000).
5. Annette Wieviorka, *Mission d'études sur la spoliation des Juifs de France, Les Biens des internés de camps de Drancy, Pitihiviers et Beaune-la-Rolande* (Paris, 2000).
6. Joseph Billig, *Le Commissariat général aux questions juives*, vol. I (Paris, 1955), vol. II (Paris, 1957), vol. III (Paris, 1960).
7. Serge Klarsfeld, *Vichy-Auschwitz : le rôle de Vichy dans la solution finale*, 2 vols. (Paris, 1983–1985); ibid., *Le Calendrier de la persécution des Juifs en France* (Paris, 1993).
8. Michael R. Marrus and Robert O. Paxton, *Vichy et les Juifs* (Paris, 1981, first published in the USA, 1981).
9. Renée Poznanski, *Être juif en France pendant la Seconde Guerre mondiale* (Paris, 1994; new edition: *Les Juifs en France pendant la Seconde Guerre mondiale*, 1997).
10. Richard H. Weisberg, *Vichy Law and the Holocaust in France* (New York, 1996).
11. Henry Rousso, "L'aryanisation économique. Vichy, l'occupant et la spoliation des juifs," Yod. *Revue des études modernes et contemporaines hébraïques et juives* 15–16 (1982).
12. Philippe Verheyde, "*L'Aryanisation des grandes entreprises juives sous l'Occupation. Contraintes, enjeux, pouvoirs. "Thèse de doctorat d'histoire, sous la direction de Michel Margairaz*, 2 vols. + 1 vol. d'annexes (Paris, 1997). A book has been published subsequently —Philippe Verheyde, *Les Mauvais Comptes de Vichy. L'aryanisation des entreprises juives* (Paris, 1999)—but quotations will be made here from Verheyde's thesis.
13. *Inventaire des archives du Commissariat général aux questions juives et du Service de restitution des biens des victimes des lois et mesures de spoliation, sous-série AJ38* (Paris, 1998).
14. Henri Amouroux, *Pour en finir avec Vichy*, vol. I: *Les oublis de la mémoire* (Paris, 1997).
15. Renée Poznanski, "Vichy et les Juifs. Des marges de l'histoire au cœur de son écriture," in Jean-Pierre Azéma et François Bédarida, eds., *Vichy et les Français* (Paris, 1992), pp. 57–67.
16. Dominique Gros, "Un droit monstrueux?," *Le Genre humain* 30–31*(Le Droit antisémite de Vichy)*, (1996): 561–575; Danièle Lochak, "Les mésaventures du positivisme ou la doctrine sous Vichy," in *Les Usages sociaux du droit* (Paris, 1989), pp. 252–285; idem, "Foreword "to Richard H. Weisberg, *Vichy, la justice et les juifs* (Paris, 1998), pp. 9–19.
17. Marc Olivier Baruch, *Servir l'État français: l'administration en France de 1940 à 1944* (Paris, 1997).
18. Yves Durand, *Le Nouvel Ordre Européen nazi (*Brussels, 1990); Cornelis J. Lammers, "Levels of Collaboration. A Comparative Study of German Occupation Regimes during the Second World War," in Robert Bohn, ed., *Die deutsche Herrschaft in den "germanischen" Ländern 1940–1945* (Stuttgart, 1997), pp. 47–70.
19. Philippe Burrin, *La France à l'heure allemande* (Paris, 1995), pp. 92–104. See also Hans Umbreit, *Der Militärbefehlshaber in Frankreich 1940–1944* (Boppard am Rhein, 1968).
20. Ulrich Herbert, *Best: biographische Studien über Radikalismus, Weltanschauung und Vernunft, 1903–1989* (Bonn, 1996), pp. 251–323.
21. Saul Friedländer, *L'Allemagne nazie et les Juifs*, vol. I, *Les années de persécution 1933–1939* (Paris, 1997), pp. 234–238.
22. Ibid., pp. 153–162.
23. Prost et al., *Aryanisation*, pp. 7–9.
24. Ralph Schor, *L'Antisémitisme en France pendant les années trente* (Brussels, 1992), pp. 145–197; Pierre Birnbaum, *Les Fous de la République, histoire politique des Juifs d'État de Gambetta à Vichy* (Paris, 1992), pp. 442–485; Centre de documentation juive contemporaine, *Le Statut des juifs de Vichy: documentation, textes rassemblés et présentés par Serge Klarsfeld* (Paris, 1990), pp. 10, 27.
25. Mattéoli, *Rapport*, p. 42.
26. Andrieu, *La Spoliation*, pp. 28–29.
27. Prost et al., *Aryanisation*, pp. 32–36.

28. One French franc in 1940 was worth about two francs today (the year 2001), that is, about $0.35; the franc in 1944 was worth half that amount. The total of the operations undertaken, though left unfinished at the end of the Occupation, is of the order of 2.5 billion French francs.
29. Mattéoli, *Rapport*, p. 56.
30. Andrieu, *La Spoliation*, p. 45.
31. Such as Poznanski, *Les Juifs*, pp. 118–125, or Jean Laloum, *Les juifs de la banlieue parisienne des années 20 aux années 50. Montreuil, Vincennes, Bagnolet à l'heure de la "solution finale"* (Paris, 1998).
32. The choice of how to present this material here has no normative function. Acts must be evaluated according to their consequences and not the intentions of their authors. In this case, "altruistic" behavior is not *a priori* any more justifiable than an attitude based upon personal interest.
33. Verheyde, "L'aryanisation", p. 452.
34. Billig, *Le Commissariat*, vol. I, p. 50.
35. Schor, *L'Antisémitisme*, pp. 136–140.
36. Paxton, *La France de Vichy*: 1940–1944 (Paris, 1973), pp. 303–309.
37. On the endless battles between traditional administrations and the new administrative entities that appeared under Vichy, see Baruch, *Servir*, pp. 201–204.
38. These new agencies were founded in the summer of 1940 and given the task of regulating the different branches of the now partly state-ruled economy. In reality, posts involving real responsibilities were filled by representatives of the major industries. Their involvement in the process of economic "Aryanization" springs from the fact that they were consulted in the nomination of provisional administrators.
39. Caisse des dépôts et consignations, *Rapport d'étape du groupe de travail sur les spoliations et les restitutions des "biens juifs"* (Paris, 1999), pp. 271–274.
40. Verheyde, "L'Aryanisation", p. 455.
41. In the French legal system notaries public have greater responsibilities and may act at a higher level than they do in the American system, drawing up contracts, etc. This important distinction makes clear their role which is recounted further on.
42. The expression (*mécanismes producteurs d'innocence*) is from Pierre Legendre, *Jouir du pouvoir. Traité de la bureaucratie patriote* (Paris, 1976), p. 238.
43. Mattéoli, *Rapport*, p. 44; Andrieu, *La Spoliation*, p. 10.
44. Baruch, *Servir*, pp. 489–527.
45. Prost et al., *Aryanisation*, p. 12. See also Joseph Barthélemy's memories, *Ministre de la Justice, Vichy 1941–1943* (Paris, 1989), pp. 313–314.
46. Marguerite Blocaille-Boutelet, "L'aryanisation' des biens," in *Le Droit antisémite de Vichy, Le Genre humain*, 30–31 (1996):243–265 (especially p. 248).
47. Étienne Verhoeyen, *La Belgique occupée: de l'an 40 à la Libération* (Brussels, 1994).
48. Pierre Laborie, "L'idée de Résistance, entre définition et sens : retour sur un questionnement," *Cahiers de l'Institut d'histoire du temps présent* 37 (1997): 15–27 (especially pp. 24–25).
49. Jerôme Carcopino, *Souvenirs de sept ans, 1937–1944* (Paris, 1953), p. 298.
50. Claire Andrieu, "L'aryanisation' et les Finances extérieures. L'activité de la direction des Finances extérieures," in *Le Droit antisémite de Vichy, Le Genre humain*, 30–31 (1996): 267–301 (especially pp. 288–295).
51. Verheyde, "L'aryanisation," p. 430–433, 467. See also Philippe Verheyde's contribution to the present volume, where he also stresses the fierce competition between French and German negotiators when discussing the possible participation of German capital in important French firms. It should be clearly understood that rivalry could coexist within the general setting defined by the official state collaboration policy.
52. Verheyde, "L'aryanisation," p. 436.
53. A summary in Raul Hilberg, *The Destruction of the European Jews*, vol. II (New York/London, 1995), pp. 629–640.
54. Pascale Froment, *René Bousquet* (Paris, 2001).

55. Henri du Moulin de Labarthète, *Le Temps des illusions, Souvenirs, juillet 40-avril 1942* (Geneva, 1946).
56. Burrin, *La France*, pp. 136–149.
57. Lochak, "Les mésaventures"; Marc Olivier Baruch, "Vichy and the Rule of Law," *Bulletin du Centre de recherche français de Jérusalem* 6 (2000): 141–156.
58. Blocaille-Boutelet, "L'aryanisation' des biens", p. 247.
59. Article 14 of the law dated 22 July 1941.
60. Andrieu, *La Spoliation*, pp. 52–57.
61. Poznanski, *Les Juifs*, pp. 353–362.
62. Billig, *Le commissariat*, vol. III, p. 75.
63. Vincent Guigueno, *L'État et l'information offerte aux Juifs spoliés (1945–1950), rapport au ministre de l'Économie, des Finances et de l'Industrie* (Paris, 1999).
64. Hannah Arendt, *Eichmann in Jerusalem. A Report on the Banality of Evil* (New York, 1964), p. 294–295.
65. Wolfgang Seibel, "Did the 'Polycratic' Nature of the National Socialist Regime Restrain or Facilitate the Persecution of the Jews? On the Necessity of Bridge hypotheses," report to the Volkswagenstiftung (Konstanz, 2000), pp. 23–24, 31–33.
66. Marc Olivier Baruch, "L'administration française entre alternance et légitimité, 1940–1947," in Serge Berstein et Pierre Milza, eds., *Axes et méthodes de l'histoire politique* (Paris, 1998), pp. 241–249.
67. Jean Guéhenno, *Journal des années noires* (Paris, 1947; reprint Paris, 1973), p. 57 (of the latter edition).

CHAPTER 12

"ETHNIC RESETTLEMENT" AND INTER-AGENCY COOPERATION IN THE OCCUPIED EASTERN TERRITORIES

Isabel Heinemann

Introduction: A "Perfectly Ordinary" Resettlement Expert

Freiherr Otto von Fircks, Christliche Democratische Union (CDU) member of the Bundestag and long-time manager of the Bund der Vertriebenen (Association of German Expellees) in Lower Saxony, had just been elected District Chairman of the CDU in Burgdorf near Hanover when, in June 1970, a leaflet appeared accusing him of participating "in Nazi crimes during the occupation of Poland."[1] Furthermore, it maintained that as leader of a compulsory resettlement force (Aussiedlungsstab) in Litzmannstadt (Łódź) the Freiherr had participated in the expulsion of Polish farm owners from the Warthegau. The leaflet was written by a Burgdorf primary school teacher named Arthur Sahm, who had chosen this way of informing the public about the Freiherr's past. The politician did not hesitate very long before lodging complaints of insult and defamation with the State Attorney's Office in Hildesheim, which in May 1971 brought charges against Sahm. Von Fircks appeared as co-plaintiff and witness at his own proceedings and announced that as an SS-Führer and leader of a so-called "Task Force" (Arbeitsstab) he had only been involved in the resettlement of ethnic Germans, so that the false portrayal in the leaflet was an insult to his honor and harmful to his work as a politician. Above all, he had been associated in this way with National Socialist acts of violence, that he had had nothing to do with. What followed was an odyssey through various courts that continued for several years until the proceedings were quietly discontinued without the defendant being acquitted.[2] Von Fircks, however, left the Bundestag in 1976, after having previously stepped down as CDU District Chairman.

What seems like a fairly normal example of postwar West German history in dealing with the National Socialist past is, however, of particular relevance for the circumstances to be discussed here. As a result of the case of Sahm and von Fircks and the comparatively lively newspaper reporting that accompanied it, the activities of the SS Resettlement Offices and Task Forces (SS-Ansiedlungs- und Arbeitsstäbe) and thereby a further aspect of the population transfers in the occupied East first attracted widespread public attention. Whereas National Socialist policies for Poland had previously been largely identified with the murders of the mobile killing squads (Einsatzgruppen) the deportation of the Jews and the mass extermination in Auschwitz, a further facet was added: the deliberate expulsion, selection and deportation of non-Jewish Poles in the context of the desired "political reorganization of the population." This was neither an act of war nor a mass crime in a narrow sense, but rather an administrative process based on the more or less smooth cooperation of various offices and staffs.

Von Fircks (b. 1912), descended from an old aristocratic Baltic family, had himself come with his family as an ethnic German from Latvia to settle in the Warthegau. There he began to work for the resettlement as a farmer, joined the SS, and was soon promoted to SS-Obersturmführer (first lieutenant).[3] In January 1940, the Freiherr wrote to a representative of the Ethnic German Welfare Office (Volksdeutsche Mittelstelle), who was also participating in the resettlement process: "The evacuation is progressing very well there [in Łódź/Litzmannstadt: I.H.]. By the 12th of February the expulsion of the Jews will be completed; then the Poles will have their turn. Occupational deployment is also going well. At any rate I can only advise coming to Łódź."[4] As leader of an SS Task Force (SS-Arbeitsstab) in Gniezno/Gnesen from early 1940 until early 1941, he coordinated not only the resettlement of ethnic Germans, but also the preceding "evacuation of the Poles and the Jews" in his district, i.e., their expulsion, transfer to concentration camps, and subsequent deportation to the General Government. Von Fircks and his successors were relatively successful in Gnesen. By the end of 1942, 10,117 people had disappeared from the Gnesen District, most of them before transportation was first stopped in March 1941, i.e., during Otto von Fircks's term of office.[5]

Recent research has shown that the idea of a "necessary Germanization" of the occupied territories and the resettlement carried out to this end represented an important background to and, at the same time, a driving force behind the National Socialist extermination policy and particularly the Holocaust.[6] For example, in order to "win back for the German people" the annexed western Polish territories by means of German settlement, Poles and Jews were ruthlessly evicted from their property. As the report by Otto von Fircks cited above indicates, the Jews were the first to be affected by the violent resettlement. They were deported in the first transports to the General Government, crowded into ghettos, and later killed in extermination camps. The Poles were forced above all to leave the rural regions of the new Eastern Gaus. They were also deported at first to the General Government, but later deprived of their property and left in their Gau or immediately sent to the Old Reich as forced labor. This expulsion of people to make room for the planned resettlement of the ethnic Germans and the problems resulting from the expulsions seemed to the population planners to prove the necessity of the most radical solutions: resettlement and extermination went hand in hand.

The SS, the police, and the civil administration usually cooperated in an effective manner in the "political reorganization of the population in the annexed territories." Without the participation of the most varied agencies, such a major project could not have been realized. The present contribution studies the part played by the race and resettlement experts of the SS in the process of resettlement and expulsion. Experts such as Freiherr von Fircks worked for the main SS office responsible, the Race and Resettlement Main Office (Rasse- und Siedlungshauptamt—RuSHA).[7] Also important are the roles played by the Gauleiter and administrative officials, the order police and, comparativly unknown in this context, the representatives of the local health authorities and labor offices. At the same time, the question arises whether and in what manner conflicts of interest were resolved—how, for example, economic considerations were weighed against ideological convictions. To assess this resettlement process as a whole, it is also necessary to clarify whether the gradual radicalization leading from "the redistribution of peoples" (*Umvolkung*) to the initiation of the "final solution" arose from polycratic conflicts of interest or more or less self-created pressures to act, and to ascertain the part played by ideological factors. In regard to the perception of the resettlement process and the role played by those responsible for it, it must be asked whether it was precisely because of the division of labor that so many more or less "civilian participants" escaped criminal prosecution and—a prominent example is again the Freiherr—were able to begin a new career in postwar Germany.

First the plans for the reorganization of the occupied territories will be briefly discussed and the measures for the expulsion of Poles and Jews and the settlement of ethnic Germans explained. Then a few examples will be given to demonstrate the actual implementation of the expulsions and the combination of ideological and pragmatic considerations involved. I will refer above all to the western Polish territories, chiefly the Warthegau, since most of the "resettlement" occurred there.

The "Political Reorganization of the Population" in the Former Polish Territories: the Expulsion of the Poles and the Settlement of Ethnic Germans

On 7 October 1939 Adolf Hitler officially appointed Reichsführer-SS Heinrich Himmler to organize the return of ethnic Germans from abroad and the Germanization of the occupied western part of Poland. Himmler was to provide for the "creation of new settlement areas through resettlement" and also for "the elimination of the harmful influence of alien segments of the population which pose a threat to the Reich and the German ethnic community."[8] Himmler then chose the title "Reich Commissioner for the Strengthening of the German Peoples" (Reichskommissar für die Festigung deutschen Volkstums—RKF) for himself and set up his own organization, the Central Office of the RKF (Stabshauptamt RKF) under Ulrich Greifelt.[9] In the following months this became the coordinating office for the entire population policy of the SS in occupied Europe.[10]

The planned Germanization of the annexed western Polish territories began first of all with the resettlement of ethnic Germans from abroad, who, in accordance with various resettlement agreements, started to arrive in the western Polish territories from winter 1939 on, above all from areas in the Soviet Union's sphere of influence.[11] In addition, Germans already living in the region were registered in the "List of Ethnic Germans" (Deutsche Volksliste—DVL), and the "evacuation" (Aussiedlung) of all Jews and as many Poles as possible was initiated. In late October 1939 the RKF decreed that the following groups of persons were to be resettled:

1. All Jews from the former Polish territories, now provinces of the German Reich.
2. All Congress Poles from the province of Danzig-West Prussia.
3. An as yet unspecified number of the especially hostile Polish population from the provinces of Poznań, South and East Prussia, and Eastern Upper Silesia.[12]

In their famous memorandum "On the treatment of the population of the former Polish territories from the point of view of racial policy" of 25 November 1939, the National Socialist population planners from the NSDAP Race Policy Office estimated a population of about 6.6 million Poles and 530,000 Jews in the occupied areas.[13] Of these, all Jews without exception and about 5.3 million Poles were to be deported to rump Poland. The Race Policy Office assumed that due to their "share of German blood" about a million people living in Poland were suitable for Germanization and could remain in the territory or be resettled in the Old Reich. The idea of assimilating a small number of Poles (in accordance, of course, with the ideology of the SS and hence based on "high racial value" and not primarily on possible "Germanness") was supported by the Reichsführer-SS Heinrich Himmler. He expressed this view in a secret memorandum "On the treatment of alien peoples in the East" of 28 May and a "Decree for the examination and selection of the population in the incorporated Eastern territories" of 12 September 1940.[14] The selection of the evacuees as "desirable" and "undesirable additions" to the German population was later actually carried out on the basis of racial criteria in the camps of the resettlement institutions.

The destination for the resettlement of undesirable expellees was provisionally to be rump Poland, now transformed into the General Government. The "removal of Jews and Poles" was placed in the hands of the Security

Police; the SS Resettlement Task Forces under the RKF (SS-Ansiedlungs- und Arbeitsstäbe) played a key role in this action. At the same time, the four Higher SS and Police Leaders of the occupied areas were appointed as deputies of the Reichsführer-SS in his role as RKF and were made responsible for the implementation of the measures in their respective areas. Parallel to this, the later Resettlement Central Office (Umwandererzentralstelle – UWZ) began to develop as the coordinating agency of the Security Police and the SD for the resettlement of Poles and Jews.[15]

The evacuation was conceived and coordinated by the RSHA using various short-term, long-term, and intermediate plans. However, the evacuation figures reached the targeted level only once, in December 1939, and afterwards consistently failed to do so.[16] By the end of January 1941, 261,517 persons had already been evacuated from the annexed western Polish areas.[17] After the so-called deportation stop in mid-March 1941—the transport capacities of the state railway were needed to prepare for the Russian campaign—a new wave of expulsions began in summer 1941. This time, however, it was not a matter of transports to the East, but rather of so-called "displacement to relatives in the same Gau." By the end of 1943, a total of 534,348 persons had been expelled from the annexed Polish territories, of whom around 350,000 were deported to the General Government, a further 200,000 being simply "displaced" or transferred to the Old Reich as labor supply.[18] It is important to note that the various plans included provision for the resettlement of specific groups of ethnic Germans. The first short-term plan was directed against the Polish intelligentsia and the Jews, but it was also designed to create living space for Baltic Germans. The intermediate plan served the sole purpose of resettling Germans from the Baltic region, whereas the second short-term plan was to enable the settlement of Germans from Eastern Poland. The third short-term plan aimed to provide enterprises for Germans from the Soviet Union, and the expanded third short-term plan was to provide additional land for the "benefit of ethnic Germans" already in the area.

The ethnic Germans from the parts of Poland and the Baltic states occupied by the Soviet Union started arriving at the end of 1939, above all in the ports of the Baltic Sea and the camps of the Warthegau. It was, therefore, no accident that the SS resettlement institutions developed in precisely these places, in Danzig, Gotenhafen, Poznań, and above all Łódź/Litzmannstadt. The Immigrant Central Office (Einwandererzentralstelle—EWZ) in Poznań, and later Litzmannstadt, a subsidiary of the Reich Security Main Office (RSHA), with its network of branch offices, was responsible for the registration and control of ethnic Germans.[19] Representatives of the Security Police and SD, the order police, the Reich Ministry of the Interior and the Reich Labor Ministry, as well as the Reich Health Executive (Reichsgesundheitsführer), evaluated the families and granted or denied naturalization, decided on their resettlement in the new Reich districts or in the territory of the Old Reich. Besides the already-named institutions, the SS race experts also participated in this "processing" or "sluicing" (*Durch-*

schleusung), as it was officially termed.[20] The "racial fitness examiners" (Eignungsprüfer) of the RuSHA office at the EWZ determined the "racial worth" of the settler families, registered it in the so-called "racial formula" (*Rassenformel*) and thereby indirectly decided their fate: the often-cited "farm in the East" was reserved for those who were rated as "racially desirable."

The registration and "processing" of the ethnic Germans took place in waves, depending on the arrival of settlers in the annexed areas. The first to come were the ethnic Germans from the Baltic region, at first from Estonia and Latvia and later from Lithuania. The so-called "processing" of people from the Baltic area began in November 1939. The next large group consisted of settlers from Eastern Poland, more precisely from the areas of Galicia, Narev, and Volhynia annexed by the Soviet Union. The third great wave consisted of ethnic Germans from the areas around Chełm and Lublin in the General Government. They were followed by ethnic Germans from Rumania and the regions of North Bukovina and Bessarabia belonging to the Soviet Union. Between October 1939 and the end of 1940 almost half-a-million ethnic Germans from abroad were moved to the annexed areas, and in the years from 1941 to 1944 another 500,000 arrived.[21]

The tension between the necessity of creating "room for ethnic Germans" and the resettlement of Poles and the deportation of the Jews has already been plausibly portrayed by Götz Aly in his monograph "*Endlösung*." Due to the pressure of resettlement and expulsion, population policy became increasingly radical. There was never any doubt about the necessity of deporting all the Jews—overall about 500,000 Jews from the occupied western Polish territories were "evacuated to the East" or, later, eliminated on the spot.[22]

In what follows a few examples of the efficient cooperation among various offices involved in the evacuation and resettlement process will be briefly discussed.

Examples of Successful Cooperation: Expulsion and Resettlement of People and their "Processing" in the Camps

After March 1940 an SS Resettlement Office (SS-Ansiedlungsstab) was set up in each Gau of the occupied parts of Western Poland; in the Warthegau, where the most extensive resettlement was expected, there were even two.[23] In each district, the resettlement offices had at their disposal an SS Task Force (SS-Arbeitsstab) to which a resettlement expert and a further thirty to forty persons belonged, mainly farmers from the Reich Food Estate (Reichsnährstand) and students doing service in the East, but also representatives of the SD, various specialists, office workers, and drivers. In early 1941 there were thirty-one SS Task Forces in the areas of Poznań and Litzmannstadt (Łódź) alone, which were ultimately responsible for implementing the local programs of expulsion and resettlement.[24] They received their instructions from the resettlement offices, which in turn were bound by the orders of the respective Higher SS and Police Leaders and the RKF.[25] At the same time they were also subject to the authority of the UWZ as the central coordinating agency of the Security Police and the SD in questions of resettlement.

The beginning of the resettlement activities of the Task Forces (SS-Arbeitsstäbe) in the western Polish territories will be briefly described here, taking as an example the Task Force in the Turek district in the Warthegau under SS-Sturmbannführer (Major) Georg Gloystein.[26] By profession a farmer, Gloystein came to the Warthegau in mid-March 1940 with an entire group of resettlement experts from the RuSHA. After extended preliminary discussions in Poznań and Łódź, with, among others, the Higher SS and Police Leader for Warthe, SS-Gruppenführer (Lieutenant-General) Koppe, "the R.u.S. Leaders [Resettlement experts from the RuSHA: I.H.] were each assigned," according to Gloystein, "a political district in order, simply put, to make it German."

Gloystein's SS Task Force (SS-Arbeitsstab) employed a total of 35 persons, consisting of general staff, transport staff, three resettlement groups, and a liaison officer for the local District Office (Landratsamt).[27] Gloystein first obtained an overview of his district, which according to SS studies had about 96,400 residents over twelve years of age, including about 4,800 ethnic Germans, 88,800 Poles, and 2,700 Jews. In all, 18,200 agricultural enterprises cultivated a total area of about 158,000 hectares, with a clear emphasis (40.2 percent) on medium-sized units of five to thirty hectares. Given this starting point, Gloystein was now faced with the task of expelling about half of the Polish population, 40,000 to 50,000 persons, in order to settle 1,900 ethnic German families from Eastern Poland on farms and in handicraft businesses.[28] If the widespread discrepancy between planning policy and the real situation is taken into account, Gloystein was successful in terms of evacuation rates: by late 1942 he had expelled 20,500 persons.[29] The RuS Führer was dependent in his work on the support of the civilian administration, which he had been immediately granted. The District Officer (Landrat), District Peasant Leader (Kreisbauernführer), and the local farmers' representative (Kreislandwirt) were, according to Gloystein, "happy that an SS Führer had finally been appointed who had the necessary knowledge to carry out the resettlement."

The next step was the registration and cataloging of villages and farms with the aim of preparing enough enterprises for the resettlement of ethnic Germans, whereby several Polish farms often had to be combined to form a single "German farmstead." The registration was carried out by smaller working groups of the SS Task Force, consisting of students and farmers.[30] The information thus acquired formed the basis for decision-making on the later evacuations of Polish farming families, for which approval by the local representatives of the Reich Food Estate and of the SD was required. The ethnic German settlers were sent to Turek by the Resettlement Office (SS-Ansiedlungsstab) in Łódź. In the Turek district the Task Force, together with the Gestapo and the police escort, arranged for the evacuation of Polish farmers to coincide with the arrival of settlers. The eviction of the farmers was intentionally held off until "the very last minute"—usually dawn on the day the ethnic Germans were to arrive—in order to deny the surprised Poles any chance of fleeing and, at the same time, to ensure that the farms would not be left unattended and the livestock untended. Then the Task Force made provisional arrangements for the new arrivals until the resettlement supervisors of the Ethnic German Welfare Office could look after them.

This resettlement procedure was carried out in all "resettlement districts," following the same pattern. A report from Litzmannstadt by the above-mentioned SS-Obersturmführer Otto von Fircks provides impressive details on how such evacuations were carried out. In the early morning of 20 March 1940, Polish families were evacuated from several villages in the vicinity of Litzmannstadt, and that same morning their farms were turned over to ethnic German settlers. Von Fircks reported:

> At three o'clock in the morning the police forces went into action; they received their final instructions for the evacuation from Hauptmann Kreuzhofer and were sent off to their destination between 3:15 and 4 a.m., partly in motor vehicles, partly on foot under the leadership of ethnic Germans familiar with the area and the trek leader (Treckführer) of the Task Force. The evacuation took place according to plan and without incident. Only in one case, in the village of Mokradolna, did a Pole succeed in escaping during the evacuation. This case is being investigated by the police.

Within a few hours the original farm owners had been expelled. They were first assembled in reception camps and taken towards evening to an "evacuation camp" in Litzmannstadt. Other members of the resettlement office had already accompanied the ethnic German settlers to their farms in the morning, and there the Higher SS and Police Leader Koppe, together with representatives of the RKF and the resettlement office, personally convinced himself of the successful course of resettlement, answered the questions of the ethnic Germans or gave them encouragement.[31]

The locally deployed police were instructed in advance by special UWZ leaflets on the implementation of the evacuations. Besides police security services, their duties included searching the evacuees for weapons, making a register of abandoned property and preventing the destruction of buildings and fixtures by the former owners during their evacuation.[32]

Georg Gloystein did not confine himself to the expulsion of the Polish rural population either, but also arranged the "resettlement" and later deportation of the Jewish inhabitants of the Turek district. The Jewish residents, who, according to Gloystein, still amounted to 2,752 persons in early 1940, were resettled between late 1940 and early 1941 in a separate "Jewish Quarter." In 1941 they were transferred to the so-called "Jewish colony of Heidemühl" in the district, from which, in mid-1942, they were directly deported to the Chełmno extermination camp.[33]

Detailed knowledge of their districts also benefited the members of the SS Task Forces during the later phases of resettlement. In May 1941 the head of the UWZ in Litzmannstadt, SS-Obersturmbannführer (Lieutenant Colonel) Hermann Krumey, required that from now on they must not only provide the names of the families to be evacuated, but also compile lists of "displacement possibilities." This meant that for each family to be evacuated the SS Resettlement and Task Forces (SS-Ansiedlungs- und Arbeitsstäbe) had to name a Polish family that could accommodate the evacuated family. This was necessary because the preparations for the war against the Soviet Union made it impossible to send transports to the General Government.[34]

Resettlement rates, however, remained far below the expected levels – as did evacuation rates. During the first phase of resettlement of ethnic Germans in Western Poland, of Baltic Germans (about 60,000 persons from Estonia and Latvia), as well as the so-called Galician and Volhynian Germans from Eastern Poland (overall around 128,000 persons), about 58,000 persons had been settled by mid-1940 in the districts of the Warthegau. By June 1941, only 225,000 out of more than 500,000 settlers had been resettled, 175,000 in rural areas and 50,000 in the towns.[35]

The cooperation between the UWZ, which was responsible for the overall planning of the settlement and resettlement, the leaders of the resettlement offices, which implemented them, and the police forces, which provided security, seems to have functioned smoothly. In late 1943 the Director of the Resettlement Central Office of Litzmannstadt (UWZ), Hermann Krumey, explicitly mentioned the especially successful cooperation in the resettlement process. He felt it would not be necessary in the future to send a UWZ representative to control the evacuation or displacement operations in the Warthegau.[36]

Naturally not everything ran smoothly. The large number of participants in resettlement operations necessitated a strict demarcation of competencies. The SS resettlement experts were occasionally annoyed by the representatives of the civilian administration, who were less well informed on racial questions, or by those who thought they were too good for the business of "getting to know the country and people" and the operations in the local areas. Thus the financial expert of the Eastern Trustee Office (Treuhandstelle Ost) in the Nessau-Hohensalza district created a distinctly negative impression when he preferred to remain in "civilized Hermannsbad"—instead of appraising the abandoned property of ethnic German settlers and visiting the corresponding "resettlement villages."[37]

Not only property was assessed. The "settlers" themselves were also registered and selected in accordance with racial and political criteria. This was the case not only for ethnic Germans entering the Old Reich from abroad, but also for the expelled Poles. In this work representatives of various offices cooperated in a "processing" involving a division of labor that will be briefly described below.

The examination of ethnic German settlers from the Baltic areas, Eastern Poland, and the Soviet Union took place either in Litzmannstadt, Poznań, the Baltic ports, or the various reception centers with the help of "flying commissions," in which representatives of all participating offices were included. At the EWZ in Litzmannstadt and Poznań the settler family passed through the following stages during the three-to-four-hour "processing": reporting office (order police), identification card and photograph office (security police), health office (Reichsgesundheitsführer), RuS-Office (RuSHA), nationality office (Reich Ministry of the Interior), and professional employment office (Reich Ministry of Labor). Sometimes there was also a Hitler Youth office (HJ-Dienststelle), a property office and a statistics office as well.

The working methods of a "flying commission" were described by a female student on Eastern service (*Osteinsatz*) as follows:

> In the waiting room the personal details are collected and the check on freedom from hereditary diseases recorded by a medical student. ... The doctor and the racial fitness examiner both examine each family one after another in order to reach a reliable overall judgment. All results are entered on cards which are coded with different colors.
>
> At the end the family must again present itself to the "High Commission," which is made up of all members of the "flying commission." If the evaluation is positive in terms of health, professional, ethnic and racial factors, theoretical assignment to a farm is made in accordance with the guidelines of the SS resettlement office, and this is the case with almost all ethnic German families.[38]

If the ethnic Germans were, however, declared racially unsuitable, they were sent for re-education to the Old Reich, where they were put to work as rural laborers. If there was evidence of "alien racial coloring" or "alien blood," the SS resettlement experts might even consider their inclusion in the program for deportation to the East.[39] As a result of the "processing," the EWZ distinguished among so-called O-cases (suitable as settlers in the East), A-cases (intended for resettlement in the Old Reich), and S-cases (racially undesirable, scheduled for deportation to the East or to concentration camps).

After their expulsion, Poles were first sent to camps run by the Resettlement Central Office (UWZ), where their fate was decided in a sorting process involving a division of labor comparable to that for ethnic Germans. The largest system of camps for "processing evacuees" was located in Litzmannstadt (Łódź). There the UWZ maintained at least six camps within the city boundaries, among them several assembly and "processing camps," a transport camp for the Old Reich, one for the General Government, and a sick ward. The SS Race and Resettlement Main Office had its own center for "stricter selection" of Poles probably suitable for "re-Germanization" (*wiedereindeutschungsfähig*) and thus "racially of high value." This camp typology already indicates a specific division of labor even within the activities of the UWZ. An internal UWZ paper described the procedure as follows: "From the assembly point the expellees are first brought to the delousing center at Dessauerstraße 11–16 in Litzmannstadt. After delousing they are taken to the processing camp at Wiesenstraße 4. Here the personal details of the Poles are recorded and their ethnic identity is checked; furthermore they are searched for weapons and food." The expellees were then "subjected to a thorough political, racial, health and work-related examination." Those classed as being of medium value were sent on a "voluntary" basis to the Old Reich as Polish rural laborers, those with a poorer evaluation "are deported by the State Police to the General Government." A small percentage of the racially superior were again selected from the groups intended for the Old Reich. "These are carefully examined by a commission of doctors, and by the Race and Resettlement Office, and then come to the Old Reich in order to be assimilated there," which meant more realistically that they were transported to the Old Reich in order to work there.[40]

The Labor Offices were highly interested in "racially good" laborers, who were now officially designated as "capable of re-Germanization." The Labor Office in Litzmannstadt also managed the transports of both those "capable of re-Germanization" and "ordinary Polish laborers" into the Old Reich.

In what follows two examples of divergences of interest and different decisions in the area of population policy in Western Poland will be discussed. A project of such ideological relevance as the racial examination of the population of the occupied territories by the SS race experts had almost inevitably to lead to conflicts with political and economic interests. First, I will discuss the racial selection of persons of German descent registered on the "List of Ethnic Germans" and then the recruitment of a specific group of "persons capable of re-Germanization," for whom there was great demand, female domestic servants.

"Labor Deployment" versus "Racial Purity": Divergence of Interests and Balancing of Interests

It was not only the ethnic Germans from abroad who had to prove their "Germanness" to the EWZ. The ethnic Germans already living in former Poland also had to apply first of all for German citizenship. A first attempt to register all local residents of "German descent" in a "List of Ethnic Germans" was undertaken in the Warthegau, beginning in fall 1939, by Gauleiter Arthur Greiser. The most important category applied was of a political nature ("declaration of loyalty to the German people"). Besides that, factors such as German language, Protestant faith, attendance of children at German schools, and German first names for children were positively rated. In contrast, Arthur Greiser did not at first want "racial attributes" to be considered as reliable grounds for judging ethnic Germanness in the Warthegau.[41] This changed, however, the moment the List of Ethnic Germans (DVL) was introduced for all incorporated Eastern territories, not only for the Warthegau, but also for Danzig-West Prussia and the enlarged provinces of East Prussia and Silesia. On 12 September 1940 Heinrich Himmler, in his "Decree on the examination and selection of the population in the incorporated Eastern Territories," ordered the introduction of "Lists of Ethnic Germans" in the four affected regions. In the decree, the Reichsführer made "racial worth" the chief criterion for recognition as a German, since it would in any case be impossible to make a clear "ethnic classification" for many persons.[42] The ultimately decisive factor for those who had not already lived as Germans in the Eastern territories before 1 September 1939, according to the Reichsführer-SS, was whether they represented a "racially valuable addition to the population." This also facilitated the inclusion of racially valuable non-Germans in the lowest group of the List of Ethnic Germans—with the aim of later Germanizing them after preliminary racial examination by the experts of the RuSHA.

Those on the List of Ethnic Germans were subdivided into four different groups. In Groups One and Two were persons who had supposedly "preserved their Germanness" or even actively defended it. They received German nationality, Reich citizenship (*Reichsbürgerschaft*) and the right to be "employed in building up the East." This meant that Himmler permitted them to remain in their homes and keep possession of their property, because they were already living "in the German East"! Group Three included people who "in the course of the years had developed ties to Polish culture," whom the Reichsführer-SS nevertheless considered to have potential for reeducation as Germans. Generally Group Three of the DVL included by far the greatest number of persons—these received German nationality, but without Reich citizenship. Those of German ancestry who had "been politically assimilated to Polish culture" were classed in Group Four and received "provisional German nationality." They became, so to speak, Germans on probation and were expected to prove themselves as Germans over a period of ten years—for example, through their political views and through activities in branches of the Party and other organizations. Himmler planned a stay of several years in the Old Reich for the members of Groups Three and Four, during which, "through intensive educational work," they would gradually be "re-Germanized and made completely German." These instructions of the Reichsführer-SS for the implementation of the List of Ethnic Germans became fully valid throughout the Reich with the promulgation of a corresponding decree of the Reich Minister of the Interior in March 1941, which adopted Himmler's categories in their entirety.[43] By mid-1941, uniform implementation of the List of Ethnic Germans procedures had been achieved in the new Reich Gaus, and a branch office of the List of Ethnic Germans had been set up in each of the eleven government districts.[44]

In connection with these homogenization measures the race experts of the SS also demanded—initially against the vehement resistance of the Gauleiter and Reich commissioners (*Reichsstatthalter*), especially of Arthur Greiser[45] and Albert Forster[46] —a large-scale racial examination of all members of Groups Three and Four of the List of Ethnic Germans, in order to "eradicate ... biologically and racially defective cases." Only those who received a racial evaluation of at least RuS III (not to be confused with Group Three of the DVL) should be permitted to remain on the List of Ethnic Germans. In this way racially undesirable persons were to be barred from acquiring rights through marriage with Germans, military service, party membership, or honorary public offices that could later render their "exclusion from the body of the German people" almost impossible.

Arthur Greiser argued that such inspections would be too expensive in wartime and would, above all, lead to political unrest. People could not be excluded retroactively from the DVL before the end of the war without risking political consequences. "Questions of nationality and race" should be dealt with separately. But such arguments were of no avail, as the Reichsführer-SS sided with the racial experts and compelled the Warthegau Gauleiter to permit a review of the members of Groups Three and Four of the DVL by RuSHA racial fitness examiners. In the Warthegau about 71,000 persons were affected. However, those who were classified as "racially unsuitable" would only lose their German identification papers "if the option of expulsion from their Gau is available," which meant that serious sanctions would be put off until after the war.[47] As a justification, Heinrich Himmler again conjured up a vision of racial threat: "Given our notion of blood it would be irresponsible to absorb Slavic blood in great quantities into our German national body by accepting Upper Silesian Poles [*Wasserpolen*], Kashubes, and German-Polish half-breeds without a racial examination. In order at least to prevent the worst damage, the defective elements must be eradicated before inclusion in the List of Ethnic Germans."[48] The sole means of detecting such "racially undesirable" persons was, however, examination by SS experts—and the Gauleiter gave in and instructed his department heads to prepare the appropriate directives or had them take over the SS proposals directly.[49]

This victory of the criterion of "racial purity" over the Gauleiter's efforts to maintain order in his Gau "during the third year of the war" must be viewed as a triumph of SS ideologists over Realpolitik. As a consequence, the selection criteria were sharpened and almost 10 percent of the 71,000 DVL members examined in the Warthegau were classified "as undesirable on racial grounds." They thus became subject to later deportation and immediate loss of rights. The persons whose elimination from the DVL was requested were reported by the RuSHA to the branch offices of the DVL with the following standard statement: "On the basis of a suitability test serious doubts have arisen as to the advisability of retaining the families (persons) named below on the List of Ethnic Germans. They represent an undesired addition to the population. Their removal from the List of Ethnic Germans is necessary for biological reasons."[50] According to the logic of the race experts, it was of the greatest importance to prevent or at least discourage these persons from reproducing. The RuSHA accomplished this by denying "racially undesired" members of the DVL 3 the mandatory marriage license and the equally necessary racial certificate (*Rassegutachten*). Anyone who received a racial rating of RuS IV or IV f (ethnically alien, "*fremdvölkisch*") was refused permission to marry. The Litzmannstadt branch office of the RuSHA sent lists of members of Group 3 of the DVL who had been classified as RuS IV or RuS IVf to registry offices and public health offices in the occupied areas so that they would not in these cases perform the marriage ceremony or issue "certificates of fitness to marry" (*Eheunbedenklichkeitsbescheinigungen*). Here too the civilian authorities followed the racially inspired decision of the SS and refused to allow the persons affected to marry.[51] Years later, this procedure was dealt with at the Nuremberg Military Tribunal VIII as an indictment for "hampering the reproduction of enemy nationals."[52]

In the other "Eastern Gaus" the racial examination of persons classed DVL 3 and 4 was somewhat less successful than in the Warthegau. East Prussia was an exception; here too the affected persons were racially selected, approximately 21,000 in all.[53] But in Eastern Upper Silesia and above all in Danzig-West Prussia, resistance by the Gauleiter impeded a speedy implementation of the racial examinations, although it is certain that the process of selection began in both areas. There are, however, no reliable figures on how far the selection had progressed there.[54] According to RKF plans, no less than 1.9 million persons were to have been selected in the two regions, an ambitious project.[55]

A special chapter of the previously mentioned "re-Germanization procedure," i.e. the deportation of "racially desirable" Poles into the Old Reich as laborers and their later "Germanization," involved the recruitment of "female Polish domestic servants." In late 1941 the Reichsführer-SS detected a serious shortage of household help in the Old Reich and tried to counter this "biological threat to the nation" through the employment of as many "racially unobjectionable" girls as possible.[56] The employment of these "girls of good race" was to enable German housewives to dedicate themselves to their maternal duties again and thereby indirectly to "redress the population balance." Furthermore, "racially valuable" laborers were definitely preferable to other forced laborers. The need was great and demand increased steadily, but Himmler and the RuSHA race experts stubbornly insisted nevertheless on a strict racial selection. The RKF Central Office was also aware of the discrepancy between the demand for household help and the number of "re-Germanizable" persons available. The head of the RKF office, Ulrich Greifelt, wrote to the Reich Minister of Labor: "I am aware that through this sort of selection of domestic labor that may be recruited for employment in the Reich and the consequent rigorous racial selection the number of employable girls in the Reich has radically diminished. I must, however, point out the extraordinary threat to our people resulting from the flooding of Germany with foreign, and especially Polish, laborers."[57] Vacant positions and the need for housemaids were directly reported by the Higher SS and Police Leaders to the RuSHA, whose racial fitness examiners examined young girls in the occupied Polish territories from a racial standpoint. For their part the RuSHA racial fitness examiners lobbied the labor offices and visited local enterprises in an effort to find "re-Germanizable Polish women." This ruthless recruiting practice often caused problems. The Gauleiter, in particular Arthur Greiser in the Warthegau, feared that the labor supply in their districts would be endangered.

Initially, the Gauleiter in the Warthegau only allowed unemployed Polish women to be summoned to the employment offices for racial examination of their "capacity to be Germanized" (*Eindeutschungsfähigkeit*). He rejected the examination of employed women by SS race experts as a threat to war production.[58] That things soon changed can be inferred from a letter of complaint to the head of the RuSHA by the head of the Warthegau Labor Office (Landesarbeitsamt), who took the case of a Polish woman as an opportunity to air his displeasure about SS recruitment practices. "On this occasion I feel obliged to point out that recently the Germanization of Polish workers already in employment has led to great difficulties." No German replacement was available for female workers recruited in this manner, he claimed, which in the end inevitably made it more difficult to fulfill the "construction and armament tasks assigned to the Warthegau."[59] Gauleiter Greiser and his officials received unexpected support from an RuSHA representative in Danzig-West Prussia, who described to the head of the Berlin office the consequences of the high-handed recruitment even among agricultural laborers and demanded an end to the practice.[60] Referring to these two statements, RuSHA Director Otto Hofmann assured the labor offices that workers would no longer be withdrawn without their consent. But a termination of the transport of persons "capable of being Germanized" to the Old Reich as a matter of principle was out of the question; nor would workers already employed be automatically exempted. The "Germanization of labor with desirable racial characteristics" by means of residence in the Old Reich still had precedence.[61] As late as the summer of 1944, "Poles capable of being Germanized," including "female Polish domestic servants," were still being transferred from Litzmannstadt to the Old Reich. From 1941 until the end of the war several thousand Polish girls, mostly still under-age, were brought to Germany to work in the households of large families (or influential SS men and Party members!). A number of surviving letters and postwar statements reveal that they were often treated like serfs.[62]

In the recruitment of "re-Germanizable" Polish laborers, especially of "Polish housemaids," the racial goals of the SS ("not to lose a drop of good blood" and "increasing the birth rate of the German people" by reducing the work of German housewives) competed with the demands of the economy and the labor market in the new territories of the Reich. The protagonists followed a different line here than in the question of the racial examination of members of Groups 3 and 4 of the DVL; they sought instead to find a balance between the different interests involved, without, however, giving up the ideological goals supported by Himmler. Although the SS race experts and the Reichsführer-SS did not abandon the most comprehensive registration of suitable persons possible, an attempt was nevertheless made to take into account the interests of the labor offices and civil administrations, which for their part provided for the employment of labor during the war.

Postscript: The "Political Reorganization of the Population" as Perceived after 1945—The Example of the SS Race and Resettlement Experts

Only a small number of persons involved in the planned "political reorganization of the population of the Eastern territories" were called to account for their actions after 1945, and by no means every participating institution was even associated with it. The above-mentioned Freiherr von Fircks is a good example. Active during the war as head of an SS Task Force (SS-Arbeitsstab), he maintained a certain continuity after the war and became a respected, successful politician representing the interests of the German expellees. It took the leaflet campaign of a committed Hessian teacher to link the Freiherr with the activities in which he had participated along with thousands of others: "National Socialist acts of violence during the occupation of Poland."

If we consider the group of about 500 SS resettlement and race experts from the Race and Resettlement Main Office who were active locally, to whom Otto von Fircks also belonged, it is clear that after 1945 only a very small number had to answer for their activities in court. At the Nuremberg Military Tribunal VIII, in the so-called "RuSHA Case," only four RuSHA members were tried for their participation in the forcible resettlements in the occupied territories of Europe: the two persons who had directed the Office during the war, a former departmental and branch office head and a somewhat randomly selected racial fitness examiner. As early as even 1954 the main defendant had been released.[63] A preliminary investigation by the Central Office of the Regional Judicial Departments (Zentrale Stelle der Landesjustizverwaltungen) in Ludwigsburg of the participation of race experts in the "special treatment" of prisoners of war and forced laborers from the East who had violated the "prohibition on sexual intercourse" with German women also came to nought.[64] The defense strategy of all the accused, who maintained that they had only participated in the resettlement of ethnic Germans and had never taken measures against Poles or other non-Germans, was as false as it was successful. Otto von Fircks had recourse to the same stereotypes years later, although he was not even prosecuted.

Apparently it was precisely the division of labor involved in the evacuations, "processing" and resettlement that made it easy to shift responsibility to other persons and institutions. The American prosecutors and the German investigators from Ludwigsburg also came to this conclusion.[65] Even when incontrovertible proof of their own actions was presented to the accused, they tried to shift responsibility for the "negative side" of the racial policy—expulsions, deportations, and extermination—to Himmler, Heydrich, and the RSHA. At the same time, they stubbornly insisted on the "positive side" of their activity—the resettlement of ethnic Germans and their local "employment in strengthening the German peoples." As long as the participation of the SS resettlement offices and SS Task Forces in violent measures to implement a "reorganization of the population" in occupied Poland remained largely unknown, this was relatively easy. It is scarcely surprising, therefore, that, in the course of the trials and other proceedings "persecution networks" sometimes became "defense networks," which cooperated in court to conceal their common role in the "resettlement process."[66]

Summary: Efficient Cooperation and Racist Ideology

The planning and realization of the "political reorganization of the population" in the incorporated Eastern territories involved a division of labor. RSHA planners and practitioners were by no means the only ones to participate in the "evacuation" of the Jews and Poles to "create living space" for ethnic Germans; race experts from the RuSHA, police forces, labor office officials, farmers and representatives of the Gau administrations were also involved. The cooperation of various different offices must have greatly facilitated the smooth functioning of each one, since the participants viewed themselves as firmly integrated into an objective administrative process.

The implementation and radicalization of the "redistribution of population," the evacuations and settlements in occupied Western Poland, are best explained with the help of a double perspective of racist ideology and cooperative practice. Deficiencies in practice, unfulfilled plans, pressure for resettlement, transport bottlenecks, and provisioning difficulties could be met by more and more radical measures, justified by an ideology of "desirable and undesirable additions to the population" which was graphically illustrated again and again in the local situation. Above all, the results of extensive racial evaluations of both Poles and ethnic Germans were offered as allegedly "objective proof" of the correctness of that ideology. In this context the Jews, as members of the "anti-race," were in principle denied any right to exist at all.

In view of their duty "to strengthen the German peoples" in the East, the participants were able to reinterpret even the most unpleasant incidents positively and at the same time to legitimate their actions as "measures for the protection of the German people" or the "Nordic race." How effective such a "positive interpretation" was for the actions and also for the self-understanding of the numerous participants and how well this could be instrumentalized for public or legal self-defense is again shown by the example of Freiherr von Fircks. Although he was not even directly threatened with sanctions as a witness and co-plaintiff, he was only able to remember his "provision for German families" and not his role in the disappearance of their Polish and Jewish counterparts.

Notes

1. Quotation from the leaflet in Heinrich Hannover, *Die Republik vor Gericht 1954–1974. Erinnerungen eines unbequemen Rechtsanwaltes*, 2nd ed. (Berlin, 1998), p. 317. I wish to thank my colleague Patrick Wagner for drawing my attention to the "Fircks Case" and placing his collection of material at my disposal.

2. For a thorough description of the proceedings and the various appeals from the viewpoint of Arthur Sahm's defense attorney, see Hannover, *Republik vor Gericht*, pp. 316–334.
3. SSO-File Otto von Fircks, BDC BAB.
4. Cited from Götz Aly, *"Endlösung." Völkerverschiebung und der Mord an den europäischen Juden* (Frankfurt, 1998, 1st ed. 1995), p. 83.
5. In comparison: From the Warthegau as a whole about 550,000 Poles and Jews were expelled and deported by the end of 1943 to make room for the resettlement of ethnic Germans. Abschlußbericht der UWZ für das Jahr 1943, gez. SS-Ostubaf. Krumey, BAB R 75/3b, pp. 103–122; Aufstellung SS Arbeitsstäbe im Bereich des SS Ansiedlungsstabes Posen. Stand vom 6.3.41, BAB R 49/3050, pp. 61–64.
6. One should consider here above all the studies by Götz Aly, but also research on the Generalplan Ost. Götz Aly and Susanne Heim, *Vordenker der Vernichtung. Auschwitz und die Pläne für eine neue europäische Ordnung* (Frankfurt on Main, 1993); Mechthild Rössler and Sabine Schleiermacher, eds., *Der "Generalplan Ost"* (Berlin, 1993); Czesław Madajczyk, ed., *Vom 'Generalplan Ost' zum Generalsiedlungsplan* (Munich, 1994).
7. On the institution, and above all, the persons working as SS Race and Resettlement experts, see my dissertation: Isabel Heinemann, *"Rasse, Siedlung, deutsches Blut." Das Rasse- und Siedlungshauptamt der SS und die rassenpolitische Neuordnung Europas (Göttingen, 2003)*.
8. Erlaß Adolf Hitlers zur Festigung deutschen Volkstums vom 7.10.1939, NO-3075.
9. In late December, 29 persons were employed at the office; their numbers grew rapidly with the intensification of the resettlement projects, however. In 1941 it was upgraded to an SS main office, the Stabshauptamt RKF.
10. A new comprehensive monograph on Himmler's policy in his role as RKF is a research desideratum. Still standard is the older presentation by Robert L. Koehl, *RKFDV: German Resettlement and Population Policy 1939–1945. A History of the Reich Commission for the Strengthening of Germandom* (Cambridge, MA, 1957). On the question of the planning and restructuring of the environment by the RKF see the dissertation by Daniel Inkelas, "Visions of Harmony and Violence" (North Western University, 1999).
11. The settlers came in waves, first from the Baltic states and Eastern Poland, later from the Soviet Union and Rumanian territory. The initial legal basis was the addendum to the Ribbentrop–Molotov Pact of 28 September 1939. Later there were further resettlement agreements with the Soviet Union and other participating states. In all, by 1944 about a million persons were moved into Reich territory.
12. Anordnung I/III Heinrich Himmlers vom 30.10.1939, *Biuletyn Glownej Komisji Badania Zbrodni Hitlerowskich w Polsce*, XII (Warsaw, 1960) p. 9f.
13. Denkschrift des Rassenpolitischen Amtes der NSDAP "über die Behandlung der Bevölkerung der ehemaligen polnischen Gebiete nach rassenpolitischen Gesichtspunkten" vom 25.11.1939, BAB R 49/75, pp. 1–40.
14. Denkschrift des RFSS, RKF vom 28.5.1940, "Einige Gedanken über die Behandlung der Fremdvölkischen im Osten," *Ursachen und Folgen, XIV: Der Angriff auf Polen. Die Ereignisse im Winter 1939–1940* (Berlin, 1969), pp. 128–131; Erlass des RFSS, RKF über die Überprüfung und Aussonderung der Bevölkerung in den eingegliederten Ostgebieten vom 12.9.1940, USHMM RG 48.005 M.
15. It developed out of the "Special Unit for the Resettlement of Poles and Jews" (Sonderstab für die Umsiedlung von Polen und Juden) at the HSSPF in Poznań. The UWZ first received its institutional form in April 1940 as an office of the RSHA and the RKF, with headquarters in Poznań, and with it the task of implementing the "resettlement of Poles and Jews" from all occupied areas. Its officials were not only responsible for the deportation of Poles from the occupied western Polish areas, but also participated on a large scale in the deportation of European Jews. On the UWZ see Phillip Rutherford's dissertation, "Race, Space and the 'Polish Question'. Nazi Deportation Policy in Reichsgau Wartheland, 1939–1941" (Pennsylvania State University, 2000).
16. In the first short-term plan of early to mid-December 1939, almost 90,000 persons were deported. The so-called "intermediate plan" of mid-February to mid-March 1940 involved

the expulsion of some 40,000 persons. In the course of the second short-term plan from April 1940 until January 1941, 133,000 persons were transported to the General Government—instead of the originally projected 600,000. Approximately 130,000 persons more were affected by the third short-term plan by January 1942. By late 1942, the third, extended short-term plan had resulted in the expulsion of a further 99,000 persons. By the end of 1943 approximately 43,000 more persons were affected.

17. See the final report by the Director of the Litzmannstadt UWZ, SS-Ostuf. Krumey, on expulsions in the context of the resettlement of Germans from Volhynia, Galicia and Chełm in the Reichsgau Wartheland of 26 January 1940, BAB R 75/6; Report by Krumey on expulsions in connection with the resettlement of Bessarabian Germans of 20 January 1942, BAB R 75/8, pp. 1–19. See also the summary in Table 15 in Czesław Madajczyk, *Die Okkupationspolitik Nazideutschlands in Polen. 1939–1945* (Berlin, 1987).
18. See Krumey's monthly report for January 1943 on the implementation of the fourth short-term plan of 8 February 1943, USHMM RG 15.007 M, 120; Krumey's final report for 1943, BAB R 75/3b, pp. 103–122.
19. The EWZ was already founded by Reinhard Heydrich, Director of the RSHA, in mid-October 1939 as a centralized office for the naturalization of ethnic Germans. The director of the EWZ was technically subordinate to the RKF and at the same time institutionally to the director of the Security Police (Sipo) and SD. After a few weeks in Gotenhafen and subsequently in Poznań, the EWZ moved to its permanent headquarters in Litzmannstadt on 15 January 1940. During its existence it had various branch offices in the occupied territories and the Old Reich, wherever there were ethnic Germans to register—above all at first in the border cities and ports of the Old Reich such as Stettin and Schneidemühl, and later in Lublin, Cracow, and Paris.
20. In September 1940, for example, 26 racial fitness examiners and RuS commanders were active at the EWZ. Der Chef des RuSHA, SS-Brigf. Otto Hofmann, an den RFSS vom 20.9.1940, SSO-file Bruno Beger, BDC BAB.
21. The figures until late 1940 were as follows: ca. 60,000 Baltic Germans from Estonia and Latvia, 128,000 Germans from Volhynia and Galicia, 30,000 Germans from Eastern Poland, 77,000 from Rumania, and 137,000 from Bessarabia and North Bukovina. EWZ records show that by late 1944 more than 1,030,000 ethnic Germans, predominantly from Eastern Europe, had been registered and racially examined in EWZ offices and by various "flying commissions." For the results of the "processing" in the EWZ Litzmanstadt by 30 November 1944, AP Łódź 204, 2/11.
22. Jews from the Reich and other countries who were in the meantime living in Litzmannstadt are not included, but only the Jewish inhabitants of Western Poland. The peak of Jewish deportations was first reached in 1942, however. In the above-mentioned evacuation transports up to summer 1941 less than half of the deported were Jewish, about 110,000 out of ca. 290,000. On the number of deported Jews from Western Poland in summer 1941, see Aly, "*Endlösung,*" p. 35.
23. With headquarters in Poznań and Łódź/Litzmannstadt. In Danzig-West Prussia the SS Resettlement Office was located in Gotenhafen and in East Prussia in Soldau. Later further SS resettlement offices were added in Alsace-Lorraine, Lower Styria, and Upper Krain, as well as in the Lublin district.
24. Record (of the Central Office of the RKF) on the coordination of the resettlement of the Ethnic Germans from the region Bug-Vistula of 6 March 1941. Aufstellung der SS-Arbeitsstäbe, BAB R 49/3050, pp. 61–64.
25. See, for example, the instructions of the Poznań Resettlement Office (SS-Ansiedlungsstab) to the leaders of the task forces in the districts 1940–41, BAB R 49/3064. The two resettlement staffs in Poznań and Litzmannstadt shared a department, where overall resettlement projects were coordinated. The director of this planning department was SS-Ustuf. Alexander Dolezalek, one of the most influential theoreticians of large-scale population movement. As a departmental head in the Reich Student Directorate (Reichsstudentenführung), he at the same time coordinated the Eastern service (*Osteinsatz*) of students in the ranks of the SS, on whom the task forces depended as auxiliary workers.

26. Georg Gloystein, b. 1893 in Dalsper, Oldenburg District, was a trained agriculturist, veteran of the First World War, and a disabled veteran. He had been a member of the RuSHA since 1936 as SS Commander and at the start of the war was active as an RuS Commander of the SS-Oberabschnitt Mitte. From March 1940 until the end of the war he served as leader of the SS Task Force in Turek, Warthegau, where he himself also managed a large estate, which he developed as an SS vocational training farm for handicapped veterans. He reported in a detailed manner on the start of his service as leader of the SS Task Force to the director of the RuSHA. Schreiben des Führers des SS-Arbeitsstabes Turek, SS-Stubaf. Gloystein, an den RuSHA-Chef SS-Gruf. Pancke vom 20.4.1940, SSO-File Georg Gloystein, BDC BAB.
27. List of personnel of the Turek SS Task Force of 13 April 1940, BAB NS 47/219.
28. Schreiben des Führers des SS-Arbeitsstabes Turek, SS-Stubaf. Gloystein, an den RuSHA-Chef SS-Gruf. Pancke vom 20.4.1940, SSO-File Georg Gloystein, BDC BAB.
29. See Krumey's final report on the UWZ's work in the Warthegau and General Government for 1943, BAB R 75/3b, pp. 103–122.
30. This preparation of farms for settlers was regarded as the main duty of the SS Task Forces. They had to take into account a variety of factors such as the "properties of the soil, size of farm, presence of stables and barn, state of the furnishings and fixtures, water supplies." The enterprises in each village were registered in so-called "village sketches," and the livestock and dead stock of each farm were summarized in "farm maps." Schreiben des Leiters des SS-Ansiedlungsstabes Litzmannstadt, SS-Ostubaf. Spaarmann, über die Selbstkontrolle der Arbeitsstäbe vom 26.3.1940, BAB R 49/3072, pp. 1–2.
31. Aktenvermerk von SS-Obersturmführer von Fircks über den Verlauf der Evakuierung der Polen und Ansiedlung am 20.3.1940, BAB R 75/3, pp. 5–6. Incidentally, the resettlements in Eastern Poland followed the same pattern (particularly in the region around Zamość in the Lublin district) and, for example, those from Alsace-Lorraine to France.
32. Merkblatt der UWZ für den Polizeibeamten zur Durchführung der Evakuierungen von polnischen Hofbesitzern vom 9.5.1940. Personal searches of evacuees were later dispensed with and the groups were enlarged to prevent the flight of Poles or destruction of property. See Merkblatt der UWZ vom Januar 1941, BAB R 75/3, pp. 7–10.
33. See the results of the final report of a preliminary judicial enquiry by the Central Office of the Regional Judicial Departments in Ludwigsburg against the members of the Łódź Gestapo Headquarters for the deportation of Jews to the extermination camps of Chełmno and Auschwitz. The same final report mentions the case of another SS Task Force Commander, SS-Stubaf. Dr. Heinrich Butschkow from the Lentschütz district in the Warthegau, who is said to have ordered and supervised the public execution of nine Jews in the Ozorkow area at the beginning of 1942. ZSt. 203 AR Z 161/67, pp. 58–59, 120–121.
34. Krumey, head of the UWZ in Litzmannstadt, 23 May 1941, on the implementation of additional resettlement through coercion in the Warthegau, BAB R 75/3b, pp. 96–98.
35. Resettlement of Vohlhynian and Galician Germans up to and including 22 May 1940 in the districts of the Warthegau. Undated Table, BAB NS 2/61, p. 26ff.
36. Der Chef der UWZ Litzmannstadt, Abschlußbericht über die Arbeit der Umwandererzentralstelle im Reichsgau Wartheland und Generalgouvernement für das Jahr 1943 vom 31.12.1943, BAB R 75/3b. p. 119.
37. Erfahrungsbericht des Leiters des SS-Ansiedlungsstabes Nessau-Hohensalza, SS-Hstuf. Plähn, an den Leiter des SS-Ansiedlungsstabes Litzmannstadt vom 2.12.1940, BAB R 49/3072, pp. 12–15. In addition, in the first months of resettlement up until July 1940 there appears to have been occasional uncertainty at the local police offices about which party and state offices should actually be called upon to participate. See the Meldung des Chefs der Stapoleitstelle Hohensalza über die Zuständigkeitsregelung zur Durchführung der Evakuierungen vom 17.7.1940 an den Chef der UWZ Posen, BAB R 75/3b, pp. 80–81.
38. The "processing" of ethnic Germans described here affected farming families already living in the Warthegau who as "Germans" claimed a larger farm than the one they already possessed. A "flying commission" was also active in examining such cases and determined the racial value and "German attitudes" of the persons involved. "Bei einer Fliegenden Kommission", Bericht der Bronia Alix Elsaß über die Tätigkeit einer Fliegenden Kommission im Warthegau, undated ca. Sept. 1940, AP Łódź L-3588.

39. See the "Anleitung zur Eignungsprüfung der Rückwanderer" des RuSHA-Chefs Hofmann vom 14.10.1939, BAB NS 2/88, pp. 89–91; Aktennotiz des SS-Hauptsturmführers Klinger aus dem Rassenamt des RuSHA vom 1.4.1940, BAB NS 2/61, pp. 52–53.
40. Internal Record of UWZ, June 1940, BAB R 75/1, pp. 12–13.
41. On the DVL in the Warthegau, see the documentation by Karol Marian Pospieszalski, *Niemiecka Lista Narodowa w "Kraju Warty"*. *Documenta Occupationis, IV.* (Poznań, 1949). The "List of Ethnic Germans" in the Warthegau was set up through the decree of the later Reich commissioner (Reichsstatthalter) on 28 October 1939, *Verordnungsblatt des Chefs der Zivilverwaltung beim Militärbefehlshaber von Posen* (1939), p. 51. An excerpt from the "Richtlinien für die Erfassung der deutschen Volkszugehörigen im Reichsgau Wartheland in the 'Deutsche Volksliste'" of November 1939 can be found in *Ursachen und Folgen, XIV: Der Angriff auf Polen. Die Ereignisse im Winter 1939–1940* (Berlin, 1969), pp. 121–125.
42. Erlaß des RFSS, RKF zur Überprüfung und Aussonderung der Bevölkerung in den eingegliederten Ostgebieten vom 12.9.1940, USHMM RG 48.005 M.
43. Verordnung über die Deutsche Volksliste und die deutsche Staatsangehörigkeit in den eingegliederten Ostgebieten vom 4.3.1941 und entsprechende Durchführungsverordnung vom 13.3.1941, RGBl. (1941, I), pp. 118–119. The decree on the implementation of the DVL already contains the instruction that only racially suitable persons could be considered for inclusion in the list, especially if their "Germanness" could not be directly proved. Erlaß des RMdI, I e 5125/41-5000 Ost, an den Reichsstatthalter in Danzig-Westpreußen und im Warthegau, die Oberpräsidenten und Regierungspräsidenten in Schlesien und Ostpreußen über den Erwerb der deutschen Staatsangehörigkeit durch ehemalige polnische und Danziger Staatsangehörige vom 13.3.1941, BAB R 49/71, pp. 14–26.
44. See Niederschrift der Sitzung am 15. Mai beim RMI über die Durchführung der Deutschen Volksliste, I e 5252 III/41 – 5000 Ost, vom 15.5.1941, AP Łódź 176/387, pp. 100–106.
45. The entries in the Ethnic German List in the Reichsgau Wartheland under the procedures used there had been almost completed already in early 1941.
46. Gauleiter Forster had also begun, like Greiser in the Warthegau, to set up his own DVL procedure in Danzig West-Prussia, which likewise relied chiefly on political evaluations and largely ignored racial criteria. Anordnung des Gauleiters und Reichsstatthalters in Danzig-Westpreußen Albert Forster zur Durchführung der Eindeutschungsaktion vom 14.12.1940, BAB R 49/76, pp. 2–29.
47. In late September 1941, the Reichsführer issued a decree on the racial examination of Section 3 of the List of Ethnic Germans in which the RuSHA received full jurisdiction for the examination of those whose German ancestry was no longer clearly documented and also of Germans with one or more non-German grandparent. Anordnung 50/1 des RKF vom 30.9.1941, BAB NS 2/153. The corresponding draft was produced by the RuSHA. Entwurf zu einer Anordnung des RFSS, RKF betreffend der rassischen Musterung des Angehörigen der Abteilungen 3 und 4 der Deutschen Volksliste. Undatiert. (1941) AP Poznań 299/1131, pp. 13–15.
48. Geheimschreiben des RFSS, RKF an den Reichstatthalter und Gauleiter Greiser über die rassische Überprüfung der Angehörigen der Abteilung 3 der Deutschen Volksliste vom 30.9.1941, AP Poznań 299/1114, pp. 3–6.
49. Erlaß des Reichsstatthalters im Warthegau, gez. i.V. Mehlhorn, an die Regierungspräsidenten in Posen, Hohensalza und Litzmannstadt vom 3.3.1942 betreffend der rassischen Untersuchung der Angehörigen der Abteilung 3 der Deutschen Volksliste, AP Poznań 299/114; Schreiben des Reichsstatthalters, gez. i.V. Höppner, an die Herren Regierungspräsidenten in Posen, Hohensalza, Litzmannstadt über die rassische Untersuchung in der Deutschen Volksliste vom 3.7.1942; Vermerk Höppners über die Besprechung mit dem Leiter der Außenstelle Litzmannstadt des RuSHA, SS-Hstuf. Dongus, vom 22.6.1942, AP Poznań 299/1131, pp. 158–159, 417–418.
50. Standard text of negative decisions by the RuSHA-Litzmannstadt to branch offices of the DVL, if the families examined had been assigned the racial values IV or IVf, AGK 167/9. The Reich commissioner, the agent of the RKF, the presidents of the administrative districts (Regierungspräsidenten) concerned, the SD departments (Leitabschnitte) and district administrators received confidential information on racial rejections through appropriate lists.

51. Schreiben des RuS-Führers Warthe, gez. SS-Ustuf. Steinhauser, an die Außenstelle Litzmannstadt des RuSHA über die Ausschließung aller IV und IV-Fälle der DVL-Überprüfungen von der Ehegenehmigung vom 18.11.1942; Schreiben des Reichsstatthalters im Warthegau, gez. i.V. Höppner, an das RuSHA über die Eheschließung von rassisch unerwünschten Angehörigen der Abteilung 3 der deutschen Volksliste; Antwortschreiben des RuSHA-Litzmannstadt vom 1.3.1943, AGK 167/47, pp. 6–8.
52. Point I, e of the charges brought at the American Military Tribunal in Nuremberg against representatives of RKF, RuSHA, Volksdeutsche Mittelstelle and the SS-Organisation "Lebensborn" (Case VIII) of 1 July 1947, *Trials of War Criminals before the Nuremberg Military Tribunals under Control Council Law No. 10. Nuremberg, October 1946–April 1949, IV* (Washington, 1950), p. 610.
53. Statistik der DVL-Kommission Ostpreußen des RuSHA von 1942, AGK 167/8, p. 8.
54. Sybille Steinbacher and Dieter Schenk are also unable to give any figures in their new studies or ignore this aspect entirely. Sybille Steinbacher, *"Musterstadt" Auschwitz. Germanisierungspolitik und Judenmord in Ostoberschlesien* (Munich, 2000); Dieter Schenk, *Hitlers Mann in Danzig: Albert Forster und die NS-Verbrechen in Danzig-Westpreußen* (Bonn, 2000). Nor does Ceslaw Madajczyk offer any statistical data on this question. Madajczyk, *Okkupationspolitik*.
55. Kleiner Umsiedlungsspiegel des RKF vom Februar 1943, BAB R 49/87, pp. 3–5.
56. An appropriate decree on the inclusion of Polish and Ukranian girls in the re-Germanization procedures was issued by Heinrich Himmler, Anordnung Nr. 51/I vom 1. October 1941, BAB R 49/73, pp. 66–67. The girls and women were examined before their transportation to Germany by SS racial fitness examiners and only those who qualified as "desirable additions to the population" (Racial group RuS I or RuS II) were assigned to work as housemaids in German households.
57. Schreiben des Leiters des Stabhauptamtes RKF, gez. Greifelt, an den Reichsarbeitsminister über den Einsatz von nationalpolnischen Hausgehilfinnen im Reichsgebiet vom 3.3.1941, USHMM RG 15007, 125.
58. Rundverfügung Nr. 5/80 des Landesarbeitsamtes im Warthegau, gez. i.A. Dr. Döpke, an die Herren der Arbeitsämter im Bezirk über die Vermittlung volkspolnischer wiedereindeutschungsfähiger Arbeitskräfte in das Reichsgebiet und die Zusammenarbeit mit der Außenstelle des Rasse- und Siedlungshauptamt-SS vom 19.1.1941, AP Poznań 299/1131, pp. 376–377.
59. Schreiben des Landesarbeitsamtes im Warthegau an das RuSHA über die Eindeutschung der Ursula Z. vom 27.7.1942, AP Poznań 299/1131, pp. 378–380.
60. Schreiben des RuS-Führers Danzig-Westpreußen, gez. SS-Stubaf. Vietz, an den Chef des RuSHA vom 1.8.1942, USHMM RG 15007, 125.
61. Brief des RuSHA-Chefs Hofmann an den RKF über die Transporte "wiedereindeutschungsfähiger Polen" ins Altreich vom 3.9.1942, USHMM RG 15.007 M, 125.
62. See the ca. 1000 letters by young "re-Germanizable" housemaids to the RuSHA branch office in Łódź (Litzmannstadt). AGK 167/20, 20a, 32, 35. Ryszard Poradowski, "Obóz 'Rasowy' przy ulicy Spornej w Łodzi w swietle relacji Wieźniów," in *Biuletyn Okregowej Komisji Badania Zbrodni Hitlerowskich w Łodzi. Instytutu Pamieci Narodowej. W 50 rocznice agresji Niemiec hitlerowskich na Polske, I* (Łódź, 1989), pp. 41–56; Bericht der Abteilung "Volkstum" aus dem RSHA an das RuSHA und den RKF über die Eindeutschung von rassisch wertvollen Fremdstämmigen vom 19.12.1942, AGK 167/38, pp. 11–21.
63. Namely Otto Hofmann. Richard Hildebrandt, who had been extradited to Poland, was executed in Bydgoszcz in 1951 for his crimes as Higher SS and Police Leader (HSSPF) Vistula. On the RuSHA trial see the document collection in the Bavarian State Archives in Nuremberg; the collection of trial documents in the BAK, All. Proz. 1, XXXIV, Rep. 501; the edition of documents *Trials of War Criminals before the Nuremberg Military Tribunals under Control Council Law No. 10. Nuremberg, October 1946–April 1949, IV and V (VIII: The RuSHA-Case)* (Washington, 1950).

64. On these grounds a few criminal proceedings against SS racial fitness examiners were initiated, which, however, were also soon suspended and did not lead to verdicts against the accused. On the preliminary judicial proceedings, see ZSt. 414 AR 122/65.
65. Closing Statement of the Prosecution, in *Trials of War Criminals*, V, p. 47f.; Vermerk der ZSt. vom 4.8.1966 über den Stand der Ermittlungen in ZSt. 414 AR 122/65, p. 634.
66. On this see my treatment of the defensive strategy adopted by RuSHA defendants at Nuremberg. Heinemann, "Rasse," pp. 565–585.

CHAPTER 13

THE "*REIBUNGSLOSE*" HOLOCAUST? THE GERMAN MILITARY AND CIVILIAN IMPLEMENTATION OF THE "FINAL SOLUTION" IN UKRAINE, 1941–1944

Wendy Lower

One of the recurring words Nazi bureaucrats in Ukraine used to describe the implementation of the "final solution" was "*reibungslos*" (smooth).[1] Often they referred specifically to the "smooth" relations between the Wehrmacht and SS-Police. On other occasions they boasted about their efficient step-by-step process of murder. To be sure, a peripheral official in Ukraine reporting to his superiors in Berlin might have been inclined to exaggerate how "free of friction" the administration of his tasks was. Indeed, recent "perpetrator" histories of the Holocaust stress the lack of conflict among regional officials vis-à-vis the "final solution." Yet the tendency of these regional studies is not to question the Nazi sense of a "smooth" process of murder. Was it the sole aim of regional leaders in the occupation administration to make the implementation of the "final solution" appear orderly? Or could their handling of the genocide be described as "frictionless"?

This case study examines how regional leaders in the military and civilian administrations of Nazi-occupied Ukraine carried out the "final solution."[2] It highlights the main administrative mechanisms and individual forces behind the Holocaust. The focus on Ukraine is particularly illuminating because the actual massacre of Jews occurred here amid the lawlessness and colonial-style methods that characterized German rule in the East. In contrast to their counterparts in the West, who operated within a relatively tight-knit structure of rule, local German leaders in Nazi-occupied Ukraine (and elsewhere in the East) were granted much more autonomy. According to the historian Theo Schulte (whose work focused on the military administration of Heeres Gruppe Mitte), "there were no clear written guidelines on Militärverwaltung comparable to those drawn up before the campaign in the West...in the East the details of policy were often disseminated by word of mouth from the Quartermaster General's office."[3] A similar scenario existed in the civilian administration in Ukraine, known as the Reich Commissariat Ukraine. Hitler deliberately granted his regional commissars extensive ruling power, leaving the day-to-day details of administering Nazi goals in their hands.[4] In other words, local leaders played an essential role in developing and implementing the Nazi system of mass murder against Ukraine's Jews, a role that has only recently come to light with the opening of the former Soviet regional archives.

The Military Administration and the Onset of the Mass Murder, June 1941–October 1941

As the Wehrmacht advanced toward Russia in the summer of 1941, the Germans divided the newly conquered eastern territory into three zones that extended from the front line westward to the rear areas. Along the front, or battle zones, and in the immediate rear areas, the army units assigned to Army Group South in Ukraine did not establish elaborate administrations. Instead, the itinerant army staffs attached to the Sixth, Eleventh, and Seventeenth Armies focused on expedient measures necessary for waging the war, which, in the Nazi *Vernichtungskrieg*, included "security cleansing operations" against Prisoners of war (POWs) and civilians. On the heels of the advancing armies came the security divisions (213, 444, 454) and their subordinate hierarchy of Kommandanturen. Known as the Army Group South Rear Area administration, this hierarchy fell under the command of General von Roques.[5]

The most important regional figures governing anti-Jewish policy in the rear area military administration were the field, city, and village commanders. The largest of these offices was administered by the Field Commander (FK) with his staff of several officers and about 100 men. The more rural outposts of the Ortskommandantur (OK) were usually manned by one officer and sixteen to twenty soldiers.[6] The OKs and FKs became the local dictators over the population, issuing streams of regulations and appointing indigenous collaborators (mayors and district leaders) to carry out Nazi orders. The Kommandanturen were assisted by Wehrmacht propaganda companies (PKs), military security units (Secret Field Police, sharpshooters, and field gendarmerie) and German SS-Police forces (Sicherheitspolizei-Sicherheitsdienst (Sipo-SD) mobile killing squads, Waffen-SS, and order police battalions).[7] As Schulte put it, "the FK and OK were the crucial point of contact where overall policy was interpreted and implemented...it was here at the grass roots level that the ruled came into contact with the ruler and that abstract theory became individual behavior mediated through the 'ordinary German soldier.'"[8]

Within the Kommandanturen administration one branch (Abteilung VII) was specifically dedicated to the "Jewish Question." According to the

August 1941 report of the Field Commander of Pervomais'k, there were four priorities in this area: (1) handling of Jewish Property; (2) marking of Jews; (3) exploitation of Jewish labor; and (4) registration and listing of the Jewish population. Ghettoization was not identified as an immediate step, and Judenräte were formed only to assist with the seizure of Jewish laborers and Jewish property. With the help of Göring's economic commandos, the Kommandanturen oversaw the distribution of rations, which became increasingly difficult for the Jews to obtain.[9]

In the realm of so-called security measures against the Jews, whom Nazi leaders had targeted in prewar guidelines as the key source of "Bolshevik" insurgency, army commanders relied extensively on the SS-Police forces. In Ukraine, Reichsführer-SS Heinrich Himmler's right-hand man was Higher SS and Police Leader (HSSPF) Friedrich Jeckeln (who was succeeded by Hans-Adolf Prützmann in November 1941). The first SS-Police units to enter the conquered territory were the mobile killing squads of Einsatzgruppe C (EGC) (special detachments Sonderkommando 4a (Sk4a) and Sk4b and task forces Einsatzkommando5 (Ek5) and Ek6) and Einsatzgruppe D (special detachments Sk10a and Sk10b and task forces Ek11 and Ek12). They were assisted by additional reserves of Waffen-SS Brigades and order police battalions (e.g. 9, 45, 303, 314, 310, 304, 315, 320, and 322).

The SS-Police units received their quarters, supplies, and food rations from the local army command, and they were obligated to report to the local army staff headquarters or the Kommandantur the actions planned against the population and POWs. The SS and police were not supposed to act independently without the consent of the military.[10] In fact, three order police battalions were assigned directly to the Wehrmacht Security Divisions to assist with "cleansing" actions.[11] By design, then, the SS-Police and the military were to coordinate their actions even though these two pillars of Nazi power were separated by independent chains of command and jurisdictional priorities as well as distinctly different institutional histories. Given the strong potential for conflict between army and SS-Police authorities, what kind of "division of labor" emerged in the field during the summer and fall of 1941, when most of Ukraine's Jewish population was subjected to military rule?

In the brief five weeks that the military occupation administration existed in western Ukraine, the local field and village commanders in L'viv and elsewhere in Galicia initiated the registration and marking of the Jewish population. They forced all Jews over the age of fourteen years to wear the "Star of David," and they plastered the "Star" on Jewish shops.[12] The Field Commander (603) of "Lemberg" also reported that his staff had posted signs on shops, public baths, and other businesses to prevent Jews from entering them.[13] A Jewish council was formed, from which the military commander demanded a sum of twenty million rubles.[14] Another standard army practice was to seize Jewish laborers and employ them in the most gruesome tasks, such as the removal of corpses from the roadways and, later, the clearing of mines.[15] Ukrainians, *Volksdeutsche* (ethnic Germans), and other locals assisted in the identification of the Jewish population. While military personnel imposed these anti-Semitic measures, SS and police units introduced more radical practices. First they sought out adult male Jews in party and state positions and other so-called radical elements to be found in the Jewish population (agitators, saboteurs, assassins). According to Operation Barbarossa guidelines and orders, the SD shot these Jews immediately.[16]

In June and July 1941, the most deadly form of military and SS-Police collaboration occurred in the pogroms and "reprisal" measures in western Ukraine. Sipo-SD chief Reinhard Heydrich had specified in his prewar guidelines for the Einsatzgruppen that pogroms should be sparked as a way of embroiling the indigenous population in Nazi plans to destroy Soviet Jewry.[17] When German and allied forces arrived in eastern Galicia and found the remains of about 5,300 People's Commissariat of Internal Affairs (NKVD) prisoners who had been massacred in at least twenty-two villages and towns, they had discovered an ideal local source of friction to ignite the pogroms. Through loudspeakers, films, posters, leaflets, and rumor campaigns, the Wehrmacht propaganda units, intelligence (Ic) officials in the armored divisions, and SS-Police denounced the Jews as the NKVD-Bolshevik perpetrators, inciting locals to lash out at all Jews and promoting an official lynch justice against male Jews.[18]

The primary instigators, the SD's mobile killing squads, often turned to the army staffs for support, mainly for the propaganda work, but also occasionally to assist with the beating and shooting of Jews. In Luts'k, where the Germans discovered murdered German prisoners of war, the military took the lead in pogrom-style reprisals. At the end of June, the OK in Luts'k had ordered 1,000 Jews to report for labor. When, on 2 July, ten dead German soldiers were discovered there, the Wehrmacht's security forces shot these Jews and a further 160 in retaliation. German order police assisted in the executions.[19] A similar incident occurred in Ternopil'. Individual soldiers volunteered to participate in the pogroms and shootings that occurred in L'viv, Sokal, and Boryslav.[20] Not all of the soldiers and officers were "willing executioners," but many who were initially curious onlookers became willing accomplices to the SD executions of male Jews.[21]

As the German and SS-Police forces plunged eastward, Nazi leaders (Hitler, Himmler, Heydrich, and Göring) pushed for an expansion of the murder "behind the lines." In mid July 1941, SS-Obergruppenführer Friedrich Jeckeln authorized the killing of women during security operations planned for the area of Novohrad-Volyns'kyy. At the end of July, Seventeenth Army Commander von Stülpnagel defined the procedure for carrying out collective reprisal actions, specifying that Jews should be the target, even Jewish youths, and that local commanders should not incarcerate hostages to have them on hand for future reprisal actions because "there will be reason to kill them soon enough."[22] Perhaps in anticipation of mass murder on an even greater scale, Jeckeln also reasserted the necessity of military-SS and police coordination in the field. Jeckeln instructed Heydrich's Einsatzkommandos to establish more contact with military headquarters and division commanders, in his words "to inform them of intended measures." Typically the SD commanders registered their activities with the intelligence officer of the army staffs. In Jeckeln's instructions he added that: "If the action is urgent, if there is no time for notification, then the report of the action will be provided subsequently."[23]

As later events would demonstrate, the sense of urgency that SS-Police leaders attached to the implementation of the "final solution" was not always shared by local military commanders (and civilian commissars). In areas east of the Dniepr River, regional military commanders sometimes found that anti-Jewish measures such as the formation of labor gangs had to be abruptly discarded because the SD had pushed through the destruction of entire Jewish communities in such a rapid manner. For example, shortly after the regional military commander in Pervomais'k outlined his four priorities for handling the "Jewish question" there, he complained about the sudden loss of Jewish workers and the independent actions of the SD killing squads.[24]

The dramatic escalation in Nazi killing actions that began in August was marked by an increase in conflicts about who was authorized to kill Jews, when the actions should occur, and how the killings should be carried out. In the wake of the mass shootings that occurred in and around Vinnytsia, Zhytomyr, Berdychiv, and Kamiianets'-Podil's'kyi, the highest-ranking army leaders issued revised guidelines about individual soldiers' participation in anti-Jewish massacres. In the Sixth Army order of 10 August 1941, Field Marshal von Reichenau stated that soldiers could comply with SD requests for assistance by serving as guards to cordon off the execution area and to prevent local civilians from entering the area.[25] The order from von Roques asserted that only officers could order executions and that the execution of Jews was to be carried out by forces of the HSSPF, not by individual soldiers.[26]

Hence during August 1941 the implementation of the "final solution" entered a new phase, in which individual perpetrator roles and agency jurisdictions were more clearly defined. As Hans Safrian observed in his study of the Sixth Army and the Holocaust: "As of August 1941, the mass murder of Jewish men, women, and children in the Sixth Army area was organized increasingly in the form of a division-of-labor cooperation between the Wehrmacht and the SS."[27] Two outstanding case studies from Zhytomyr illustrate the actual forms of this cooperation.

When stationed in Zhytomyr, members of Einsatzgruppe C and the Sixth Army collaborated in the search for "better" mass-shooting procedures and killing methods. On 7 August 1941 the local field commander's office along with Wehrmacht propaganda units and members of Sk4a staged a public execution of two Jews (Wolf Kieper and Moishe Kogan), who had been denounced as "Cheka" men. This Holocaust "spectacle," which German propaganda units documented in a series of shocking photographs, was recently highlighted in the traveling German exhibit "The German Army and Genocide." What the Wehrmacht PKs did not photograph and has not been analyzed by scholars is the scene that unfolded after the hanging.[28]

After local SS-Policemen hanged Kieper and Kogan in Zhytomyr's main square, Ukrainian auxiliaries and military field police forced over four hundred male Jews onto trucks and drove them to the horse cemetery. Here German soldiers beat the Jews with clubs and other objects before the order police and Ukrainian auxiliaries brought them in groups of ten to twelve to the edge of a pit. The Jews were lined up facing the firing squad of Waffen-SS riflemen, and the order to fire was probably given by their platoon commander, Grafhorst. After some time, the shootings were halted because SS and army officials (including a Sixth Army staff doctor) observed that not every victim who fell into the pit was dead. An impromptu meeting of SD and Wehrmacht officials was called. It included Sonderkommando 4a chief, SS-Standartenführer Blobel, the Wehrmacht doctor, and a military judge named Dr. Artur Neumann. They decided that the riflemen should aim for the heads. This method soon proved to be inadequate because it was too "messy"; nevertheless the executions continued until all the Jews had been killed. Afterwards Blobel and his men met again with local army officials. They discussed the fact that this "type of shooting was intolerable for both victim and firing-squad members."[29]

In early August 1941, around the time of the Kieper-Kogan hangings, the senior staff doctor with the Sixth Army, Dr. Gerhart Panning, approached Blobel with a special request. When the Sixth Army was stationed in Zhytomyr (if not earlier at Luts'k), close relations had developed between Sk4a and members of the Sixth Army medical staff. The commander of Sk4a, Colonel Paul Blobel, and some of his fellow executioners had sought medical attention from the staff. They received injections to calm their nerves after the massacres. Panning, who had learned about the German capture of certain Russian explosives (dumdum bullets), was investigating the possible injuries German soldiers might suffer from this illegal ammunition. To determine the possible effects of the Soviet ammunition on German soldiers, Panning decided that the explosives should be tested on human beings. Panning asked Blobel for some "guinea pigs." They agreed to use Jewish POWs.[30]

Oberstabsarzt Panning did not have the official authorization to order Blobel's men to carry out this murderous experiment, yet Blobel was willing to oblige. The experiment offered Blobel the possibility of "advancing" the implementation of the "final solution," and of maintaining "smooth" relations with the Wehrmacht. Additionally, Blobel handpicked certain men for this gruesome job so that they would become the increasingly hardened killers that he needed to carry out the "final solution." Dr. Panning, on the other hand, acted under the guise of "medical research." In fact, Panning's local reputation as a "researcher" spread to Berlin a few weeks later. On 12 September Helmuth James von Moltke, the Abwehr's international law expert, wrote to his wife about Panning's experiments with Jewish victims, stressing that the incident was "the height of bestiality and depravity and there is nothing one can do."[31]

The Blobel-Panning collaboration in Zhytomyr reveals several facets of the implementation of the "final solution" under the military administration. In particular, their close cooperation demonstrates how the otherwise independent interests of two agencies in the field converged around the Holocaust. On the face of it, such cooperation between a vicious commando chief and a doctor from the Prussian military establishment seems rather odd.[32] Blobel was a notoriously well-connected Nazi and vicious anti-Semite. He was an SD careerist who demanded that all of his underlings—cooks, drivers, typists, etc.—bloody their hands in the murder. His superiors praised his total loyalty and reliability. In fact, Himmler later recognized Blobel by granting him the task of covering up the genocide as head of special top secret commando 1005. Yet Blobel, who was also known for his choleric outbursts, held a degree in architecture from one of the best art schools in Germany. In other words, he was not only (as his personnel file stated) a "born criminal investigator," "of unconditional reliability," but also a technically minded architect, "very predisposed to the practical."[33] Thus Blobel appreciated pragmatic solutions, and in this regard he saw eye to eye with the senior staff doctor Panning, who was director of the Forensics Institute in the Military Medical Academy in Berlin. Basically unrestrained by institutional and legal structures, Blobel and Panning were free to "refine" killing methods against the Jews and to conduct heinous experiments with Jewish "guinea pigs."

Such outstanding examples of cooperation illustrate the significance of individual initiative, behavior, and interaction in the field. In an even more familiar case of conflict, which emerged between Blobel's men and the Sixth Army staff in Bila Tserkva, the radicalizing effect of administrative structures is especially evident. Here the main conflict between SD and Wehrmacht personnel centered not on killing methods per se, but on the uneasiness that surrounded the shooting of children. No matter how distasteful and psychologically taxing local officials had found the "messy" shooting methods they experienced in Zhytomyr and elsewhere across Western Ukraine, they accepted in principle the killing of male Jews, who were portrayed in militantly political and anti-Semitic terms as the "criminal" Bolshevik enemy. At Bila Tserkva, local SD and Wehrmacht officials confronted something new—the mass execution of "innocent" Jewish infants and children.

Not long after the Jewish population of Bila Tserkva had been registered in mid August 1941, the Field Commander Riedl called in members of Sk4a to assist with the executions.[34] Blobel dispatched a subunit of his killing commando to the town, led by SS-Obersturmführer August Häfner. When Häfner arrived in Bila Tserkva, he found the registered Jews in a school-type building at the edge of town, where they had been brought by the military's Secret Field Police (GFP). Besides a few German soldiers, young Ukrainian militiamen armed with clubs and rifles guarded the building. The GFP handed over about 70 of the adult Jews to Häfner's killing commando, and Waffen-SS marksmen shot them. Then several hundred more were gunned down, leaving the children who remained in the building orphaned. The crying of the abandoned infants and children was heard by nearby Wehrmacht units, whose chaplains filed a complaint on 20 August to the general staff officer of Infantry Division 295, Lieutenant Colonel Helmuth Groscurth. Groscurth wrote up a report that eventually landed on the desk of the Commander of the Sixth Army, Field Marshal von Reichenau.

Groscurth was not convinced that the killing of Jewish children was properly authorized, so he insisted that the issue be brought to the attention of his superiors. Since the commander of Groscurth's division "was not capable of making this decision on his own," the case was brought to a higher level, to Sixth Army headquarters (AOK6). Groscurth's intervention caused a delay in the killing *Aktion* and prompted a meeting of local leaders on the next day (21st August). Field Commander Riedl hosted the meeting with Blobel and his subunit commander Häfner, an Abwehr (intelligence) officer from AOK6, Captain Luley, and Groscurth. The action had been mismanaged, they concurred, because it had caused a stir among the local soldiers, thereby jeopardizing troop discipline. They branded the chaplains a couple of "troublemakers." Then Riedl asserted the Nazi ideological rationale for the execution of Jewish children. He urged that "this brood must be stamped out" without any further "unnecessary" delays. Blobel agreed. When they moved to plan the next course of action, Blobel assured them that von Reichenau also wanted the children killed. Apparently this type of second-hand verbal approval sufficed, because the conveners then proceeded with the assignment of the personnel and resources needed to carry out the massacre.

Thus what proved to be decisive was not the existence of a written order to authorize the killing of Bila Tserkva's Jewish children. By this time, the participants in this critical meeting had already committed mass murder, had witnessed it, or had received other top-secret orders and instructions to kill more Jews. To be sure, Riedl's and Blobel's direct influence (representing the more extreme anti-Semites) was decisive. Yet additional forces were also present, especially the Nazi administrative momentum to "finalize" the *Aktion* in an orderly manner. On 26 August, von Reichenau fumed about the Bila Tserkva massacre, stating that it was simply not "organized properly."[35] He also wrote that, once such an *Aktion* is started, it should be carried out in an expedient manner. Reichenau disregarded the core issue in this conflict, the butchery of children, and instead stressed that killing actions should continue as planned in a frictionless way.[36]

The Bila Tserkva incident illuminates another important aspect of the SD-Wehrmacht dynamic. The Army had the power to dispute SD actions, to intervene, and even to protest them in an influential manner, but they opted instead for a relationship of mutual compliance. After the war, Blobel's right-hand man, August Häfner, summed it up best when he reflected on the SD-Wehrmacht relationship at this time: "The Security Police could not step back vis-à-vis the Wehrmacht and conversely General Field Marshall von Reichenau could not step back vis-à-vis the Security Police."[37]

As of summer 1941, a burgeoning number of SS-Policemen found themselves cast in the role of executioner. At Bila Tserkva, these killers demonstrated that they were capable of finding ways to adapt to the genocide, in large part by allocating certain "unpleasant" tasks to non-Germans, but also by "improving" their mass-shooting methods. After the Bila Tserkva incident, Sk4a commanders took another, more "orderly" approach to the genocide by keeping Jewish mothers with their children. Sk4a commando leader Heinrich Huhn, who along with Ukrainian militiamen killed 561 Jewish children in Radomyshyl on 6 September, recounted that at the subsequent ghetto liquidation at Zhytomyr on 19 September: "The women were allowed to hold their children in their arms" (*Die Frauen durften ihre Kinder auf den Armen halten*).[38] Nazi killers such as Huhn believed that this was a more efficient and even "humane" approach. Thus, with each killing action, regional officials in the army and SS-Police advanced their genocidal methods and overcame conflicts. They gained experience as perpetrators, and as "policy administrators".

Nowhere in Ukraine was this developing Nazi expertise in mass shooting as a killing "process" manifested to such a staggering degree as at Babi Yar on 29–30 September 1941.[39] In Kiev, SS-Police leaders Jeckeln and Blobel along with military city commander, Eberhard, decided to skip the registration procedure and ordered the Jews to gather near the killing site.[40] There German guards formed a corridor through which forty to fifty Jews were forced to walk toward the ravine, suffering beatings and blows to the head along the way.[41] Then German SS-Police and Ukrainian guards forced the Jews to remove their clothes, since the Germans had determined from previous actions that the clothes could be used for other purposes, such as for the needy ethnic Germans.[42] It is not evident at Babi Yar, but the Wehrmacht commanders at Mariupol' and in Kryvyi Rih took over the task of collecting, cleaning, and distributing Jewish clothing, linens, dishes, etc. In the Zhytomyr ghetto massacre a week prior to Babi Yar, the Volksdeutsche Mittelstelle (Ethnic German Liaison Office) asserted its control over the Jewish belongings.[43]

After the Jews at Babi Yar were forced to remove their clothes and give up their valuables, members of the order police, known as "packers" led halfnaked Jews into the ravine. SS-Policemen pushed the Jews face down on top of the bloody corpses of the victims who had preceded them. Then SD marksmen from Blobel's unit came along and shot the Jewish victims in the neck. There were three groups of marksmen (about twelve in each group) traversing the ravine at one time.

Standartenführer Blobel and Obergruppenführer Jeckeln established a rotation of duties whereby SD commandos changed from shooting to loading of ammunition to guarding the Jews near the ravine. During two days, from 6:00 a.m. until 6:00 p.m., Blobel's men, with the help of order police battalion 45 and indigenous auxiliaries, massacred 33,771 Jewish men, women, and children in this manner. Afterwards Sk4a assigned some locals to cover up the bodies with soil and lime chloride. To seal off the grave site, the Germans blew up the walls of the ravine with explosives. The last task in this entire "killing process" was the handling of Jewish valuables. For several days Sk4a members smoothed out bank notes totaling millions, packed them into sacks and, as one participant recalled, "sent them off somewhere" (perhaps to the Beutestelle in Berlin).[44]

Indeed, Babi Yar demonstrates how systematic the Nazi approach to mass shooting had become during the summer of 1941. According to Einsatzgruppe C's report, the Babi Yar killings were so efficiently organized that the Jews believed they were going to be resettled right up to the last moment. Certainly Blobel's Sk4a unit of less than one hundred men manifested its developing expertise in mass murder at the ravine. At another level, the Nazi perception of an "orderly massacre" provided the perpetrators with a psychological buffer, a false sense of "civilized behavior" in the midst of the barbaric bloodshed. Furthermore, the perpetrators wanted a local *Aktion* to go smoothly because its completion meant that the Germans were one step closer to achieving their goal of making Nazi territory "free of Jews." Yet by October 1941, even after having reached a high level of proficiency as mass murderers, Nazi officials remained dissatisfied. As the Einsatzgruppe C chief reported, despite the "efficient organization" of Babi Yar and the fact that "approximately 75,000 Jews have been liquidated in this manner, it has nevertheless become apparent that this method will not provide a solution to the Jewish problem."[45]

As many as 300,000 Jews were killed under the Wehrmacht administration in Ukraine. By the end of January 1942, most of the larger Jewish communities from the Zhytomyr region and eastward to Kharkiv had been totally decimated.[46] The SS-Police's primary role as the executioners was manifested in this initial phase of the Nazi "final solution." Yet the regional military apparatus also played its part. The Kommandantur oversaw the registration and marking of the Jews and of Jewish property, the collection of arbitrary taxes, formation of Jewish forced-labor battalions, and the distribution of Jewish rations. Wehrmacht propaganda units broadcast anti-Semitic declarations and turned some executions into public spectacles. Newly reopened movie houses were furnished with a special film sent from Berlin, "Der ewige Jude."[47] In short, regional leaders in the military and SS-Police carved out their respective roles in the "final solution," and they did so in a relatively "frictionless" manner. As SS-Police and Wehrmacht forces arrived in the eastern parts of Ukraine, historic Jewish communities began to disappear from the map within a matter of days and weeks.

Nearly all of the estimated 350,000 Jews who survived this first killing wave resided in the western regions of Volhynia-Podolia.[48] This area of conquered Ukrainian territory was placed under commissariat rule after 1st September, thus ushering in a new phase of the Holocaust in Ukraine. During this phase, the prevailing Nazi desire for a "smooth" implementation of the "final solution" reappeared in more elaborate forms of administrative coordination, which were centered in the office of the commissar.

The Administration of the "Final solution" in the Reich Commissariat Ukraine, 1941–1944

Unlike the mobile military administrations that swept across Ukraine in the summer and fall of 1941, the Reich Commissariat Ukraine was presumed to be a permanent governing structure. It consisted of five (later expanded to six) regional entities, known as General Commissariats. Within a Commissariat, such as the Zhytomyr General Commissariat, there were about twenty-five subdistricts, or district commissariats (Gebietskommissariate). Numerous public and private agencies also spanned across Ukraine's rural landscape, including the Reich Post, the Reich Railway, and agricultural leaders from Hermann Göring's Four Year Plan, as well as private construction companies like the Firma Jung, which was contracted by the Organisation Todt (OT) to build up Ukraine's roadways and canals.

Within this web of Nazi public and private agencies, the most prominent regional figurehead was the General Commissar. He was responsible for the welfare and fate of the entire civilian population in his region, including the Jews, and empowered to enforce police measures against civilians. The commissars were surrounded by a clique of deputies, a regional SS-Police leader and, in some cases, a special advisor on Jewish matters. Together they kept the General Commissar abreast of the local "Jewish question."

One of the first actions taken by the commissars in Volhynia-Podolia was the ghettoization of the Jews. In Letichev, District Commissar Frieber deliberately scheduled this upheaval on Rosh Hashana, 21 September 1941.[49] While the commissars gained a well-deserved reputation as the leaders of local terror campaigns against the Jews, the actual day-to-day implementation of the Nazi terror involved several departments in the commissariat office. The welfare, medical, and nutrition analysts made sure that Jews were left to die of starvation and disease in the ghettos and camps. In Zwiahel (Novhorad Volyns'kyi) and other areas populated by ethnic Germans, the commissars handled the redistribution of Jewish belongings to the *Volksdeutsche*.[50]

Although the commissars faced stiff competition from SS-Police officials over the fate of Jewish plunder, they were often quite effective in asserting control over the seizure and distribution of Jewish property and goods. According to the General Commissar of Zhytomyr, all Jewish property went first to the commissar's office. Any Ukrainian militiaman who had plundered Jewish goods previously had to hand it over to the commissars.[51] Seized belongings like sewing machines, bedding and clothing were stored in a local booty depot. Army officials, members of the OT, *Volksdeutsche*, and others privileged by the Nazi system filed written requests – often pleas – to the commissar's office to obtain these goods. Jewish flats and furniture were rented to Dutch and German businessmen in Zhytomyr. The commissars' accountants tallied Jewish gold, silver, and currency. It was deposited in the operating budget along with other "Jewish contributions."[52] During 1942–43, the commissar's distribution of the plunder became more bureaucratic; receipts were issued showing the property's Jewish provenance.[53]

On the eve of impending massacres the commissar held a briefing (a so-called *Einsatzbesprechung*) about the "Jewish Question." He brought together his leading advisors to discuss the number of Jews left in the area, their exact location, the commissar's local labor needs, and the timing of the next mass-shooting. Sometimes local army commanders and OT specialists participated in such meetings. The commissar and the district SS-Police leader coordinated all the necessary personnel and material needed to carry out the ghetto liquidations and massacres, down to the assignment of POWs or collective farm-workers to dig the mass graves.[54]

Among the various agencies stationed in the civilian occupied zones, the closest interaction occurred between the commissars and the SS police. According to Hitler's (and Himmler's) orders, each commissar was assigned an SS-Police leader who was "directly and personally" responsible to him.[55] Thus "on paper" the commissars could issue orders to the local SS-Police forces. In practice, however, the more senior the SS-Police leader, the more difficult it became for the commissar to control his counterparts in the SS-Police. After all, the SS-Police was the "executionary power" behind the "final solution."[56] An independent SS-Police chain of command running from Himmler down to the lowest-level gendarme station chief remained in place, and ultimately all SS-Policemen were loyal to their Reichsführer, not to one of Rosenberg's commissars, whom Himmler disparaged as a "a bunch of overpaid bureaucrats."[57]

During the summer of 1942, for example, Zhytomyvs' General Commissar Klemm was forced out of his position and sent back to the Reich because he had resisted the encroachment of the SS-Police into his region's politics. While this conflict was raging, Klemm's office reported to Berlin that local agencies worked together "smoothly" in the construction of Hitler's secret bunker in Vinnytsia.[58] The Klemm incident made it clear to local leaders that inter-agency conflicts were to be avoided; stirring up such "problems" might mean a demotion or a transfer to the front.

Still, tension between the regional-level commissars and SS-Police officials surfaced when Himmler and the Reich Commissar for Ukraine Erich Koch pushed through the final liquidation of Ukraine's ghettos in the second half of 1942. At the commissars' convention in Luts'k on 29–31 August the commissars learned of Koch's "personal wish" for the "final solution" to be carried out "one hundred percent." Consequently, the General Commissar for Volhynia-Podolia promptly asked the SD outposts in his region to accelerate the actions against the Jews so that the ghettos would be destroyed within five weeks.[59] In Brest, the city commissar Franz Burat resisted the liquidation of the ghetto because he needed the Jewish labor force. As Christopher Browning's research has shown, Burat and his ally in the SS-Police, Friedrich Rohde, argued to their superiors that the Jewish workers were more valuable than the meager food rations they consumed. But the attempt to resist was futile. In mid October 1942, the Brest ghetto was attacked by SS-Police forces. After several days of mass shootings and "Jew hunts," the combined forces of local SS-Policemen, mobile Order-Police battalion 310 and the 48th motorized police company had killed 20,000 Jews.[60]

Outside major centers like Brest, relations between the rural commissars and gendarme stations were generally less antagonistic. The fewer traces of conflict at this level suggest that in the most remote outpost of Nazi rule the mere shortage of personnel usually encouraged cooperation. Two examples from the Volhynian district of Zdolbuniv typify the ideological affinity and administrative coordination that existed at the lowest levels of Nazi rule in Ukraine.

On a hot summer evening in August 1942, two members of the Ukrainian Schutzmannschaft were patrolling the Zdolbuniv ghetto when they spotted a Jewish girl named Hanka Prussack. She was sitting on a bench outside her house. Because it was after the official curfew time, the two Ukrainian auxiliaries beat her with their rifle butts until she lay lifeless. Hungarian soldiers stationed nearby heard the cries of Prussack and came to her aid. But they were too late. The outraged soldiers then lashed out at the Ukrainian auxiliaries, beating them so badly that they had to be hospitalized. The incident created a big stir within the commissariat administration because the "prestige" of the German government had been lowered by the Ukrainian auxiliaries' actions. To counter this embarrassment, the commissar's office declared that Hanka had been slain by a Jewish ghetto member and demanded that the Judenrat deliver the "Jewish murderer" or ten Jewish hostages. The Jewish elder protested to the Germans, but to no avail. Believing that the rest of the Jewish community would be spared death, the Judenrat complied with the German demand for hostages and gave ten Jews to the Germans. At least seven of them were placed in the custody of the district SS-Police leader Joseph Paur. The district commissar, Georg Marschall, who believed that the only possible solution to the Jewish problem was to "remove them all," ordered Paur to kill these Jews.[61] One Jewish prisoner was able to run away during the shooting, but members of the gendarme post of Zdolbuniv killed the rest.[62]

About this time, in the summer of 1942, district SS-Police leader Paur had also arrested a local Jewish man named Gelman for an alleged violation of the Nazi law against the slaughtering of livestock. Paur, who was stationed in the same building as the district commissar Marschall, reported the violation to the commissar. Either Marschall or his deputy ordered Paur to execute Gelman publicly in order to terrorize the rest of the population. When Paur forwarded this order to his subdistrict gendarme post in Mizoch, where the alleged violation had occurred, Paur added that the Judenrat must assist in the execution. On the day scheduled for the hanging, Paur drove with his gendarme colleagues from to Zdolbuniv to Mizoch. With the Jewish council present, the gendarmes hanged Gelman. In this case, the district SS-Police outposts did not feel it necessary to bring Gelman to the SD. The matter was worked out locally by the district SS-Police leader and the commissar, who asserted their own terror tactics.

As these examples demonstrate, the decentralization of the "final solution" did not result in administrative chaos. On the contrary, the fact that such ad hoc collaboration occurred at the district level of rule demonstrates the totality of what Raul Hilberg has termed the "machinery of destruction." Yet the killings in Zdolbuniv also show that in the Reich Commissariat Ukraine this machine was not operated by automatons and desk murderers, but rather by functionaries with clear ideological and careerist ambitions.

Eventually, the direct involvement of public and private German agencies became so significant that the SD officials stationed in the Reich Commissariat (who were small in number) found it unnecessary to conduct searches for Jews in hiding.[63] As it turned out, Ukrainian and *Volksdeutsche* auxiliaries, German railroad workers, postal employees, construction foremen, foresters, and other local recruits turned the genocidal hunt for Jews into a bloodthirsty sport.[64] Jews who were not killed on the spot were brought to the SD office, where they underwent "special treatment." In Kiev's SD headquarters, the head of the Judenreferat (Department IVb) did not investigate whether his "prisoner" had committed a crime. He needed only to confirm the Jewishness of his "suspect," since being a Jew was deemed a crime punishable with death. The Judenreferat did not have to obtain countersignatures on the death sentences against Jews, which were required in other cases. Instead, the departmental chief, SS-Hauptsturmführer Hans Schumacher (a former member of Ek5), or his boss, the Commander of the SD in Kiev, Erich Ehrlinger (a former member of Ek1b), gave the Judenreferat the "nod" of approval.[65] The SD bureaucrats and commanders sought as much as possible to avoid placing their own signature on the death sentences of "innocent" Jews. In accepting a superior's nod of approval and not the requisite countersignature, these Nazi officials recognized the secret, criminal nature of the "final solution" while they upheld some semblance of an orderly "civilized" bureaucratic procedure.

In Kiev, executions of SD-held prisoners occurred weekly, if not more often, and usually on Saturday mornings. Kiev's SD Commander, Erich Ehrlinger, met with his adjutant to approve the final execution list, to determine the exact date and time, and to assign who would do the guarding, driving, and shooting. These assignments were posted on a bulletin board in the office. The execution commando consisted of eight to ten men. The Jewish prisoners, often families of men, women, and children, were gathered in the courtyard of the Gestapo prison, forced into gas vans or onto trucks and driven to the mass graves at the edge of the city. Commander Ehrlinger stood by the pits. Occasionally he grabbed a weapon and shot the Jews "to set a good example" or to "speed up the process." Between February 1942 and August 1943, about 365 Jews were gassed or shot by the SD in Kiev.[66]

Although the Sipo-SD played a central role in the genocide, the more numerous stationary and mobile Order-Police units and their indigenous auxiliaries became the "foot soldiers" of the "final solution" in Ukraine. On 12 March 1942, the Commander of the Gendarmerie in the Zhytomyr Commissariat wrote to his order policemen in the district offices that "from now on when it is totally clear why an execution should occur, it is not necessary to obtain approval; however in each case a short report of the act/event is to be lodged with superiors."⁶⁷ In effect, Nazi SS-Police leaders gave their subordinates at the lowest levels a license to kill Jews. In Koziatyn and Ruzhyn, for example, the gendarme chiefs routinely reported ex post facto the shooting of small numbers of Jews whom they found hiding in the forest and fields. In Zdolbuniv, the gendarme posts submitted lists of prisoners to their district headquarters. These lists showed the prisoners' name, race, and any valuables seized. When district gendarme chief Paur looked over the list and saw "Jew," he marked that name for execution. The gendarme post implemented the order without the involvement of the commissar, the nearest SD office, or central authorities in Berlin.⁶⁸

The last major feature of the Nazi administration of the "final solution" in the Reich Commissariat Ukraine was the use of forced labor in the extermination process, known as the "*Vernichtung durch Arbeit* (extermination through labor)." This approach was formalized in the Wannsee Protocol of January 1942, which stated that Jews could provisionally be used in heavy-labor projects like road building and worked to death. As of 1942, Jews from Galicia, Transnistria, Hungary, and Poland were brought to Ukraine for such purposes. Most struggled for their lives in the SS-Police labor camp system along Ukraine's southern border with Romania.

In the "*Vernichtung durch Arbeit*" campaign, one of the key organizational links between the SS-Police and private concerns was the OT, which was a militarized labor organization responsible for building military installations and transportation routes.⁶⁹ OT personnel handed over the exhausted or sick Jewish laborers to the SS-Police. OT engineers and foremen did not have the "power of public office" to carry out an execution, but occasionally they transgressed this Nazi law. For example, in March 1943, a military–SS and police tribunal in Proskurow (Luts'k) sentenced foreman Johann Meisslein to prison for ordering the execution of two Jewish female laborers.⁷⁰

The Meisslein case shows that as the number of agencies involved in the genocide expanded, SS and police officials maintained that they alone were empowered to order the execution of Jews. The foreman could exploit he Jewish laborers and hand them over to the SS-Police to be killed, but the formal order to carry out the murder was supposed to come from the SS-Police. According to Hermann Kaienburg's work on this underexamined aspect of the Holocaust in Ukraine, as many as 25,000 Jews died in the OT–SS and police construction of the autobahn.⁷¹

Conclusion

In his seminal work on the Holocaust, Raul Hilberg introduced the metaphor of a machine to explain the Nazi administrative process behind the "final solution." The key operator of this machine, as Hilberg demonstrated, was the middle-ranking bureaucrat, who "no less than his highest superior was aware of currents and possibilities."⁷² Like the Berlin-centered bureaucrats in Hilberg's analysis, the regional leaders in Ukraine "displayed a striking pathfinding ability in the absence of directives, a congruity of activities without jurisdictional guidelines, a fundamental comprehension of the task even when there were no explicit communications."[73] The regional leaders not only translated Nazi aims into concrete plans of action, but a significant number bloodied their own hands in the implementation. Empowered by their superiors to murder Jews, they took the initiative to develop local "systems" and methods for killing over 1 million Jews in Ukraine.

The Nazi implementation of the "final solution" was an ongoing invention of central and peripheral leaders. Hitler, Himmler, and Heydrich defined the aim of the "final solution'" and they constructed an administrative framework to administer the policy. Yet, in its implementation, the "process" of mass murder developed from the ground up, often after "on the spot" decision-making about how to proceed with the massacre in the most efficient manner. In other words, the technicians and operators of the "final solution" apparatus—men like SD commando chief Blobel, Sixth Army judge Neumann, Oberstabsarzt Panning, and Kiev's Stadtkommandant Eberhard—developed a callously efficient, purposeful (*"zweckmäßig"*) approach to mass shooting. By early 1942, nearly all of Ukraine's Jews east of the Zhytomyr region had been gunned down by Nazi SS-Policemen and collaborators in the local militia and army administration.

During the second phase of the "final solution" in Ukraine, the commissars imposed their own individual styles of terror against the Jews—hence the mosaic of local Holocaust histories that comprise the Nazi "final solution" in the region. Commissars like Marschall were generally university-degreed, middle-ranking bureaucrats and Nazi ideologues, who suddenly found themselves in positions of extreme power. Like the SS-Police killing commanders who preceded him during the 1941 sweep, Marschall understood his local anti-Jewish actions within the broader context of a "final solution." Ultimately, the test of a regional leader's "success" was his ability to garner and exploit all the local possibilities (e.g., the use of Ukrainian auxiliaries) for bringing about the destruction. When the commissar declared his region *"judenfrei"* he also sought approbation from his superiors for a job "well done."

In Nazi-occupied Ukraine, the most remarkable administrative pattern was one of ad hoc collaboration. Ironically, factors that might otherwise have caused conflicts or resistance to the "final solution," such as personnel shortages and the isolation of the rural outposts, actually furthered the Holocaust. Nevertheless, there were certain aspects of the genocide, like the loss of Jewish labor and the distribution of Jewish valuables, that sparked infighting among local German leaders. The commissars, who had ambitious plans for building up regional transportation systems, housing, and industry, wished to capitalize as much as possible on "free" Jewish labor. In the end, however, the ideological consensus surrounding the "final solution" proved stronger than the economic rationale for keeping Jewish laborers alive.

Regional leaders and functionaries who felt uneasy about the massacres found ways to adapt to the genocide. Even at the lowest levels of the Nazi hierarchy, one could play one's part in the "final solution" without dirtying one's own hands, as Ukraine's Sipo-SD Commander Dr. Thomas reassured his deputy in late 1941. In other words, one could avoid officially authorizing the murder through oral orders and gestures like nodding, or one could find more bloodthirsty types among the Germans and indigenous population to do the most gruesome task, killing children. Regional leaders in the military and civilian administration sought to develop a "frictionless" killing process, one that afforded them some psychological distance from the killing, one that was efficient enough for large-scale massacres, and one that would impress superiors. But what they actually produced were bloody scenes of human butchery, scenes that the Nazi euphemism *"reibungslos"* certainly belies.

Notes

* The opinions expressed in this chapter are solely those of the author and are not to be construed as constituting the opinions of the United States Holocaust Memorial Museum.

1. This common bureaucratic term appeared in the reports of SS-Police, military, and commissariat officials. The term also captured the attention of Jürgen Matthäus in "Reibungslos und Planmäßig: Die Zweite Welle der Judenvernichtung im Generalkommissariat Weissruthenien (1942–1944)," *Jahrbuch für Antisemitismusforschung* 4 (1995): 254–274. Also see Raul Hilberg, *Sources of Holocaust Research: An Analysis* (Chicago, 2001), pp. 104–105.
2. For the earliest in-depth treatment of the bureaucracy's role, see Raul Hilberg, *The Destruction of the European Jews* (New York, 1985 [1961]) and "The Bureaucracy of Annihilation," in Francois Furet, ed., *Unanswered Questions: Nazi Germany and the Genocide of the Jews* (New York, 1969). See also the structural analysis of the Third Reich by Hans Mommsen, *Beamtentum im Dritten Reich* (Stuttgart, 1967), and the sociological study by Zygmunt Bauman, *Modernity and the Holocaust* (Ithaca, 1989).
3. Theo Schulte, *The German Army and Nazi Policies in Occupied Russia* (New York, 1989), p. 54.
4. Adolf Hitler, *Secret Conversations 1941–1944*, trans. Norman Cameron and R.H. Stevens (New York, 1979), p. 479.
5. For a more detailed overview of the military structure in Ukraine, see Dieter Pohl's "Schauplatz Ukraine: Der Massenmord an den Juden im Militärverwaltungsgebiet und im Reichskommissariat 1941–1943," in Norbert Frei, Sybille Steinbacher, and Bernd C. Wagner, eds., *Ausbeutung, Vernichtung, Öffentlichkeit: Studien zur nationalsozialistischen Verfolgungspolitik* (Munich, 2000), pp. 125–162. Erich Friderci replaced von Roques in November and December 1941.
6. Schulte, *German Army*, p. 66.
7. For the active role of the Army's propaganda and security units in anti-Jewish measures in Zhytomyr, see Wendy Lower, "Nazi Colonial Dreams: German Policies and Ukrainian Society in Zhytomyr, 1941–1944" (Ph.D. dissertation, American University, Washington D.C., 1999). For Kodyma, see records of the 30th corps, and postwar testimony of General von Salmuth and others, in the Nuremberg Military Tribunal (NMT) High Command Case 12, X, pp. 1228–1230.
8. Schulte adopts Jürgen Förster's concept from "New Wine in Old Sins?: The Wehrmacht and the War of 'Weltanschauungen,' 1941," in Wilhelm Deist, ed., *The German Military in the Age of Total War* (Leamington Spa, 1985), p. 319. See Schulte, *German Army*, p. 68.
9. The FK (676) Pervomaisk records from August 1941, held at the USHMM, Osobyi (Moscow) collection RG 11.001m13/ 92/1275-3-661. The marking of the Jews and for-

mation of labor gangs was undertaken by FK 676 in Drohobycz, and special shops for Jews established in Sambor by the FK, July 1941. See FK 676 reports in this USHMM collection, 1275-3-661. Similar measures were outlined in the widely distributed "Merkblatt über Sofortaufgaben der Ortskommandanturen," KTB SD454, Anlage zum Div. Befehl Nr. 59, NARA RG242/ T-315/R 2216/000091-94. Jewish rations were reduced to the amount allotted to children (if rations were available at all); see 4 November 1941 order no. 44, NARA RG 238/ PS-1189/ Box 26.

10. Raul Hilberg, "Wehrmacht und Judenvernichtung," in Walter Manoschek , ed., *Die Wehrmacht im Rassenkrieg: Der Vernichtung hinter der Front* (Vienna, 1996), pp. 24–25.
11. The three battalions were 82, 311, and 318. From the war diary (KTB) SD 454 it is evident that Orpo battalion 82 (from Breslau) was consistently deployed for actions against Jews and POWs, SD 454 KTB NARA RG 242, T-315/R 2215/000385-469. On the deployment of order-police battalions in the East, see the Himmler order of 21 May 1941, in *Der Krieg gegen die Sowjetunion 1941–1945: Eine Dokumentation zum 50. Jahrestag des Überfalls auf die Sowjetunion* (Berlin, 1991), pp. 99–100.
12. Roques order of 21 July 1941, NARA RG 238/ NOKW-1601.
13. FK 603 Tätigkeitsbericht Lemberg, 31 July 1941, USHMM (Osobyi) RG 11.001m13/92/ 1275-3-663.
14. Dieter Pohl, *Nationalsozialistische Judenverfolgung in Ostgalizien 1941–1944* (Munich, 1997), pp. 46–47.
15. The Jewish labor gangs were put to use on the roadways, first to clear rubble and corpses from the roads; see FK 675 Vinnitsa, August 1941,USHMM(Osobyi) RG 11.001m13/92/1275-3-662; in mine-clearings, at Kiev, 29th Infantry Corps to 99th Infantry Division (AOK6), 22 September 1941, NARA RG 238/NOKW-1323; and at Kharkov, NOKW-184.
16. See "Guidelines for the Conduct of Troops in Russia," in KTB SD 454, NARA RG 242/ T-315/2215/000711-13. Also see, Jürgen Förster's "The Relation Between Operation Barbarossa as an Ideological War of Extermination and the Final solution," in David Cesarani, ed., *The Final solution: Origins and Implementation* (New York, 1996), p. 93.
17. See Richard Breitman's *The Architect of Genocide: Himmler and the Final solution* (Hanover, 1991), pp. 167–177.
18. Leaflets with anti-Semitic messages, in KTB AOK 17, NARA RG 242/ T-501/R674/8308414; released Ukrainian POWs who returned to their villages identified local Jews and hanged them with a vengeance, described in the report of Ortskommandant Wosnessensk, cited by FK (193) Nikolaev Lagebericht of 18 August–September 1941, USHMM (Osobyi) RG 11.001m113/92/1275-3-662. Also see Pohl, *Ostgalizien*, pp. 54–67.
19. Hans Safrian, "Komplizen des Genozids: Zum Anteil der Heeresgruppe Süd an der Verfolgung und Ermordung der Juden in der Ukraine 1941," in Manoschek, ed., *Die Wehrmacht im Rassenkrieg*, p. 102.
20. Pohl, *Ostgalizien*, pp. 59–60.
21. The involvement of individual soldiers in pogroms (in Galicia) was discouraged by von Roques; see his memo, "Befriedungsmaßnahmen," 29 July 1941, NARA RG 242/ T-501/R5/000475-476.
22. AOK 17 order of 30 July 1941 regarding procedure for handing over suspicious persons from intelligence officer (Ic/AO), the army's liaison to the SD kommandos, NARA RG 238/NOKW-1593.
23. On authorization to kill "female agents or Jews who have placed themselves at the use of the Soviets" in Zwiahel (Novohrad-Volyns'kyi) see HSSPF Jeckeln's instructions for joint SS-Police and military cleansing operations, dated 25 July 1941, in NARA RG 242 T-501/R 5/000559-60. See also, NARA RG 23/NOKW-1165 for joint First SS Brigade and AOK6 "cleansing" operations. Heydrich order of 17 July 1941 expanding the killing of all male Jewish prisoners, 17–45 years, reprinted in Peter Klein, ed., *Die Einsatzgruppen in der besetzten Sowjetunion 1941–42: Die Tätigkeits-und Lageberichte des Chefs der Sicherheitspolizei und des SD* (Berlin, 1997), pp. 331–334.

24. On the loss of Jewish labor, see FK Pervomais'k report of 21 September 1941, USHMM (Osobyi) RG 11.001m13/92/ 1275-3-661; and OKIV/839, Uman 30 August 1941,USHMM RG 11.001m13/92/ 1275-2-663. On local relations with the SD and the rapid massacres, see OK Nowo Ukrainka Lagebericht 1–14 September 1941, USHMM RG 11.001m13/92/1275-3-663/ 92 and OK Nikolejew, 11 September 1941, Nikoleav Oblast records, USHMM RG 31.008m/1432-1-1/ fiche 2. The military handed over 4,669 Jews to the SD in Nikoleav, NARA RG 238/NOKW-1464.
25. Von Stülpnagel's orders focused on maintaining troop discipline to keep peace with the Ukrainians, AOK 17 Ic.AO "Behandlung der Bevölkerung und Aufrechterhaltung der Disziplin," 24 August 1941, KTB AOK 6, NARA RG 242/ T-312/R 674/8308378; Von Reichenau's order of 10 August 1941, "Exekutionen durch den SD," Anlage KTB SD 454, NARA RG 242/ T-315/R 2215/000959. Also see Keitel's memo on "Jews in the Eastern Territories," 12 September 1941, NARA RG 242/ T-77/R 1028/6500510.
26. Commander Rear Army South, War Diary, Az. III Tgb.Nr. 3/41 geh., 1 September 1941, in KTB SD 454, NARA RG 242/ T313/R 2216/000081.
27. Safrian, "Komplizen des Genozids," in Manoschek, ed., *Die Wehrmacht im Rassenkrieg*, p.108.
28. The scene was precisely sketched by an eyewitness Wehrmacht soldier, probably drawn after the war. The eyewitness also claimed that the SD kommando photographed the killing but the film was destroyed by the commanding officer of the killing unit. See USHMM Photo Archives, #431.278, W//S #79780, Zhitomir, Source: Schweizerisches Bundesarchiv.
29. Statements of August Häfner, 10 June 1965 and 8 February 1966, of Ernest Wilhem Boernecke, 5 November 1965 and Heinrich Huhn, 13 September 1962, Trial against Kuno Callsen et. al, ZSt, AR-Z 419/1962. Häfner statements in Ernst Klee, Willi Dreßen, and Volker Rieß, eds., *The Good Old Days: The Holocaust as Seen by its Perpetrators and Bystanders* (New York, 1991), p. 114.
30. Statements of Kurt Friedrich Hans, 30 September 1965 and 12 August 1965, Callsen Trial, ZSt, AR-Z 419/1962.
31. See Gerhart Panning's "Wirkungsform und Nachweis der sowjetischen Infanteriesprengmunition," (mit 12 Abbildungen) in *Der deutsche Militärarzt*, January 1942. Library of Congress microfilm #0184. Panning died in March 1944. See von Moltke's letter in Beate Ruhm von Oppen, ed., *Letters to Freya, 1939–1945* (New York 1990), p. 160. See also, Alfred Streim *Die Behandlung sowjetischer Kriegsgefangener im "Fall Barbarossa"* (Heidelberg, 1981), pp. 135–137 and Friedrich Heber, *Gerichtsmedizin unterm Hakenkreuz* (Leipzig, 2002), pp. 274–278.
32. For a more in-depth analysis of the influence of Prussian tradition and values on the Nazi system, see Hans Mommsen, "Preussentum und Nationalsozialismus," in Wolfgang Benz, Hans Buchheim and Hans Mommsen, eds., *Der Nationalsozialismus: Studien zur Ideologie und Herrschaft* (Frankfurt on Main, 1993), pp. 29–41.
33. Paul Blobel's personnel record of 7 October 1935, reprinted in Henry Friedlander and Sybil Milton, eds. *Archives of the Holocaust: An International Collection of Selected Documents*, 11 (New York, 1989), p. 70.
34. Hans Safrian and Bernd Boll, "Auf dem Weg nach Stalingrad: Die 6. Armee 1941–42," in Hannes Heer and Klaus Naumann, eds., *Vernichtungskrieg: Verbrechen der Wehrmacht 1941 bis 1944* (Hamburg, 1995), p. 275.
35. Ibid., p. 153.
36. Helmut Krausnick and Harold Deutsch, eds., *Helmuth Groscurth: Tagebücher eines Abwehroffiziers, 1938–1940* (Stuttgart, 1970), p. 541.
37. "Die Sicherheitspolizei konnte gegenüber der Wehrmacht nicht zurück und Generalfeldmarschall von Reichenau umgekehrt gegenüber der Sicherheitspolizei," August Häfner statement of 13 October 1965, Callsen Trial, ZSt 207 AR-Z 419/62.
38. Heinrich Huhn statement of 13 March 1966, Callsen Trial, ZSt 207 AR-Z 419/62.
39. The leading role of the SD Kommandos was made clear in the OK and FK reports from , Kryvyi Rih, and Nikoleav. See in particular the Nikolajew report, OK I/853 "Einsatz der Juden," 11 September 1941, Nikoleav Oblast records, USHMM RG 31.008m/1432-1-1/ fiche 2.

40. See Pohl, "Schauplatz," p. 137 and Klee, Dreßen, and Rieß, *The Good Old Days*, pp. 63–68.
41. Testimony of survivor, Dina M. Proniceva, 9 February 1967, reprinted in Peter Longerich, ed. *Die Ermordung der europäischen Juden: Eine umfasssende Dokumentation des Holocausts 1941–1945* (Munich, 1989), pp. 124–127. Additional survivor testimonies are in Erhard Roy Wiehn, ed., *Nothing is Forgotten: Jewish Fates in Kiev, 1941–1943* (Konstanz, 1993).
42. For the Zhytomyr ghetto action, see the Einsatzgruppe C Ereignismeldung of 7 October 1941, in Yitshak Arad, Shmuel Krakowski and Shmuel Spector, eds., *The Einsatzgruppen Reports: Selections from the Dispatches of the Nazi Death Squads' Campaign Against the Jews in Occupied Territories of the Soviet Union July 1941–January 1943* (New York, 1989), pp. 171–174. The OK in Mariupol reported (29 October 1941) that, after the SD killed 8,000 Jews there, his office seized Jewish property and clothing given to the military hospital, POW camps, and ethnic Germans, in Illrii Illr'evich Kondufor, Vasilii Nikolaevich Nemiatyi and Instytut istorii partii, eds., *History Teaches a Lesson: Captured War Documents Expose the Atrocities of the German-fascist Invaders and their Henchmen in Ukraine's Temporarily Occupied Territory during the Great Patriotic War (1941–1945)* (Kiev, 1986), p. 45.
43. A Nazi system for handling Jewish property was not developed at this early stage in the genocide. See Martin Dean's chapter in this volume and "Jewish Property Seized in the Occupied Soviet Union in 1941 and 1942: The Records of the Reichshauptkasse Beutestelle," *Holocaust and Genocide Studies* 14 (Spring 2000): 83–101. In Kryvyi Rih, the military (OK 538) seized gold and other precious metals, which were applied to the local Wehrmacht operating budget; see OK (538) report dated 14 September 1941, USHMM (Osobyi)/RG 11.001m13 92/1275-3-665.
44. Klee, Dreßen and Rieß, *The Good Old Days*, p. 67. See report of Orpo battalion 314 about killings and confiscations of Jewish monies, 24 January 1942, BA Berlin-Lichtefeld, R 2104/25. I am grateful to Martin Dean for this document.
45. Einsatzgruppe C, Ereignismeldung no. 128, 2 November 1941. NARA RG 242/ T175/233.
46. Pohl, "Schauplatz," p. 159; Aleksandr Kruglov, *Unichtozhenie evreiskogo naseleniia Ukrainy v 1941–1944: khronika sobytii* (Mogilev, 1997), p. 96.
47. See the September and October 1941 RK and OK reports from Kryvyi Rih, USHMM (Osobyi)/RG 11.001m13 92/1275-3-665.
48. About 530,000 Jews in eastern Galicia were placed under the rule of the Generalgouvernement, and another 185,000 Jews along the southern border fell under Romanian control mainly inTransnistria.
49. See Vladimir Goykher's memoir, *The Tragedy of the Letichev Ghetto* (New York, 1993). Shmuel Spector, *The Holocaust of Volhynian Jews, 1941–1944* (Jerusalem, 1990), pp. 116–187.
50. Lagebericht from Gebietskommissar, Zwiahel, dated 20 May 1942, BAK R6/310.
51. General Commissar Klemm's order of 12 December 1941, Zhytomyr State Archive, Ukraine (hereafter ZSA), P1182-1-6/170.
52. See the accounting records (17 November 1941- 28 February 1942) of Gebietskommissar Dr. Bluemel in Tschudnow, ZSA, P1537-1-282. General Commissar Klemm ordered all commissars to report Jewish currency and gold to the finance department, 24 July 1942, ZSA, P1151-1-9.
53. Locals who had plundered furniture after the massacres of 1941 also came forward with "unofficial receipts" to claim that they had purchased the items from the Jews. See the inventory commission, files of the director, Herr Plisko, ZSA, P1152-1-16.
54. Case against the Kasatin district commissariat, "Abschlussbericht" ZSt II AR-Z 137/67, pp. 20–22 and Case against the Litin district commissariat, "Abschlussbericht" ZSt II AR-Z 135/6, pp. 561–563.
55. Hitler orders of 17 July 1941 on the administration in the East, NARA RG 242/ T-454/100/000680.
56. RmfdbO memo (Otto Brautigam's file) "Richtlinien für die Behandlung der Judenfrage," 4 February 1942, NARA RG 242/ roll 154/MR 334, EAP 99/447.

57. Himmler's criticism of Rosenberg's staff, Himmler letter to G. Berger, August 1942 NARA RG 242/ T-175/66/2582327. On the senior-level conflicts over *Ostpolitik*, see Alexander Dallin, *German Rule in Russia, 1941–1945: A Study of Occupation Policies* (New York, 1955) and Timothy Mulligan, *The Politics of Illusion: German Occupation Policy in the Soviet Union, 1942–43* (New York, 1988).
58. See General Commissar's Lagebericht dated 3 June 1942, BAK R6/310. I am grateful to Dieter Pohl for this document. Zhytomyr's SSPF Otto Hellwig memo about Klemm's complaints to the SS-Police, 20 July 1942, ZSA, P1151-1-706.
59. Records of the General Commissar of Volhynia-Podolia in the Polish Main Commission for the Investigation of Nazi Crimes, Zbior Zespolow Szczatkowych Jednostek SS I Policji-Sygnatura 77, memo to SD outposts 31 August 1942. Documents in Martin Dean's possession.
60. Christopher Browning, *Nazi Policy, Jewish Workers, German Killers* (Cambridge, 2000), pp. 130–139.
61. See Douglas K. Huneke, *The Moses of Rovno: The Stirring Story of Fritz Graebe, A German Christian who Risked his Life to Lead Hundreds of Jews to Safety During the Holocaust* (New York, 1985), p. 33.
62. See Case 553, *Justiz und NS-Verbrechen: Sammlung deutscher Strafurteile wegen Nationalistischer Tötungsverbrechen 1945–1966* (Amsterdam, 1976–77). As of 1952, Paur was the director of the crime unit in Neustadt am Aisch. He retired in 1960 and was arrested and sentenced to seven years in prison in 1964.
63. In Zhytomyr, an area of 70,000 square kilometers (an area larger than the combined U.S. states of New Hampshire, Vermont and Massachusetts), there were six SD outposts. In Volhynia Podolia there were five.
64. Records of the Gebietskommissare in Berdychiv, esp. the case of three Jewish workers (the Horrowitz brothers and Moses Landau) from 17 July 1942, ZSA, P1465-1-1. See also Case 26, *Justiz und NS-Verbrechen* and Huneke, *Moses of Rovno*, p.82.
65. See Klein, *Die Einsatzgruppen. pp. 81–82.*
66. Case 526, *Justiz und NS-Verbrechen*, p. A-35-37.
67. KdG Zhytomyr, 12 March 1942, ZSA, P12151-1-9.
68. See Case 553, *Justiz und NS-Verbrechen*. Reports of Jews killed by the district SS-Police offices in Kasatin and Rushin, ZSA, P1182-1-36 and P1182-1-6.
69. See *Handbook of the Organisation Todt* (MIRS, London, March 1945).
70. "Feldurteil" Gericht der Kdtr.des Bereiches Proskurow (FK183), 12 March 1943, Prague Military Archive Various SS Records, carton B142. I am grateful to Jürgen Matthäus for this document.
71. Hermann Kaienburg, " Jüdische Arbeitslager an der 'Strasse der SS,'" *1999. Zeitschrift für Sozialgeschichte des 20. Jahrhunderts* 11 (1996): 38.
72. Raul Hilberg, *The Destruction of the European Jews* (New York, 1985), p. 996.
73. Ibid., p. 993.

PART III

DECENTRAL INITIATIVE AND VERTICAL INTEGRATION

CHAPTER 14

INTRODUCTION: A BUREAUCRATIC HOLOCAUST – TOWARD A NEW CONSENSUS

Michael Thad Allen

During the first third of the twentieth century, many became aware that a "new man" had begun to play a disproportionate role in shaping the twentieth century, one who was neither a bourgeois nor a worker. This was the mid-level manager, the white-collar worker, or the petty administrator (however we choose to label him). Siegfried Kracauer and Hans Speier were among the first to explore this new work culture. They were conscious that the growing complexity of industrial society had created new salaried employees, but that, however much these might influence the means of production directly, they did not own them. They could never count as classic entrepreneurs, least of all among entrepreneurs. They gained their positions through educational credentials, and yet they did not count among the classically trained, humanistic professions, again, least of all among doctors, lawyers, or professors. Like the blue-collar worker, they were creatures of a new, intensifying division of labor in modern corporations, and yet they struggled above all to distinguish themselves from the proletariat. Thus they did not count as workers, least of all among manual laborers. The new white-collar men or "pink-collar" women seemed neither fish, flesh, nor fowl. Speier labeled them (in German the *Angestellten*) "value-parasites"; Kracauer accused them of "spiritual homelessness."[1] If many did not know quite what to make of this "new man" or "new woman," they seemed equally unsure whether their debut on the world-historical stage boded anything good for humankind.

Speier's work in particular greatly influenced the American sociologist C. Wright Mills, who was responsible for translating the writings of Max Weber for an American audience. In 1951 Mills also wrote *White Collar*, exploring the new work world of the twentieth-century office. Given the powerful influence of Max Weber's interpretation of bureaucratic rationalization on Mills, it is no surprise that he blamed modern organizations with their new division of labor for a malaise of alienation and stunted moral development: "Among white-collar people, the malaise is deep-rooted; for the absence of any order of belief has left them morally defenseless as individuals and politically impotent as a group ... white-collar man has no culture to lean upon except the contents of a mass society that has shaken him and seeks to manipulate him to its alien ends."[2] By the 1950s, it seems, the trepidation of Speier or Kracauer had turned to outright hostility. By the 1960s Hannah Arendt would make a failed vacuum-oil salesman-cum-petty administrator a central trope. *Eichmann in Jerusalem*, arguably the single most influential history of the Holocaust, held the mid-level manager and bureaucratic organization accountable for the Nazi genocide.

American intellectuals needed little prompting from immigrants such as Speier or Arendt in order to engender their own native contempt for mid-level managers and office workers. In the nineteenth century we already have Herman Melville's Bartleby the Scrivener, and Lewis Mumford labeled the white-collar worker the "penny-in-the-slot automaton."[3] Even as many begrudgingly accorded these new workers a singular place in industrial society, few ever identified with them. They are usually simply subsumed among that often invoked category, the "middle class" or "petit bourgeois," which, as Arno Mayer once noted, "has had a harder time commanding scholarly attention than either the power-elite or the proletariat: it has no patronage to dispense; it is not seen as a revolutionary threat; and it lacks the romance of utter wretchedness ... that commands empathetic scrutiny."[4]

More often than not, the agency of this class is not so much explained as assumed not to exist. An intensified division of labor is held responsible for the white-collar workers' spiritual emptiness. They are undeniably specialists, deeply embedded in hierarchies to which they contribute but which they cannot conceive or control alone. They receive orders and convey them further along chains of authority. Rather than acting in any direct, personal relationship with employees, they are paid salaries to manage from afar. In the process they depersonalize and deskill even themselves. Unlike the (often overly idealized) classic entrepreneur, they do not and cannot own the means of production. Therefore they have supposedly remained incapable of pursuing any personal moral vision, and they also seem to escape personal responsibility. Thus "organization men" supposedly submit their individual will to the purely instrumental calculation of organizations, and for this reason many condemn their soullessness; worse, they stand accused of imposing their own soullessness upon the rest of the world. Variants of this view can be found in contemporary popular books like John Ralston Saul's *Voltaire's Bastards*, which makes the mid-level manager the butt of disaffection with nothing less than the Enlightenment in general.[5]

Whereas Speier and others had influenced American social scientists before and during World War II, in the 1950s and 1960s American intellectuals quickly reexported their discontent with the mid-level manager back to

Germany. In these decades, American managerial techniques traveled to Europe as part of Marshall Plan aid and, before that, as part of the military occupation—not only to Germany but to Japan as well. German managers also resumed the brisk industrial tourism that had characterized the prewar period. They visited American corporations in search of ideas, technology, and organizational innovations. American subsidiaries also moved into the West German market. With this exchange, discontent with American corporate bureaucracy seems to have quickly followed.[6]

For example, Vance Packard's *The Pyramid Climbers* was reprinted repeatedly in German translation, starting in 1963, a year after its American publication. Although Packard's intent was to reform American-style management, he nevertheless directed a scathing critique at what he punningly called the "Bland New Leaders" of the modern economy: "The human managers are expected to be at all times absolutely logical and at no time humanly emotional"; he referred to them as "component parts of the management machinery."[7] The manager as a "cog" in the bureaucratic machine is now a well-established cliché, but Packard did not coin it. Rather, he had drawn it from repeated interviews with the chief executive officers of American corporations, who complained about their own employees in the bureaucratic edifices that they themselves had erected!

Thus, if German and American scholars of the Holocaust have made repeated reference to "cogs in the machinery" of bureaucratic organizations, it is at least partly due to the common preoccupation among cultural elites with white-collar workers in the immediate postwar era.[8] Hans Mommsen and, earlier, Raul Hilberg both identified a "self-operating" machinery of death that led to the Holocaust, attributing causal force to the division of labor and technical rationality in modern society. In doing so, they share in a much larger trend that has heaped scorn on the new white-collar world of twentieth century industrial society. Not a few critics have blamed bureaucratic capitalism for the decay of modern society in general, with the Holocaust as perhaps the cardinal sin in that degeneracy.

The chapters presented below should prompt us to ask whether that traditional interpretation accurately represents the "desk murderer" (*Schreibtischtäter*), without whom, as the older literature rightly points out, the unique "technocratic" nature of the Holocaust would have scarcely been possible. Perhaps one poignant insight might be drawn from another American observer of the new middle classes, Richard Hoffstadter. Hoffstadter once challenged C. Wright Mills, "You have somehow managed to get into your portrait of the white-collar man a great deal of your personal nightmare, writing about him as though he must feel as you would feel if you were in his position."[9] Have Holocaust studies not committed a similar, understandable error? Have we not somewhat too easily condemned the mentality of the Adolf Eichmanns? Have we fundamentally misunderstood their world as if they lived it as we presume we would have, that is, by being alienated? The chapters in this section challenge us to strive for a more complex understanding of the Holocaust than metaphors of "cogs" or ideal types of thoughtless "bureaucratic twerps" might allow.[10]

To strive for a more comprehensive understanding of these perpetrators is not to excuse, explain away, or "identify" with them. Rather, the opposite is true: to assume that a mechanistic division of labor must have coerced the likes of Eichmann to overcome his moral "resistance" to killing transposes, in a curious backhanded way, our own motives onto him—it assumes that he likely wished to do otherwise, as we hope any sane, rational citizen should have. To acknowledge the commitment, the mixture of petty bureaucratic routine and an almost electric excitement, is to face squarely the strangeness of Eichmann and so many others like him. There can be no doubt, as Arendt or Raul Hilberg proposed from the beginning, that bureaucracies and their staffers were responsible for a new kind of evil in modern society. But, rather than presupposing the alienation of bureaucrats and their amoral malaise, these chapters admirably inquire into the real motivations of perpetrators.

The Eichmanns of the world are present here in other incarnations: Gerald Feldman's Allianz director Eduard Hilgard, or Wolf Gruner's civil servants from the Third Reich's major cities. Each shows the active role that bureaucrats played. They were not reactive or constrained but, more often than not, proactive; their scope for action and command was enhanced by modern organizations; and they used the increasing range of their authority to accelerate or radicalize policies of discrimination and, eventually, genocide.

Wolf Gruner demonstrates how, with distressing repetition, this occurred over and over again in the municipal governments of German cities, and, as such, his essay is part of the recent wave of regional studies that seeks to look beyond the spectacular and thuggish policies of the Nazi Party, the SS, or the SA. Though we have much information on the "ordinary men" of the SS, these were never "ordinary institutions." This, Gruner aptly notes, cannot be said of the municipal civil servants of Germany's diverse cities. This might be the last place we would look for radical policies, and it has been. Yet otherwise petty civil servants developed "an entire catalogue of exclusionary measures," anticipating, sometimes by several years, national laws.

To highlight only one example, after the incendiary Nuremberg Party Rally, the Minister of the Interior Wilhelm Frick and the Economics Minister Hjalmar Schacht actually saw the need to put a brake on escalating racial violence and public displays of anti-Semitism at the municipal level. A lower-level bureaucrat had prompted them to do so, in this case in response to the fiery oratory of Kurt Fiehler, the mayor of Munich and head of the NSDAP's Main Office for Municipal Policy. Fiehler, in his turn, often had to respond to pressure from below. In general, at least until 1938, local mayors and town councils were eager to achieve more than national policy prescribed. They were not so much "working toward the Führer" (*dem Führer zuarbeiten*) as so often supposed; they often felt pressure to "work toward" their own constituencies within German society. Official policies were often adopted at the national level only after extensive experimentation (often competitive) among different municipalities. Local authorities, not Reich or even necessarily Party authorities, also first initiated forced-labor programs for Jews, undertook spontaneous "cleansing," and began to threaten the Jews' economic existence.

Gruner's study would seem to prompt us to reconsider the prevalent preoccupation with National Socialist "polycracy." As more than a generation of solid scholarship has demonstrated, the National Socialist regime was notoriously fractious. Competing hierarchies often existed side by side to accomplish the same task, and this meant that the division of labor, both horizontally and vertically, continually witnessed a steady accretion of functions and layers. It has commonly been assumed that this caused great inefficiency within modern organizations. But, at least for some functions, the increasing fragmentation of institutions seems to have enhanced cooperation rather than conflict. As Wolfgang Seibel's most recent work demonstrates, when the civil authorities of the Vichy regime dealt with separate and competing German occupation authorities, room for initiative increased. The same was true of the SS's concentration-camp industries and other administrative functions.[11]

The insurance executives discussed by Feldman present a different aspect of "polycracy." They tried to take advantage of divergent rivalries within the Third Reich in order to profit and avoid liability. In Feldman's particular case of Allianz and its actions following the *Reichskristallnacht*, insurance executives went out of their way to find means to deny liability for Jewish claims, and did not hesitate to rely upon Hitler's expressed will (as recorded by Joseph Goebbels) that "The insurance companies will not pay [the Jews] a thing." As the problem of liability evolved, however, it became clear that Jews were not the only ones owed payment; so too were foreign owners of commercial property. This was not to mention the involvement of foreign insurers and reinsurance firms, from whom the Nazi state would have been quite glad to receive moneys, as well as publicly chartered insurance companies backed by Nazi Party hacks, who sought to protect the "common interest" from the "self-interest" of private insurers. In short, this was a polycratic morass, one populated by, among others, the SS, Goebbels, and Hermann Göring.

Eduard Hilgard seems to have been motivated at first to protect the honor and international prestige of his industry in general and his firm, Allianz, in particular. He pressed to make payments, knowing that payments to Jews would be forbidden by the likes of Göring; meanwhile, he did not expect Göring and the SS to combine in suggesting that the private insurance industry make good on its payments so that they could be confiscated in turn by the Reich. The *Reichskristallnacht* expropriated the property of Germany's insurance companies and the Jews at the same time. During and after these negotiations, insurance industry spokesmen believed themselves (not the Jews) to be the victims of Nazi policy. In such an atmosphere, one did not have to be an ardent National Socialist to instrumentalize specific issues for personal or institutional gain.

Feldman argues that Hilgard was not a radical anti-Semite. Motives remain frustratingly ambiguous, even opaque. Allianz executives were unlikely to consider extermination of the European Jews a worthy cause, unlikely even to consider it within the ken of historical possibility, but once they accepted the normality of anti-Semitic policies they were willing enough to take it up for their own ends. Gruner, on the other hand, suggests that the constant reinforcement of discrimination implies, at the very least, a passive acceptance of anti-Semitism and repeatedly emphasizes that German officials had the freedom to act otherwise. Mayors could have used their authority to shield their local Jews; in fact, in some few cases in some few cities they did. This not only points up the sad fact of how remarkable true civil courage was in the Third Reich, but it also shows that choice was possible—or at least far less constrained by bureaucratic structure than often presumed.

In all cases motives varied, as in any modern society, but there would seem to be several constants. First, the vast majority of German officials and bureaucrats acted to instrumentalize radical anti-Semitism in order to achieve ulterior motives. On the other hand, these motives seem to have constantly reinforced anti-Semitic policy. Lastly, bureaucrats could act as they did due to the fact that the regime never seems to have experienced any serious deficit of support in any vital segment of the population; to the contrary, there was widespread acceptance ranging from passively condoning local excess to ardent participation.[12] To the "ordinary German," after all, local officials were the regime. Bureaucratic activism was either popular or, at the very least, not unpopular.

Many traditional interpretations of the division of labor have questioned why there was no "resistance" to the Holocaust by mid-level managers or low-level functionaries: "Why did so many who participated in the series of events that led directly and indirectly to the extermination of the Jews fail to withdraw their contribution either through passive resistance or any form of resistance whatsoever?"[13] The alienation within modern bureaucracies has offered a powerful explanation. The complex division of labor necessary to carry out the Holocaust is presumed to have served a primary function in inuring otherwise placid, upstanding citizens to the horror of genocide. Organizations atomize individuals, preempt their conscious moral engagement, and thus facilitate their participation. For example, Christopher Browning and others have argued that the SS introduced factory-style gassing in order to spare the common SS soldier the gut-wrenching brutality of face-to-face murder. Indeed, leaders of SS shooting squads as well as Rudolf Höss, the Kommandant of Auschwitz, claimed that the scale of murder demanded extra layers of organization and technology between killers and victims. It was a psychological necessity: "Now we had discovered the gas and the process for gassing," remarked Höss.

> Now I was finally calmed that we would be spared these bloodbaths, that the victims too would be spared until the last minute. It was exactly this that had worried me the most as I thought of Eichmann's descriptions of the Einsatz Kommandos mowing down Jews with machine guns and machine pistols. Horrific scenes were supposed to have played out: [victims] fleeing as they were shot at, the killing of the wounded, above all women and children. The

frequent suicide among the ranks of our own Kommandos, among them those who could not bear wading through all the blood any more. Some had also gone crazy. The majority of these Einsatz Kommandos had to rely upon alcohol to help them through the work.¹⁴

The very scenes that Höss described did, in fact, "play out" throughout German-occupied Eastern Europe.

On the other hand, Christopher Browning's *Ordinary Men* may be taken as a good example of how more or less irrelevant the division of labor was in overcoming "resistance." Browning pinpoints exactly those junctures in which members of Reserve Police Battalion 101 had a choice and elected not to shoot. He purposefully urges us to take the most charitable view of the "shooters," that they must have had to cope with "the demands of conscience." Browning is very similar to Arendt in this regard, who believed that the Nazi killers had first to " overcome" the animal pity by which all normal men are affected in the presence of physical suffering.¹⁵ Even if we start from the idealistic assumption that the resistance of "ordinary men" should be the norm; that, if left to their own devices, they would not have participated in shootings. Even if we discount evidence that demonstrates acts of cruelty in which perpetrators ratcheted up the inhumanity of their deeds when expressly ordered not to do so; if we purposely interpret data in such a way as to give Nazi shooters every benefit of the doubt when they proclaimed their own lack of motivation or intention to participate in killings (i.e. after the war); still Browning's research shows that, in the end, only a maximum of 20 percent and more likely only 10 percent ever chose not to kill Jews even when presented with the explicit latitude to choose not to do so. Although an increasing division of labor did tend to distance the Police Battalion 101 from visceral, face-to-face murder over time, nonetheless, "Segmentation and routinization, the depersonalizing aspects of bureaucratized killing, cannot explain the battalion's initial behavior."¹⁶ Whatever role hierarchical bureaucracy played in the Holocaust, it is very unlikely that it primarily served to attenuate "resistance" or any innate abhorrence.

We might take as another example Jean-Claude Pressac, *Die Krematorien von Auschwitz. Die Technik des Massenmordes*. Pressac's central question concerns the complicity and conscious knowledge of SS engineers and architects as well as private corporations in the construction of the gas chambers. At what point, he asks, would it have been absolutely impossible for the "technocrats" of extermination to have avoided direct knowledge of the murderous purpose of their technology despite the bureaucratic nature of their tasks? He concludes that no later than the late summer/early fall of 1942 could even the most petty-minded engineer, like Kurt Prüfer of the furnace manufacturer Topf & Söhne, have remained ignorant of the Holocaust.¹⁷

Pressac, like Browning, starts from the implicit assumption that bureaucracies functioned primarily to remove individuals from knowledge of the overarching consequences of their work. In the end, however, he too demonstrates that—even if we purposely indulge all credulity—perpetrators nevertheless must have known what they were doing. Furthermore, they showed eager initiative even when they clearly did not have to. Prüfer's firm, Topf & Söhne, for example, suggested, in the absence of any prompting, a warm forced-air ventilation system for the gas chambers of Birkenau. This simple technical innovation demonstrates that the firm knew that the basement morgues of Birkenau's crematoria II and III were no longer used to "store" the bodies of the dead (a purpose demanding cool air) and clearly indicates that the firm knew that Zyklon-B pellets activate only at relatively warm temperatures. As with Browning's Police Battalion 101, so too with the "technocrats of extermination" at Auschwitz—an increased division of labor may have distanced them from direct murder, but this fact never seems to have been a necessary condition to secure their willing participation.[18]

The primary question concerning the Holocaust as a crime based on the division of labor is not "How did the division of labor overcome 'resistance?'" but, rather, "What interrelationship existed between centralized authority and spontaneous initiative at the local level?" Wolf Gruner's investigation of municipal governance raises this question as well, as have Christopher Browning's most recent explorations of bureaucracy. These suggest that local initiative and hierarchical, bureaucratic authority were mutually complementary.[19] Centralized organizations relied upon the agency of local, more or less independent actors as a source for their own innovation. "Polycracy" actually helped increase the effectiveness of central authority in this way. At the local level it led to many, sometimes competing, sometimes complementary policies. Central agencies selected from among them. In Gruner's study this role was played by the German Gemeindetag (Council of Municipalities) and the Reich Ministry of the Interior.

If we acknowledge that the bulk of recent literature has been leading to a new consensus, these essays help us approach the division of labor in the Holocaust in a new way. Namely, bureaucracies under National Socialism were not so much instrumental in overcoming "resistance" to the Holocaust among "ordinary Germans"; nor did they foster the "banality of evil"; rather, they served to channel and recombine the enthusiasm of local functionaries. The abiding question remains, then, not why there was so little resistance, but why there was so much participation. Perhaps the fact that the barbarous utopia of National Socialism so often met with cooperation and complicity rests in the nature of its grandiloquent dreams of a Thousand Year Reich, vistas of historic destiny, and loudly proclaimed "final solutions." These were as prevalent and seemingly all-encompassing as they were vague. The absence of concrete programmatic substance only enhanced the division of labor within the Nazi regime by spurring multiple initiatives, which could be understood, in the eyes of ambitious white-collar workers, as so many virtuous iterations of the "Führer's" will. It is a tragic but conspicuous fact that the centralized bureaucracies of the Holocaust never lacked initiatives to choose from.

Notes

1. Hans Speier, *German White-Collar Workers and the Rise of Hitler* (New Haven, 1986), quote: p. 9. Speier's essays appeared first before 1934; Mill's work would culminate in *White Collar* by 1951. The Nazis had suppressed the publication of Speier's work in 1934, and his essays did not appear in any accessible form in German until Jürgen Kocka finally had the full manuscript published in 1977. Mills had read them in manuscript form. Second quote from Siegfried Kracauer, *Die Angestellten* (Frankfurt on Main, 1971, reprint from 1929), quote: p. 91.
2. Cited after Olivier Zunz, *Making America Corporate 1870–1920* (Chicago, 1990), pp. 2–3. C. Wright Mills, *White Collar: The American Middle Classes* (Oxford, 1951), pp. xv, xvii, and "The Morale of the Cheerful Robots," pp. 233–235.
3. Lewis Mumford, *Technics and Civilization* (New York, 1963, reprint from 1934), p. 177.
4. Arno Mayer, "The Lower Middle Class as Historical Problem," *Journal of Modern History* 47 (1975): 409.
5. John Ralston Saul, *Voltaire's Bastards: The Dictatorship of Reason in the West* (New York, 1992).
6. On Europe in general see Charles Maier, *In Search of Stability: Explorations in Historical Political Economy* (Cambridge, 1987), pp. 121–152. On France see Richard Kuisel, *Seducing the French: The Dilemma of Americanization* (Berkeley, 1993), pp. 70–102, and Kristin Ross, *Fast Cars Clean Bodies: Decolonization and the Reordering of French Culture* (Cambridge, 1996). On Japan see Simon Partner, *Assembled in Japan: Electrical Goods and the Making of the Japanese Consumer* (Berkeley, 1999), pp. 51–66. On Austria see Reinhold Wagnleitner, *Coca-Colonization and the Cold War: The Cultural Mission of the United States in Austria After the Second World War* (Chapel Hill, 1994). On Germany see Volker Berghahn, *The Americanization of West German Industry 1945–1973* (Cambridge, 1986), pp. 26–39, 230–259.
7. Vance Packard, *The Pyramid Climbers* (New York, 1962), p. 11. Translated as *Die Pyramiden-Kletterer*, this book was printed in 1963, 1965, 1966, 1968, and later. Likewise David Riesman's *The Lonely Crowd: A Study of the Changing American Character* (New Haven, 1950) was printed in West Germany in 1956 and reprinted in 1958, 1960, 1961, 1964, and 1970.
8. This is dealt with at greater length in the epilogue of Michael Thad Allen, *The Business of Genocide: The SS, Slave Labor, and the Concentration Camps* (Chapel Hill, 2002).
9. Zunz, *Making America Corporate*, p. 3.
10. David Schoenbaum used such language in his comment on Walter Laqueur, "Hannah Arendt in Jerusalem: The Controversy Revisitied," in Lyman Legters, ed., *Western Society after the Holocaust* (Boulder, 1983), p. 128.
11. Wolfgang Seibel, "A Market for Mass Crime? Inter-Agency Competition and the Initiation of the Holocaust in France, 1940–1942," *International Journal of Organization Theory and Behavior* 5 (2002): 219–257. I have also dealt with "Polykratie" at greater length in my epilogue to *The Business of Genocide*. See also Peter Hayes, "Polycracy and Policy in the Third Reich: The Case of the Economy," in Thomas Childers and Jane Caplan, eds., *Reevaluating the Third Reich* (New York, 1993), pp. 190–210.
12. See Robert Gellately, *Backing Hilter: Consent and Coercion in Nazi Germany* (Oxford, 2001).
13. Hans Mommsen, "Die Realisierung des Utopischen. Die 'Endlösung der Judenfrage' im 'Dritten Reich,'" in idem., *Der Nationalsozialismus und die deutsche Gesellschaft* (Reinbek, 1991) p. 186.
14. Rudolf Höss, Meine Psyche, Werden, Leben, u. Erleben, IfZ, 13/4: 87. Compare Christopher Browning, *Fateful Months: Essays on the Emergence of the "Final Solution"* (New York, 1985), pp. 57–67. Matthias Beer, "Die Entwicklung der Gaswagen beim Mord an den Juden," *Vierteljahrshefte für Zeitgeschichte* 35 (1987): 403–411.
15. Christopher Browning, *Ordinary Men: Reserve Police Battalion 101 and the Final Solution in Poland* (New York, 1992), p. 185.

16. Arendt, *Eichmann in Jerusalem: A Report on the Banality of Evil* (New York, 1963), p. 106. This is a popular quotation. See Zygmunt Bauman, *Modernity and the Holocaust* (Cambridge, 1989), p. 20.
17. Browning, *Ordinary Men*, p. 162.
18. Jean-Claude Pressac, *Auschwitz: Technique and Operation of the Gas Chambers* (New York, 1989), pp. 69–96. See Topf & Söhne to Bischoff, 5/2/43, "Be- und Entlüftungsanlage im Krematorium II! "State Auschwitz Museum, AuII BW 30/34. This is a response from Topf & Söhne to a request that the Central Building Directorate of Auschwitz had made some time before (unspecified when in the letter).
19. I have also dealt with this more extensively in "Technocrats of Extermination: Engineers, Modern Bureaucracy, and Complicity," in Ronald Smelser, ed., *Lessons and Legacies of the Holocaust IV* (Evanston, 2002), pp. 100–122.
20. Note the evolution from Browning's thought through earlier essays such as those on the gas vans (cited above) and, for example, "Bureaucracy and Mass Murder: The German Administrator's Comprehension of the Final Solution," in *The Path to Genocide: Essays on Launching the Final Solution* (Cambridge, 1995), pp. 125–144.

CHAPTER 15

LOCAL INITIATIVES, CENTRAL COORDINATION: GERMAN MUNICIPAL ADMINISTRATION AND THE HOLOCAUST

Wolf Gruner

Introduction

For many years the NSDAP and, more specifically, the Gestapo were regarded as the sole driving force behind the persecution of the Jews. From this perspective local politics played virtually no part at all, and if reference was made to the local level, historical research reduced its share either to acts of violence of the SS and SA or to the controlling influence of the party and the Gestapo over local measures.[1] Until the 1990s municipal administrations were hardly ever seen in an active role as the initiators of persecution, although it has long been possible to find references to their persecutory activities in some monographs[2] and even detailed accounts of the initiation and implementation of exclusionary measures in some local studies of particular cases.[3]

Now, it can in the meantime be proved that from 1933 not just a few, but many towns and local communities introduced anti-Jewish restrictions systematically. Mayors and local officials often devised proscriptive measures years ahead of the state regulations, or went far beyond instructions from above in order to discriminate socially, politically, and culturally against the Jewish population.[4] In Hanover, the municipal inspector Ernst Schwertfeger and his officials were probably more feared than the security police because of their activities in connection with the establishment of "Jewish houses" during the war.[5] An inquiry among survivors in Leipzig reveals a similar situation. When in the 1960s the chief public prosecutor of the German Democratic Republic (GDR) investigated the activities of the "Judenreferent" (Officer for Jewish Affairs) of the Gestapo, the Jews questioned could not remember this man from the Gestapo, but all recalled with horror the two officials from the municipal administration.[6]

Active municipal involvement played a decisive part in the dynamic growth of persecution in the 1930s. In the implementation of Nazi "Jewish policy" it was as precisely the local authorities who had substantial room for maneuver. In 1933 the NS regime under Hitler had indeed postulated the goal of expelling the Jews from Germany, but for a long time afterwards it did not formulate any concrete guidelines on the way this goal was to be reached. It was only in 1938 that the NS leadership centralized and coordinated its "Jewish policy." Various new laws and decrees were introduced for the Reich, which had long been part of everyday practice in many towns.[7] As an explanation of the radical nature of this racist local policy, the hypothesis frequently and excessively advocated in the research of the last decades that competition for power among the authorities in a polycratically structured NS State was the cause of the increasing severity of persecution is obviously of little use. The findings presented below show that, up to 1938, in the main phase of their anti-Jewish initiatives, the towns were very seldom involved in conflict with other state or party agencies on questions of competence.

This was, not least, the result of the rapid infiltration of National Socialism into the municipalities. In the process of establishing the NS dictatorship, most of the old mayors were replaced or state commissioners appointed. A number of the new heads of the municipalities were "veterans" of the National Socialist movement, such as Dr. Karl Fiehler in Munich, Dr. Friedrich Krebs in Frankfurt on Main, or Dr. Julius Lippert in Berlin. The aggressive but by no means general replacement of persons was complemented by the dissolution of many town councils and new municipal elections in Prussia.[8] In addition, the newly appointed heads of the municipalities initiated large-scale "purges" in the municipal administrations. Municipal officials and other salaried employees, both political opponents of the new system and Jewish Germans, were compelled to leave the local administrations before the enactment of the infamous "Professional Civil Service Law" (*Berufsbeamtengesetz*) and to an even greater degree after it came into force. Very soon many local-government officials were not only members of the NSDAP but also held offices in the party.[9] The NSDAP quickly gained influence over the local administration at both the personal and the institutional level. The legal basis for this development was provided in January 1935 by means of the German Municipal Code (Deutsche Gemeindeordnung), in which elections and job advertisements were replaced by the appointment of officials. The party now had the right to select town councilors and to have a say in the appointment of mayors and deputy mayors. As the communities were understood to be part of the state administration, they were placed under the supervision of the Reich Ministry of the Interior and its Department of Municipal Affairs.[10] Nevertheless, as so-called self-governing bodies, they continued to enjoy substantial freedom of action at the local level. The towns and other local authorities also became compulsory members of the German Council of Municipalities (Deutscher Gemeindetag), which was established in May 1933 as a result of the "coordination" (*Gleichschaltung*) of the old central organizations of the municipalities. It was presided over by Karl Fiehler, the Mayor of Munich, who was also chiefhead of the NSDAP's Head Office for Municipal Affairs (Hauptamt für Kommunalpolitik), a man who had taken part in Hitler's putsch in 1923 and was a fellow prisoner in Landsberg. His deputies, first the Berlin District Mayor Herbert Treff and later the Mayor of Halle/Saale, Professor Johannes Weidemann, were longstanding members of the NSDAP. Other party activists took over posts as honorary presidents of the regional councils of the municipalities, for example the Nuremberg mayor Willy Liebel in the Bavarian Regional Council and the Berlin State Commissioner Lippert in the Prussian Regional Council.[11] By means of such double roles the party created a local political network, which also operated effectively in the central and regional committees and and working groups of the German Council of Municipalities. In the course of the 1930s the German Council of Municipalities was to distinguish itself as the supraregional institution in the NS state that coordinated the anti-Jewish policies of the town councils.[12] The more than 50,000 mayors, 100,000 deputy mayors, and 250,000 town councilors in the Reich[13] operated independently with discretionary power, both in the shaping of daily local politics and in the planning and implementation of specific anti-Jewish initiatives.

Local-Government Initiatives

Most of the general accounts of the persecution of the Jews begin with the description of the activities of the SA and SS in the second half of March 1933 against Jews employed in stock exchanges, district courts, and universities, and Jewish businessmen. The early anti-Jewish measures adopted by various local administrations are seldom mentioned. Evidence, however, has long been available in the extensive local literature on the persecution. One example is the treatment of Jewish suppliers by the municipalities. As early as 18 March the Mayor of Cologne ordered the exclusion of "Jewish" firms from the award of contracts for municipal departments and companies in which the town was involved. Existing contracts were to be cancelled. Even the municipal museums were informed of this decision.[14] The award of contracts to Jews was prohibited on 24 March in Munich,[15] 28 March in Oldenburg,[16] and 29 March in Bremen.[17] The Mayor of Düsseldorf, Robert Lehr, declared on 30 March that the town would no longer take the stores and businesses of Jewish Germans into account when purchasing goods, that it would no longer employ Jewish lawyers, and, furthermore, that it would suspend Jewish doctors, chemists, and pharmacists. Existing contracts were to be cancelled.[18] By 31 March similar measures had been taken in Wuppertal, Essen, Harburg-Wilhelmsburg, Karlsruhe, and Dortmund.[19] The prohibition of official connections between municipal employees and Jewish firms in Frankfurt on Main, Münster, and Mülheim served the same purpose.[20] Berlin, Frankfurt on Main, Mülheim, Münster, Cologne, Dortmund, Remscheid, Speyer and Karlsruhe "purged" their departments, institutions and works by the end of March. "Non-Aryan" municipal officers were suspended from duty, salaried employees and workers dismissed.[21] The mayors could justify their decisions by reference to the program of the NSDAP, which forbade the employment of Jews in public offices, whether in the Reich, the individual states (*Länder*) or the municipalities.[22]

It was only after the official nationwide Boycott Day on 1 April 1933 that the first anti-Jewish laws were promulgated. Among them was the infamous Professional Civil Service Law, which not only "legitimized" the illegal dismissals by the municipal administrations, but also—and more importantly—provided in its "Aryan paragraph" an instrument of definition and selection for the future. The number of local-government initiatives did not decline as a result in the following months; instead, a new wave of exclusionary measures followed up to the summer of 1933. In April the municipal authorities (*Magistrat*) in Göttingen accepted the motion of the members of the NSDAP brought in the town council (Bürgervorsteherkollegium) that the town and the municipal works should no longer award contracts to Jewish firms.[23] In the advertisements of the Berlin Supply Office and the Electricity Board the "Aryan paragraph" was now applied not only to firms submitting tenders but also to their suppliers.[24] The Cultural Department of the town of Munich did not, in the meantime, even permit artists of "Semitic descent" to take part in a competition on the design of the municipal fountains.[25]

The exclusionary actions rapidly spread to other areas of local-government policy. Mayors prevented subsidies to the nurseries of Jewish communities or, as in Berlin and Remscheid, refused to permit the rent of public buildings by Jewish clubs.[26] Even more common in this phase were local-government initiatives that made it difficult for Jewish residents to use public facilities or even excluded them entirely: From June 1933 Jews in Altenburg in Thuringia were excluded from pawnbroking[27]; from August on, Jews in Munich were no longer allowed to participate in public auctions in the municipal pawnshop.[28] From September Jews in Nuremberg were not even allowed to enter the municipal pawnshop.[29] In all of the latter initiatives the exclusion from the use of public facilities went hand in hand with indicated deliberate economic restrictions. The same is true of the anti-Jewish restrictions introduced by the summer in municipal markets and fairs in big cities like Berlin and Frankfurt on Main, but also in many small communities in Brandenburg, Saxony, and the Rhineland.[30] In many places prohibition of the use of public baths by Jews was now also introduced. Between April and August 1933 regulations to this effect were launched in Speyer, Tübingen, Plauen, Straubing, Trebnitz, Nördlingen, Nuremberg, Erlangen, Fulda, Beuthen, and Berlin. The corresponding arrangement for Munich was even reported on in August in the *Völkischer Beobachter*.[31] The German Council of Municipalities began to support and coordinate such local-government initiatives.[32] These prohibitions published by the town halls were of exemplary importance in three ways: first, because they stigmatized all Jewish Germans without distinction; secondly, because they were actions of a state authority for all citizens to see; and, thirdly, because public signs were put up to lend force to the decisions. In August the town councils in Ober-Rossbach (District of Neustadt an der Aisch) and Großgründlach in Franconia prohibited even entry to their communities for all "people of alien race."[33]

In the late summer of 1933 the NS leadership attempted to curb the uncontrolled enforcement of restrictions. Martin Bormann ordered the repeal of measures not sanctioned by law, in particular those refusing the right to enter public baths, to enter communities at all, or to trade in markets.[34] This decree of 12 September had, however, very little effect, as many of the towns evidently—and rightly—regarded it as a purely tactical move. In fact, the communities neither repealed their previous regulations nor refrained from making new ones.[35]

The towns reacted in the same way to the edict issued a short time before by the Reich Minister of Economic Affairs requiring equal treatment of Jewish and non-Jewish firms.[36] Some towns, for example Cologne and Bremen, did, in fact, withdraw their directives forbidding the award of municipal contracts to Jews.[37] But it is very doubtful whether this had any practical effect on the local restrictions. In Frankfurt on Main the directives from above were formally acknowledged, without any actual revision of policy. The municipal trade department (Wirtschaftsamt) described the procedure adopted as follows: "As far as the official measures are concerned, Jewish firms are permitted to submit tenders for public contracts; the tendency in practice, however, will probably be to take them into account far less than previously when awarding the contracts."[38] In December 1933 the town of Munich withdrew its restrictions only for foreign companies.[39] In Hamburg the regulations excluding Jews were at first repealed, but a year later the repeal was revoked. In spite of the legally binding regulations of the central government, the mayor instructed the senators on 22 October 1934 not to undertake any business whatever with "non-Aryan firms."[40] As a result of such developments, in Berlin more than thirty anti-Jewish regulations of the Municipality were in force in 1935.[41]

In the early summer of 1935 a further wave of municipal initiatives began, due to a change in the policy of the NS leadership, anti-Jewish rioting, and a campaign in the media initiated and controlled by the government. Its main feature was a massive introduction of measures forbidding the use of public baths. After the beginning of the summer season, such measures were discussed in Frankfurt on Main, Ludwigshafen am Rhein, Trier, and the radium baths in Landeck in Silesia.[42] The announcement in the *Völkischer Beobachter* of 19 July that the Mayor of Breslau had forbidden German Jews the use of several public baths and similar reports in other local newspapers soon had a massive copycat effect, both in big towns such as Stettin, Berlin, Leipzig, Bremen, and Chemnitz[43] and in many smaller communities in Swabia and Westphalia.[44] On 1 August 1935 the town council of Gladbeck in the district of Recklinghausen passed an entire package of measures in the "fight against Jewry": (1) Prohibition of the use of municipal baths and sports grounds. (2) Prohibition of the acquisition of houses and building sites. (3) Prohibition of the acquisition of existing businesses and firms or the opening of new ones. (4) The erection of signs at the city limits with the inscription "Jews unwelcome in this town." (5) Segregation of Jewish and "Aryan" children in schools. (6) Prohibition of selling at the weekly market for Jewish merchants. (7) Loss of support from public funds for "national comrades" who maintain connections with Jews. (8) Publication on the bulletin board in the town hall of the names of "national comrades" who maintain connections with Jews. (9) Ban on the acceptance of marriage loan coupons and municipal vouchers by the owners of Jewish businesses. (10) Identification of "non-Aryan" shops and businesses. (11) "Establishment of a separate room for Jews in St. Barbara's Hospital".[45] These decisions have been treated as unique in local history, because they went "far beyond the measures encountered in other towns."[46] But a closer examination of the evidence reveals the inaccuracy of this estimate. Münster and the local authorities in Straußberg and Dallgow near Berlin and Gauting in Bavaria all issued similar catalogs of segregationist measures.[47]

These massive local-government activities soon led to protests both at a national and a state (*Land*) level, as some of the measures, such as the prohibition of property deals or the right to stay in particular places, went far beyond the limits set by the state at this time. In a letter to the Prussian Minister of the Interior written at this time we find: "The fight against Jewry should be carried out in accordance with the directions of our Führer and the government and not in the way imagined by some head of a local council or mayor who has gone berserk."[48] For this reason the topic also played its part in the well-known conference of 20 August 1935, arranged by the Reich Minister of Economic Affairs, Hjalmar Schacht. At this meeting the Reich Minister of Justice, Gürtner, criticized the local authorities for "ignoring the instructions of the government."[49]

In spite of this criticism at ministerial level, however, further anti-Jewish activities occurred in many communities. To take only one example, the participation of Jews in lending, borrowing, and auctioning in municipal pawnbroking offices was restricted by the towns of Recklinghausen, Heidelberg, Düsseldorf, and Duisburg between the middle of August and the middle of September 1935.[50] The wave of new exclusions received official support in spite of the line taken by the NS government. At the Nuremberg party conference Karl Fiehler, who was both Mayor of Munich and one of the national leaders (Reichsleiter) of the NSDAP, explicitly welcomed the new "racial laws" as guidelines for local political actions.[51] But only a few days later, on 23 September, the Ministers Frick and Schacht officially determined that "all defamatory measures and offensive signs, bans on visits to theatres or swimming pools, picketing in front of Jewish businesses, and chanting anti-Jewish slogans should be forbidden."[52] The new prohibition of such "individual actions" only came into force, however, in the middle of December 1935.[53]

But in spite of its own instructions the NS leadership in fact supported unofficially a further radicalization of anti-Jewish policies at the local level.

In the next three years new forms of discrimination were introduced in many places. Many welfare offices reduced the benefits for the Jewish poor and municipal hospitals and shelters for the homeless isolated the Jewish sick and homeless.[54] Some communities forbade not only official contacts but even personal relationships of municipal officials and salaried employees with Jews. Some towns issued restrictions on the use of public facilities by Jews for the first time, while others added further bans on using libraries and sports grounds or visiting theatres, museums, and zoos.[55] In Stuttgart, where the mayor, Karl Ströhlin, had prevented bans on the use of the public swimming pools as late as summer 1935, the town council, in the fall of 1936, now not only forbade the use of the swimming pools, but also excluded Jews from admission to municipal old people's homes and from attendance at schools for nursery teachers. In the Stuttgart hospitals Jews were, in future, to be segregated, municipal employees were ordered not to buy in Jewish shops, and Jewish merchants were to be refused admission to municipal markets and fairs. The town broke off all business relations with Jews.[56]

By the spring of 1938 other big cities had introduced dozens of new exclusionary regulations, although there were no official instructions from above, let alone national laws to cover them.[57] The extent of the anti-Jewish measures adopted by local authorities can be illustrated by the example of the exclusion from auctions and pawnbroking in municipal pawnshops. An inquiry by the German Council of Municipalities reveals that of the fifty-nine major cities that had their own pawnbroking offices twenty, including Dresden, Leipzig, Dortmund, Cologne, Mainz, Munich, and Wuppertal, had, by the beginning of 1938, excluded Jews from pawnbroking but not from participation in auctions. Conversely, eleven other authorities had forbidden the participation of Jews in auctions but not in pawnbroking. In Nuremberg, Leipzig, and Baden-Baden Jews were not allowed to enter the pawnshops at all.[58] Inspired by this inquiry, Berlin, Aachen, and Wiesbaden followed suit.[59] Since the beginning of the NS regime, therefore, more than half of the municipal pawnshops had introduced restrictive measures and less than half had undertaken nothing. This state of affairs after five years of NS rule shows, first, that anti-Jewish activities in local communities were not isolated actions but a mass phenomenon and, secondly, that municipal authorities had great freedom in the formulation and implementation of their "Jewish policies."

In the course of 1938, however, the "innovative" role of the local authorities in the process of persecution was decreasing. As the failure of the previous policy of expulsion gradually became clear after the annexation of Austria, the NS leadership reached an agreement after the November pogrom to segregate the Jews who could not be driven out in communities completely isolated from German society. To this end anti-Jewish policy was to be controlled in future by Göring. There was now a strict division of labor in accordance with which the Reich Security Main Office (Reichssicherheitshauptamt) took over responsibility for the supervision and establishment of separate Jewish communities with separate facilities, the Ministry of Labor for compulsory labor, and the Ministry of Economic Affairs for compulsory "Aryanization." The Municipalities were expected to organize the isolation of Jewish residents in "Jewish houses"(Judenhäuser).[60]

Some towns made arrangements of their own before this law came into force. The city-administration of Nuremberg had called upon house owners to give Jewish tenants their notice shortly after the pogrom, and preparations for similar steps were made in Munich, Dresden, Kassel, and Duisburg.[61] At the end of April 1939 the "Law on Leasing to Jews" (*Gesetz über Mietverhältnisse mit Juden*) legalized these initiatives by transferring to the town authorities alone the right to concentrate Jews in specified housing, "if necessary by force."[62] In many places the systematic eviction of Jews now began.[63] The speed with which such clearances were carried out depended on the degree of commitment of the municipal administrations involved. Leipzig and Dresden had already "purged" whole city-districts of Jews by the end of 1939; Göttingen, in contrast, only began to set up "Jewish houses" in the fall of 1940 and Hanover even waited until the early summer of 1941.[64] Normally everything was arranged by the municipal housing departments; in Düsseldorf, however, it was the Trade Department and in Leipzig the Office for the Promotion of House Building.[65]

At the same time the Municipalities were already involved in other parts of the new program of persecution. Here again, towns developed initiatives that went beyond the discriminatory activities required by the central government. When, for example, in early 1939 the Mayor of Kelkheim/Taunus heard about the introduction of compulsory labor for Jews, he asked for the supply of Jewish labor for road-building. He received from the Employment Office of the State of Hesse twenty unemployed men recruited in Frankfurt, for whom he organized a "camp" in the ballroom of the local inn, which was then regularly inspected by the town councilors. The men of the "Jewish crew" (*Judenkolonne*) received the lowest wages, were not allowed to move about freely, and were strictly separated from the local residents, although there were no corresponding official guidelines on these points.[66] Innumerable German municipalities, or more precisely their building, gardens, park, and other departments, employed thousands of Jewish forced laborers, in cemeteries, rubbish dumps, and fairgrounds, for the construction of streets, parks, sports grounds, and stadiums, for cleaning streets or removing snow, and for work in municipal power stations and gasworks.[67] Some of the municipalities paid the Jewish forced laborers the minimum wage for unskilled workers, which was about RM 0.40—0.50, others made purely token payments between RM 0.10 per hour and RM 0.50 per day, and others paid nothing.[68] At the beginning of 1942 the Mayor of Frankfurt on Main even complained to the German Council of Municipalities that the reduced "standard wage for Jews" introduced in Hesse for private businesses did not apply to the hundred Jewish forced laborers employed by the town. The result was a national decree in June 1942 enabling the reduction of the minimum wage for unskilled laborers for Jews employed in public service. In this way all of the other city administrations in the Reich profited from Frankfurt's successful protest.[69]

In the implementation of anti-Jewish measures that were not their responsibility the local authorities also had plenty of room for additional forms of discrimination. After the outbreak of the war, for example, the municipal food and trade departments (Ernährungs- und Wirtschaftsämter) made it even more difficult than before for the Jewish residents to get their food rations, which had in any case been reduced, either by introducing strictly limited shopping hours or by establishing a small number of separate shops.[70] A number of towns attempted to participate in the "Aryanization" policy of the central government and to acquire "Jewish" property as cheaply as possible.[71] In most cases the municipalities and their departments worked together with the authorities concerned relatively smoothly.

The Interaction between Local Authorities

The persecutory policies of the local authorities were of a relatively spontaneous nature in the first months of 1933, but they soon came to be characterized by mutual arrangements and cooperation. From the summer of 1933 the German Council of Municipalities played an increasingly important role in the coordination of anti-Jewish measures. In an extensive correspondence dealing with all the areas of persecution the local authorities conferred with their central organization on the "legality" and practicability of their initiatives, and the German Council of Municipalities itself published surveys of activities in the towns, thus providing specific information and enabling an exchange of views on the implementation of persecutory measures between them.[72]

In the course of the 1930s direct contact between local authorities also increased. Following written inquiries in Chemnitz and Halle/Saale in the summer of 1938, for example, the Deputy Mayor of Leipzig, Haake, found out that these towns no longer allowed Jewish clubs to use the municipal gymnasiums and then adopted the same policy.[73]

The exchange of information also functioned directly between municipal departments of different towns. In 1937 the Leipzig Parks and Gardens Department made inquiries to the corresponding departments in Berlin, Hamburg, Cologne, Frankfurt on Main, Breslau, and Königsberg, asking whether they also forbade Jews the use of the public benches in the parks.[74] The study of the persecution policies of other towns was not, moreover, restricted to correspondence. Personal observations were also made: for example, in 1941 members of the Munich Housing Department visited the town of Mannheim in order to gain experience in the "clearance" of "Jewish housing for the victims of bombing."[75]

There existed also direct contacts between the mayors of towns. Many of them met regularly in the committees of the German Council of Municipalities. Questions of persecution appeared always on the agenda of the eighteen special committees in which representatives of the ministries, the German Council of Municipalities, and the local authorities discussed social, political, or economic aspects of local-government policy. Municipal departmental experts regularly discussed initiatives in the working groups organized on a regional and national level by the German Council of Municipalities from 1934 on. In addition the German Council of Municipalities also convened working committees on an ad hoc basis to discuss topical issues, and in 1939 it established five war committees for mayors and regional administrators (Landräte).[76]

The discussions in the committees of the German Council of Municipalities made a fundamental contribution both to the multiplication and the unification of anti-Jewish ideas at the local-government level. Here is just one example of this. At the conference of the "Working group on administrative issues of the mayors of towns belonging to the government district of Stettin" in 1935 the use of municipal facilities by Jews was discussed. The head of the Party Regional Office (Gauamtsleiter), Czirniok, argued before those present that Paragraph 17 of the German Municipal Code permitted restrictions. He referred in this context to the town of Stettin, which only allowed the Jews to use selected swimming pools on certain days. Those present decided that the office of the German Council of Municipalities for Pomerania should pass on "such local statutes" to other local authorities as models for future policy.[77]

Ministerial civil servants took part personally in many of the committee meetings of the German Council of Municipalities. The latter debated the results of such discussions internally with the relevant agencies of the Reich through its office in Berlin. In this way permanent pressure was put on the ministries to extend anti-Jewish policies. On 13 March 1936, for example, the provincial office of the German Council of Municipalities in Schleswig-Holstein informed the Berlin office that at the last meeting of the "Southern Working Group on Administrative Issues of the Towns of the District" their mayors had reached an agreement on the principles for the treatment of sick Jews: (1) Long-term Jewish patients in municipal hospitals and convalescent homes should be isolated from other patients. (2) In case of accident Jews should be admitted and fully treated, which meant de facto that in other cases sick Jews could be refused admittance. The provincial office requested the opinion of the office of the German Council of Municipalities in Berlin, as it was a question of principle.[78] The council informed the provincial office that an application had already been made to the Ministry of the Interior requesting a "definitive clarification of the question of the right of Jews to use hospitals and other facilities of the communities."[79]

The German Council of Municipalities had directed this general inquiry to the ministry when, from the end of 1935, the independent actions of individual local authorities had again been forbidden and their segregationist activities often seemed to contradict official policy. The Ministry of the Interior submitted the draft of a decree supporting the position of the local authorities to the Führer's deputy, but in spring of 1936 the latter requested that the ministry "should refrain from pursuing...a general regulation for the time being, as the Jewish question (was) not ready for such a solution at the moment." But although there was neither an official decree nor even a placet from the ministry, the German Council of Municipalities now answered all of the towns that submitted inquiries on this issue as follows: It is true that the central ban on individual activities is still in force, but it is our opinion that, nevertheless, "the individual communities are not forbidden to restrict the use of public baths by Jews." According to the German Municipal Code, they were entitled to regulate admission to their facilities autonomously. The German Council of Municipalities used this line of argument to "legitimize" various actions restricting the right of Jews to use municipal baths, markets, and libraries.[80] The German Council of Municipalities, therefore, played "the role of a mediator" between the local and central levels with enormous freedom of action.[81]

Although in this case it proved impossible to arrive at a swift central solution by means of a national law, other exclusionary initiatives undertaken by the towns were soon officially "legalized." At the end of July 1937 the Ministry of the Interior allowed at least those town officially classified as health resorts and spas to introduce restrictions on the use of their amenities by Jews for certain times and localities. From facilities that did not specifically serve health purposes, such as sports grounds, gardens, and restaurants, the Jews could henceforth be totally excluded.[82] In July 1938 they were forbidden to stay in health resorts at all.[83] On 1 March 1938 the Ministry of Economic Affairs had excluded "Jewish" firms from the award of public contracts.[84] In May the Ministry of the Interior decreed that Jewish patients could be refused admission to municipal hospitals, and in June that Jewish patients in the hospitals should be segregated.[85] At the end of July 1938 Jews were legally excluded from auctioneering, which at the same time amounted to a "legalization" of the restrictions on Jewish activities in the municipal pawnshops.[86]

The anti-Jewish policies of the municipal administrations led in many cases to contacts with the local NSDAP or its agencies, for example the German Labor Front. The contacts mostly concerned interventions of the party in local-government affairs or suggestions on exclusionary measures. But even in the early period of the Nazi regime conflicts were rare, as the towns exercised sole power in all areas of local politics and their mayors, as in Munich, were themselves often top officials in the party.[87] In 1934, for example, the NSDAP in Frankfurt on Main submitted a number of requests to the town to forbid the use of municipal facilities by Jewish clubs. The sports department then demanded a decision from the mayor, who had hitherto permitted the use of the facilities, although he charged excessive prices.[88] Friedrich Krebs, himself active in the NSDAP since 1922, decided to continue leasing, but found a compromise that served both sides. Leasing to Jews was to be permitted as long as there were no "detrimental effects" and the facilities were not needed by "German" clubs.[89]

Contrary to the widespread belief that the NSDAP always advocated the most radical ideas, evidence it is clear that some party organizations had difficulty in keeping up with the persecutory mania of some local administrations. In the summer of 1936 the Mayor of Plauen asked the party for its opinion on the possible exclusion "of Jews from the use of the municipal library and reading room and from admission to the museum, the municipal theatre," and other cultural facilities. The District Office (Kreisleitung) of the NSDAP played the issue down and queried the need for special regulations at all as the Jews made so little use of these amenities anyway.[90] Other agencies of the party that might have become involved, such as the Security Service of the SS or the Regional Offices for Municipal Affairs (Gauämter für Kommunalpolitik), lacked for many years both the personal resources and the authority at local level to influence the specific forms of municipal persecution of the Jews. Only in two towns was the NSDAP able to establish organizations of its own that attempted step by step to take control of Jewish policy, the "Anti-Jewish Defense Section" (Judenabwehrstelle) of the district office in Dresden from the mid 1930s on, and the "Department of the Party Regional Leader's (Gauleiter) Representative on Aryanisation" in Munich at the end of the 1930s.[91]

No less rare than the evidence in the archives for a real or guiding influence of local party agencies are the proofs of a general, let alone successful, intervention of other local authorities in the municipal Jewish policies. For this reason, in some towns, special agencies were created within the municipal administration that took over the tasks of the state. In Leipzig an "Office for the Promotion of House Building" was founded, which, at the end of 1939, centralized the "processing of all Jewish affairs" under its own aegis, including matters originally within the competence of Reich authorities at local level. Apart from the clearance of houses, the office also controlled the "Aryanization" of businesses, forced-labor services, and the separate distribution of food and coal. In Frankfurt on Main the municipal "Official for Jewish Welfare" fulfilled a similar function.[92]

It was only in Berlin that a special state office succeeded in taking over a particular sphere of Jewish policy from the municipal administration. "The reshaping of the capital of the Reich (*Neugestaltung der Reichshauptstadt*)" under the auspices of Albert Speer and his "General Construction Inspectorate" was given top priority, and it was empowered by law to intervene in the eviction of Jewish tenants.[93] In the other towns in Germany the control of the municipal administration over the "creation of Jewish ghettos" long remained unchallenged. The party and the Gestapo were excluded from this field, as the Gestapo in Munich pointed out in a letter of complaint to the municipal trade board: "The Law of 30.4.1939 does not permit the Gestapo for the time being to intervene decisively in this area. It is rather the task of the local authority."[94] This demonstrates that both the development and the radical nature of these persecutory measures depended on the degree of commitment of the municipal administration concerned.[95]

It was only two years later that the Reich leadership of the NSDAP began attempting to break the municipal monopoly of the process of "ghettoization." In spring 1941 it insisted on the introduction of a "uniform national arrangement for the clearance of Jewish housing" by means of confiscation. Through its regional law offices (Gaurechtsämter) the party put direct pressure on mayors and town councils, for example in Hamburg, Düsseldorf, and Jena.[96] In Frankfurt on Main the NSDAP regional leader instructed the regional housing commission to take over the "utilization of Jewish housing by national comrades," a task delegated from May 1941 to the Officialer for Jewish Welfare, whose office had been placed under Gestapo control the year before.[97] In the course of the preparations for deportation from summer 1941, the regional leaderships were joined by the Reich Security Main Office (Reichssicherheitshauptamt) and local Gestapo agencies in organizing the process of "ghettoization" in various communities.[98]

In the shaping of their anti-Jewish policies from 1933 the municipalities regularly came into contact with the local agencies of national institutions. In the district courts, for example, they fought—often successfully—against the victims of municipal discriminatory measures that were not covered by the law. From the mid 1930s Jewish tenants brought actions against illegal notice given by municipal housing departments and from 1939 Jewish workers challenged the right of the towns to cut wages and social-security contributions for conscripted labor.[99] The municipal administrations usually cooperated smoothly with the local employment offices and the armament units of the Armed Forces (Rüstungskommandos der Wehrmacht), at first in organizing forced labor and later, in cooperation with the Gestapo, in the deportations. The municipal administration of Frankfurt on Main handed over its Jewish forced laborers after informal discussions and even transferred many of them from places of work central to the war effort to jobs in civil society in order to facilitate their deportation.[100]

Conflicts only seem to have occurred when the aims and ambitions behind the persecution collided. The demand of the municipalities from 1936/37 for the exclusion of the Jews from public welfare were fulfilled by a central decree after the pogrom of 19 November 1938. Breslau, Chemnitz, Düsseldorf, and Cologne immediately stopped the payment of assistance to the Jewish poor and referred them to Jewish institutions. The security police intervened against the municipal actions in many places. Although Berlin and Vienna were among the first to approve radical exclusion, the two cities were among the last to implement the policy because of resistance by the Gestapo. At first sight this seems paradoxical, but, whereas the welfare offices were only interested in the short-term success following the exclusion, the Gestapo thought much more strategically. It wanted to avoid the financial collapse of the Jewish institutions, which would result from a run on them by the thousands of Jewish poor, as the religious community had to guarantee the maintenance of a separate welfare and school system after the pogrom and also provide the financial means for emigration. Here two different persecutory aims collided. The varying results of the conflict in the towns depended on the specific local balance of power.[101] This contradicts the thesis of Matzerath that mayors and regional administrators (Landräte) were degraded to the level of mere stooges of the Gestapo.[102] Another case is revealing similar results. After the beginning of deportation in 1941 quite a number of municipalities tried to buy up the property of the Jewish communities as cheaply as possible. In many places the Gestapo—in one case in Frankfurt on Main Heydrich personally—prevented these transactions and demanded higher sums from the towns concerned, arguing that the wealth of Jewish organizations should explicitly serve the purposes of the "final solution."[103] Here again the cause was an open conflict between the interests of the security police and those of the municipalities.

Local-Government Interests

It was precisely at the local level that practical administrative interests influenced in a particularly strong way the planning and implementation of persecution by municipal officials. From 1933 the redistribution of municipal resources was based on financial arguments, whether it was a question of abolishing the subsidies for Jewish clubs and other organizations or of reducing public assistance to poor Jews. The initiative taken by the town of Frankfurt on Main in summer 1933 to remove Jewish children from the town schools can be seen in this context. This initiative, which the German Council of Municipalities passed on to the relevant ministry in 1934 as "an issue requiring a fundamental revision" of policy in regard to the creation of separate schools for Jews, was justified by claiming that the interests of the municipalities could only be protected "if the cost of maintaining these special schools were carried by the Jewish religious communities alone."[104]

According to the racist logic of the municipalities it would be possible by excluding the Jews to create more organizational capacity for the "Aryan population" in institutions such as schools, nurseries, swimming pools, etc. The towns achieved a similar effect by "Aryanizing" the property of Jewish institutions and their facilities. After the pogrom the acquisition of synagogues and cemeteries destined for demolition played an important part. In 1939 the local-government of Görlitz wanted to build a municipal baths on a plot of land of the destroyed synagogue bought for a minimal price. In 1941 the municipalities and the German Council of Municipalities demanded the classification of Jews as "enemies of the Reich" so that they could then take advantage of an order by Hitler permitting the free acquisition of building sites. In this they were successful. From 1942 the NS state allowed many towns to take over the property of expelled Jews, on which accommodation for municipal officials, temporary housing, homes for infants, schools, and mental homes were then to be built.[105]

Until the end of the war the redistribution of housing "de-tenanted" (*entmietet*) in the course of the "ghettoization" was, moreover, an important social and political instrument in regard to the general population, other authorities, and private enterprise. A memorandum of the Municipal Housing Office in Frankfurt on Main published as early as the beginning of February 1939 states:

> The "original" Jewish housing that is now becoming available cannot generally be taken into account in the attempt to satisfy the still lively demand for very cheap small flats, but can be considered as a means of meeting, at least partially, the need for more spacious accommodation for the offices of the armed forces which will be coming to Frankfurt, for branches of industry, etc. The impoverished Jews who have come into the city recently have for the most part taken poor-quality accommodation in the old part of the town. The vacation of this housing is a precondition for the implementation of the restoration plans mentioned in what follows.[106]

This quotation makes it abundantly clear that social policy and town planning were to be realized at the expense of the Jewish inhabitants.

As in Frankfurt, the municipal administration in Vienna was also interested in the provision of small flats for selected young "Aryan" families.[107] Those responsible received specific inquiries and even clearance applications from "veterans" and municipal employees.[108] In Berlin the housing of Jews was intended at first to satisfy the needs of those tenants whose homes were demolished during the implementation of Speer's plans for the reshaping of the capital city.[109] Later "Jewish accommodation" was used as a reservoir for disabled veterans, recipients of the Knight's Cross, and large families.[110] In Munich in 1939 many of the more than 1,400 "de-tenanted" flats were reserved at first, as in Berlin, for tenants whose housing had been demolished, then in 1940 for returning emigrant families, and in 1941 for large families and "social emergencies." At the same time more and more prominent persons from "the party, the state, the armed forces, and artistic circles" were given such flats.[111] Hamburg, Münster and other towns gave Jewish housing to bombed-out families.[112] After the beginning of the allied air attacks the Mayor of Frankfurt on Main placed 260 flats of Jewish tenants at the disposal of the police responsible for the homeless (Obdachlosenpolizei), 85 of which were cleared immediately for those whose houses had been destroyed, the remainder being reserved for future cases. Furthermore, from May 1941, the "Officialer for Jewish Welfare" offered Jewish housing on a systematic basis to national comrades who were looking for accommodation. Apart from providing 400 flats cleared to this end, he also cooperated with the Municipal Housing Department in securing additional quarters for the armed forces, the Reichsarbeitsdienst (Reich Labor Service), the NS-Volkswohlfahrt (National Socialist People's Welfare), the municipal hospital, and the youth office.[113]

The accommodation seized from Jewish tenants relieved the municipalities of the need to construct new housing or other facilities, which hardly ever occurred.[114] Especially during the war, the distribution of housing was a particularly effective social and political instrument. It was not without good reason that the mayors of Baden assembled in the German Council of Municipalities at the beginning of 1941 discussed together the purposeful utilization of the housing of the Jews deported to France in the autumn of 1940.[115]

The interiors of Jewish homes were also subject to "Aryanization." Here again the towns were among the most interested parties. Shortly after the beginning of the deportations in Germany, in October 1941, the Mayor of Münster, Hillebrand, discussed the "imminent removal" of the Jews with the party regional leadership (Gauleitung), the Gestapo, and the Finance Department, in order to "evaluate" experience gathered from other governmental districts. The topics of conversation included problems connected with the allocation of cleared housing and the sale or auctioning of the possessions left behind.[116] In Hamburg the Social Service Department later received furniture and household effects owned by the deported Jews, public libraries acquired private libraries and the municipal art gallery was given various paintings.[117] The curators of municipal museums and mayors in Frankfurt on Main and Hanover also made efforts to "Aryanize" the art and coin collections of the emigrants and the deported.[118]

Conclusions

The towns and their officials enjoyed an enormous freedom of action in their anti-Jewish policies, which has hitherto been overlooked in research. There appear to be three main reasons for this: (1) Structurally the municipalities formed part of the state administration and from 1933 on they were placed under the authority of the Reich Ministry of the Interior. But they continued to be regarded as self-administered and responsible for the affairs of the communities. (2) Organizationally they were linked together by the German Council of Municipalities and its committees. Its coordinating activities and its support even against the decisions of ministries promoted local-government initiatives and helped to "legitimize" them. (3) Until 1938 the Nazi leadership did not provide the municipalities with concrete guidelines for their persecution policies.

These favorable preconditions permitted the towns to influence decisively the shape of persecutionJewish policies at the local level in the NS regime for years. Among the first spontaneous anti-Jewish measures, staffing policies played a major part; many towns "purged" their administrations even before the April boycott and the passing of the Professional Civil Service Law. Other fields of early discriminatory activities were the redistribution of municipal resources and the reorganization of municipal capacities. Jewish businessmen received no new contracts and were forbidden to enter municipal pawnshops and markets. Jewish organizations lost their subsidies or had to pay more for the use of municipal facilities. Jews were forbidden to enter municipal baths and even entire communities. In spite of several governmental instructions issued from summer 1933, many towns did not revoke the prohibitions, which were not covered by the law; in other towns they were formally abolished but informally maintained. This was tacitly tolerated by the Nazi leadership. At the same time municipal "Jewish policies" found more and more imitators due to the exchange of information between the towns and the coordinating activities of the German Council of Municipalities.

In the summer of 1935 a new wave of local exclusionary activities began. Many communities had in the meantime introduced extensive restrictions on the participation of the Jews in municipal life. Although, after the promulgation of the Nuremberg Laws, the NS leadership again officially forbade individual actions precisely because some of the municipal prohibitions were too radical, the existence of a kind of informal division of labor between the local and the central levels is unmistakable. In the years 1936 and 1937 the local administrations extended the prohibitions, above all in connection with the use of facilities such as baths, libraries, and pawnshops. The Jewish poor were discriminated against, the Jewish sick isolated. The German Council of Municipalities not only defended such "illegal" municipal initiatives against the objections of the ministries but also called for the passing of corresponding laws to cover them in the name of the towns. The activities of the German Council of Municipalities led, moreover, to a standardization of the local forms of discrimination. In more and more towns there were more and more similar anti-Jewish prohibitions; in many places there existed in the meantime extensive catalogs of exclusionary measures. As far as the persecution of the Jews at local level is concerned, particularly in the municipalities, the topos of the quiet years from 1934 and 1936/37 must, therefore, be dismissed once and for all as a legend.

Up to 1938 local-government measures usually anticipated the corresponding laws by years. But then the situation changed in 1938. In the summer of that year the municipalities lost their "innovative" role in the persecution of the Jews, as the NS state then for the first time centralized and coordinated the separation of the Jewish population, issuing laws to accelerate the process. After the pogrom of November 1938 and the introduction of division of labor in the implementation of now centralized persecution policies, with one measure the municipalities did, however, gain new responsibility; municipal housing departments had to plan and organize the establishment of "Jewish houses." (*Judenhäuser*). In addition a number of towns developed initiatives of their own in limiting the provision of food supplies, excluding Jews from public assistance, exploiting Jewish forced labor, and "Aryanizing" Jewish property.

Until the end of the 1930s, a considerable number of the anti-Jewish policies of the NS state were, therefore, developed at the local level. Local discrimination originated mainly in the municipal administrations and only rarely in the party or the Gestapo. Often the entire administration of a town participated in the persecution of the Jews: the departments responsible for building and planning, transport and trade, finance and nutrition, parks and gardens, welfare and housing, legal matters and statistics, the registry, and tax and property offices were all active from 1933 in excluding Jewish Germans from the life of the community. The departments concerned with culture, the maintenance of cemeteries, sport, youth, and pawnbroking, and the maintenance of cemeteries, which did not exist everywhere, also participated in these policies. These findings apply, furthermore, not only to the administration as such, but also to the various municipal works and institutions. Power stations, gasworks, waterworks, street-cleaning and refuse-collection departments, real estate and forestry departments, the transport services, municipal baths, hospitals, markets, abattoirs, shelters for the homeless, and, last not least, municipal theatres, museums, and libraries introduced anti-Jewish regulations independently, in consultation with, or on the orders of their municipal superiors. Many departments employees also lined their pockets by acquiring Jewish property.

The innumerable anti-Jewish measures adopted by the towns and other communities can only be ascribed very broadly to particular phases. The points of time at which local-government restrictions were introduced differed too widely. Plauen in Saxony, for example, forbade Jews to use the municipal library as early as the end of 1937, whereas Berlin only introduced a similar ban in 1939, and Vienna, which was known to be particularly radical, as late as 1941.[119] What is more, there were often substantial differences even between the different departments of one municipal individual administration as regards the extent and the vehemence of their anti-Jewish activities. According to the German Municipal Code the deputy mayors, as representatives of the mayor, bore full responsibility for the administrative areas under their control and this allowed them to exercise a strong personal influence over the policies of those departments. This can be proved in the cases of the head of the Social Service Department in Hamburg, Oskar Martini, and of the head of the Welfare Service Department in Munich, Friedrich Hilble, neither of whom, incidentally, was a member of the NSDAP long after 1933.[120]

Systematic and comparative detailed studies will be needed in order to decide whether the different approaches of individual departments reflected the degree of commitment of the departmental head alone or whether additional factors played a part, for example the influence of other institutions. The interaction of the local-governments with other authorities will, therefore, have to be analyzed much more precisely than has hitherto been the case. The research results presented to date show that, in the question of the persecution of the Jews politics at the local level was characterized much more by cooperation than by conflicts over competence between the local authorities and the local party offices. The towns often avoided potential conflicts from the start by exchanging information or reaching agreements either directly with the agency affected in each particular case or indirectly through the German Council of Municipalities. Conflict only arose from 1938 with the beginnings of centralization in the policies of persecution. Differences occurred between local-governments and the Gestapo because their policies were dictated by different interests. This usually resulted in more moderate rather than more radical measures. For the area of local-government over the whole period it seems inaccurate, therefore, to claim that rivalry between the local leaderships of different agencies led to a "cumulative radicalization," which found an outlet in the persecution of the Jews.[121]

It was not least the general lack of conflict between institutions that gave the local administrations an undisputed freedom of action in the pursuit of their anti-Jewish policies at least until 1939 and often until well into the war. This fact provided wide scope for the individual commitment of the mayors and their officials and, consequently, for personal responsibility. The dynamics of anti-Jewish local politics can in some many cases be traced back to the personal anti-Semitic motivation of individual mayors, councilors, or heads of department. Quite apart from the NS activists, many non-party members also held opinions of an authoritarian and/or racist kind. The reason for the large number of local initiatives must, however, be sought outside ideological positions. In the case of many officials and salaried employees who were not explicit Nazis, individual interests clearly brought a swift adaptation to the dominant thinking, whether it was the wish for social advancement or only the desire to protect their jobs.[122] But this kind of opportunism can only explain the general lack of personal resistance to the anti-Jewish policies of the local administrations and the consequent widespread participation of municipal staff. A large number of officials, however, developed anti-Jewish ideas and implemented the prohibitions without revealing any recognizable racist attitudes. The motivating force was often obviously the desire to serve the "interests" of the local-government. For such persons the potential availability of resources and finance and of Jewish labor and possessions for the purposes of municipal planning, budgeting, and the provision of services seems to have provided both the motivation and the legitimization of their anti-Jewish actions.

During the war many municipal officials then applied their practical experience to the administration of the countries occupied by Germany. Hans Cramer, the Mayor of Dachau after 1933, became mayor of the Polish town of Wloclawek and later city commissioner (Stadtkommissar) of Kowno (Kaunas) in Lithuania.[123] Franz Schönwälder, the former Mayor of Breslau, was appointed Mayor of Sosnowitz in Eastern Upper Silesia in January 1940. There he developed new initiatives for the ghettoization and deportation of the Jews and the "utilization" of their property.[124] The Mayor of Dresden, Emil Zörner, first became City Chief Official (Stadthauptmann) of Cracow in Poland and then Governor of the district of Lublin, one of the regional centers of the mass murders perpetrated against the Jews.[125]

After 1933 a countless number of the over 400,000 mayors and city employees in Germany took part actively or passively, directly or indirectly in the persecution of the Jews. Many of them acted independently and at their own discretion to promote the reorganization of urban life, sector for sector, in accordance with racist criteria. Because detailed political directives from above were lacking and because of institutional arrangements for the division of labor, the municipalities enjoyed enormous freedom of action at the local level, which their officials usually used to the disadvantage of the Jewish inhabitants. In its promotion of anti-Jewish activities, municipal policy frequently anticipated central policy and was, therefore, a driving force behind the persecutory measures, which has been totally underestimated in research. Particularly in the years before 1938, but often even later, it played a decisive part in the shaping of anti-Jewish policy and therefore of Jewish life in the Nazi state.

Notes

1. Horst Matzerath, *Nationalsozialismus und kommunale Selbstverwaltung*, (Stuttgart, 1970). Most recently, Peter Longerich, *Politik der Vernichtung. Eine Gesamtdarstellung der nationalsozialistischen Judenverfolgung* (Munich, 1998); and Michael Wildt, "Violence against Jews in Germany 1933–1939," in David Bankier, ed., *Probing the Depths of German Antisemitism. German Society and the Persecution of the Jews 1933–1941* (New York/Jerusalem, 1999), pp. 181–212.
2. See Karl Schleunes, *The Twisted Road to Ausschwitz. Nazi Policy towards German Jews 1933–39* (London, 1972); Kurt Pätzold, *Faschismus, Rassenwahn, Judenverfolgung. Eine Studie zur politischen Strategie und Taktik des faschistischen Imperialismus 1933–1935* (Berlin, 1975).
3. *Dokumente zur Geschichte der Frankfurter Juden* (Frankfurt on Main, 1963); Peter Hanke, *Zur Geschichte der Juden in München zwischen 1933 und 1945* (Munich, 1967); Hans-Joachim Fliedner, *Die Judenverfolgung in Mannheim 1933–1945*, 2 vols. (Stuttgart, 1971); Günther von Roden, *Geschichte der Duisburger Juden* (Duisburg, 1986); Josef Werner, *Hakenkreuz und Judenstern. Das Schicksal der Karlsruher Juden im Dritten Reich*, 2nd revised and expanded ed. (Karlsruhe, 1990); Wolf Gruner, *Judenverfolgung in Berlin 1933–1945. Eine Chronologie der Behördenmaßnahmen in der Reichshauptstadt*, ed. by Reinhard Rürup (Berlin, 1996).
4. For more details see Wolf Gruner, "Die NS-Judenverfolgung und die Kommunen. Zur wechselseitigen Dynamisierung von zentraler und lokaler Politik 1933–1941," *Vierteljahrshefte für Zeitgeschichte*, 1, no. 48 (2000): 75–126.
5. Hans-Dieter Schmid, "'Finanztod.' Die Zusammenarbeit von Gestapo und Finanzverwaltung bei der Ausplünderung von Juden in Deutschland," in Gerhard Paul and Klaus-Michael Mallmann, eds., *Die Gestapo im Zweiten Weltkrieg. "Heimatfront" und besetztes Europa* (Darmstadt, 2000), pp. 141–154, especially p.145.
6. Günther Wieland (former GDR Chief Public Prosecutor) in an interview with the author on 8 September 1998 in Berlin.
7. See Gruner, "NS-Judenverfolgung."
8. In towns with more than 200,000 inhabitants only four out of 28 mayors remained in office until summer 1933. For all communities with over 20,000 inhabitants the figure is 96 out of 252. After the Prussian municipal elections of 12 March the majorities shifted in favour of the NSDAP; in the non-Prussian communities the composition of the local authorities was adjusted in accordance with the elections to the Reichstag; see in general Matzerath, *Selbstverwaltung*; Jeremy Noakes, "Oberbürgermeister und Gauleiter. City Government between Party and State," in Gerhard Hirschfeld and /Lothar Kettenacker, eds., *Der "Führerstaat." Mythos und Realität. Studien zur Struktur und Politik des Dritten Reiches* (Stuttgart, 1981), pp. 197–201.
9. For details on Munich see Helmuth M. Hanko, "Kommunalpolitik in der 'Hauptstadt der Bewegung' 1933–1935," in Martin Broszat, *Bayern in der NS-Zeit*, vol. 3 (Munich, 1981), pp. 329–442, especially pp. 329–369.
10. The use of the German Municipal Code to increase the influence of the NSDAP over local-government staffing policy has been pointed out by Hans Mommsen, *Beamtentum im Dritten Reich. Mit ausgewählten Quellen zur nationalsozialistischen Beamtenpolitik* (Stuttgart, 1966), p. 33. On this point in general see Matzerath, *Selbstverwaltung*; Noakes, Oberbürgermeister und Gauleiter; Hanko, "Kommunalpolitik in der 'Hauptstadt der Bewegung.'"

11. Bundesarchiv Berlin (BAB) R 2 Research (former BDC), O. 850, fol. 8–10: Bericht Oberste Leitung der NSDAP-Parteiorganisation/Kommunalpolitische Abteilung an Organisationsamt (September 1933); and BAB R 2 Pers. (former BDC), PK: Jeserich, Kurt, unfol.: Geheime Denkschrift (1938), pp. 1–5.
12. Wolf Gruner, "Der Deutsche Gemeindetag und die Koordinierung antijüdischer Kommunalpolitik im NS-Staat. Zum Marktverbot jüdischer Händler und der 'Verwertung jüdischen Eigentums,'" in *Archiv für Kommunalwissenschaften*, II. Halbjahresbd., 37 (1998), pp. 261–291 [in English: Wolf Gruner "The German Council of Municipalities (Deutscher Gemeindetag) and the Coordination of Anti-Jewish Local Policies in the Nazi State," *Holocaust and Genocide Studies*, Vol. 13, no. 2 (1999): 171–199]; idem, "Die öffentliche Fürsorge und die deutschen Juden 1933–1942. Zur antijüdischen Politik der Städte, des Deutschen Gemeindetages und des Reichsinnenministeriums," *Zeitschrift für Geschichtswissenschaft*, 7, no. 45 (1997): 597–616. [in English: "Public Welfare and the German Jews under National Socialism. On Anti-Jewish Policies of the Municipal Administrations, the German Council of Municipalities and the Reich Ministry of the Interior (1933–1942)," in Bankier, *Probing the Depths of German Antisemitism*, pp. 78–105].
13. On the figures: BAB NS 25, Nr. 95, foBl. 129: Speech by Fiehler "Nationalsozialistische Kommunalpolitik" (undated, ca. 1936); Landesarchiv (LA) Berlin, Rep. 142/7, 0-5-53/ Nr. 1, vol. 3, unfol.: Fernschreiben Deutscher Gemeindetag, aufgenommen am 14. März 1942.
14. Horst Matzgerath, ed., *Jüdisches Schicksal in Köln 1918–1945. Katalog zur Ausstellung des Historischen Archivs der Stadt Köln/NS-Dokumentationszentrum* (Cologne, 1989), p. 157.
15. Hanke, *Juden in München*, p. 100.
16. According to Frank Bajohr, *"Arisierung" in Hamburg. Die Verdrängung jüdischer Unternehmer 1933–1945* (Hamburg, 1997), p. 97.
17. Regina Bruss, *Die Bremer Juden unter dem Nationalsozialismus* (Bremen, 1983), pp. 49–50.
18. Frank Sparing, *Boykott, Enteignung, Zwangsarbeit. Die "Arisierung" jüdischen Eigentums während des Nationalsozialismus* (Düsseldorf, 2000), pp. 26–27; Pätzold, *Faschismus*, p. 65.
19. Dirk van Laak, "Die Mitwirkenden bei der "'Arisierung.' Dargestellt am Beispiel der westfälisch-rheinischen Industrieregion 1933–1940," in Ursula Büttner, ed., *Die Deutschen und die Judenverfolgung* (Hamburg, 1992), p. 236; Uwe Lohalm, *Fürsorge und Verfolgung. Öffentliche Wohlfahrtsverwaltung und nationalsozialistische Judenpolitik in Hamburg 1933 bis 1942* (Hamburg, 1998), p. 16; Werner, *Hakenkreuz*, p. 73; Ulrich Knipping, *Die Geschichte der Juden in Dortmund während der Zeit des Dritten Reiches* (Dortmund, 1977), p. 35.
20. Gerhard Bennertz, "Die Geschichte der Jüdischen Kultusgemeinde in Mülheim a. d. Ruhr in der ersten Hälfte des 20. Jahrhunderts im Grundriß," *Zeitschrift des Geschichtsvereins Mülheim a. d. Ruhr*, 58 (1983): 24; Wolfgang Wippermann, *Das Leben in Frankfurt zur NS-Zeit*, vol. I: *Die nationalsozialistische Judenverfolgung* (Frankfurt on Main, 1986), pp. 157–158;, Gregor Zahnow, *Judenverfolgung in Münster* (Münster, 1993), pp. 37–38.
21. Gruner, *Judenverfolgung in Berlin*, pp. 17–21; Josef Walk, ed., *Das Sonderrecht für die Juden im NS-Staat. Eine Sammlung der gesetzlichen Maßnahmen–Inhalt und Bedeutung* (Heidelberg/Karlsruhe, 1981), I/29, p. 8; Knipping, *Juden in Dortmund*, p. 23; Horst Matzerath, "Bürokratie und Judenverfolgung," in Büttner, *Die Deutschen und die Judenverfolgung*, pp. 105–129, especially p. 110; Hannes Ziegler, "Verfemt-Verjagt-Vernichtet. Die Verfolgung der pfälzischen Juden 1933–1945," in Gerhard Nestler and /Hannes Ziegler, eds., *Die Pfalz unterm Hakenkreuz. Eine deutsche Provinz während der nationalsozialistischen Terrorherrschaft* (Landau/Pfalz, 1993), pp. 325–356, especially p. 333; Werner, *Hakenkreuz*, p. 58.
22. Program fofr 1920, in Walter Hofer, ed., *Der Nationalsozialismus. Dokumente 1933–1945*, new revised ed. (Frankfurt on Main, 1988), pp. 28–31.

23. Alex Bruns-Wüstefeld, *Lohnende Geschäfte. Die "Entjudung" der Wirtschaft am Beispiel Göttingens*, ed. by Geschichtswerkstatt Göttingen (Hanover, 1997), p. 70.
24. Gruner, *Judenverfolgung in Berlin*, pp. 22–23.
25. Hanko, "Kommunalpolitik in der 'Hauptstadt der Bewegung,'" p. 407.
26. On Berlin: Gruner, *Judenverfolgung in Berlin*, pp. 22–23; on Remscheid: BAB R 36, Nr. 2051, foBl. 13: OB Remscheid (Stadtturnrat Dr. Borgmann) an DGT Berlin vom 20. Oktober 1934.
27. According to the *Jüdische Rundschau* of 26 June 1933; *Das Schwarzbuch – Tatsachen und Dokumente. Die Lage der Juden in Deutschland*, ed. by Comité des Délégations Juives–Reprint of the edition Paris 1934 (Frankfurt on Main, 1983), p. 477.
28. According to the *Münchner-Augsburger Abendzeitung* of 11 August 1933; Hanke, *Juden in München*, p. 104.
29. According to the *Vossische Zeitung* of 22 September 1933; *Das Schwarzbuch*, p. 477.
30. *Das Schwarzbuch*, p. 348; Kurt Düwell, *Die Rheingebiete in der Judenpolitik des Nationalsozialismus vor 1942* (Bonn, 1968), p. 95. On this point in general see Gruner, Der Deutsche Gemeindetag, pp. 267–274 [idem, "The German Council of Municipalities," pp. 174–179].
31. Gruner, "NS-Judenverfolgung," pp. 85–86; *Das Schwarzbuch*, pp. 468–470; and Walk, *Sonderrecht*, I/225, p. 48.
32. On this point in general see Gruner, Der Deutsche Gemeindetag, pp. 261–291 [idem, The German Council of Municipalities, pp. 171–199]; idem, "NS-Judenverfolgung," pp. 84–88.
33. According to the *Fränkische Tageszeitung* of 8 August 1933 and the *Frankfurter Zeitung* of 22 August 1933; *Das Schwarzbuch*, p. 475.
34. Hans Mommsen and Susanne Willems, eds., *Herrschaftsalltag im Dritten Reich. Studien und Texte* (Düsseldorf, 1988), p. 429, Dock. Nr. 2: Anordnung Bormanns an die Gauleitungen vom 12. September 1933.
35. For more details see Gruner, "NS-Judenverfolgung," p. 86.
36. Kurt Pätzold, ed., *Verfolgung, Vertreibung, Vernichtung. Dokumente des faschistischen Antisemitismus 1933–1942* (Leipzig, 1983), p. 58, Dock. Nr. 15: RWM an Industrie- und Handelstag vom 8. September 1933.
37. Matzerath, *Jüdisches Schicksal in Köln*, p. 157; Bruss, *Bremer Juden*, pp. 49–50.
38. *Dokumente Frankfurter Juden*, IV 2, p. 180: Denkschrift des Wirtschaftsamtes vom 17. Februar 1934.
39. Hanke, *Juden in München*, p. 103.
40. Lohalm, *Fürsorge und Verfolgung*, p. 15.
41. Gruner, *Judenverfolgung in Berlin*, pp. 17–36.
42. *Dokumente Frankfurter Juden*, VII 26, pp. 360–361: Sportamt an OB am 6. April 1935; BAB R 36, Nr. 2060, fol. 9: OB Ludwigshafen an DGT am 20. Mai 1935; ibid, fol. 12: OB Trier/Stadtamt für Leibesübungen an DGT/Abt. III am 6. Juli 1935; ibid, fol. 14: Städt. Badverwaltung Bad Landeck an DGT Berlin am 12. Juli 1935.
43. Gruner, "NS-Judenverfolgung," pp. 94–95.
44. BAB NS 25, Nr. 85, fol. 12: NSDAP-Reichsleitung/HA für Kommunalpolitik "Vertrauliche Berichtsauszüge" vom 5. September 1935, VII. Sendung 1935 (Druck), p. 3.
45. Reprint of the document in Werner Schneider, *Jüdische Heimat im Vest. Gedenkbuch der Jüdischen Gemeinden in Recklinghausen* (Recklinghausen, 1983), p. 204.
46. Ibid.
47. Gruner, NS-Judenverfolgung, p. 95.
48. Brandenburgisches Landeshauptarchiv (BLHA) Potsdam, Pr. Br. Rep. 2 A I Pol, Nr. 1919, foBl. 81: Schreiben an das Preußische Ministerium des Innern vom 20. August 1935.
49. Mommsen and Willems, *Herrschaftsalltag im Dritten Reich*, Do. Nr. 12, p. 444: Protokoll der Sitzung im RWM am 20. August 1935.
50. LA Berlin, Rep. 142/7, 4-10-3/Nr. 23, unfol.: Handschriftl. Vermerk über Ergebnis der Umfrage DGT/Abt. IV (Schlüter) vom 25. Februar 1938, p. 3; ibid, OB/Leihamt Düsseldorf an DGT Berlin am 4. März 1938; ibid, OB Heidelberg an DGT Berlin am 4. März 1938; Walk, *Sonderrecht*, II/3, p. 131.

51. Speech made on 16 September 1935, in *Die Nationalsozialistische Gemeinde*, 3 (1935), pp. 552–554.
52. Quoted from Pätzold, *Faschismus*, pp. 279–280.
53. BLHA Potsdam, Pr. Br. Rep. 2 A I Pol, Nr. 1919, fol. 291: Runderlaß-Gestapo vom 19. Dezember 1935 in Erlaß der Gestapo Potsdam vom 7. Januar 1936.
54. Gruner, "Fürsorge," pp. 597–616 [idem, "Public Welfare," pp. 78–88]. For more details see the new book of the author: Wolf Gruner, *Öffentliche Wohlfahrt und Judenverfolgung. Wechselwirkungen lokaler und zentraler Politik im NS-Staat 1933–1942* (Munich, 2002).
55. Gruner, "NS-Judenverfolgung," pp. 103–106.
56. Roland Müller, *Stuttgart zur Zeit des Nationalsozialismus* (Stuttgart, 1988), pp. 292, 296.
57. Gruner, "NS-Judenverfolgung," pp. 104–105.
58. LA Berlin, Rep. 142/7, 4-10-3/Nr. 23, unfol.: Ergebnis der Umfrage DGT/Abt. IV vom 25. Februar 1938. See Gruner, Der Deutsche Gemeindetag, pp. 278–279 [idem, The German Council of Municipalities, p. 182].
59. LA Berlin, Rep. 142/7, 4-10-3/Nr. 23, unfol.: Handschriftl. Vermerke auf Ergebnis der Umfrage DGT/Abt. IV vom 25. Februar 1938, pp. 1–2; ibid, OB Aachen an DGT Berlin am 15. März 1938.
60. For more details see Gruner, "NS-Judenverfolgung," pp. 98–103, 107–111.
61. Ibid., p. 117.
62. *Reichsgesetzblatt* I 1939, p. 864.
63. The first reference to this is provided in Konrad Kwiet, "Nach dem Pogrom. Stufen der Ausgrenzung," in Wolfgang Benz, ed., *Die Juden in Deutschland 1933–1945* (Munich, 1988), pp. 545–659, especially pp. 633–659.
64. Gruner, "NS-Judenverfolgung," pp. 117–118; Bruns-Wüstefeld, *Lohnende Geschäfte*, p. 109; Marlies Buchholz, *Die hannoverschen Judenhäuser. Zur Situation der Juden in der Zeit der Ghettoisierung und Verfolgung 1941 bis 1945* (Hildesheim, 1987).
65. StadtA Düsseldorf, IV 459, fol. 257: Berichtsvorlage Wirtschaftsamt Düsseldorf für Ratsherrensitzung (undated, ca. mid July 1939); Manfred Unger and Hubert Lang, eds., *Juden in Leipzig. Eine Dokumentation zur Ausstellung anläßlich des 50. Jahrestages der faschistischen Pogromnacht vom 5. 11.–17. 12. 1988* (Leipzig, 1988), pp. 180–183: Faksimile OB Freyberg an Sachsischen Wirtschaftsminister am 18. Juli 1940.
66. See Wolf Gruner, "Terra Inkognita? Die Lager für den '"jüdischen Arbeitseinsatz"' 1938–1943 und die deutsche Bevölkerung," in Büttner, *Die Deutschen und die Judenverfolgung*, pp. 131–159, especially pp. 131–133 [in English: "Terra Inkognita?—The Camps for "'Jewish Labor Conscription'" 1938–1943 and the German Population," *Yad Vashem Studies* XXIV, Jerusalem (1994): 1–3].
67. For a detailed treatment see Wolf Gruner, *Der Geschlossene Arbeitseinsatz deutscher Juden. Zur Zwangsarbeit als Element der Verfolgung 1938 bis 1943* (Berlin, 1997).
68. Ibid., pp. 144–145.
69. For more details see Wolf Gruner, "Der Geschlossene Arbeitseinsatz und die Juden in Frankfurt on Main 1938–1942," in Monica Kingreen, ed., *"Nach der Kristallnacht". Jüdisches Leben und antijüdische Politik 1938–1945 in Frankfurt on Main* (Frankfurt on Main/New York, 1999), pp. 259–288.
70. Gruner, "NS-Judenverfolgung," p. 116.
71. Gruner, *Der Deutsche Gemeindetag*, pp. 274–291 [Gruner, *The German Council of Municipalities*, pp. 179–199]. Wolf Gruner, "Die Grundstücke der 'Reichsfeinde'. Zur 'Arisierung' von Immobilien durch Städte und Gemeinden 1938–1945," in *"Arisierung". Volksgemeinschaft, Raub und Gedächtnis*, edited for the Fritz Bauer Institut by Irmtrud Wojak and Peter Hayes (Frankfurt on Main, New York, 2000), pp. 125–156.
72. Further details in Gruner, "Fürsorge," pp. S. 597–616 [idem, "Public Welfare," pp. 78–105]; idem, "Der Deutsche Gemeindetag," pp. 261–291 [idem, "The German Council of Municipalities," pp. 171–199]; idem, "Die Grundstücke der 'Reichsfeinde,'". pp. 125–156.
73. StadtA Leipzig, Kap. I, Nr. 122, fol. 124RS: Schul- und Bildungsamt Leipzig an HVA Leipzig am 27. Juli 1938.

74. Ibid., fol. 32: Rundschreiben Park- und Gartenamt Leipzig vom 15. September 1937; ibid., fol. 40: Ergebnis der Umfrage (undated).
75. Yad Vashem Archive (YV) Jerusalem M1DN, Nr. /119, fol. 82–84: Vermerk Städtischer Wohnungsnachweis München vom 28. Januar 1941.
76. LA Berlin, Rep. 142/7, 0-1-10/Nr. 1, unfol.: "Der Deutsche Gemeindetag" von Dr. Schlempp (1. Juli 1941), p. 6.
77. BAB R 36/, Nr. 2060, fol. 35: Bericht der Tagung am 4. November 1935 in Altdamm.
78. LA Berlin, Rep. 142/7, 3-10-11/Nr. 72, unfol.: DGT Schleswig-Holstein an DGT Berlin am 13. März 1936. Restrictions on the admission of Jews to hospitals were also discussed at a conference in Wesermünde; StadtA Göttingen, Sozialamt, Acc.Nr. 407/77, Nr. 47/1, unfol.: Niederschrift über die Tagung der Arbeitsgemeinschaft für Verwaltungsfragen der hannoverschen Stadtkreise am 31. August 1938.
79. LA Berlin, Rep. 142/7, 3-10-11/Nr. 72, unfol.: DGT/Abt. III an DGT Schleswig-Holstein am 25. März 1936.
80. Gruner, "Der Deutsche Gemeindetag," pp. 270–271 [idem, "The German Council of Municipalities," pp. 176–177] and idem "NS-Judenverfolgung," pp. 96–97.
81. For an assessment of the significance of mediating agencies see Wolfgang Seibel, "Staatsstruktur und Massenmord. Was kann eine historisch-vergleichende Institutionenanalyse zur Erforschung des Holocaust beitragen?" *Geschichte und Gesellschaft*, 4, no. 24 (1998): 539–569, especially pp. 556–557.
82. Pätzold, *Verfolgung*, pp. 138–139, Dock. Nr. 94: RMdI-Schnellbrief vom 24. Juli 1937.
83. Helmut Eschwege, ed., *Kennzeichen J. Bilder, Dokumente, Berichte zur Geschichte der Verbrechen des Hitlerfaschismus an den deutschen Juden 1933–1945* (East Berlin, 1981), p. 381: RMdI-Erlaß vom 11. Juli 1938.
84. BLHA Potsdam, Pr. Br. Rep. 41 Birkenwerder, Nr. 9, fol. 201–202.
85. Gruner, "NS-Judenverfolgung," pp. 105–106.
86. "Bekanntmachung der neuen Fassung des Gesetzes über das Versteigerungsgewerbe vom 12. Februar 1938," *Reichsgesetzblatt* I 1938 I, p. 202.
87. On Munich see Hanko, "Kommunalpolitik in der 'Hauptstadt der Bewegung,'" pp. 410–411.
88. The town had increased the rent fourfold for Jewish applicants; *Dokumente Frankfurter Juden*, VII 23 A, p. 356: Sportamt an OB am 4. Juni 1934.
89. Ibid., VII 23 B, p. 357: OB-Verfügung vom 14. Juni 1934.
90. BAB, Zwischenarchiv Dahlwitz-Hoppegarten (ZDH), ZA VI/, Nr. 3852, A. 12, fol. 7+RS: OB Plauen/Schulamt an NSDAP Kreisleitung am 10. September 1936; ibid., fol. 7RS: Kreisgeschäftsführer an OB Plauen am 19. September 1936.
91. Gruner, "NS-Judenverfolgung," pp. 122–123.
92. Ibid.
93. He named the districts that were to be "purged". Later his department organized several clearance programs; Wolf Gruner: "Die Reichshauptstadt und die Verfolgung der Berliner Juden 1933–1945," in Reinhard Rürup, ed., *Jüdische Geschichte in Berlin. Essays und Studien* (Berlin, 1995), pp. 229–266, especially pp. 241–248. See the recent detailed account in Susanne Willems, "*Der entsiedelte Jude*". *Albert Speers Wohnungsmarktpolitik für den Berliner Hauptstadtbau* (Berlin, 2002).
94. YV Jerusalem, M1Dn/Nr. 111 B, fol. 482: Stapoleitstelle an OB/Gewerbeamt München am 13. Juli 1939.
95. In individual cases, for example in Düsseldorf and Leipzig, the towns cooperated with the NSDAP district offices in the establishment of "Jewish houses"; Gruner, "NS-Judenverfolgung," pp. 118–119.
96. *Die Geschichte der Juden in Hamburg 1590–1990*, vol.. 1: *Vierhundert Jahre Juden in Hamburg*. Eine Ausstellung des Museums für Hamburgische Geschichte vom 8.11.1991 bis 29.3.1992 (Hamburg, 1991), p. 475, Doc. Nr. 312: Rechtsamt an NSDAP-Gaurechtsamt Hamburg vom 15. April 1941; BAB/ZDH ZA I, Nr. 7928, A. 4, unfol.: NSDAP-Gau Thüringen/Kreisrechtsamt Jena an OB/Wohnungsamt am 20. März 1941; StadtA Düsseldorf, IV 12314, fol. 59: NSDAP-Gaurechtsamt (Dr. Wagner) an OB Düsseldorf am 7. April 1941. Cf. the initiative of the regional leader (Gauleiter) in Hanover at the end of

March 1941 for the evacuation of Jewish housing and the accommodateion of the Jews in huts; Buchholz, *Die hannoverschen Judenhäuser*, p. 27.
97. *Dokumente Frankfurter Juden*, XIII 3, S. 473: Gestapo-Beauftragter bei der Jüdischen Wohlfahrtspflege an Gestapo Frankfurt on Main 22. Oktober 1941.
98. Gruner, "NS-Judenverfolgung," pp. 118–119.
99. On housing issues see: Karl Christian Führer, "Mit Juden unter einem Dach? Zur Vorgeschichte des Gesetzes über Mietverhältnisse mit Juden," 1999. *Zeitschrift für Sozialgeschichte des 20. und 21. Jahrhunderts*, 7 (1992): 51– 61. For actions on rents and the rulings in 1938 in Berlin; see Buchholz, *Die hannoverschen Judenhäuser*, p. 8; Gruner, "Reichshauptstadt," p. 238. See also the various examples of the legal decisions on forced labor in 1939/40 in Gruner, *Der Geschlossene Arbeitseinsatz deutscher Juden*.
100. Gruner, "Der Geschlossene Arbeitseinsatz und die Juden in Frankfurt on Main," p. 279.
101. Gruner, "Fürsorge," pp. 607–610; [idem, "Public Welfare," pp. 91–101]; for more details on this topic see Gruner, *Öffentliche Wohlfahrt und Judenverfolgung*; see also Gruner, *Zwangsarbeit und Verfolgung. Österreichische Juden im NS-Staat* (Innsbruck, 2000), pp. 25, 103–104.
102. Matzerath, "Bürokratie," p. 118.
103. Gruner, *"Die Grundstücke der 'Reichsfeinde,'"* pp. 142–143.
104. YV Jerusalem M1DN, Nr. 92, fol. 11: DGT Berlin an Magistrat Frankfurt on Main am 9. September 1933; ibid., fol. 20–21: DGT an Preuß. Minister für Wissenschaft am 17. Oktober und Antwort vom 29. Oktober 1934.
105. Gruner, *"Die Grundstücke der 'Reichsfeinde,'"* pp. 125–156.
106. *Dokumente Frankfurter Juden*, IX 6, pp. 402–403: Denkschrift des Bauamtes vom 6. Februar 1939.
107. Gruner, *Zwangsarbeit und Verfolgung. Österreichische Juden im NS-Staat*, p. 143.
108. Various examples of the correspondence on this in Österreichisches Staatsarchiv/Archiv der Republik Wien, Baldur von Schirach, Box 14.
109. Gruner, *"Reichshauptstadt,"* pp. 241–248.
110. *Dienstblatt der Stadt Berlin*, 1942/Teil III, p. 145, Nr. 143: Rundverfügung Planungsamt vom 24. Dezember 1942.
111. YV Jerusalem M1DN, Nr. 261, fol. 18–19: Tätigkeits- und Abschlußbericht der "Dienststelle des Beauftragten des Gauleiters für die Arisierung" zum 30. Juni 1943, pp. 14–15.
112. Karl-Heinz Roth, "Ökonomie und politische Macht: Die "'Firma Hamburg'" 19030–1945," in Angelika Ebbinghaus and /Karsten Linne, eds., *Kein abgeschlossenes Kapitel: Hamburg im ""Dritten Reich""* (Hamburg, 1997), pp. 15–176, especially p. 112; Susanne Freund, "'Arisierung'" in Münster—dargestellt anhand ausgewählter lebensgeschichtlicher Zeugnisse," in Alfons Kenkmann and Bernd-A. Rusinek, eds., *Verfolgung und Verwaltung. Die wirtschaftliche Ausplünderung der Juden und die westfälischen Finanzbehörden* (Münster, 1999), pp. 41–66, especially p. 63.
113. *Dokumente Frankfurter Juden*, XIII 3, pp. 472–473: Gestapo-Beauftragter bei der Jüdischen Wohlfahrtspflege an Gestapo Frankfurt on Main am 22. Oktober 1941.
114. Interestingly enough, the permanent complaints of many of the NSDAP regional offices (Gauämter) for local-government policy in 1940 and 1941 on the lack of new municipal housing in spite of the acute need for it contained no demands for the "de-tenanting" of "Jewish housing"; BAB NS 25/, Nr. 1094: Tätigkeitsberichte der Gauämter für Kommunalpolitik an das Hauptamt in München.
115. StadtA Freiburg im Breisgau C4 VI/28, Nr. 1, unfol.: Protokoll der Sitzung der Oberbürgermeister der Stadtkreise (DGT-Landesdienststelle Baden) vom 27. Februar 1941, pp. 9–10.
116. According to Gerd Blumberg, "Etappen der Verfolgung und Ausraubung und ihre bürokratische Apparatur," in Kenkmann and Rusinek, eds., *Verfolgung und Verwaltung*, pp. 15–40, especially p. 36.
117. Bajohr, *Arisierung in Hamburg*, p. 333. On Göttingen see Bruns-Wüstefeld, *Lohnende Geschäfte*, pp. 111–112.

118. Gruner, "Der Deutsche Gemeindetag," p. 286 [idemGruner, "The German Council of Municipalities," pp. 187–188]; Schmid, "Finanztod," p. 146. See for detailed accounts: Monica Kingreen, "Raubzüge einer Stadtverwaltung. Frankfurt on Main und die Aneignung 'jüdischen Besitzes,'" in Wolf Gruner and Armin Nolzen, eds., *Beiträge zur Geschichte des Nationalsozialismus*, Vol. 17: *Bürokratien. Initiative und Effizienz*, (Berlin, 2001), pp. 17–50.
119. BAB/ZDH ZA VI/, Nr. 3852, A. 12, foBl. 15RS+16: Vermerk Stadtbücherei Plauen vom 12. Februar 1938 und Umlauf vom 18. Dezember 1937; Gruner, *Judenverfolgung in Berlin*, p. 65; Central Zionist Archives Jerusalem, Sp 26/, Nr. 1191g, unfol.: Bericht über die Tätigkeit der IKG Wien 19. Mai 1938–1944/45, p. 36.
120. On this point in general see the detailed study of the author: Wolf Gruner, *Öffentliche Wohlfahrt und Judenverfolgung*.
121. Hans Mommsen, "Hitlers Stellung im nationalsozialistischen Herrschaftssystem," in his collection of essays, *Der Nationalsozialismus und die deutsche Gesellschaft. Ausgewählte Aufsätze* (Reinbek, 1991), pp. 67–101, especially pp. 81–82.
122. See Hanko, "*Kommunalpolitik in der 'Hauptstadt der Bewegung,'*" p. 331.
123. Jürgen Matthäus, "Das Ghetto Kaunas und die '"Endlösung"' in Litauen," in Wolfgang Benz and Marion Neiss, eds., *Judenmord in Litauen. Studien und Dokumente* (Berlin, 1999), pp. 97–112, especially p. 104.
124. Sybille Steinbacher, "*Musterstadt*" *Auschwitz. Germanisierungspolitik und Judenmord in Ostoberschlesien* (Munich, 2000), pp. 267–271, pp. 310–311.
125. Markus Gryglewski, "Zur Geschichte der nationalsozialistischen Judenverfolgung in Dresden 1933–1945," in Norbert Haase, Stefi Jersch-Wenzel and Hermann Simon, eds., *Fotografien und Dokumente zur nationalsozialistischen Judenverfolgung in Dresden 1933–1945* (Leipzig, 1998), pp. 87–150, especially p. 109.

CHAPTER 16

THE *REICHSKRISTALLNACHT* AND THE INSURANCE INDUSTRY: THE POLITICS OF DAMAGE CONTROL

Gerald D. Feldman

The subject of this chapter is somewhat at odds with the basic theme of this book since it addresses the dilemmas of the German insurance business in trying to escape the costs of involvement in the expropriation of German insurance assets and its exploitation of the National Socialist regime's division of labor and its polycratic organization to attain this goal of nonparticipation or limited participation. Let me make clear from the outset that this has nothing whatever to do with resistance to National Socialist measures against the Jews even if some of the actors from the insurance industry involved personally deplored those measures. Rather, it has to do with the techniques and arguments employed by the insurance industry to save money and distance itself from participation in a costly engagement in radical anti-Jewish measures. Indeed, as will be shown, the defence of those interests could be turned into a legitimation of and moral contribution to the regime's anti-Semitic measures.

The November Pogrom and the Air Ministry Meeting of 12 November 1938

There is by now a substantial literature on the origins and course of the November pogrom, so that the general and most relevant aspects can be quickly stated here. The pogrom was launched in the wake of the shooting on 7 November of the Legation Secretary at the German Embassy in Paris, Ernst vom Rath, by the distraught Herschel Grynszpan, whose family had been among the 16,000 Polish Jews expelled to Poland under the most miserable circumstances in late October. Vom Rath died on the late afternoon of 9 November, and Hitler received the news while participating in the "Old Fighters" (party veterans) dinner in Munich. Hitler had been in an intransigent mood on the "Jewish question" for some time, and Propaganda Minister Goebbels was anxious to restore his status, tarnished of late by his propaganda failures and extramarital affairs. The idea of a pogrom and of a more radical policy toward the Jews had been in the air for months in Party and SD circles. In any case, Hitler decided to take Goebbels off the leash, and he informed the assembled party leaders at the dinner that "spontaneous" actions in response to the vom Rath assassination, some of which had already begun on 8 November, were not to encounter interference. Thus was unleashed the "Night of Broken Glass" of 9–10 November 1938, a Party and SA orgy of vandalism, burning, looting, and sadistic mistreatment of Jews throughout the Reich that led to the destruction of 267 synagogues and 7,500 businesses, the murder of 91 Jews, and a wave of arrests in which 30,000 Jews were dragged for usually brief but always terrifying incarcerations into concentration camps, thereby producing further deaths and suicides. Although Goebbels personally ordered an end to the "demonstrations" on the front page of the *Völkischer Beobachter* on 10 November, vandalism and violent actions continued in some places as late as 13 November.[1]

Goebbels coordinated his actions, including the termination of the pogrom, very closely with Hitler, and cheerfully noted in his diary that he found Hitler "totally radical and aggressive." Much damage had been done, but Hitler was unconcerned since, as Goebbels noted in reporting their conversation in Munich on 10 November in his diary entry of the next day: "The Führer wants to take very sharp measures against the Jews. They must themselves put their businesses in order again. The insurance companies will not pay them a thing. Then the Führer wants a gradual expropriation of Jewish businesses and to give the owners paper payment for them that we can void any time."[2] This diary entry is of immense importance for two reasons. First, in the general sense, it demonstrates that some of the most important actions soon to be taken reflected the express wishes and intentions of Hitler. Secondly, with specific reference to insurance, it shows that Hitler was well aware that insurance claims might be made in connection with the pogrom but had preempted any serious discussion of payment by ordering that the Jews were not to receive insurance compensation.

Needless to say, the leadership of the insurance business was also well aware that the fire, glass, and burglary and theft branches especially had a problem on their hands. In some respects, it was an old problem since as far back as 1932 the insurance companies were trying to get the Nazis to understand that the breaking of the windows of Jewish businesses did not harm the Jews but rather the insurance companies, which had to cover the damage, while it benefited the French and Belgian glass industries. They did so in 1933 in connection with the anti-Jewish boycott and other actions against Jewish enterprises. They also ruminated whether they had such liability in cases where the insurance policies in question did not make provision for civil unrest, although the issue was whether such individual instances of damage as there were qualified as civil unrest.³ However, a good argument could be made that the government should pay the costs in any case. Thus, in December 1933, the Reich Economic Court had ruled that such damages taking place during the anti-Jewish boycott of 1 April 1933 constituted a domestic disturbance and fell under the compensation provisions of the Tumult Damage Law.⁴

By 1938, however, conditions had changed, and the insurers were no longer sure what to do about actions taken against Jewish businesses that took place in the spring of that year and foreshadowed what was to happen in November. On the one hand, the organization of glass insurers was nervous enough about recurring incidents to advise its members not to replace broken windows immediately but rather to use wooden boarding and makeshift measures until the wave of actions against Jewish stores died down. On the other, it no longer felt it could use the press or other public means to point out the counterproductive nature of the actions against Jewish property openly, and it certainly did not feel it could take the Nazi regime to court to make it pay for a Nazi-caused tumult.⁵ The anti-Jewish outbursts in the spring, however, were as nothing compared to the massive violence and destruction unleashed in November, that certainly were a civil disturbance to any sentient person.

Ironically, by this time nearly all German insurance policies had eliminated domestic coverage against civil disturbance, and this because the government had insisted that the New Germany did not have civil disturbances! Thus, the Reich Supervisory Board for Insurance told the Reich Group for Insurance on 28 April 1938 "that in the National Socialist State the marketing of riot insurance and the mention of riot, domestic or civil unrest, disturbance of the peace, mob action, plundering, strikes, lockouts, and sabotage in the general insurance conditions of the other insurance branches is insupportable." ⁶ Strictly speaking, therefore, the insurers were "home free," since they no longer covered civil disturbances and thus could claim nonliability to their customers and refer them to the courts and the government with respect to payment. For obvious reasons, this was not possible, and the insurance companies had a problem on their hands, one that was compounded by the fact that foreigners, both non-Jewish and Jewish, had also suffered damage, that foreign insurance companies insuring property in Germany were unlikely to want to pay for damages when it was a notorious fact that the firemen and police stood by and let the events of 9–11 November take place, and that there were some foreign insurers and reinsurers involved as well.

It was a situation filled with potential dangers for the insurance business, and it would have to bring the entire network of relationships in business and government at its disposal to limit the damage it was liable to suffer. The first of these was the insurance industry organization itself. Thus, on 11 November, the leader of the Reich Group for Insurance, the Allianz director Eduard Hilgard, sent a most revealing confidential letter to the organization of private insurers, pointing out that the damage, the amount of which still could not be determined, had been very great, and that one could also not determine "whether the damages are subject to compensation under the terms of the policies." This being the case, "it seems absolutely necessary that the insurance companies proceed in the handling of this matter according to totally uniform principles, which have to be adopted in agreement with the relevant authorities and party agencies." Hilgard therefore asked that they take measures as quickly as possible to insure that no company do anything to prejudice this unified stance. On the one hand, it was necessary to acknowledge all incoming reports of damages. On the other, it was important that "no payments for damages occur before further instructions are received concerning the handling of these reports." Finally, Hilgard asked that he be supplied with ongoing information about the extent of the damages, which he needed for his reports to the Reich Economics Minister.[7]

Hilgard certainly was fully aware that protection against civil unrest had been virtually eliminated from insurance policies, but he also knew that legal norms were not the order of the day and that it was quite easy to fall victim to competing interests and agendas within the regime. Hilgard also knew that the authorities were in a position to exercise dictatorial authority with respect to the payment or nonpayment of insurance. This was not only because it was a government-inspired pogrom that had created the complicated situation in the first place and that one of the unique characteristics of such a regime is that it is in a position to arbitrarily "solve" the problems it arbitrarily creates. It was specifically because § 81a of the Reich Insurance Decree gave the government the power to set aside existing clauses in the general insurance conditions if it deemed such action "in the public interest."[8] The insurance industry was in no position to make autonomous decisions on its liability with the confidence that it could fight for its position in court. It would inevitably have to come to terms with the authorities and party agencies. Finally, it is important to note that the private insurance industry was in a constant struggle with the publicly chartered insurance companies, which had the support of the party radicals, especially the vicious Gauleiter of Pomerania, Franz von Schwede-Coburg, and Joseph Goebbels' brother Hans, who headed a major company in the Rhineland. The conflict was particularly intense at this time, and the sense of insecurity in the Reich Group must have been very high.[9]

Unquestionably, however, the person most irritated by the pogrom was Hermann Göring, who as head of the Four-Year Plan had been planning a steady and "peaceful" expropriation of Jewish assets and had a profound distaste for "spontaneous" actions that damaged Jewish assets and threatened to drain the economy of foreign exchange. For these reasons, he was furious at Goebbels but also anxious not only to limit the damage to the economic interests of his program but also to take advantage of the events of the pogrom to speed up the expropriation of Jewish assets, eliminate the Jews from German economic life, and drive them out of the country. These concerns led to him summon the infamous meeting of some 80–100 high government and party officials in the Reich Air Ministry on 12 November

1938.¹⁰ One of those called to the meeting, albeit only for a brief portion as an expert to inform Göring and the assemblage of the insurance implications of the pogrom, was Hilgard. The latter found himself sitting between Göring and Goebbels and directly across from Reinhard Heydrich, the Chief of the Security Police and Security Service, who was Reichsführer-SS Himmler's right-hand man, and from Kurt Daluege, the Chief of the Order Police. To add to the memorableness of the occasion, Göring's aides expressed to Hilgard the hope that he would help to "finish" Goebbels "off entirely" just before Hilgard entered the room.¹¹

Göring was absolutely committed to making sure that insurance companies did not fulfill any obligations to Jews and, apparently assuming that the insurance companies had liability even in the case of a domestic disturbance, he offered to issue a decree absolving the insurance companies of all liability and asked that the relevant ministries cooperate in this endeavor. At the same time, however, he expressed interest in taking advantage of any foreign reinsurance monies that might be owing because of the damage. This expectation, in fact, was utterly ridiculous since how could one collect reinsurance when the direct insurers were being absolved of paying any insurance? Hilgard explained to Göring that very little reinsurance was involved, but he then pursued a strategy that was to get him into great difficulty. Fearful of bringing up the simple and true argument that the insurance companies had very little liability because almost all had got rid of their clauses covering civil unrest and were actually most worried about lawsuits and embarrassing claims by foreigners, Hilgard asked Göring that the insurance companies be allowed to pay any obligations that they did have in connection with the pogrom. It was necessary to maintain confidence in the German insurance business, and failure to meet contractual obligations would constitute a "black spot on the coat of honor of the German insurance industry." Göring's initial reaction to this suggestion that the insurance companies meet such liabilities was to reiterate that he would issue a decree that would provide relief, but when Hilgard indicated a desire to discuss this, Heydrich chimed in with the idea that the insurance companies should pay out their obligations and that the money would then be confiscated. In this way the companies could formally save face. Hilgard's response to this, and Göring's interruption, along with Hilgard's interjection in the midst of Göring's remarks were most revealing:

> Hilgard: What Obergruppenführer Heydrich just said is what I actually also consider the right way, first to use the apparatus of the insurance industry to determine, to regulate, and also to pay out, but then to give the insurance industry the possibility, in some kind of fund ...
> Göring: One moment! You have to pay out in any case because Germans are damaged. But you receive a legal ban against making the payments directly to the Jews. You must also pay the damages that you would have had to pay to the Jews, but not to the Jews but to the Finance Minister. (Hilgard: Aha!) What he does with it is his business.¹²

The only sensible way to interpret Hilgard's "Aha!" is that Göring had hoisted Hilgard on his own petard. The latter apparently hoped that the insurance companies could make what was tantamount to fictional payments where they had liability and then get their money back from the state. While there is no direct evidence that Hilgard anticipated that this money would come from the Jews, his agreement with the scenario sketched out by Heydrich, who was aware of Göring's plan to levy a billion mark fine on the Jews, could be interpreted as indicative of Hilgard's thinking. Heydrich stated: "Field Marshal, I was going to make the proposal that one settles on a specific percent of the reported assets—a billion marks is to be collected—in my view 15 percent and then raises this percent somewhat so that all the Jews pay the same amount and then give the insurance companies the money back from this amount."[13] Göring, however, had obviously changed his mind with respect to the liability of the insurance companies. Where at the beginning of the meeting he indicated a desire to relieve them of all obligation, Hilgard's request that the companies be allowed to fulfill such obligations as they may have had caused Göring to change his mind and to interrupt Hilgard before the latter had a chance to clarify his point. Göring now had no intention of letting Hilgard off the hook or of giving any money back to anyone: "No I am not thinking at all of giving the money back to the insurance companies. The insurance companies are liable. No, the money belongs to the state. That is absolutely clear. That would be a gift to the insurance companies. They have made a generous request. They will fulfill it. You can count on it!"[14] Göring was in a ruthless mood, and he intended to collect from everyone: Jews and insurance companies. Hilgard thus left the meeting with what was potentially a very big bill to be paid by the insurance business.

The Politics of Damage Control

Beginning on 12 November, that is, within hours of the meeting in the Air Ministry, there began a new flood of anti-Jewish legislation that distinguished itself from past measures by vastly accelerating their despoliation, exclusion from German economic life, and social and personal isolation. Most important from the perspective of the insurance issue were the three decrees issued on 12 November itself. The first of these, the "Decree for the Restoration of the Appearance of the Streets around Jewish enterprises," placed the burden of cleaning up and repairing damage from the pogrom on the Jews and mandated the confiscation by the state of any insurance to which Jews of German citizenship could make claim. The second decree imposed an Atonement Tax of one billion marks on Jews of German citizenship. Of great significance in connection with this decree, however, was the Implementation Decree of 21 November. It ordered that all Jews with assets of RM 5,000 or more be obligated to pay 20 percent of their assets in four payments between 15 December 1938 and 15 August 1939. Especially significant for the insurance question, however, § 7 of the Implementation Decree provided that payments of insurance in connection with the pogrom to Jews with German citizenship and stateless Jews were to be made directly to the Revenue Offices and to be credited against their levy on assets. Insofar as such payments exceeded the latter, however, they were to be confiscated by the Reich anyway. Finally, there was the "Decree for the Exclusion of Jews from German Economic Life," which barred Jews from owning or running any enterprises after 1 January 1939.[15]

As should be obvious, the meeting in the Air Ministry had left Hilgard with an extremely unpleasant and unanticipated problem on his hands, namely, that Göring and the government now appeared to be anticipating substantial payment of the damages from the insurance companies as well as from the Jews. When he returned to his office, he immediately arranged for a meeting with his colleagues in the Reich Group, but even before it was held he received a call from the official in the Reich Finance Ministry (RFM) Göring had put in charge of the matter, probably Ministerial Director Johannes Schwandt, who was to be Hilgard's bête noire during the coming months, telling him that Göring "expects a payment of 20 million marks, with which he will then be satisfied." Hilgard and his colleagues had no intention of paying any such sum if they could help it, but they were fully aware that they would have little chance of winning a legal battle "since our real opponent in court would not be the damaged Jews but rather the almighty Göring, who had pronounced the seizure of all Jewish claims by means of a decree."[16] It is not very likely that Hilgard ever believed that the insurance industry could take the government of the Third Reich to court over this issue or that the government would engage in a formal law suit but, as will be shown, the potential for a variety of legal suits of other types was built into the situation. Avoiding law suits at home and abroad was a very important determinant of both industry and bureaucratic behavior in the coming negotiations.[17]

If Hilgard was going to prevent Göring from having his way, he would have to mobilize his contacts in the ministries, above all the Reich Economics Ministry (RWM), which was charged with implementing the decree on repairing the damages arising from the pogrom. Hilgard would also have to keep his "troops" in line. Thus, on 18 November, the various insurance organizations were informed about his collaboration with the RWM and their members were instructed to provide detailed information on the damages and on who had suffered them—German Jews, non-German Jews, "Aryans," foreigners. The injunction against paying any damages was reiterated and the Reich Group announced its intention of working closely with the various business managers of the insurance branch organizations in assuring a uniform approach to the problem.[18] During the next few days, however, the confusion grew because of the RWM's Implementation Decree of 21 November. Three days later, the Reich Group informed its members that no payments were to be made to Jews despite the issuance of the Implementation Decree and, on 29 November, pointed out that the Implementation Decree said nothing about "whether" the insurance companies were obligated to pay the damages but only stated that "in so far" as Jews were successful in claiming such obligations, the sums were to be paid to the Finance Ministry. In the meantime, the Economics Minister had reserved his decision about the actual obligations in question and would probably only come to a determination after the extent of the damages had been established.[19]

Hilgard now viewed it as his chief task to persuade the RWM that the insurance companies were neither legally liable nor financially capable of covering the damages and, further, that holding them liable made no sense in terms of the goals and purposes of the decrees of 12 November. He stated the views of himself and his colleagues in a memorandum to Ministerial Director Lange of the RWM of 6 December 1938.[20] In his covering letter, Hilgard called for a uniform settlement of the issues and urged that the RWM hold a discussion with the relevant insurance-industry leaders as well as Reich Justice Ministry (RJM) officials. He left open the question as to whether the Finance Ministry needed to be asked to join as well, which was quite understandable given the interest of the Finance Ministry in supporting Göring's idea of making the insurance companies liable and collecting their money.

The memorandum itself was signed by Director Hans Goudefroy of Allianz, who served as the legal expert for the Reich Group, and by Hilgard himself. They began by narrowly defining the relevant damages under the two decrees relevant to the issue—the Decree for the Restoration of the Appearance of the Streets and the Atonement Tax Implementation Decree of 21 November. They took the position that only those damages were relevant that directly affected the appearance of the streets and involved businesses and homes. Thus, damages to the interior of businesses and houses, as well as damages to synagogues and Jewish schools and other institutions, did not fall under the decrees. They applied a similarly narrow construction to § 7 of the Implementation Decree, reiterating that it did not establish liability but only stated that, if liability existed, then insurance payment was to go to the Revenue Office and be counted in the Atonement Tax payment. They then turned to the central question: did liability exist? Unsurprisingly, the answer was negative and was based on the Reich Court decision of 8 June 1923 in the Porto Alegre case, in which an angry mob responded to the German sinking of a Brazilian ship in April 1917 by storming and destroying various German businesses. Those claiming damages from the insurance companies tried to argue that they were entitled to compensation because the disturbances were not directed against the Brazilian government or officials and thus did not qualify as civil disturbances. The court, however, ruled that a civil disturbance existed when "portions of the populace, which do not have to be considered numerically insignificant, are set in motion in a way that disturbs the public peace and order and exercise violence, be it against persons, be it against things." In the view of the authors, this fitted the situation of 8–10 November perfectly, as was amply demonstrated in his view by Goebbels's call for a cessation to the demonstrations of 10 November in which he called for an end to the "demonstrations and reprisals" taken against Jewry and Jewish property in "justifiable and understandable anger" over the murder of vom Rath. From this Goudefroy and Hilgard triumphantly concluded that "therefore the damages of 8–10 November were the result of civic or internal disturbances and are consequently not liable to compensation."

The two insurance executives did not intend to leave any stone unturned, however, and went on to argue that, even if the conditions defining a civic disturbance were not fully satisfied by the events in question, nevertheless the sense of the general insurance conditions in excluding compensation for civil disturbances, acts of war, earthquakes, and the like was to protect the insurers from liability for "elementary events," and this was the sort of event Goebbels described when he wrote in an article of 12 November on "The Grünspan Case"[21] that the events in question were "an eruptive outburst of the anger of the population." Thus, if the pogrom was not a civil disturbance, then it was something like an earthquake.

Goudefroy and Hilgard showed themselves to be quite masterful in carrying the logic of the pogrom and the decrees arising from it to their brutal and vicious conclusions. Thus, "Aryan" owners of destroyed Jewish properties could not suffer damages or lay claim to insurance payment because the Jews had the responsibility to make the repairs. They were most emphatic, however, about that lack of Jewish entitlement to compensation:

> Through the decrees of 12 November 1938, all of Jewry, therefore also German and stateless Jewry, has been pronounced guilty of the Paris murder and thereby of a provocation against the German people. When the provocateur brings about the event provoked, then he must accept being treated like the perpetrator himself. It will not do to treat the politically condemned Jews as being legally guiltless with respect to insurance. As a consequence, it is justifiable to raise the objection that the German and stateless Jews were responsible for being intentionally, or at the very least being grossly negligent in bringing about the insurance case. Thereby, however, all insurance claims are rendered inapplicable.

It was not enough to argue that the collective guilt of the Jews for the murder of vom Rath deprived them of all rights to insurance, however. Goudefroy and Hilgard found it necessary to go further by insisting that paying the Jews insurance would be "a violation of good morals" since it would involve payment of those who had been found guilty of a crime: "The act of reprisal against the Jews has the character of a punishment approved by the state. It would contradict the general sense of justice in the highest degree if the German insurance companies would have to remove this atonement placed upon the Jews." Yet this is precisely what would happen. Thus, if one compared two Jews, each with RM 100,000 in assets and with damages of RM 20,000, the first having no insurance and the second having insurance, then the former would have to pay RM 20,000 in damages out of his own pocket plus RM 16,000 in Atonement Tax on his remaining assets, while the latter would pay RM 20,000 in Atonement Tax but nothing for damages if he were compensated by insurance. Thus, the RM 16,000 difference would be covered by the insurance companies. This already unsatisfactory result, however, would be made even more "unbearable" if the money in question came from a mutual insurance enterprise, which would then have to raise the money from its members, "for in this case the Aryan members of the enterprise must pay the punishment imposed on the Jews."

This memorandum is a monument to the sophistry, casuistry, and perversion of business and personal ethics that were coming to characterize businessmen like Hilgard and Goudefroy in the pursuit of their interests under the conditions created by National Socialism. This said, it is important to recognize that the issue was not one of paying damages to Jews since direct insurance payments for pogrom damages to Jews were manifestly out of the question. Nevertheless, as the brutal example employed at the end of the memorandum demonstrates, the authors were prepared to argue that the liability of the insurers was especially undesirable because it might have the effect of relieving the Jews somewhat of the burdens imposed on them by the decrees. If the chief goal was the avoidance of insurance payment to the government, Goudefroy and Hilgard nevertheless did not shy away from reinforcing their position by arguing that insurance-company liability would detract from the punishment being visited upon the Jews. Promoting the efficacy of anti-Semitic measures was thus an integral part of their argumentation against insurance-company liability.

Nearly every major ministry was by this time engaged in trying to control the damage and complications created by the pogrom—except for the German Jews, of course. On 8 December, a meeting was held in the Interior Ministry at which representatives of the Ministries of Justice, Economics, Finance, and Propaganda appeared, along with officials from the Foreign Office and SS, to determine the extent to which the Reich might be liable for the pogrom damages. The RWM was able to present an estimate by Hilgard of the damages, thus providing an overview of the scale of the problem. By this time, it was very clear that certain groups would have to be compensated for the damages for political reasons—Jewish and non-Jewish foreigners and non-Jewish German citizens—and that public funds would have to be used for at least the immediate handling of some cases. Furthermore, some property belonging to "Aryans" had been damaged because the perpetrators believed it belonged to Jews, had belonged to Jews or belonged to persons of "mixed blood" or to persons who were politically suspect without being Jews. There was an entire category of persons who were indirectly damaged because they had just invested all their assets in purchasing Jewish property or had sold goods to Jews who were now completely bankrupt and in no position to get compensation. The big question was how to settle claims quickly, and avoid court trials and publicity. Here the government already had a mechanism at its disposal in the form of a law decreed on 13 December 1934 on the "Settlement of Claims in Civil Law," which permitted the Minister of the Interior to terminate claims made to the courts in connection with compensation for damages arising from "the National Socialist Uprising and Renewal of the State" and to adjudicate such cases itself in accordance with the "healthy feeling of the people."[22] Needless to say, it was a law aimed primarily at preventing Jews from taking the National Socialist regime and its minions to court for acts of vandalism and injustice. Its potential usefulness with respect to stifling court proceedings in cases brought by Jews and non-Jews in connection with the pogrom is easily apparent. Thus, at the 8 December meeting, a decision was made to centralize such decisions in the Justice Ministry so as to insure uniformity of practice and maintain budgetary control. In the National Socialist state, however, "uniformity of decision making" was really a formula for discriminatory practice so that only "Aryan" hardship cases would receive compensation and it would be possible to distinguish between foreign Jews who had been foreign citizens for a long time and those who had recently emigrated. The Gauleiter would be asked for advice, as provided under the 1934 law, and non-Jews interrelated with Jews would be denied compensation. Indeed, as the 14th Decree for the Implementation of the Law on the Settlement of Claims in Civil Law of 18 March 1939, which was specifically issued to deal with compensation for damages arising from the events of November 8 and the following days, made clear, such compensation would only be given on the basis of need and after political criteria were met. These emergency measures, however, still left open the question of insurance company liability, that is, whether payments by the Reich were purely subsidiary or whether they were to be the primary source of compensation. While the position of the insurance companies was reported to those assembled on 8 December, responsibility for dealing with the issue was turned back to the Reich Economics Ministry.[23]

Ministerial Councilor Daniel of the RWM, while basically friendly to the position of the insurance companies, was above all anxious to keep the discussion of the issue confined to a small circle and was very anxious to avoid any public discussion of whether or not the damages were the result of tumult and thus free of insurance obligation. He worried that it might indeed prove difficult to avoid court cases. Small and medium-sized firms, whose existence was threatened by the potentially high costs, would certainly do everything in their power to save themselves if held liable, and it would be impossible to prevent foreign insurers and reinsurers from questioning any government decision refusing to recognize the pogrom as a tumult.[24]

Daniel sought to clarify the matter at a meeting with the insurers and other governmental officials on 16 December under the chairmanship of Ministerial Director Gottschick of the RWM.[25] By this time, the reported damages, which later turned out to be exaggerated, had risen to RM 60 million, RM 45 million for fire damage, RM 8–10 million for glass, and the rest for burglary. They expected court cases to be brought in by foreign insurers claiming non-liability because of tumult. Hilgard came in well prepared to argue the case for non-liability for German insurers as well. In the case of burglary insurance, there was no liability because the goods had been stolen after the windows had been broken rather than by those who had done the initial damage. As for the fire and glass damage, it was the result of civic unrest. Also, the Jews had already replaced almost all the glass that had been broken, as was required by decree, so that the obligation of insurers to replace the glass no longer existed. More generally, and quite plausibly, Hilgard argued that he had never told Göring at the meeting of 12 November that the insurance companies would pay in every case, but only "that the companies would remain faithful to their contracts and would pay in those cases in which they were legally bound to compensate."[26] A false impression had been created that Hilgard had accepted full liability. Once again, he and his colleagues reiterated that the costs were unaffordable. The small mutual glass insurers would have to ask for additional payments from their members that would exceed by many times the normal premium, and even the larger fire-insurance companies would be hard pressed. As in the memorandum of 6 December, so now, the industry representatives argued that payment should not be made for reasons of economic policy, namely, that "the Aryan insured would not understand the Aryan community of the insured being the bearer of the burden in the last analysis."[27] They warned that foreign reinsurers would refuse to pay, so that the German insurance companies would have to sue them in foreign courts. When asked if the insurance companies also refused to pay for damages to "Aryans" and foreigners, Hilgard remained consistent. From the standpoint of the law and liability, there was no difference between the Jews and the foreigners. Returning to the proposal first made by Heydrich at the 12 November meeting at which he had so eagerly grasped, Hilgard suggested that, if the authorities thought it important to regulate the damages done to "Aryans" and foreigners, then one had in effect to invent a scenario that would appear acceptable while at the same time be economically palatable to the insurers: "The insurers regulate all the demonstration damages including the Jewish damages without prejudice to their favorable legal situation. But the Reich obligates itself internally to replace 100 percent of the expenditures of the companies. Approximately RM 30 to 50 million will be necessary that the Reich could pay out of the [Jewish—GDF] contribution."

The position of the insurance companies was now quite clear. They deemed themselves free of all obligation but were willing to participate in a make-believe acceptance of obligations provided their payments were reimbursed by the state, largely through the money collected from the Jews. In the discussion among the ministerial officials following the departure of Hilgard and his colleagues, one of the RWM officials argued that it was "unbearable" to place the damage costs on the insurance companies and that, as intended in the Implementation Decree of 21 November, the costs were to be covered by the Jewish indemnity. The problem, as all admitted, however, was that the decrees issued in the wake of the pogrom were contradictory and confusing. It was unclear whether the Decree for the Restoration of the Appearance of the Streets was intended to mandate payment by the insurers and thereby exclude application of the civil-unrest clause in policies or not, and while the Justice Ministry felt that the civil unrest clause was applicable, it was very unhappy with the decree's formulation. Potentially, this left the determination to the courts, which was precisely what one wished to avoid. The RJM was especially distressed by the Implementation Decree of 21 November issued by the Finance Ministry, about which the Justice authorities had not been consulted despite Finance Ministry claims to the contrary written into the preamble of the decree, under which the insurance payments could be counted in partial payment of the Atonement Tax. In the RJM's view, "the goal must be to free the insurance companies and extract the contribution without exception from the Jews."[28]

When it came to the *modus operandi*, however, the RJM wished to issue a decree making the insurance companies liable, thus obviating the need for discussions in the courts, but then in reality spare the insurance companies the need to pay by taking the money from the Jewish contribution. The only thing the insurance companies would have to pay under such an arrangement was the money owed to "Aryan" Germans and to foreigners, a sum the officials thought manageable for the insurance firms. This in no way satisfied either the RFM or the Four Year Plan representatives at the meeting. The former questioned whether the insurance companies, aside perhaps from some of the smaller glass companies, really were so badly off and felt that additional evidence was necessary, while the latter went further and argued that the assumption of insurance-company liability governing the various decrees could not be set aside. Insofar as § 7 of the Implementation Decree was concerned, this was interpreted as creating a measure of equity among the Jews so "that the small Jewish businessman, whose windows have been shattered, should not come away worse off than the rich Jew, whose villa remained untouched. For this reason one decided that the payments from the insurance claim should be counted toward the contribution."[29] Neither the RWM nor the RJM could accept this position, which in their view created legal insecurity. The by now infamous § 7 only made sense if the insurance companies were liable, and this was not the case, as the companies were in a position to demonstrate. Another way had to be found and, since there was no agreement, the RWM took it upon itself to draft a new decree, which would be submitted to the other ministries in an effort to solve the problem.

Needless to say, the insurance-industry leaders were well aware, even in the benighted Germany of 1938–1939, that they were complicit in a very shady endeavor, not in the sense that they were directly cheating Jews of insurance entitlements but rather in the sense that they were aiding and abetting the cover-up of government activities generally viewed as criminal in the civilized countries with which Germany still consorted. This can be seen most clearly from an extraordinarily frank letter Hilgard sent to Reich Economics Minister Funk on 17 December 1938 as a follow-up to the meeting of the previous day, which was intended as a last-minute appeal to avoid insurance company liability.[30] Hilgard spoke for both the private- and public-sector insurers in rejecting the idea that the insurance companies should pay for the punishment meted out on the Jews.

Once again Hilgard cited the Porto Allegre case, which demonstrated that the disturbances did not have to be directed against the government to count as disturbances, but he warned especially against the idea, suggested in the previous day's discussion, that the government could simply pass a law setting aside the court's decision. It would call forth, Hilgard warned, "a storm of outrage abroad." As evidence he cited an article in the British *News Chronicle*, which reported that many German insurance companies were facing bankruptcy because the damages to Jewish synagogues and businesses amounted to over 50 million pounds. Most German insurers, according to the article, carried reinsurance in England, but the English insurers were well aware that the Germans themselves had eliminated insurance for domestic disturbances from their policies, that the damage was done with the "quiet approval" of the government, and that "the [British] insurers can demonstrate that the police and the fire department did not do their duty, so that the insurers did not receive the measure of official protection that is the precondition for reinsurance." He pointed out that Swiss insurers were also involved, and that it was not in the interest of the State to have such questions brought to trial. Also, the reinsurers would expect the German insurers to demand that the terms of their own policies with regard to civic unrest be effectuated. Thus, the entire industry as well as the state would be embarrassed if liability were made an issue.

While Hilgard emphasized the alleged plight of small insurers, he warned very emphatically in the name of the entire industry against letting the question hang on whether or not the existence of individual firms were endangered by liability, "for it is self-evident that, if, for example, Allianz has to pay damages in the amount of perhaps 6 million as a result of the anti-Jewish demonstrations, it will not be toppled over. But one must be clear about the fact that every mark that is to be paid for this by the German insurance firms must somehow work out to the disadvantage of the other Aryan insured." There was therefore only one solution, namely, the one he had advocated in the meeting on the previous day, that the amount of insurance involved be taken from the Jewish contribution. About 50 million in damages had been reported, and if one assumes that the synagogues and other Jewish religious buildings are "not worthy of reconstruction," then one was left with about 40 million in damages. This was a sacrifice worth making to avoid the "very heavy psychological damages" that he had discussed. He further proposed that the insurance companies undertake the regulation of the damages and then be paid back in full measure. Hilgard did not omit to mention that the use of the insurance apparatus in this way involved considerable administrative costs to the insurance companies in any case, and he pleaded with Funk "not to deny the German insurance business these fully justified demands and to do everything to keep catastrophic harm away from the German insurance industry."

Particularly heavy artillery from the side of the insurers now entered the fray in the person of Kurt Schmitt, former General Director of Allianz, Reich Economics Minister in 1933–1934, and now General Director of the Münchener Rückversicherungs Gesellschaft. Schmitt sent a strictly confidential letter to Justice Minister Franz Gürtner on 20 December. It was clearly intended to move the discussion of the 9 November damages up in the hierarchy of both the industry and the government, a privilege Schmitt could allow himself as a former minister. Schmitt claimed that he had assumed that the decree transferring Jewish damage claims to the Reich had been issued so "as to prevent any discussion of the actual and legal issues related to this question." Now apparently "certain circles" in the government were actually planning to call on the insurance companies to pay. Schmitt insisted that, "under the existing laws," the companies had no liability because of the civil disturbance involved. Schmitt made it clear that he did not think it very wise to raise questions about this:

> Now the very determination as to whether there has been such a violation of the public order or not is unpleasant. But even if this were to be denied, the obligation to compensate would still not be a practical issue because of the possibilities for suits. I can certainly spare myself going into details about this and need only to point out that it would be unbearable if, for example, foreign insurance companies or reinsurers made the question of perpetration or the behavior of the police and the fire department a subject of court proceedings. It is an especially unpleasant complication of the present case that in many instances foreign insurance companies are involved as direct insurers and reinsurers, and according to foreign press reports one can expect that they would refuse to pay voluntarily. In this situation, there is only one practical way of forcing the insurance companies to pay, namely the issuance of a special law. I consider this idea, after the Jews have in general already been obligated to bear the costs of the damages, to be so impossible that I do not have to say a word about it. I believe that a more unusual and unjust special tax and intervention in existing legal relationships could hardly be thinkable.

Apparently, what was being done to the Jews was more "thinkable," and the peculiar juxtaposition of the "normal" and the "bizarre" in the relationship between the insurance business and the government at this point was heightened by the Christmas and New Year wishes with which Schmitt ended his letter. In any case, Schmitt noted that he was anxious to bring this "delicate complex of questions" to Gürtner's attention.[31]

The insurance industry was now mobilizing itself. While Gürtner, following a suggestion by Schmitt, invited Director Alois Alzheimer of Münchener Rück to take up discussions with councillor Hans Thees of the Justice Ministry, Hilgard had a circular sent on 27 December informing the industry of the line he was taking in dealing with the government, thereby making the position he and Goudefroy had taken the official position of the industry. On 4 January 1939, Alzheimer met with Thees and other officials and not only reiterated the by now usual arguments, but also indicated that the insurers would be prepared to accept liability de facto for "Aryans" and foreigners. The domestic reinsurers would also take on the obligation and, while one could try to get foreign reinsurers to take a similar stance, court cases had to be avoided. The bad news was that a number of insurance companies were already being taken to court and, when Thees asked that the RJM be regularly informed of all such cases, Alzheimer suggested that they make contact with Director Goudefroy of Allianz, who had apparently been given the job of serving as watchdog in this area.[32]

Finally, on 10 January, Hilgard sent a new memorandum to the Reich Economics Minister setting forth his position in detail and making concrete proposals for a solution.[33] What is interesting about this latest memorandum was the extent to which it gave priority to anti-Semitic considerations in making the case against insurance-company liability. Thus, because it would be counted toward the Atonement Tax, payment by the insurers would involve a shifting of the punishment to "purely German insurance communities." It would "weaken the profitability of German insurers in favor of the Jews and contradict the healthy feeling of justice among all national comrades to the highest degree." At the same time, the Reich would get no additional money because the payment would be credited to the contribution. To be sure, the Jews were also not entitled to compensation because of the civil disturbance involved, and Hilgard quite openly stated that there could be no legitimate charge against the companies for making "unjustified savings" by not paying the damages. Indeed, they were making a "significant sacrifice, if they voluntarily compensate the 'Aryan' insured and thereby would take away the Reich's obligation to compensate." Also, the German insurers could count on the foreign reinsurers to "leave them in the lurch," and foreign reinsurers would claim the right to go to court if they felt themselves victims of special legislation that undermined the basic standards written into insurance contracts. The long-term effect would be to undermine the international relations of the industry and its value for the procurement of foreign exchange. Hilgard saw no contradiction between his proposals and the decrees sequestering such insurance claims as may have existed and, picking up on an argument used by Schmitt, viewed the sequestration of insurance claims as necessary "in order to take away from the Jews the legitimacy to launch complaints and to bring the events of 8–10 November before the courts." It was also necessary to prevent "sensational trials before foreign courts" and prevent foreign Jews from using the issue "in a tendentious manner against the German Reich." He therefore proposed the following way of dealing with the problem: "The leader of the Reich Group Insurance announces in agreement with the relevant ministries that the insurance enterprises are not obligated to pay the direct or indirect damages to domestic or stateless Jews in connection with the events of 8–10 November 1938. However, the German insurance enterprises are obligated to compensate insured Jews of foreign citizenship and Aryans."

In the meantime, the pressure for a solution was increasing. On the one hand, foreign insurers and reinsurers were making inquiries with their German colleagues about the situation, and the bad press Germany was getting for the pogrom in general also contained reports that German insurance companies were threatened with bankruptcy because of the pogrom's costs. While dangers of insolvency were hotly denied, responses to more general inquiries were vague, generally stating that matters had not yet been decided and sometimes indicating that civil commotion clauses made liability unlikely.[34] On the other hand, the courts were already hearing some cases, and Hilgard urged the insurance companies to settle foreign claims immediately and generously, while explicitly disclaiming any liability "so that the payments could not be viewed as prejudicial with respect to claims made by domestic Jews."[35]

How much were the insurance companies paying and how large were the potential claims of German and stateless Jews? At the turn of 1938–1939, the insurance companies had some sense of actual and potential sums involved. Insofar as total damages in all insurance categories except health and accident were concerned, what appears to have been a final estimate at the end of January 1939 came to RM 49.5 million, 46.1 million of which was suffered by Jews and the remaining 3.4 million in almost equal total measure by German "Aryans" and Jewish and non-Jewish foreigners. Glass was by far the most important category, amounting to 2.1 million.[36] Given the international complications involved, one may reasonably assume that the amounts were paid out promptly, although it is worth noting that Hilgard, undoubtedly acting under instructions connected with the impending war, issued very secret instructions on 25 July 1939 that no payments were to be made to Poles.[37]

The balance of the potential claims could be made by German Jews. According to the breakdown of damages provided by the insurance companies, they suffered RM 38.2 million in fire damage, RM 4.4 million in glass damage, and RM 3.1 million in theft and break-in. When Hilgard reported the final liabilities of the companies to German Jews to Ministerialrat Daniel of the RWM on 30 January 1939, however, these came to fire damages of RM 19,622,329 and break-in and theft damages of RM 3,566,763. The purpose of Hilgard's report was to provide the RWM with that statistical material needed to inform Göring and the Finance Ministry of the sums involved and to plead the case for the insurance companies not being held liable. Hilgard well understood that it was in his interest to keep the final figures presented to the government as low as possible, since the more Göring and the RFM thought they might lose, the more they would push for the imposition of liability. At the same time, he and his allies in the RWM were very aware that his figures on German-Jewish claims were potentially much higher than what was being reported. Many Jews had not bothered, but might if they knew the companies were liable, while others were in concentration camps and could not apply.[38]

This, of course, only heightened the importance of lowering the potential liability. The circumstances of Germany's Jews were of help here, since Hilgard spoke only of claims made by the Jews up to the time of his letter rather than of potential claims. Also, the ministerial officials had asked to report only such claims as might be legally incontestable. There were some Jews who did have insurance against public disturbance, the total sum involved coming to RM 38,000, and they could possibly have made claims. Excluding them from the reported claims was tantamount to denying them payment, a rather ironic, not to say hypocritical, position in view of the fact that the insurers considered the pogrom a public disturbance. In any case, the figures Hilgard now reported were almost ten million short of the amount estimated for fire and theft and break-in because they included only actual claims and those viewed as incontestable in court. This did not end the whittling down of the final sum, however. Hilgard proceeded to argue that RM 16,055,566 of the fire insurance and RM 79,000 of the break-in and theft insurance pertained to synagogues and other Jewish institutional buildings. If one subtracted these amounts, then the amount of insurance that could be claimed was RM 3,566,763 in fire insurance and RM 2,995,239 for break-in and theft, making a total of RM 6,522,002. This was the amount, Hilgard argued, that the Reich would lose if it accepted his proposal. While Hilgard's global figures did not include the publicly chartered insurance companies, which had greater liability in their contracts and were most responsible for insuring synagogues and such buildings, Hilgard urged that those companies be freed of any such liability as well, "since here one is dealing with the destruction of public property not worthy of protection."[39] This was, to say the least, a remarkable notion since the insurance companies had issued policies on these buildings and collected premiums.

Furthermore, while Hilgard's sleight of hand was neatly aided by his use of anti-Semitic screed, it is significant also to note that there was one important branch of insurance simply left out of his calculations and argumentation, namely, the glass-insurance branch, where German Jews had suffered RM 4,430,000 in damages. The companies involved were already liable for RM 2.1 million in damage to "Aryans" and foreigners. Apparently, Hilgard and the RWM were by this time very confident of their case that liability for glass damages would ruin many of the small mutual companies and severely damage others. These costs would simply be left to the Jewish obligation to clean up and restore the appearance of the streets. Potential benefits from insurance-company liability in the form of a reduction of the Atonement Tax by the amount of insurance paid on a Jew's behalf to the Revenue Office would not be allowed to come into play with respect to glass damages. Indeed, the Economics Ministry was strongly supportive of Hilgard's position, happy that the amount had been reduced to "only" RM 6.5 million, pleased that the companies were going to pay off "Aryans" and foreigners, satisfied that the glass companies were not included since they were supposed to replace damages in kind anyway and were not included in the Implementation Decree of the Atonement Tax under which insurance payments for the damages were to be credited against the tax, and happy to have the civic-unrest question relegated to the sidelines.[40]

Nevertheless, it was to be months before the matter was settled, and there was to be a good deal of hard bargaining along the way, especially with the

Finance Ministry, the details of which cannot be discussed here. Hilgard became increasingly emboldened in his resistance to the RFM, thanks to the possibilities opened up by the recently promulgated 14th Decree to the Law on the Settlement of Civil Law Claims of 13 March 1939, which was directly concerned with the pogrom damages and enabled the Interior Ministry to close down court cases and settle claims according to its own guidelines. Under § 3 of this decree, German and stateless Jews were not entitled to receive any compensation through such mediation by the Interior Ministry, so that the Justice Ministry or the Interior Ministry could literally throw such cases out of court without a hearing. Hilgard believed that the insurance companies would do well in remaining cases brought before the Interior Ministry, a not unreasonable conclusion since his colleague Goudefroy was constantly reporting all cases taken to court connected with the pogrom to the Justice Ministry in the hope that they would be suspended and handled under the 13 March decree.[41]

The wily and tenacious Hilgard persistently demonstrated his skills as a behind-the-scenes operator in the politics of the Third Reich. By early July, Schwandt of the RFM had cut his demands to 3 million, but Hilgard would have none of it, arguing that the statute of limitations on claims for break-in and theft had passed so that the legal situation of the insurers was better than before. When Schwandt threatened to pass a law forcing the insurers to pay, Regierungsrat Segelcke of the RWM broke the impasse by pointing out that, while a law was not likely at this point and the legal situation was favorable to the insurers, Hilgard ought really to voluntarily offer a "certain compensatory payment," which he "would very much welcome in the interest of the reputation of the insurance industry." After further discussion, Hilgard offered "at the most" RM 1.5 million to the Finance Ministry, a sum that Schwandt declared "only of interest to the RFM if at least one-quarter of the damages reported by the Jews are thereby covered."[42] Hilgard was asked to supply the necessary information as well as an accounting of the amounts paid out to foreigners and German "Aryans."

While there does not appear to be a record of the exact figures and information supplied by Hilgard, the RM 1.5 million figure seems to have been the accepted point of departure. Synagogues and Jewish buildings and glass damages had been eliminated from that calculation from the very outset. Indeed, the total amount of such claims seems to have been less than anticipated because, as Hilgard reported, of "the correction of some damage reports." Whatever the case, Hilgard managed to pay even less than he had promised, since in the final accounting with the government on 14 October 1939, he reported a total payment from the Reich Group to the treasury of RM 1,297,988, 1,074,828 of it coming from the private insurers of the "old Reich," 190,010 coming from the publicly chartered companies, and 17,988 from the Ostmark (Austria). Thus, Hilgard seemed to have managed to save yet another RM 200,000. The RM 1.3 million paid to the treasury did not, of course, include the sums paid directly to "Aryans" and foreigners, although money undoubtedly was saved on the Poles.[43]

This extra benefit to the insurers probably was the outcome of the charade that the insurers and the ministerial officials had concocted to deal with the insured Jews. The projected lump sum payment to the Treasury was not without its complications since it was intended to be in lieu of insurance claims to German Jews and Germans in the categories of fire and theft. The Reich Group, therefore, instructed its members on 3 August to plan to make fictional payments to Jews who had made claims in the amount of 50 percent of their claim for fire and theft. They were also to make believe that they were compensating glass insurance if the customer happened to have a comprehensive policy for fire and/or theft insurance as well. No letter would be sent to Jews who only had glass insurance. The basis of the calculation would not be explained to the customer, and all claims had to be presented by 15 August. The model for such a letter to Jewish insurers was as follows:

> *To the Jewish policyholder.*
> *Re: Fire insurance policy No. ...*
>   *Break-in and Theft insurance policy No. ...*
>   *Glass-Insurance policy No. ...*
> *(non-applicable categories to be crossed out)*
>   *On the basis of the above insurance policy(ies) a sum in the amount of*
>   *RM ....*
>
> Is granted to you due to the events of November 1938 on the basis of an understanding with the Reich Finance Ministry and the Reich Economics Ministry, the Reich Justice Ministry and the Reich Interior Ministry without recognizing a legal obligation in view of the doubtfulness of the case. The payment of the sum is made on the basis of § 2, para. 2 of the Decree on the Restoration of the Appearance of the Streets at Jewish businesses of 12 November 1938, Reich Legal Journal I, p. 1581, and the Implementation Decree for the Atonement Tax of the Jews of 21 November 1938, Reich Legal Journal I, p. 1638, directly to the Reich.
>
> You are entitled to deduct the above-mentioned sum from the last partial payment due on 15 August 1939 on the basis of the Decree on the Atonement Payment of Jews of German Citizenship of 12 November 1938, Reich Legal Journal I, p. 1579.
>
> No further claims against us exist on the basis of the existing insurance policies as a result of the events of 8–10 November 1938.[44]

The Role of Networks

Thus ended this extraordinary exercise in state-sanctioned collective moral turpitude, but it also illustrated the corruption of the very meaning of business morals in connection with the despoliation of the Jews. The only "proper" position for the insurers was to insist that the entire pogrom was a public disturbance and that they owed nothing, as was in fact held by the courts after the war with respect to Jewish claimants. This, however, because of the vagaries of § 7 of the Implementation Decree of November 21 to the Atonement Tax, would have deprived the Jews of any relief whatever. Of more relevance to our purposes here, however, is that the entire story proved a highly significant illustration of the role played by networks in the economic history of the Holocaust. It pitted the insurance industry against Göring's Four-Year Plan Office and the Finance Ministry, which sought to collect as much as possible from the insurance industry as well as the Jews. Thanks to the organization of the Reich Group and the leadership and negotiating skills of Hilgard, the industry demonstrated remarkable discipline in following its leader, and Hilgard was thus able to mobilize the more sympathetic Reich Economics Ministry and Reich Justice Ministry and, through Goudefroy, keep abreast of developments in the courts and thus have unpleasant cases settled by the also sympathetic Interior Ministry. In this way, the demands of Göring and the RFM were constantly whittled down. In the process, however, Hilgard and his colleagues constantly argued their case in terms that legitimized the pogrom and the arguments used by Goebbels and the regime to defend it. The damage controlled was the damage to the insurance industry, not of course to the Jews, and the price the insurance industry had to pay was payment to foreigners, in order to prevent international complications, and engagement in a charade what helped further to undermine their inhibitions about complicity in the crimes of the regime.

Notes

1. Saul Friedländer, *Nazi Germany and the Jews*. Vol. I. *The Years of Persecution, 1933–1939* (New York, 1997), pp. 257–279; Wolfgang Benz, "Der Rückfall in die Barbarei. Bericht über den Pogrom," in Walter H. Pehle, ed., *Der Judenpogrom 1938. Von der 'Reichskristallnacht' zum Völkermord* (Frankfurt on Main, 1988), pp. 13–51.
2. *Die Tagebücher von Joseph Goebbels*, edited by Elke Fröhlich, assisted by Jana Richter (Munich, 1998), part 1, vol. 6, p. 182.
3. Rundschreiben (RS) Abteilung Glas-Versicherung, Allianz u. Stuttgarter Verein, 8. Aug. 1932, 4. Nov. 1932, 30. März 1933, 1. April 1933, Firmenhistorisches Archiv der Allianz AG (FHA), S 17.22/180.
4. Peter Longerich, *Politik der Vernichtung. Eine Gesamtdarstellung der nationalsozialistischen Judenverfolgung* (Munich/Zürich, 1998), pp. 36, 595.
5. RS Deutscher Glasversicherungs-Verband, 20. Juni 1938, Archiv des Gesamtverbandes der Deutschen Versicherungswirtschaft, e.V. (GDV), RS/45; Bericht betr. Judenaktion in Berlin vom 17. 6. bis 21.6.38, Sonderarchiv Moscow (SM), 500-1-645, Bl. 32–37.
6. Reichsaufsichtsamt an die Wirtschaftsgruppe Privatversicherung, 20. April 1938, Historisches Archiv der Münchener Rückversicherungs-Gesellschaft, München (MR), G 1/1. See the Beiratssitzung der Fachgruppe Feuerversicherung, 28 June 1938, SM 1458/1/178/Bl. 92–111; Beiratssitzung, Fachgruppe Glasversicherung, 26 October 1938, SM 1458/1/225/Bl. 70–71. See the various RS of the RAA and Allianz of 1937 in Bundesarchiv Koblenz (BAK) B280, 12285/Bl. 49–51.
7. Wirtschaftsgruppe Privatversicherung der Reichsgruppe Versicherungen an die Fachgruppen, 11. Nov. 1938, GDV, RS/46.
8. See the discussion in Andre Botur, *Privatversicherung im Dritten Reich. Zur Schadensabwicklung nach der Reichskristallnacht unter dem Einfluß nationalsozialistischer Rassen- und Versicherungspolitik.* [Berliner Juristische Universitätsschriften. Zivilrecht, Bd. 6] (Berlin/Baden-Baden 1995), pp. 71–73. This is an outstanding study. The author, however, did not have access to the Moscow Sonderarchiv files.

9. This conflict is discussed at considerable length in Gerald D. Feldman, *Allianz and the German Insurance Business, 1933–1945* (New York/Cambridge, 2001).
10. Stenographische Niederschrift von einem Teil der Besprechung über die Judenfrage unter Vorsitz von Feldmarschall Göring im RLA am 12. November 1933, 11 Uhr, in: International Military Tribunal, Urkunden und Beweismaterial, vol. 4, Document 1816-PS, pp. 499–540 (hereinafter cited as Document 1816-PS).
11. Eduard Hilgard, "Mein Leben in der Allianz" (unpublished memoirs), FHA, NL2/7, p. 107.
12. Document 1816-PS, p. 511.
13. Ibid., p. 516.
14. Ibid.
15. Joseph Walk, ed., *Das Sonderrecht für die Juden im NS-Staat*, 2nd ed. (Heidelberg, 1996), p. 253ff.
16. Hilgard, "Mein Leben," p. 110, FHA., NL 2/7.
17. See Hilgard's interrogation of 14.7.47 in Institut für Zeitgeschichte (IfZ), OMGUS (FINAD), 2-57-6.
18. RS Wirtschaftsgruppe Privatversicherung, 18.11.38, GDV, RS/15. The call for speedy transmittal of such information was reiterated in an RS of 21.11.38, ibid.
19. RS Wirtschaftsgruppe Privatversicherung, 24.11.38 and 29.11.38, GDV, RS/20.
20. Hilgard to Lange, 6.12.38 and his memorandum of 5.12.38, "Bestehen Versicherungsansprüche deutscher oder staatenloser Juden auf Grund der Vorgänge vom 8.–10. November 1938?" in SM, 1458-1-98, Bl. 147-153.
21. *Völkischer Beobachter*, 12 November 1933.
22. RGBl, I, 1934, S. 1235-1236; I, 1939, S. 614, and Walk, *Sonderrecht*, I-487, pp. 99, 288.
23. Vermerk über das Ergebnis der Besprechung im RMdJ. Am 8. Dezember 1938 zur Frage der Gewährung von Schadenersatz für Verluste, die im Zuge der Aktion gegen die Juden am 8., 9. und 10. November 1938 entstanden sind, Bundesarchiv Berlin (BAB) R 30.01/10788, Bl. 356-360. For die Vierzehnte Verordnung zur Durchführung und Ergänzung des Gesetzes über den Ausgleich bürgerlich-rechtlicher Ansprüche vom 18. März 1939, see RGBl, I, S. 614 and "Wiedergutmachung von Schäden aus den Aktionen vom 8. November 1938 und den folgenden Tagen," Reichsminister des Innern an die Landesregierungen, 28. März 1939, BAB R 18/3746b.
24. Vermerk Ministerialrat Dr. Daniel, 9.12.38, SM, 1458-1-98, Bl. 164-165.
25. The meeting was originally scheduled for the 14th. There are two reports on the meeting, the first by Ministerialrat Hans Thees of the Justice Ministry, the second by Regierungsrat Segelcke of the RWM. The former is to be found in BAB R 30.01/10788, Bl. 353-354, the latter in SM, 1458-1-98, Bl. 169-172.
26. SM, 1458-1-98, Bl. 169.
27. Ibid., Bl. 170.
28. Vermerk Thees, BAB R 31.01/10788, Bl. 373 and complaints of the RJM about non-participation in the Impelementation Decree of Nov. 25, 1938, BAB, R 31.01/10787, Bl. 118. See also Botur, *Privatversicherung*, pp. 185–186.
29. Vermerk Segelcke, SM 1458-1-98, Bl. 171.
30. For the discussion and quotations that follow, see Hilgard an Funk, 17. December 1938, SM, 1458-1-98, Bl. 177-182.
31. Schmitt an Gürtner, 20.12.38, BAB R 30.01/10788, Bl. 361–362.
32. Gürtner an Schmitt, 21.12.38, ibid., Bl. 363, and RS Wirtschaftsgruppe Privatversicherung v. 27.12.38, Bl. 377, Vermerk Thees, 4.1.39, Bl. 381–384.
33. Hilgard an den Herrn Reichswirtschaftsminister, 10.1.39, ebd., Bl. 388–390.
34. See, for example, the correspondence between Münchner Rück and its London correspondent, Dr. C.E. Golding, 24 and 30 November 1938, between B.B. Fischer of the Royal Exchange Assurance and A. Martini of 1and 14 December 1938, and the correspondence with the L'Union des Propriétaires Belges between March and May 1939 in MR, G 1/8.
35. Schreiben Hilgard an die Wirtschaftsgruppe, 1. Februar 1939, BAB R 30.01/10788, Bl. 479. and Oberlandsgerichtspräsident Bergmann an den RJM, 31. Januar 1939 und Ver-

merk, 4. Februar 1939, BAB R 30.01/10788, Bl. 415–416. See also Rundschreiben der Wirtschaftsgruppe Privatversicherung, 2. Februar 1939, GDV, RS/19.
36. Aufstellung, 26 January, 1939, SM, 1458-1-98, Bl. 236. This is a more accurate estimate of potential insurance company liability than that employed at the 12 November meeting in the Air Ministry of RM 225 million, taken over by Avraim Barkai in his important "Schicksalsjahr 1938. Kontinuität und Verschärfung der wirtschaftlichen Ausplünderung der Juden," in Pehle, ed., *Der Judenpogrom 1938*, p. 115. Hermann Graml also speaks of 225 million in his *Reichskristallnacht. Antisemitismus und Judenverfolgung im Dritten Reich* (Munich, 1988), p. 178.
37. See RS Wirtschaftsgruppe Privatversicherung, 25. Juli 1939, GDV, RS/16.
38. Autenrieth an das RWM, Ministerialrat Dr. Daniel, 21. Dezember 1938, SM, 1458-1-98, Bl. 217-218. For Hilgard's use of these figures, see Hilgard to Daniel, 30. Januar 1939, ibid., Bl. 238-239.
39. Hilgard to Daniel, 30 January 1939, ibid.
40. Schreiben Lange an den RJM und RFM, Feb. 3, 1939, BAB R 30.01/10788, Bl. 425-426.
40. Vermerk Daniel, 16. Mai 1939, SM, 1458-1-98, Bl. 273-274. Botur, *Privatversicherung*, pp. 197–202, did not have this information on the RFM demands at his disposal, which explains his puzzlement over the sums at which Hilgard and the RFM finally arrived. See, however, his excellent discussion of the 14th Decree, pp. 202–210.
42. Niederschrift über die Sitzung des Beirats der Fachgruppe 7 am 28. Juni 1939, SM 1458-1-147, Bl. 71, and Vermerk, 6. Juli 1939, SM 1458-1-98, Bl. 277.
43. Reichsgruppe Versicherung an den Herrn Reichswirtschaftsminister, 14. Oktober 1939, ebd. Bl. 290, and Wirtschaftsgruppe Privatversicherung an alle Feuer- und Glas-Versicherungsgesellschaften, 13. November 1939, GDV, RS/16.
44. Reichsgruppe Versicherungen an die Wirtschaftsgruppe Privatversicherung und die Wirtschaftsgruppe "Öffentlich-Rechtliche Versicherung," 3. August 1939, SM 1458/1/98/Bl. 283-285 and BAB R 30.01/10789, Bl. 91–93.

Part IV

"Structure," "Agency," and the Logic of Radicalization

CHAPTER 17

MORE THAN JUST A METAPHOR: THE NETWORK CONCEPT AND ITS POTENTIAL IN HOLOCAUST RESEARCH*

Jörg Raab

Introduction

What the contributions to the present volume reveal, in accordance with earlier findings,[1] is that the persecution and annihilation of European Jewry under Nazi rule was a division-of-labor-based crime in the sense that the core group of perpetrators, under tight control of central agencies, notably the Reichssicherheitshauptamt, relied on a highly differentiated structure of institutional and individual actors. While some of these structures had been deliberately created, others were integrated in the persecution machinery according to local circumstances and opportunities. The "society of organizations"[2] as such delivered large parts of the infrastructure of the Holocaust.[3]

The present volume attempts to both enrich the empirical illustration and to enhance our theoretical understanding of the Holocaust as a division-of-labor-based crime. What, then, can be said about the general nature of division of labor and how it was, presumably, related to networks of persecution during the Holocaust?

Division of labor, without further qualifications, remains a vague term. It may, in fact, occur at an individual, an organizational, an interorganizational, a societal, and even an international level. In general, four types of division of labor can be identified: by function or task, by object, by place, or by clients.[4] Division of labor by function or task is also often labeled as functional differentiation. Division of labor makes specialization and standardization of tasks possible, which create economies of scale and as a consequence lead to enormous gains in efficiency and productivity or—for that matter—in destructive capabilities. However, no matter what specific type of division of labor at what level is applied, coordination or reintegration of the various units performing different tasks is mandatory in order to achieve the overall goals and reap the efficiency gains.

Integration can be achieved on the one hand, through functional-organizational mechanisms of coordination. Here direct mutual coordination (formal and/or informal communication, integrating committees, liaison individuals, or groups)[5] and standardization of behavior or programming (ex ante coordination)[6] can be distinguished. Hierarchical coordination can be seen as a special form, in which personal command is based on a formal hierarchy.[7] On the other hand, integration can also be achieved through cognitive-cultural mechanisms. These are generally shared beliefs within a society outside the organization (common values, common culture, common socialization) and shared beliefs within the organization (common visions, shared norms of cooperation, unity of purpose, corporate identity).

A second mechanism which is more intentional and easier to create, is the orientation towards common goals. As Renate Mayntz puts it: "the overall task of an enterprise works as a motive of coordination, which counters the centrifugal tendencies of specialization and segmentation."[8]

Consequently, division of labor inevitably requires reintegration and coordination. In this chapter, I argue that the network concept can be used as an overarching framework to analyze functionally differentiated actor systems of persecution within the Holocaust and their reintegration. Especially when several rather distinct organizational entities produce specific outputs together, the network concept is a very useful way to think about, analyze, and categorize those systems.

The network concept has had a huge reception in the social sciences in the last twenty years, and network analysis is regarded as one of the major innovations in sociology in the last decades. The broad application of the network concept is inevitably accompanied by a multitude of meanings and understandings of the term. In this chapter, four meanings are distinguished: network as an analytical tool; network as a social structure; network as a governance form; and network as theory. After having presented these perspectives, I will evaluate their respective relevance to Holocaust research.

It is important to acknowledge that "structural analysis" does not mean to deny intention or ideology as crucial determinants of the Holocaust; in the end it is people and not structures that murder, but it is these structures that enable or restrict actions with certain intentions. What is more, these structures can never be completely and most often only marginally shaped, even in dictatorial regimes. But ultimately all approaches and concepts are only useful if they contribute additional knowledge in answering "the real question: precisely how genocide could happen, how an unbalanced, paranoid hatred and chiliastic vision became reality and implemented as horrific government practice."[9]

Networks of Persecution —Mapping the Analytical Framework

The term "network" has been one of the most widely used notions in the social sciences for the last two decades. In a very broad definition it can be understood as a set of social entities linked directly or indirectly by various ties. Besides a general metaphorical use, at least four concepts attached to the term "network" can be identified in the literature.[10] First, the concept of "network" is applied as an empirical tool to describe social structure. Secondly, network is used as a label for a specific type of social structure. Thirdly, it is a concept to describe and analyze forms of governance, i.e., forms of coordinating social activity. Fourthly, it is used as a notion to summarize different theses within the first three meanings. These theses could form a network theory, i.e., a consistent body of variables about the development, structure, functions, functioning, dissolution, and consequences of networks. Needless to say, these concepts are not independent of each other, but distinguishing the concepts for heuristic purposes can lead to additional insights. In the following, these four meanings of "network" are briefly elaborated.

Network as an Empirical Tool

Network analysis as an empirical tool has been one of the major innovations in the social sciences in the last thirty years and has recently been applied more and more in policy analysis as well. The current concepts and methods for structural analysis emerged at the end of the 1960s, when a group led by Harrison C. White at Harvard University achieved a major breakthrough, and spread widely during the 1970s, although basic concepts of sociometry and graph theory had been developed since the 1930s. Two reasons have led to the success of network analysis as a paradigm and an empirical tool. First, concepts were based on relations rather than attributes. By concentrating their attention on the ties between social entities, rather than on the qualities possessed by them, it forces social scientists to think in terms of constraints and options that are inherent in the way social relations are organized.[11] Network analysis is therefore based on an "anticategorical imperative, which rejects all attempts to explain human behavior or social processes solely in terms of categorical attributes of actors, whether individual or collective."[12] At the center of analysis, therefore, are not attributes such as age, gender, social status, political affiliation, religious beliefs, ethnicity, or psychological predisposition, but the relations between social entities as a means of explaining why people behave the way they do and why certain outcomes come about.[13] In the context of this research, it is a strategy that focuses less on factors like the number of German troops, the number of German SD/Gestapo personnel, the personality and ideology of leading figures, on the German as well as on the indigenous and Jewish side or geographical conditions. Rather, the center of attention is the multiple relations between actors directly or indirectly participating in the persecution of the Jews and the prominence of these actors, as well as the frequency and density of their interactions.

The two basic components of all network analyses are a set of objects (called nodes, positions, or actors) and a set of relations among these objects (called edges, ties, or links).[14] In the context of Holocaust research, nodes could be leading figures of the German security apparatus and the occupation administration, as well as representatives of the indigenous police forces and administration. It is also possible, however, to conceptualize nodes as whole organizations or parts of organizations, such as the different departments of the German occupation administration, the central agencies in Berlin, the Jewish Council, the indigenous ministries, etc. Ties that could be interesting to investigate in Holocaust research are communication linkages, command and control relations, conflicts, or joint involvement in actions against the Jewish population.

Network analysis is not a neutral statistical method and it is not a theory but an empirical tool to describe social structure on the basis of relations between social entities.[15] It is nonetheless analytically formal in that it mandates systematic and replicable routines, requires strict coding rules, and has an internal logic or algorithm that produces descriptive or inferential results.[16] Its wide applicability has meanwhile been demonstrated in a variety of disciplines, such as anthropology, social psychology, political science, economics, sociology, epidemiology, and history, to name but a few. The strength of the methodology is based on the availability of the following tools:

1. well-developed data collection procedures;
2. conceptualizations, i.e., methods for analyzing and measuring the structural properties of whole systems (centralization, hierarchization, density, etc.) and of the social positions of the single social entities within these systems (centrality, clique membership, prestige, structural equivalence, etc.); and
3. the availability of sophisticated statistical procedures to calculate these measures, which are meanwhile implemented in standard calculation and visualization software.

Based on this "toolbox," the principal achievement of network analysis "has been to transform a merely metaphorical understanding of the embeddedness of actors in networks of social relationships into a more precise and usable tool for social analysis."[17] It is now possible to operationalize and measure the relational properties of social systems and the encompassing units by collecting data on virtually any social relation between these units of interest to the researcher, which can be summarized as follows:[18]

1. Transaction relations: actors exchange control over physical or symbolic media.
2. Communication relations: linkages between actors are channels by which messages may be transmitted from one actor to another in a system.

3. Boundary penetration relations: the ties between actors consist of constituent subcomponents held in common, for example, corporation boards of directors with overlapping members.
4. Instrumental relations: actors contact one another in efforts to secure valuable goods, services or information, such as a job, an abortion, political advice, recruitment to a social movement.
5. Sentiment relations: perhaps the most frequently investigated networks are those in which individuals express their feelings of affection, admiration, deference, loathing, or hostility toward each other.
6. Authority/power relations: these networks, usually occurring in complex formal organizations, indicate the rights and obligations of actors to issue and obey formal commands.

Usually, social entities in a system are connected by several types of ties. In network analysis a network is regarded as a set of actors connected by one type of tie (toft). Thus analyzing political or economic systems, we find several networks among the same set of actors, which can have a quite different form, depending on the tie.

The main instrument for collecting network data for research on temporary social structures is the questionnaire, where people are asked about their personal relationships or are asked as representatives about the relationships of their organizational bodies. But relational data has also been gathered by monitoring electronic communication, analyzing cross-ownership of companies in annual reports, and using membership lists of organizations or archival records of enlistment, marriage, and trade relations. The methods and substance of data collection in historical-sociological analysis will be reviewed in more detail below.

Network as Social Structure

One of the fundamental assumptions in network analysis is the belief that structures have a certain stability, which leads to its rather static character. When applying the "network" notion in the analysis of economic, political, and social processes and outcomes, it is assumed that after some time actors have built more or less stable exchange relations, which are not changed fundamentally by "superficial" everyday events.[19] In most cases the nodes within a policy network represent corporative or collective political or administrative actors, such as ministries and government agencies, or societal actors, such as associations and unions, or even private actors, such as companies that occupy specific positions or roles. Very often, these actors are formal organizations or parts of them. "Network" in this respect, however, is seen as a social structure with very specific features. In policy making it is regarded as an arrangement characterized by a predominance of informal communicative relations, a horizontal as opposed to a hierarchical pattern of relations, and a decentralized pattern of actors' positions.[20] In economic sociology, networks are often seen as horizontally structured systems of production and exchange, with a predominance of informal ties and loosely coupled relations, in contrast to a tightly coupled, rigid, hierarchical organization. The difference between the two usages of "network" is that in the first instance it is possible to conceptualize any social structure (even pure hierarchies) as a network and apply the analytical toolbox of network analysis. In the second instance "network" is meant as a structure with very specific features. For Holocaust research, that means that we will not necessarily find a network with a horizontal structure and loosely coupled relations, because a multitude of actors are involved. Rather, a close analysis has to reveal what the social structure actually looked like, if possible based not only on one type of relationship but on various ones. The more information the researcher has about different relationships, the more accurate the analysis will be, because cases could occur in which a social system has a quite dense and decentral communication structure but at the same time a quite hierarchical command and control structure.

Network as a Form of Governance

Starting with Williamson's *Markets and Hierarchies* in 1975, in which the author elaborated Coase's basic ideas about the determinants for the organization of economic activities, a rich body of literature has developed on different forms of governance over the last two decades.[21] For some time transaction costs as the major explanatory factor to explain special forms of social organization were applied only in economics. It was only a few years ago that the discussion in economics, organization theory, and political science converged in a common literature. Central to it were the questions about the factors that lead to hierarchical, network, or market arrangements and about the conditions under which the different forms have comparative advantages.[22] A broad discussion thereby developed on the questions whether networks are simply a combination of elements of market and hierarchy—and could therefore be placed on a continuum somewhere between market and hierarchy—or whether they are better understood as unique forms of governance in their own right.[23]

Central to the concept of network as a form of governance is the understanding of network as an emergent organizational entity, i.e., as a new form of social organization, which is more than the sum of the actors and their links and which is more than a combination of elements of hierarchy and markets. Networks can be more than a short stop between market and hierarchy: they can represent a qualitatively new type of governance through a combination of elements of the other two basic coordination mechanisms. These elements are the existence of a plurality of autonomous actors, as found within markets, and the capability to pursue collective goals through deliberately coordinated actions, which is one of the major elements of hierarchies.[24] In this approach "network" is conceived and interpreted as a discrete form of governance, and together with market and hierarchy, as an ideal type of coordination. The characteristics of this ideal type are seen not

Table 17.1 Forms of Governance: Market, Hierarchy, and Network in Comparison

Form of Governance	Market	Hierarchy	Network
Basis of legitimacy	Contract: property rights	Employment: rights of order and direction	Exchange
Mechanism of control/coordination	Price	Authority/rules	None
Type of conflict resolution	Exit	Loyalty	Voice
Can collective goals be achieved?	No	Yes	Yes
Mode of decision making	Decentralized, "invisible hand"	Central	Multilateral
Status of actors	Autonomous, independent	Dependent	Autonomous but interdependent
Dominant orientation of actors	Self-interest	Achievement of organizational goals	Solution of a common problem
Dominant type of differentiation	Segmentation (supply and demand)	Functional and structural differentiation (levels of hierarchy)	Functional differentiation (division of labor by task)
Dominant type of integration	Exchange of goods, services and money	Common organizational goal, formal rules	Common topic/problem, exchange/pooling of resources and information
Social structure	Atomized	Vertical	Horizontal
Functional logic	Competition	Order/obedience, sub-/superordination	Negotiation

Sources: Parts of the table were adapted from Powell, "Neither Market Nor Hierarchy: Network Forms of Organization," *Research in Organizational Behavior* 12 (1990) p. 300, and Helmut Willke, *Systemtheorie III: Steuerungstheorie* (Stuttgart/Jena, 1995), p. 137, who describe the characteristics and functioning of the three ideal types of governance in detail.

only in a specific structural feature of the system of production and exchange, but also in the mode of conflict resolution, the basis of legitimacy, the general (cognitive) orientation and incentives of the actors, etc., as is shown in Table 17.1.

It is claimed by the proponents of this approach[25] that it is possible not only to achieve more conceptual clarity but also to develop a refined analytical instrument, with which actor coordination in concrete policy or economic systems can be modeled as a specific mixture of these basic forms.[26]

The integration of the discussion in economics, organization theory, and political science had two consequences. First, scholars had a less normative and more flexible notion for the description of new arrangements in policy making. Secondly, the discussion on and comparison of markets, hierarchies, and networks, which was taken from economics, had a strong functionalist and economic flavor.[27] A major concern was effectiveness and efficiency and the classical questions of political science were more and more superseded. In empirical policy network studies one rarely reads about power and influence, legitimacy, interests, democracy, etc. This was substantively different in the early network studies. They focused explicitly on the analysis of political structures, especially on power structures.[28] Therefore, it is necessary to separate the discussion on network as a governance form, network as a specific social structure, and network as an analytical tool to address questions of power, influence, and responsibility more accurately, which are a special concern in Holocaust research. With network as an analytical tool, influence and power can be operationalized in terms of centrality or prestige of actors on the basis of the respective types of tie. On the other hand, thinking in terms of governance and not only in terms of social structure opens up a new perspective. Systems of governance made up of different organizations, whether their features come close to a network or rather represent a mixed type, can be seen as an organization of a "higher order"[29] or as an "emergent"[30] form of organization, which produce outcomes that cannot be attributed to any single organization alone. Moreover, the process and therefore the outcome cannot be completely controlled by any individual organization. This is an idea that has some similarities to the ones expressed in the concept of "cumulative radicalization."[31] namely that interaction effects create results that were not foreseen and cannot be controlled by any single organization. However, that does not mean that these results necessarily go against the goals or convictions of these actors.

The different views on networks have great implications not only for the analysis of the structure and the processes but also for the evaluation of the outcome. In the context of Holocaust research, this goes right to the question of ultimately personal responsibility and the question of the comparative importance of intentions versus structures. This question will be explored in more detail below.

Network as Theory

If one agrees with the thesis that a network is a discrete emergent social entity that is more than just the sum of its integral parts, one can follow the usual path of generating scientific knowledge.[32] First the phenomenon is discovered and described. Then definitions are formulated and the search for categories starts. In a second step scholars look for explanatory factors of the phenomenon. In a third step the research perspective changes. The former *explanandum* is turned into the explanatory factor (*explanans*) to analyze and explain either classical phenomena or new phenomena that are linked to the newly discovered fact. In the last three decades an extensive literature has developed on social networks in general and on inter-organizational and policy networks in particular. This literature describes and categorizes networks as the perceived new phenomenon, searches for explanatory factors, and tries to explain the consequences.

The formulated hypotheses of all three steps form a theoretical body, although in a strict sense a theory is characterized by its dependent variable. To become a single body a set of consistent hypotheses has to be formulated. In most instances in the social sciences several competing theories and approaches exist for the description and explanation of social phenomena. Therefore, it is likely that in the future we will find a theory of network governance, a network theory of organizations,[33] a contingency theory of networks,[34] an institutionalist theory of networks, a constructivist theory of networks,[35] etc. As Emirbayer and Goodwin state:[36] "There moreover remains the question as to how structures of all types—cultural as well as societal—interrelate with social action itself and with the very potential for human agency. These questions require that we consider, in turn, the influence that cultural and societal formations have upon social actors and the transformative impact that social actors, for their own part, have upon cultural and societal structures."

Therefore, "network" could serve as an integrating framework, in which—on the basis of social actors and their relations—a wide array of questions about structure and agency could be dealt with, which is also a core issue for Holocaust research.

In the following, however, I will mainly come back to the first three understandings of "network." It is used as an analytical tool, as a social structure, and as a form of governance. I will further evaluate how these concepts could add knowledge about the structural conditions of the persecution of Jews during Nazi rule in Germany and Europe.

Networks of Persecution—Historical Evidence

What is the historical evidence presented in the preceding empirical chapters of this book that networks of persecution existed? There is ample evidence that a great variety of distinct organizational entities contributed directly and indirectly to the persecution of the European Jews. The group of core perpetrators in the SS/Gestapo apparatus was strongly dependent on the knowledge, organizational capacity or simply manpower of other organizations whose primary goal was not the destruction of European Jewry. This was the case in decision making as well as in the implementation of anti-Jewish measures.

Gerald D. Feldman describes impressively how many organizations and organizational entities were involved in the decision process about how to deal with the damage of the *Reichskristallnacht* and potential claims by Jews and third parties. He names among others the interest group of the German insurance industry, the large insurance companies such as Allianz and Münchner Rückversicherung, and various Reich ministries and agencies, as well as the SD. Philippe Verheyde describes the division of labor between German and French, as well as among French organizations, to achieve the expropriation of Jewish entrepreneurs in France.

Dieter Ziegler reports how different actors from banks, Gauwirtschaftsberater, Gauleiter and the Gestapo each had their part in the (regional) economic persecution. Alfons Kenkman and Martin C. Dean give an impressive account of how the knowledge, organizational capacities, and professionalism of various specialized organizations came into play in order to "secure" the financial assets of the Jews for the Nazi state. The Gestapo had by no means the knowledge and manpower necessary to monitor the financial transactions of the Jews, strip them off their financial and real-estate assets, and then administer and commercialize them. The same holds true for the numerous agencies playing their specialized role in the eviction and deportation of Poles and the resettlement of *Volksdeutsche* (ethnic Germans) in the Warthegau, as described by Isabel Heinemann.

Even in the "Wild East" we see division of labor between various organizations such as police and SS units, the civil administration, the Reich Finance Ministry, the military, Einsatzstab Rosenberg (Reich Leader Rosenberg's Special Task Force), and Treuhandstelle Ost (Trustee Office East), as well as the SS Economic Administration Main Office (SS-WVHA) as Dean portrays the situation in the occupied Soviet territories.

The situation in the Ukraine, as Wendy Lower states, was characterized by a division of labor between the SS and SD and different military units that provided the "logistics" for the mass killings. One can therefore conclude that division of labor, mainly by task or function (functional differentiation), was a general structural feature in the whole persecution process, although it seems to have varied widely between different regions and different segments of the persecution apparatus. The economic persecution reveals a higher functional differentiation than the physical one and it was in general more pronounced in the Reich and the Western European countries than in the East. But it seems nonetheless that, in general, functionally differentiated actor systems, which are a prerequisite for the development of networks, existed throughout the persecution apparatus.

What, then, is said in the contributions in this volume about how these systems of persecution were (re)integrated? Given the devastating outcome, there must have been a fair amount of coordination and reintegration despite the notion of the National Socialist state as a "polycratic"[37] regime or even as "organized chaos."[38] In fact, almost all the contributions in this volume emphasize the cooperation and high coordination capacity, rather than overlapping competencies and endless power struggles. Even in cases where conflicts developed, as reported by Feldman for the insurance case or by Lower for the persecution of Jews in the Ukraine, in the end a consensus or at least a solution was reached that satisfied the core perpetrators.

There is not one example in this volume where such conflicts would have led to a long-term delay of anti-Jewish measures or even a permanent blockage in a stalemate situation. Is this simply because there was the (long) shadow of hierarchy in the shape of Himmler and ultimately Hitler or even the rather manifest power position of the security apparatus that was able to bring dissenters in line? This was probably an important factor that should not be underestimated. But it is not the full picture. Especially in the economic persecution the different contributions in this volume suggest that the officials within the security apparatus had to maneuver cautiously and negotiate with their counterparts in the financial administration. Once this relationship was stabilized it created a firm axis around which the other organizations were grouped, forming a highly effective network of persecution on the basis of various communication relations from which there was hardly any escape.

The axis between the financial and the security apparatus was supported by the fact that the officials in the financial bureaucracy, as reported by Kenkmann, were at least indifferent toward the fate of Jews. The same seems to be true for many of the Wehrmacht officers (see the contribution by Lower). The cognitive factor, therefore, should not be underestimated. It appears that in the overwhelming number of cases officials outside the immediate security apparatus were either indifferent, opening up leeway for negotiations on secondary goals (length of the use of the Jewish labor force, "medical experiments," etc.), or anti-Semitic themselves. It is therefore not surprising that the ideological consensus surrounding the "final solution" proved to be stronger than the other rationales for keeping Jews alive, as Lower states in her contribution.

Interpersonal relationships that developed "on the spot" forming informal networks were another form of integration. They seem to have been of importance especially in instances in which institutional structures were rather weak, as was the case in the remote outposts in the East or in areas that had only recently been occupied. The contributions in this volume suggest that the personal relationships in these situations were stronger than potential conflicting interests. In fact, mutual participation or knowledge of corruption and enrichment, as reported by Frank Bajohr, which resembles a situation of mutual hostage taking, might have strengthened these informal personal relations.

It seems, however, that despite some important parallels presented here the mode and extent of integration and the subsequent structure differed extensively. Therefore, the structure of the different persecution systems cannot easily be comprehended and understood at first sight. This is especially the case in those instances in which economic and physical persecution are temporally and organizationally intertwined, enhancing the number of actors that are involved at the same point in time. Especially in these instances, the application of a systematic and theoretically guided framework, as suggested here with the network concept, should result in valuable additional knowledge.

There are some hints in the contributions to this volume that in some instances a structure might have developed that is similar to a network as a rather horizontally structured social system, as well as features of a network as a form of governance, especially for the economic side of persecution. Nonetheless, empirical evidence from case studies on the physical persecution[39] suggests that it was rather the classical hierarchical-bureaucratic form of coordination that secured reintegration. The network approach, however, provides concepts and tools for taking a fresh look at old data and collecting new data in order to find out what different forms of coordination seemed to have reintegrated systems that are generally described as rather chaotic. It should further clarify how hierarchic these systems really were. In doing this, a much more finely grained analysis should be possible in identifying differences in the persecution apparatus, categorizing different types, and linking them with different levels of "outcome effectiveness."

Applying Network Analysis in Holocaust Research: Methodological Problems and Possible Solutions

Operationalization and Data Sources in Historical Network Analysis

As was demonstrated in the previous section, there is ample evidence that the persecution apparatus was a complex system whose structural features presumably varied between regions, between different segments of the persecution apparatus, and over time. It is therefore promising to apply the network concept as an analytical tool to gain a more detailed picture of the assumed interorganizational structures.

Although network analysis is a promising tool within historical analysis, only a few studies exist in which it is applied and only very few studies in which researchers were able or willing to produce quantitative results. The main field of application lies in historical sociology in research on social/protest movements and local community networks. Besides the rather limited empirical work, there is—to my knowledge—only one article, by Charles Wetherell[40] that deals explicitly with historical social network analysis. In a review article for *Historical Methods*, Erickson[41] makes some comments about the application of social network analysis in historical research and the special data restrictions that come with it. Wetherell names several reasons why there is little work in this area, which is mostly done by sociologists and not by historians. The most important reason in the context of this research is the "formidable data requirements"[42] that social network analysis demands. For a "whole network approach" information is needed on relations between all entities within a social system, if possible for various types of ties and for various time spans. For historical analysis which is usually plagued by missing, incomplete, or inaccessible historical records, "social network analysis remains an inherently problematic enterprise."[43]

One of the most commonly used operationalizations for learning something about structures in historical network analysis is personal interlinkages. Here, data is created from a multitude of sources (membership lists, diaries, biographical dictionaries, residential registration, and conscription registers) that connect both individual persons and organizations (dual-mode data).[44] In one of the most noticed studies in which historical network analysis was applied, Gould uses data on the cross-enlistment of men in military units of the national guard of other Paris *arrondissements* to explain the different resistance levels during the uprising in 1871.[45] In a variety of studies, membership or sponsor lists are used to map structures and explain developments of protest movements over time, as Osa does for Poland[46] or Bearman and Everett for protest movements in the United States from 1961 to 1983 (cosponsoring of protest rallies).[47] Rosenthal et al. used biographical dictionaries to identify women reformers in nineteenth-century New York State (1840–1914) and the interorganizational structure within the women's movement.[48] In one of the classics of historical social network analysis, Padgett and Ansell used data previously collected by historians for more descriptive studies to analyze the structural position that supported the rise of the Medici in Renaissance Florence.[49]

This brief review shows that network analysis has been applied to learn about social structures in very different periods and cultural backgrounds, on very different scales, and to answer very different empirical and theoretical questions. It has become apparent that, in order to gain relational information about social structures in the past, researchers have to make creative use of the available sources.

Networks of Persecution: Data Sources, Possible Operationalization, and Method

The first step in any network analysis is to determine the boundaries of the network, i.e., the identification of the relevant actors that should be included as the nodes in the analysis. The task is to determine first which of the existing organizations were directly or indirectly involved in the economic and/or the physical persecution. For matters of practicability it might be necessary to restrict the analysis to a number of "cases," for example, to certain regions/cities or to a limited number of decision or implementation sequences.

Unfortunately, it seems at this point that only a few of the operationalizations of the links which were used in historical network analysis to date are of great use for the research proposed here. Furthermore, the data sources generally used in historical network analysis, such as lists, do not resemble those available or useful in the research undertaken here. The biggest challenge, therefore, is to make use of material that is available—letters and radio messages between the different German and indigenous actors involved in the persecution, reports, diaries of functionaries, or the interrogation protocols and court transcripts of the trials of war criminals. The only chance to learn something systematically about the structure between the actors participating in or contributing to the physical and economic persecution of the Jewish population is to extract – relational information – written records. However, the following problems still exist in this regard. The population of the originally existing documents cannot be identified, the population of the still existing documents is unknown, and it is only possible to make informed guesses as to how reliable some of the documents are. Furthermore, the number of available documents could still be too big for a full data collection, so that despite the first two problems it could be necessary to draw samples. To handle this problem, it is suggested that the data collection be based on a limited number of events or cases for which a sufficient but not overwhelming documentation still exists, rather than on randomly sampling across the board. One could, for example, select specific deportations or the "Aryanization" of "representative" companies and collect the data from documents dealing with these processes.

The accuracy and reliability of judicial records and interrogation protocols for the data-collection processes is another problem.[50] First, it seems that even for experienced historians insurmountable mountains of documents exist.[51] These documents are qualified further as being full of gaps in recollection, mistakes, lies, wrong accusations, and statements of self protection,[52] although Tuchel provides a more optimistic view for cases in which the interrogations were conducted by experienced prosecutors and judges.[53] Every researcher therefore has to decide whether and how to include this type of source. One should take into account, however, that, contrary to conventional historical analysis, the data, once entered into the "big" data pool, cannot be easily reconnected to the original source and therefore researchers should be rather cautious.

These problems are well known to historians. For social scientists, however, who would like to make at least some limited generalizations, they are even more grave. In the context of this research it is impossible to determine whether a tie between two actors actually did not exist or whether it could just not be established by looking at the existing documents. Strictly speaking, it is only possible to make a statement about an existing tie, if information in documents indicates it, not about an absent tie.

It is however possible to collect relational data from written texts through content analysis, as well as using other information in these documents in this respect.[54] For example, addresses, distribution lists/carbon copies, and handwritten supplements are often a rich source of relational data. In a next step, this information can be aggregated into broader relational categories, such as "joint participation," "conflict," "order," "information exchange," etc. If sufficient data collection can be achieved on one or several of these types of ties, it is possible to proceed with a quantitative network analysis and use its full potential. The actors and the links between them could be coded in matrices (one for every type of tie). These matrices are, then, the basis for the computation of measures to determine the centrality, status, or specific structural positions of actors as well as certain properties of the whole actor system, such as density or centralization. These measures can then be interpreted, for example, in terms of coalition formation, the power of different actors, or the differentiation and integration of the persecution apparatus.

Conclusion: Networks of Persecution—The Potential of Network Analysis

When looking at networks of persecution from a social-science standpoint, one can distinguish four different perspectives: network as an analytical tool, network as social structure, network as governance form, and network as theory. Using these concepts and techniques can help to shed some light onto previously overlooked aspects of the Holocaust. Using network as an analytical tool and applying quantitative network analysis can help to answer questions or verify/falsify hypotheses about structural features of the networks of persecution, as well as the positions of the different actors involved. How were different segments of the functionally differentiated persecution apparatus reintegrated? Were the SS/Gestapo apparatus and, in the case of the occupied countries, the German actors really the most central and the indigenous actors the peripheral ones? How dense were these structures and did they vary over time? Did certain actors have specific structural positions as intermediaries? What form did the power structure have—was it really a strict hierarchical one, with the actors of the security apparatus dominant? What can therefore be inferred about the discretional leeway the actors had on average in the system?

Although considerable problems remain, especially in the realm of data collection, methodological solutions exist to cope with them if the necessary resources are available and/or the research strategy is adapted to the existing sources. If it is not possible to carry through the whole analysis because of lack of data or representativeness of the documents, the application of the conceptual framework will at least sharpen the analysis by using the rigor and precision that comes with the attempt at quantification.[55] It will raise new questions and will oblige the researcher to work creatively with the historical documents. The systematic search for the form and extent of division of labor and the modes of integration and coordination will reveal gaps previously overlooked. This in turn will trigger off a more intensive search for information on the actors and their relations than a traditional historical analysis would probably pursue.

Taking the perspective of networks of persecution as a social structure with specific features sharpens the focus for the question whether it is possible to actually talk about networks in the form of a rather horizontal, loosely coupled system of interdependent actors, instead of a highly centralized and highly hierarchical system.[56] Taking this approach one step further and looking at the networks of persecution as complex systems of coordination beyond the mere relations between the actors opens up yet another perspective. Systems of governance made up of different organizations, whether their features come close to a network or rather represent a mixed type of hierarchy/network/market, can be seen as an organization of a "higher order"[57] or an "emergent"[58] form of organization, which produce outcomes that cannot be attributed to any single organization alone. Moreover, the process and therefore the outcome cannot be completely controlled by any individual organization. This opens up the question of the "effectiveness" of the persecution apparatus. "Effectiveness" could be determined by measuring deportation rates and the extent of "Aryanization" as different outcomes of decision making and implementation within different systems of governance. In short, it allows one to shift the level of analysis from the single organization or the mere sum of organizations to more or less integrated systems of action. An interesting question in this respect will be to what extent it was necessary for the governance system to be integrated through common goals or a shared perspective of the "problem," as a network-like governance form would reveal, or whether a combination of complementary goals has the same integrative effect. The framework of governance mechanisms that was presented here could therefore be a very useful tool in explaining differences in outcomes and effectiveness in terms of different forms of organization of the persecution.

That leads to the last understanding of "network as theory." It is an ongoing attempt to unite structure with agency. "Network" could hereby serve as a uniting framework in operationalizing and measuring structure in network analytical terms and reconcile it with concepts and assumptions of agency (beliefs, ideology, rational choices). Developing and testing such an overarching analytical framework in Holocaust research could be beneficial for both social science and historiography. The anti-Jewish policy of these years, with its life and death decisions, represents an extreme case, in which ideology, beliefs, rational choices, and structures are much more pronounced than in the day-to-day politics of democratic societies, and might therefore reveal some very valuable insights for social and political theory. For historiography it could be a framework to further help overcome the old and in the meantime sterile debate[59] between structuralists and intentionalists in Holocaust research.

Notes

* Support for this research was provided by a grant from the Volkswagen Foundation for the project "Holocaust and Polycracy in Western Europe 1940–1944" and by the provision of the research infrastructure by the School of Public Administration and Policy, University of Arizona.

1. Hans G. Adler, *Der verwaltete Mensch. Studien zur Deportation der Juden aus Deutschland* (Tübingen, 1974); Michael Zimmermann, "Gestapo und die regionale Organisation der Judendeportationen. Das Beispiel der Stapo-Leitstelle Düsseldorf," in Gerhard Paul and Klaus-Michael Mallmann, eds., *Die Gestapo. Mythos und Realität* (Darmstadt, 1995), pp. 357–372.
2. Charles Perrow, "A Society of Organizations," *Theory and Society* 20 (1991): 725–762.
3. Zygmunt Bauman, *Modernity and the Holocaust* (Ithaca, 1989).

4. Luther Gulick, "Notes on the Theory of Organization," in Luther Gulick and Lyndall Urwick, eds., *Papers on the Science of Administration* (New York, 1937), pp. 3–13.
5. Paul R. Lawrence and Jay W. Lorsch, *Organization and Environment. Managing Differentiation and Integration* (Boston, 1967).
6. James G. March and Herbert A. Simon, *Organizations* (New York, 1958).
7. Lawrence and Lorsch, *Organization*, p. 12.
8. Renate Mayntz, *Die soziale Organisation des Industriebetriebes* (Stuttgart, 1966), p. 17.
9. Ian Kershaw, *The Nazi Dictatorship. Problems and Perspectives of Interpretation* (London, 1985), p. 90.
10. I owe this basic idea to Patrick Kenis; it can also be found in Franz U. Pappi, "Policy-Netze: Erscheinungsformen moderner Politiksteuerung oder methodischer Ansatz," in Adrienne Héritier, ed., *Policy-Analyse. Kritik und Neuorientierung (PVS-Sonderheft)* (Opladen, 1993), pp. 84–96.
11. See Willy van Poucke, "Network Constraints on Social Action: Preliminaries for a Network Theory," *Social Networks* 2 (1979): 181.
12. Mustafa Emirbayer and Jeff Goodwin, "Network Analysis, Culture, and the Problem of Agency," *American Journal of Sociology* 99 (1994): 1414.
13. Ibid.
14. David Knoke, *Political Networks. The Structural Perspective* (Cambridge, 1990), p. 8.
15. Patrick Kenis and Volker Schneider, "Policy Networks and Policy Analysis: Scrutinizing a New Analytical Toolbox," in Bernd Marin and Renate Mayntz, eds. *Policy Networks. Empirical Evidence and Theoretical Considerations* (Boulder, Colorado, 1991), pp. 25–62.
16. Larry J. Griffin and Marcel van der Linden, "Introduction," in idem, eds., *New Methods for Social History* (Cambridge, 1998), p. 8.
17. Emirbayer and Goodwin, "Network Analysis," p. 1446.
18. David Knoke and James H. Kuklinski, *Network Analysis* (Beverly Hills, 1986), p. 12.
19. Adrienne Windhoff-Héritier, "Policy Network Analysis," in Hans Keman, ed., *Comparative Politics. New Directions in Theory and Method* (Amsterdam, 1993), p. 144.
20. Kenis and Schneider actually talk about "the predominance of informal, decentralized and horizontal relations." Using the analytical distinction between network as social structure and network as governance form, one notices that they are actually talking of structure and that it should be formulated as above, because it is hard to imagine a "decentralized relation" (Kenis and Schneider, "Policy Networks," p. 32).
21. Oliver Williamson, *Markets and Hierarchies: Analysis and Antitrust Implications* (New York, 1975).
22. The integration of the discussion was driven forward among others by Hollingsworth: Joseph R. Hollingsworth and Leon N. Lindberg, "The Governance of the American Economy: the Role of Markets, Clans, Hierarchies, and Associative Behaviour," in Wolfgang Streeck and Philippe C. Schmitter, eds., *Private Interest Government: Beyond Market and State* (London, 1985), pp. 221–254; Joseph R. Hollingsworth, Phillipe C. Schmitter and Wolfgang Streek, eds., *Governing Capitalist Economies: Performance and Control of Economic Sectors* (Oxford, 1994); Joseph R. Hollingsworth, "Coordination of Economic Actors and Social Systems of Production," in Joseph R. Hollingsworth and Robert Boyer, eds., *Contemporary Capitalism – The Embeddedness of Institutions* (Cambridge, 1997), pp. 1–55.
23. Walter W. Powell, "Neither Market nor Hierarchy: Network Forms of Organization," *Research in Organizational Behavior* 12 (1990): 295–336.
24. Renate Mayntz, "Policy-Netzwerke und die Logik von Verhandlungssystemen." in Héritier, ed., *Policy-Analyse*, pp. 39–56.
25. For example Volker Schneider and Patrick Kenis, "Verteilte Kontrolle: Institutionelle Steuerung in modernen Gesellschaften," in Patrick Kenis and Volker Schneider, eds., *Organisation und Netzwerk* (Frankfurt on Main/New York, 1997), pp. 9–44.
26. Ibid., p. 20.
27. Charles Perrow, "Markets, Hierarchies and Hegemony," in Andrew H. Van de Veen, ed., *Perspectives on Organization Design and Behaviour* (New York, 1981): 371–386.

28. See, for example, the community power studies of Edward O. Laumann and Franz Urban Pappi, "New Directions in the Study of Community Elites," *American Sociological Review* 38 (1973): 212–230; Edward O. Laumann, Peter V. Marsden, and David Prensky, "The Boundary Specification Problem in Network Analysis," in Ronald S. Burt and Michael J. Minor, eds., *Applied Network Analysis* (Beverly Hills/London, 1983), pp. 18–34.
29. Gunther Teubner, "Die vielköpfige Hydra: Netzwerke als kollektive Akteure höherer Ordnung," in Patrick Kenis and Volker Schneider , eds., *Organisation und Institutionelle Steuerung in Wirtschaft und Politik* (Frankfurt on Main, New York, 1996), pp. 535–562.
30. Fritz W. Scharpf, ed., *Games in Hierarchies and Networks* (Boulder, Colorado, Frankfurt on Main, 1993).
31. Hans Mommsen, "Der Nationalsozialismus. Kumulative Radikalisierung und Selbstzerstörung des Regimes," *Meyers Enzyklopädisches Lexikon* (1976): 785–790.
32. I owe this idea to Patrick Kenis.
33. Patrick Kenis and David Knoke, "A Network Theory of Interorganizational Relations. Conference Paper," *EGOS Conference* (Maastricht, 1998), pp. 42.
34. Candace Jones, William S. Hesterly, and Stephen P. Borgatti, "A General Theory of Network Governance: Exchange Conditions and Social Mechanism," *Academy of Management Review* 22 (1997): 911–945.
35. Harrison C. White, *Identity and Control* (Princeton, 1992); Emirbayer and Goodwin, "Network Analysis"; Mustafa Emirbayer and Ann Mische, "What is Agency?" *American Journal of Sociology* 103 (1998): 962-1023. Although theae authors do not use this term, their questions and arguments could be placed in such a category in a crude distinction of approaches.
36. Emirbayer and Goodwin, "Network Analysis."
37. Peter Hüttenberger, "Nationalsozialistische Polykratie," *Geschichte und Gesellschaft* 2 (1976): 417–442.
38. Johannes Houwink ten Cate and Gerhard Otto, *Das organisierte Chaos. "Ämterdarwinismus" und "Gesinnungsethik." Determinanten nationalsozialistischer Besatzungsherrschaft* (Berlin, 1999).
39. Adler, *Der verwaltete Mensch;* Zimmermann, "Gestapo und regionale Organisation."
40. Charles Wetherell, "Historical Social Network Analysis," *International Review of Social History* 43 (1998): 125–144.
41. Bonnie H. Erickson, "Social Networks and History: A Review Essay," *Historical Methods* 30 (1997): 149–157.
42. Wetherell, "Historical Network Analysis," p. 125.
43. Ibid.
44. Ronald Breiger, "The Duality of Persons and Groups," *Social Forces* 53 (1974): 181–190.
45. Roger V. Gould, *Insurgent Identities. Class, Community, and Protest in Paris from 1848 to the Commune* (Chicago/London, 1995).
46. Maryjane Osa, "Mobilizing Structures and Cycles of Protest: Post Stalinist Contention in Poland, 1954–1959," *Mobilization* 6 (2001): 140–161.
47. Peter S. Bearman and Kevin D. Everett, "The Structure of Social Protest, 1961-1983," *Social Networks* 15 (1993): 171–200.
48. Naomi Rosenthal et al., "Social Movements and Network Analysis: A Case Study of Nineteenth-Century Women's Reform in New York State," *American Journal of Sociology* 90 (1985): 1022–054.
49. John Padgett and Christopher K. Ansell, "Robust Action and the Rise of the Medici, 1400–1434," *American Journal of Sociology* 98 (1993): 1259–1319.
50. Dieter Pohl, *Von der "Judenpolitik" zum Judenmord. Der Distrikt Lublin des Generalgouvernements 1939–1944* (Frankfurt on Main, 1993).
51. Trials that produced up to 30,000 pages are a reality: Wolfgang Scheffler, "NS-Prozesse als Geschichtsquelle. Bedeutung und Grenzen ihrer Auswertbarkeit durch den Historiker," in Wolfgang Scheffler and Werner Bergmann, eds., *Lerntag über den Holocaust als Thema im Geschichtsunterricht und in der politischen Bildung* (Berlin, 1998), p. 18.
52. Pohl, "*Judenpolitik*," p. 11.

53. Johannes Tuchel, "Die NS-Prozesse als Materialgrundlage für die historische Forschung. Thesen zu Möglichkeiten und Grenzen interdisziplinärer Zusammenarbeit," in Jürgen Weber and Peter Steinbach, *Vergangenheitsbewältigung durch Strafverfahren. NS-Prozesse in der Bundesrepublik Deutschland* (Munich, 1984), pp. 134–144.
54. Jörg Raab, "Networks of Persecution: A Suggestion on How to Analyze Inter-Organizational Networks in the Holocaust. Conference Paper," *XXII Sunbelt Conference* (New Orleans, 2002), p. 39.
55. Harold D. Lasswell, "Why Be Quantitative?" in Harold D. Lasswell and Saul K. Padover, eds., *Language of Politics* (New York, 1949), pp. 40–54.
56. The theoretical and methodological framework suggested here has been applied to analyze the decision and implementation process surrounding the deportation of Jews who had converted to the Christian faith in the Netherlands in the summer of 1942. Wolfgang Seibel and Jörg Raab, "Verfolgungsnetzwerke. Zur Messung von Arbeitsteilung und Machtdifferenzierung in den Verfolgungsapparaten des Holocaust," *Kölner Zeitschrift für Soziologie und Sozialpsychologie* 55 (2003): 197–230.
57. Teubner, *"Die vielköpfige Hydra."*
58. Scharpf, *Games in Hierarchies.*
59. Ulrich Herbert, "Vernichtungspolitik. Neue Antworten und Fragen zur Geschichte des 'Holocaust'," in Ulrich Herbert, ed., *Nationalsozialistische Vernichtungspolitik 1933–1945. Neue Forschungen und Kontroversen* (Frankfurt on Main, 1998), p. 22.

Chapter 18

Restraining or Radicalizing?
Division of Labor and Persecution Effectiveness

Wolfgang Seibel

Organized Chaos and Effective Persecution—An Unexplained Paradox

Starting with Franz L. Neumann's "Behemoth,"[1] the history of theoretical reasoning on Nazi Germany and division-of-labor-based mass crime is closely connected to characterizations of Nazi dictatorship as "polycratic" or even as "organized chaos."[2] German occupation administration during World War II in particular is usually portrayed as an example of disorganized and ineffective governance.[3] How can we explain, then, the building of an effective terror apparatus stretching all over German-controlled Europe? Obviously, the question is most challenging with respect to the persecution and annihilation of European Jewry.

Issues of organization and intent in what then became Holocaust research have been discussed since the late 1970s under the heading "functionalism" versus "intentionalism."[4] While "intentionalists" insisted on the ideological intent of mass murder as a crucial explanatory factor, "functionalists" pointed to the fragmented structure of Nazi rule and the quasi-chaotic character of administration as a source of "cumulative radicalization."[5] Recent research, as documented in the present volume, has substantially enhanced the understanding of both the structural and the intentional side of the Holocaust. The persecution apparatus comprised not only the SS and Gestapo machinery, which always attracted the bulk of related general and scholarly interest,[6] but also a vast variety of "regular" public and private agencies—municipal registration offices, housing authorities, fiscal authorities, railroads, banks, insurance companies, etc.—as has been revealed especially through research on the economic side of anti-Jewish policy and persecution.[7]

Moreover, research on how different segments of tactical and strategic German warfare and occupation policy interacted with the mass murder of Jews has enhanced our knowledge of the political and institutional embeddedness of the Holocaust.[8] Finally, there is sufficient evidence, indeed, that the "polycratic" nature of the institutional conglomerates involved, driven by inter-agency competition and rivalry, did not necessarily impede but sometimes actually accelerated the persecution.[9]

The question of what was "intended" by those participating in the persecution and how those intentions were related to the respective institutional environment remains nonetheless disputed. Recent research appears both to confirm and to cast doubt on Daniel J. Goldhagen's[10] thesis on Hitler's "willing executioners." Without tens of thousands of "executioners," who were to be found in the numerous public and private institutions that participated in the different domains of persecution, the Holocaust would not have been possible. Nor can it be doubted that there was an intentional logic linking the economic and the repressive police measures of persecution. The destruction of the economic basis of individual civil existence was an integral component of the anti-Jewish policy of the National Socialist government.

However, taking division of labor seriously when it comes to the unique nature of the Holocaust as organized mass crime implies acknowledging an extended motivational basis of the persecution beyond anti-Semitic ideology. As we know from related classics—Adam Smith and Émile Durkheim in particular—the separation of individual motives and common goals is the dominant effect of division of labor. Individual members or participants do not have to care about the overall goals of complex organizations in order to make organizations powerful tools in the hands of functional elites. Moreover, the separation of individual motivation and common-goal attainment is a much more efficient mechanism of human-resource mobilization than common goals shared by any single individual. There is good sense in acknowledging that division of labor created a similar kind of mobilization within the machinery of persecution during the Holocaust. Division of labor and the selective perception it entailed not only created a taken-for-granted effect but also provided an opportunity for the pursuit of a variety of selfish but not necessarily ideological intentions. What is more, the more dependent the perpetrators on human and organizational resources outside their immediate control, the less reliable, in their own perception, was anti-Semitism as a motivating force.

Current research, part of which is represented in the present volume, thus invites us to reconsider the discussion of the respective significance of structural and agency-related factors for the initiation and implementation of the persecution and destruction of European Jewry by Nazi Germany.

Two Rival Assumptions

What made the "intentionalism" versus "functionalism" debate "sterile" (to cite Herbert[11]) was not only a lack of empirical information but also a lack of hypotheses on causal linkages between structural properties of the persecution apparatus and different logics of agency. Taking the intentional side of organized mass crime seriously implies building hypotheses on how structural properties of the persecution apparatus were linked to the individual motivation of perpetrators and their helpers, which can be done in the form of two rival assumptions:

1. Division of labor as a structural feature of the persecution apparatus might have restrained the persecution of the Jews due to high coordination costs for the persecutors, limited sanction possibilities, and enhanced room for maneuver for divergent action strategies of competing authorities.
2. Division of labor as a structural feature of the persecution apparatus might have radicalized the persecution of the Jews due to enhanced opportunities for selective perceptions and selective incentives of subsidiary actors (or "helpers") and enhanced opportunities to suppress moral sentiments through utilitarian motives.

What follows is devoted to the operationalization of the above assumptions and the empirical evidence supporting each of them.

Persecutors, Helpers, and Division of Labor

Acknowledging division of labor as a structural feature of the persecution apparatus implies assuming that the persecution apparatus directed against the Jews was run by a core group of perpetrators who did not entirely control the human and organizational resources necessary for persecution. This, in turn, implies the distinction of two groups of actors, the persecutors and their helpers.

Persecutors can be defined as actors taking the political and administrative initiative for persecution. Helpers can be defined as actors on whose cooperation the persecutors were dependent in the implementation of their initiative. Certainly, this is an ideal-typical classification. The distinction of persecutors and helpers is, nonetheless, justified by the fact that the persecutors were dependent on subsidiary actors whose compliance with crime and mass murder could not be taken for granted. Ironically, persecution apparatuses represented solely by persecutors and committed accomplices would not have been sufficiently robust. The persecutors, depending on third-party resources, had good reasons to count on universal rather than particularistic motives of potential helpers. Those motives had to be strong and universal enough to ensure compliance with measures of persecution even in the absence of anti-Semitism or immediate sanctions and coercion.

A universal and thus robust motive is utility maximization. Certainly, no action is truly based on merely utilitarian motives but those motives are the most foreseeable and the risk of miscalculating the action orientation of average people is most reduced if we assume them to observe some kind of utilitarian preference scale.[12] In avoidance of some common misunderstandings regarding the role of utilitarian motives of Holocaust perpetrators, however, it is imperative to differentiate the relevant units and levels of analysis. It would be misleading to assume, as has been convincingly stated,[13] that the mass murder of the Jews was part of a means-end rational master plan designed to reconcile racist goals and economic necessities. However, while utilitarian motives cannot sufficiently explain the planning of the Holocaust at the macro-political level, they can be considered the most robust motivational forces at the personal level. After all, the persecutors had good reasons for taking utilitarian rather than ideological motives into account when assessing the probability of compliance among helpers whose cooperation was indispensable but whose commitment to the murderous goals was uncertain.[14]

In an attempt to assess the causal linkage between the structural properties of the persecution apparatus and the action orientation of both persecutors and helpers, one may treat the features of the persecution apparatus as an opportunity structure for utility maximization of those initiating persecution for ideological reasons and those without an initial will to persecute—let alone murder—the Jews. One has, then, to identify structural peculiarities of the persecution apparatus, as well as the subjective expected utility[15] of both persecutors and helpers connected to those peculiarities. This may lead to hypotheses on causal linkages between structural and intentional factors, thus bridging the gap between "micro"-motives of persecutors and helpers and the "macro"-effects of overall persecution effectiveness.[16]

One may assume that persecutors would consider as a utility the control over their helpers as well as the defense or enhancement of their power in general. One may assume that helpers would consider as a utility the protection against sanctions of the persecutors, the defense or improvement of their own power position, personal enrichment, and, finally, preservation of professional selective perceptions and protection against cognitive dissonances resulting from disparities between moral norms and actual behavior.

Most of the above assumptions are trivial. This holds especially for the striving of the persecutors for power and control at the lowest possible costs and the striving of the helpers for protection against sanctions and for personal or institutional advantages. These premises are further supported by utilitarian theories of obedience to norms as dependent on the subjectively evaluated probability of sanctions[17] and obedience to orders by subordinates as dependent on the control possibilities of the order givers according to the "principal–agent" theorem (see below). It is the assumption that helpers generally sought protection from cognitive dissonances that is less trivial since it means assuming a minimal capacity for moral judgment. What one may take for granted is that the capacity for moral judgment was drastically reduced on the German side by anti-Jewish persuasions, let alone Nazi propaganda.[18] By the same token, however, residual moral distinctions clearly remained intact,[19] which implies that the helpers' compliance with anti-Jewish persecution created cognitive dissonances in Festinger's sense.[20] Accordingly, one may assume that the helpers perceived the chance to avoid those psychic costs as a utility.

In a second step, we need to identify the structural peculiarities of the persecution apparatus to which, according to the general hypotheses, the individual motivation of persecutors and their helpers was linked in one way or the other. Assuming that the persecutors were dependent on helpers implies division of labor as the main structural phenomenon shaping the persecution apparatus. Division of labor can be defined as the extent to which the actors participating in the persecution performed different activities.

Empirically, "division of labor" refers to a variety of configurations. As already mentioned, those initiating the persecution were under any circumstances dependent on third-party resources. For instance, the Gestapo, as well as the Nazi agencies initiating "Aryanization," already relied in Germany proper on a ramified structure of subsidiary institutional actors, who, in their respective areas of expertise and competencies, contributed their share to the complex task of persecution in both the economic and the repressive police field. Some of the resulting inter-organizational linkages, such as the technical assistance of banks or the railroad agencies, did not involve rivalry. Some, however, did involve rivalry in terms of competencies and influence, whose effect on the action orientation of persecutors and helpers has to be taken into account.

Measuring structural indicators such as "division of labor" in a historical context represents one of the major challenges to future research. The issue here is to build hypotheses, both empirically and theoretically grounded, on

Table 19.1 Presumed Effect of Division of Labor on the Utility Expectation of Persecutors and Helpers.

Actors	Utility expectation	Effect of division of labor in the persecution apparatus on utility expectation
Persecutors	Oversight/supervision of the "helpers"	(−)
	Defense/improvement of power position	(−)
Helpers	Defense/improvement of power position	(+)
	Enrichment	(+)
	Preservation of professional selective perception, protection from cognitive dissonances	(+)

(+) = positive effect on the relevant utility expectation; (−) = negative effect on the relevant utility expectation causal linkages between division of labor as crucial structural properties of the persecution apparatus and the action-orientation of persecutors and helpers. Figure Table 19 depicts a set of relevant hypotheses.

Division of Labor and Persecutor-Helper Interaction

According to the above assumptions, an increase in division of labor did not rank high in the persecutors' preference scale. Instead, centralization and tight vertical integration of the organizational apparatuses at their disposal were in the natural interest of the persecutors. There is, indeed, strong empirical evidence in support of a related hypothesis.

The organizational history of the persecution apparatuses of the Nazi regime is characterized by the continuous process of hierarchical integration of the SS and Gestapo machinery. The main stages, here, were the *Verreichlichung* (extension of Reich jurisdiction) of the *Länder* (state) police forces, the organizational separation of the police from the general administration, the fusion of the police with Nazi party organizations (SS/Sicsherheitsdient (SD)) and, in September 1939, the integration of all repressive functions in a single agency, internally named Reichssicherheitshauptamt (RSHA, Reich Security Main Office), with dependencies in all parts of occupied Europe.[21] Both the overcoming of initial differences of interests between the NSDAP and local or state economic administration in the "Aryanization" process[22] and the smooth cooperation of the Gestapo and the numerous branches of regular administration in the preparation and implementation of the deportations[23] fit in here.

Wherever these tightly integrated organizational structures could not be imposed, the persecutors were dependent on what, from their own point of view, were second-best solutions. Mobilizing compliance among helpers whose action could not be controlled by hierarchical means was crucial. The mechanisms of non-hierarchical control were thus at least as important as mechanisms of hierarchy and vertical integration as far as the actual power of the persecutors is concerned.[24] According to the assumptions presented in Table 19.1, an increase in division of labor, while restricting the immediate control of persecutors, entailed considerable potential for mobilizing compliance among helpers. In what follows, basic mechanisms of both hierarchical and non-hierarchical control, along with related empirical illustrations, are presented to understand the effectiveness of persecution apparatuses.

Reciprocal Interdependencies and "Veto Points"

As pioneer students of organizational behavior have pointed out, the control and coordination capacity of superiors depend not only on the mere number of units to be coordinated, but also on the nature of the tasks to be shared and the type of relationship among the respective units.[25] A classic scheme is Thompson's classification of coordination problems[26] distinguishing "pooled," "sequential" and "reciprocal" interdependencies, implying an increasing need for coordination. According to the Thompson scheme, division of labor in interlocking decision-making systems creates reciprocal interdependencies requiring permanent interaction, which is obviously harder to manage than the common use of resources or linear sequences of decision making. An equivalent to Thompson's "reciprocal interdependence" is the "veto point" phenomenon discussed in the political-science literature.[27] The ability to veto implies power, and it suffices for just one of the participating actors to say "no" to render decision making ineffective. The more veto points, the more "polycratic" and potentially more ineffective the related processes of decision making.

Reciprocal interdependence and related veto points are especially essential to occupation regimes,[28] and it is here that its importance for Holocaust research is salient. As far as German occupation regimes during World War II are concerned, the degree of interdependence and the impact of veto points differed according to a multiplicity of empirical factors—largely unknown, so far—among which the institutional setting of the occupation regimes was prominent. Different types of occupation regimes accorded different degrees of discretionary power to native actors. The relative power of native actors was greater in Western Europe than it was in Eastern Europe, and in Western Europe itself it was greater in France than, say, in the Netherlands or Norway. In an occupied country such as France, Germans and native key actors indeed found themselves in a relationship of reciprocal dependency—an asymmetrical reciprocity, of course.

Both the term and the accusation of "collaboration" only make sense if based on the assumption that native actors did not use the veto points at hand in an effort to obstruct the occupier.[29] The trailblazing character of Robert Paxton's study[30] on Vichy France, for instance, was due to its demonstration that Vichy did have a choice. Vichy could have said "no,", particularly so in the "Jewish question."[31] The central accusation has since then been that the État Français used its room for maneuver neither in the interest of the country in general nor specifically in the interest of the Jewish community.[32]

Principal-Agent Issues

A standard interpretation of hierarchical control is the principal–agent theorem,[33] whose main assumption is that those subjected to orders ("agents") react opportunistically to what their superiors or "principals" want them to do. To combine low control costs with high compliance of agents is defined as the key problem of principals and, when it comes to the impact of institutional settings, it is usually assumed that the control capacity of principals correlates positively with low degrees of organizational fragmentation, since higher degrees of fragmentation tend to protect agents against sanctions, with the agents adjusting their utility expectations accordingly.[34]

Obviously, the principal–agent theorem can be plausibly applied to occupation regimes. While in the literature a shirking problem (the temptation of the agent to be unfaithful to the principal) is assumed already for enterprises or bureaucracies in democratic constitutional states, it can definitely be assumed for an occupation regime and especially so when the occupying power demands compliance with immoral action. Moreover, if information asymmetries and scarcity of resources are assumed to restrict the control capacity of principals in enterprises or bureaucracies, the assumption holds all the more for occupiers lacking both extensive knowledge of the occupied country and administrative infrastructure. Conversely, the occupier's resource dependency implies room for maneuver of native actors.[35]

The resource problem also holds for the persecution of the Jews in German-occupied Europe. Since the persecutors were dependent on the cooperation of helpers, different administrative and political conditions in different territories under German rule resulted in different degrees of discretionary leeway of native agencies, which necessarily included freedom of action for "helpers" in the persecution apparatuses and related opportunities to expand their relative power. Whether or not native agents used these advantages for "shirking" in the sense of non-compliance with the German principals was crucial to the effectiveness of persecution.

Bargaining, Log-Rolling

Assuming that helpers had a choice to comply or not to comply with mass crime does not necessarily imply that helpers perceived that choice as a moral issue. However, what the helpers presumably did, regardless of moral judgment and political persuasion, was to take into account the high priority assigned to the "Jewish question" by the Nazi regime in general and by the SS and Gestapo in particular. Under the conditions of an occupation regime, for instance, native actors could be tempted to bargain for concessions of the Germans in important fields of native policy by means of compliance with the occupying power's anti-Jewish policy. Such log-rolling, as it is termed in the language of political economy,[36] presupposes negotiating power on the part of the relevant participants—a situation peculiar to "veto player" effects of political institutions and typical of both the "polycratic" nature of Nazi dictatorship and occupation regimes.[37]

There is indeed empirical evidence in support of the assumption that bargaining and log-rolling were mobilizing factors of helpers' compliance during the Holocaust. This holds not only with respect to the relationship of German and native agencies in the occupied territories but also with respect to inter-agency relationship in Germany proper. As long as the Germans were geo-politically strong, i.e., far into 1942, the logic of log-rolling was likely to imply compliance with German anti-Jewish policy since advantages from refusal were uncertain, a calculation whose terms began to change at the turn of 1942/43 with the increasing probability of German defeat. Again it is the French example that fits well with this assumption. After the fall of

1942 the hitherto smoothly collaborating Vichy government shifted to a tactic of latent obstruction of the German deportation policy.[38] Jonathan Steinberg[39] and Meïr Michaelis,[40] using the Italian example, describe a similar logic and its impact on the fate of the Jews in Italy and in the European territories under Italian control.

However, a logic of log-rolling could also occur in the relationships between rival German agencies. The contemporary witness Bargatzky[41] describes how the *Gruppe Justiz* (Justice Division) of the *Militärbefehlshaber in Frankreich* recommended the spoliation of Jewish assets as an alternative to the confiscation of French cultural goods.[42] In his memoirs of this period he cites from a memorandum which he himself prepared in 1940/41, a note that according to the Hague Convention on Land Warfare the confiscation of private property by occupying forces is prohibited, a prohibition that, however, is limited in the case where "the security of the occupying power would be endangered by the unrestricted use of the private property." "In the course of total war," the memorandum continues, "such a danger can, e.g., arise if elements hostile to the occupying power possess a specific influence on the economic provision of the occupied territory."[43]

As the author himself concedes, the wording ("elements hostile to the occupying power") was compatible with Nazi language justifying the persecution of the Jews. Not only was the memorandum a plea for forced spoliation of Jewish property, but it also justified the economic persecution of the Jews on a seemingly nonideological international-law basis. What the rhetoric veiled, however, was a political bargain intended to save French art and museum possessions from the plundering of art works by the *Einsatzstab Reichsleiter Rosenberg* (Reich Leader Rosenberg's Special Task Force), literally a plundering agency hunting for any kind of valuables all over German-occupied Europe,[44] and by Hitler's de facto deputy, Göring. So even a certain anti-Nazi mood and related bargaining with the persecutors could not only be combined with anti-Semitism but could also indirectly intensify the persecution of the Jews.

Enrichment and Defense or Improvement of Power Positions

That the persecution apparatus provided an opportunity structure for self-enrichment, increasing with the degree of division of labor and the number of participants, is a plausible assumption. The empirical proofs are depressingly numerous.[45] Here too, however, persecution was apparently codetermined by institutional incentives and inter-agency rivalry.

A case in point is the tense relationship between the Gestapo and the fiscal administration as it arose with the implementation of the *11. Verordnung zum Reichsbürgergesetz* (Eleventh Ordinance supplementing the Reich Citizenship Law) of 25 November 1941. The ordinance's target group was the deported Jews or Jews to be deported, who, after they had moved their regular domicile "abroad"—i.e., after having been deported—thereby lost both their citizenship and their property. Section 2 of the ordinance stipulated: "A Jew loses his German citizenship (a) if, once this ordinance becomes effective, his regular domicile is abroad, (b) if and when he subsequently moves his regular domicile abroad." Section 3 specified: "The property of the Jew will accrue to the German Reich once he loses his German citizenship pursuant to this ordinance."

The formulation "accrue to the German Reich" (*verfällt dem Reich*) provided the basis for the automatic jurisdiction of the Reichsfinanzministerium (Ministry of Finance) and the fiscal authorities in contrast to the customary formulation, used up until the Eleventh Ordinance, "collection of assets" (*Vermögenseinziehung*), which still had its legal source in the *Notverordnung zum Schutz von Volk und Staat* of 28 February 1933 (Emergency Decree for the Protection of the People and the State) from which the Reichssicherheitshauptamt derived the jurisdiction of the Gestapo. The preparation of the Eleventh Ordinance was characterized by a "tug of war between the Reich Finance Ministry and the Gestapo"[46] about who was entitled to appropriate the assets.[47] Finally, however, a compromise was reached. In a circular (*Runderlaß*) to the *Oberfinanzdirektionen* (higher fiscal authorities) of 9 December 1941 the Reichsfinanzministerium pointed out: "Since their [the Jews': WS] property *accrues* to the German Reich, it will no longer be *collected*."[48] What the bureaucratic language indicated was that the authority in charge was the fiscal administration, while the SS/SD reserved the right to skim off 25 percent% of the liquidated property for financing the deportations.[49]

This sort of rivalry, as well as the final compromise, fits the interpretive scheme of a National Socialist "polycracy" and its radicalizing effect (see also contributions to Part 1 of the present volume). In the perception of the Reichsfinanzministerium officials the key issue was the observance of traditional budget law standards and thus the avoidance of shadow budgets. Presumably, the civil service aristocracy of the fiscal administration was inclined to instruct the parvenu agency, the *Reichssicherheitshauptamt*, about how things had to be done in an ordinary state. Weinert[50] reports on similar attitudes in the *Reichsrechnungshof* (Reich Accounting Office), while Adler[51] describes similar rivalries between the fiscal administration on the one hand, and Himmler's agencies in his capacity as *Reichskommissar für die Festigung deutschen Volkstums* (Reich Commissioner for the Strengthening of Germandom) and the *Haupt-Treuhandstelle Ost* (HTO, Trustee Office East), on the other, in the spoliation of assets and household possessions of deported Jews in Austria and the "Protectorate of Bohemia and Moravia." Conversely, subordinate functionaries even of Himmler's nonpolice-related administrative offices liked to flex their muscles before the fiscal administration, pointing out that if necessary they would have to report to the superior administrative office (in the final instance thus to Himmler, Heydrich, or Kaltenbrunner). This explains the irritated tone of the correspondence documented by Adler[52] and the ambition of the SS/Gestapo to get rid of the nagging fiscal administration. Where the Gestapo saw the opportunity, it did just this—in Austria, for example, by founding its own sales organization for looted Jewish property under the acronym "Vugestap" (for *Verkauf jüdischen Umzugsgutes Gestapo* (Sale of Jewish Removal Goods — Gestapo)).[53]

Selective Professional Perception, Reduction of Cognitive Dissonances

The assumption according to which division of labor within the persecution apparatuses increased the chances of helpers to preserve their selective professional perception and to find protection against cognitive dissonances is supported by behavioral studies of organizational decision making. According to this strand of literature, organizational structures are robust to the extent to which they become independent of the intentional actions of participants. As Barnard has pointed out,[54] organizational stability requires an equilibrium between inducements provided by the organization and contributions of participants. The equilibrium is all the more stable the more a "zone of indifference" emerges within which the contributions of participants—their compliance with the organizational purposes—are relatively independent of the inducements, positive or negative, that the organization has to offer. The indifference is supported by organizational norms and routines that form the essential premises of decision making and are taken for granted in everyday organizational life, thus reducing cognitive complexity and mitigating the tension between demands for decisions and the limited intellectual capacities of rational decision making,[55] at the expense, however, of selective perception.[56]

Professional routines represent the most common pattern of selective perception.[57] Cognitive and motivational indifference toward organizational purposes is thus not only an effect but also a prerequisite for the stabilization of any organization. Moral indifference is not necessarily involved—it may or may not shape the mentality of organizational members. Moral indifference toward organizational purposes is, however, basically supported by organizational structures as such.[58]

These assumptions are clearly compatible with Hannah Arendt's[59] banalization thesis since they point to the cognitive effects of organizational structures based on a division of labor.[60] While acting within these structures, helpers could share the illusion that, within the framework of their limited task, they were acting normally. This kind of selective perception and the resulting taken-for-granted effect have been portrayed by many authors as a key explanation of the mobilizing effect of formal organization when it came to the mass murder of European Jewry.[61]

Selective perceptions as such, however, do not explain the compliance with actions whose immoral character is obvious. The classic experiments on the causes of immoral behavior, especially Stanley Milgram's study of obedience to immoral orders[62] and Leon Festinger's studies of coping with conflicts between competing behavioral norms,[63] support the assumption that division of labor facilitates the suppression of moral scruples by way of self-deception. As Milgram has shown, obedience to immoral orders depends on the psychological support of the social environment such as the aura of scientific research or the status of the order giver.

Accordingly, when it comes to the organizational basis of mass crime, one may assume that both the legal form of the persecution and the usual professional environment were highly effective in stimulating the helpers' compliance. In the perception of the helpers, it presumably made a difference whether orders to destroy the civil existence of Jewish fellow citizens were issued by highly reputable agencies, such as the local tax authority or the local court, or, in the occupied territories, by native authorities as opposed to the Gestapo and other agencies of the German occupier.[64]

Festinger's experiments confirm that individuals basically strive to achieve consistency of values and actual behavior and that inconsistencies create emotional tension ("cognitive dissonances"), which, in turn, requires patterns of mitigation. Among those patterns, illusions and self-deceptions are crucial.[65] The difference between persecutors and helpers is that the latter were running a higher risk than the former in terms of value-versus-behavior inconsistency. Accordingly, helpers were dependent on intended ignorance about what they were actually doing.[66] The division of labor within the persecution apparatuses, rather than creating illusions in the first place, enhanced the opportunities of intentional ignorance based on—but not produced by—selective perceptions.

Thus, acknowledging the impact of division of labor on the strength of perpetrators does not diminish the role of personal responsibility but rather sharpens the understanding of the kind of responsibility that is actually required. Individuals are responsible not only for what they are doing but also for what they allow themselves to perceive. Formal organizational structures with division of labor at their core do shape perceptions but they do not absolve individuals from responsibility for what they want to know and what they prefer to ignore. Using organizational structures as an opportunity to ignore what it is ethically imperative to perceive is as immoral as committing immoral acts itself.

Reaggregating the Hypotheses

In summarizing the previous section, one may conclude that division of labor within the persecution apparatuses had an ambivalent impact on the strength of perpetrators. What one may presume is that the decreasing control capacity of persecutors due to division of labor was counterbalanced by an increase of compliance on the helpers' side. While division of labor restricted hierarchical control and enhanced the dependence of SS/Gestapo agencies on third-party resources, those resources were mobilized through opportunities of subsidiary but indispensable actors to enrich themselves, to enhance their relative power position, and to protect themselves against cognitive dissonances.

To SS/Gestapo agencies, then, losing direct control due to an overly ramified structure of the persecution apparatus did not necessarily mean a loss of persecution effectiveness. One may even assume that overcentralization of the persecution apparatuses would have been counterproductive since it would have caused unsolvable bottleneck problems in terms of control at the center and counterincentives to comply at the periphery. This implies that a medium degree of division of labor was, presumably, what served the persecutors best.

Certainly, when assessing the impact of "structures" as opposed to ideological intentions, the role of political culture in the broadest sense has to be taken into account. The degree of general anti-Semitism in a given country under German occupation, the culture of obedience to formal law, and the general belief in the legitimacy of governmental action have restrained or facilitated the persecution of the Jews. Ironically, though, it is ideology and political culture that deliver strong reasons to investigate structural determinants of the persecution process. Acknowledging the ambivalent impact of division of labor on the strength of perpetrators may not only explain why the persecutors could rely on third-party resources even in the absence of direct control but may also contribute to an explanation of different degrees of Jewish victimization in cross-national comparison, which, in a pure political-culture perspective, would remain highly counterintuitive.

For instance, anti-Semitism was undoubtedly a source of compliance both in the ranks of the German military administration in Belgium and France and in native agencies.[67] The pronounced anti-Semitism of the Vichy government and the Commissariat générale aux questions juives—a de facto ministry for anti-Jewish policy—can be cited as the most infamous examples in Western Europe. The Vichy government issued the first anti-Jewish ordinances without any German initiative.[68] The Netherlands, by contrast, had no significant anti-Semitic tradition. What is more, it was in the Netherlands, in February 1941, that the only political strike against anti-Jewish repression was organized throughout German-occupied Europe (and ruthlessly suppressed by the Germans).[69]

And yet it was not in France that the Jewish community suffered the greatest losses in Western Europe but in the Netherlands. While in France approximately 25 percent of the Jews were eventually deported, the deportation rate in the Netherlands amounted to approximately 76 percent.[70] Certainly, due to the respective occupation regimes, the persecutors, the SS and Gestapo agencies in particular, were in a strong position in the Netherlands and in a weaker position in Belgium and France.[71] What current research also reveals, however, is that the structural position of native actors made them act in accordance with what was perceived as the national, institutional, or personal interest.

Compliance and noncompliance with the anti-Jewish policy of the German occupants was contingent on both professional attitudes and utility expectations connected to the respective structural position.[72] Both French and Dutch officials pursued a policy of the *moindre mal* and, accordingly, made concessions to the Germans where losses remained calculable and compensatory gains seemed to be achievable. In these bargaining processes, losses at the expense of the Jews were particularly calculable since they were restricted to a particular societal group, while the perception of the national, institutional, or personal interest was, in turn, shaped by the structure of both the occupation regime in general and persecution apparatuses in particular.

The outcome was opportunism in the pure sense. Pierre Laval, freshly reinstalled as head of the Vichy government, did not hesitate to approve the deportation of several thousands of Jewish infants of non-French origin in the summer of 1942, but refused to let Jews be denaturalized and subsequently deported in August 1943 with the prospects of a *Pax Germanica* fading away and the Germans being increasingly dependent on human and industrial resources in occupied Western Europe.[73] Dutch bureaucrats took professional pride in establishing a sophisticated central register that meticulously listed every Jewish resident in the Netherlands according to the racial classification imposed by the Germans.[74] Both French and Dutch officials complied with the spoliation of Jewish property in an effort to maintain control over the native economy and to prevent further interference by the Germans.[75] French banks, though, in early 1942 stopped collaborating in raising a levy of one billion francs imposed on the Jews in the occupied zone as soon as they realized that public collaterals of a loan contract were insufficient.[76]

What these cases illustrate is, again, that division of labor had no deterministic impact on the strength of perpetrators but rather created an opportunity structure for immoral behavior while not suspending moral imperatives. However, once those imperatives had been replaced by utilitarian motives—ranging from crude enrichment to the idea of improving one's nation's fate under the condition of hostile occupation—the loss of moral judgment led to mere complicity.

Conclusion: The Overdetermination of Persecution

The persecution and annihilation of the Jews under Nazi rule was the result of deliberate, intentional planning on the basis of racist anti-Semitism in a particularly aggressive or "elimininationist"[77] form. The ideological intention of those initiating the "final solution," however, explains neither the scale nor the steady radicalization of persecution and mass murder that makes the Holocaust unique in history. It is the successful and sustainable mobilization of human and organizational resources that caused the scale and scope of persecution. Recent research, including the one documented in the present volume, has revealed how widespread and ramified participation in the persecution was. Neither the motivation of those involved nor the integration of the persecution apparatus would have been possible on the basis of coercion or ideology alone. Much more robust motives must be taken into account, in particular a broad variety of utility maximization on the part of those who did not initiate the persecution but nonetheless decisively supported its implementation.

Regardless of robust utilitarian motives—above all, the avoidance of sanctions and the improvement of individual and institutional positions—which made the persecution sustainable and decisively contributed to its steady radicalization, it has to be stressed that it was anti-Semitism that not only triggered the persecution but also delivered the indispensable ideological basis of its implementation. Anti-Semitism, as Helen Fein[78] has put it, was the ideology excluding a particular societal group from the universe of moral obligation and thus caused a fundamental moral indifference among German elites, as well as among rank-and-file bureaucrats and bystanders, toward the gradual escalation of persecution.[79]

This, however, does not necessarily imply anti-Semitism as a shared belief of those involved in the persecution. Even if it was not shared, though, anti-Semitism served as a signaling mechanism transmitting a clear message as to what was desired by the persecutors and, accordingly, could be usefully observed by their helpers. The racist agenda was known to everyone and it could be used opportunistically according to individual or institutional ambitions. Regular administration agencies, such as the fiscal authorities, while intensifying the spoliation of Jewish assets, even displayed an anti-SS and anti-Gestapo attitude, just as Vichy authorities did in a similar anti-German vein—in an attempt to maintain or to regain jurisdiction over what obviously ranked high in the persecutors' preference scale. Individual and institutional utilitarianism and racist ideology, in a broad variety of configurations, were mutually reinforcing determinants of the persecution and it is this overdetermination that explains much—if not most—of the Holocaust's scale and dynamics. However, the utilitarian motives causing the scale and sustainability of the persecution were shaped by the respective structural position of the actors involved. It is here that structure-related and agency-related analyses have to be linked.

Notes

1. Franz L. Neumann, *Behemoth. The Structure and Practice of National Socialism 1933–1944* (London, 1944 [1941]).
2. See Martin Broszat, *Der Staat Hitlers. Grundlegung und Entwicklung seiner inneren Struktur* (Munich, 1969); Karl-Dietrich Bracher, *Die deutsche Diktatur. Entstehung, Struktur, Folgen des Nationalsozialismus* (Cologne/Berlin, 1969); Karl-Dietrich Bracher, "Nationalsozialismus, Faschismus, Totalitarismus—Die deutsche Diktatur im Macht- und Ideologiefeld des 20. Jahrhunderts," in Karl Dietrich Bracher, Manfred Funke, and Hans-Adolf Jacobsen, eds., *Deutschland 1933–1945. Neue Studien zur Nationalsozialistischen Herrschaft* (Düsseldorf, 1993), pp. 566–590; Jane Caplan, *Government without Administration. State and Civil Service in Weimar and Nazi Germany* (Oxford, 1988); Manfred Funke, *Starker oder schwacher Diktator? Hitlers Herrschaft und die Deutschen* (Düsseldorf, 1989); Hermann Graml, "Wer bestimmte die Außenpolitik des Dritten Reiches? Ein Beitrag zur Kontroverse um Polykratie und Monokratie im NS-Herrschaftssystem," in Manfred Funke, Hans-Adolf Jacobsen, Hans-Helmuth Knütter and Hans-Peter Schwarz et al. eds., *Demokratie und Diktatur* (Düsseldorf/ and Bonn, 1987), pp. 223–236; Gerhard

Hirschfeld and Lothar Kettenacker eds., *Der "Führerstaat": Mythos und Realität. Studien zur Struktur und Politik des Dritten Reiches* (Stuttgart, 1981); Johannes Houwink ten Cate and Gerhard Otto eds., *Das organisierte Chaos. "Ämterdarwinismus" und "Gesinnungsethik"*. *Determinanten nationalsozialistischer Besatzungsherrschaft* (Berlin, 1999); Peter Hüttenberger, "Nationalsozialistische Polykratie," *Geschichte und Gesellschaft* 2 (1976): 417–442; Gerhard Schulz, "Neue Kontroversen in der Zeitgeschichte: Führerstaat und 'Führermythos,'" *Der Staat* 22 (1983): 262–280; Klaus Hildebrand, "Monokratie oder Polykratie. Hitlers Herrschaft und das Dritte Reich," in Hirschfeld and Kettenacker, "*Führerstaat,*" pp. 73–97; for an overview see Hans-Ulrich Thamer, "Monokratie—Polykratie. Historiographischer Überblick über eine kontroverse Debatte," in Houwink ten Cate and Otto, eds., *Das organisierte Chaos*, pp. 21–34.)
3. Wolfgang Benz, Johannes Houwink ten Cate, and Gerhard Otto, eds., *Die Bürokratie der Okkupation. Strukturen der Herrschaft und Verwaltung im besetzten Europa* (Berlin, 1998); Werner Röhr, "System oder organisiertes Chaos? Fragen einer Typologie der deutschen Okkupationsregime im Zweiten Weltkrieg," in Robert Bohn, ed., *Die deutsche Herrschaft in den "germanischen" Ländern 1940–1945* (Stuttgart, 1997), pp. 11–46; Hans Umbreit, "Nationalsozialistische Expansion 1938–1941. Strukturen der deutschen Besatzungsverwaltungen im Zweiten Weltkrieg," in Michael Salewski and Josef Schröder eds., *Dienst für die Geschichte. Gedenkschrift für Walther Hubatsch* (Zürich/Göttingen, 1985), pp. 163–186; Hans Umbreit, "Auf dem Weg zur Kontinentalherrschaft," in Militärgeschichtliches Forschungsamt, ed., *Das Deutsche Reich und der Zweite Weltkrieg*, vol. 5.1:. Bd. 5, *Erster Halbband: Kriegsverwaltung, Wirtschaft und personelle Ressourcen 1939–1941* (Stuttgart, 1988), pp. 3–345.
4. See Christopher R. Browning, *The Path to Genocide. Essays on Launching the Final Solution* (Cambridge/New York, 1992), pp. 86–124; Philippe Burrin, *Hitler and the Jews. The Genesis of the Holocaust* (London, 1994), pp. 20–24; Ulrich Herbert, "Vernichtungspolitik. Neue Antworten und Fragen zur Geschichte des "Holocaust," in idem ed., *Nationalsozialistische Vernichtungspolitik 1933–1945. Neue Forschungen und Kontroversen* (Frankfurt on Main, 1998), pp. 9–66; Hirschfeld and Kettenacker, "*Führerstaat;*" Michael R. Marrus, *The Holocaust in History* (New York, 1987), pp. 34–36.
5. Hans Mommsen, "Der Nationalsozialismus. Kumulative Radikalisierung und Selbstzerstörung des Regimes.," in *Meyers Enzyklopädisches Lexikon*, vol. 16 (Mannheim, 1976), pp. 785–790.
6. See Jens Banach, *Heydrichs Elite. Das Führerkorps der Sicherheitspolizei und des SD 1936–1945* (Paderborn, 1998); Richard Breitman, *Der Architekt der "Endlösung": Himmler und die Vernichtung der europäischen Juden* (Paderborn, 1996); Ruth Bettina Brirn, *Die Höheren SS- und Polizeiführer. Himmlers Vertreter im Reich und in den besetzten Gebieten* (Düsseldorf, 1986); George C. Browder, *Foundations of the Nazi Police State. The Formation of Sipo and SD* (Lexington, 1990); George C. Browder, *Hitler's Enforcers. The Gestapo and the SS Security Service in the Nazi Revolution* (New York/Oxford, 1996); Hans Buchheim, Gerhard Paul, eds. et al., Martin Broszat, Hans-Adolf Jacobsen and Helmut Krausnick, *Anatomie des SS-Staates*, 2 vols. (Munich, 1976); Robert Gellately, "Situating the 'SS-State' in a Social-Historical Context: Recent Histories of the SS, the Police, and the Courts in the Third Reich." ," *Journal of Modern History* 64 (1992): 338–365; Gerhard Paul and Klaus-Michael Mallmann, eds., *Die Gestapo. Mythos und Realität* (Darmstadt, 1995); Friedrich Wilhelm, *Die Polizei im NS-Staat. Die Geschichte ihrer Organisation im Überblick* (Paderborn, 1997).
7. Gerard Aalders, *Roof. De ontvremding van joods bezit tijdens de Tweede Wereldoorlog* (The Hague, 1999); Avraham Barkai, *Vom Boykott zur "Entjudung". Der wirtschaftliche Existenzkampf der Juden 1933–1943* (Frankfurt on Main, 1987); Frank Bajohr, "*Arisierung*" *in Hamburg. Die Verdrängung der jüdischen Unternehmer 1933-1945* (Hamburg, 1997); Commission Buysse [Commission d'étude sur le sort des biens des membres de la Communauté juive de Belgique spoliés ou délaissés pendant la guerre 1940–1945], *Rapport final: Les Biens des victimes des persécutions anti-juives en Belgique* (Brussels, 2001); Commission Mattéoli [Mission d'étude sur la Spoliation des Juifs de France], *Rapport final de la "Mission d'étude sur la spoliation des Juifs en France,"* (Paris,

2000); Helmut Genschel, *Die Verdrängung der Juden aus der Wirtschaft im Dritten Reich* (Göttingen, 1966); Harold James, *The Deutsche Bank and the Nazi Economic War Against the Jews. The Expropriation of Jewish-owned Property* (Cambridge, 2001); Gerhard Kratzsch, *Der Gauwirtschaftsapparat der NSDAP. Menschenführung, "Arisierung", Wehrwirtschaft im Gau Westfalen-Süd. Eine Studie zur Herrschaftspraxis im totalitären Staat*, (Münster, 1989); Johannes Ludwig, *Boykott, Enteignung, Mord. Die "Entjudung" der deutschen Wirtschaft* (Hamburg, 1989); Jonathan Steinberg, *Die Deutsche Bank und ihre Goldtransaktionen während des Zweiten Weltkrieges* (Munich, 1999).

8. Götz Aly, *"Endlösung". Völkerverschiebung und der Mord an den europäischen Juden* (Frankfurt, 1995); Christopher R. Browning, *Nazi Policy, Jewish Workers, German Killers* (Cambridge, 2000); Christoph Dieckmann, "Der Krieg und die Ermordung der litauischen Juden," in Herbert, ed., *Vernichtungspolitik*, pp. 292–329; Christian Gerlach, *Krieg, Ernährung, Völkermord. Forschungen zur deutschen Vernichtungspolitik im Zweiten Weltkrieg* (Hamburg, 1998); Christian Gerlach, *Kalkulierte Morde. Die deutsche Wirtschafts- und Vernichtungspolitik in Weißrussland 1941 bis 1944* (Hamburg, 1999); Jörg Gutberger, *Volk, Raum und Sozialstruktur. Sozialstruktur- und Sozialraumforschung im "Dritten Reich"* (Münster, 1996); Susanne Heim und and Götz Aly, *Vordenker der Vernichtung. Auschwitz und die deutschen Pläne für eine europäische Neuordnung* (Frankfurt on Main, 1991); Ulrich Herbert, "Die deutsche Militärverwaltung in Paris und die Deportation der französischen Juden," in idem, ed., *Vernichtungspolitik*, pp. 170–208; Rolf-Dieter Müller, *Hitlers Ostkrieg und die deutsche Siedlungspolitik. Die Zusammenarbeit von Wehrmacht, Wirtschaft und SS* (Frankfurt on Main, 1991); Jörg Friedrich, *Das Gesetz des Krieges. Das deutsche Heer in Rußland 1941–1945. Der Prozeß gegen das Oberkommando der Wehrmacht*, 2nd ed. (Munich, 1996).

9. See contributions by Gerard Aalders, Marc-Olivier Baruch, Martin C. Dean, Wolfgang Dierker, Jonathan Petropoulos, Philippe Verheyde, and Dieter Ziegler in the present volume.

10. Daniel J. Goldhagen, *Hitler's Willing Executioners* (New York, 1996).

11. Herbert, *Vernichtungspolitik*, p. 22.

12. This refers to what John Rawls calls the problem of the "original position" and the "veil of ignorance": What can be assumed to be the most general preferences of individuals who, in an original position, are ignorant even about the most basic characteristics of the particular society they live in? See John Rawls, *A Theory of Justice*, revised ed. (Cambridge, 1999 [1971]), pp. 118–192. "Even though the parties are deprived of information about their particular ends," Rawls concludes, "they have enough knowledge to rank their alternatives. They know that in general they must try to protect their liberties, widen their opportunities, and enlarge their means for promoting their aims whatever these are" (Rawls, *Justice*, p. 143).

13. Browning, *Nazi Policy*; Peter Longerich, *Politik der Vernichtung. Eine Gesamtdarstellung der nationalsozialistischen Judenverfolgung* (Munich/Zurich, 1998).

14. A significant example is what the *Judenreferent* of the SD (Sicherheitsdienst) in Paris, Dannecker, wrote to his opposite number in the German military administration in January 1941: "It turned out that the cultivation of opposition to the Jews among the French is hardly possible on the basis of idealism, while in the case where economic advantages present themselves consent to the anti-Jewish struggle is more likely to be obtained." [*Es hat sich gezeigt, daß die Züchtung einer Judengegnerschaft bei den Franzosen auf ideeller Basis kaum möglich ist, während im Falle des Sichbietens wirtschaftlicher Vorteile eine Billigung des antijüdischen Kampfes eher erfolgen wird.*]—Der Beauftragte des Chefs der Sicherheitspolizei und des SD für Belgien und Frankreich, Dienststelle Paris, an den Chef der Militärverwaltung Frankreich, Verwaltungsstab [The Representative of the Chief of the Security Police and the SD for Belgium and France, Paris Office, to the Chief of the Military Administration of France, Administrative Staff], note of 28 January 1941, II B 2, Dan [Dannecker]/Wa (Centre de Documentation Juive Contemporaine [CDJC], V-64, cited in Serge Klarsfeld, *Vichy—Auschwitz. Die Zusammenarbeit der deutschen und französischen Behörden bei der "Endlösung der Judenfrage" in Frankreich* (Nördlingen, 1989), p. 363.

15. For an overview on what is, awkwardly enough, being called subjective-expected-utility (or SEU) theory, see Siegwart Lindenberg, "Homo Socio-oeconomicus: The Emergence of a General Model of Man in the Social Sciences," *Journal of Institutional and Theoretical Economics* 146 (1990): 727–748.
16. See James S. Coleman, *Foundations of Social Theory* (Cambridge, 1990), pp. 1–23, for the general problem of micro-foundation of structure-related assumptions.
17. Gary S. Becker, "Crime and Punishment: An Economic Approach," *Journal of Political Economy* 76 (1968): 169–217.
18. See Rainer C. Baum, *The Holocaust and the German Elite. Genocide and National Suicide in Germany, 1871–1945* (Totowa/London, 1981); Goldhagen, *Willing Executioners*.
19. Even in Germany proper the delicate balance of knowledge, concealment and camouflage of anti-Jewish measures, the deportations in particular, played an important role. The rhetoric of "evacuation," "outward migration," "expulsion," or "resettlement" (*Evakuierung, Abwanderung, Abschiebung* or *Umsiedlung*) used by the administrations in connection with the deportations of Jews did not constitute mere euphemisms employed with a clear knowledge of the actual fate of the deportees (this was, of course, its function in the perpetrators' perspective); they presumably also supported the self-deception of the numerous administrative personnel involved in the deportation measures. If the moral discernment of these actors had been entirely suspended, this rhetoric, or at least its consistent employment, would not have been necessary. That the helpers in the persecutory actions against the Jews recognized the immoral nature of these actions and thereby of their own cooperation, or that they could have recognized this immorality if they had wanted to recognize it, is for Western Europe in particular, well documented: Stéphane Courtois and Adam Rayski, *Qui savait quoi? L'extermination des juifs, 1941–1945* (Paris, 1987); Herbert, *Vernichtungspolitik*, pp. 48–63; Steinberg, *Deutsche Bank*, pp. 79–89; Marrus, *Holocaust*, pp. 157–164; Michael R. Marrus and Robert O. Paxton, *Vichy et les Juifs* (Paris, 1981), pp. 478–491; Hans Mommsen, "Die Realisierung des Utopischen. Die 'Endlösung der Judenfrage' im Dritten Reich," *Geschichte und Gesellschaft* 9 (1983): 381–420; Hans Mommsen, "Was haben die Deutschen vom Völkermord gewußt?" in Walter Pehle and Uwe Dietrich, eds., *Der Judenpogrom 1938. Von der "Reichskristallnacht" zum Völkermord* (Frankfurt on Main, 1988); Nanda Van der Zee, *Om erger te voorkomen. De voorbereiding en uitvoering van de vernietiging van het Nederlandse jodendom tijdens de Tweede Wereldoorlog* (Amsterdam, 1997).
20. Leon Festinger, *A Theory of Cognitive Dissonance* (Stanford, 1957).
21. Banach, *Elite*; Richard Breitman, *Architekt*; Birn, *Die Höheren SS- und Polizeiführer*; Browder, *Foundations*; idem, *Gestapo*; Buchheim, Broszat, Jacobsen and Krausnick et al., *Anatomie*; Gellately, "SS-Sate"; Paul and Mallmann, *Gestapo*; Wilhelm, *Polizei*.
22. Bajohr, *"Arisierung"*; Kratzsch, *Der Gauwirtschaftsapparat der NSDAP*, pp. 150–163; Ludwig, *Boykott, Enteignung, Mord*.
23. Hans G. Adler, *Der verwaltete Mensch. Studien zur Deportation der Juden aus Deutschland* (Tübingen, 1974), pp. 323–437; Michael Zimmermann, "Eine Deportation nach Auschwitz. Zur Rolle des Banalen bei der Durchsetzung des Monströsen,"" in Heide Gerstenberger and Dorothea Schmidt, eds., *Normalität oder Normalisierung? Geschichtswerkstätten und Faschismusanalyse* (Münster, 1987), pp. 84–96; Michael Zimmermann, "Die Gestapo und die regionale Organisation der Judendeportationen. Das Beispiel der Stapo-Leitstelle Düsseldorf," in Paul and Mallmann, *Gestapo*, pp. 357–372.
24. Wolfgang Seibel, "The Strength of Perpetrators—The Holocaust in Western Europe, 1940–1944," *Governance – An International Journal of Policy, Administration, and Institutions* 15 (2002): 211–240, and contribution by Jörg Raab in the present section.
25. Peter M. Blau and William Richard Scott, *Formal Organizations* (San Francisco, 1962); Jeffrey Pressman and Aaron Wildavsky, *Implementation: How Great Expectations in Washington are Dashed in Oakland or, Why It's Amazing that Federal Programs Work at All. This Being a Saga of the Economic Development Administration as Told by Two Sympathetic Observers Who Seek to Build Morals on a Foundation of Ruined Hopes* (Berkeley, 1963); James D. Thompson, *Organizations in Action* (New York, 1967); Joan Woodward, *Industrial Organization. Theory and Practice.* (London, (1965).

26. Thompson, *Organizations*.
27. George Tsebelis, Veto Players. How Political Institutions Work (Princeton, 2002).
28. See Cornelis J. Lammers, "The Interorganizational Control of an Occupied Country," *Administrative Science Quarterly* 33 (1988): 438–457.
29. See Hirschfeld and Seibel in the present volume.
30. Robert O. Paxton, *Vichy France. Old Guard and the New Order, 1940–47* (New York, 1972).
31. See Marrus and Paxton, *Vichy*.
32. Regina M. Delacor, "*Ausländische Juden—Opfer 'nationaler Prophylaxe'? Zur Verstrickung des État Français in die 'Endlösung der Judenfrage' 1942–44*," unpublished conference paper, Colloque "La France et l'Allemagne en Guerre (Novembre 1942–Automne 1944)" (Paris, 1999); Julian Jackson, *France–The Dark Years 1940–1944* (Oxford, 2001); Serge Klarsfeld, *Die Endlösung der Judenfrage. Deutsche Dokumente 1941–1944.* (Paris, 1977); idem, *Vichy—Auschwitz*; Ian Ousby, *Occupation. The Ordeal of France, 1940–1944* (London, 1997); Marrus and Paxton, *Vichy*; Richard H. Weisberg, *Vichy Law and the Holocaust in France*, (New York, 1996).
33. From the abundant literature, see the basic works of Sanford J. Grossman and Oliver Hart, "An Analysis of the Principal–Agent Problem," *Econometrica* 51 (1983): 7–45; Bengt Holmström, "Moral Hazard and Observability," *Bell Journal of Economics* 10 (1979): 74–90; John W. Pratt and Richard Zeckhauser, *Principals and Agents: The Structure of Business* (Boston, 1985); Stephen Shavell, "Risk Sharing and Incentives in the Principal and Agent Relationship," *Bell Journal of Economics* 10 (1979): 55–73.
34. Randall L. Calvert, Mathew D. McCubbins, and Barry R. Weingast, "A Theory of Political Control and Agency Discretion," *American Journal of Political Science* 33 (1989): 588–611; David Epstein and Sharry O'Halloran, "Administrative Procedures, Information, and Agency Discretion," *American Journal of Political Science* 38 (1994): 697–722; Edward P. Schwartz and Michael R. Tomz, "The Long-Run Advantages of Centralization for Collective Action: A Comment on Bendor and Mookherjee," *American Political Science Review* 92 (1997): 685–697.
35. Lammers, "Interorganizational Control," pp. 438–457.
36. Peter Bernholz, "Logrolling, Arrow-Paradox and Cyclical Majorities," *Public Choice* 15 (1973): 87–95; William H. Riker and Steven J. Brams, "The Paradox of Vote Trading," *American Political Science Review* 67 (1973): 1335–1347.
37. That "polycratic" or "polyarchic" structures encourage bargaining and logrolling is a longstanding commonplace in political science theory: See Robert A. Dahl and Charles E. Lindblom, *Politics, Economics, and Welfare. Planning and Politico-Economic Systems Resolved into Basic Social Processes* (New York, 1953), pp. 272–348.
38. Klarsfeld, *Vichy-Auschwitz*, pp. 161–274; Marrus and Paxton, *Vichy*, pp. 446–458.
39. Jonathan Steinberg, *All or Nothing: The Axis of the Holocaust: 1941–1943* (London/New York, 1991)..
40. Meir Michaelis, "The Holocaust in Italy: Areas of Inquiry," in Michael Berenbaum and Abraham J. Peck, eds., *The Holocaust and History. The Known, the Unknown, the Disputed, and the Reexamined* (Bloomington/Indianapolis, 1998), pp. 439–462.
41. Walter Bargatzky, *Hotel Majestic. Ein Deutscher im besetzten Frankreich* (Freiburg, 1987), pp. 73–75.
42. Bargatzky—after 1945 a high-ranking civil servant in the Federal Government and from 1967 until 1982 President of the German Red Cross—was from July 1940 on *Kriegsverwaltungsrat* in Paris.
43. Bargatzky, *Majestic*, p. 73.
44. See Joseph Billig, *Alfred Rosenberg dans l'action idéologique, politique et administrative du Reich hitlérien. Inventaire commenté de la collection de documents conservés au C.D.J.C. provenant des archives du Reichsleiter et Ministre A. Rosenberg* (Paris, 1963).
45. The enrichment of banks, real-estate brokers, notaries, shipping agencies, assessors, or even of former neighbors through the the spoliation of Jewish property has been extensively documented not only for Germany, but also for the territories under German occu-

pation. See Aalders, *Roof*, pp. 149–236; Adler, *Der verwaltete Mensch*, pp. 589–644; Johannes Bähr, *Der Goldhandel der Dresdner Bank während des Zweiten Weltkriegs* (Leipzig, 1999); Bajohr, *"Arisierung,"* pp. 265–324; Franziska Becker, *Gewalt und Gedächtnis. Erinnerungen an die nationalsozialistische Verfolgung einer jüdischen Landgemeinde* (Göttingen, 1994); Alex Bruns-Wüstefeld, *Lohnende Geschäfte: Die "Entjudung" der Wirtschaft am Beispiel Göttingens* (Hanover, 1997); Caisse des Depôts et Consignations [Groupe de travail sur les spoliations et les restitutions des "biens juifs"], *Rapport d'étape, Janvier 1999* (Paris, 1999); Commission Buysse, *Rapport final*; Commission Mattéoli, *Rapport final*; Wolfgang Dreßen, *Betrifft: "Aktion 3". Deutsche verwerten jüdische Nachbarn* (Berlin, 1998); Steinberg, *Die Deutsche Bank*; Zimmermann, "Die Gestapo," pp. 357–372.
46. Barkai, *Boykott*, p. 194.
47. See Dean, *Collaboration in the Holocaust: Crimes of the Local Police in Below Russia and Ukraine, 1941–1944* (Basingstoke, 2000) 2001; Stefan Mehl, *Das Reichsfinanzministerium und die Verfolgung der deutschen Juden 1933–1943* (Berlin, 1990), pp. 89–98).
48. RMF – O 5205 – 98 VI, cited in Joseph Walk, ed., *Das Sonderrecht für die Juden im NS-Staat. Eine Sammlung der gesetzlichen Maßnahmen und Richtlinien—Inhalt und Bedeutung*, 2nd ed. (Heidelberg/Karlsruhe, 1996), p. 359; [my italics, WS].
49. Circular of the Reichssicherheitshauptamt, RSHA—IV B 4 a/1033/41—39, 3 December 1941, cited in Walk, *Sonderrecht*, p. 358.
50. Rainer Weinert, *"Die Sauberkeit der Verwaltung im Kriege". Der Rechnungshof des Deutschen Reiches 1938–1946*, (Opladen/Wiesbaden, 1993).
51. Adler, *Der verwaltete Mensch*, pp. 598–603.
52. Ibid., pp. 601–603.
53. Ibid., pp. 592–594.
54. See Chester I. Barnard, *The Functions of the Executive. Thirtieth Anniversary Edition* (Cambridge, Massachusetts, 1968 [1938]), pp. 56–59; Herbert A. Simon, *Administrative Behavior. A Study of Decision-Making Process in Administrative Organization*, 2nd ed. (New York, 1957).
55. Simon, *Adminstrative Behavior*, 2nd ed., 15th pr. (New York, 1970), pp. 61–109; James G. March and Herbert A. Simon, *Organizations* (New York/London, 1958), pp. 137–172.
56. DeWitt Dearborn and Herbert A. Simon, "Selective Perception. A Note on the Departmental Identification of Executives," *Sociometry* 21 (1958): 140–144.
57. See Konrad Jarausch, *The Conundrum of Complicity. German Professionals and the Final Solution*, United States Holocaust Memorial Museum: Joseph and Rebecca Meyerhoff Annual Lecture [held 11 June 2001] (Washington D.C., 2002), and the contribution by Michael Th Allen in the present volume.
58. Zygmunt Bauman, *Modernity and the Holocaust* (Ithaca, 1989), pp. 18–27; John Lachs, *Responsibility and the Individual in Modern Society* (Brighton, 1981), pp. 22–34.
59. Hannah Arendt, *Eichmann in Jerusalem. A Report on the Banality of Evil* (New York, 1963).
60. See Charles Perrow, *Complex Organizations. A Critical Essay*, 3rd ed. (New York, 1987), pp. 128–131.
61. Uwe Dietrich Adam, *Judenpolitik im Dritten Reich* (Düsseldorf, 1973); Guy B. Adams and Danny L. Balfour, *Unmasking Administrative Evil* (London, 1998), pp. 53–72; Adler, *Der verwaltete Mensch*; Michael Thad Allen, *The Business of Genocide. The SS, Slave Labor, and the Concentration Camps* (Chapel Hill, 2002); Bauman, *Modernity*, pp. 18–27; Mommsen, "Realisierung des Utopischen"; James C. Scott, *Seeing like a State. How Certain Schemes to Improve the Human Condition Have Failed* (New Haven/London, 1998), pp. 76–83; Zimmermann, "Deportation nach Auschwitz."
62. Stanley Milgram, *Obedience to Authority: An Experimental View* (New York, 1974).
63. Festinger, *Cognitive Dissonance*.
64. In a circular of 1 November 1940, the head of the division of economic affairs of the German Military Commander in France, Dr. Elmar Michel, explained why French rather than German authorities should assume the task of eliminating the Jews from the French econ-

omy: "[In this way] the co-responsibility of the French will be achieved and the French administrative apparatus will be at our disposal. Accordingly, as long as important German interests are not at stake, primarily French provisional administrators [of Jewish businesses] have to be nominated. What is desired in principle is the replacement of Jews by Frenchmen in an attempt to let the French people benefit economically from the removal of the Jews and to avoid the impression that the Germans just want to put themselves in place of the Jews." [Es wird auf diese Weise die Mitverantwortung der französischen Stellen erreicht und es steht der französische Verwaltungsapparat zur Verfügung. Es werden dementsprechend, wenn nicht wichtige deutsche Interessen in Frage kommen, auch in erster Linie französische kommissarische Verwalter eingesetzt. Grundsätzlich wird die Ersetzung der Juden durch Franzosen erstrebt, um so auch die französische Bevölkerung wirtschaftlich an der Verdrängung der Juden zu beteiligen und den Eindruck zu vermeiden, als wollten sich nur die Deutschen an die Stelle der Juden setzen.]—Der Militärbefehlshaber in Frankreich, Wi I 426/40, 1. November 1940 (Centre de Documentation Juive Contemporaine, Paris, CL-1).—The author of the circular, Michel, in 1949 became head of division and *Ministerialdirektor* in the Federal Ministry of the Economy under the minister and future West German chancellor Ludwig Erhard: see Willi A. Boelcke, *Die deutsche Wirtschaft 1930–1945. Interna des Reichswirtschaftsministeriums* (Düsseldorf, 1983), p. 353.

65. Festinger, *Cognitive Dissonance*, pp. 264–266.
66. See Timur Kuran, *Private Truths, Public Lies. The Social Consequences of Preference Falsification* (Cambridge, Massachusetts, 1995), for the paradox of intentional ignorance.
67. Herbert, *Vernichtungspolitik*; Joseph Billig, *Le Commissariat Général aux questions juives (1941–1944)*, 3 vols. (Paris, 1955, 1957, 1960).
68. Weisberg, *Vichy Law*.
69. See Louis De Jong, *The Netherlands and Nazi Germany* (Cambridge, Massachusetts, 1990), pp. 27–50.
70. Approximate rates of Jewish victimization, 1939–1945 (according to Wolfgang Benz, ed., *Dimensionen des Völkermordes. Die Zahl der jüdischen Opfer des Nationalsozialismus* (Munich, 1996; percentages refer to deportation and/or mass murder): France 25%, Belgium 43%, The Netherlands 76%, Denmark 8%, Norway 42%, Poland 78%, Soviet Union 69%, Czechoslovakia (Bohemia and Moravia, Slovakia, on the basis of territories in 1939) 72%, Hungary 69%, Greece 81%, Yugoslavia 79%, Italy 25%.
71. Seibel, "Strength of Perpetrators."
72. See Aalders, *Roof*; Marc-Olivier Baruch, *Servir l'état français. L'administration en France de 1940 à 1944* (Paris, 1997); idem, *Das Vichy-Regime. Frankreich 1940–1944* (Stuttgart, 2000).
73. Marrus and Paxton, *Vichy*, pp. 446–458.
74. Bob Moore, *Victims and Survivors. The Nazi Persecution of the Jews in the Netherlands 1940–1945* (London, 1997), pp. 194–199.
75. See Aalders, *Roof*; Commission Mattéoli, *Rapport final*.
76. Billig, *Le Commissariat générale*, vol. 3, pp. 219–220; Caisse des Dépôts et Consignations, *Rapport d'étape*, p. 93.
77. Goldhagen, *Willing Executioners*.
78. Helen Fein, *Accounting for Genocide: National Responses and Jewish Victimization during the Holocaust* (New York, 1979); idem, *Genocide: a Sociological Perspective* (London, 1993).
79. Baum, *German Elite*.

NOTES ON CONTRIBUTORS

Gerard Aalders is a Senior Researcher at the Netherlands Institute for War Documentation (NIOD). His recent publications include: *Bij Verordening. De roof van het joodse vermogen in Nederland en het naoorlogse rechtsherstel. Bijlage 3 van het Eindrapport van de Contactgroep Tegoeden WO II* [*The Looting of Jewish Assets in the Netherlands and Post-War Restitution*], The Hague, 2000; and a trilogy on the looting and restitution of Jewish Property: *Roof. De ontvreemding van joods bezit tijdens de Tweede Wereldoorlog*, The Hague, 1999 [English edition: *Nazi Looting. The Plunder of Dutch Jewry during the Second World War*, Oxford and New York, 2004]; *Berooid. De beroofde joden en het Nederlandse restitutiebeleid sinds 1945* [*Destitute. The Robbed Jews and the Dutch Restitution Policy since 1945*], Amsterdam, 2001; *De nazi-roof van 146 duizend kilo goud bij De Nederlandsche Bank* [*Jackdaws. The Nazi-looting of 146,000 Kilo's of Monetary Gold from the Central Bank of the Netherlands*], Amsterdam, 2002.

Michael Thad Allen is currently Visiting Associate Professor at the University of Connecticut. He has published extensively in business history, the history of technology, and the history of the Holocaust. His recent publications include "Modernity, the Holocaust, and Machines without History," in a volume he edited with Gabrielle Hecht, *Technologies of Power*, Massachusetts, 2001: 175–214; and "The Devil in the Details: The Gas Chambers of Birkenau, October 1941," *Holocaust and Genocide Studies* 16 (2002): 189–216. He is also the author of *The Business of Genocide: The SS, Slave Labor, and the Concentration Camps*, North Carolina, 2002, which was awarded the German Studies Association-DAAD book prize for 2002–2003 and the Southern Historical Association's Smith Prize for the best book in European history, 2001–2002.

Frank Bajohr is a Senior Researcher at the Institute for Contemporary History at Hamburg University. His research focuses on the history of the Third Reich and the persecution of the Jews. His recent publications include: *Parvenüs und Profiteure. Korruption in der NS-Zeit* [*Parvenues and Profiteers. Corruption during the Nazi-Era*], Frankfurt am Main, 2001; *"Aryanisation"* in Hamburg. *The Economic Exclusion of Jews and the Confiscation of their Property in Nazi Germany*, New York, 2002; "Unser Hotel ist judenfrei". *Bäder-Antisemitismus im 19. und 20. Jahrhundert* [*Our Hotel* is judenfrei. *Spa-Antisemitism in the 19th and 20th Century*], Frankfurt am Main, 2003.

Marc Olivier Baruch is a directeur d'études à l'École des hautes études en science sociales in Paris. A civil servant himself, his work mainly focuses on administration and government in twentieth-century France. The majority of his research was concerned with the French civil service during the Second World War: *Servir l'Etat français. L'administration en France de 1940 à 1944*, Paris, 1997. He recently edited a thorough study on the purges in France after the Second World War: *Une poignée de misérables. L'épuration de la société française après le Seconde Guerre mondiale*, Paris, 2003 and is currently working on government and administration in dictatorial political systems.

Martin C. Dean is an Applied Research Scholar at the Center for Advanced Holocaust Studies, United States Holocaust Memorial Museum, Washington, DC. He was previously Senior Historian with the Metropolitan Police War Crimes Unit in London. His research focuses on the implementation of the Holocaust in Eastern Europe and the confiscation of Jewish property. His recent publications include: *Collaboration in the Holocaust: "Crimes of the Local Police in Belorussia and Ukraine, 1941–44,"* London and New York, 2000; "Der Raub jüdischen Eigentums in Europa" [The Robbery of Jewish Property in Europe]. In: Constantin Goschler and Philipp Ther (eds), *Raub und Restitution: Arisierung und Rückerstattung des jüdischen Eigentums in Europa*, Frankfurt am Main, 2003: 26–40; "The Development and Implementation of Nazi Denaturalization and Confiscation Policy up to the Eleventh Decree to the Reich Citizenship Law of November 25, 1941." In: *Holocaust and Genocide Studies* 16 (2002): 217–242.

Wolfgang Dierker is Director of Government and Public Affairs for Hewlett-Packard Germany, Berlin. He earned a Ph.D. from the University of Bonn in 2000 and has done research on the history of National Socialism. His recent publications include: *Himmlers Glaubenskrieger. Der Sicherheitsdienst der SS und seine Religionspolitik 1933–1941* [*Himmler's* Glaubenskrieger. *The Sicherheitsdienst of the SS and its Religion Policy, 1933–1941*], Paderborn: Schöningh 2002; "'Ich will keine Nullen, sondern Bullen'. Hitlers Koalitionsverhandlungen mit der Bayerischen Volkspartei im März 1933" ["I don't want *Nullen* but *Bullen*". Hitler's Negotiation for a Coalition with the *Bayerische Volkspartei*, March 1933], *Vierteljahrshefte für Zeitgeschichte* 50 (2002): 111–148.

Gerald D. Feldman is a Professor of History at the University of California, Berkeley and is Director of the Institute of European Studies and the Center for German and European Studies. He has written books and articles on Germany in the First World War, the inflation and hyperinflation, and the

Weimar Republic. He has most recently turned his attention to the business history of the Third Reich. His major book-length publication in this field is *Allianz and the German Insurance Business, 1933–1945*, New York and Cambridge, 2001. He has also written numerous articles dealing with financial institutions in National Socialist Germany. He is presently working on a history of the Austrian Banks between 1938–1945.

Christian Gerlach is an Assistant Professor of History at the Department of History, National University of Singapore. His research is devoted to: the German occupation of Eastern Europe during the Second World War, German economic policy, the Holocaust and other German mass violence, as well as international development policy and the world food problem of the 1970s. Recent publications include: *Kalkulierte Morde: Die deutsche Wirtschafts- und Vernichtungspolitik in Weißrußland 1941–1944* [*Calculated Murder. German Economic and Annihilation Policy in White Russia*], Hamburg, 1999; *Krieg, Ernährung, Völkermord: Forschungen zur deutschen Vernichtungspolitik im Zweiten Weltkrieg* [*War, Food, and Genocide. Studies on German Annihilation Policy during World War II*], 2nd ed., Zurich and Munich, 2001; "The Wannsee Conference, the Fate of German Jews, and Hitler's Decision in Principle to Exterminate All European Jews." In: *Journal of Modern History* 70: 4 (1998): 759–812.

Wolf Gruner was E. Desmond Lee Visiting Professor of Global Awareness at Webster University, St. Louis, Missouri, U.S.A. until 2003 and is now Postdoc. Fellow of the S. Fischer-Stiftung at the Institut für Zeitgeschichte-Außenstelle, Berlin. His historical research focuses on the Holocaust in Europe and state discrimination of indigenous people in Latin America. Recent publications include: *Öffentliche Wohlfahrt und Judenverfolgung. Wechselwirkungen lokaler und zentraler Politik im NS-Staat (1933–1942)* [*Public Welfare and Persecution of the Jews*], Munich, 2002; "The Factory-Action and the Events at the Berlin Rosenstrasse. Facts and Fiction about 27 February 1943 – Sixty Years Later," in: *Central European History* 36 (2003): 179–208. *Forced Labor of Jews. Economic Needs and Nazi Racial aims in Germany, Austria, the Czech and Polish Territories. A comparative view*, Cambridge, 2004; "Anti-Jewish Policy in Nazi Germany 1933–1945. From Exclusion and Expulsion to Segregation and Deportation. New Perspectives on Developments, Actors and Goals." In: *The Comprehensive History of the Holocaust: Germany*, ed. by Yad Vashem Jerusalem, Nebraska, forthcoming.

Isabel Heinemann is Wissenschaftliche Assistentin at the History Department of Freiburg University. Her main fields of expertise are the history of National Socialism and contemporary U.S.-American history. She has worked extensively on the various aspects of NS racial policy in occupied Europe and now prepares a comparative study of the American family in the twentieth century. Her recent publications include her dissertation, "'Rasse Siedlung, deutsches Blut'. Das Rasse- und Siedlungshauptamt der SS und die rassenpolitische Neuordnung im besetzten Europa" [*The* Rasse- und Siedlungshauptamt *and the Racist Reshaping of Occupied Europe*], Göttingen, 2003; "'Until the Last Drop of Good Blood'. The Kidnapping of 'Racially Valuable' Children and Nazi Racial Policy in Occupied Eastern Europe," in A. Dirk Moses (ed.), *Genocide and Settler Society. Frontier Violence and Stolen Indigenous Children in Australian History*, (in print); "Towards an 'Ethnic Reconstruction' of Occupied Europe: SS Plans and Racial Policies," *Annali dell Istituto Storico in Trento XXVII* (2001), pp. 493–517; "Another Type of Perpetrator: The SS Racial Experts and Forced Population Movements in the Occupied Regions," *Holocaust and Genocide Studies* 15: 3 (2001). pp. 387–411.

Gerhard Hirschfeld is Director of the Library of Contemporary History and Professor of Modern History at the University of Stuttgart. His research interests concern the cultural and social history of the First World War, and comparative history of the Nazi occupation of Europe and The Netherlands in the twentieth century. His most recent publications include "Der Völkermord im Zwanzigsten Jahrhundert —Plädoyer für eine vergleichende Betrachtung" [Genocide in the Twentieth Century. A Plea for a Comparative Perspective]. In: *Völkermord—Friedenswissenschaftliche Annäherungen*, Baden-Baden, 2001, pp. 78–90; "Nazi Germany and the East," in: *Germany and the East*, ed. by E. Muehle, Oxford, 2003, pp. 67–90; *L'umanità offesa. Stermini e memoria nell'Europa del Novecento* (with Gustavo Corni), Bologna, 2003; Enzyklopädie Erster Weltkrieg [Encyclopedia World War I] (with Gerd Krumeich and Irina Renz), Paderborn et al. (2nd ed.) 2004.

Alfons Kenkmann was Director of the municipal historical site "Villa ten Hompel" in Münster (1998–2003) and has been a Professor of Didactics of History at the University of Leipzig, since 2003. Recent publications include: *Wilde Jugend. Lebenswelt großstädtischer Jugendlicher zwischen Weltwirtschaftskrise, Nationalsozialismus und Währungsreform* [*Wild Youth. Deviant Juvenile Behaviour in between World Economic Crisis, the NS-system and Monetary Reform*], Essen, 1996 (2nd ed. 2002); *Verfolgung und Verwaltung. Die wirtschaftliche Ausplünderung der Juden und die westfälischen Finanzbehörden* [*Prosecution and Administration. The Economic Depredation of the Jews and the Fiscal Authorities in Westphalia*] (with Bernd-A. Rusinek), Münster, 1999; *Im Auftrag. Polizei, Verwaltung und Verantwortung*, [*On Behalf of ... Police, Administration and Responsibility*] (with Christoph Spieker), Essen, 2001.

Wendy Lower earned her Ph.D. at American University in Washington, DC. Her contribution to this volume is based on her dissertation, "Nazi Colonial Dreams: German Policies and Ukrainian Society in Zhytomyr, Ukraine 1941–1944." Dr Lower has lectured and taught Holocaust history at Georgetown University, University of Maryland and the United States Holocaust Memorial Museum. Her research has been published in the journals, *Holo-*

caust and Genocide Studies and *German Studies Review*. She was Director of the Visiting Scholars Program at the United States Holocaust Memorial Museum's Center for Advanced Holocaust Studies (2000–2004) and is currently Assistant Professor of History at Towson University, Maryland.

Jonathan Petropoulos is the John V. Croul Professor of European History at Claremont McKenna College in Southern California, where he also serves as director of the Gould Center for Humanistic Studies and the Associate Director of the Center for the Study of the Holocaust, Genocide, and Human Rights. He is the author of *Art as Politics in the Third Reich*, North Carolina, 1996, and *The Faustian Bargain: The Art World in Nazi Germany*, Oxford, 2000, and co-editor of *A User's Guide to German Cultural Studies*, Michigan, 1998. He has also served as Research Director for Art and Cultural Property on the Presidential Commission on Holocaust Assets in the United States, where he helped draft the report, "Restitution and Plunder: The U.S. and Holocaust Victims' Assets" (2001). Jonathan Petropoulos has helped organize art exhibitions, including "Degenerate Art: The Fate of the Avant-Garde in Nazi Germany," which opened at LACMA in 1991, and he has served as a consultant for a number of Holocaust victims trying to recover lost artworks. He is currently completing a book on German royal families during the Third Reich.

Jörg Raab is Assistant Professor of Policy and Organization Studies at the University of Tilburg, Netherlands. His research is mainly devoted to organization theory; especially inter-organizational networks, quantitative network analysis and visualization of social networks as well as governance mechanisms in the state, economy and society. Recent publications include: "Privatisierungsnetzwerke" [Privatization Networks] (with Wolfgang Seibel). In: Wolfgang Seibel et al.: *Verwaltete Illusionen. Die Treuhandanstalt und ihre Nachfolgeeinrichtungen 1990–2000*, Frankfurt am Main and New York, 2004; "Dark Networks as Problems" (with H. Brinton Milward), *Journal of Public Administration Research and Theory* 13: 4 (2003): 413–440; "Verfolgungsnetzwerke. Zur Messung von Arbeitsteilung und Machtdifferenzierung in den Verfolgungsapparaten des Holocaust" [Persecution Networks. On the Measurement of Differentiation of Power and Division of Labor within the Persecution Apparatuses of the Holocaust] (with Wolfgang Seibel). In: *Kölner Zeitschrift für Soziologie und Sozialpsychologie* 55 (2003): 197–230; "Where Do Policy Networks Come From?", *Journal of Public Administration Research and Theory* 12: 4 (2002): 581–622; *Steuerung von Privatisierung. Eine Analyse der Steuerungsstrukturen der Privatisierung der ostdeutschen Werft- und Stahlindustrie 1990–1994*, Wiesbaden 2002.

Wolfgang Seibel is a Professor of Political and Administrative Science at the University of Konstanz whose research focuses mainly on issues of politics and organization, public administration and non-governmental organizations in particular, in German political history. His recent publications include *The Nonprofit Sector in Germany*, (with Helmut K. Anheier), Manchester, 2001; *Verwaltete Illusionen. Die Treuhandanstalt und ihre Nachfolgeeinrichtungen 1990–2000* [*Administered Illusions. The Treuhandanstalt and her Successors, 1990–2000*], Frankfurt am Main and New York, 2004; "The Strength of Perpetrators—The Holocaust in Western Europe, 1940–1944," *Governance—An International Journal of Policy, Administration, and Institutions* 15 (2002): 211–240; "A Market for Mass Crime? Inter-Institutional Competition and the Initiation of the Holocaust in France, 1940–1942," *Journal of Organization Theory and Behavior* 5 (2002): 219–257; "Verfolgungsnetzwerke. Zur Messung von Arbeitsteilung und Machtdifferenzierung in den Verfolgungsapparaten des Holocaust" [Persecution Networks. On the Measurement of Differentiation of Power and Division of Labor within the Persecution Apparatuses of the Holocaust] (with Jörg Raab). In: *Kölner Zeitschrift für Soziologie und Sozialpsychologie* 55 (2003): 197–230.

Philippe Verheyde is Maître de Conférences of Economic History at University of Paris VIII-Saint-Denis. He has studied the economic aryanisation process in France during the Second World War. His current research continues to analyse relationships between political and economical powers during the two world wars. His most important publications are: *Les mauvais comptes de Vichy. L'aryanisation des entreprises juives* [*The Faulty Accounts of Vichy*], Paris, 1999; *La Caisse des dépôts et consignations, la Seconde Guerre mondiale et le XXe siècle* (co-author and direction) [The *Caisse des dépôts et consignations*, World War II and the 20th Century], Paris, 2002; "L'implication du Comité d'organisation des industries du bois dans le processus d'aryanisation" [The Involvement of the *Comité d'organisation* of the timber industry in the "aryanization" process], in: *L'organisation de l'économie dirigée sous Vichy: les CO*, Presses universitaires de Caen, 2004 (forthcoming).

Dieter Ziegler is a Professor of Business and Economic History at Ruhr Universität Bochum. His academic areas of interest are: the history of banking, transport history, the history of European industrialisation, and the business history of the Third Reich. Recent publications include: *Die deutsche Wirtschaftselite im 20. Jahrhundert* [*The German Economic Elite in the 20th Century*], Essen 2003 (edited with Volker Berghahn and Stefan Unger); *Banken und "Arisierungen" in Mitteleuropa während des Nationalsozialismus* [*Banks and "Aryanization" in Central Europe during Nazi Rule*], Stuttgart 2002; "Nationalsozialisten im Kampf um die Beute. Der 'Arisierungsfall' der Engelhardt Brauerei AG" [National Socialists Struggling for Prey. The "Aryanization Case" of the Engelhardt Brewery], in: W. Abelshauser, et al. (eds), *Wirtschaftsordnung, Staat und Unternehmen. Neuere Forschungen zur Wirtschaftsgeschichte des Nationalsozialismus*, Essen, 2003.

INDEX

A
Aachen, 275
Abetz, Otto, 193
about this book: acknowledgments, 8; focus, 3–4; organization, 6–7
Abs, Hermann Josef, 53
Adler, Hans, 88, 96
Adolf Weinmüller, Munich, 112, 113
Alibert, Raphaël, 72
Allianz Insurance, 262, 263, 297, 302, 308–12, 330
Altenburg, Thuringia, 272
Aly, Götz, 18, 218
Alzheimer, Alois, 309, 310
L-Ameublement, Groupement Nationale de, 77
Amouroux, Henri, 191
Amsterdam Stock Exchange, 146, 180–82
Ancestral Heritage Society (*das Ahnenerbe*), 105
Andreae, Fritz, 50
Andrieu, Claire, 201, 204
anti-Semitism: economic persecution, escalation in France (1941), 195–97; of employees of big banks, 61–63; of French Vichy regime, 190, 196; insurance company liability and, 310–14; redemptive, 33, 125; as state ideology, 4; terror during National Socialist power seizure, 120; violence and individual enrichment, 120–22
Arendt, Hannah, 1, 8n.2, 37, 132, 163, 209, 260, 262, 350
Arnhold Brothers, 47, 52, 53, 54
Aron, Raymond, 35, 36, 192
art, looting of, 103–14; cooperation and networks, 112–14; orders and initiatives, 108–11; rivalry and competition, 111–12
Art Looting Investigation Unit, 113
Art Protection Unit (Kunstschutz), 106
'aryanization': of business property, 51–59; and collaboration, 81–85; corruption and, 122–25; in France, 198–209;

Franco-German industrial and commercial relations and, 75–78, 85–86; of German economy, 173; and Germanization, 78–81; interventions in firms, large and small, 75–76, 81; of Jewish business, 2, 3, 4, 14, 15, 16–17, 18, 44–65, 66n.13; process of, 110; state networks of economic, 69–75; Vichy French government and, 69–75, 83, 85–86. *see also* 'dejewification'
assets, confiscation of Jewish: in Austria, 173–74; in occupied USSR, 89–92, 97–99; within the Reich, 92–99, 160–63, 173–74
assets, looting of Jewish: amounts in Netherlands, 184–87, 188n.24; in Germany and Austria, 173–75; in the Netherlands, 168–87; types and dimensions in Netherlands, 174–84
Assets, Office for the Collection of (Dienststelle für die Einziehung von Vermögenswerten), 161
Assets, Ordinance on the Disposition of Jewish, 124
Atonement Tax, 48, 300, 302, 304, 310, 312, 314
'Atonement' through 'Jewish Wealth Levies,' 156–57
Auschwitz, 160, 264, 266
Austria, 105–106, 109; 'annexation' of, 16, 29–30, 121, 172, 275

B
Babi Yar, 244–45
Baden-Baden, 275
Baeck, Leo, 121
Baer, Richard, Irmgard and family, 152–53, 155–56, 158–60, 163, 165n.27
Baltic States, 90–91, 218, 221, 287
Bankhaus Lippmann, 107
banking: 'aryanization' of business property, 51–59; 'dejewification' of German economy and the big banks, 47–48, 60,

64, 66n.13; Jewish employees of big
  German banks, 48–51; Reich intervention
  in affairs of big banks, 59–65; role of big
  banks under National Socialism, 44–65
Banque de France, 194
Bartel, Gustav, 106
Barthélemy, Joseph, 202
Bauman, Zygmunt, 132
Bavaria, 271
Bayerische Staatsgemäldesammlungen, 109–10
BBC Radio, 202
BdS (Befehlshaber der Sicherheitspolizei und
  des SD), 1, 193
Behemoth (Neumann, F.L.), 340
Beiersdorf AG, 58
Belarus, 90
Belgium, 106, 110, 129, 168, 169–70, 352
Belgrade, 129–30
Berdychiv, 240
Berlin, 57, 58, 89–91, 93, 109, 120–21,
  270–73, 275, 277, 278, 280, 281, 283;
  Chief Constable Graf Helldorff, 127;
  'dejewification' of retail trade in, 123;
  Gau leadership in, 121; State Police
  Headquarters in, 126
Berlin Supply Office, 272
Berliner, Ludwig, 50
Berthoud, Jacques, 82, 84
Bessarabia, 218
Best, Werner, 193, 200
Biala-Podlaska, 128
Bichelonne, Jean, 82, 200
Biela Tserkva, 244–46
Bielefeld, 152–53, 156, 158–60
Billig, Dr Joseph, 190
Birkenau, 266
Blanke, Dr (*Kriegverwaltungsrat*), 86n.23, 193
Blitzkrieg, 145
Blobel, SS-Standartenführer Paul, 241–45, 251
Blum, Leon, 71
Blutordensträger ('Blood Order'), 122
Boegner, Pastor Marc, 82
du Bois, Comité d'Organisation des
  Industries, 77
Borislav, Ukraine, 239
Borisov, Byelorussia, 17
Bormann, Martin, 21, 112, 273
Bouquet, René, 204, 207
Bouthillier, Yves, 200
Bouts, Dirk, 110–11
Brandenburg, 272
Brecht, Berthold, 93
Bremen, 79, 271, 273
Breslau, 104, 121, 273, 277, 281, 287
Brest, 247–48
Brod, Max, 93
Browning, Christopher, 247, 264, 265, 266
Brüning, Reichskanzler Heinrich, 59, 63

Brussels, 107
Buchenwald, 156
Buchheim, Hans, 37
Buchner, Ernst, 109–11
Bühler, Dr Albert, 178
Bukovina, North, 218
Burat, Franz, 247
Bürckel, Josef, 112, 121, 122
Burrin, Philippe, 146
Busch, Alfred, 65
Byelorussia, 17

C
Carbonne-Lorraine, 82
Cassirer, Dr & Co., 58
Cathala, Pierre, 79, 83
CDC (Caisse des Dépôts et Consignations),
  191, 196, 197, 200, 202, 203, 208
CDJC (Centre de Documentation Juive
  Contemporain), 190
CDU (Christliche Democratische Union), 213
CGQJ (Commissariat Général aux Questions
  Juives), 71, 72, 77–78, 79, 83, 190–91,
  195–97, 199–200, 203, 205–206, 208
Charlottenburger Wasser- und Industriewerke,
  51
Chaussures André group, 79, 81, 84
Chelm, 218
Chelmno extermination camp, 220
Chemnitz, 273, 277, 281
Chirac, Jacques, 189
Church Policy Dept. (SD), 29
collaboration and 'aryanization,' 81–85
Cologne, 132, 149, 163n.1, 271, 272, 275,
  277, 281
Commerzbank, 47, 49, 50–52, 55–57, 59, 60,
  62, 64, 68n.58
corruption: and 'aryanization,' 122–25; and
  extermination policy, 125–34; under
  National Socialism, 118–34; in occupied
  territories, 15–18, 127–34
Couve de Murville, Maurice, 204
Cracow, 106, 128, 287
Cramer, Hans, 287
Crannach-Sichart, Dr Eberhard von, 113
Currency Protection Commando
  (Devisenschutzkommando), 106, 107, 112

D
Dallgow (near Berlin), 274
Daluege, Kurt, 301
Danat Bank, 59, 63, 64
Dannecker, Theodor, 26, 33, 34, 192, 199
Danzig-West Prussia, 131, 216, 217, 223,
  226–27
Darwinism, institutional *see* polycracy
De Bijenkorf, 181
de Gaulle, Charles, 192
de Pellepoix, Louis Darquier, 200

Decree on Functions (Joint Directive, SS and Secret State Police), 28–30
'dejewification': of German Economy, 47–48, 60, 64, 66n.13; of retail trade in Berlin, 123. *see also* 'aryanization'
Denmark, 168
deportation, 160–62, 182, 183
Detmold, 151
Deutsche Ausrüstungswerke (DAW), 16, 19n.9
Deutsche Bank, 46, 47, 49, 50–53, 56, 57, 59, 60, 62, 64, 68n.58
Dienststelle Mühlmann, 105–6, 106–7
Dietrich, Maria Almas, 113
division of labor: bargaining, 347–48; cognitive dissonances, reduction of, 350–51; diversity within, 3–4; helper-persecutor interaction and the, 345–51; horizontal and vertical dimensions of, 141; 'intentionalism' *vs.* 'functionalism,' 340, 342; log-rolling, 347–48; networks and, 4, 5; organized chaos and effective persecution, paradox of, 340–42; organized mass crime and, 1–4; overdetermination of persecution, 353–54; persecution effectiveness and, 340–54; persecutors, helpers and the, 342–45, 345–51; power positions and, 348–50; principal/agent issues, 346–47; professional perception, selective, 350–51; reaggregating the hypotheses, 351–53; reciprocal interdependencies, 345–46; vagueness of term, 321–22; 'veto points,' 345–46
Dniepr River, 240
Dorotheum, Vienna, 112
Dortmund, 151, 158, 271, 275
Drancy concentration camp, 189, 190, 199
Dresden, 275, 276, 280, 287
Dresdner Bank, 44, 46–61, 63, 64, 68n.55, 181
Duisburg, 274, 276
Durkheim, Émile, 341
Düsseldorf, 149, 162, 271, 274, 276, 281
Düwel, Wilhelm, 126
DVL (Deutsche Volksliste), 216, 223–27, 233n.41

E
Earthegau, 218
East Frisiaesland, 126
Eastern Trustee Office (Treuhandstelle Ost), 221
Eberhard, Stadtkommandant Kiel, 244, 251
Economic Investgation, Bureau of (Wirtschaftsprüfstelle), 180
Ehrlinger, Erich, 249
Eichmann, Adolf, 1, 32, 34, 170, 192, 261, 262
Eichmann in Jerusalem (Arendt, H.), 260
Eichwede, Wolfgang, 110

Einsatzgruppen (mobile killing squads), 31, 127, 128, 239–41, 242–45
Elbing, 121
Electricity Board, 272
Eleventh Decree, property confiscation under, 95, 96, 98, 161–62, 348–49
Endlösung (Aly, G.), 218
Enemy Property Control Administration, 106
Engelhardt brewery group, 58, 68n.45
EPA Einheitspreis AG, 58
Erlangen, 272
ERR (Einsatzstab Reichsleiter Rosenberg), 106, 107, 110, 111–12, 114, 176, 330, 348
Essen, 271
Ethnic German Welfare Office (Volksdeutsche Mittelstelle), 214, 220, 244, 246
EWZ (Einwandererzentralstelle), 217, 218, 221–22, 223, 231n.19
Exclusion of Jews from German Economic Life, Decree for the, 301
expropriation of Jewish property, 14–18
extermination policy and corruption, 125–34
Eyck, Jan and Hubert Van, 110–11

F
FA (Finanzämter), Finance Offices, 92–93, 94
The Faustian Bargain (Petropoulos, J.), 110
Federal Archive Law, 105
Fein, Helen, 354
Festinger, Leon, 350, 351
Fiedler, Martin, 109
Fiehler, Dr Karl, 270, 271, 274
Fiehler, Kurt, 262
Finance Ministry, French, 196, 200, 204
Finances Extérieures, Direction des, 82
financial bureaucracy, 148–63; and Holocaust as topics of historical research, 149; structure and officials of, 149–53
Fircks, SS-Obersturmführer Otto von, 213–15, 220, 228, 229
Firma Jung, 246
Fischböck, Hans, 169, 170, 172, 178, 179
Fischer, Theodor, 114
'Flight Tax' (*Reichsfluchtsteuer*), 14, 48, 62, 93, 94, 151, 153–55
Forster, Albert, 131
Fournier, Pierre-Eugène, 71, 194
France, 69–86, 106–108, 110–12 168; acknowledgment and 'repentance' in, 189; cooperation with occupying forces in, 143–46; economic anti-Semitic persecution, escalation of (1941), 195–97; Gaullist Free France, 202; Nazi objectives with regard to Jews in, 207–208; occupation regime in (1940), 191–95; political vision, serving the country, 203–205; profit strategies in, 199–201; rationalities at work in, 198–206; *Révolution nationale* in, 192; 'special

funds' in Northern, 129; spoilation of Jewish property (1940–44), 189–209; unoccupied, 45; valorization of professional abilities, 201–203; values and passions in, 205–206; Vichy government in, 144–45, 189–209, 346, 348, 352, 353
Franco-German industrial and commercial relations, 75–78, 85–86
Franconia, 123
Frankfurt am Main, 270, 271, 272, 273, 276–77, 279–84
Freiburg, 56
French-Jewish businesses, 16–17
Frick, Wilhelm, 21, 262, 274
Fridenson, Patrick, 85
Friedländer, Saul, 33, 125
Frisch, Walter, 53–54
Führer Decree (May, 1940), 171
Fuhrermuseum in Linz, 107, 175
Führer's Prerogarive (*Führervorbehalt*), 107, 111, 112
Fuld, H. & Co., 58
Fulda, 272
Fürth, Commerzbank in, 57

G
Galaries Lafayette, 79, 81, 82, 83, 198
Galeries Barbès, 77, 81
Galicia, 218, 221, 238, 239, 250
Gauting, Bavaria, 274
Gay, Peter, 153
Gelsenkirchen, 151
German Council of Municipalities (Deutscher Gemeindetag), 270–71, 272, 275, 276–79, 282, 284–86
German Expellees, Association of (Bund der Vertriebenen), 213
German Municipal Code (Deutsche Gemeindeornung), 270, 279, 286
Germanization and 'aryanization,' 78–81
Gerzon Brothers, 181
Gestapo, 2, 3, 4, 14, 104–105, 113, 141, 142, 144, 156, 171, 219, 269, 330, 345, 349, 350; corruption in extermination policy, 125–26, 128, 129, 131; and financial administrators, 92–95, 97, 98; Jewish persecution (1933–39), 20–37; and local authorities, 280–82, 285, 286
GFP (Secret Field Police), 242
Giebel, Hilarius, 58
Gillet-Thaon firm, 80, 86n.23
Gladbeck, Recklinghausen, 273–74
Globocnik, Odilo, 16, 112
Glubokoye (Glebokie), 90
Gniezno/Gnesen, 214
Goebbels, Hans, 298
Goebbels, Joseph, 106, 112, 113, 132, 263, 296, 299, 302–303, 315
Goeth, Amon, 105

Golddiskontbank, 49, 50, 59, 158
Goldhagen, Daniel J., 45, 108, 341
Göring, Hermann, 16, 63, 64, 83, 106–107, 111–12, 129, 157, 173, 175, 176, 239, 246, 263, 298–301, 348
Görlitz, 282
Gotenhafen, 217
Göttingen, 149, 272, 276
Göttsche, Claus, 126
Goudefroy, Hans, 302, 303, 304, 310, 313, 315
Goudstikker art dealership, 111
Graz, Austria, 130
Greifelt, Ulrich, 216, 226
Greisler, Arthur, 129, 143, 223, 224, 225, 226
Groscurth, Lieut. Col. Helmuth, 243
Großgründlach, Franconia, 273
Grynszpan, Herschel, 295
Guéhenno, Jean, 209
Gürtner, Franz, 274, 309
'gypsies' (Sinti and Roma), 104, 148

H
Haberstock, Karl, 112, 113
Häfner, SS-Obersturmführer August, 242, 243
Hagen, Herbert, 27, 28, 34
Hague Convention of Land Warfare, 171–73, 192, 348
Halle/Saale, 271, 277
Hamburg, 57, 108, 120, 123, 126, 132, 149, 273, 277, 281, 283, 284, 286
Hannsen, Ministerialdirigent Walter, 110
Hanover, 269, 276, 284
Hanover-Braunschweig Gau, 121
Hans Lange, Berlin, 112
Harburg-Wilhelmsburg, 271
Hardy & Co., 47, 52, 53
Harster, Dr Wilhelm, 179
Hartung, Ulrike, 110
Heidelberg, 274
Heidemühl, 220
Heising, Heinrich, 150–52, 161–62
Helena Rubinstein, 80, 81, 82, 84
Helldorff, Berlin Chief Constable Graf, 127
Herbert, Ulrich, 37
Hess, Rudolf, 21
Hesse, State of, 276–77
Heuss, Anja, 110, 111
Heydrich, Reinhard, 21–23, 26–31, 33, 94, 105, 111–12, 228, 239, 251, 282, 299–300, 306, 349
Hilberg, Raul, 132, 163, 190, 249, 250–51, 261, 262
Hilble, Friedrich, 286
Hilgard, Eduard, 262, 263, 297–98, 297–301, 303–304, 306–308, 310–13, 315
Himmler, Heinrich, 16, 17, 105, 106, 111, 112, 131, 133–34, 142, 169, 215, 216, 251, 299, 331, 349; confiscation of

Jewish valuables, 91, 94–96; 'ethnic resettlement,' 224–28; 'final solution' in Ukraine, 238, 239, 242, 247; persecution of Jews (1933–39), 20–22, 26, 29, 31, 35
Hirsch, N.V. & Co, 181
Historical Methods, 332
Hitler, Adolf, 13, 16, 17, 22, 32, 35, 37, 45, 63, 95, 107, 109–13, 173, 175, 215, 239, 247, 251, 282, 296, 331
Hitler's Willing Executioners (Goldhagen, D.), 45, 108
Hofer, Walter Andreas, 107, 113, 176
Hoffstadter, Richard, 261
Hofmann, Otto, 227, 234n.63
Holland *see* Netherlands
Holocaust: coordination of persecution apparatuses, 2; division of labour and the, 1–4; extermination of economic existence of Jews, 2–3; and financial bureaucracy as topics of historical research, 149; housing redistribution, 282–84; interaction between local authorities, 277–82; local-government initiatives, 271–77; local-government interests, 282–84; municipal involvement, 270–71, 284–88; occupation politics and the, 3; organizational forms of persecution, 3–4; organized mass crime and the, 5–6; plundering, 'wild' enrichment and the, 132–34; radicalization of policy and the, 13–14; recent research findings, 2–4; self-initiative of local and regional authorities, 3; warfare strategies and tactics, interrelation with the, 3
Höss, Rudolf, 264–65
HTO (Haupttreuhandstelle Ost), 107, 131, 349
Huhn, Heinrich, 244
Hungary, 17–18, 250

I
insurance industry: anti-Semitism and insurance company liability, 310–14; compensation, Jewish entitlement to, 303; damage control, politics of, 300–14; Kristallnacht and the, 295–315; networks, role of, 314–15; November (1938) pogrom and the, 295–300
Italy, 168

J
J'accuse (Zola, E.), 189
Jakob, Dr Arthur, 131
Jeckeln, Friedrich, 238, 239, 240, 244
Jena, 281
'Jew' defined, 176–77
Jewish Affairs Dept. (SD), 30
Jewish auctions (*Judenauktionen*), 104
Jewish Councils (*Judenräte*), 128
Jewish Emigration, Central Office for, 105

Jewish Punitive Tax (*Judenvermögensabgabe*), 94–95, 122, 151, 156–57
Jewish Removal Goods, Office for the Sale of, 104–105
'Jewish Transports' (*Judentransporte*), 126
Johannes Jeserich AG, 58
Judicial Departments, Central Office of the Regional, 228, 232n.33
Julius Berger Tiefbau AG, 58

K
Kaienburg, Hermann, 250
Kaltenbrunner, Ernst, 35, 349
Kam'yanets'-Podil's'kyy, 240
Karlsruhe, 271
Kassel, 276
Kattowitz, 129, 131
Kaufmann, Hugo, 50
Kaunas (Kowno), Lithuania, 287
Kelkheim/Taunus, 276
Kieper, Wolf, 240–41
Kiev, mass executions at, 249
Klarsfeld, Serge, 191
Kleemann, Wilhelm, 48
Klemm, General Commissar, 247
Knochen, Helmut, 71, 192, 193, 199
Koblenz, 25–26
Koch, Erich, 127, 247
Koechlin, Baumgartner & Cie, 80
Kogan, Moishe, 240–41
Köhler, Ingo, 47, 67n
Königsberg, 277
Koppe, SS Lieutenant-General, 219, 220
Kracauer, Siegfried, 259–60
Krebs, Dr Friedrich, 270, 279–80
Die Krematorien von Auschwitz (Pressac, J.-C.), 265
Kreuter, Alexandre, 79
Kripo (Police Criminal Investigation Dept.), 29, 105
Kristallnacht, 94, 109–10, 112, 156–57, 183, 263, 295–315, 330
Krumey, Lieut.-Col. Hermann, 220–21
Künsberg, Eberhard Baron von, 106
Kryvyy Rih, 244

L
La Laurencie, General de, 70
La Samaritaine, 76
Lammers, Hans, 91, 112
Landeck, Silesia, 273
Lasch, Karl, 105
Lasker-Schuler, Else, 93
Laval, Pierre, 79, 83, 202, 205, 353
Law for the Restoration of the Professional Civil Service, 49, 50, 51, 59–60, 61, 63, 65, 150, 270, 272, 284
Law on Leasing to Jews, 276

Law on Settlement of Claims in Civil Law, 305, 313
Lebenswert ('life value'), 32
Lehr, Robert, 271
Leipzig, 269, 273, 275, 276, 277, 280
Lemberg, 128
Letichev, 246
Lévy-Finger Paint Company, 82
Liebel, Willy, 271
Limberger, Gisela, 107
Lindener, Kurt, 137n.75
Linz, 130, 175; Special Assignment (Sonderauftrag Linz), 107–108, 112
Lippert, Dr Julius, 270
Lippmann, Rosenthal & Co (Liro), 146, 178–79, 180–82, 185–86
Liquidation of Enterprises, Netherlands Company for the, 180
Littmann family, 104
Lódz (Litzmannstadt), 131, 137n.75, 213–14, 217, 218–22, 225, 227, 231n.17
Loeb, Rudolf, 53
Lohse, Dr Bruno (Reichskommisar in Ostland), 90, 107, 113–14
Lorentz, Bernhard, 46, 62
Lorenz, Dr Walter, 131
Louvain, 111
Lübeck, 126
Lublin, Poland, 16, 218, 287
Ludwigshafen am Rhein, 273
Lust, Georg, 51
Luts'k, 239, 247
L'viv, 238, 239

M
Mädel, Dr, 96, 97
Mainz, 275
Maison de Bonneterie, 181
Mannesmann Röhren Werke, Düsseldorf, 80
Mannheim, 57, 93, 277
Mariupol, 244
Markets and Hierarchies (Williamson, O), 326
Markus Schiff-Markus Nelken & Sohn, 52
Marrus, Michael, 191
Marschall, Georg, 248, 251
Marshall Plan, 260–61
Martini, Oskar, 286
Marx, Else and Hugo, 110
Mattéoli Commission, 189, 190, 191
Maurras, Charles, 72
Mayer, Arno, 260
Mayntz, Renate, 322
MBF (Militärbefehlshaber in Frankreich), 70, 78, 79, 83, 192, 193, 195, 197, 203, 205
Mein Kampf (Hitler, A.), 35
Meisslein, Johann, 250
Melville, Herman, 260
Mendelssohn & Co., 52, 53, 56
Meyer, Emil, 65

Michaelis, Meïr, 348
Michel, Elmar, 70, 71
Miedl, Alois, 111, 114
Milgram, Stanley, 350–51
Mills, C. Wright, 259–60, 261
Mir, Belarus, 90
Misocz, 248
Moabit-West FA, 94, 95
Moltke, Helmuth James von, 241
Mommsen, Hans, 37, 45, 150, 261
Moore, Bob, 170
Moser, Dr Walter, 131
Mühlmann, Dr Kajetan, 105–106, 106–107, 113, 175
Mülheim, 271
Müller, Heinrich, 26, 27
Mumford, Lewis, 260
Münchener Rückversicherung, 309, 330
Munich, 105, 112, 120, 127, 270–77, 279, 280, 283, 286
Münster, 161, 271, 274, 283, 284; Regional Tax Offices at, 151–52, 155, 158–60, 161–62
Mutschmann, Martin, 53

N
National Socialism: art prundering program under, 103–14; corruption through 'economic assistance' within, 15–18; corruption under, 118–34; Jewish persecution (1933–39) under, 20–37; political power sources within, 13–14; role of big banks under, 44–65; structure of movement, 118–20
Nederlandsche Bank, 175
Neimann, Erich, 58
Nessau-Hohensalza district, 221
Netherlands, 106–107, 111, 130, 192, 352; administrative apparatus for looting, foundation of, 178–79; amounts of looting, 184–87, 188.24; civil government during occupation, 169–71; cooperation with occupying forces in, 143, 144, 145–46; definition of Jew, 176–77; deportation to Westerbork, 182; direct looting (at gunpoint), 176; First Liro Decree, 181–82; German attack on the, 169; indirect looting, 175–76; law-abiding nature of Dutch society, 172; organized looting in the, 168–87; registration, 177–78; Second Liro Decree, 175, 182; sequestration of Jewish assets, 179–81; stamps to avoid deportation, 183; types and dimensions of looting, 174–84
networks: analytical method, 333–35; analytical tools, 324; concept and potential in Holocaust research, 321–36; data sources in network analysis, 324–25, 332–35; as empirical tools, 323–25; as

governance forms, 326–28; insurance industry, role in, 314–15; mechanisms for integration of, 322; network analysis, application in Holocause research, 332–35; operationalization in network analysis, 324–25, 332–33, 333–35; of persecution, historical evidence, 329–32; of persecution, mapping the analytical framework, 323–29; of persecution, potential of network analysis, 335–36; as social structures, 325–26; as theoretical entities, 328–29
Neumann, Dr Artur, 241, 251
Neumann, Franz L., 340
News Chronicle, 308
NKVD (People's Commissariat for Internal Affairs), 239
Nördlingen, 272
Norguet, René, 84
Norway, 129, 168, 170–71, 184, 192
Nouvelles Galaries group, 76
Novohrad-Volyns'kyy, 239, 246
NSBO (Nationalsozialistische Betriebszellenorganisation), 49, 51
NSDAP (Nationalsozialistische Deutsche Arbeiterpartei), 2, 21, 22, 66n.19, 118–25, 129, 135n.13, 152, 169, 216, 262, 269–72, 274, 279–81, 345
NSV (Nationalsozialistische Volkswohlfart), 121, 152
Nuremberg, 44, 57, 271, 272, 274–76
'Nuremberg Laws,' 25, 50, 59, 194, 285
Nuremberg Military Tribunal VIII, 226, 228

O
Ober-Rossbach, 273
Oberfinanzpräsident (OFP), Berlin, 94, 95, 96
Oberg, SS General Carl-Albrecht, 193
Ohlendorf, Otto, 31
Oldenburg, 126, 271
Olso, 129
OMGUS (US Office of Military Government for Germany), 53, 65n.1
Omnia Treuhänd organization, 180
Ordinary Men (Browning, C.), 265
Orenstein & Koppel, 58
organized mass crime: division of labour and, 1–4; moral indifference and, 6; moral judgment and, 5; structure of, 5–6
OT (*Organisation Todt*), 143, 246, 247, 250
Ottoman Empire, 18

P
Packard, Vance, 261
Palatinate, 26
Panning, Dr Gerhart, 241, 242, 251
Papeteries Braunstein, 79, 81, 82, 83
Papeteries de la Chapelle, 79
Paris, 107, 198

Paris-France group, 76, 81
Parvenüs und Profiteure (Bajohr, F.), 112
Pau, France, 110
Paul Knopp firm, 77
Pauley, Bruce, 109
Paulsen, Peter, 105
Paur, Joseph, 248, 250
Paxton, Robert, 191, 346
Pervomaysik, 238, 240
Pétain, Philippe (Marshal de France), 72, 190, 191, 192, 201, 205, 207
Petropolous, Jonathan, 14, 16
Pillau, 121
Plant, Max, 125–26
Plauen, 272, 280, 286
Pohl, Oswald, 91
Poland, 15–16, 105–107, 142–43, 168, 213–15, 250, 287; efficient cooperation in, 229; 'ethnic resettlement' in, 213–29; expulsion and resettlement in, 218–23; FRG perceptions of population reorganization in, 228–29; political reorganization of the population in, 215–18; racial purity, labor deployment and balance of interest in, 223–27; racist ideology in, 229
polycracy, 2, 3, 12, 88, 98, 103–14, 118, 263, 330, 340, 349
Pomerania, 278, 298
Porto Allegre, Reich Court case of the, 302, 308
Posen, 105
Posse, Dr Hans, 107, 112, 176
POWs (Prisoners of War), 237, 238, 241, 247
Poznan, 129, 131, 216–19, 221, 231n.25
Poznanski, Renée, 191
Prague, 127
Pressac, Jean-Claude, 265
Presser, Jacob, 170
'processing' (Durchschleusung), 217–18
Professional Civil Service Law, 49, 50, 51, 59–60, 61, 63, 65, 150, 270, 272, 284
property, looting of Jewish, 14–18; deportation and utilization of property, 160–62; emigration control, 155–56; financial bureaucracy and, 148–53; foreign-exchange controls, 153–55; 'Jewish Wealth Levies,' 151, 156–57; monitoring of wealth, 157–60; plundering after Kristallnacht, 156–57; 'Reich Flight Tax,' 151, 153–55; surveillance of accounts, 157–60
Proskurow, 250
Protestant Federation of France, 82
Prüfer, Franz, 126
Prüfer, Kurt, 265
Prussack, Hanka, 248
Prussia, 123, 216, 223, 270, 271, 274
Prützmann, Hans-Adolf, 90–91, 238
The Pyramid Climbers (Packard, V.), 261

Q
Quaatz, Reinhold, 48, 50

R
race defilement, accusation of ('Blutschande'), 54, 67n.38
Race Policy Office, 216
'racial certificate' (*Rassegutachten*), 225
'racial formula' (*Rassenformel*), 218
Radio Oranje, 180
Radomyshyl, 244
Rath, Ernst vom, 157, 295–95, 303
Rauter, Hanns Albin, 169, 179
Rechtswahrerbund (National Socialist Lawyers Association), 152
Recklinghausen, 274
Reich Accounting Office, 128, 349
Reich Air Ministry, 298–300
Reich Association of German Civil Servants, 152
Reich Association of Jews in Germany, 125–26
Reich Citizenship Law, 50–51, 162
Reich Economic Court, 297
Reich Economic Ministry (Wirtschaftsministerium), 49, 50, 53–55, 61, 79, 152, 273, 276, 298, 301–302, 304–307, 309–13, 315
Reichenau, Field Marshal von, 240, 243
Reich Finance Ministry (RFM), 91–98, 105, 109, 112–13, 130, 149, 154, 156–58, 160–61, 301, 307, 310–11, 313, 315, 330, 349
Reich Food Estate (Reichsnährstand), 218, 219
Reich Group for Insurance, 297, 298, 301, 302, 313–15
Reich Health Executive (Reichsgesundheitsführer), 217
Reich Insurance Decree, 298
Reich Interior Ministry, 270, 279, 284, 304–305, 313, 315
Reich Justice Ministry, 302, 304, 305, 307, 313, 315
Reich Post Office, 156, 246
Reich-Ranicki, Marcel, 152
Reich Supervisory Board for Insurance, 297
Reichsbahn (state railroad), 3, 156, 246
Reichsbank, 64, 91, 92, 175
Reichscommissariat Ostland and Ukraine, 89–92, 143
Reichshauptkasse Beutestelle (War Booty Office), 89, 91
Reichskreditgesellschaft, 53
Reichskristallnacht *see* Kristallnacht
Reichsrechnungshof (German Auditor General), 14
Reichsvereinigung (RV) der Juden, 96–97
Reichzentrale für jüdische Auswanderung (Reich Central Office for Jewish Emigration), 14
Remscheid, 271, 272
Restitution Affairs, Court of (US occupation zone), 124–25
Restoration of Streets around Jewish Enterprises, Decree for the, 300–301, 302, 306–307
Rhineland, 272
Ribbentrop, Joachim von, 192–93
Richter, Hermann, 65
Riga, 91
Ritscher, Samuel, 51
RKF (Reichskommissar für die Festigung Deutschen Volkstums), 216, 217, 218, 220, 226, 230n.10
Rochlitz, Gustav, 113–14
Rohde, Friedrich, 247
Röhm, Ernst (and the 'Röhm affair'), 21, 23, 108–9
Roques, General von, 237, 240
Rosenberg, Reichsleiter Alfred, 91, 106, 111, 176, 247
Rosenthal & Co, 107
Rothschild Schloss Wildhof, 109
Rousso, Henry, 191
RSHA (Reichssicherheitshauptamt), 1, 20, 30, 31, 95, 96, 105, 125–26, 133, 170, 192, 217, 228, 229, 275–76, 281, 321, 345, 349
RuSHA (Rasse- und Siedlungshauptamt), 142, 215, 218, 219, 221, 224–29
Rüstungsinspektion (armaments inspection board), 77

S
SA (Sturmabteilung), 21, 49, 51, 120, 122, 269, 271
Saar-Pfalz Gau, 122
Safrian, Hans, 240
Sahm, Arthur, 213–14
St Nazaire Penhoët, Ateliers et Chantiers de, 79, 81, 83
Saul, Rohn Ralston, 260
Saxony, 272, 286
SCAP (Service du Contrôle des Administrateurs Provisoires), 71, 72, 74, 83, 193–94, 197, 200
Schacht, Hjalmar, 49, 63, 264, 276
Schallert, Willibald, 126
Scherbenfonds ('debris funds'), 121–22
Schippel, Hans, 51
Schirach, Baldur and Henriette von, 130
Schleswig-Holstein, 278
Schloss Neuschwanstein, 110
Schmidt, Fritz, 169
Schmitt, Kurt, 63, 311
Scholz, Robert, 112
Schönwälder, Franz, 287
Schreibtischtäter (desk murderers), 109, 261
Schulte, Theo, 236
Schumacher, SS-Hauptsturmführer Hans, 249

Schuschnigg regime, 109
Schwede-Coburg, Franz von , 298
Schwertfeger, Ernst, 269
Schwob d'Héricourt family, 80
Sciaky group, 76–77, 81
SD (Sicherheitsdienst), 1, 2, 14, 104–106, 143, 168, 170, 179, 217–19, 239, 240, 242–44, 247, 249–51, 330; functions and organizational structure, 21–24; Inlandsnachrichtendienst (Domestic Intelligence) of the, 24; working relationships with Gestapo, 20, 24–31
SDHA (Sicherheitshauptamt), 23, 33
Serbia, 129–30
Service des Domaines, 196, 202
Seyss-Inquart, Arthur, 106, 112, 130, 169, 170–72, 175, 179, 180
Siegen, 150
Siegfried Falk, 52–53
Silberberg family, 104
Silesia, 131, 216, 223, 225, 226
Singer, Kurt, 34–35
Sipo-SD, 237, 239, 249, 252
Six, Franz Alfred, 24, 27, 31
Smith, Adam, 341
Société Cotonnière du Nord et de l'Est, 79–80, 81
Société Nationale de Chemin de Fer (SNCF), 194
Sokol'niki, 239
Solmssen, Georg, 50
Sonderbehandlung (special treatment), 143
Sonderkommandos (Special Commandos), 108
Sonderstab Bildende Kunst (Special Staff for Visual Arts), 112
Sosnowitz, 131, 287
Soviet Union *see* USSR
Sozialforschung, Institut für (Hamburg), 108
Speer, Albert, 280, 283, 292n.93
Speier, Hans, 259–60
Speyer, 271, 272
SS (Schutzstaffel), 2, 3, 4, 14–17, 105, 141–44, 170, 215–17, 226, 227, 240, 269, 271, 345; corruption in extermination policy, 120–22; and financial administrators, 91, 92, 94; Jewish persecution (1933–39), 20–37; political practice in Jewish policy of, 31–37
SS-Police, 236–39, 241, 244–48, 250–52, 330
SS-Resettlement Offices and Task Forces (Andsiedlungs- und Arbeitsstäbe), 213, 214, 217–19, 221–23, 228, 232n.30
SS-WVHA (Economic Administration Office), 91, 92, 330
Staatsschutzkorps (State Security Corps), 22
Stalingrad, 150
Steinberg, Jonathan, 348
Steinthal, Max, 50

Stettin, 273, 278
Stoltzenfus, Nathan, 45
Straubing, 272
Straußberg, 274
Streccius, Alfred, 192
Ströhlin, Karl, 275
Stübs, Gerhard, 126
Stülpnagel, Karl-Heinrich von, 190, 239
Stülpnagel, Otto von, 74, 83, 192
Stürmer Publishing House, 123
Stuttgart, 57, 275
Styria, Lower, 130
Swabia, 273

T
'tax-evasion warrants' (*Steuersteckbrief*), 154
Teichler, Richard, 105
Terboven, Gauleiter Josef, 129, 170
Terropil', 239
Theresienstadt, 97, 160
Thiel, Carl, 79
Thuringia, 123
Topf & Söhne, 265, 266
Transnistria, 250
Treblinka, 16
Trebnitz, 272
Treff, Herbert, 271
Treuhandverwaltung für das Deutsch-Niederländische Finanzabkommen, 79
Trier, 273
Trunk, Isaiah, 128
Tübingen, 272
Tumult Damage Law, 297
Turek district, 220

U
UGIF (Union Générale des Israélites de France), 197, 198, 202
Ukraine, 89–92, 127, 143, 330; administration of 'final solution' in, 246–50; Babi Yar, systematic approach to mass shooting at, 244–45; Bila Tserkva, murder at, 242–44; decentralization of 'final solution' in, 248–49; 'final solution,' implementation in (1941-44), 236–52; forced labour in extemination process, 250; mass murder, onset (1941) in, 237–46; military administration in, 237–46; regional figures governing anti-Jewish policy in, 237–38
Ulmo Ironworks, Rimaucourt, 78, 81
Unto Caesar (Voigt, F.A.), 36
Urbig, Franz, 62
USSR, 111, 142, 143, 218; German-occupied territories of, 15, 17, 31, 89–92
utilization of Jewish property by Nazia, 14–18
UWZ (Umwandererzentralstelle), 219, 221, 220, 221, 222

V

Vahrenkamp, Wilhelm, 105
Vallat, Xavier, 71, 72, 195, 196, 207, 208
Van Leer, Bernard, 80, 82
Vernichtung durch Arbeit (annihilation through labor), 143, 250
Vichy, 69–75, 83, 85–86
Vichy and the Jews (Marrus, M. and Paxton, R.), 191
Vienna, 105–106, 109, 112, 281, 283, 286
Vierjahresplan Agency, 107
Vileyka, 92
Vinnytsia, 240, 247
Voegelin, Eric, 35, 36–37
Voigt, Frederick A., 35, 36
Volhynia, Belarus, 90, 218, 221
Volhynia-Podolia, 245, 246, 247, 248
Völkischer Beobachter, 272, 273, 296
'*Volksstaat*', Germany as Hitler's, 18
Voltaire's Bastards (Saul, J.R.), 260
Voss, Dr Hermann, 107, 176
Vugetsa (Vermögenssumzugsgut Gestapo), 104–105
Vught transit camp, 182
VVRA (Vermögensverwaltungs- und Rentenanstalt), 178, 179, 180–81, 185–86

W

Waffen-SS, 105, 238, 241, 242
Wagner, Gauleiter Adolf, 112
Wannsee Conference (1942), 182
Wannsee Protocol, 250
Warsaw, 16, 128
Wartheland Reichsgau, 129, 131, 142, 213–15, 219, 221, 223, 225–27, 330
Wassermann, Oscar, 49
Weber, Christian, 122
Weber, Max, 132, 162, 259
Wehrmacht, 90, 108, 127, 129–30, 133, 143, 236–40, 243–45, 331
Weidemann, Professor Johannes, 271
Weimar Republic, 63, 118, 150
Weisberg, Richard, 191
Weser-Ems Gau, 122
Westerbork transit camp, 182, 183
Westphalia, 148, 149–62, 163n.2, 273
Wetherell, Charles, 332
Wetzell, Carlos, 80, 84
White, Harrison C., 323
White Collar (Mills, C.W.), 259–60
Wiesbaden, 275
Wimmer, Friedrich, 169, 170
Wisliceny, Dieter, 27
Wloclawek, Poland, 289
Wolf, Martin, 27
Wuppertal, 271, 275
Württemberg-Hohenzollern Gau, 123

Y

Yugoslavia, 168

Z

Zamosc Jewish Council, 128
Zdolbuniv, 248, 249, 250
Zhytomyr, 89, 240–42, 244, 246, 249, 251
Zinßer, Hugo, 65
Zöorner, Emil, 287
Zweig, Arnold, 93
Zwiahel (Novhorod-Volyns'kyy), 246

Schuschnigg regime, 109
Schwede-Coburg, Franz von, 298
Schwertfeger, Ernst, 269
Schwob d'Héricourt family, 80
Sciaky group, 76–77, 81
SD (Sicherheitsdienst), 1, 2, 14, 104–106, 143, 168, 170, 179, 217–19, 239, 240, 242–44, 247, 249–51, 330; functions and organizational structure, 21–24; Inlandsnachrichtendienst (Domestic Intelligence) of the, 24; working relationships with Gestapo, 20, 24–31
SDHA (Sicherheitshauptamt), 23, 33
Serbia, 129–30
Service des Domaines, 196, 202
Seyss-Inquart, Arthur, 106, 112, 130, 169, 170–72, 175, 179, 180
Siegen, 150
Siegfried Falk, 52–53
Silberberg family, 104
Silesia, 131, 216, 223, 225, 226
Singer, Kurt, 34–35
Sipo-SD, 237, 239, 249, 252
Six, Franz Alfred, 24, 27, 31
Smith, Adam, 341
Société Cotonnière du Nord et de l'Est, 79–80, 81
Société Nationale de Chemin de Fer (SNCF), 194
Sokol'niki, 239
Solmssen, Georg, 50
Sonderbehandlung (special treatment), 143
Sonderkommandos (Special Commandos), 108
Sonderstab Bildende Kunst (Special Staff for Visual Arts), 112
Sosnowitz, 131, 287
Soviet Union *see* USSR
Sozialforschung, Institut für (Hamburg), 108
Speer, Albert, 280, 283, 292n.93
Speier, Hans, 259–60
Speyer, 271, 272
SS (Schutzstaffel), 2, 3, 4, 14–17, 105, 141–44, 170, 215–17, 226, 227, 240, 269, 271, 345; corruption in extermination policy, 120–22; and financial administrators, 91, 92, 94; Jewish persecution (1933–39), 20–37; political practice in Jewish policy of, 31–37
SS-Police, 236–39, 241, 244–48, 250–52, 330
SS-Resettlement Offices and Task Forces (Andsiedlungs- und Arbeitsstäbe), 213, 214, 217–19, 221–23, 228, 232n.30
SS-WVHA (Economic Administration Office), 91, 92, 330
Staatsschutzkorps (State Security Corps), 22
Stalingrad, 150
Steinberg, Jonathan, 348
Steinthal, Max, 50

Stettin, 273, 278
Stoltzenfus, Nathan, 45
Straubing, 272
Straußberg, 274
Streccius, Alfred, 192
Ströhlin, Karl, 275
Stübs, Gerhard, 126
Stülpnagel, Karl-Heinrich von, 190, 239
Stülpnagel, Otto von, 74, 83, 192
Stürmer Publishing House, 123
Stuttgart, 57, 275
Styria, Lower, 130
Swabia, 273

T
'tax-evasion warrants' (*Steuersteckbrief*), 154
Teichler, Richard, 105
Terboven, Gauleiter Josef, 129, 170
Terropil', 239
Theresienstadt, 97, 160
Thiel, Carl, 79
Thuringia, 123
Topf & Söhne, 265, 266
Transnistria, 250
Treblinka, 16
Trebnitz, 272
Treff, Herbert, 271
Treuhandverwaltung für das Deutsch-Niederländische Finanzabkommen, 79
Trier, 273
Trunk, Isaiah, 128
Tübingen, 272
Tumult Damage Law, 297
Turek district, 220

U
UGIF (Union Générale des Israélites de France), 197, 198, 202
Ukraine, 89–92, 127, 143, 330; administration of 'final solution' in, 246–50; Babi Yar, systematic approach to mass shooting at, 244–45; Bila Tserkva, murder at, 242–44; decentralization of 'final solution' in, 248–49; 'final solution,' implementation in (1941-44), 236–52; forced labour in extemination process, 250; mass murder, onset (1941) in, 237–46; military administration in, 237–46; regional figures governing anti-Jewish policy in, 237–38
Ulmo Ironworks, Rimaucourt, 78, 81
Unto Caesar (Voigt, F.A.), 36
Urbig, Franz, 62
USSR, 111, 142, 143, 218; German-occupied territories of, 15, 17, 31, 89–92
utilization of Jewish property by Nazia, 14–18
UWZ (Umwandererzentralstelle), 219, 221, 220, 221, 222

V

Vahrenkamp, Wilhelm, 105
Vallat, Xavier, 71, 72, 195, 196, 207, 208
Van Leer, Bernard, 80, 82
Vernichtung durch Arbeit (annihilation through labor), 143, 250
Vichy, 69–75, 83, 85–86
Vichy and the Jews (Marrus, M. and Paxton, R.), 191
Vienna, 105–106, 109, 112, 281, 283, 286
Vierjahresplan Agency, 107
Vileyka, 92
Vinnytsia, 240, 247
Voegelin, Eric, 35, 36–37
Voigt, Frederick A., 35, 36
Volhynia, Belarus, 90, 218, 221
Volhynia-Podolia, 245, 246, 247, 248
Völkischer Beobachter, 272, 273, 296
'*Volksstaat*', Germany as Hitler's, 18
Voltaire's Bastards (Saul, J.R.), 260
Voss, Dr Hermann, 107, 176
Vugetsa (Vermögenssumzugsgut Gestapo), 104–105
Vught transit camp, 182
VVRA (Vermögensverwaltungs- und Rentenanstalt), 178, 179, 180–81, 185–86

W

Waffen-SS, 105, 238, 241, 242
Wagner, Gauleiter Adolf, 112
Wannsee Conference (1942), 182
Wannsee Protocol, 250
Warsaw, 16, 128
Wartheland Reichsgau, 129, 131, 142, 213–15, 219, 221, 223, 225–27, 330
Wassermann, Oscar, 49
Weber, Christian, 122
Weber, Max, 132, 162, 259
Wehrmacht, 90, 108, 127, 129–30, 133, 143, 236–40, 243–45, 331
Weidemann, Professor Johannes, 271
Weimar Republic, 63, 118, 150
Weisberg, Richard, 191
Weser-Ems Gau, 122
Westerbork transit camp, 182, 183
Westphalia, 148, 149–62, 163n.2, 273
Wetherell, Charles, 332
Wetzell, Carlos, 80, 84
White, Harrison C., 323
White Collar (Mills, C.W.), 259–60
Wiesbaden, 275
Wimmer, Friedrich, 169, 170
Wisliceny, Dieter, 27
Wloclawek, Poland, 289
Wolf, Martin, 27
Wuppertal, 271, 275
Württemberg-Hohenzollern Gau, 123

Y

Yugoslavia, 168

Z

Zamosc Jewish Council, 128
Zdolbuniv, 248, 249, 250
Zhytomyr, 89, 240–42, 244, 246, 249, 251
Zinßer, Hugo, 65
Zöorner, Emil, 287
Zweig, Arnold, 93
Zwiahel (Novhorod-Volyns'kyy), 246